A VOLUME IN THE SERIES,

COMMUNISM IN AMERICAN LIFE

CLINTON ROSSITER, *General Editor*

THEODORE DRAPER

American Communism
AND
Soviet Russia

THE FORMATIVE PERIOD

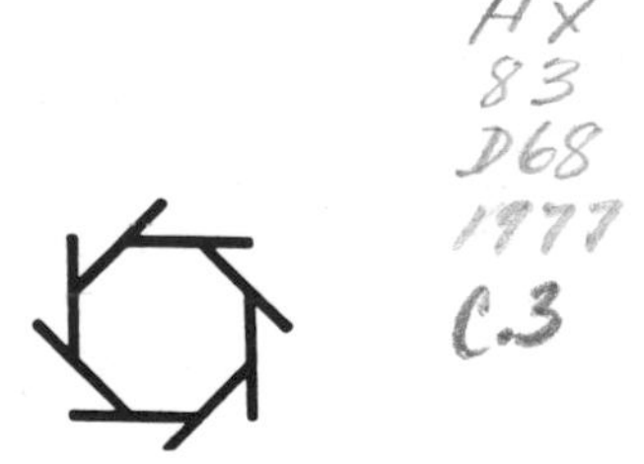

OCTAGON BOOKS

A DIVISION OF FARRAR, STRAUS AND GIROUX

New York 1977

Reprinted 1977
by special arrangement with Theodore Draper

OCTAGON BOOKS
A DIVISION OF FARRAR, STRAUS & GIROUX, INC.
19 Union Square West
New York, N.Y. 10003

Library of Congress Cataloging in Publication Data

Draper, Theodore, 1912-
American communism and Soviet Russia.

Reprint of the ed. published by Viking Press, New York, in series: Communism in American life.
Includes index.
1. Communism—United States. I. Title. II. Series.

[HX83.D68 1977] 335.43'0973 76-51212
ISBN 0-374-92334-5

Manufactured by Braun-Brumfield, Inc.
Ann Arbor, Michigan
Printed in the United States of America

To Evelyn with love

Note

This book is one of a series of studies of Communist influence in American life. The entire survey has been made possible through the foresight and generous support of the Fund for the Republic. All of us who have taken part in it are grateful for this exceptional opportunity to study the most confused and controversial problem of the age and to publish the results exactly as we find them.

CLINTON ROSSITER

Contents

Introduction 3

1. The New Day 9
2. The Farmer-Labor United Front 29
3. Roads to Chicago 52
4. The Parting of the Ways 75
5. The La Follette Fiasco 96
6. How to Win a Majority 127
7. Bolshevization 153
8. Party Life 186
9. Politics and Trade-Unionism 215
10. Ruthenberg's Last Wish 234
11. Lovestone in Power 248
12. American Exceptionalism 268
13. The Turning Point 282
14. The Sixth World Congress 300
15. The Negro Question 315
16. The Birth of American Trotskyism 357

17. The Runaway Convention 377
18. How to Lose a Majority 405

Notes 445
Acknowledgments 533
Index 535

American Communism
AND
Soviet Russia

Introduction

When I began this work, I knew little of the history of the first ten years of the American Communist movement. I assumed that the "real" history of American Communism had begun with the economic depression of the early nineteen-thirties. Originally I conceived of writing the whole story in one volume, of which the opening chapter would briefly outline the party's "prehistory" from 1919 to 1929.

But the more I studied the party's actions and policies from 1930 to 1945, the period on which I had intended to concentrate, the more dissatisfied I became. It gradually became clear to me that the controlling forces and motivations of the chief characters in the story could not be understood from the actions and policies of the Popular Front and war years. At every crisis and turning point, such as the outbreak of war in 1939 or the downfall of Earl Browder in 1945, the leaders seemed to be responding to influences and pressures out of the distant past rather than in the immediate present.

What were those influences and pressures? And how far in the past?

With some reluctance, I began to search for a deeper understanding of the entire movement by learning more about the party in the late nineteen-twenties, then in the early nineteen-twenties, and finally about its remote origins. It was for me a voyage of discovery because I found scholarly exploration almost completely lacking, sources uncollected and often unknown, and most of the available material encrusted with personal bias and political propaganda.

On closer investigation, I came to value the importance of the formative period for its own sake. Again and again I encountered key characters begging to be resurrected, intriguing mysteries waiting to be solved, and neglected aspects of our national history needing to be explored. But the compelling reason that urged me on was undoubtedly what the past could teach about the future.

Thus I came to the conclusion that the time had not yet come for the kind of one-volume history that I had originally contemplated. There was too much spadework to be done; there were too many missing characters to be resurrected; there were too many mysteries to be solved. If the work was worth doing at all, it was worth doing it by digging beneath the surface.

The more I dug, the more I became convinced that the first decade of the American Communist party's existence was the basic one for an understanding of its fundamental nature. In later years, its power and policies changed enormously. In the long perspective, however, the changes proved to be superficial and transitory. The historical task, as I saw it, was not merely to record the changes, important as they were, but to seek the underlying reality that has outlasted all the changes of line and leadership.

In human terms, the search took me back to the founding generation of American Communists. This founding generation, despite its numerical shrinkage over the years, has retained effective control of the party for four decades. It has made and unmade all the changes directly or through younger men loyal to it. It has never relaxed its grip of the top leadership, and in a Communist party the top leadership is, in all important respects, the only part that makes effective decisions. In its main line, therefore, a history of the Communist party is chiefly a history of its top leadership.

The founding leaders were not born Communists; they could not join an already fully formed and hardened movement. Most of them came out of other radical movements with different traditions; they were made Communists at the same time as the Communist movement itself was in the making. This molding process of both the movement and the leaders consumed an entire decade. Once it was completed, they could not as a group tear themselves away from their origins, no matter how far they seemed to move away from them in quest of mass influence. Those who tore themselves away from the origins invariably tore themselves loose from the movement.

For this molding process to have penetrated so deeply and persisted so tenaciously, it must have been extraordinarily intense and thorough. The decade that it took to be completed was, as far as the inner life of the party was concerned, savage in its intensity and brutal in its thoroughness. In *The Roots of American Communism,* I was able only to begin the study of this process. In this volume, I have attempted to study it as a whole. I have conceived of this volume, however, as completely independent and self-contained. Those who have not read *The Roots of American Communism* will find its substance in the first chapter of the present volume; those who have read it may find the chapter useful to refresh their memories; in addition, the material is presented in a new form indispensable for the logical unfolding of all that follows.

The title, *American Communism and Soviet Russia,* suggests what I consider to be the essence of the whole process, and this essence is fundamentally my subject. Whatever has changed from time to time, one thing has never changed—the relation of American Communism to Soviet Russia. This relation has expressed itself in different ways, sometimes glaring and strident, sometimes masked and muted. But it has always been the determining factor, the essential element. That this is so is evident in all four decades of the party's history; why it is so is buried in the history of the party's first decade. It has seemed to me worthwhile to devote an entire volume to the why; then the rest of the story need cause no wonder or confusion.

But if there is one area of this subject most difficult to get at with accuracy and authority, it is that of American Communist–Soviet Russian relations. Fortunately, the Communist movement was far less inhibited in the early years than in the later ones. If anyone took the trouble to read all that the Communists here and abroad published in their newspapers, magazines, books, and pamphlets in their first ten years, he could arrive at a fair approximation of the truth. I doubt whether any of my observations or conclusions would be materially changed if I had limited myself to documentary sources.

But no one who wishes to know the Communist movement more intimately and deeply can be satisfied with published sources only. At the most critical points, they are completely useless or worse than useless because they may cover up the real sequence of events. They can be read most intelligently if the reader already knows more than they offer to tell him.

When I began this work, I had never seen a copy of a special type of documentary source material in this field—the confidential Minutes of the top committees. By the time I had finished, I had amassed for the period 1919–29 alone about a thousand pages of such Minutes of the Political Committee, Secretariat, and Trade Union Committee of the party, and of the National Committee of the Trade Union Educational League, about four-fifths of them of the all-important Political Committee. These minutes were mimeographed in a limited number of copies and usually stamped "Read and Destroy." Luckily, there is a good fairy that works for historians and, with enough time and patience, turns up the most unlikely and carefully hidden source materials.

These Minutes, though not complete, enabled me to obtain information and gain insights that could be found nowhere else. I do not know of any other historical work on any Communist party that has been based in such large part on these rarest and most highly prized of all Communist documents. In addition, I have been able to utilize other mimeographed and typewritten material, the originals of which were available in Moscow only, such as the stenographic record of the first discussion in Moscow in 1928 on the "right of self-determination of the Negroes in the Black Belt." In this case, one of the participants had brought back with him a carbon copy which he had completely forgotten for thirty years and which he came upon while looking for something else of interest to me.

Even this combination of documentary sources, however, may leave something to be desired. A certain number of incidents and discussions were never put down on paper in any form. Many events lack color and definition unless the formal documents are supplemented by the impressions and interpretations of those who took part in them. For historians of other political parties this vacuum is usually filled by memoirs of the leading figures. In the Communist party, the memoir literature is relatively scarce, and such memoirs as there are usually reveal little after the author has joined the party. The historian of Communism must find a substitute for such memoirs by means of interviews and correspondence. I have spent many hours, and in some cases days, with quite a few of the *dramatis personae* of these pages. I have tried to give them credit for their contributions in the Notes and Acknowledgments.

All these sources have their advantages and shortcomings. In the end, the only safeguard is to work from such a wealth of material that one source may check and correct another. I have also thought that the best way to put the entire subject on a firm footing is to provide the reader with the fullest possible notes. In this way no one need take anything for granted or on trust; it is possible for anyone to know the nature of the evidence and guide himself accordingly. There seems to have been a scholarly prejudice against work in the field of American Communism—as if sound methods of research could not be applied to it. Perhaps this treatment may encourage others by showing that the material is there and it is our task to find it.

1

The New Day

"THE WORLD is on the verge of a new era. Europe is in revolt. The masses of Asia are stirring uneasily. Capitalism is in collapse. The workers of the world are seeing a new life and securing new courage. Out of the night of war is coming a new day." [1] *

Thus began the first Manifesto of the newly formed Communist Party of America in September 1919. Its aspirations, faith, and certainty belonged to a long, inspiring, self-destructive, and ever-renewing tradition of revolutionary idealism. For a brief moment, the founders of American Communism were destiny-intoxicated men, appointed to end misery and oppression, break the chains of war, halt the exploitation of man by man, and create a new social order based on justice, freedom, and equality.

But to become a social force, revolutionary idealism must be transmuted into an ideological doctrine and an organized movement. The leap from the ideal to the doctrine, and from the doctrine to the movement, has been too much for all the great revolutionary doctrines and movements of the last century—socialism, syndicalism, anarchism, and communism. All have passed through a cycle of exaltation and disenchantment. All came as fresh, liberating visions; all became stale, imprisoning dogmas. Somewhere between the revolutionary ideal and the social force, a miscarriage took place.

This is the study primarily of a movement, less of a doctrine, and

* Numbered reference notes begin on page 445.

least of all of an ideal. Ideals can often bring people into—and take them out of—revolutionary movements, but ideals play little part in the day-by-day organizational drudgeries, political maneuvers, and struggles for power. Yet the eternally frustrated pursuit of the ideal gives revolutionary movements a special dimension and peculiar fascination for their devotees, as well as for some outsiders. Without it, much that is tragic would merely be sordid.

But no one can study the Communist movement without getting enmeshed in doctrinal problems and disputes. The early Communists grew out of the Marxian Socialist movement, and their pre-Communist period was largely spent struggling over the true interpretation of the Marxian doctrine. In the dark years before the seizure of power in Russia, only the promise of the doctrine gave them the strength and hope to carry on in the face of seemingly hopeless odds. After the seizure of power, the doctrine gave them a "principle of legitimacy" without which their dictatorship would have rested on nothing more than brute force. Other systems legitimatize themselves by reason of historical continuity or democratic sanction. Of necessity, the Communist movement validates itself by means of its own doctrine. It posits communism as the path of an inevitable historical process which objectively serves the interests of the workers and ultimately all mankind. The reasoning is elliptical: Communism gives the Communists the right to impose their rule on the masses.

In theory, Marx, Engels, and Lenin provided their disciples with guides to action; in practice, they provided them with too many guides to too much action. They wrote over long periods for many different situations at various stages of their development. For three-quarters of a century, they handed down a vast stock of apt quotations for any conceivable policy, prowar and antiwar, sectarian and opportunist, dictatorial and democratic. In some areas they left an embarrassment of riches and in others an embarrassing void. Like all scriptures, their writings have needed interpretation and application to "changed conditions" and different "objective circumstances." The same words could not mean or imply the same things in places and times as far apart as the Great Britain of the middle nineteenth century with which Marx and Engels were primarily concerned, the Russia after the turn of the century which Lenin had chiefly in mind, and the United States in the third decade of the twentieth century in which American Communism was formed.

Thus the Communist movement has been massively built on shifting sands of doctrine. It is filled with uneasy tensions within the doctrine, and between the doctrine and the reality. In no other country have these tensions been as great as in the United States. According to the doctrine, the revolution should have come first in a capitalist state with an advanced industrial system and a large, organized proletariat. The United States most nearly conformed to these classical specifications. According to the reality, however, in the United States capitalism was most dynamic, the class structure most fluid, and the proletariat least class-conscious. In large part, therefore, the story of American Communism has been one of struggle between doctrine and reality. This struggle has taken many forms with varying degrees of success. But even the greatest success of American Communism has been tainted by the fact that it has succeeded in coming closest to the reality by departing furthest from the doctrine.

As a result, American Communism has been torn between the conflicting demands of political orthodoxy and mass influence. In the ideal Communist world, piety and power would always go together. But in the United States, where the Communists must compete in the open political market, they have most often obtained power at the price of piety and piety at the price of power. Political orthodoxy, however it may be defined at the moment, has invariably condemned them to sectarianism, isolation, and impotence. Opportunism has invariably paid off in increased membership, sympathizers, and influence. The pendulum has regularly swung from sectarianism to opportunism and back again in an effort to correct the imbalance between political orthodoxy and mass influence. But this imbalance has never been corrected; it has merely been shifted from one extreme to the other.

Other revolutionary movements in the United States had faced similar problems. But one other factor has been uniquely Communist and has made the Communist movement unique. Only the Communists have belonged to a centralized, disciplined international organization. The Socialists, anarchists, and syndicalists had considered themselves integral parts of international movements, but their organizational ties were purely nominal. No American Socialist, anarchist, or syndicalist had ever imagined that decisions could be made for him in Berlin, London, or Paris. With the American Communists, for the first time, the questions arise: Who makes the fundamental decisions? What final authority interprets the Communist doctrine and applies it to the American reality? What supreme power determines the permissible limits of political orthodoxy and mass influence?

The answers to these questions cannot be found solely or even primarily in the American Communist party. We must search for them in the interrelation between the American Communist party and the Communist International, and in the interrelation between the Communist International and the Russian Communist party. We must study an American movement whose seat of power was not located in the United States. No other American political movement presents such complex and difficult problems of decision-making and organizational control. We might well go abroad in search of the intellectual influences that helped to shape other American political movements, but we would hardly ever leave the country to account for their continuous development and day-by-day operations. In the case of the Communist movement, however, we must constantly go far afield in order to understand what was happening at home. We must regularly shuttle back and forth between New York or Chicago and Moscow. We must always know what was simultaneously occurring in the Communist International and the Russian Communist party. The route may sometimes seem long and circuitous, but if we refuse to be content with half the story, and the more superficial half at that, there is no other way.

Doctrine and reality, political orthodoxy and mass influence, inner development and outer control—the entire history of American Communism has consisted of variations on these themes. They can be recognized at the inception of the movement. They ring out firmly and clearly at every crisis. They run through and bind together the complex and far-flung jumble of tactics and events.

Doctrine and reality

The first fledgling doctrine of American Communism derived in the main from two revolutionary traditions—socialism and syndicalism. They were represented organizationally by the Socialist Labor party, formed in 1877, the Socialist party, formed in 1901, and the Industrial Workers of the World (I.W.W.), formed in 1905. For half a century, the radicals and revolutionists in these organizations had fought and split over a series of interlocking issues—political or economic action; the "pure and simple" trade-unionism of the American Federation of Labor or the revolutionary "dual unionism" of the I.W.W.; violent overthrow of capitalism or peaceful gradualism; orthodox Marxism or "revisionism"; emphasis on immediate demands or on the ultimate goal; class struggle or class collaboration; proletarian revolution or middle-class reformism. The traditional Left Wing by and large regarded political action, or "parliamentarism," with contempt; it extolled the "direct action" of economic struggle. It despised the American Federation of Labor and glorified the I.W.W. It entertained grave doubts about the ultimate efficacy of peaceful methods and did not shrink from contemplating violent ones if necessary. It identified itself with orthodox Marxism, the ultimate goal, class struggle, and proletarian revolution. To be sure, the Left and Right Wings cannot be neatly sealed off from each other. Some of the most violent strikes of the late nineteenth and early twentieth centuries were waged by A.F. of L. unions. The Socialist Labor party leader, Daniel De Leon, included peaceful political methods and trade-union dualism in his system.[2]

The early Communists inherited most of these traditional Left-Wing preconceptions. They considered the class struggle a political struggle in the sense that it aimed at the conquest of political power. But they approved of political or parliamentary activity only for the purpose of propaganda, and regarded the industrial forms of "mass action," especially mass strikes and demonstrations, as far more important. They wrote off the A.F. of L. as a "bulwark of capitalism" and heartily endorsed the "revolutionary industrial unionism" of the I.W.W. The early Communist infatuation with force and violence was sometimes implied in the term "mass action," sometimes openly expressed in terms of "armed insurrection and civil war." They contemptuously spurned immediate demands, Marxist "revisionism," class collaboration, middle-class reformism.[3]

But the first American Communists also inherited important influences from other revolutionary traditions. One influence came from the Dutch Left Wing, which was represented personally in the United States from 1915 to 1918 by a politically minded engineer, S. J. Rutgers. It was from the Dutch that the Americans borrowed the vague and elastic term "mass action," which for some years, before the Russian influence became paramount, served them as the key to all the mysteries of revolutionary thought and action. Another influence came from the Lettish (or Latvian) immigrant movement, the stronghold of the Left Wing in the Socialist party of Massachusetts. The Lettish Socialist federation was most instrumental in setting up the first Left Wing organization generally regarded in the direct line of American Communist ancestry, the Socialist Propaganda League, founded in Boston in October 1915. A third influence, even in advance of the Bolshevik revolution, emanated from a number of Russian émigrés who came to the United States during the First World War, the most notable of whom were Madame Alexandra Kollontay, Nikolai Bukharin, and Leon Trotsky. Rutgers, the Letts, and the Russians, as well as other Left Wing émigrés, such as the Japanese Sen Katayama and the Irish James J. Larkin, worked together closely and their influence far exceeded their numbers.[4]

The Bolshevik revolution in Russia of November 1917 did not immediately displace these older traditions. The incipient American Communists did not at first recognize the novel features of the Bolshevik revolution and the Leninist ideology. In the beginning they saw them in their own image, and embraced them as the embodiment of their own previous ideas. The American Communist leader, Charles E. Ruthenberg, explained Bolshevism early in 1919 not as something "strange and new," but as the consequence of the same type of education and organization that the Socialist movement had been and was carrying on in the United States. The Socialist-syndicalist background of his thought crept into his description of the Bolshevik state as a "Socialist industrial republic." [5]

This conglomeration of influences went into American Communism at its inception partially as a result of the peculiar flair of its first outstanding ideological propagandist, Louis C. Fraina, for soaking up ideas from different sources. Self-taught, doctrinaire, precocious, Fraina typified the fanatically dedicated young Left Wing intellectual. First a disciple of Daniel De Leon in the Socialist Labor party, he took over the Dutch Left Wing mystique of "mass action" and embraced the cause of the Russian Bolsheviks early in 1917, even before their seizure of power. As long as the development of the Left Wing was primarily propagandistic in nature, his key roles in the literary organs of the Left Wing gave him a position of primacy. In 1914 the influential *New Review* took him on its board of editors—in such distinguished company as Max Eastman, Floyd Dell, and Walter Lippmann—and he had come to dominate the paper and to swing it to the extreme Left by the time it suspended publication in the summer of 1916. The following year, Fraina edited the two new organs of the Left Wing—*The New International* by himself and *The Class Struggle* with Louis B. Boudin and Ludwig Lore. He went on to edit *The Revolutionary Age* in 1918–19, the first collection in English of the writings of Lenin and Trotsky in 1918, and the first issues of the official Communist organ, *The Communist,* in 1919. He wrote most of the early manifestoes and programs, which clearly bore the marks of his personal intellectual development—from the "industrial government of the working class" to "mass action" to "the dictatorship of the proletariat." And after ten years of revolutionary activity he was in 1919 only twenty-five years old.[6]

Postwar Europe influenced the pre-Communist American Left Wing in another, more pervasive way. The revolutionary wave that swept over Europe between 1917 and 1919 seemed to portend the long-awaited world revolution. After the Russian revolution of 1917 came the Hungarian, Austrian, and Bulgarian revolutions of 1918. At the war's end, German Kaiserdom toppled, and for a time a revolutionary socialist regime seemed more likely than a bourgeois republic to replace it. Abortive Soviet regimes arose in Hungary, Finland, and Bavaria in 1919. "New Soviet governments will arise as the months go by and it will not be long until the eastern [western] boundary of Soviet Europe is the Rhine," Ruthenberg wrote in the spring of 1919. "Can capitalism stop the Soviet movement there? It is not likely. The Soviet movement will sweep forward and onward until the Soviet Republic of the World comes into being." [7]

At home, a token of the same unrest appeared to justify the most extravagant revolutionary expectations. The Seattle general strike, the Lawrence textile strike, the Butte mine walk-out, the Boston police strike, the national coal strike, the great steel strike, and lesser labor disputes involved more workers in 1919 than the total number involved during the next six years. In Butte, Montana, and Portland, Oregon, short-lived "Councils" or "Soviets" of "workers, soldiers, and sailors" scared the wits out of local guardians of law and order. A recent historian of this period has written: "By the autumn of 1919 millions of Americans had come to believe that the country was faced by the menace of revolution, although genuine revolutionaries constituted almost no threat of any kind and the great strikes were for the most part expressions of legitimate grievances." [8]

Nevertheless, the newly converted American Communists stopped short of believing that conditions in the United States in 1919 contained the stuff of immediate revolution. The industrial unrest that year had been set off by the soaring cost of living in a booming economy, not by a mass revolt against an exhausted and demoralized system. The Manifesto of the Communist party in 1919 recognized that the war had strengthened American capitalism, whereas it had weakened European capitalism, but confidently predicted that the collapse of capitalism in other countries "will play upon and affect events in this country." From this basic premise, it went on to characterize the prospect in the United States: "While this is not the moment of actual revolution, it is a moment of struggles pregnant with revolution." [9] The "psychological attitude of 1919" was ruefully recalled by Ruthenberg: "The proletarian world revolution had begun. The workers were on the march. The Revolution would sweep on. In a few years—two, three, perhaps five—the workers of the United States would be marching step by step with the revolutionary workers of Europe." [10]

Thus, from the outset, the tension between doctrine and reality in the American Communist movement was expressed in terms of two kinds of realities—the European, which came closest to fulfilling the doctrine, and the American, which lagged furthest behind. The early Communists worked out an American revolutionary perspective by hitching it to a European revolutionary perspective. They saw the American revolution through European lenses because they devoutly believed that the collapse of American capitalism was only a few steps behind the collapse of European capitalism.

This was one way of getting around the problem of a revolutionary movement in a country exceptionally unripe for revolution. Yet if revolution depended on an end to the development of the productive forces, as Marx believed,[11] the United States was further from revolution than any country in history. If revolution depended on the unwillingness of tens of millions of people to live in the old way any longer, as Lenin claimed,[12] the United States was ripe for many forms and degrees of discontent, but they were less directed at overthrowing the existing order than at squeezing more out of it individually. At bottom, this deviation between reality and doctrine has compelled American Communism to resort to revolutionary fantasies or to nonrevolutionary pretenses.

Orthodoxy and influence

Mass influence triumphed in its first encounter with political orthodoxy, but not for long. The opening skirmish took place during the very birth of an American Communist party. In June 1919, the foremost Left Wing leaders came together for the first time at a national conference in New York City to consider ways and means of forming a Communist party. For three days, the ninety-four delegates from twenty states hotly debated the question: Should they form an American Communist party immediately, or should they wait for the outcome of the Socialist party's convention in Chicago only ten weeks later? The delegates who most flaunted their Bolshevik orthodoxy demanded immediate action. Those more interested in mass influence held out for delay in order to capture the Socialist party, which had shot up from about 80,000 members in 1917 to almost 110,000 in 1919. This gain was largely due to a sudden influx, inspired by the Bolshevik revolution, into the party's "foreign-language federations," particularly the Slavic ones. In May 1919 seven of these semiautonomous federations—the Russian, Lithuanian, Ukrainian, Polish, Hungarian, South Slavic, and Lettish—had been expelled by the Socialist party's Right-Wing-controlled National Executive Committee, and this action had precipitated the calling of the National Left Wing Conference. At the conference, however, the foreign-language leaders, who pressed for immediate action, were outvoted by the English-speaking delegates, who favored delay. The minority retaliated by staging a walk-out and issuing a call for a national convention in Chicago at the beginning of September to set up a Communist party. The majority elected a National Council to pursue the policy of capturing the Socialist party.

The issues in this split, the prototype of all future Communist splits, were posed in such a way that the predominantly foreign-language group represented extreme political orthodoxy and the English-speaking majority the broadest mass influence. The Russian federation's spokesman, Alexander Stoklitsky, declared contemptuously: "The builders of the Communist Party dare not run after masses whose hearts must be softened by the injustice of the N.E.C. We do not care for a Communist Party minus communist principles." [13] To this thrust, the Americans had no conscience-satisfying answer, owing to their still superficial, naïve belief that the Russian Bolsheviks had never sacrificed principles to power and that the smaller the revolutionary party, the purer its revolutionary doctrine and spirit.

Five weeks after the Left Wing conference, therefore, the majority of the English-speaking National Council, including Ruthenberg and Fraina, changed sides. The taunt of opportunism, fear of isolation from the foreign-language federations, and the sky-rocketing prestige of the Russian federation's leaders induced them to capitulate. A minority of the National Council, headed by John Reed and Benjamin Gitlow, refused to back down. They intensely resented the bullying methods of the Russian federation's leaders and remained loyal to the old line of first going to the Socialist convention. Fortuitously, these "Americans" were ranged against the "Russians"—not the Russians in Russia, but the Russians in America who owed their temporary accession of power and glory to the Russians in Russia who had made everything Russian seem powerful and glorious to the success-starved American Left Wing.

These prenatal splits explain why the American Communist movement was divided at birth into two rival parties, the Communist party of America and the Communist Labor party of America, both organized in Chicago in the first days of September 1919. The C.P., with Ruthenberg as National Secretary and Fraina as International Secretary and Editor, included the bulk of the foreign-language federations. The C.L.P., with Alfred Wagenknecht as Executive Secretary and John Reed as one of the International Delegates, contained more native-born American radicals.

Of the future Communist leaders, Charles E. Ruthenberg, Alexander Bittelman, Jay Lovestone, Bertram D. Wolfe, William W. Weinstone, Juliet Stuart Poyntz, and others started their Communist careers in the C.P.; Benjamin Gitlow, Arne Swabeck, Max Bedacht, William F. Dunne, James P. Cannon, Ella Reeve Bloor, and others began in the C.L.P. The C.P. claimed 58,000 members for itself and admitted only about 10,000 for the C.L.P., but the maximum figure for those who signed up in both parties after the founding conventions was probably closer to 40,000, with the C.P. two or three times as large as the C.L.P. In the C.P. at its inception, East Europeans made up over 75 per cent of the total membership, the Russians alone almost 25 per cent, and English-speaking members only 4 per cent. Yet the C.L.P. brought the native-born or English-speaking quota of both parties up to no more than 10 per cent.

In the beginning, American Communism was not very different in its methods and make-up from other American radical movements. The first conventions were wide open, the discussions free, the leaders democratically chosen. The organizational model was taken over from the parent Socialist party. Except for references to "Soviets" and "dictatorship of the proletariat," its programs still reflected more of the movements of the past—socialism and syndicalism—than of the movement of the future, communism. One can only speculate on what might have happened if American Communism had been permitted to develop by itself. In the nature of world communism, it could not much longer have remained isolated from the Communist International, or, as it was familiarly called, the Comintern, which had been founded in March 1919, six months earlier than the two American Communist parties. But the American government first interfered with the free development of the American Communist movement, and thereby forced it in its first months to depart from the traditionally open operation of American radical movements.

The so-called Palmer raids of January 1920 inaugurated a new phase in the Communist tug-of-war between orthodoxy and influence. The anti-Communist drive culminated two years of official persecution of the entire radical movement. Homes, headquarters, and meetings were broken into, thousands of arrests were made, and aliens were deported en masse. In the end, few Communists actually served prison sentences, the chief victims being Ruthenberg, Gitlow, and three others in New York, and Ludwig E. Katterfeld in Chicago. The raids immediately drove both Communist parties underground. They adopted conspiratorial methods, and their memberships melted away. By 1920 the two parties were reduced to no more than 10,000 members altogether, and even this figure was cut almost in half in the next two years. With underground conditions came an underground mentality. More than ever, American Communists could identify themselves with Russian Bolshevism, which had been nurtured in Czarist conditions of illegality and conspiracy. The romantics and illusionists made a necessity into a virtue by telling themselves that illegality was the natural habitat of a real revolutionary movement. The next three years, 1920–22, may be called the dark age of American Communism, during which it seemed to leap from a promising beginning to premature senility. The shock of official persecution, the isolation of the underground, and the demoralizing inner life of the faction-ridden movement combined to make its survival questionable.

A succession of splits paralyzed the underground Communist movement, but essentially they were always the same split. In April 1920, a minority group led by Ruthenberg demanded unity with the C.L.P., belatedly rebelled against the foreign-language domination, and bolted from the C.P. A leaflet to railway strikers helped to cause this break. The foreign-language majority insisted on calling for armed insurrection. Ruthenberg's group protested that, much as it also believed in "open insurrection and armed conflict" in the party's program, it did not consider them appropriate in a leaflet to striking railwaymen. *"They will compromise principles and tactics in order to get 'contact with the masses,' "* the anti-Ruthenberg extremists thundered back.[14]

Toward the end of May 1920, Ruthenberg's group joined with the C.L.P. to form a new United Communist party. A year later, in May 1921, this split was temporarily healed by a merger of the U.C.P. and the original C.P. into another Communist Party of America. Toward the end of 1921, the Communists also benefited from two windfalls—the adhesion of William Z. Foster's small group of Chicago trade-unionists, organized in the Trade Union Educational League (T.U.E.L.) and the merger with a larger group of Socialist officials and propagandists—among them J. Louis Engdahl, Alexander Trachtenberg, and Moissaye J. Olgin—previously organized as the "Workers' Council."

The Communist Party of America maintained a semblance of unity for only a few months. This time the issue of orthodoxy or influence took the form of the question—to have or not to have a "legal party"? So deeply ingrained was the underground mentality that no official Communist openly proposed giving up the existing illegal party. The problem was whether to have both an illegal and a legal party, with the former in control of the latter, or to maintain only a simon-pure illegal party. The split materialized as a result of a decision by the dominant Communist leadership to go ahead with the organization of an open, legal party. A half-hearted effort, called the American Labor Alliance, was made in July 1921. It was replaced by a broader, more successful organization, the Workers Party of America, in December 1921, with James P. Cannon as Chairman and Caleb Harrison, soon replaced by Charles E. Ruthenberg, as National Secretary.[15] Into it came the Workers' Council and a second large contingent from the Socialist party's foreign-language federations, including the largest, the Finnish, and one of the most active, the Jewish. Unlike the underground Communist party, the Workers party's program made no mention of Soviets, the dictatorship of the proletariat, or armed insurrection. Its statement of purpose was calculated to attract the greatest possible number of radicals: "to educate and organize the working class for the abolition of capitalism through the establishment of the Workers' Republic." After the Workers party was set up, a Left Opposition of the underground Communist party broke away in January 1922 in protest against the Workers party's watered-down program. This opposition also called itself the Communist party of America and, to add to the confusion, set up its own "legal apparatus," the United Toilers of America, the following month. The official organ of the United Toilers, *Workers' Challenge,* was edited by Harry M. Wicks.

Nor was this the last split. Within the Communist-Workers party combination, another serious rift opened. After his release from prison in the spring of 1922, Ruthenberg took over the post of secretary of the Workers party. He saw no further reason for the existence of the underground Communist party, which merely served the function of controlling the Workers party, already wholly controlled by Communists. This dispute whipped up one of the more celebrated of the early factional storms—the struggle between the "Geese" and the "Liquidators." * The former rose to defend the honor and protect the existence of the original underground party, the latter to substitute the above-ground Workers party for the underground Communist party. In effect, the American Communist movement of 1922 was rent into three factions and two parties.

These splits, the last of the formative period, were patched up in practice by the end of 1922 but continued formally until the spring of 1923. The official abdication of the underground took place at the third convention of the illegal Communist party of America in New York on April 7, 1923. It went through the motions of dissolving itself in favor of the legal Workers party which then functioned as the American Communist party in everything but name.

Thus political orthodoxy and mass influence had fought four major battles in as many years—over the premature split in the Socialist party in 1919, the unification of the first two Communist parties in 1920, the monopoly of the illegal party in 1921, and the substitution of the legal for the illegal party in 1922. The battles had seesawed, now favoring one tendency, now the other. Yet it would be a mistake to think of the sectarians and opportunists as truly irreconcilable enemies. They were, in fact, symptomatic of the dualism in communism, of its peculiar combination of rigidity and flexibility, each of which accounts for some of its strength and some of its weakness. In individual Communists, as in the movement as a whole, the two tendencies struggle for supremacy. The same leader may represent sectarianism in one period and opportunism in another. Two seemingly incompatible factions may call off their feud and fall into line as soon as a higher authority has decided the issue between them,

* The "Geese" harked back to Roman history. The story goes that one of this faction's leaders, Abram Jakira, was accused by William F. Dunne of cackling like a goose, whereupon Jakira's fellow-factionalist, Israel Amter, recalled that geese had saved Rome and they would yet save the American Communist party. Lovestone allegedly shouted: "All right, then; from now on you're the Goose Caucus."

The "Liquidators" went back to post-1905 Russian history. It was Lenin's favorite epithet for the Mensheviks who advocated a broad Russian Labor party, a step which he claimed implied an end to the independent existence of the Russian Social Democratic Workers party.

only to change places on another issue at a later date. Though it is often hard to distinguish where political differences end and purely factional struggles for power begin, the Communist movement is so constituted that a struggle for power must take the form of a political difference, and that difference is invariably posed in terms of sectarianism versus opportunism, Left versus Right. If there were no political differences, they would have to be invented, and indeed have been.

Development and control

The case of John Reed strikingly illustrates the Russian genesis of American Communism. Politically, his role was brief and superficial; symbolically, its significance was deep and lasting. Upper-class, Portland-born, Harvard-educated, he came home in the spring of 1918 after six months in Russia, the first American radical eyewitness of the Bolshevik revolution. The Russian experience turned Reed from an anarchist sympathizer into a fervent Communist, and he propagated the new faith in lectures, articles, and his best-known book, *Ten Days That Shook the World.* He owed his Communist faith to a Russian experience which he attempted to reproduce in the United States. He was not the only one. Robert Minor, a famous radical cartoonist and another anarchist sympathizer, and William Z. Foster, an equally famous radical trade-unionist and ex-syndicalist, also came to communism, by somewhat different paths, after direct contact with Soviet Russia.

The other early American Communists went through a similar experience, but vicariously. Ruthenberg did not go to Russia to become a Communist, but he testified: "It was the Russian Revolution—the Bolshevik Revolution of November 7, 1917—which created the American Communist Movement"; and he also declared: "Without the Russian Revolution there would have been no Communist Movement in the United States." [16] As late as 1923, James P. Cannon, who did not become a Communist in Russia either, put it: "The Russian

Revolution is going forward to victory in America as in every other country." [17]

Although American Communism owed its very existence to Soviet Russia and the Russian revolution, for over a year the immediate influence of Soviet Russia on American Communism was minimal. The instrumentality of this influence, the Comintern, was not fully organized until its Second Congress in the summer of 1920. This congress adopted the Statutes and Twenty-One Points of admission which gave the Comintern its permanently monolithic character; they empowered the Comintern to issue binding "instructions" and to send its representatives to affiliated parties. A resolution passed at the second convention of the Communist Party of America in 1920 showed how intimately the individual parties, the Comintern, and Soviet Russia were viewed together: "The Communist Parties of the various countries are the direct representatives of the Communist International, and thus indirectly of the aims and policies of Soviet Russia." [18]

The Second Congress of the Comintern issued an ultimatum to force the unification of the American Communist and United Communist parties. When this did not help, the Comintern, in the spring of 1921, sent a delegation to the United States, consisting of Charles E. Scott (the party name of Carl Jansen or Charles Johnson, a Lettish Communist, formerly of Roxbury, Massachusetts), Louis C. Fraina, one of the American delegates to the Second Congress, and Sen Katayama, the Japanese exile who had become a Comintern official. This delegation brought the warring parties together into the Communist party of America in May 1921.

The Second Congress also initiated a far-reaching change of policy in the American party. It instructed the American Communists to work in the A.F. of L. instead of seeking to destroy it. The full impact of this change of line hit the American Communists with the publication of Lenin's little book, *"Left-Wing" Communism: An Infantile Disorder,* written in the spring of 1920 but not available in an American translation until the beginning of 1921. This textbook of

Leninist tactics was the product of his recognition that the world Communist movement had failed to win over the masses of Western Europe and America and could do so only by adopting more flexible methods. He declared war on the "ultra-Left" for refusal to see the necessity of "compromise" and "manoeuvre," for resistance to participation in "bourgeois parliaments," and for opposition to working in "reactionary trade unions." The Comintern's instructions and Lenin's influential booklet led the Communist party of America in May 1921 to write into its program for the first time a formal disavowal of the dual-union, antipolitical American Left Wing tradition.

The Comintern again resorted to strong-arm measures to unify the rival American Communist parties in 1922. It sent a second delegation to the United States, headed by a Pole, H. Valetski (or Walecki), as plenipotentiary representative, a Hungarian, Joseph Pogany, and a former Socialist Labor party member from Buffalo who had returned to Russia in 1917, Boris Reinstein. These three attended and escaped from the underground convention near Bridgman, Michigan, in August 1922, which was betrayed by one of the delegates, a special agent of the Department of Justice, and raided by government agents. Valetski soon succeeded in breaking the last resistance to unity. He intimidated a convention of the Communist–United Toilers opposition in September 1922 into unconditionally accepting his terms. The problem of the legal party versus the underground was settled at the Comintern's Fourth Congress in November 1922. Two of the Liquidators, Cannon and Bedacht, after an interview with Trotsky, persuaded the Russians to throw their weight behind the full legalization of the American Communist movement. In written instructions, the Comintern ordered the illegal and legal American parties to merge as soon as possible, and these orders were carried out in full by the spring of 1923.

By this time, the party's rank and file and leadership had changed. The first figures of the Workers party in March–June 1922, before unification, had given it a total membership of only 8339. After unification the following year, the number had doubled. The Russian proportion had dropped to about 7 per cent because so many

Russians had been deported to their homeland or had given up their membership; the Finns now accounted for almost 45 per cent; the English-speaking share still hovered at around 5 per cent, with another 45 per cent capable of using English as a second language. Of the early leaders, John Reed had died of typhus in Russia in the fall of 1920, the first important American victim of disillusionment with Communism, short of an organizational break. After a series of bizarre mishaps and misfortunes, Louis C. Fraina had dropped out of sight in the fall of 1922, to return to public life years later under another name, Lewis Corey.

Afterward, Ruthenberg gave the Comintern credit for the unity, as he had given the Bolshevik revolution credit for the existence, of the American Communist movement:

> In the bitter factional struggles which tore asunder the Communists [*sic*] organizations during 1920 and 1921, it was the Communist International which appeared as the unifying influence. It was the demand and influence of the Communist International which unified the United Communist Party and the Communist Party in 1921. It was the representative of the Communist International who in 1922 led back into the Party the opposition which split away in the struggle over the founding of the open party.

And he concluded:

> Had there been no Communist International, no deciding and directing body with authority to pass upon question[s] of principles and tactics for the revolutionary workers in the United States and to direct their movement into the right channels, the factional struggle might well have resulted otherwise than it did. It is not an exaggeration to say that if there is today in the United States one party—the Workers Party—in which all the Communist groups are united, it is because of the persistent effort and tactful guidance of the International.[19]

Moscow's domination was bitter medicine for some of the stronger European parties; it was soothing syrup for the weak American party. The Americans virtually begged for dictation from Moscow as a means of solving internal problems which they could not solve alone; they were genuinely grateful to the Russians in the Comintern for forcing unification and legalization upon them. For American Communism, then, there was no Chinese wall between inner development and outer control; one led gradually to the other by a process of which we are only at the beginning. The American Communist movement did represent a "new day" in the history of American radicalism, but not in the sense that its founders had foreseen or intended.

2

The Farmer-Labor United Front

WHILE the American Communists were caged in the underground, the American scene did not remain the same.

The boom of 1919 gave way to the depression of 1920–22. Prices tumbled, wages sank, bankruptcies multiplied. More than a third of those employed in construction and coal mining and over a fifth of those in manufacturing and transportation were thrown out of work. The farmers in the corn, wheat, and cotton belts suffered most. Farm prices in 1921 plunged to one-third of what they had been in 1920. Hard times gripped the country under the Republican administration of Warren Gamaliel Harding, elected in 1920 as the guarantor of "normalcy."

Moreover, the Communist movement was not the only expression of postwar radicalism in the United States. The Farmer-Labor movement, which arose at the same time, was also partially inspired from abroad, in this case by the postwar Reconstruction Program of the British Labour party, which had favored a "new social order." A machinists' strike in Bridgeport developed into a "labor party" in five Connecticut towns in the summer of 1918. President John Fitzpatrick and Secretary Edward N. Nockels of the Chicago Federation of Labor adopted the cause of a labor party in November of that year. An American Labor Party of Greater New York was organized by local unions in January 1919. Similar movements were set in motion in Pennsylvania, North Dakota, Minnesota, Ohio, and other states. These local groups came together in November 1919 in Chicago to organize a national Labor Party of the United States, which, to attract farm support, changed its name to Farmer-Labor party the following July. In the presidential election of 1920, Parley Parker Christensen, a radical lawyer from Utah, received about a quarter of a million votes on the Farmer-Labor ticket, most of them in Washington, Illinois, and South Dakota.

In its first stages, the Farmer-Labor movement was a child of the local trade unions. Its main strength was concentrated in the West. It was loosely socialistic in general tendency, though it owed more to agrarian Populism than to Marxian socialism. The Chicago-based Labor party of 1919 demanded the nationalization of all public utilities, basic industries, natural resources, and banking and credit systems, as well as workers' participation in the management of industry. It went its own way, largely outside the established radical and trade-union paths. In this formative period, it contended with the hostility of the Communists, who still opposed anything but Russian-style revolution, the lukewarm sympathy of the Socialists, who considered it premature, and the antagonism of the A.F. of L.'s national leaders, who felt that it endangered their traditionally "non-partisan" political policy.

Against such opposition, the Farmer-Labor party appeared helpless. But just as it showed signs of early exhaustion, it rallied as a result of a belated burst of interest from an unexpected quarter—the railway unions. Half a million railway workers were summoned to strike against wage cuts, despite the most sweeping injunction ever issued in a labor dispute. Inasmuch as the government and courts were deeply implicated in the railway crisis, the unions were driven into a mood for political as well as economic action. Led by William H. Johnston, a former Socialist, then head of the International Association of Machinists, the sixteen railway unions began to flirt with the idea of forming a new political party to the Left of the two old parties. They took the first step by calling a Conference for Progressive Political Action in Chicago in February 1922, four months before the railway strike. The Farmer-Labor party, the Socialist party, and other groups, including the largest farmers' organizations, participated. The conference went on record to organize state and local groups to elect candidates pledged to the principles of "genuine democracy" in agriculture, industry, and government.[1]

The Communists were not represented at this conference. Not only were they not invited, but they were not yet ready to accept such an invitation if it had been offered to them. The first program of the Communist party in September 1919 had dismissed the Labor party as "a minor phase of proletarian unrest" which the trade unions had organized in order "to conserve what they have secured as a privileged caste." It concluded severely: "There can be no compromise either with Laborism or reactionary Socialism." [2] The Communist Labor party refused to "associate" with any other groups "not committed to the revolutionary class struggle." [3] Preoccupied with their own problems of unity and legalization in 1920–21, the underground Communists paid relatively little attention to the Farmer-Labor movement. They disdainfully regarded it as a watered-down, trade-union-sponsored version of reformism, and if the reform Socialists were bad, the Farmer-Laborites were worse.[4]

It is most unlikely that the American Communists, left to themselves, would have changed their attitude toward the Farmer-Labor movement when they did—if ever. But they were not left to themselves.

Lenin's advice

The first hint of the coming change did not ostensibly concern the American Communists at all. In the summer of 1920, Lenin was asked whether the British Communist party, then in process of formation, should affiliate with the British Labour party. Most of the early British Communists had denounced the Labour party for so long that they suffered anguish at the idea of joining it. To their surprise, Lenin strongly advised them to do so, on condition that they would be permitted to carry on "free and independent Communist activity." [5] The entire question was hotly debated at the Comintern's Second Congress in 1920, at which Lenin's views of course prevailed.

During the Second Congress, Lenin brought up the subject of a Labor party for the United States in an interview with Louis C. Fraina. The latter argued against it, in line with the prevailing American Communist point of view, and Lenin did not insist.[6] The Americans were hotly criticized at the Second Congress for their anti-A.F.-of-L. trade-union policy but not for their anti-Labor-party policy. It was not clear, moreover, whether what Lenin had said about the British Labour party applied to the situation in the United States. He had emphasized that the loose organization of the British Labour party was "very peculiar," with the implication that the same tactics might not be possible elsewhere.[7] In any case, the American Communists did not see or want to see any analogy between Lenin's advice to the British Communists and their own circumstances, and the fact that Lenin had discussed the matter with Fraina was not even known to the other American leaders.

At the Comintern's Third Congress in 1921, however, Lenin again took the initiative. In a conference with the entire American delegation he raised the question of whether the formation of a Labor party would not facilitate the work of the American Communists. The delegates took his advice to heart and brought back the news of his interest in a Labor party, but nothing was done about it immediately.[8] Toward the end of 1921, Parley Parker Christensen, the recent Farmer-Labor candidate for president, obtained two interviews with Lenin in Moscow during a world tour, and probably gave him a glowing account of the Farmer-Labor movement's prospects.[9]

Later, one of the most prominent American Communists, Alexander Bittelman, admitted that Lenin's advice to the British Communists had been the starting point of the American change of line:

> And only after the party became more intimately familiar with the United Front tactics of the Communist International, and particularly, with Lenin's advice to the British Communists, to fight for admission into the Labor Party, did the C.E.C. [Central Executive Committee] finally feel justified in adopting a complete thesis which committed the party to a labor-party policy.[10]

The concept of the united front derived from another of Lenin's suggestions to the British Communists: he urged them to wage a campaign for an electoral agreement with the leadership of the British Labour party. He based this recommendation on the weakness of the British Communists and the strength of the Labour party. His purpose, as he disclosed with disarming candor, was not designed to strengthen the Labour leadership. On the contrary, he declared that he wanted to "support" them "in the same way as a rope supports one who is hanged." [11] He reasoned that, if the Labour leaders accepted the Communist offer, they would open up the Labour party to Communist propaganda, and if they rejected it, they could be exposed as enemies of working-class unity. In effect, he hoped to achieve by the *offer* of support what he could not achieve by outright attack. Since the Labourites were hardly likely to cooperate in their own destruction, the Communists expected to gain more by agitating for the agreement than by achieving it.

When Lenin first planted this seed of the united front, he had in mind only one of the weakest Communist parties, the British. Eastern Europe was still viewed with revolutionary optimism. The Red Army had marched on Warsaw in the summer of 1920 and sought to take over Poland without benefit of any semblance of the united front. But when this attack failed, and even more so when the German Communist rising in March 1921 collapsed, the Comintern's leadership began to take a greater interest in Lenin's advice to the British Communists.

It now appeared that the entire European Communist movement was much further from power than the Russians had once imagined. Thus the British seed sprouted into a long-range, world-wide "strategic maneuver," as Zinoviev called it—the united front.[12]

The decline of the postwar revolutionary wave, the increasing recovery of European capitalism, and the internal crises suffered by the inexperienced, jerry-built Communist parties outside Russia made the new line necessary. These parties had been formed mainly by splitting the old Social-Democratic and syndicalist movements. The splits had been justified on the ground that only the revolutionary elements unencumbered by reformists and compromisers could make the imminent revolution. As the prospect of the Western revolution faded, the splitting tactics backfired on the Communists who found themselves thrown on the defensive for disrupting the existing working-class organizations. The united front was one of those abrupt Communist about-faces which constitute an admission of error and guilt but are made in such a way as to enable the Communists to benefit the most from their own confession. In this case, the Communists sought, not without success, to transfer the onus of splitting to the parties and organizations the Communists had been splitting.

As a simple slogan, the united front possessed a sure-fire popular appeal and satisfied one of the deepest instinctive needs of the working class. But by the time the Comintern had worked it out in detail, the new policy was far from simple. The first codification of the united front in 1922 stated:

> The tactics of the United Front imply the leadership of the Communist vanguard in the daily struggles of the large masses of the workers for their vital interests.[13]

In order to enable the Communists to gain the leadership of what was ostensibly a "united" movement, three different types of united fronts were distinguished—"from below," "from above," and a combination of the two.

A united front "from below" was, in practice, set up under Communist leadership to attract mass support outside the Communists' own ranks. Only the united front from below was fully authorized and approved by the Comintern. A united front "from above" was wholly made by Communist leaders with the leaders of other workers' organizations. This type was ruled out as never permissible. In certain circumstances, particularly if the Communists found themselves in a hopeless minority, as in England, the Comintern made allowances for a combination of the united front from above and below, "as a method of agitation and mobilization of the masses, and not as a method of political coalition with the Social-Democracy."

In other words, negotiations with leaders of other parties were permissible in order to get at the masses behind them but not in order to achieve a political agreement from top to bottom.[14] The irrepressible Karl Radek once accused the Comintern leaders of using the united front to "unmask" the Social-Democrats, not to unite with them.[15]

Thus the original Communist conception of the united front must be placed in its historical context to be understood realistically. As long as the Russian Bolsheviks thought that they retained the offensive in the battle against world capitalism, it was never contemplated. It was devised as an expedient to get the Communists off the defensive onto the offensive. Only a series of painful defeats induced them to adopt such an expedient. If the Red Army had captured Warsaw in 1920, the head of the Comintern, Zinoviev, once acknowledged, the united front would not have become necessary.[16] Another Russian delegate to the Comintern, Bukharin, explained: "Such questions and slogans as, for instance, the united front or the workers' government or the capital levy, are slogans that are based on very shifting ground. This basis consists of a certain depression within the labor movement." [17] A high Russian Comintern official, Manuilsky, pointed out that "the application of the united front tactics worked out by the Third and Fourth Congresses of the C.I. [Communist International] applied to the period of the decline of the revolutionary wave of 1918–1919" and did not apply to a period of a rising wave.[18]

Hence the united front was one thing in theory and another in practice. In theory it was supposed to issue "from the depths of the working masses themselves"; in practice it was required to submit to "the leadership of the Communist vanguard." This duality in the Communist version of the united front, more than anything else, has been responsible for the most tragic experiences in the labor and radical movements of the twentieth century.

Debut in Cleveland

It took the American Communists about a year to make up their minds about the Farmer-Labor united front. After the Comintern had introduced the policy of the united front in December 1921, the Americans had met it with passive resistance. Like many European Communists, they at first resented the idea that Communists were ever obliged to go on the defensive or resort to shifty maneuvers.

The first American "thesis" on the united front was not adopted until May 1922. It recognized the Labor party—the Communists did not accept the farmers in the title until the following year—as the specific American form of the political united front but regarded it as only a "propaganda slogan" without practical implications.[19] In the middle of October 1922 the American Communists finally came out with an unequivocal endorsement of the Labor party in a pamphlet, *For a Labor Party*. Though it served the purpose of unquestionably committing them to the Farmer-Labor movement, it still fell short of giving the Communists a practical program of action. It assumed that the Labor party would be based on and formed by the organized Labor movement as a whole and not by part of it. The pamphlet also insisted upon a pure "class party," which it defined as one that clearly set forth its goals from the outset as "the abolition of wage slavery, the establishment of a workers' republic and a collectivist system of production." [20]

The Communists made their turn just before the second Conference for Progressive Political Action, held in Cleveland in December 1922. They were so anxious to get into the larger movement that they did not wait for an invitation. When Ruthenberg tried to present his credentials for the Workers party, however, he was quickly rebuffed. The credentials committee, controlled by the more conservative railway unions, refused to seat him, on the ground that the Communists' belief in dictatorship was incompatible with the conference's democratic aims. Ruthenberg received the support of the Chicago Farmer-Labor party's delegates and of practically no one else. Fortunately for the Communists, the conference also disappointed the Farmer-Laborites. When the latter tried to commit the C.P.P.A. to the immediate formation of a national party, the vote went 64 to 52 against them, chiefly because the railway unions were unwilling to go so far and so fast without more support from the A.F. of L. The Farmer-

Laborites withdrew in disgust from the C.P.P.A. The Communists, still thinking of a Labor party of the entire labor movement, tried to dissuade them from leaving immediately and unsuccessfully pleaded with the Farmer-Laborites to stay in, make another fight at the next conference, and then pull out with more support.[21]

Ironically, the Farmer-Laborites played into the hands of the Communists by refusing to take their advice. As long as the railway unions constituted the Right Wing of the amorphous third-party movement, the Farmer-Laborites represented the Left Wing, with the Communists hanging onto their coat-tails, a relatively minor factor at the extreme Left. By breaking away from the railway unions, the Farmer-Laborites upset this balance of forces. They placed themselves in the position of the Right Wing in relation to their new allies, the Communists, who promptly pre-empted the position of the only real and true Left Wing.

Ruthenberg was pleased. "At the Cleveland Convention," he recorded cheerfully, "the Workers' Party made its first appearance in the life of the American workers and farmers as a definite force." [22] Even so, the convention was a historic occasion less for what it had achieved than for what it had implied. For the first time on the American scene, the Communists had tried to play politics on a broad scale. The C.P.P.A. had frustrated them, but the Farmer-Laborites had more than compensated them. By voting for the admission of the Communists, the Farmer-Laborites had publicly taken them back into the fold of the Labor movement from which they had been excluded or had excluded themselves. For a Communist party which could not decide to come up from the underground until the end of 1922, this was no small gain.

The Communists moved quickly to consolidate their new position. "After the December meeting of the C.P.P.A.," Bittelman related, "we began thinking in terms not of propaganda alone but also of organizational and political manoeuvres *designed to bring about the actual formation of a Farmer-Labor Party*. The tactical means to this end was to be an alliance or United Front between the Chicago Federation of Labor and Fitzpatrick's Farmer-Labor Party on the one hand and the Workers Party with its sympathizing organizations on the other hand." [23]

Not for another dozen years, not until they were to make a similar jump onto the bandwagon of the New Deal in the nineteen-thirties, were the American Communists presented with so favorable an opportunity to become a major political force as this alliance offered them in the first six months of 1923. If they did not fail the second time, one reason was the expensive lesson they learned the first time.

Before Chicago

The decision to shift the basis of the Farmer-Labor united front from the entire labor movement to the relatively small portion represented by the Chicago Federation of Labor was made by the Communists' top leadership in New York. But, after three years of isolation and sectarianism, it was ill prepared to carry out the new line of united front. A Leftist element opposed the Labor party in principle, and the dominant group, headed by Ruthenberg, lacked the experience and personal ties for complex organizational and political maneuvers.

Into this novel, difficult, and promising situation stepped the intriguing and mysterious figure of Joseph Pogany, alias John Pepper. After coming to the United States in the summer of 1922 with the Comintern delegation of Valetski and Reinstein, Pogany changed his name to Pepper and stayed on indefinitely. At the convention near Bridgman, Michigan, that August, he was unanimously elected to the Central Executive Committee as one of the two "non-factional" members; the other was William Z. Foster. In a matter of months, the key Political Committee appointed Pepper its secretary.[24] Fresh from Moscow, he knew all about the united front, among many other things. Within three months of his arrival, he wrote the pamphlet, *For a Labor Party*.[25]

While the New York leadership, with the help of Pepper, could expound on Communist policy in the Farmer-Labor movement, it did not have the trade-union or political connections to carry out its policy. The New Yorkers lacked the necessary ties to the Chicago Federation of Labor leaders who controlled the existing Farmer-Labor party. But a strong Communist group in Chicago occupied a peculiarly strategic position for winning over both the Farmer-Labor party and the trade unions. In fact, the two could not be separated as objects of Communist policy. The Chicago trade unions had taken the lead in creating the Farmer-Labor movement and only those Communists familiar to the trade-union leaders were welcomed in their political movement.

The Chicago Communist leadership was made up of young trade-unionists who satisfied these requirements. The District Organizer, Arne Swabeck, served as delegate from the local painters' union to the Chicago Federation of Labor. The Industrial Organizer and former District Organizer, Charles Krumbein, was a delegate from the steam-fitters' union to the federation. Jack Johnstone was one of the painters' delegates and Andrew Overgaard one of the machinists'. Earl Browder doubled as managing editor the *The Labor Herald,* the monthly organ of the Trade Union Educational League, and as member of the Workers party's District Executive Committee in Chicago. They had one foot in the trade unions and the other in the party; they were fairly typical of the more indigenous American radical tradition; they were men in their early thirties, about ten years younger than Foster, who was still concentrating on building up the T.U.E.L.

In March 1923, the Farmer-Labor party of Chicago broke away from the C.P.P.A. and decided to call a convention to organize a national party of workers and farmers. In April the Workers party received an invitation to attend. The convention was set for July 3 in Chicago.

The New York leadership of the Workers party thereupon designated a Chicago committee of three, Swabeck, Krumbein, and Browder, to meet with a committee of the Farmer-Labor party, composed of John Fitzpatrick, Edward N. Nockels, and Jay G. Brown.

Fitzpatrick, a heavy-set former blacksmith, Irish in origin, was a free-wheeling American radical of the old school. He had opposed American participation in the First World War, had spoken out as an ardent friend of the Russian revolution, had defied steel barons and A.F. of L. bureaucrats. But he was primarily a militant trade-unionist, willing to experiment in national politics only as long as the outlook seemed favorable. With Nockels, his close personal friend and the secretary of the Chicago Federation of Labor, Fitzpatrick made the federation's final decisions. Brown, the Farmer-Labor party's secretary, worked most closely with the Communists, but could not stray very far from Fitzpatrick and Nockels. The Farmer-Labor leadership also included Robert M. Buck, a professional "progressive" journalist who edited the Farmer-Labor party organ, *The New Majority,* and Anton Johannsen, chairman of the Organization Committee of the Chicago Federation of Labor, a "short, round and jolly" ex-anarchist who knew the revolutionary movement from the inside and had strongly influenced such prominent prolabor intellectuals as Lincoln Steffens and Hutchins Hapgood.[26]

Meanwhile, in New York, Pepper increasingly made himself the spokesman of Communist policy. In a series of articles in the New York Communist organ, *The Worker,* he expounded the theory and practice of the united front and especially the duties of party members in other organizations. One of these articles took the form of a debate with the Socialist writer, Upton Sinclair, who had been asked by *The Worker*'s editor for his views on the admission of the Workers party to the Labor party. Sinclair appealed to all working-class groups to abandon their factional disputes, join in the new party, and "obey the rules of the game." Pepper used this occasion to issue a public reminder that the Communists believed in the dictatorship of the proletariat, "the role of force in history," and Soviets, which made it impossible for them to live in the same political party as "Tammany Hall Socialism." In another article, he held forth on the necessity for all Communists who belonged to other labor organizations to consider the interests of their party more important than the special interests of the organizations, and to carry out their party's policies regardless of their personal conviction on individual points. "In face of danger, we must not forget that a Communist Party is always an army corps surrounded by dangers on all sides—a Communist should not abandon his party, even if he thinks that the Party is in the wrong," Pepper proclaimed. "Every militant Communist should write on his shield: 'My Party, right or wrong, my Party!' "[27]

Fitzpatrick and Nockels had worked amicably with Swabeck, Krumbein, and Browder and knew where they stood with them, but Pepper and the New Yorkers were unknown quantities. The type of thinking represented by Pepper's articles made the Chicago trade-union leaders wonder where Communist policy might take them.[28] The Chicago Communists soon sensed a change in attitude.

Swabeck recalls: "At the very first meeting Fitzpatrick started out by bluntly saying: 'Let's get the record straight—we are willing to go along, but we think you Communists should occupy a back seat in this affair.' "[29]

Johannsen also warned Browder and Johnstone privately: "If you keep your heads, go slow, don't rock the boat, then the Chicago Federation will stand fast. But if you begin to throw your weight around too much, the game will be up."[30]

While Fitzpatrick feared that the Communists were getting out of hand, the New York Communists feared that the Chicago Communists were too close to him. The Chicagoans realized that a break in the alliance threatened and tried to stave it off. They appealed for help to the Workers party chairman, James P. Cannon, who happened to be passing through Chicago on a lecture tour, and he sent off a "serious warning" to the New York national office against further endangering relations with Fitzpatrick's group.[31] The reply from Ruthenberg, on June 4, went just the opposite way—it peremptorily ordered Swabeck, Browder, and Krumbein to stay out of further discussions on arrangements with the Farmer-Laborites.[32] Ruthenberg and Pepper hurried to Chicago to crack down on the Chicago committee.[33]

This move by the New York Communist leadership coincided with Fitzpatrick's own growing misgivings about the forthcoming Chicago convention, only a month away. By the beginning of June, he knew that most of the national unions, the Socialist party, and the A.F. of L.'s top officials were going to boycott the convention. He was bombarded from all sides with warnings that the Communists were not acting in good faith and were preparing to "pack" the meeting.

Disappointment with the response and pressure from hostile forces caused Fitzpatrick to entertain second thoughts about the convention. Early in June he proposed to the Communists that the original plan for the gathering should be revised. Instead of organizing a new party immediately, he suggested merely drawing up a program to be referred to the respective organizations by the delegates, setting up an organization committee to rally more support for the new party, and holding another convention to form the party at a more favorable moment. This proposal avoided a break with the Workers party, which was to be represented on the organization committee along with other national organizations. It clearly indicated that Fitzpatrick wanted to play for time and postpone an irrevocable decision. But the maneuver to delay certainly represented a wavering on his part and placed the ultimate creation of the new party in doubt.

Fitzpatrick's proposal presented the Communists with a dangerous temptation. It lured them on to demand immediate action on the new party, thrust Fitzpatrick aside, and supersede his group in the leadership of the larger movement. They had been making unforeseen headway in rounding up delegates to the forthcoming convention. If they accepted Fitzpatrick's proposal, they might allow the advantage to slip out of their hands. On the other hand, they confronted the danger of isolating themselves by splitting with Fitzpatrick. They had gone far in a remarkably short time in their first political alliance with non-Communist forces, and they faced the question of how far they could go alone.

The question was thrashed out at a full meeting of the Central Executive Committee. When Ruthenberg realized that a split with Fitzpatrick impended, he drew back, took the position that the Communists could not afford a split at that stage of the development of the Farmer-Labor movement, and recommended going along with Fitzpatrick a while longer. Pepper went to the opposite extreme. He insisted on plunging ahead with the original plan for the convention, even at the expense of a split with Fitzpatrick, if a half-million organized workers and farmers were represented at Chicago on July 3. Foster tried to steer a middle course. He wanted to make the support of a sufficient number of national unions the condition for going ahead without Fitzpatrick.

In this crucial trial of strength, Pepper won. He carried the entire committee except Ruthenberg, Foster, and Katterfeld, the latter being a spokesman for the extreme anti-Farmer-Labor-party Leftist tendency.[34] This vote made Pepper the real leader of the American Communist movement less than a year after his arrival in the United States.

Once the decision was made, the Communists closed ranks. The Chicagoans grumbled and crumbled. As the convention neared, Fitzpatrick removed himself further and further from his impatient allies. When they tried to meet with him two days before the convention, he adamantly refused.[35]

Foster later admitted that the decisive split had taken place before the convention:

> The latter merely registered the break that had already occurred. The last word that the Workers Party could get from you [Fitzpatrick] before the gathering convened (received through high officials of the Farmer-Labor Party) was that you were determined not to go along with the Workers Party under any circumstances.[36]

Nothing of this struggle behind the scenes came out in the open. The majority of delegates arrived in Chicago expecting to organize a new party without delay. Instead of fighting publicly, Fitzpatrick sulked privately.

The Chicago convention

Several hundred delegates, claiming to represent some 600,000 organized workers and farmers, came to Chicago for the Farmer-Labor convention on July 3, 1923. The organizations represented included 4 national trade unions, the most important of which was the Amalgamated Clothing Workers; 4 state farmers' organizations; 3 national political bodies—the Farmer-Labor party, the Workers party, and the Proletarian party; 125 fraternal societies; and 247 local farmers' and trade-union branches.[37]

Only 10 delegates were officially allotted to the Workers party, compared with approximately 50 for the Farmer-Laborites. But the Communists had other ways of getting in. Dozens of Communists attended as delegates from local trade unions. Others managed to represent such organizations as the Lithuanian Workers' Literature Society, the Rumanian Progressive Club, and the United Workingmen Singers. Pepper and Ruthenberg later admitted that the Communist delegates numbered about 200,[38] and the Communists therefore went into the convention with from one-third to almost one-half of all the delegates.[39] Since the Workers party claimed only 13,970 members in July 1923, this percentage of Communist delegates amounted to an extraordinary showing for a relatively small organization in a convention at which about 600,000 were supposedly represented.[40] For the first time, the Communists demonstrated their superiority in the technique of electing delegates to a united front.

Fitzpatrick's group made one last effort to shake off the Communists. In a surprise move, the Farmer-Laborites attempted to devote the first day to a convention of their own party instead of the broader one. The Communists realized that this plan was designed to freeze them out. The day before the convention opened, the Communists called on the Farmer-Laborites to seat only the delegates of their regularly affiliated per-capita-paying organizations, a small fraction of those attending the Chicago convention. Communist sources claim that the Farmer-Laborites agreed.[41]

On July 3, however, a move was made to seat all the local and central labor-body delegates not previously affiliated with the Farmer-Labor party, excluding only the Workers party and other "international" organizations. The Communists counterattacked with a motion to seat all delegates, including themselves. The vote overwhelmingly favored the Communists, who promptly moved to adjourn the session in favor of the general meeting the next day.[42]

This preliminary victory helped to give the Communists delusions of grandeur. It convinced them that they could win the support of the great majority of delegates without or against the Fitzpatrick forces. Pepper seemed vindicated; his star ascended to the highest point of his American career. The prospect of running away with the convention intoxicated all the Communists present, even those who had previously betrayed the greatest apprehensions, including Ruthenberg and Foster, both members of the Communist steering committee.[43]

The Communist steam-roller proceeded to flatten all opposition. The Communist delegates were organized in groups of ten, each with its appointed captain to keep the others in line.[44] Strategically placed throughout the convention floor, they took the unorganized delegates by storm. The Communists put in their man, Joseph Manley, as secretary of the key organization committee and outvoted the opposition 26 to 3 in the committee on Manley's report. Fitzpatrick's aide, Robert M. Buck, twice pleaded with the Communists to withhold their motion for the immediate formation of a new party.[45] They refused to be deterred.

At the end of the second day, July 4, Ruthenberg pushed through a move, against heavy opposition from Fitzpatrick's side, for the immediate organization of a new party—the Federated Farmer-Labor party—one word added to the old name to indicate that the new party was based on organizational affiliations rather than individual membership. Henceforth, the Communists and their sympathizers backed the F.F.-L.P., the old-line progressive trade unionists the F.-L.P.

On the third and last day, July 5, Fitzpatrick vainly tried to stem the tide. He made no effort to hide his grief and bitterness:

> I know Brother Foster and the others who are identified and connected with him, and if they think they can attract the attention of the rank and file of the working men and women of America to their organization, I say to them and to this organization, that is a hopeless course, and they cannot do it.
>
> Then what have they done? They have killed the Farmer-Labor Party,

and they have killed the possibility of uniting the forces of independent political action in America; and they have broken the spirit of this whole thing so that we will not be able to rally the forces for the next twenty years!

Fitzpatrick for the first time at the convention attacked the Workers party by name:

I know, as a practical proposition, that the minute the Workers' Party is identified with this movement, that then that will be the battering ram that is going to be used against every group. And I say that it is just like going up a blind alley. There is a stone wall at the other end. And if you do this, you are going to meet that stone wall, because you are not making an appeal to the hopes and aspirations of the men and women in the width of the country. You are putting the Farmer-Labor Party in the other fellow's hands—to blow you off the face of the earth. And then our activities are at an end.

Foster tried to turn away Fitzpatrick's wrath with soft words. He recalled that they had gone through "some good battles" together and gave Fitzpatrick credit for "the courage of his convictions." He had never disagreed with him "until right here."

Then Foster taunted Fitzpatrick for doing just what the latter had condemned the C.P.P.A.'s Cleveland conference for doing—postponing a decision—and went on to pit his judgment against Fitzpatrick's:

And I hope the leaders here will decide to go along with this great movement—and I don't hesitate to say that if they submit the question to their own rank and file, they will decide to go along with this movement.

Ruthenberg gave the official Communist reply. Against Fitzpatrick's appeal to the reality of American life, he invoked the special power of the Communist doctrine to determine that reality:

We are Communists—I am a Communist—and we do not guess at things. We analyze the economic conditions and the political facts, and our policies are based upon the political life of this country and of the working class. And we believe that today, as never before, there has grown out of the experiences of this life an understanding of the need for a political party, representative of the farmers and workers, to take its place in the political arena of this country. And we say this party will be a success, if we seize the opportunity—not merely because of our propaganda ability, not only because of our promulgation of the idea, but because it is in the life of the American workers and farmers today, growing out of the aggression of the government against them, out of their everyday experiences in the class struggle.

After denying that the Communists wanted to dominate the convention, Ruthenberg claimed for them only what they had earned:

> We know that it was our efforts, our work in the trade unions, our propagandizing, our leaflets, our newspapers, our speakers, our organizers, who to a large extent made possible this Convention. And because of that, we took the liberty of interposing with our organization of the militant self-sacrificing workers who are ready to give their strength and money to this cause, and who can be the motive force pushing it forward and spreading it out and making it a real mass movement. We know that—and we are not hiding it.[46]

On the last day, the Communists made a tactical concession by accepting the constitution and platform of the old Farmer-Labor party for the new Federated Farmer-Labor party. Fitzpatrick's supporters replied that in this case they saw no need for a new party, and countered by inviting the assembled groups—barring the Communists—to affiliate with them. They belatedly discovered that the Communists did not advocate "lawful means to bring about political changes" and did accept the leadership of an international organization "whose propaganda and doctrines advocate the overthrow of the government of the United States by other than legal and constitutional methods, such as the Third International." [47] Communist oratory plus Communist organization overwhelmingly defeated this move. It apparently obtained only about fifty votes or approximately 10 per cent.[48] In the final vote, a number of Farmer-Labor delegates bolted from Fitzpatrick's party to vote with the Communists. The most important breakaway was the strong Washington state organization.[49] Fitzpatrick, crushed, walked out. An independent liberal observer reported that those Farmer-Labor delegates who walked out with him did so largely out of personal loyalty.[50]

Outwardly, no Communist triumph could have been more complete. Not only did the Communists have their way about the immediate formation of the new party, but, to advertise their control, they appointed as National Secretary a well-known Communist, Joseph Manley, then an avowed Pepper follower and Foster's son-in-law.[51] One of the Farmer-Labor bolters, William Bouck of the Western Progressive Farmers of the state of Washington, was made chairman. A Socialist writer counted at least 14 of the 33 members of the F.F.-L.P.'s National Executive Committee as known Communists and a few of the remaining 19 as probable ones.[52]

Ruthenberg himself boasted: "It [Workers party] assumed the position of leadership and the first mass party of the American workers—the Federated Farmer-Labor Party—was formed." [53]

Otherwise, little distinguished the new Federated Farmer-Labor party from the old Farmer-Labor party. The programs, written by Ruthenberg himself, were practically identical.[54] Most of the eleven points in the platform of the F.F.-L.P. were just the kind of moderate reforms that the Communists had previously scoffed at—a federal eight-hour work day, living wage, unemployment compensation, ban on child-labor, compulsory education, soldiers' bonus, workers' and maternity insurance. Two points were more general, but borrowed bodily from the old Farmer-Labor programs: nationalization of all public utilities and means of communication and transportation, and increasing control by workers and farmers of the management and operation of industries through their economic organizations.[55] In effect, the program was almost pure reformism, spiced with dabs of syndicalism and Populism. To avoid scaring anyone away, none of the phrases dear to the Communists of this period, such as the "revolutionary overthrow of capitalism," was permitted. Robert Morss Lovett thought that it was "such a complete summary of ameliorative proposals that it reads like a satire." [56] All in all, it was quite a performance for a party whose reason for existence had recently been the extermination of reformism, compromises, and illusions.

The lesson of Chicago

The recriminations were loud and bitter.

Fitzpatrick cried out that what the Communists "have done is on the level of a man being invited to your house as a guest and then once in the house seizing you by the throat and kicking you out the door." [57] The official organ of the Farmer-Labor party served notice that the Communists "were not the kind of folks other kinds of folks could live with in peace and harmony. But more important than that, they had demonstrated that they hadn't the slightest conception of the principle of human conduct that requires deliberation and care in bringing strange groups together and trying to make teammates of them." [58]

The Communists reserved their hottest fire for Fitzpatrick. Ruthenberg charged that he "had gotten 'cold feet' because of fear of the Gompers' machine." [59] Pepper jeered at him as one of the "political corpses of well-intentioned leaders" which paved the road to revolution.[60] Foster accused him of "treason" to the Labor party movement.[61] (A few years later, the Communist organ called Fitzpatrick one of the "fascist leaders" of the Chicago Federation of Labor.[62])

The lamentation of the Farmer-Laborites that the Communists were invited "guests" who took over the party was not very convincing. The original call to the meeting did not say that the Farmer-Labor party was simply holding an ordinary convention of its own; it invited "all" labor, farm, and political groups to sent representatives to devise means "for knitting together the many organizations in this country." [63] The Communists "helped liberally to finance the convention," as guests are not generally expected to do.[64]

In fact, the new party started as the property of the Chicago Farmer-Laborites; it then became a joint enterprise of the Farmer-Laborites and the Communists; and finally the Farmer-Laborites felt that it was more reprehensible or less embarrassing to be ousted by Communist guests than by Communist partners.

The Communist case against Fitzpatrick was based on an alleged agreement with the Farmer-Laborites made two weeks before the convention.[65] But Ruthenberg admitted that this "agreement" had not been made with Fitzpatrick, the only one who could make a binding agreement; it was never acknowledged by the Farmer-Laborites; and even if there had been some kind of agreement two weeks before the convention, there certainly was no agreement two days before.[66]

Neither the Farmer-Laborites nor the Communists could afford to bring the real issues into the open. Fitzpatrick could not afford to admit that he had been quite willing to accept the Communists as junior partners, and that he had woefully misjudged the opposition of the Socialists, the major national unions, and the A.F. of L. leadership. On their part, the Communists could not afford to admit that Fitzpatrick had good reason to feel double-crossed, since he had been led to believe at the outset by the Communists that they would follow his lead, and that the momentum of their drive for delegates had lured them into overestimating their own strength and underestimating Fitzpatrick's final power of decision. It seems most unlikely that Fitzpatrick would have gone so far with the Communists, or that they would have gone so far without him, if either had foreseen the ultimate consequences.

The Chicago disaster broke Fitzpatrick's spirit. Not only had his plans misfired, but the Communists had made him look foolish. He had walked out of the C.P.P.A. meeting in December 1922 because he wanted immediate action on the formation of a new party. Seven months later, he had to walk out of his own convention because he did not want immediate action on the formation of a new party. In the entire labor movement, only his organization had been willing to sponsor the Communists, and in the most public and humiliating way it had been forced to admit error. The rest of the A.F. of L. laughed at Fitzpatrick for his naïveté, and the Communists cursed him for his "betrayal."

Hopelessly disillusioned, Fitzpatrick went far beyond merely putting an end to his old friendship with Foster and breaking with the Communists; he also broke with all that the Communists had come to stand for—amalgamation of craft unions and the Labor party, which the Communists had appropriated from progressive trade-unionists like himself.

The end was tragic: Fitzpatrick fought the Communists by abandoning his own old ideals and objectives, which were set back more than a decade because the progressives behind him did not distinguish between fighting the Communists and fighting the objectives which the Communists had taken over from them.

In its inception, the Farmer-Labor–Communist alliance had not been a one-sided affair. The Communists had been able to use the Farmer-Laborites because the latter had tried to use them. The first stage of the alliance seemed to favor the Farmer-Laborites. But the decisive factor was the relation of forces between the allies. Once the Farmer-Laborites opened the doors of their movement to the Communists, superior organization gave the Communists the upper hand. A large but loose movement could not cope with a small but disciplined one.

This experience showed for the first time that the Communists could make progress in the United States in the measure that they could make alliances with forces stronger than themselves. Without associations, tie-ups, or deals with larger liberal, farm, labor, or minority groups, the Communists have stewed in their own juice. The Communist appeal by itself, in its own terms, has never attracted a mass following. The escape from isolation and the development of more widespread Communist influences have invariably come as a result of liaisons between the Communists and movements which they had previously despised.

In this respect John Fitzpatrick was the lineal predecessor of John L. Lewis and Henry A. Wallace.

3

Roads to Chicago

For a party that had been treated not so long before as the pariah of the labor movement, the Communist capture of the Chicago convention in July 1923 represented a remarkable achievement. Even if we discount some of it as the result of "packing" a convention, the ability to carry out such an operation amounted to no small organizational feat and took Fitzpatrick's experienced machine by surprise. After three years of sectarian isolation and internecine warfare, the Communists had succeeded in a few months in breaking out into the open, putting into effect a totally new political line, striking up a working alliance with the most promising militant force in the trade-union movement, and winning over enough of their ally's own followers to take over the joint enterprise. The Chicago experience showed that, given the right circumstances, the Communists were capable of making a speedy and spectacular comeback.

This coup came off because a large section of the Farmer-Labor movement still thought of the Communists as an integral part of a broad, amorphous Left Wing, peculiar in some respects perhaps, but not outside the family of traditional American radicalism. The official persecution of the Communists had gained them much sympathy in Left Wing circles and many free-lance radicals were glad to take them back into the fold. The Communists' allegiance to the Soviet Union constituted no bar, because good will toward the Soviet Union extended far beyond Communist ranks. The policy of the united front seemed to give the Communists a basis for working with other groups, and it was still too new and untried for non-Communist Left-Wingers and progressives to have learned the difference between the appearance and the reality.

If the four-year-old Communist movement had traveled far to get to the Chicago convention, a far longer and more tortuous journey had been made by the Communist leaders who dominated the convention—Ruthenberg, Pepper, and Foster. Each of them took a different road to Chicago and approached American Communism from a different direction.

Ruthenberg

For Charles E. Ruthenberg, the road began in Cleveland, Ohio, where he was born in 1882. His parents were German immigrants who had arrived in the United States only four months before his birth. His father, a cigar-maker in the old country and a longshoreman in the new, is said to have brought Socialist sympathies with him. Young Charles received an elementary education at a German-Lutheran school, after which, at the age of fourteen, he worked in a bookshop during the day and attended a business college in the evening. Two years later, his father died, his schooling came to an end, and he went to work as a carpenter's helper in a picture-molding factory. After a year, he transferred to the business office and, for the next eighteen years, moved up in a variety of white-collar jobs—bookkeeper, salesman, and sales manager for a book company, salesman for a roofing company, head of the estimate department of a roofing company, and office manager for a garment manufacturer. His admiring Communist biographer reports that he was "the most efficient office executive and purchasing agent" the garment company ever had.[1]

In his early twenties, Ruthenberg considered himself an ardent follower of Cleveland's "reform mayor," Tom Johnson, a peculiar combination of streetcar magnate and disciple of Henry George.[2] At about the same time, according to an interview in a Cleveland newspaper, Ruthenberg thought of becoming a minister but was led by the study of evolution and sociology into embracing socialism,[3] which attracted him at the outset as an evolutionary process in fulfillment of Tom Johnson's municipal reform movement.[4] He joined the Socialist party in Cleveland in 1909 and immediately threw himself into organizational activity. He was elected within a few months to the City Central Committee; and the Cleveland local made him its organizer and secretary in 1913 on a volunteer basis and as a paid, full-time official in 1917. He became the party's perennial candidate—for state treasurer in 1910, mayor of Cleveland in 1911, governor of Ohio in 1912, United States senator in 1914, and mayor again in 1915 and 1917. In the Cleveland local, then a stronghold of the Left Wing, he moved rapidly away from his Tom Johnson period of evolutionary reform to the traditional Left Wing position of emphasizing the ultimate revolutionary goal instead of "municipal reform tactics." [5]

Ruthenberg stepped out on the national stage of the Socialist party as a delegate to the conventions of 1912 and 1917. At the first, he identified himself with the cause of William D. Haywood, and voted with the Left Wing minority against a constitutional clause repudiating sabotage and violence. At the St. Louis convention in 1917, he acted as the chief floor leader of the Left Wing and served on the committee of three which drafted the antiwar resolution. For his opposition to the war, he went to prison for ten months in 1918. He again demonstrated his outstanding determination and courage during a May Day demonstration in Cleveland in 1919. In the face of bloody attack by mounted police and army tanks, he stood his ground, insisted on speaking, and suffered arrest.

By 1919, at the age of thirty-seven, he had spent ten years of hard work and had earned increasing recognition in the Socialist movement. He had won widespread respect for his ability and had paid a high price for his beliefs. When he wrote, "The Communist Party came into existence in the United States, as elsewhere, in response to the ferment caused in the Socialist parties by the Russian Revolution," he was telling his own story as much as the party's.[6] He qualified as secretary of the first Communist party because no other native-born American could match his record of organizational experience and achievement. He made up in steadiness what he lacked in brilliance. Reserved in manner, distant and courteous in his personal relations, a quiet, moderating influence on those around him, he always remained "the most efficient office executive" rather than the creative, inspiring political leader.

"Someone in the party has to remain cool and calm and be orderly, efficient and economical," he wrote to a close personal friend just before his death in 1927. "That seems to be my role." [7]

Within Ruthenberg himself, the struggle between doctrinal orthodoxy and mass influence went on unceasingly. His first impulse usually favored the masses. The pattern of his behavior was set as early as the summer of 1919 in the split between those who insisted on forming a pure Communist party immediately and those who wanted to wait a few months in order to capture the Socialist convention. First he voted against immediate action, then moved over to the other side and accepted the secretaryship of the foreign-language-controlled Communist party, although the rest of the Ohio delegation went with the more Americanized Communist Labor party. Two years later, he implied that the American party had been organized prematurely "in hip-hip-hurrah fashion" and might better have waited another year or two.[8] In the spring of 1920 he repented by splitting off from the Communist party and uniting with the Communist Labor party. During this realignment, he clearly recognized the dual forces pulling at each other within the Communist movement. His group, then in the minority, wrote of its opponents:

> The majority members of the committee considered themselves "great theorists." They constantly talked about the word "principle," but never about how to relate Communist principles to the working class movement of this country and to make these principles a living reality in action.

And his group thought of itself in these terms:

> They believed that a Communist Party should be, not a party of closet philosophers, but a party which participates in the every day struggles of

the workers and by such participation injects its principles into these struggles and gives them a wider meaning, thus developing the Communist movement.[9]

After he was released in the spring of 1922 from his second prison term of a year and a half, Ruthenberg assumed command of the fight against the underground existence of the party. He scoffed at those who held that it should come out into the open only when it could advocate "armed insurrection" in its program. Ruthenberg and Bedacht wrote that, if they had to choose between armed insurrection in the program or coming out openly as a party, they would choose an open party without armed insurrection in its program.[10] Ruthenberg's view ultimately prevailed, and Communist programs were henceforth tailored to fit the needs of legality.

Ruthenberg's closest associate, Max Bedacht, was born in Munich, Germany, in 1883, one year after Ruthenberg's birth. He left school at the age of thirteen to be apprenticed to a barber; four years later he went to work in Switzerland, and there he was converted to socialism. He came to the United States in 1908, worked as a barber in New York for two more years, and then edited German papers in Detroit and San Francisco. In 1919, when the California delegation was refused admission to the Socialist convention and went over to the Communist Labor party, Bedacht was elected to the C.L.P.'s National Executive Committee. After John Reed's death at the end of 1920, Bedacht took Reed's place as the C.L.P.'s representative to the Comintern. He returned from Moscow in 1921 an enthusiastic partisan of the new line of reaching the masses, and thereafter served as Ruthenberg's lieutenant in closest personal rapport with him. Though Bedacht held many different positions in his long career as a Communist leader, he was primarily an old-fashioned radical agitator, at his happiest before a crowd.[11]

The Communist invasion of the Farmer-Labor movement again showed the gap between Ruthenberg's first impulse and final decision. He undoubtedly shrank from the split with Fitzpatrick's group and tried to stave it off. But he was too weak to resist Pepper and ended by joining forces with him.

No man could rise to the top in the Communist movement without a taste and talent for factional in-fighting, and Ruthenberg was no exception to this rule. He fought more honorably than the others, but he fought. He came to feel that the secretaryship belonged to him and made all the necessary maneuvers to hold on to it. He chafed at many of Moscow's instructions and interventions without ever making a stand against them.

Some men are the same in all movements, and some act differently in different movements. Ruthenberg probably belonged to the second type.

Pepper

For John Pepper, the road to Chicago started in his native Hungary during his former incarnation as Joseph Pogany.[12] As Pogany, he had been a professional journalist who had worked on the staff of the official organ of the Hungarian Social Democratic party. When the war ended and the Hapsburg monarchy was overthrown, he organized the disillusioned war veterans into a Soldiers' Council with himself at the head.

Meanwhile another Hungarian journalist, Bela Kun, who had been a war prisoner in Russia, was sent back home by the Bolsheviks to organize a Communist revolution. To the dismay of the newly born Hungarian Communist party under Kun, Pogany used the Soldiers' Council to support the liberal regime of Count Michael Karolyi; he even arrested some of the Communist leaders.[13] As the Communist pressure increased, however, Pogany suddenly switched sides. He was one of the five Social Democrats who signed a unity pact with the Communists which led to the overthrow of the Karolyi regime and the formation of a Hungarian Soviet government in March 1919.[14] Pogany was rewarded with the post of Commissar of War. A year and a half after the Bolshevik revolution in Russia, history seemed to be repeating itself; Pogany was called the "Hungarian Trotsky." This high point in Pogany's revolutionary career lasted only three weeks. The Communists did not trust him and eased him out in favor of one of their own men. When the Hungarian Soviet regime came to an end on its one hundred and thirty-third day, he occupied a relatively minor propaganda position.[15]

The downfall of the Hungarian Soviets in the summer of 1919 was the real beginning of Pogany's strictly Communist career. Despite the way the Communists had treated him, he decided to throw in his lot with them, and with Kun and others succeeded in making his way to Moscow. This defeated Hungarian group proceeded to play a peculiarly strategic role in the Comintern, which desperately needed non-Russian personnel in its higher echelons. Though there was much misgiving in Moscow about the way the Hungarians had mishandled their own revolution, they were given numerous opportunities to mishandle other people's revolutions. In the group that went to work for the Comintern were Kun and Pogany. Together with a Pole, Guralsky, they constituted the Comintern's delegation to Germany, which was at least partially responsible for the disastrous rising in March 1921.[16] Pogany was thus personally involved in two of the greatest defeats suffered by the Communist movement in Europe in the period immediately following the Russian revolution.

By 1922, the Comintern was thoroughly fed up with its band of unlucky, quarrelsome Hungarians, who, ever since the post mortem held in Moscow after their debacle, had been divided into bitterly warring factions. Finally, a Comintern commission was appointed to investigate the matter, and it recommended that the Hungarian factionalists should be dispersed outside Moscow.[17] The chief targets of this punishment were Ladislaus Rudas and Joseph Pogany, representing the opposing factions. Rudas shifted to philosophical work and later became one of the chief teachers of the American students at the Lenin School in Moscow. Pogany suspected that the United States might be more fertile territory for his talents.[18] When the Comintern decided to send a delegation to the United States in the summer of that year, he talked his way into it.

Pogany's background, then, was not at all what he led the Americans to believe. He was no Old Bolshevik. As the so-called organizer of the Hungarian Red Army, he was a very feeble imitation of Trotsky. In Hungary and again in Germany, he had had nothing but disasters to his credit. He was actually *persona non grata* in Moscow. He came to the United States only because the Comintern was anxious to send him as far away as possible. It was no accident, therefore, that he did not return to Russia with the other two representatives, Valetski and Reinstein. His mission to the United States was a form of exile, and this was true of other "Comintern representatives" after him.

But Joseph Pogany transformed into John Pepper dazzled the American Communists. The short, stocky, dark, bespectacled, thirty-six-year-old Hungarian arrived with a Comintern delegation and knew the inner workings of the Comintern as no American did. With his ability to talk for hours at a time on almost any conceivable subject—at first in German, and within a few months in English—and with an abundant supply of old-world charm when he chose to turn it on, he impressed the provincial Americans as the typical Central European revolutionary intellectual. He could tell fascinating stories of his great days as Commissar of War of the Hungarian Soviet Republic which had been, after all, the second one in history, even if it had failed to survive. He referred familiarly to the greatest heroes of the Russian revolution, to Lenin and to Trotsky and, above all, to Zinoviev, the master of the Comintern, who had protected Pogany's faction until Lenin turned against both Hungarian factions. He exuded unlimited self-confidence and unhesitatingly handed down incontrovertible decisions. He treated the Americans as political children who desperately needed the benefit of his vast knowledge and brilliant intellect, and a surprising number of American Communists agreed with him. Being in the United States illegally, he behaved conspiratorially, an additional source of glamour. Though it seems that his specific mission to the United States had been limited to working in the Hungarian federation and on the Hungarian Communist paper, *Uj Elöre,* it soon became clear to him that the Americans needed him for bigger things.[19] He could not be expected to disillusion the many American Communists who, without quite knowing what his exact status was, took for granted that a man who spoke with such superb authority and superlative arrogance must be the "Comintern representative" (or, more familiarly, the "Comintern rep"). In any case, this was the role which Pepper played in the United States, whether or not he was properly commissioned to do so.

To do him justice, Pepper had a keen mind, a fertile imagination, an indefatigable curiosity, in addition to a lofty disdain for scruples. He worked hard at understanding the country, much harder than most of the American Communists did. In a matter of weeks, the Hungarian who had fled from his own country in the wake of an unsuccessful revolution assumed the role of teaching the backward Americans how to make their revolution. Some rebelled at his brazenness, but the most important American Communists came under his spell and for many months none dared to challenge his authority. His amazing, if temporary, success was partly due to the fact that he was able to give so many Americans a sense of inferiority, and partly a result of the overwhelming prestige which his alleged influence in the Comintern conferred on him. But the man had enough ability to make his bravado seem warranted. When the Communist writer, Michael Gold, thought of outstanding Communist "thinkers" in 1923, the first three that came to his mind were Max Eastman, William Z. Foster, and John Pepper.[20]

Pepper was not content merely to be the power behind Ruthenberg's throne. A facile journalist, he poured out articles and pamphlets, one of which, *For a Labor Party,* became the American Communists' first best-seller.[21] In both *The Worker* and *The Liberator,* then the weekly and monthly organs of the party, he wrote so much and so often that he made himself the party's foremost spokesman.

One of Pepper's articles was entitled, "Be American!" In it, he complained bitterly that the majority of the Workers party consisted of foreign-born workers, that a "great part" were not citizens and spoke only their native language with at most a smattering of English. In another article he repeated the charge: "The Workers Party is not enough American." Pepper was annoyed because this was not the best human material for a Hungarian to use in making an American revolution.[22]

Pepper also commanded a strong personal following within the top leadership. After his "non-factional" election to the Central Executive Committee at the underground Bridgman convention in the summer of 1922, which had narrowly favored the so-called Goose faction's support of the illegal party, Pepper decided to throw his weight on the side of unification into a single, legal party. So successful were his efforts on behalf of a legal party that he received most of the credit for inducing the Goose faction to surrender. Instead of punishing its chief leaders, he made their political rehabilitation his mission. As a result, he converted Amter, Gitlow, Minor, and others into personal admirers and protégés, and they in turn enabled him to build a personal political machine within the party. His most precocious and appreciative pupil, however, was the former Liquidator, Jay Lovestone. When Pepper was appointed secretary of the top Political Committee, and when he bested Ruthenberg in the vote on the split with Fitzpatrick before the Chicago convention, he established his ascendancy over Ruthenberg and wielded more power than anyone else in the top leadership. From the summer of 1923 to the end of the year, Pepper was the *de facto* leader of American Communism.

Foster

In some ways, William Z. Foster had furthest to go to the Farmer-Labor convention in Chicago. His journey began in Taunton, Massachusetts, in 1881. His father, an English-hating Irish immigrant, washed carriages for a living. His mother, a devout Catholic of English-Scotch stock, bore twenty-three children, most of whom died in infancy. When young Bill was six, the family moved to Philadelphia and stayed there for the next ten years. The boy grew up in a slum where, as he later described it, "indolence, ignorance, thuggery, crime, disease, drunkenness and general social degeneration flourished." He quit school and began to work at the age of ten to help support the family. After several boyhood jobs, he left Pennsylvania, at the age of nineteen, to see the world through the eyes of a slim, wiry, migrant worker. For a few months he drove a trolley in New York. He took a job as a cook in a Texas railway yard. He tried the seaman's life for three years and homesteading in Oregon for another three. For about a dozen years altogether, he belonged to the army of "floating workers" on the railroads—as car inspector, car carpenter, airbrakeman, common laborer. He hoboed his way up and down and across the country. He personified the American proletariat as few radical leaders have ever done.[23]

In the first forty years of his life, Foster changed his politics almost as freely as his jobs. A street speaker in Philadelphia introduced him to socialism in 1900, and he joined the Socialist party the following year. His active Socialist period, however, occurred in Oregon between the years 1904–1909. There he came under the influence of the Left Wing, then a major force in that state, and joined an extremist group headed by a physician, Dr. William F. Titus, who preached an uncompromising version of faith in the revolutionary class struggle and scorn for all reforms.[24] The expulsion of this Left Wing drove him out of the Socialist party in 1909, and for a few months the following year he went over to a short-lived Wage Workers party. His next stop in 1910 was the I.W.W., the beginning of his syndicalist period.

Politics, work, adventure, were at this stage lumped together for Foster. He hoboed, but he was no ordinary hobo. He farmed, logged, mined, railroaded, but he was no ordinary farmer, logger, miner, or railroader. He went from radical organization to radical organization, but he was no ordinary radical. He was goaded on by an incessant drive to make something more of himself than an ignorant, downtrodden, submissive product of a Philadelphia slum. Early in 1910, after his interest in the I.W.W. had been aroused, he took another unusual step. With a hundred dollars as his capital, he hoboed his way to New York, crossed the Atlantic, and spent the next year in

France and Germany observing the syndicalist and socialist movements.

This experience determined his political course for the next ten years. He came back home convinced of the futility of the I.W.W.'s official doctrine of revolutionary dual unionism; he then adapted the French syndicalist policy of "boring from within" to the situation in the United States in terms of working inside the A.F. of L.[25] The I.W.W.'s reaction was one of boredom, and in 1912 Foster formed his first personal organization, the Syndicalist League of North America, to push his ideas. The Syndicalist League survived two years. He replaced it in 1915 with the International Trade Union Educational League. That existed for about a year.

Foster himself practiced what he preached. He joined an A.F. of L. union, the Brotherhood of Railway Carmen of America, in Chicago and in 1915 became business agent of its Chicago district council. From this time dated his collaboration with John Fitzpatrick of the Chicago Federation of Labor. After a term as business agent, Foster looked for larger fields to conquer and in 1917 hit on an organizing campaign of the Chicago packing-house workers. With Fitzpatrick as chairman and himself as secretary, Foster formed an organizing committee which signed up over 200,000 workers. One of its organizers was Jack Johnstone, another ex-I.W.W. who believed in boring from within the A.F. of L. The successful packing-house campaign made Foster for the first time a national figure. The following year, he set out to apply the packing-house organizing technique on a far greater scale to a key industry—steel. He put together another committee with the same team—Fitzpatrick as chairman and Foster as secretary. One of this committee's organizers was Jay G. Brown, later secretary of the Farmer-Labor party. In the fall of 1919, Foster led 365,000 steel workers in one of the major strikes of the decade. Despite defeat, its scope and ferocity enhanced Foster's fame as a trade-union organizer. From then on, he had almost nowhere to go but down.

After the steel strike, Foster took stock. He maintained that the existing trade-union movement did not need revolutionizing; it was revolutionary already. He wrote:

> The trade unions will not *become* anti-capitalistic through the conversion of their members to a certain point of view or by the adoption of certain preambles; they *are* that by their very makeup and methods.[26]

In this fashion, Foster obliterated the traditional line between revolutionary and nonrevolutionary trade unions. His view made the A.F. of L. as revolutionary in practice as the I.W.W., but on a far larger scale. This theory enabled Foster to square his A.F. of L. present with his I.W.W. past; it permitted him to tell a Senate committee in 1919, without putting too great a strain on the truth, that his views were "in the main" in harmony with those of Samuel Gompers; and it also enabled Gompers to vouch for him.[27]

Foster spent the next two years refining and enlarging this essential idea. He embodied it in his third personal organization, formed in November 1920—the Trade Union Educational League. The full-fledged Fosterite theory was set forth in a pamphlet, *The Railroaders' Next Step*, written in March 1921, just before his first trip to Russia. It was inspired by the unprecedented unrest prevalent in the railroad crafts, but Foster went much further than the railroaders' problems. He generalized on their experience for the entire labor movement and thereby produced a distinctive theory.

According to the Foster of 1921, the conservative unions were working toward the same goal as the radical unions. That goal was industrial unionism. The conservative unions were merely taking a different path, a path that was "unconscious," "evolutionary," and "inevitable." In the "more or less lengthy evolutionary process," he saw three distinct phases: isolation, federation, and amalgamation. In the first phase, craft unions acted independently. In the second phase, they made alliances with other craft unions. In the third, "they gradually fuse themselves together into a unified body along the lines of their industry." The third phase led directly to industrial unionism.[28] One of Foster's followers, Jay Fox, wrote reassuringly: "Amalgamation will proceed in an orderly fashion. There need be no violent disturbance of the existing organizations, with their long-established customs, dues systems, etc. The processes can go ahead in a steady progress." [29]

The end of the process, Foster predicted, would be the social revolution. He ended on a note of orthodox syndicalism:

> At heart and in their daily action the trade unions are revolutionary. Their unchangeable policy is to withhold from the exploiters all they have the power to. In these days, when they are weak in numbers and discipline, they have to content themselves with petty achievements. But they are constantly growing in strength and understanding, and the day will surely come when they will have the great masses of workers organized and instructed in their true interests. That hour will sound the death knell of capitalism. Then they will pit their enormous organization against the parasitic employing class, end the wages system forever and set up the long-hoped-for era of social justice. That is the true meaning of the trade union movement.[30]

None of Foster's ideas was really original. He had picked up the basic idea of boring from within during his first trip to Europe in 1910–11, and Gompers had used the term "amalgamation" as early as 1888.[31] Amalgamation had been proceeding in the clothing, railway, and machinists unions without Foster's help.[32] But previous amalgamationists had not fitted it into a revolutionary philosophy. Foster, who had a knack for adapting existing ideas for his own purposes, succeeded in making a peculiar hodgepodge of conservative, progressive, and revolutionary trade-unionism. He glamorized the purely organizing function of conservative unionism; he sensationalized the amalgamation policy of "progressive" unionism; and he tried to string them together on a revolutionary thread. He excluded only one existing tendency from his system—revolutionary dual unionism. On it he conferred chief blame for the backwardness of the American labor movement.[33]

Pre-Communist Fosterism was careful to offend the susceptibilities of the A.F. of L. as little as possible. The T.U.E.L. carefully attempted to avoid the traditional pitfalls that had brought previous rivals of the A.F. of L. to grief. It attacked dual unionism with the zeal of a recent convert. It issued no membership cards, collected no dues, and gave out no charters. To join, it was merely necessary to belong to a bona-fide trade union, accept the principles of the T.U.E.L., and subscribe to its official organ, *The Labor Herald.*[34] If the A.F. of L. was unconsciously but inevitably revolutionary, there was no reason why a good revolutionary could not be a good A.F. of L. man. The T.U.E.L. had something for everybody. It was revolutionary and evolutionary; it was dedicated to industrial unionism, but it was not going to upset the apple cart of craft unionism; it held out the soothing prospect of going by easy stages from craft unionism to industrial unionism, and from industrial unionism to the overthrow of capitalism.

At the height of Foster's organizing success and trade-union prestige, the Communists wanted no part of him. They scorned his panacea of boring from within as a betrayal of revolutionary trade-unionism. In the midst of the steel strike, they scoffed at him as "E.Z." Foster because he refused to take the hard road of dual unionism.[35] They condemned him mercilessly because he testified before a Senate committee that he had sold Liberty Bonds during the war.[36] As long as the Communists agreed with the I.W.W. in rejecting Foster's position, his T.U.E.L. had no chance of gaining a mass following or even a substantial body of revolutionary militants.

At the age of forty, then, Foster had demonstrated remarkable gifts as a labor organizer; he had worked out a theory of nonrevolutionary revolutionary trade-unionism; and he had a personal organization with a small but devoted group of disciples. Yet he found himself in a difficult position. After the steel strike, he marked time as an active organizer. Conservative trade-unionists rejected his theory because it was too revolutionary, and revolutionary trade-unionists rejected it because it was too conservative. His third organization, T.U.E.L., seemed doomed to remain, like the other two, an empty shell.

Cannon, Browder, and Foster

In the midst of this lull in Foster's career, the American Communists changed their trade-union line. Lenin's injunction to work in "reactionary trade unions" hit them with full force early in 1921. At the same time, the Comintern took steps to form a new trade-union international, the Red International of Labor Unions, otherwise known as the Profintern. The original plan called for an alliance with the syndicalists to compensate for the Communist weakness in the West-European and American trade-union movements. Foster suddenly fitted into both national and international Communist schemes. The Communist change of line transformed his supreme vice—the policy of boring from within the A.F. of L.—into his most precious virtue. Whether he could be converted into a Communist or would choose to remain an unorthodox syndicalist, the Profintern's organizers wanted him to attend its first congress in Moscow.

The Communists made the first overtures to Foster. Cannon says that he went to see Foster early in 1921 and found him "still hesitant and evasive" about Soviet Russia and the proletarian revolution.[37] But that spring the first Comintern delegation, composed of Scott, Fraina, and Katayama, arrived in the United States with instructions to round up an impressive group of American delegates to attend the Profintern's first congress. As a result of this mission the paths of Cannon, Browder, and Foster crossed at a crucial moment for themselves and American Communism.

Cannon, Browder, and Foster had much in common compared with most of the New York Communist leaders.

Cannon's parents had come from England and had settled in Rosedale, Kansas, then a suburb of Kansas City, where he was born in 1890. Browder's forebears had come from the British Isles over a hundred years before the American Revolution, and his parents had lived in Wichita, Kansas, at the time of his birth in 1891. When the Browder family moved to Kansas City in 1912, Cannon and Browder frequented the same radical circles. Like Foster, they had started out politically in the Socialist movement. All three had dropped out, one after the other, Foster first, then Cannon, and finally Browder. Like Foster also, Cannon went into the I.W.W. but rejected Foster's boring-from-within deviation.

This clash between orthodox and unorthodox syndicalism also came between Cannon and Browder. For a time they worked together on a Kansas City labor paper, *The Toiler,* published by one of Foster's followers, Max Dezettel. When the paper took Foster's line against the I.W.W.'s traditional dual unionism, Cannon withdrew and became one of the I.W.W.'s traveling organizers. Browder first met Foster during one of the latter's hoboing trips across the country organizing for the Syndicalist League and was influenced by him without formally joining the organization. An accountant by profession, Browder carried out Foster's policy by joining the local Bookkeepers, Stenographers, and Accountants union, which elected him its president in 1914.

Unlike Foster, Browder refused to compromise on the war issue and served two jail sentences between 1918 and 1920 on charges of conspiring against the draft law and non-registration. The Bolshevik revolution of 1917 made Communist converts of both Browder and Cannon, and reunited them politically. In the spring of 1919, between Browder's two prison sentences, they collaborated on a Kansas City weekly, *The Workers' World,* then one of the few pro-Communist papers in the Midwest. When Browder, its first editor, went back to jail for his second term, Cannon took over until he was arrested for agitating against a government injunction in a Kansas coal strike and the paper, after nine months, came to an end. Another long-time Communist who contributed to the paper was Ella Reeve Bloor, then the Socialist party's organizer in Kansas City.

While Browder served his second prison term, Cannon helped to organize the Communist movement in the Midwest. The Communist Labor party appointed him its secretary for the Kansas-Missouri district in 1919, and the United Communist party sent him as its organizer to the St. Louis–Southern Illinois district in 1920. Later that same year, he edited the U.C.P.'s organ in Cleveland, also called *The Toiler,* but was soon called to New York to take part in the top leadership of the U.C.P.'s successor, the Communist Party of America. Meanwhile, Browder was released from prison in November 1920 and moved from Kansas City to New York. He obtained a job as head of the bookkeeping department of a wholesale firm, joined the local Communist unit, and looked forward to a few years of quiet comfort.[38]

At this juncture, the Comintern delegation appeared on the scene, looking for someone to organize a broad American representation to the Profintern's founding congress. The New York Communist trade-union specialist, Joseph Zack, a recently arrived immigrant tailor, lacked the background for the task.[39] Cannon, fresh from the Midwest, thought of his Kansas City colleague, Browder, and recommended him. Despite his private plans, Browder could not resist the offer. On a cross-country tour for delegates, he stopped in Chicago and delivered an invitation to the most famous radical trade-unionist in the country, Foster, who also could not resist. Still enough of a syndicalist to have qualms about the venture, however, Foster agreed to go to Moscow only as an "observer." Browder himself headed an American delegation of seven, including one official I.W.W. delegate, to the Profintern congress, which took place in July 1921.[40]

Like John Reed before him, Foster went to Russia an observer and there became a participant. The articles he wrote in Russia indicate why he decided to throw in his lot with the Communists. For one thing, he was tremendously impressed with the ubiquitous power of the Bolshevik party.[41] Throughout the vast, chaotic land, he saw men like himself, some of them former syndicalists, running everything, in the factories, in the army, in the government. The Russian revolution also gave him reason to believe, as it had done earlier to the first American Communists, that a minority could win over the American masses and thus take a short-cut to the American revolution. Of "militants" like himself, he wrote:

The Russian revolution has taught them that the great masses will probably never become clear-headedly revolutionary, but that they will follow the lead of an organized conscious minority that does know the way.[42]

Above all, he has stated, he was first attracted to the Communist party by "Lenin's stand on the trade union question," which happened to coincide with his own.[43] The Comintern's ban on dual unionism made his T.U.E.L. the logical, ready-made instrument for Communist activity in the American trade-union movement. A pact was struck between the T.U.E.L.'s leader, Foster, and the Profintern's leader, A. Lozovsky (S. A. Dridzo), and for many years thereafter Lozovsky served as Foster's chief mentor and protector in Moscow. In the subsequent arrangement, Browder moved from New York to Chicago to edit the T.U.E.L.'s official organ and act as liaison with the party leadership. With the Profintern behind him and the American Communists in the T.U.E.L., the bargain did not seem at all unequal to Foster. He gave all the credit for his good fortune to the Comintern:

> To the Third International, and particularly to the Russians at the head of it, is due the credit for breaking the deadly grip of dual unionism in the American labor movement.[44]

Before he went to Moscow, Foster's chief stock in trade had been amalgamation. After he came back from Moscow, he added to his repertoire the Labor party, the defense of the Soviet Union, and the dictatorship of the proletariat. Foster at first merely superimposed these political objectives on his trade-union philosophy. In effect, the Communists accepted his trade-union policy, and he accepted their political program. But he still believed that trade-unionism took precedence over politics: "It may be accepted as an axiom that whoever controls the trade unions is able to dictate the general policies, economic, political and otherwise, of the whole working class." [45]

First, Foster helped to convert the Communists to his trade-union policy. Then he spent the rest of his life being converted by them.

Foster after Moscow

For about a year Foster's deal in Moscow paid off. The T.U.E.L. came to life at the beginning of 1922. It had consisted of "little more than a few scattered groups" before it launched its monthly organ, *The Labor Herald,* in March of that year.[46] The first serious Communist penetration of the American labor movement began March 19, 1922. On that day, Foster and Johnstone, on behalf of the T.U.E.L., introduced a pro-amalgamation resolution in the Chicago Federation of Labor without consulting the Federation's leaders.[47] The Communists had a strong bloc of twenty-eight delegates in the Chicago Federation, almost one-fifth of the total, and pushed through the resolution by a three-to-one vote.[48]

The Chicago Federation's resolution gave the signal for a nationwide pro-amalgamation campaign. By the following year, the score in favor of amalgamation stood at sixteen state federations, fourteen national unions, scores of central labor bodies and thousands of local unions.[49] "It was a veritable landslide," Browder rejoiced.[50] The T.U.E.L.'s National Committee reported that the amalgamation movement was "running like wildfire." [51] In the Comintern's organ, Foster spread the glad tidings that "fully half" of the American labor movement "has been led to declare itself" in favor of industrial unionism.[52] Samuel Gompers rushed to Chicago, denounced amalgamation as a Communist plot, and accused Foster of wanting "to become the Lenine of America." [53] In retaliation for the pro-amalgamation resolution, the A.F. of L. cut off its contribution of half the Chicago Federation's expenses.[54]

The Communists also began to entrench themselves and to wield increasing influence in the unions themselves. By the fall of 1922, the T.U.E.L.'s National Committee reported: "At the present time, the League has groups and connections in practically all the important industrial centers of the United States and Canada" and "already it is wielding a decisive influence in shaping the policies of Labor." [55]

"Decisive" was undoubtedly overoptimistic, but the influence was incomparably greater than previously. For the most part, however, Foster's strategy consisted of backing progressive opposition elements rather than attempting to challenge the existing leaderships with his own forces alone. The first candidate for top union office to get the T.U.E.L.'s support and to run on the T.U.E.L.'s platform was William Ross Knudsen, who opposed the incumbent, William H. Johnston, for the presidency of the International Association of Machinists in 1922. Knudsen went down the line for the Profintern, industrial unionism, and the "workers' republic" and, in a union of almost 200,000, received about 30 per cent of the votes.[56] In the miners' union, the T.U.E.L. backed Alexander Howat, President of the Kansas mine district, against the International President, John L. Lewis. Early in 1922, Lewis expelled Howat by a handful of votes, and Howat thereafter furnished the Communists and their causes with a militant progressive trade-union ally.[57] Other strength was claimed in the printing and needle trades and especially in the railroad unions.[58] "Like a flame sweeping through a dry forest, the program of the League is making its way through the trade unions," one of Foster's aides exulted.[59] For the T.U.E.L., 1922 was a year of "truly wonderful growth," another declared.[60]

At this stage, Foster's gratitude to Fitzpatrick overflowed publicly. He paid tribute at the end of 1922 to Fitzpatrick as "one of the sturdy oaks of the labor movement. Honest, capable and fearless, he is deeply hated by the labor-crushing elements in Chicago." [61]

Foster was still feeling his way in the Communist movement. His impulse was to stay aloof from the common variety of inner-party affairs and to devote himself to what he considered in the long run more important—the trade-union field. He conceived of himself as playing approximately the same role in the Communist movement as Eugene Victor Debs had played in the Socialist movement—the independent leader whose power derived from his popular following rather than from the party officeholders. Foster hid and even denied his Communist ties until 1923; his theory of winning the leadership of the existing trade unions by strictly trade-union methods still dominated his public image and statements. In the spring of 1922, he ridiculed those radicals who believed in winning over the workers "with talk" and advised them to keep their mouths shut more often, do more "day-by-day detail work," and convince the masses that they were good union men. "Let the militants offer a practical program, participate in labor's everyday struggles with concrete demands, let them learn how to handle masses and his [their] task of radicalizing the unions will be accomplished soon," he said.[62] Early the following year he counseled: "You must not be oppositionists on principle. Don't carry on an anti-Gompers' fight. That was the mistake of the old Socialist Party." [63] His approach was matter-of-fact, down-to-earth, straightforward.

One of the early women Communists compared him with other radical leaders: "Foster does not possess the overpowering gigantic force of De Leon, the emotional sweep of Haywood, nor the great emotional sweep of Debs. His power is centered on an elemental simplicity for interpretation, combined with a dynamic force for 'putting it across.' " And she added, "Listening to Foster, one does not feel as if in the presence of the mighty." [64]

At first Foster dealt at arm's length with the top Communist leadership through the medium of Browder, who shuttled between Chicago and New York. But the magnet of Communist power soon proved too strong and Foster decided to do his own political chores. Since the reserved Ruthenberg and the earthy Foster could never get along, a clash of ambitions menaced the party.

Pepper at first intrigued Foster as much as he did everyone else. Always on the look-out to strengthen his personal influence, Pepper lost no time in cultivating Foster. He paid effusive tribute to Foster in the party organ as "a man who is at once blood of the blood, flesh of the flesh, of the working masses; a worker himself, a trade unionist, a revolutionist, a Marxian and a Communist" [65]—an appreciation which rather overshot the mark. When disagreement arose in the Central Executive Committee over the advisability of splitting with Fitzpatrick at the Chicago conference, Foster's position came much closer to Pepper's than to Ruthenberg's, because Foster agreed with Pepper on the possibility of a split and merely posed different conditions. At Chicago, in effect, Foster chose between Fitzpatrick and Pepper, and though he soon regretted his brief honeymoon with Pepper, he could never go back to Fitzpatrick; without ties to Fitzpatrick's group, he could seek leadership only within the Communist party.

In Moscow the following year, Foster tried to explain why Pepper had seduced him in Chicago: "It is true that I was somewhat inexperienced in communist tactics, but Pepper, who allowed everyone to assume that he was representing the Comintern in America, was so enthusiastic that he voted one hundred per cent for everything that was undertaken in Chicago, and those of us who do not enjoy an international reputation were disposed to accept as correct communist tactics everything to which Pepper said *yes* and *Amen.*" [66] In his *History of the Communist Party of the United States,* Foster admits his share of the blame for the split with Fitzpatrick.[67]

The roads that led Ruthenberg, Pepper, and Foster to Chicago differed enormously. As people, they differed just as much. They cannot be pressed into the same psychological or intellectual mold. Yet, despite these differences, they came to resemble one another politically more than they would ever admit. As they fought one another, they adopted the same weapons and learned from one another how to wield them most effectively. Those who stayed in the Communist movement long enough became interchangeable parts of the same machine; they submitted to a system which used them all in the same way and subjected all to the same pressures of conformity. More than anyone else perhaps, Foster exemplified this process, because he had so far to go to become a Communist and then outlasted all the other Communists of his generation.

4

The Parting of the Ways

THE Federated Farmer-Labor party came into the world stillborn. As soon as the delegates left Chicago and scattered across the country, the Communists found they had won a Pyrrhic victory. They had been skillful enough to seize control of the convention, but they were not strong enough to pump life into the movement. The vast majority of the 600,000 members the delegates had claimed to represent faded away when it became clear that the Communists controlled the party.

The Communist secretary of the F.F.-L.P., Joseph Manley, later admitted that the Workers party had furnished the "overwhelming bulk" of the membership and finances. Only the Workers party had paid the nominal per capita tax to the F.F.-L.P. The Workers party had turned over its Chicago organ, *The Voice of Labor,* to the F.F.-L.P., which had renamed it the *Farmer-Labor Voice,* but the Workers party had continued to pay all expenses as before.[1] Only 100,000 members were represented in the organizations that had actually affiliated to the F.F.-L.P., most of them "on paper only."

"They could just as readily have been affiliated to any united front committee set up by the Workers Party," Manley stated.[2] Another Communist leader declared that the F.F.-L.P. had consisted of "ourselves and our nearest relatives." [3]

At first Foster did not fully realize how much the great Chicago victory had cost him. For a few weeks, he entertained the hope that one or all of his three main propaganda campaigns—for amalgamation, the Labor party, and recognition of Soviet Russia—would "shatter the Gompers machine." He saw the forthcoming A.F. of L. convention in Portland, Oregon, as the beginning of the end for Gompers' leadership.[4]

Then the bottom fell out of the T.U.E.L. Or, as Browder put it, the "storm broke" [5] and wiped out all the T.U.E.L.'s hard-won gains. The Progressive-Communist alliance in the unions was replaced by a Progressive-conservative alliance. The new Fitzpatrick policy made its appearance at the convention of the Illinois State Federation of Labor in September 1923. The Farmer-Labor party was overwhelmingly rejected, amalgamation repudiated, the recognition of Russia reversed. Fitzpatrick and his closest associates went down the line against all three causes, formerly dear to them.[6] The original Farmer-Labor party of Chicago wasted away, and the Chicago Federation of Labor gradually re-embraced Gompers' "nonpartisan" political policy.[7]

Without the cover provided by the alliance with Fitzpatrick, the Communists were isolated and defenseless. A wave of expulsions hit them in the unions. Membership in the T.U.E.L. was generally outlawed. The A.F. of L. convention at Portland, Oregon, in 1923 shattered Foster's influence, not Gompers'. The convention set an example for Communist expulsions by unseating William F. Dunne, a leading Communist representing the Butte, Montana, trade unions, by a one-sided vote of 27,837 to 108, with 643 abstentions. The expulsion motion was presented by Philip Murray, then vice-president of the United Mine Workers of America. Not a single voice was raised at the convention in favor of amalgamation.[8] The debacle, Foster later acknowledged, practically made the T.U.E.L. "an underground organization in nearly every trade union in the country." [9]

More than three decades later, at the American Communist convention in 1957, Foster spoke of the two greatest mistakes in American Communist history. He declared that the first had been made in 1923 when the Communists split with their allies in the Farmer-Labor movement, and the second in 1949 when they split with their allies in the C.I.O.[10] After so many years, the mistake of 1923 still haunted him because the isolation of the Communists in the nineteen-twenties so closely resembled in cause and effect the isolation of the Communists in the nineteen-fifties.

Hangover or fool's paradise

In 1923, Foster learned the lesson that every Communist trade-unionist learns sooner or later—that Communist trade-unionism exists at the mercy of Communist politics.

The original arrangement which had brought Foster into the Communist movement seemed to have separated the two. It gave Foster command of the Communist trade-union field through the T.U.E.L. with headquarters in Chicago, and it gave Ruthenberg command of the over-all political field through the Central Executive Committee with headquarters in New York. This division of labor worked well as long as the T.U.E.L. benefited from Communist support; it broke down as soon as Communist politics made the T.U.E.L. one of its victims. Foster had given the Communists the power to tear down as well as to build up his organization, and if he adhered to the initial deal restricting him to the trade-union field, he was back where he had started, a general without an army.

Ironically, Foster's Chicago associates, Swabeck, Krumbein, and Browder, had tried to save him from the consequences of a break with Fitzpatrick. Browder, in particular, had stuck out his political neck against Pepper. Immediately after the break with Fitzpatrick at a meeting of the Communist leadership in Chicago, he had denounced the split and had offered a motion that Pepper be invited to go back to Moscow. The motion was seconded by William F. Dunne, but no one else spoke for it, and it was never put to a vote.[11] Browder paid for his temerity by being left out of the Chicago District's delegation to the Workers party's national convention at the end of the year.[12] The ties that bound Browder and Foster were more complex than appeared on the surface. Browder worked as Foster's subordinate; he recognized Foster as the "organizer and directing head" and "logical leader of the new movement." [13] But he watched Foster vacillate and miscalculate; he had taken part far more openly than Foster had in Communist party politics; and the memory of Foster's political shortcomings rankled.

For a more successful revolt against Pepper, someone closer to the top leadership and more adept at party in-fighting was needed—someone, for example, like Jim Cannon.

Except for having sent off his letter to the New York leadership in support of the Chicago group's position, Cannon had stayed out of subsequent developments in the Communist–Farmer-Labor tug-of-war. While all the other Communist leaders were congregating at the Chicago convention, he had been assigned to speak at a picnic in Portland, Oregon, a circumstance which he did not think had been accidental.[14] Cannon knew nothing about the split with Fitzpatrick until he had read about it in a Pacific Coast newspaper. Owing to these circumstances, Cannon occupied a peculiarly strategic position in the inner-party struggle. As chairman of the party, he ranked high enough in the official hierarchy to tangle with Pepper or Ruthenberg. He had spent six months in Moscow and could not be hoodwinked by Pepper on that score. He had just crossed the country and could speak with authority about the state of the nation, the labor movement, and the party itself.

And Cannon was canny. He "had all the magnetism, the shrewdness, the punch, the bag of tricks of the typical American politician," wrote the Negro poet Claude McKay, after observing him in Moscow.[15]

To Cannon, Pepper's policy was paralyzing the party. Cannon had no illusions about its strength. His lecture tour had given him a vivid impression of how big the country was and how few the Communists were. He could not see the Communists leading a mass movement by themselves. Alone, Cannon's skepticism would not have made much difference. But if Foster felt the same way, the combined forces of the party's chairman and its trade-union leader could not be ignored.

As Cannon tells the story, he had stopped off at Duluth, Minnesota, shortly after the Chicago convention, for one of his last lectures. Foster was also there to attend a combination trade-union conference and picnic. They spent the afternoon discussing the situation under a shade tree in a corner of the picnic grounds. At first, Foster professed to be optimistic about the prospects of the Federated Farmer-Labor party. Cannon was more dubious, and Foster soon admitted that he himself was troubled. When Cannon pressed him for an explanation of his own role at the Chicago convention, Cannon recalls that Foster said to him, in substance: "You know, it's a funny thing. When people who all want the same thing get together in a closed room, they tend to see what they want to see and they can talk themselves into almost anything. In the party caucus at the convention, so many of our people, carried away by the enthusiasm of the moment, spoke so emphatically about our strength here, there and everywhere, including the Chicago Federation of Labor, that I got carried away myself and was convinced against my will and better judgment." Then Foster added: "The trouble is, we've got the hangover, but the others in New York are still living in a fool's paradise. Something has to be done to change this course, or we will soon fritter away all the gains of our trade-union work up to now." [16]

According to Cannon, this conversation was the beginning of the Foster-Cannon Opposition in the party. No commitments were made, but the factional seeds had been planted. Foster needed someone to goad him into waging a bitter, ruthless party war. He was no match for Ruthenberg or Pepper in a no-holds-barred ideological battle or in lining up allies for a factional campaign of envelopment. Cannon needed Foster's popular appeal, and Foster needed Cannon's factional ability.

The battle of the theses

Another man might have been shaken into temporary silence by the embarrassing turn of events after the Chicago convention. But not Pepper. He tried to bluff his way out by brazenly converting every Communist defeat into a triumphal victory. He insisted that the Federated Farmer-Labor party was a "real mass party" of the American Left Wing.[17] When Dunne was expelled from the Portland convention of the A.F. of L., Pepper called it "the greatest victory for the cause of Communism." [18] And he obtained Ruthenberg's backing in the coming struggle for power against Cannon and Foster.

At the meeting of the Workers party Executive Council on August 24, 1923, Pepper and Ruthenberg introduced a joint resolution to chart the future of the controversial Federated Farmer-Labor party. This resolution, known as the Pepper-Ruthenberg "August theses," insisted on going ahead with the F.F.-L.P. It held out the hope of enrolling 250,000 workers and 50,000–80,000 farmers by the end of the year. It admitted that such a party would represent only the Left Wing of the labor movement, but offered the additional inducement that it could become the nucleus for either a "mass party of labor" or "a mass Communist party." The authors made clear that they were interested in the F.F.-L.P. only as long as, and to the extent that, it served the interests of the Workers party:

> We will carry on the struggle for the labor party so long as we can increase the influence and strengthen the Workers Party organization through this campaign. When situations arise in which the interests of the Workers Party conflict with the goal of the formation of the labor party we must unhesitatingly sacrifice the labor party.

Instead of admitting failure, therefore, Pepper and Ruthenberg suddenly pulled out of their hats an embarrassment of riches—a big Left-Wing party, a mass Labor party, or even a mass Communist party. For one mirage, they had substituted three.

The "August theses" also launched a full-scale attack on three types of Communist opposition to the F.F.-L.P. These were identified as "former Leftists" who secretly opposed the idea of a Labor party on principle; trade-unionists who feared to lose their former Progressive allies by making an aggressive fight for the F.F.-L.P.; and others who shunned responsibility and lacked confidence in the party. The Leftist opposition was quickly dismissed as "not dangerous today" and "disorganized." Without naming names, the other two groups—

the leaders of which were easily identified as Foster and Ludwig Lore —were characterized as the "opposition from the Right" and the real danger. The trade-unionists came in for the biggest bombardment:

> This opposition holds important strategical points of the Party in its hands, which is fully justified. It is most closely connected with the trade union work of our Party. Without its active, 100% warm support and cooperation, the organizing of the Federated Farmer-Labor Party cannot be carried out. These comrades are skeptical, oppose the carrying out of important instructions of the C.E.C. On every question we have to negotiate with them for weeks, so that we lose most precious time thereby, and in this way the effectiveness and efficiency of the policy and instructions of the C.E.C. are diminished and impaired.[19]

The "August theses" were carried 9 to 3. Foster, Cannon, and Bittelman voted against them. The new Opposition was officially born.[20]

Of the minority of three, however, only Cannon dared at this stage to trade punches with Pepper. They squared off and let fly with articles in the *Daily Worker*.

Cannon led off cautiously. In his first article, he paid lip-service to the party line but warned his comrades "to watch carefully where we are going" and "not to let our enthusiasm lead us to overestimate the rate of radical development, and rush into premature actions." [21] He warmed up in the second by observing that "we seem to be organizing our enemies faster than we are organizing our friends" and "we still throw more bluffs and make more noise than our strength warrants." [22]

This was too much for Pepper. "A part of our most active and industrious comrades who have been rendering the best service to the Party in the fight for a standing in the labor movement, and in the fight in the trade unions, do not understand today the policies of the Party in the question of the Labor Party," he shot back. "They identify the Party too closely with the trade unions, and if not in their theory, yet in their practice, they wish that the Party would not be a political party, but simply a left wing of the trade union movement." [23]

In retaliation, Cannon presented an Opposition program. This amounted to nothing less than a demand for a return to the pre-Chicago-convention policy. He deplored the break with the Progressive wing of the trade-union movement and looked forward "to the possibility of a rapprochement." [24] In a subsequent article, he explained: "The progressive movement remains practically the same as before, and our attitude towards it, prior to Chicago, which was essentially correct, still holds good." [25]

This was full-scale sedition. "At a meeting of the Political Committee shortly afterwards, with Foster present," Cannon recalls, "Pepper singled me out for the brass-knuckles treatment. He sought, by a combination of denunciation and ridicule, to put an end to my critical opposition forthwith. I didn't care for that treatment and said so." Foster indicated that he was reconsidering the whole Chicago experience. He told Cannon after the meeting that he was quite worried about the situation, especially the danger that all their trade-union positions would crumble. "I don't recall him saying so specifically," Cannon adds, "but I think it was at that time that Foster made his basic decision to throw his full energy into the party and to fight it out with Pepper for the leadership." [26]

At every such turning point, the American heresy reared its head, and now it was Cannon's turn to express it:

> The American movement has no counterpart anywhere else in the world, and any attempt to meet its problems by the simple process of finding an European analogy will not succeed. The key to the American problem can be found only in a thorough examination of the peculiar American situation. Our Marxian outlook, confirmed by the history of the movement in Europe, provides us with some general principles to go by, but there is no pattern, made to order from European experience, that fits America today.[27]

But Pepper had no equal at weaving and side-stepping in a fight. His agile brain and glib tongue ceaselessly manufactured new theories, new historical analogies, new quotations.

In *The Liberator* of September 1923 he announced majestically: "The revolution is here. World history stands before one of its greatest turning-points—America faces her third revolution." But now it was neither a Communist nor a Farmer-Labor revolution. It was "the LaFollette revolution" of "the well-to-do and exploited farmers, small businessmen and workers." He went on grandiosely: "It will contain elements of the great French Revolution, and the Russian Kerensky Revolution. In its ideology it will have elements of Jeffersonianism, Danish cooperatives, Ku Klux Klan and Bolshevism. The Proletariat *as a class* will not play an independent role in this revolution." At the same time, Pepper peered even further into the future: "After the Victory of this LaFollette revolution, there will begin the *independent* role of workers and exploited farmers, and there will begin then, the period of the *fourth* American revolution—the period of the proletarian revolution." [28]

Pepper viewed LaFollette as a kind of American Kerensky who should be encouraged to take power away from the big capitalists in behalf of the middle class and then should be overthrown by the American Bolsheviks in behalf of the proletariat. As he put it the following month, the Communists were to support "the real people's movement—the LaFollette revolution" and at the same time "to criticize pitilessly" its half-measures and hesitancy.[29] The entire conception was plainly an American version of the two Russian revolutions of 1917.

Pepper's sudden enthusiasm for LaFollette had one great tactical merit. The Wisconsin senator was coming up strongly as the great hope of the vast majority of American liberals and progressives. Though no official announcement had been made, his candidacy for the presidency in the next year's election was already taken for granted, but it was still questionable whether he would capture the Republican nomination or start a new party. Only by supporting LaFollette could the Communists get back into the mainstream of the labor movement which was almost solidly behind him. The Farmer-Labor bandwagon having collapsed under him, and largely because of him, Pepper was all set to jump on the LaFollette bandwagon.

Pepper's analysis of the LaFollette movement also showed that his

American education was progressing. When he first came to the United States in 1922, he had thought in terms of two classes—the capitalists and the proletariat—and had ruled out the American middle class as a hopeless factor with no future. A year later, he had drastically revised this view of the American middle class. It was now so strong and dynamic that it was capable of achieving a successful revolution against the big capitalists. If Pepper had been too pessimistic about the American middle class in 1922, however, he became too optimistic about it in 1923. Yet he had lost his oversimplified picture of American society. He had caught a glimpse of a relatively fluid social structure in which it was possible in his own mind for such seemingly incongruous elements as Jeffersonianism, Danish co-operatives, the Ku Klux Klan, and Bolshevism to be jumbled together in a strange, new American ideology.

This was not the end. Pepper soon came forth with an even more daring theory. He started, as usual, with a perfectly valid fact, the farm crisis of the early twenties, from which he drew the conclusion that agriculture was the weakest link of American capitalism, and hence that the farmers had become the most revolutionary class in the United States.

He wrote: "It is of vital interest to our party to win over and influence as great a mass as possible of native-born English-speaking workers. But it is highly improbable that we can win over in the near future the majority of this labor aristocracy corrupted by imperialism. The farmers as a class present a different picture than the working class." [30]

In a matter of weeks, then, Pepper's interest had shifted from the working class to the middle class to the farmer. As always he overreached himself. The farmers' revolution deceived him just as much as the LaFollette revolution had done. Every time Pepper came across a new fact about his new country, his agitated brain worked on it until he had conceived a stupendous new theory. Before his enemies could recover from one, he hit them with another.

Even those who hated Pepper the most could not resist a sneaking admiration for him. Cannon describes one vivid scene.

He was illegally in the country; it was dangerous for him to appear anywhere in public, or even to become personally known and identified by too many people; and he had had only about a year to study the English language. Despite that, at one tense general membership meeting in Chicago, where the fight broke out in real earnest, and we were concentrating heavy fire on his regime, he appeared at the meeting, unannounced, to give us a fight. Facing a hostile crowd, which was excited to the brink of a free-for-all, he took the floor to debate with us—in English!—and his speech dominated the debate from his side of the meeting. It was a magnificent performance that failed.[31]

To break the deadlock, the Political Committee resorted to a device that always implied a lack of confidence by the American Communists in their ability to solve their own problems by themselves: it invited the dissenters to submit opposing theses to the Comintern.[32] Ruthenberg unsuccessfully tried to head off a war of theses. He arranged to have Foster, Pepper, and himself appointed as a special committee to work out a joint thesis. This attempt to reduce the mounting tension failed, and the Foster-Cannon combination came out in November 1923 with its own declaration of policy, the ideological debut of the new faction. It closely followed the line of Cannon's recent articles.

Foster and Cannon unequivocally condemned the split at the July 3 conference at Chicago. They accused the Communist top leadership of pursuing a "false policy" which had inevitably led to the split. They demanded a return to the former Communist-Progressive alliance. At great length they recited the disastrous effects of the Federated Farmer-Labor party, and held it responsible for the "heavy losses" and progressive isolation suffered by the Communists. By duplicating the Workers party, they charged, it was blocking the way to a mass Farmer-Labor party as well as to a mass Communist party. In effect, they proposed dropping the pretense of the F.F.-L.P. and working openly as Communists with the goal of restoring the *status quo ante* in the Farmer-Labor movement.[33]

Pepper and Ruthenberg countered with their own "November theses" which showed them in a compromising mood. The main problem they faced was what to do about the growing Third-Party movement and the declining Farmer-Labor movement. They attacked the Third Party under Senator LaFollette as "backward-looking" because it belonged to the trust-busting tradition of American progressivism, but said a good word for it because it weakened and split the "united capitalist class." They reduced the Federated Farmer-Labor party to the status of an "instrument of propaganda" for the idea of an "all-inclusive mass farmer-labor party" and named the F.F.-L.P. as only one of the groups that might call a national Farmer-Labor convention for the 1924 presidential elections. They adopted a very flexible election policy of supporting Farmer-Labor, Socialist, or Third-Party candidates, whichever had the best chance to win.

Only one type of candidate was not even contemplated by them—the Communist. They held out for maximum support to the F.F.-L.P., but made the more important practical concession of limiting organization of the F.F.-L.P. to places where it would not bring about a split in the Left Wing.[34]

The Pepper-Ruthenberg "November theses" were conciliatory enough to induce Cannon and Foster to withdraw their own proposals and avoid a head-on collision at the Workers party's third national convention the following month. Superficially, the party's political unity was restored. But Cannon and Foster had no intention of withdrawing their bid for power.

Cannon's *combinazione*

Foster and Cannon alone were no match for Pepper and Ruthenberg. The former were strong in Chicago but weak in New York, and Chicago alone gave them no more than a strong base of operations. The situation obviously called for alliances in the party as well as outside. In the preliminary stages, Foster was content to let Cannon, who was more intimately acquainted with the leading Communists and their exploitable grievances, take the lead. As the faction's chief organizer as well as its original ideologist, Cannon succeeded in a remarkably short time in forming a loose coalition of all the discontented elements, held together less by how much they agreed with one another than by how much they disagreed with Pepper.

The Jewish federation, the third largest, was one of the party's festering sores. In it two groups were locked in combat, one led by Alexander Bittelman, then the federation's secretary, and the other by Moissaye Olgin, editor of the Jewish organ, *Freiheit.* Bittelman, a member of the party's top Executive Council, had joined Cannon and Foster to vote against the Pepper-Ruthenberg "August theses." Fortunately for Cannon, Pepper had made a bitter enemy of Olgin by installing a "commissar" on the paper over Olgin's head. Pepper's choice, Gitlow, was scarcely qualified to cope with a coterie of high-powered Jewish intellectuals, and Olgin's angry resignation enabled Cannon to pull off a factional coup by gaining the confidence of both the Bittelman and Olgin groups.[35]

Cannon's next triumph was a tie-up with Ludwig Lore, editor of the party's German organ, *New Yorker Volkszeitung,* and chieftain of the German federation. Then almost fifty, Lore had started his long and prominent career in the Socialist movement in his native Germany; he had represented a German-style orthodox Marxism in the United States after emigrating in 1903; and he had lent his name and influence to the pro-Bolshevik Left Wing in the formative period of American Communism. But Lore had never been able to function in the Communist movement before the Workers party was formed at the end of 1921.[36] Though the Workers party had soon evolved into a regular Communist party, Lore had never been housebroken and continued to comment in the *Volkszeitung* on the events of the day with a unique lack of inhibition. He did not hesitate to criticize the Comintern's blunders, and Zinoviev's high-handed methods especially annoyed him.

Pepper had insisted on putting Lore on the Communist steering committee at the Chicago Farmer-Labor convention in order to build up some credit with him, but Lore had been the only member of the committee to vote against the split with Fitzpatrick, which logically should have lined him up afterward with Cannon and Foster.[37] Never an easy man to classify, Lore had then turned around and had voted for the Pepperite "August theses," which Cannon and Foster had opposed. After this, he sternly disapproved of a "Third Party alliance" with LaFollette, though that was one of the few things upon which Cannon, Pepper, Foster, and Ruthenberg agreed. As the national convention neared, Lore decided to back Foster and Cannon for the leadership because they appealed to him as indigenous labor leaders who could win a mass following, and because Pepper's methods resembled Zinoviev's too closely to please him.

Lore's sphere of influence far exceeded the German federation. Olgin stood close to him politically, as did the Jewish needle-trades leaders, Charles S. Zimmerman and Rose Wortis, and the first director of the New York Workers School, Juliet Stuart Poyntz, the most influential of the women near the top leadership.

In the end, Cannon's coalition ranged from the party's extreme Left to its extreme Right. The former was typified by Alfred Wagenknecht, one of the few unreconstructed Leftists, who considered himself a victim of discrimination in the distribution of leading posts. The latter was represented by the Finnish federation, which controlled the largest single bloc of votes in the party, about 45 per cent of the total.

Most of the 6583 Finnish members in 1923 were Midwest farmers whose main interest was in cooperatives, one of which, with a membership of 15,000, they controlled. The federation published three daily papers, the largest of which was *Tyomies,* with a circulation of 12,000, as well as a weekly for women and a semimonthly magazine.[38] Its secretary-treasurer, Fahle Burman, Swedish by origin and a former organizer of the Western Federation of Miners, lined up with the Foster-Cannon group and shared its practical attitude toward trade-union and other problems.[39] Like Lore, the cooperative-minded Finns had been drawn into the Workers party because it had appeared broad enough to tolerate considerable differences; then they had come under attack from the Pepper-Ruthenberg group for being different.

Of all the associations struck up by Foster in the struggle against Pepper and Ruthenberg, the one with Bittelman proved to be the most enduring and important. Superficially, Foster and Bittelman made a curious combination. The Irish carriage-washer's son and the

Jewish immigrant from Russia seemed as unlike as two people could be. One was a proletarian Midwestern trade-unionist who knew much more about strike strategy than Marxist theory. The other was a Marxist pedant and a product of the typical Russian-Jewish school of revolution—early Socialist training in the Jewish Bund, two years in Siberia, emigration to the United States in 1912, activity in the Jewish Socialist federation, and attraction to the Russian revolution.[40] Then in his early thirties, Bittelman already personified one of the principal types in the gallery of Communist leaders—the doctrinaire "theoretician." He and Foster clung to each other for many years, with intervals of rivalry, because one complemented the other.

Foster's attitude toward the New York Communists was double-edged. He had contempt for their estrangement from the American working class about which, he felt, they talked much and knew little. But he suffered from inferiority in their favorite pastime of theorizing and intellectualizing. Pepper could overwhelm him with analogies and precedents from European history or with just the right quotations from Marx, Engels, and Lenin. Foster's answer to Pepper was Bittelman.

Bittelman spoke and read Russian. He avidly followed the Russian press for the latest twists and turns of policy and the ups and downs of leading personalities. He functioned at his best as a pundit in top committees, laboriously composing long-winded, excessively abstruse inner-party documents in which the Comintern would find every comma in the expected place. Outside his immediate circle in New York, he was for years barely known, except as a name, to the rank and file. At the end of the nineteen-twenties, after a decade of uninterrupted party warfare, Ella Reeve Bloor assured Foster that "no one, through the country," knew two of his co-factionalists, one of them Bittelman.[41]

With Bittelman, Lore, Wagenknecht, and the Finns behind them, the "trade-union faction" of Foster and Cannon set out to give the "political faction" of Pepper and Ruthenberg a lesson in party politics. A preliminary victory was scored by the Foster-Cannon forces in a controversy over the location of the party headquarters. The

Chicago district committee proposed moving the headquarters from New York to Chicago on the ground that the party's mass activities centered in Chicago. After resisting the move, the New Yorkers capitulated. The national headquarters opened in Chicago on September 1, 1923, and remained there for almost four years.[42]

Foster's revenge

The third convention of the Workers party took place in Chicago, December 30, 1923, to January 2, 1924. It was attended by 53 delegates claiming to represent a membership of 15,233.[43] Unlike some previous and subsequent conventions, it was not attended by a Comintern delegation or representative and had to be content with a letter from the Comintern.

This letter congratulated the Workers party on correctly applying the united front in the United States; it assured the Americans that the opposition from Gompers, the Socialists, and "a few so-called 'progressive' trade-union leaders of the Middle West" created "the best basis for the United Front policy." It praised the organization of the Federated Farmer-Labor party as "an achievement of prime importance," but showed some awareness of reality by recognizing that the F.F.-L.P. had organized "only a small portion of the militant workers and farmers," and by calling for a larger "United Front of all proletarian and farmers' parties and organizations." [44]

Even before the convention opened, it was clear that Lore controlled the balance of power. According to Ruthenberg, he influenced about fifteen delegates, and the two major groups divided the rest.[45] Lore himself told of a desperate attempt by Lovestone, representing the Pepper-Ruthenberg group, to win him over:

> Before I left New York for the Chicago convention, just a year ago, I was told by a mutual friend that Lovestone would meet me at the Chicago railroad depot on my arrival. Lovestone, who had been obliged to get out of bed at 4 o'clock of a very unpleasant December morning in order to meet me, dangled, after a few preliminaries, a most enticing list before my eyes, a list of names in the handwriting of Comrade Ruthenberg. My

name stood at the head of the slate that the Ruthenberg-Lovestone-Pepper group was prepared to propose to the convention. I informed Lovestone that I had one main purpose at this convention, to oppose the LaFollette alliance with all my might.[46]

On the crucial issue of the "Third Party alliance," Pepper made a second attempt to bid for Lore's support or at least to neutralize him. The convention's "theses," acceptable to both the Pepper-Ruthenberg and Cannon-Foster groups, left the door wide open for a Communist–Farmer-Labor alliance with the LaFollette movement. Lore could have been defeated in an open vote. But at a secret session, Pepper started the discussion by springing a surprise. He tried to save Lore's face—or so Lore interpreted his move—by recommending that the disputed section should be withdrawn and referred to the Comintern for decision. The convention adopted Pepper's suggestion by a vote of 43 to 0, with 10 abstentions. Nevertheless, Lore refused to be bought at this price, and his group unanimously decided to support Pepper's enemies in the struggle for power.[47]

Meanwhile, Foster and Cannon organized a caucus of delegates held together by a common dislike for the policy that had resulted in the split with Fitzpatrick's forces. This caucus combined with Lore's band to beat down the Pepper-Ruthenberg group on two other fighting issues. When the Pepper-Ruthenberg group attempted to censure the Chicago district committee for having accepted Fitzpatrick's leadership, the vote went 37 to 15 in favor of the Chicagoans. Another Pepper-led sortie against Foster's leadership of the Trade Union Educational League was relegated to the incoming Central Executive Committee. On the other hand, the convention endorsed the old leadership's action at the July 1923 convention and hailed the formation of the F.F.-L.P. as a "victory for the Party." [48]

The final tussle toppled Pepper from power. With Lore's support, Foster and Cannon won control of the top leadership. It was not complete control, because Ruthenberg remained as Executive Secretary. Foster assumed the chairmanship, replacing Cannon in that post, and Cannon moved over to the post of Assistant Secretary. The Foster-Cannon-Lore coalition controlled the new Central Executive Committee by a margin of 8 to 5, and the Political Bureau by 4 to 3.[49] Lore was rewarded by the Fosterites with a seat on the C.E.C. Bittelman soon replaced Pepper as secretary of the Political Bureau.[50] The new majority also moved in to take over the most important districts. Swabeck remained District Organizer in Chicago, and another member of the Chicago team, Krumbein, was shifted to New York to replace William W. Weinstone as District Organizer.[51] Cannon's personal followers included Martin Abern, National Secretary of the Young Workers League, and Max Shachtman, editor of its semimonthly organ, *The Young Worker*. The Communist youth organization claimed a membership of 4000 and duplicated the factional divisions of the party on a smaller scale.[52]

Pepper shrewdly pointed out the convention's contradictions. It had approved the old leadership's Farmer-Labor policy and had elected a new leadership which disagreed with that policy. In the new leadership, one group criticized the former leadership from the Right in opposition to the split with Fitzpatrick, and the other group criticized it from the Left in opposition to an alliance with LaFollette. But Pepper consoled himself with the thought that the party had averted a split such as had formerly resulted from a bitter clash of policies and power.[53] One reason for the avoidance of a split was the new majority's willingness to maintain Ruthenberg as Executive Secretary. A clean sweep of the old regime might have precipitated a much more vindictive postconvention struggle for survival.

Ruthenberg also made a peace offering to the victorious Foster-Cannon caucus. As he saw it, three tendencies had developed in the party. The first sprang from the old "impossibilist" wing of the Socialist party, so called because it had believed that all reforms were impossible under capitalism and had advocated Socialist propaganda and education only. This tradition now expressed itself in the opposition to the united front and the Third Party alliance, he held, and it was represented from different sides by Lore on the Right and Wagenknecht on the Left. The second tendency originated with those Communists who came from the trade unions and the I.W.W. Ruthenberg charged that it overstressed the industrial side of the party's work, neglected the farmers and unorganized workers, and obstructed the Federated Farmer-Labor party. He mentioned Foster's name in this connection. The third tendency advocated, against the first one, fighting the actual class struggle, and, against the second, subordinating the industrial program to political struggles. Ruthenberg cited himself and Pepper as its exemplars. He contended that the leadership of the third tendency had been overturned by an "abnormal" alliance between the first and second tendencies; and he called for a renewal of the alliance between the second and third tendencies, to which he attributed the party's progress of the past year.[54]

Self-serving as this analysis was, it exposed some of the open nerves in the party. The two major groups, represented by Ruthenberg and Foster, could not get along separately and could not get along together. They needed each other and yet rubbed each other the wrong way. Logically, Ruthenberg and Foster should have found a way to work together and spare the party a mean and costly factional struggle. But once Ruthenberg saw Foster as his potential successor, he solidified his pact with Pepper, whose support he could not afford to lose. Different temperaments and backgrounds undoubtedly played a large part in this estrangement. Nevertheless, Ruthenberg and Foster had things of greater importance in common—the urge for mass influence, the organizer's sense of reality, the concern for actions more than words.

It is hard to see what could have permanently kept them so far apart, other than their rivalry for power. The way each side had tried to play off Lore against the other showed how little there was to choose between them in methods. Ruthenberg had gladly accepted Lore's support in August 1923 and had sent Lovestone to dangle an "enticing list" before Lore's eyes on the eve of the convention. But if Lovestone's attempt to buy off Lore had lacked delicacy, the alliance between Foster and Lore was not on a much higher plane of principle. Lore had voted for Foster, with whom he disagreed on the issue of the LaFollette alliance just as much as he disagreed with Ruthenberg. Foster had joyfully accepted the right vote for the wrong reason, and cashed in on Lore's belief, which was not without foundation, that he could influence Foster more than he had been able to influence Pepper. Ruthenberg thereupon expressed horror that Foster should have allied himself with the same Lore whom he had tried to make an ally and hinted broadly that the two of them should gang up on Lore. Foster, of course, preferred to have Lore as his junior partner than to go back to the old arrangement in which he was Ruthenberg's junior partner.

The Workers party's third convention at the beginning of 1924 was another milestone in Foster's development as a Communist. In three years, he had progressed from a Communist neophyte to the majority leader of the top leadership. He had, at first timidly, then more and more boldly, ventured out of the trade-union sanctuary where he felt most secure; and, thanks largely to Cannon's expert reconnoitering, he had successfully stormed, on the first attempt, the inner political fortress of the party's old guard, the Central Executive Committee.

Foster's latent political ambitions had been whipped up by unforeseen circumstances. He had previously counted on his trade-union strength to give him influence in Communist politics, but he had not anticipated that Communist politics would make or break his trade-union influence. When the C.E.C. determined the fate of his T.U.E.L., he could no longer content himself with control of the T.U.E.L.—he had to gain control of the C.E.C. With the T.U.E.L. in ruins because of Communist politics, he became a Communist politician ostensibly to regain the lost ground. And though for many years he still regarded trade-unionism as his special province, the quicksand of Communist politics dragged him in deeper and deeper, until he became indistinguishable from the men he set out to replace.

To them, however, he hardly qualified as a Communist leader of first rank. They were willing to recognize his credentials in one field only, that of trade unions, and even there they blamed him for the T.U.E.L.'s predicament. They had been accustomed to think of him as a trade-union specialist with a thin, hasty veneer of Communist ideology, and the circumstances of his victory gave them no reason to change their minds. The credit for outmaneuvering them belonged to others: Cannon had managed the coup; Lore had delivered the decisive votes; and the Finns had brought up the rear with big battalions of farmers whose dues the New Yorkers were glad to take but whom they contemptuously regarded as hopelessly Right-Wing country bumpkins. Without Foster's glamour as a mass leader, this combination might not have held together, but it was composed of such heterogeneous and even contradictory elements that it gave Foster's victory the ripe odor of political opportunism and encouraged the losers to stage a comeback by pressing the attack against its weakest link—Lore.

For Foster personally the Workers party's third convention marked the end of his strictly trade-union career. It plunged him into the maelstrom of Communist politics and power from which he had held himself publicly aloof in his first two years in the party. By building his power in the C.E.C. on the wreckage instead of on the growth of the T.U.E.L., he made the transition contrary to his original plan. The parting of the ways between Foster and Ruthenberg at the end of 1923 blighted the life of the party for the rest of the decade. The groups that formed around them congealed into fully formed factions which fought on one issue after another, exchanged places on issues, forgot what they had been fighting about, broke up partially, and formed again.

For years, the leaders of American Communism were haunted by a great "if": What would have happened to the Farmer-Labor movement, the Trade Union Educational League, and the inner life of the Workers party, if they had refrained from breaking with Fitzpatrick's forces in July 1923?

5

The LaFollette Fiasco

AFTER the split with Fitzpatrick, the miscarriage of the Federated Farmer-Labor party, and the tailspin of the Trade Union Educational League, the Communists were down but not out. The "Third Party alliance" gave them the rare opportunity of playing the same game twice.

The concept of this alliance arose out of Communist doctrine as it was understood and practiced in this period. According to this doctrine, the LaFollette movement represented a third party of the petty bourgeoisie as distinguished from the two parties of the big bourgeoisie, the Republican and the Democratic. To the extent that it signified a split between the petty bourgeoisie and the big bourgeoisie, the Communists welcomed it. On the other hand, they did not wish to be tainted by or accept any direct responsibility for a petty-bourgeois party, which, they insisted, could solve no problems for the working class but would inevitably mislead and betray it. To get around the difficulty of belittling the LaFollette movement and yet refraining from breaking with it, they conceived of an "alliance" between the Third Party, representing well-to-do farmers and small businessmen, and the Farmer-Labor party, representing workers and exploited farmers. They did not ask LaFollette whether he wanted to have Communist allies, but as long as he did not repudiate them publicly, a tacit understanding with a portion of LaFollette's following was possible.

As usual, Pepper was ready with a theory. His "theory of two splits" maintained that it was necessary to split the petty bourgeoisie from the big bourgeoisie, and also to split the working class from the petty bourgeoisie. The Third Party could be supported to do the first job, the Farmer-Labor party to do the second one.[1]

"The creation of a Third Party is a revolutionary fact," Pepper explained, "but it is a counter-revolutionary act to help such a Third Party to swallow a class Farmer-Labor party." [2]

Sometimes the policy was set forth as a matter of principle, sometimes as a practical maneuver. Ruthenberg's statements shuttled from one to the other. "But the birth of a Third Party will weaken the centralized capitalist power," he wrote. "It will place the petty bourgeoisie definitely in opposition to that centralized power. That is an event of great revolutionary importance. The Workers Party is ready to throw all its strength into the balance to bring about this situation." [3] At the same time he disavowed LaFollette in such a way that the Communists could keep their political skirts clean without isolating themselves from the masses behind LaFollette. After vowing that "we will unquestionably support LaFollette in the election campaign along with the masses of workers and farmers who are behind the Farmer-Labor Party movement," he gave this justification for the commitment:

> We are against LaFollette. We know that the political victory of the workers and exploited farmers lies over the dead body (politically) of LaFollette. We will say this to the working class of this country. If, in spite of what we say, the masses of workers and exploited farmers who are not yet Communists, insist upon nominating LaFollette and placing their hope upon him, we will not desert them in the struggle. We will go along with them and vote for their candidate, but at every stage of development we will point out that their hopes are illusions.[4]

With this basic approach the new ruling triumvirate of Foster, Cannon, and Bittelman had no quarrel. Their statement of policy, which they had the votes to make official, reiterated the theory of the two splits, the "Third Party alliance," the "class Farmer-Labor Party," and all the rest. But Foster had a special reason for getting behind the Third Party alliance. He still looked at such political maneuvers primarily from a trade-union point of view and he was chiefly interested in their effect on the A.F. of L. He expected the A.F. of L.'s rank and file to back LaFollette's candidacy while its bureaucracy continued to support the two old parties, and in this split he saw the best possibilities for the T.U.E.L.'s comeback.

"The split from the old parties will tear loose great masses of organized workers from their allegiance to the capitalist parties and their own leaders who are agents of these parties," the triumvirate predicted. "It will upset the balance of power in the A.F. of L. and open the door for a general development of the trade unions in all directions." [5]

Only Lore and Olgin, in the name of their group, came out in opposition to an electoral alliance with the Third Party of LaFollette. They argued that the Workers party was too weak to engage in such a complicated maneuver, that the economic situation did not warrant expectation of a mass political revolt, and that the Communists should follow "a direct and obvious class line" by steering clear of "dubious political deals with the petty bourgeoisie." [6]

At the other extreme, some Workers party branches embraced the Third Party so enthusiastically that they organized "LaFollette for President" clubs. By rebuking them as well as Lore's group, Ruthenberg adopted his favorite stance of avoiding extremes and striking a balance between political orthodoxy and mass influence.

The Farmer-Labor united front of 1923 had been a simple operation compared to the Third Party alliance of 1924. The one had posed relatively few political problems within a narrow sector of the labor movement but had come to grief over the issue of organizational control; the other raised far more complex political problems in relation to the working class, farmers, and middle class in an organizational form which the Communists could not even aspire to control.

"Unquestionably the policy which we must follow is a difficult one," Ruthenberg admitted. "It is not easy to strongly criticize and give support at the same time." [7]

The ambivalence toward LaFollette's candidacy in 1924 strikingly anticipated the Communists' ambivalence toward Franklin D. Roosevelt's candidacy twelve years later.

From Chicago to St. Paul

After Fitzpatrick's disillusionment, Chicago rapidly receded in importance as the Communists' center of operations in the Farmer-Labor movement. But their credit had not been exhausted elsewhere. A significant segment of the Farmer-Labor movement in the predominantly agricultural states still wanted to organize a new party for the presidential election of 1924. This sentiment was strongest in the Northwest, which had contributed the most important breakaway from Fitzpatrick at the Chicago convention in July 1923. Pepper's theory about the revolutionary potential of the American farmer conveniently coincided with the practical need of the Communists to seek new allies in the farm belt.

The theory and the need directed the Communists' attention to Minnesota. In 1922 the Minnesota Farmer-Laborites had scored a major upset by breaking through the traditional two-party system. They had sent Dr. Henrik Shipstead, a dentist by profession, to the United States Senate, had elected two of the state's ten members of the House of Representatives, and had gained control of the State Legislature. At a special election on July 15 the following year, the Farmer-Labor candidate, Magnus Johnson, had won the governorship by a big majority. Johnson's victory, soon after the Chicago convention of July 3, particularly attracted Pepper's attention. He analyzed it as a "real *people's movement* against capitalism" rather than a "class movement." Pepper justified instructions to the Minnesota Communists to vote for Johnson on the ground that the Communists could not separate themselves from a mass movement "even if these masses had lower middle class illusions, and even if they stood under petty bourgeois leadership." [8]

In the same month, July 1923, the left hand of the Communists did not seem to know what the right hand was doing. In Chicago, the left hand had split recklessly with Fitzpatrick's group. In Minnesota, the right hand had given "critical support" to the Shipstead-Johnson group. But the contradiction was more apparent than real. In Chicago the Communists imagined that they were strong enough to seize control. In Minnesota they knew that they were not. What the left or right hand did, then, depended on who had the upper hand.

The Minnesota Communists could not make a direct alliance with the Farmer-Labor party's top leadership. The next best thing was an alliance with a group of lesser leaders, among whom the key figure was William Mahoney, a former Socialist and Farmer-Labor veteran who edited the *Minnesota Union Advocate,* official organ of the St. Paul Trades and Labor Assembly. Harry M. Wicks was sent to negotiate with Mahoney, but Wicks and the local Communists could not get along together, and most credit for the successful effort went to a young Minneapolis machinist, Clarence A. Hathaway.[9]

Hathaway was an example of local talent available for promotion into the top Communist leadership. His mother was the daughter of Swedish immigrant parents, his father an English-American carpenter. Clarence was born in St. Paul in 1892, attended high school for three years, and at the age of nineteen was apprenticed as a machinist. He spent the years of World War I in England, where he was converted to socialism, and after his return to the United States in 1919 found his way into the Communist movement in Detroit. For some years, however, he was primarily known as a trade-unionist and official of the International Association of Machinists, first as secretary of the Michigan machinists' district in 1920–21, and on returning to Minnesota, as business agent of District 77 in 1922–24 and vice-president of the Minnesota Federation of Labor in 1923. In that year, he was made secretary of the Farmer-Labor party in Ramsay County; and as the year ended, the Minnesota Communists sent him as a delegate to the Workers party's third convention. His trade-union and political experience made him an invaluable Communist asset in the Minnesota united front maneuvers. Thirty-one years old in 1923, Hathaway was no grim pedant. He played and talked a good game of baseball; his personality was gay, warm, and slightly unstable. In the Communist factional line-up then taking shape, he identified himself with the Cannon wing of the Foster-Cannon entente.[10]

District No. 9 of the Workers party, with headquarters in Minneapolis, contained 1765 members in 1923, most of them Finns interested in little more than their cooperatives. English-speaking Communists like Hathaway were so rare that he claimed to be the only Communist connection with the Minneapolis Farmer-Labor party. Shipstead and Johnson would have nothing to do with him, but Mahoney welcomed his cooperation. Out of their joint efforts came, in September 1923, a new organization in Minnesota, the Farmer-Labor Federation, based on individual membership, unlike the older Farmer-Labor party which was primarily an electoral machine. In effect, the federation was a united front of a type by now familiar between Communists and "Left" Farmer-Laborites. Ruthenberg flatly stated that the Farmer-Labor Federation was organized "largely through the efforts of our party." [11]

The next step was a conference called by the Farmer-Labor Federation in St. Paul, November 15–16, 1923. The Communists participated in the conference through the Federated Farmer-Labor party which in this way still served a useful purpose. The conference set itself the goal of uniting the various Farmer-Labor groups throughout the country in preparation for the 1924 election. This conference opened the second stage of the Communist experiments with the Farmer-Labor united front in 1923–24. In the first stage, the Communists' allies had come from the trade-union wing of the Farmer-Labor movement centered in Chicago; in the second stage, they came from the agrarian wing centered in St. Paul.

LaFollette's shadow

But wherever the Communists turned within the Farmer-Labor movement, the shadow of LaFollette fell across their path. The new Communist allies were even more fervently pro-LaFollette than the old. Mahoney differed from LaFollette's other followers chiefly in his desire to see LaFollette at the head of a Farmer-Labor ticket instead of a more general Third Party ticket. For the Communists to make any headway with the Mahoney type of Farmer-Laborite, a price was necessary—support in one form or another of LaFollette's candidacy. The St. Paul conference compelled them to settle this price before November 15, 1923. The Workers party's Executive Council met two days earlier to determine policy for the Communist delegates to the conference.

Foster submitted the following motion: "That if the conference takes up the question of candidates, we shall support the nomination of LaFollette."

Ruthenberg offered a negative formula: "That we propose that nominations be left to the convention (we are not for LaFollette, but if the convention nominates him we will not split on that account)." [12]

Ruthenberg's motion was adopted by a vote of 9 to 2. In practical effect, the two motions scarcely differed. Ruthenberg's more devious approach was mainly a face-saving device to enable the Communists to have their LaFollette cake and eat it too. They knew that in the end they could not break with LaFollette without breaking the united front.

This settled, the November 15 conference decided to call a convention in St. Paul on May 30, 1924, to nominate candidates and adopt a platform. Meanwhile, LaFollette's own backers went forward, ignoring the St. Paul plans. The pro-LaFollette Conference for Progressive Political Action met in St. Louis on February 11–12, 1924, and issued a call for a nominating convention at Cleveland, Ohio, on July 4.

As the time for these conventions neared, Mahoney became increasingly unhappy about the May 30 meeting. Before committing himself, he wanted to know the final decision on LaFollette's candidacy. To the Communists, his vacillation meant that, in a choice between LaFollette and Farmer-Laborism, he would choose LaFollette. The date of the St. Paul convention suddenly took on the significance of a determination to go ahead with a Farmer-Labor candidacy with or without LaFollette and with or without Mahoney. Pepper, once more the extremist, made May 30 a holy symbol. When Mahoney protested, "There is nothing sacred about May 30," Pepper retorted, "But there is something sacred about May 30, Mr. Mahoney! May 30 is the date and the symbol of the class party!" [13]

But Pepper could no longer impose his will on Communist policy. The Fosterites shrank from the prospect of another split, and they outvoted Pepper in the top committee 4 to 3—Foster, Browder, Dunne, and Cannon versus Pepper, Ruthenberg, and Lovestone.[14] In revenge, Ruthenberg threatened to appeal the decision to the Comintern, and the two sides agreed to send a delegation to Moscow for a showdown.[15]

Meanwhile, Mahoney could not wait for Moscow. He wanted to postpone the May 30 convention to June 20 in order to get closer to the C.P.P.A.'s July 4 convention. Ruthenberg and Foster persuaded him to call a conference in St. Paul on March 12 to adjust the question of the date. Among themselves, the Communists continued to differ. Pepper refused to budge from his "sacred" May 30 even at the risk of isolation. But this time, Pepper was isolated. Ruthenberg was willing to settle for June 20 if the Communists failed to get five state Farmer-Labor parties for May 30, a condition with little likelihood of fulfillment, and Ruthenberg's compromise won, 6 to 1.[16]

At the meeting on March 12, the Communists narrowly avoided a split. For a while no agreement on the date seemed possible. Finally it was set for June 17. In addition the Communists joined in recommending to the forthcoming convention a course of action which would leave the way open for support of the candidates and platform that the C.P.P.A. might adopt on July 4. A new organization committee was set up, with Mahoney as chairman and Hathaway as secretary.[17]

After this meeting, the confusion was immense. Here were two conventions, less than three weeks apart, ostensibly called to nominate presidential condidates. In the first one, the Farmer-Laborites made no effort to hide their desire to support the candidate of the second one. The Communists did not want to come out for the Farmer-

Laborite candidate and did not want to come out against him. A way out of this maze was proposed by Ruthenberg on May 2:

> We shall nominate in the convention [on June 17] a candidate in opposition to LaFollette and cast our vote for such a candidate. We must, however, be careful to see to it that this manoeuvre does not defeat LaFollette, for to nominate another candidate and permit LaFollette to become the candidate of the July 4 convention in opposition to our nominee would be to destroy the class farmer-labor party as a mass organization.[18]

The Fosterite majority preferred a less circuitous formula and voted down Ruthenberg's proposal in favor of a resolution by Foster that concluded:

> if he is nominated, pledging our support but stating our Communist attitude toward LaFollette.[19]

Again the difference was more apparent than real. As Foster later revealed, Ruthenberg time and again "gave Mahoney, of the Minnesota farmer-labor party, to understand that if the Workers Party made any opposition to the candidacy of LaFollette in the approaching conferences and convention it would be purely formal, to keep the record clear." [20]

Clear or not, such was the record until the May preceding the two conventions.

And then came voices from afar.

The curse of Trotskyism

After months of silence, the Comintern spoke. All through the crisis with Fitzpatrick, the Comintern had been of little help to the American Communists. Its letter at the end of 1923 to the Workers party's Third Convention had shown little awareness of the real situation caused by the split with Fitzpatrick. But in the spring of 1924 as the Americans were entangled in their negotiations with Mahoney, the Comintern proceeded to take a lively interest in American politics. The occasion was an enlarged meeting of its Executive Committee (E.C.C.I.), otherwise known as a "plenum," held in April-May 1924. This plenum gave the American factions an opportunity to settle their differences in Moscow just before the St. Paul and Cleveland conventions.

Each of the three main factions was represented by an American delegate to the plenum. Fresh from his victory at the Workers party's Third Convention, Foster looked forward to his second appearance in Moscow as the new majority leader. Ruthenberg decided that it was more important for him to organize the St. Paul convention than to spend weeks discussing policy in Moscow, and Pepper went instead. Lore could not be persuaded to make the trip, and Olgin substituted for him.

The American delegates arrived in Moscow in the midst of the turmoil and upheaval that had erupted in the Russian Communist party after Lenin's death in January 1924. The struggle for power was being waged on the one side by a triumvirate composed of Zinoviev, head of the Comintern and the Leningrad party organization, Kamenev, head of the Moscow party organization, and Stalin, General-Secretary of the Russian party; and on the other side by Trotsky, Commissar of War. The most prominent member of the ruling triumvirate and Lenin's heir apparent, Zinoviev, was a man of outward grandiosity and inward sleaziness, accustomed to use the Comintern as his personal fief. Of the four, the man who occupied least place in the consciousness of the Americans was Stalin.

It appears that Stalin made his debut in the American Communist press as late as 1921 with an article on the national question, reprinted from the Russian Press Service.[21] Foster's book of 155 pages about his first visit to Russia in 1921 contained a chapter on "Some Revolutionary Leaders," starting with Lenin, Trotsky, Zinoviev, and Bukharin, and listing twelve more names, but Stalin's was not among them.[22] Before 1924, Stalin seems never to have spoken in the Comintern, though he is mentioned as a Russian delegate on two occasions.[23] The first article on Stalin in the American press did not appear in a Communist publication. It was written by a fellow traveler, Anna Louise Strong, for *Hearst's International* of April 1924. She wrote, "As far as Lenin can be said to have any successor, Stalin inherits his place." No one took her seriously.[24]

The father of American anti-Trotskyism, as of so much else, was Pepper. His feud with Trotsky went back to the Comintern's Third Congress in 1921, at which he had engaged in a polemic against Trotsky, with a temerity unusual at so early a period, on the nature of the revolutionary perspective. Pepper had hotly challenged Trotsky's view, then similar to Lenin's, that the bourgeoisie had won a "breathing space," and had made himself a spokesman of the "Leftist" Zinovievist position that the Communists should continue to base themselves on "civil war and crises." [25] Trotsky had struck back at Pepper with some of his most scathing invective and the wound had never healed. When Pepper came to the United States the following year, he brought with him his antagonism to Trotsky and imbued his American disciples with it.

Trotsky later paid his respects to Pepper in these terms: "As for Pepper, he is the consummate type of the man who knows how to adapt himself, a political parasite." [26]

Trotsky's first influential sympathizer in the American party was Lore. He had befriended Trotsky during the latter's short stay in New York in 1917 and had refused to conceal his admiration for Trotsky even after it had become politically dangerous. With far more enthusiasm than accuracy, Lore had reported the Foster-Cannon-Lore victory at the Workers party's Third Convention to his *Volkszeitung* readers as a Trotskyist victory. Lore's predilection for Trotsky—rather than for Trotskyism, which still lacked sharp definition—and his animosity toward Zinoviev fed each other. On one occasion, after Zinoviev had observed that the Comintern expected a welcome surprise from the American labor movement, Lore dared to question whether Zinoviev's information about the United States came from reliable sources. On the fifth anniversary of the founding of the Comintern in March 1924, he infuriated the Comintern's apologists with a typical Loreism.

> The Third International changes its tactics, nay, even its methods, every day, and if need be, even oftener. It utterly disregards its own guiding principles, crushes today the theses it adopted only yesterday, and adapts itself in every country to new situations which may offer themselves. The Communist International is, therefore, opportunistic in its methods to the most extreme degree, but since it keeps in its mind the one and only revolutionary aim, the reformist method works for the revolution and thus loses its opportunistic character.[27]

Pepper was the first to exploit the possibilities of amalgamating the factional struggle in the Russian party with the factional struggle in the American party. Through Trotsky, he saw that he could strike at Lore, and through Lore, at Foster. He went into action immediately after the first official condemnation of Trotsky at the Russian party's thirteenth conference in January 1924. The following month, Pepper nominated himself to write an article for *The Liberator* endorsing the "Old Guard Bolsheviks," as the Russian triumvirs Zinoviev, Kamenev, and Stalin called themselves. Cannon objected on the ground that he did not know enough of the facts.[28]

In March, Pepper for the first time openly combined the anti-Trotsky campaign with the anti-Lore campaign. He opened fire on Lore with a bill of particulars against Lore's writings, and tagged on a subsidiary motion to "endorse fully the policy of the majority of the Russian C.E.C. and Conference of the Russian Party." Never before had such a bold attempt been made to utilize the Russian factional struggle as a weapon in the American factional struggle. In this maneuver, Pepper could not lose. If the Fosterites voted against Trotsky, they would displease their ally, Lore. If they balked at repudiating Lore, they could be charged with shielding Trotsky, about whom they knew little and cared less. In self-preservation, the Fosterites managed to ward off Pepper's blow by a 4-to-4 vote in the Executive Council.[29]

Later that month, Pepper pressed the attack again. In the larger Central Executive Committee, he made a short, simple motion "to endorse the Old Guard in the Russian Communist Party controversy." Once more Foster was compelled to fight back defensively; he offered an amendment to the effect that the American party was "not called upon to take a position on the merits of the controversy" because the Russian party conference had already settled it. Instead, Foster asked the party press to print all the documents of the controversy for discussion, and condemned any attempt to make it a factional issue in the American party; the Fosterite majority in the C.E.C. pushed through his proposal.[30] In the "discussion" that took place in the *Daily Worker,* Zinoviev appeared in twenty-three issues, Stalin in six, Kamenev in four, and Trotsky in three—a margin of thirty-three to three against Trotsky.[31]

The term "Old Guard" curiously linked the Russian and American factional struggles. In Russia, it was used by the Zinoviev-Kamenev-Stalin regime to get across the idea that Trotsky had been a comparative late-comer in the Bolshevik party. In the United States, it was used by the Pepper-Ruthenberg group as a reminder that Foster had been a comparative late-comer in the American Communist movement. The American "Old Guard" tried to cash in on the victory of the Russian "Old Guard," but there was more to it than that. Ruthenberg and his followers sincerely believed that Foster was an upstart, a barely reformed syndicalist, a threat to the real founders of the party and true guardians of the Communist faith. Little as Trotsky and Foster resembled each other in any other respect, their similarity as late-comers inspired the deposed American "Old Guard" to regain power by putting the curse of Trotskyism on Foster.

Foster's foes refused to let go of a good thing. The Thirteenth Congress of the Russian party took place in May 1924, while Foster, Pepper, and Olgin were still in Moscow. In advance of this congress, Charles E. Scott, then the American representative to the Profintern, sent a telegram to Ruthenberg suggesting a message to the Russian congress endorsing the "old Bolsheviks." Ignoring the last decision of the C.E.C. against taking a position on the Russian controversy, Ruthenberg despatched a telegram on his own responsibility: "Our Party supports the leadership of the old Bolsheviks and trusts they will continue to guide your work"—and later boasted about it.[32]

To their consternation, the three American delegates in Moscow found that the only policy on which all of them agreed, the "Third Party alliance," had become a political football in the Russian factional struggle. They learned that Trotsky had made the Comintern one of his main targets of criticism on the ground that it had been pursuing a soft, opportunistic policy, and that he had singled out as one of the worst examples of this evil the American party's proposed alliance with LaFollette.[33] To cut off this line of attack, Zinoviev had decided to execute a "Left turn." The new order of the day banned any form of cooperation with liberal or Social-Democratic parties. The Comintern now wanted the British Communists to fight against the MacDonald Labour government, the French Communists to attack Herriot's "Left Bloc" regime, and the German Communists to break off all relations with the German Social-Democrats. If MacDonald and the German Social-Democrats were outlawed as enemies, how could LaFollette, who had never paid lip service even to socialism, qualify as an ally of the Communists?

Pepper's "exile"

Foster pathetically described his unexpected tribulations with the Third Party alliance:

> It was my hard task to defend it in the Comintern. No sooner did I hit Europe and explain it to the first revolutionist I met than I encountered a drastic condemnation of it as the most dangerous opportunism. And so it continued all the time I was on the continent. Never on my whole trip, in Russia and elsewhere, did I meet a single Communist who did not wholeheartedly repudiate this proposition. The action of the Comintern presidium was unanimous in rejecting it as a manoeuvre unfit for the Workers Party to make.[34]

Foster learned fast. When he recovered from his embarrassment, he moved to the Left so quickly that he outdistanced the Comintern leaders. They demanded complete disassociation from LaFollette, but they had not yet reached the point of cutting loose from the Farmer-Labor movement. Foster made a leap into the more extreme position. He argued that, if a split with the pro-LaFollette Farmer-

Laborites took place at the St. Paul convention on June 17, there would be no one left but the Communists and their closest sympathizers. Hence he proposed that, if the Farmer-Labor party failed to have a "mass character," as it certainly would, the Workers party should run its own candidates. Zinoviev and the other Comintern leaders accepted this amendment.[35] But Foster still had far to go to get a high mark from his superiors. Radek, then head of the Comintern's American Commission, spoke sharply about him: "As far as the work of Comrade Foster is concerned, I believe that we may have serious difficulties with this comrade." [36]

Logically, Lore should have reaped the benefit of the Comintern's anti-LaFollette decision. But the "coincidence," as one of Pepper's disciples, Amter, called it deprecatingly,[37] added the Comintern's discomfiture to all the other counts against Lore. The Comintern considered it inopportune to demand his immediate punishment and merely called for an "ideological campaign" against Lore's tendency.[38] Nevertheless Lore's days in the Communist movement were clearly numbered.

Pepper, Foster, and Olgin were subjected to the strongest pressure to denounce Lore. Pepper needed no urging, but Foster was Lore's ally and Olgin was Lore's collaborator. In this situation, it was incumbent on Foster and Olgin to outdo Pepper in demonstrating their anti-Loreism. They were equal to the task. Foster introduced the motion to censure Lore for his past misdeeds.[39] Olgin was prevailed on to break with Lore and go home to compose a series of bitter tirades against him.[40] By turning on Lore, Olgin successfully passed the Comintern's test of loyalty to itself above everything.

A gifted writer, linguist, and scholar, Olgin became the dean of Jewish Communist intellectuals in the United States but he had much to live down. The Bolshevik revolution of 1917 had at first dismayed him. He had written a book in which he had called the Mensheviks "more realistic" and the Bolsheviks "more dogmatic," and a magazine article in which he had accused Lenin, whom he had called the "Great Inquisitor of Russian Social Democracy," of blocking "the road of the Russian revolution by calling forth a reaction" and "in reality weakening the strength of democratic Russia."[41]

Like many Jewish Communist intellectuals of the time, Olgin was an assimilated Russian in his culture and outlook. He could not give up his Russian orientation after he came to the United States in 1915 at the age of thirty-seven. A pilgrimage to Soviet Russia had preceded his conversion to communism and his entrance into the Workers party in 1921. He could not bear the thought that his anti-Communist record might bar him from his intellectual homeland. Not quite attuned to the new order, however, he had made a second grave blunder by joining forces with Lore.

When Olgin broke with Lore and denounced his former associate, he showed that he had the stuff of which long-time Communist leaders were made. The lesson was not lost on him. In the nineteen-thirties, he wrote the official anti-Trotskyist manual.[42] He devoted himself to defending the party line, whatever it was, or to smelling out what it was going to be. If any of his friends fell into bad grace with the party, he demanded the privilege of denouncing him. With his great talents, he needed only a defect in character to rise to the top.

For Foster, one feature of his second journey to Moscow was pure, unadulterated joy. Pepper had asked the Comintern to remove Foster's faction from power in the American party by adding four more minority members to the Central Executive Committee and by turning over full control of the *Daily Worker* to the reinstated Pepper-Ruthenberg majority.[43] Foster retaliated by demanding the removal of Pepper from the American scene. The Comintern assuaged some of Foster's distress by turning down Pepper's demands and granting his request.

When Pepper's American disciples learned of his "exile," they wailed with rage. Ruthenberg, Lovestone, Bedacht, and Minor sent off long testimonials to the Comintern attesting to Pepper's extraordinary services to the American party.[44] In the *Daily Worker,* Lovestone called Pepper's forced retirement from the American scene the "virtual deportation" of "a comrade who has been of greater service to the Communist International in general and to the Communist movement in particular than all of the demagogic, hypocritical defamers of him and his associates."[45] Gitlow assailed it as "a crime against the party" because "no single man has rendered the American party as much valuable service as did Comrade Pepper."[46]

But Pepper did not need their commiseration. He soon made his Russian "exile" just as profitable as his American "exile" had been. He attended the Comintern's Fifth Congress only a few weeks later as a ranking American delegate, and delivered the report of the key Political Commission.[47] He was subsequently appointed chief of the Comintern's newly formed Information Department.[48] Pepper in Moscow could do almost as much damage to the Fosterites as he had done in New York or Chicago. He was excellently placed in the Comintern to give his American faction the inside information that would do it the most good. Instead of getting rid of Pepper, Foster had merely shifted him to another battle front.

Back home Foster tried to make the most of the Comintern's rejection of Pepper's demands:

> We all know that the C.I. is a real international and that it does not hesitate to reorganize a central executive committee in any country if such action is necessary in order to put the party involved back into Bolshevik control. Now if the claims of the [Pepper-Ruthenberg] minority were true the duty of the Comintern would have been clear, and we know it would have performed that duty relentlessly by removing the present C.E.C. from power.[49]

Again Foster crowed too soon. Radek foreshadowed the ultimate fate of Foster's majority by referring to Ruthenberg's group as "the element of Communist consciousness."[50] The American factions bandied about what the Russian leaders said about them in Moscow to prove whether they were in or out of favor. Foster played up Pepper's unsuccessful demands and Lovestone countered with Radek's unfavorable remarks. No one questioned the fundamental principle that an American Communist leadership could be made and unmade in Moscow, and by using it against Pepper and Ruthenberg in 1924, Foster paved the way for his own undoing a year later.

Foster also came back from Moscow far wiser in the ways of the Russian factional struggle. After his return, the C.E.C. endorsed the "Bolshevik group" in Russia by a vote of 12 to 1, the lone hold-out being Lore. Ruthenberg rubbed it in:

Evidently Comrade Foster had learned while there that the Communist International did not look with favor on parties which refused to take a position on such a vital question as the controversy in the Russian Communist Party.[51]

In fact, all the Americans had learned so much in Moscow that soon afterward, at the Comintern's Fifth Congress, the American delegation was given the honor, in the company of the German, French, and British delegations, of presenting the anti-Trotskyist resolution.[52] By the end of 1924, Foster and Ruthenberg sent jointly signed cables to the Russian party denouncing Trotsky.[53]

Within twenty-four hours

The Comintern handed down its final decision on the American question in Moscow on May 20, 1924.[54] Foster returned from Moscow on June 1 and read it, top secret, to the Central Executive Committee.[55]

The consternation it created was later described by Bittelman:

All our tactics, all our literature, all of our slogans formulated during the months of January to May were based on this general idea of the third party alliance and then at a certain moment the Communist International said to our party, you cannot do it, and the Central Executive Committee was confronted, comrades, with a very critical situation. I am sure every member of the Central Executive Committee will be able to recall now very vividly the situation we found ourselves in at that particular moment. We were confronted with the necessity of completely reorienting ourselves practically within 24 hours, and comrades, a reorientation which was to take place [not] in the close study of your library, not in your own room, a reorientation of a political party on the open political arena, under the very fire of the enemy, because you must remember that at about the same time LaFollette and Gompers opened their attack on the June 17 convention and the Communists.[56]

The Comintern came out for a break with LaFollette in such a way as to enable the Communists to run their own candidates. It suggested that the Farmer-Labor party should offer to support LaFollette on condition that he would accept its full program and give it control over his campaign and finances. After LaFollette had inevitably rejected these terms, the Communists could use his refusal in order to repudiate him. A break with the pro-LaFollette elements in the Farmer-Labor movement would unquestionably ensue, whereupon the Communists could run their own candidates in the coming presidential election.[57]

Eight days after the Comintern had reached its decision, LaFollette made public a letter to Attorney General Herman L. Ekern of Wisconsin in which he denounced communism and excluded the Communists as "the mortal enemies of the progressive movement and democratic ideals." [58] Since the Comintern's decision was still a tightly guarded secret, the American Communists were able to counterattack as if LaFollette had forced them into it.[59]

The Third Party alliance, then, came apart at both ends almost simultaneously. Mahoney immediately showed the effects of LaFollette's letter and began to sound like a second Fitzpatrick. He wrote: "The presence of an organized revolutionary group within the [Farmer-Labor] party and constantly striving to control and direct it, is causing many to question the wisdom of tolerating such activity," and "The thing that causes most irritation and distrust is the existence of a small group carrying on their intrigues and plots to control." [60] By the time the June 17 convention approached, Mahoney was fighting in the arrangements committee to exclude Communist delegates.[61]

By declaring the Third Party alliance dead, LaFollette and the Comintern deprived the June 17 convention in St. Paul of its reason for existence. Foster entertained doubts about the whole enterprise, but Ruthenberg had invested too much in it to let go and was determined to hang on to the Farmer-Labor movement without the Third Party alliance. He redoubled his efforts to make the Farmer-Labor movement a success and greeted LaFollette's attack as a blessing in disguise: "The road is now clear for the Farmer-Labor Movement to march forward." [62]

Ruthenberg's efforts mainly consisted of manufacturing counterfeit Farmer-Labor parties. Manley revealed that he and the local Communist organizer had hatched the Farmer-Labor party of North Dakota. Swabeck disclosed that the convention of the Illinois Labor party was packed with Communists or close sympathizers. Hathaway, at the center of the organizing activity for the St. Paul convention, confessed that in most states the Farmer-Labor conventions were "made up of delegates of [Communist] party branches only." According to Manley, the Communists spent at least $50,000 to subsidize so-called Farmer-Labor organizations, conventions, and publications.[63]

Under these circumstances, the fact that the St. Paul convention met at all was another triumph for Communist persistence and organization. It was attended by over 500 delegates from nearly 30 states.[64] The same issue arose that had wrecked the Chicago convention the year before. The Communists demanded a national Farmer-Labor party immediately, and Mahoney's group favored postponement. This time the Communists gave way to Mahoney. But with a Comintern decision at their backs the Communists could not compromise on the decisive issue of LaFollette. At the convention the pro-LaFollette sentiment outside Communist ranks was so strong that Foster raised the question whether it was worth going on. The majority of the Communist top leadership could not bear the embarrassment of calling off the convention midway and decided to go ahead even if the outcome had to be disowned afterward. In the confusion, even the factional line-up crumbled.[65]

Though the convention refused to turn itself into a full-fledged political party, it went on to nominate candidates. Mahoney, who knew that LaFollette did not want any dealings with the convention, proposed leaving the nomination open in order to make possible LaFollette's support at a later stage.[66] In obedience to the still secret Comintern decision, Foster declared that the Communists could accept LaFollette as the Farmer-Labor candidate only if he agreed "to accept the party's platform and its control over his electoral campaign and campaign funds." [67] A subterfuge gave all sides a way out of this impasse. Duncan MacDonald, a mine-union official, was nominated for President, and William Bouck, the Washington state chairman of the Federated Farmer-Labor party, for Vice-President. MacDonald later revealed that he had consented to the arrangement "with the express understanding that it be only provisional, contingent on the outcome of the Cleveland conference of the LaFollette group." [68] This unusual "understanding" was merely a face-saving device. Foster admitted that LaFollette "could have controlled St. Paul for the mere asking." [69] Bittelman stated that "nearly everybody in the convention with the exception of our own delegates was in favor of LaFollette being the presidential nominee." [70] In effect, MacDonald had agreed to become a stand-in for three weeks—one of the most fleeting presidential candidates on record.

The Conference for Progressive Political Action met in Cleveland on July 4. It drew its strength from liberal and progressive groups, international unions, state federations of labor, cooperative societies, and the original Farmer-Labor and Socialist parties. A repentant Mahoney tried to get in but was punished for actively participating in the St. Paul convention despite LaFollette's condemnation. Foster, Ruthenberg, and Manley observed the proceedings for the Communists. They could not resist the evidence before their eyes that the convention's candidates for President and Vice-President, Senators Robert M. LaFollette of Wisconsin and Burton K. Wheeler of Montana, had overwhelmingly captured the imagination and won the support of the liberal and labor movements. They saw their own erstwhile Farmer-Labor allies clamoring to climb onto the LaFollette bandwagon.

Foster and Manley reacted immediately; they came to the extreme conclusion that LaFollettism had then and there liquidated Farmer-Laborism. Ruthenberg agreed about the liquidation but refused to take the next step that Foster urged on him—to withdraw MacDonald and Bouck in favor of outright Communist candidates.

The Communist top leadership met on July 8 to act on Foster's proposal. At first Ruthenberg demurred. But the Comintern's decision had provided for the contingency of a split between the Communists and their St. Paul Farmer-Labor allies. It had instructed the Communists to act independently in their own name or to launch a campaign in the name of the Farmer-Labor party, depending mainly on how far they would succeed in maintaining "contact with the working masses represented at the June 17th Conference." After July 4, Foster could demand an open Communist election campaign because contact with the working masses had obviously broken down. Ruthenberg finally conceded. Only three votes were cast against Foster's motion.[71] The three hold-outs, Lovestone, Engdahl, and Browder, made a highly unusual combination. Lovestone and Engdahl refused to go along with Ruthenberg, and Browder with Foster, though Browder later changed his mind and admitted his "error." [72]

Bittelman boasted:

> To have changed within one day, almost, fundamentally, our main political line under the very fire of the enemy without in the least demoralizing our ranks, was proof not only of the political flexibility of the Central Executive Committee, but also of the discipline and Communist quality of the party as a whole.[73]

So it was. It required a special Communist flexibility, discipline, and quality to believe, or seem to believe, fundamentally one thing one day and the opposite the next day. Of all the changes of line, about-faces, zigzags, and 180-degree turns the American Communists have made, this one will always hold a place of honor as the first of such magnitude.

The new line of July 8 was carried out at full speed. Within forty-eight hours, the Communists announced their candidates, William Z. Foster for President and Benjamin Gitlow for Vice-President. So great was their haste that the fifty-five members of the National Committee elected at St. Paul on June 17 could not be consulted or polled.

Instead, five of the seven members of the smaller National Executive Committee met on July 10 to issue a statement withdrawing MacDonald and Bouck and endorsing Foster and Gitlow. At least three of these five were open Communists.[74]

On that same day, fifty hastily assembled Communist delegates came together in a Workers party gathering in Chicago to inaugurate the Foster-Gitlow campaign. Those few Farmer-Laborites who had gone along with the Communists to the end were taken by surprise and complained bitterly of a betrayal of confidence.[75] In the final accounting, the Communists put the Farmer-Labor movement to death as if it were their private property, something they had never admitted while it had shown signs of life.

Mahoney went the way of Fitzpatrick. Browder soon denounced him as "the agent of forces of capitalist exploitation in Minnesota" and "agent of the bankers." [76] And Mahoney helped to bar the Communists from the Farmer-Labor Federation in March 1925. To erase the "Communist taint," as the Minnesota movement's historian puts it, the federation changed its name to "Association." [77]

After the Comintern's decision and especially after July 8, the full force of the American Communists' wrath was turned on LaFollette. They assailed him as an "utter failure," a "reactionary," a "menace," a "tool of big business," an "enemy of labor," the "candidate of political gangsters," and the "enemy of immigration." [78] Ruthenberg condemned LaFollette as more reactionary than the Republican candidate, Calvin Coolidge, or the Democratic candidate, John W. Davis, because LaFollette's attacks on the "private monopoly system" would "halt and destroy this basis for the socialization of industry." [79] Foster and *Daily Worker* editorials characterized the LaFolletteites as the future American fascists.[80] "Our biggest task today is to combat and destroy the LaFollette illusion," Foster wrote two weeks before the election.[81] All of this, however, did not prevent Calvin Coolidge from implying that LaFollette represented communism in the election.[82]

It was a far cry from the days of Pepper's third American revolution—the LaFollette revolution.

The morning after

Coolidge received 15,720,000 votes, Davis 8,380,000, LaFollette 4,825,000, and Foster 33,300.

The election returns in November 1924 fatally disappointed the Progressives. The Socialist–trade-union–farm coalition fell apart immediately, and the party itself was soon buried without pomp or ceremony. When Senator LaFollette died the following year, all hope of resurrecting a third party in that generation died with him. It was twenty-four years before Henry A. Wallace attempted, in alliance with the Communists, to head another third party in a presidential election, and he made a far worse showing.

For the Communists, the vote in 1924 was a nonfatal disappointment. Unlike the Progressives, they could hold on and wait for a better day. Yet they could not hide from themselves that they had squandered one rich opportunity after another, had tried to maneuver everyone else and had only succeeded in maneuvering themselves back into the rut of isolation and sectarianism. The injury they did to themselves was second only to the injury they did to the Farmer-Labor movement.

How did the Communists defeat themselves? What had led them astray?

In part they were betrayed by their own ideas. The Communists had insisted on making the Farmer-Labor party a proletarian "class" movement and the LaFollette Third Party a middle-class movement. This dogma had led them to demand the organizational separation of the two movements. Not without relief, they had obeyed the Comintern's decision to break up the alliance, and they had turned on LaFollette with pent-up fury, as if to cleanse themselves of a secret sin. The Comintern's decision had made them feel guilty of having played fast and loose with their ideology, and as compensation for their loss of mass influence they fell back into the comfortable bosom of their doctrine.

Before the election, Bittelman had given the orthodox Communist definition of what the parties represented:

Socialist-LaFollette-Gompers alliance—Small bankers, merchants, and manufacturers. More or less well-to-do farmers. The so-called liberal petty bourgeoisie, and the labor aristocracy and labor bureaucracy who have submitted to a bourgeois point of view.

Workers Party—Class conscious workers, the wage-earning proletariat, and the poorest sections of the farmers.[83]

After the election, however, he studied the returns and made the unexpected discovery:

That the LaFollette movement, objectively a movement of the petty bourgeoisie, was not supported in the elections in any large measure by the petty bourgeoisie, but by the workers of the east and middle west and by the poor farmers in the northwest.[84]

And Foster also observed of LaFollette's vote:

Undoubtedly most of this came from trade unionists and others of the more advanced sections of the workers and poor farmers.

Foster even admitted that the Communists' own membership had "displayed a strong instinct" to go with the masses in the LaFollette movement. He added picturesquely: "The sweep of the LaFollette movement shrivelled the tender plant of the farmer-labor party movement like a hot blast from the desert." [85]

The doctrine held that LaFollette represented the petty bourgeoisie, and the Communists the workers and poor farmers. But the election returns showed that the petty bourgeoisie chose to be represented by Coolidge or Davis, the workers and poor farmers by LaFollette. The reality stubbornly refused to be governed by the theory. From this divergence flowed much of the Communists' confusion. They contended that the Farmer-Labor movement, not LaFollette, represented the Leftward trend, that there was a necessary contradiction between the two, and that LaFollette had insidiously seduced Leftward-moving workers and poor farmers away from the Farmer-Labor movement. In reality, LaFollette represented the most extreme mass

Leftward trend in American politics for almost a decade. After LaFollette, there would not be anything comparable for two more national elections, and it would require a major depression to bring it about—without a Farmer-Labor movement. The oversimplification of social classes in the United States gave the Communists a rationale for doing their best to kill the biggest Leftward political movement of the decade and for gloating over its grave.

Nevertheless, by themselves, the American Communists had exhibited a "strong instinct" to stay within the orbit of the LaFollette movement or at least to avoid an open clash. The Communist leadership, from Pepper to Foster, had wholeheartedly agreed on it, and on this issue the anti-LaFollette tendency under Lore had been a hopeless minority. Nothing in the United States, from the broad mass of workers to the Communist rank and file to the Communist leadership, had demanded or had desired a break with LaFollette. Yet, faced with the choice of resisting the Comintern or defying the entire American labor movement, the Communist membership, and its own better judgment, the American Communist leadership unhesitatingly chose to obey the Comintern.

Once the decision was made, there were no regrets. The Comintern enjoyed such power and prestige that it could impose its will on the American Communists and make them like it. Indeed the overnight adaptation to the Comintern's decisions became the special mark of the real Communist. As Bittelman put it, "the quick change in tactics" proved that "we are well on the road to become a real Leninist party." [86]

Another cause of the Communist failure in the election was economic. After the depression of 1921, the Communists needed another depression in 1924 to drive the masses of workers and farmers to the Left, and what they needed they managed to see.

Pepper discovered that an economic depression had started in the second half of 1923 and was "evoking and deepening the general discontent." Early in 1924 Lovestone gave assurances that "our capitalists can at best only hope to delay for a short period the serious economic troubles that are impending for the country" and that "these economic troubles are pregnant with fundamental political changes." By midsummer, he saw "pitch blackness" ahead for the American economy. Browder wrote a pamphlet, *Unemployment,* in 1924, in which he predicted 6,000,000 jobless for the winter of 1924–25, or more than in 1921. Gitlow outbid him with seven to eight million unemployed by the winter of 1925.

Foster's political and economic prognosis early in 1924 showed how closely politics and economics were bound together in Communist thinking. "We may look, during the oncoming months, for a great sharpening of the struggle between the reactionary and revolutionary forces, and forever greater demands being made upon the left-wing's claim to leadership," he wrote. "The basic cause of these developments will be the business depression now looming on the industrial horizon." [87]

But the Communists saw an economic mirage. Recovery went forward in 1923 and 1924. Rising agricultural prices in 1923 caused the Western farmers to lose much of their interest in political insurgency. Boom and complacency worked for the Republicans in the 1924 election. Unluckily for both Farmer-Laborism and LaFollette Progressivism, they were geared to hard times and were tested politically in relatively good times. Writing in the Comintern's organ in the spring of 1925, Browder admitted that the "huge economic depression" the Communists had expected in 1923 had not materialized but hastened to predict another "breakdown of the capitalist system of production definitely in the near future for the United States." [88]

A revealing controversy on the revolutionary outlook in the United States in 1924 was conducted by Scott Nearing and Foster. Nearing, a Socialist economics teacher whose dismissal from the universities of Pennsylvania and Toledo had made him a wartime *cause célèbre,* criticized the Communists for overestimating their own strength and assuming "a following that does not exist." The chief trouble, as he saw it, came from the virtual absence of revolutionary sentiment among American-born workers and farmers, and its restriction to certain foreign-born workers, especially those of Slavic origin, whose numbers were destined to be reduced heavily by the new immigration laws. Like Lore, he argued that a small, weak revolutionary movement had no business attempting big political maneuvers like the LaFollette alliance, and advised it to preserve its "stern integrity, strict discipline, and live revolutionary ideals." In conclusion, he observed of Foster and Pepper:

> As a matter of tactics, you and he are following a policy based on Russian experience, which is quite unfitted to cope with the situation you confront in the United States, and which will drive your party to ruin if you pursue it.[89]

Foster's answer unwittingly suggested what he had understood by communism and what had appealed to him in it. He refused to agree that the American workers lacked revolutionary sentiment. There was, he insisted, "a great volume of discontent" which was "mostly unconscious, blind, stupid, timid and easily misled," but nevertheless, "the raw stuff of which revolutions are made." Then he cast light on this stage of his thinking:

> Revolutions are not brought about by the type of far-sighted revolutionaries that you have in mind, but by stupid masses who are goaded to desperate revolt by the pressure of social conditions, and who are led by straight-thinking revolutionaries who are able to direct the storm intelligently against capitalism.[90]

This controversy did not prevent Nearing from joining the Communist party some time later and staying in it for the rest of the decade.

Foster also engaged in a bitter polemic with the venerated Socialist leader, Eugene Victor Debs. When Debs came out for LaFollette, Foster chided him for his "complete capitulation." Debs fired back that Foster and the Communists had also played along with LaFollette but that, unlike them, he had no "Vatican in Moscow" to guide him. This barb stung Foster into proclaiming:

> We make no apology for accepting the guidance of the Third International. On the contrary, we glory in it.[91]

The old Foster had come into the Communist movement to teach it something about American realities, but the new Foster had to be taught about them in Moscow. Subsequently, he looked back at his trip to Moscow in 1924 and declared:

> I am convinced that the Communist International, even though they were five thousand miles away from here, or even six thousand, understood the American situation far better than we did. They were able to teach us with regard to the American situation.[92]

A similar transformation had taken place in Cannon. When Pepper had forced the split with Fitzpatrick in 1923, Cannon had dared to stand up against him and protest against transferring European patterns to peculiar American situations. But when the Comintern forced a split with LaFollette in 1924, he did not stand up against it, though the stakes were similar and the consequences even more profound. Just before the 1924 election, Cannon spoke of the real Leninist nucleus that had developed in the American party, and the speech illuminated what had made the change in him:

> It is characteristic of such comrades that they regard the adherence of our party to the Communist International not as a formal affair, but as an inseparable part of its being, which shapes and colors all of its activities, something that penetrates into the very marrow of its bones. For them, the word of the Communist International is decisive in all party questions. It is as one of such comrades that I wish to speak here tonight.[93]

Ironically, their Russian teachers were not as sure of themselves as they sometimes pretended to be. At the Comintern's Fifth Congress in 1924, Zinoviev sadly admitted: "We know England so little, almost as little as America." [94]

Step by step, the molding process went on, and the LaFollette experience was a giant step. It brought about one of the decisive confrontations of the divergent elements that had gone into the making of American Communism. The urge to expand its mass influence, the desire to seek an accommodation with the American reality, and the need to obey the impulses of its inner development were wrapped up in the Third Party alliance. To be sure, the Comintern had been responsible for the initial impetus in this direction. It had introduced the united front to the Americans and had thereby set them on the path that had led to the Third Party alliance.

But the Comintern was a capricious master; it gave and it took away. It played the united front like an accordion, contracting or expanding it with little reference to the American situation. At worst its policies reflected its own internal rivalries. At best it laid down a "general line" on the basis of a predominantly European perspective. It looked at America as if it were an appendage of Europe and made American policy as an afterthought of European policy. A Right or Left turn in Europe was inevitably accompanied by a Right or Left turn in America. Whichever it was, the Comintern could not be challenged; it was the repository of the infallible doctrine and the supreme court of political orthodoxy. In the end it made no difference how the accordion was played; inner development was always subject to, and only another form of, outer control.

The American leaders submitted to this process or did not long remain leaders. Partly they were prisoners of their own doctrine of "monolithism." Whenever discipline and conviction clashed, one or the other had to give way, and the monolithic nature of the Comintern, embodied in its statutes and Twenty-one Points of admission, guaranteed the victory of discipline.

On these occasions, Pepper was fond of reminding his American disciples of an aphorism by his master, Zinoviev: "Discipline begins where conviction ends." [95]

But if discipline wins out often enough, conviction loses its force and meaning. After a while, discipline never ends and conviction never begins. Yet it would be a mistake to underestimate the ability to believe whatever the Comintern made it expedient to believe. The problem of conviction arose whenever the Comintern changed its line, but, after all, the old line was just as much Comintern-inspired as the new one. The choice was not so much between a pro-Comintern and an anti-Comintern line as between two Comintern lines, yesterday's and today's. A conviction which had been derived from the Comintern could be changed by the Comintern without much urging.

But there was always the first time. For Foster, the first time occurred in 1924. Unlike Ruthenberg, Cannon, Bittelman, and the rest, he had held himself aloof from the Communist movement in its first period because he had disapproved of the party line in the field of his primary interest. The Communists had stretched out their hands to him, had cried *mea culpa* for having disagreed with him, and had changed their trade-union policy to coincide with his own. Then for two years he had labored single-mindedly in his trade-union vineyard, little changed from the past in his emphasis on practical work and organizing techniques encumbered with a minimum of revolutionary "talk." While he had faltered once by countenancing the split with Fitzpatrick, he had recovered and attempted to retrace his steps. Even his bid for power in the party had been justified as a fight for his old policy, and the Third Party alliance had won his enthusiastic approval as the last chance to get back into the mainstream of the labor movement. From his first trip to Moscow in 1921 to his second trip in 1924, there was some consistency and continuity in Foster's record.

But the break with LaFollette, wholly at the behest of the Comintern, violated and betrayed everything he had stood for. Not his entrance into the Communist movement but this turning point three years later constituted the real break with the previous course of his own inner development. It made him a Communist, not because of the party line, but irrespective of it. Though he still had far to go to convince some of his fellow Communists that he was ideologically and politically equal to them, he had demonstrated something far more important for his future career—the ability to change, or appear to change, his convictions as often as the party line demanded. He behaved as if, by becoming a Communist, he had exhausted all the individuality and rebelliousness that he had stubbornly cultivated as a Socialist and syndicalist, as if he had made the decision to end all decisions.

6

How to Win a Majority

THE Farmer-Labor movement's revenge was ironic. Dead, the movement disturbed the Communists more than it had disturbed them alive.

After having done more than their share to kill the Farmer-Labor movement, the Communists could not bury it in their own minds. They proceeded to hold an inquest which dragged on for months and tore the party again into wildly wrangling factions. For about half a year, the factions had been restrained from fighting openly by the Comintern's pre-election decision of May 1924. But the decision did not tell them what to do after the election. Between Comintern decisions, the American Communists were still permitted to do their own thinking, and this privilege reopened the Pandora's box of factionalism.

Immediately after the election, the new struggle broke out over the ghostly question of the Farmer-Labor movement. Was it dead or merely dormant? If dead, what should the Communists do next?

Foster's majority said that the Farmer-Labor movement was dead beyond recall and was not useful any more even as an "agitational slogan." A mass trade-union basis, the argument ran, was indispensable for a real Farmer-Labor movement. Such a basis was now totally lacking and inconceivable for a considerable period. Therefore, instead of wasting any more time on it, the Communists should concentrate all their efforts on building their own party.[1]

Ruthenberg's minority replied that the Farmer-Labor movement was only temporarily dormant and the old slogan, "For a class Farmer-Labor party," was just as good as ever. According to this reasoning, disillusionment with LaFollette was inevitable. When it came, interest in the Farmer-Labor movement was bound to revive. Farmer-Laborism was still the best means for speeding up the development of a mass Communist party.[2]

The "discussion" was long and painful. It lasted from the second week in November 1924 to the middle of January 1925. All the dirty linen of Communist policy for months past was washed in public. The historian has a special reason for being grateful to it; without it the whole story of the Farmer-Labor and LaFollette episodes could not be told.

In these contests, each faction had its acknowledged champion. The generals of the opposing groups, Foster and Ruthenberg, viewed themselves as potential leaders of the entire party or at least felt some need to play that role. Though they missed few opportunities to torment each other, they left the most extreme partisanship to their chiefs of staff, Bittelman and Lovestone respectively. Bittelman's inexhaustible appetite for logic-chopping and hair-splitting ran wild in these periodic spasms of open discussion. His pre-eminence was recognized by a pro-Ruthenberg District Organizer, John J. Ballam, who conferred on him the title of "chief rabbi." [3] On the other side of the trenches, Lovestone had rapidly replaced Pepper as Ruthenberg's strong man. For a time, Lovestone had isolated himself by opposing the switch from the Farmer-Labor party to the Workers party in the 1924 election. But he had staged a speedy comeback and Foster gave him credit for having won over the entire Ruthenberg faction to his point of view on the Farmer-Labor question.[4]

After eleven weeks of intense controversy and mutual vilification, nothing was decided. At the very outset, Ruthenberg's group had proposed submitting the question to the Comintern for decision. Foster's group, confident of its majority at home, objected, and the Foster-controlled Central Executive Committee asked the Comintern for permission to hold a party convention in January 1925 to settle the issue. But the Comintern decided to take up the new American dispute at its approaching Fifth Plenum, instructed both factions to send delegates to Moscow, and postponed the American convention until it had rendered its verdict.[5]

So the main scene of the American battle was again transferred to the Russian capital.

Stabilization and socialism

As the American delegates headed eastward, they drove into doctrinal winds that, unknown to them, had shifted sharply.

While the American Communists had been wrestling with the problems of the Farmer-Labor and LaFollette movements, the Russian Communists had been struggling with issues of a far more general nature—the state of world capitalism and the fate of socialism in Russia.

These issues had arisen because the Russian Communists could not live indefinitely on the stock of ideas inherited from the Bolshevik revolution of 1917. As the years passed, one of the most central of these ideas, the imminence of the world revolution, which had nerved the Russians to make their own revolution, could not be held with the old faith and ardor. Even though Lenin had expressed second thoughts by the end of 1920, other leading Bolsheviks had shown less willingness to compromise with reality. The Russian delegation to the Comintern, made up of Zinoviev, Bukharin, and Radek, had offered resistance to the defensive policy, partly by encouraging offensive actions, such as that in Germany in March 1921, or by resorting to vaguer and less pessimistic formulas. As head of the Comintern, the "General Staff of the World Revolution," Zinoviev had a special stake in the old creed. His Comintern position was made incomparably more important by the imminent world revolution than by a revolution indefinitely postponed. But the world situation had also helped the offensive theory to persist. The French occupation of the Ruhr in 1923 had created such economic chaos and popular embitterment in Germany that the Comintern's hope of a revolution in the heart of Europe had temporarily revived, only to sink lower than ever before.

By 1924 even Germany, with the help of the Dawes Plan, had made strides toward recovery, but no one would have known it from the Comintern's reaction. The Fifth Congress, the first after Lenin's death, which met in the summer of 1924, stubbornly refused to recognize the signs. Zinoviev set forth its basic assumption: "A stabilization of the world economic situation is out of the question." The Comintern's chief economist, Eugen Varga, confidently predicted a severe American crisis and European economic deterioration in 1924–25. Zinoviev insisted that the German situation was still "pregnant with revolution" and put the "problem of power" on the agenda of the most important European countries.[6] On the basis of this prognosis, he attacked the "Right" as the main enemy and took the sting out of Trotsky's demands for an even more aggressive revolutionary policy.

If Zinoviev had chosen to see more stabilization in the world economic situation and less pregnancy in the German revolutionary situation in the first half of 1924, he would undoubtedly have regarded the American Communists' alliance with LaFollette with greater equanimity. An erroneous estimate of the European situation as well as the exigencies of the Russian factional struggle had motivated the Comintern to demand the break with LaFollette.

Belatedly the Comintern agreed that the capitalist system had gained a more extended lease on life, which it called "partial and temporary stabilization." This term recognized the recovery of Western capitalism but qualified it as a mere postponement of the inevitable final breakdown. The promulgation of "partial stabilization," about a year and a half after the facts had warranted it, was one of the chief purposes of the Comintern's Fifth Plenum in March 1925.

In Communist doctrine, however, "partial stabilization" raised a peculiarly troublesome question. If, as the Russian Bolsheviks had believed, the world revolution was necessary to build socialism in Russia, did the postponement of the world revolution mean the postponement of socialism in Russia?

The question was later posed in its sharpest form by Stalin: "Can our revolution mark time for an indefinite period, pending the victory of the revolution in the West?" [7] Until April 1924 Stalin had answered this question in the orthodox way—that the "organization of socialist production" could not be achieved in a single country and required the efforts of "the proletarians of several advanced countries." But in December 1924 he revised this traditional conception in favor of a new formulation that the victorious proletariat in a single country "can and must build a socialist society." At first he made no effort to deny the import of the change, but after a while he resorted to verbal sleight-of-hand to divert attention from his embarrassing about-face.[8]

Trotsky accepted Stalin's challenge with alacrity. The Stalinist revision of the old program of socialism through world revolution gave him an issue with which to carry the battle to the entire Communist world. Trotsky refused to separate victory over the Russian bourgeoisie from victory over the world bourgeoisie. He insisted that Russia could not reach the productive level required by socialism if it developed outside the world economy. He contended that the new and heretical doctrine of "socialism in one country" would inevitably lead to the betrayal of the world revolution and the transformation of the Comintern into an auxiliary of the Soviet state.[9]

Much of the great debate turned on what Lenin had said. To give his revision the appearance of Leninist orthodoxy, Stalin contended that Lenin had believed in "socialism in one country." But he could not produce a single text from Lenin before 1915 that lent itself in any way to his argument and for his next text he was obliged to jump all the way to 1921. In his quotations from 1921 on, however, Stalin was more persuasive, because these reflected Lenin's disillusionment with the expected world revolution and his increasing preoccupation with Russia's isolated economic development.

The Opposition had no trouble pointing out the incongruities: it was most unlikely that Lenin had written for so many years before 1921 without touching more than once on such a crucial point as socialism in one country; texts from Lenin before 1921 on the necessity for a world revolution to save the Russian revolution were numerous; and there were Stalin's own unlucky, contradictory formulations of April and December 1924. Trotsky, however, tended to manipulate quotations from Lenin in reverse. His preference ran to the earlier ones which had played up the world revolution, and he encountered more difficulty with the later ones which had played it down.[10]

Apart from these appeals to authority, the debate was vitiated by ambiguities in the conception of socialism. Was it merely equivalent to an advanced, nationalized technology? Or was it predicated on a harmonious development of technology, standard of living, personal and political freedoms—the emancipation of society from all oppression, not the substitution of the state oppressor for the private oppressor? According to Stalin, Russia by itself could achieve a technological basis that would reach and surpass that of Western capitalism without the help of a Western revolution. According to Trotsky, Russia needed the material and cultural assistance of socialist regimes in the West to establish the technological basis as well as the fuller harmonious socialist society. In the end, Stalin showed that a nationalized economy could rival Western technology by means of police methods and mass oppression that made a monstrous mockery of everything previously understood by socialism except its technological basis. Trotsky expected Stalinist Russia to result neither in socialism nor in advanced industrialization of the Western type; he was right about the first but not about the second, and therein lay both his strength and his weakness.

In the world Communist movement, the theory of "socialism in one country" formally abolished the dependence of the Russian revolution on the Western revolution which had formerly existed in theory. It freed the Russian Communists from the old doctrine that the survival, let alone the ultimate success, of their revolution would depend on the victory of the Western revolution. It provided a new orthodoxy to rationalize the dependence of the Western revolution on the Russian revolution.

This doctrinal conflict was accompanied by a factional realignment among the Russian Communists. Behind the scenes, a rift between Zinoviev and Kamenev on the one hand and Stalin on the other took place in 1925. After its victory over Trotsky the year before, the triumvirate could devote more attention to its own rivalries, and Stalin's hold on the party machine had given his partners increasing cause for alarm. As the triumvirate drifted apart, it was replaced by the duumvirate of Stalin and Bukharin on a platform of "socialism in one country."

In the political spectrum of the Russian party leadership at this time, Bukharin occupied a position on the Right; Trotsky stood on the Left; Stalin maneuvered in the center; and Zinoviev and Kamenev wavered between the Left and the Center. Bukharin had not always been a Rightist. In previous years, he had been the outstanding theoretical exponent of "Left Communism" and one of Trotsky's most ardent admirers. But the changing times had also changed him. He had compensated for his past excesses by going to the opposite extreme and had drawn more drastic implications than anyone else had from the concepts of "partial stabilization" and "socialism in one country." He came to believe in an extended period of capitalist stabilization and in building socialism in Russia at a very gradual pace with a minimum of social dislocation by encouraging the peasantry and discouraging forced industrialization. For the time being, as the party's leading theorist and its most beloved personality, he suited Stalin's needs well in the struggle against Zinoviev and Trotsky.

The Americans en route to Moscow could not know the inside story of these Russian developments. But they could not escape their repercussions.

The Fifth Plenum

The high-powered American delegation to the Fifth Plenum, which opened on March 21, 1925, was composed of Foster, Cannon, and John Williamson (of the Young Workers League) for the majority; Ruthenberg, Lovestone, and Pepper (already there) for the minority.

In Moscow the delegates who had traveled with legal passports used their own names—Cannon and Williamson were the only Americans who could do so. Ruthenberg adopted the pseudonym "Sanborn"; Foster, "Dorsey"; and Lovestone, "Powers," and they are so listed in the official record of the plenum.[11]

They quickly plunged into the work of an American Commission which conducted a month-long debate on the future of the American Farmer-Labor movement, the sins of Loreism, and other long-festering problems. The chairman of this commission was the Finnish Communist leader, Ottomar V. Kuusinen, and its secretary the Swiss, Jules Humbert-Droz, both members of the Comintern's top Secretariat. These private sessions gave each of the Americans an opportunity to state his case and to blow off steam, and they enabled the Comintern officials to acquaint themselves with the most intimate details of the American situation before making a decision.

But the Americans were also assigned to other commissions which, like parliamentary and congressional committees, did most of the real work and brought in reports to be rubber-stamped by the full plenum. On this occasion, Cannon and Pepper were appointed to the important political commission responsible for the general line, Ruthenberg and Foster to the commission on trade-union unity, Foster and Lovestone to the one on the peasant question, and one or two others to the mandate, Czechoslovak, Yugoslav, Dutch, Italian, and colonial commissions.[12] These commissions permitted the Americans to gain an insight into the Comintern's policies in other fields and countries and to take soundings of the changing line and the relationship of forces.

The first important event at the open plenum was Zinoviev's report. It set the line on the basic question of "partial stabilization":

> Yes, the bourgeoisie has obtained a breathing spell. Today we see that the bourgeoisie's breathing spell continues longer than we thought, even if, seen in historical perspective, two or three years, yes, even five to ten years, are a trifle.[13]

For the Communist parties, the chief feature of this plenum was the slogan of "Bolshevization." As Zinoviev interpreted the term, it merely summed up the application of Leninism to different situations, and he specifically warned against the mechanical transference of Russian experience to other countries.[14] But even this caution against making Bolshevization the same as Russification showed how far the pendulum had swung. The question had once been to what extent Russia could imitate the West. It had now become to what extent the West could imitate Russia. Zinoviev himself rarely practiced what he preached, and in any case not he but his successor was able to put the slogan into practice.

But Zinoviev did not dominate this plenum as he had previously dominated Comintern meetings. Two of the longest and most significant reports, one extolling conciliation of the peasantry and the other indicting Trotskyism, were delivered by Bukharin. Some American delegates had obviously begun to take their cues more from him than from Zinoviev. After Bukharin had finished eulogizing the role of the peasantry, Lovestone echoed the same sentiments in terms of the American farmer. And after Bukharin had demolished Trotskyism, Ruthenberg backed him up by inveighing against Loreism—the so-called American manifestation of Trotskyism—without neglecting the opportunity to charge that the Fosterite majority had wavered on the issue. Not to be outdone, Foster arose to protest his innocence of Trotskyism and to clear his skirts of Loreism by pointing out that when the Ruthenberg group was in the majority, it had never attacked Lore. Of the seven speakers on the subject who followed Bukharin, not one defended Trotsky.[15]

The brunt of defending a pro-Labor-party policy was shouldered by Pepper. In one of his flights of creative fancy, Pepper divided the history of the Communist International into three periods, past, present, and future—the Central European, the Far Eastern, and the Far Western. He defined social democracy as the specific problem in the first, the revolutionary national movement in the second, and the Labor party in the third. He peered into the future and pronounced: "I believe that the policy of the C.I. will be dominated ever more powerfully by England, the United States of America and Latin America." [16]

Cannon protested that an American labor party, however desirable, was premature without mass trade-union support. He appealed against Pepper's speculative powers to the real powers in the Comintern: "We hope that the support of our Russian comrades will save us from mistakes and blunders, and thereby save us from becoming the victim of theoretical experiments." [17]

Gradually Cannon realized that the odds favored Pepper. "I soon got the chilling impression, and I think Foster did too, that the position of our faction was far weaker in Moscow than at home, and that we couldn't do anything about it," he relates. "The other faction had the advantage there. With Pepper as an active representative, busy in the apparatus of the Comintern, the Ruthenberg faction seemed to have the inside track." [18]

Meanwhile, at home, everyone in the American party waited anxiously for some sign of the outcome in Moscow. Delegates wrote to their friends and adherents to keep them abreast of the tide of battle. As conflicting reports criss-crossed the Atlantic, rumors and questions circulated in the higher echelons of the party in New York, Chicago, and points west. Had the Comintern really determined to reorganize the American leadership? Was the Farmer-Labor policy in or out? Why was the Comintern's decision delayed and when would it come?

There was nothing conspiratorial or enigmatic about this situation. At the end of March, the *Daily Worker* published a cable from Moscow which began:

> American commission will soon render political decision based on which both factions can and must work together and through which party unity will be secured. Minority must absolutely submit to discipline and decisions of central executive committee.

The cable was signed as follows:

Majority Delegation
Minority Delegation
American Commission
HUMBERT-DROZ [19]

The four short lines at the end of the cable could have enabled any informed observer to infer what was going on in Moscow. In addition, a joint statement by the top committees of the Workers party and Young Workers League stated: "Within a few days the decision of the Comintern will have settled all controversial points." [20]

This "Decision of the Communist International on the American Question" caught the entire American leadership by surprise for the second time in two years. The Comintern, it indicated, had taken a second look at the Farmer-Labor and LaFollette movements and had arrived at an attitude sharply at variance with its previous one.

The Comintern now gave LaFollette credit for "an important victory" in the election, an implied rebuke to those American Communists who had pooh-poohed the Progressive vote. Despite this optimistic estimate, the decision added: "That does not mean that the tactics of the Workers party were not correct. They were correct. Our party only met with a defeat which was not to be avoided under the given circumstances."

The about-face was even more clearly implied in the Comintern's new view of the Farmer-Labor movement. Foster's position that it had no immediate future was tersely denounced as "incorrect." The American Communists were enjoined to do their "utmost to further this movement." Only two concessions were made to Foster's point of view—that the slogan should be changed from Farmer-Labor to Labor party, and that any organizational steps toward a Labor party should have a "firm mass basis of trade union support," defined as at least 500,000 organized workers.

On the main issue, however, Ruthenberg's position was not only pronounced "right" but even criticized for not going far enough. The Comintern called for a much broader Labor party under much less radical leadership than any American Communist had ever dared to contemplate: "It is very possible that in America, at first there will be for a time at the head of the labor party similar reformist labor traitors to those in England, or worse. Nevertheless, the formation of such a party may for a time represent a definite step forward in the American labor movement, and the Communist party is obliged to participate in this party." [21]

Had this been the Comintern's attitude in 1923 and 1924, there would have been no pressure from Moscow to break with Fitzpatrick or LaFollette. By implication, the line for the future was a crushing criticism of the line of the past. The 1925 decision represented a fine example of a peculiar Comintern practice: it implied that something had gone wrong without openly admitting error. If the Comintern could have treated such matters humorously, it might have said that its earlier policy had been correct but that the opposite policy would have been even more correct.

Foster had guessed wrong again. He had turned against the Farmer-Labor movement after the Comintern's decision of May 1924 but, unlike the Ruthenberg-Lovestone group, he had failed to turn in favor of the Farmer-Labor movement before the Comintern's decision of April 1925. His old enemy, Pepper, was singled out for special praise in the Comintern's new decision. His old ally, Lore, was denounced in the strongest terms as the representative of a non-Communist tendency and a "definite decision" on the Lore question was demanded at the next American convention.

And again Foster did not flinch. He and his group meekly accepted the Comintern's new line as they had the old one. They formally agreed with Kuusinen's criticism that they had based themselves "on superficial temporary phenomena." Foster even gloated that the Russians had criticized Ruthenberg's group for "yielding too much" to his own group on the question of a Labor party, and he contended that the best pro-Labor-party arguments had been advanced by Zinoviev, Stalin, and Kuusinen.[22]

Politics and tactics were not the only things discussed in Moscow.

Ruthenberg's political victory in the Comintern's decision created a most awkward situation in the American party leadership. It placed Foster's majority in the equivocal position of being politically weaker but organizationally stronger than its rivals. Usually the Comintern refused to countenance this contradiction; this time Zinoviev decided to overlook it. At a conference with Foster and Cannon, Zinoviev tried to determine in advance what the division of power at the next American convention should be. He proposed that "the new central committee is to be so elected at the party conference that the Foster group obtains a majority, and the Ruthenberg group is represented proportionately at least by one-third." Foster, of course, accepted the proposal jubilantly.

But Ruthenberg refused to go along, and Zinoviev was no longer able to impose his will.[23] Two or three days later, Zinoviev announced a change of mind. In another meeting with Foster and Cannon, he explained that opposition to his proposal had developed on "constitutional grounds." His new attitude was studiously impartial. On only one point was he adamant—Lore must go. Toward the claims of majority support by the two major factions, he refused to commit himself: "The future will show which of the two has deceived itself. We can only wish both wings the best of good luck." [24]

Between Zinoviev, who had tried to insure Foster's continuing control, and those who wanted to put Ruthenberg back into power, a deceptive-looking compromise was arranged. It took the following form:

> The Party Congress will be held at an early date. All disputed questions which may arise between the two groups in the Party Central Committee in the interval, and which cannot be agreed upon, are to be settled in a parity commission under the chairmanship of a neutral comrade. This commission shall also control the actual conduct of the Party discussion.
>
> The Executive Committee is of the opinion that the Party Congress, in a calm atmosphere, free from all fractional passions, should elect the Party Central Committee from among the comrades of both groups. The group which will be in the minority at the Party Congress must in any case be assured a large representation in the Central Committee.[25]

On the face of it, this arbitrament judiciously abstained from playing favorites. It left the election of the American leadership to the forthcoming convention, and tried to protect whichever side became the minority. But it introduced two new and ambiguous elements, the "parity commission" and the "impartial chairman." No American could qualify as impartial, and the Comintern intended to send one of its own representatives to play the role. The American delegates left Moscow not quite knowing where the Comintern stood or what they might expect.

The essential element

Back home, both factions immediately plunged into a struggle to control the coming convention. Though the Comintern ostensibly had favored neither, each exerted itself to prove that it favored the Comintern more than the other did. Ruthenberg's group claimed that the Comintern's decision on the Labor party had clearly vindicated its previous position. Foster's group insisted that the Comintern's demand for broad mass support had obviously justified its own past policy. Both sides campaigned for delegates on their interpretation of the Comintern's decision.

Meanwhile, the convention was delayed because the "impartial chairman" had failed to arrive and the parity commission could not be formed without him. This quandary called for cablegrams to the Comintern to decide the issue of going ahead with or without him. Bittelman proposed sending the following:

PARITY COMMISSION NOT CONSTITUTED BECAUSE ABSENCE OF ESSENTIAL ELEMENT NO DEFINITE INFORMATION REGARDING ARRIVAL IN VIEW OF THIS CEC REQUESTS PERMISSION TO PROCEED WITH ORGANIZATION TO BE SUBJECT TO APPROVAL OF PARITY COMMISSION WHEN FULLY CONSTITUTED.

Ruthenberg retaliated with another cablegram:

PARITY SITUATION SUCH THAT CONVENTION ARRANGEMENTS BY PARITY COMMISSION ESSENTIAL FOR FUTURE OF PARTY PROTEST AGAINST ACTION BEFORE FULL CONSTITUTION OF PARITY COMMISSION WHICH WILL BE POSSIBLE IN ONE WEEK ACCORDING TO INFORMATION RECEIVED.[26]

Bittelman's proposal was favored five to two in the Executive Council. But Ruthenberg had the more reliable information about the imminent arrival of the missing chairman.

The "essential element" was Sergei Ivanovich Gusev, the most important Russian Communist ever sent by the Comintern on a mission to the American Communist movement. He was an authentic Old Bolshevik, who had served in November 1917 as secretary of the Military Revolutionary Committee of Petrograd which had directed the actual Bolshevik uprising and seizure of power, and he had fought afterward in the civil war as a member of the supreme Revolutionary Military Council headed by Trotsky. Gusev was the author of the first Communist manual on civil war. In this period some of the most important Bolshevik feuds had been nurtured, arising out of differences in military policy or clashes of rival ambitions. In the gravest of these disputes—the one between Stalin and Trotsky on the conduct of the southern front, and a later feud on fundamental military doctrine between a group headed by Frunze and another headed by Trotsky—Gusev had always sided against Trotsky.

At a very early stage, then, the Comintern representative was known as an embittered enemy of Trotsky and a consistent supporter of Stalin. Gusev had been transferred from the Russian party's Central Control Commission to the Comintern in one of Stalin's first moves to wrest control of the International from Zinoviev. A factional struggle in the German party had already received Gusev's attention at the recently concluded Fifth Plenum. His mission represented the first direct Stalinist intervention in the American Communist movement.[27]

Gusev, a soft-spoken, roly-poly man in his fifties, came to the United States via Mexico. He stayed in Mexico City for several weeks, assiduously studied English, and learned enough in a short time to cross the border at Laredo, Texas, with an Elks button in his lapel, posing as an American businessman.

In Chicago he adopted the pseudonym of "P. Green," spoke sparingly in a slow, methodical English or German, and ended all discussions with a finality that precluded further disagreement. He was wooed and cultivated on all sides, a game at which Ruthenberg's men came out far ahead. He spent hours interrogating the various leaders, sizing up their strong and weak points, learning from and through them about the strange American land. He told them stories of his military and revolutionary past, gravely handed out advice, and hinted darkly of the great shake-up coming in the Comintern's highest ranks.

Soon after his arrival in Chicago, the parity commission was set up —Foster, Cannon, and Bittelman for the majority; Ruthenberg, Lovestone, and Bedacht for the minority; and Gusev as the "impartial chairman." In theory, the delegates to the coming convention were freely chosen and free to make up their own minds on policy and leadership. But the delegates could have their minds made up for them by an agreement in advance between the top leaders of the rival factions. In the parity commission, Gusev insisted on hammering out "unanimous" resolutions to make the convention less unpredictable. Of seventeen resolutions presented at the convention, fifteen were adopted unanimously in the commission.

Policy was relatively easy. The real crisis always came in determining the leadership. The election of delegates in the districts had let loose another frenzy of factionalism, despite all previous vows of penance and reform. In Cleveland and in Philadelphia, two separate organizations existed. Chicago and New York seemed to be heading toward a similar split. From all over the country came charges and countercharges of fraud, padding of membership rolls, gerrymandering, and every form of electoral skulduggery known to the district organizers of Tammany Hall.

Ruthenberg's group decided to acknowledge defeat in advance. The parity commission allocated thirteen seats in the next Central Executive Committee to Foster's group and eight to Ruthenberg's. It also assured the latter of not less than one-third on all executive organs of the party.[28]

With most of the resolutions unanimous and the division of power fixed, the convention was fully "prepared."

The Fourth Convention

The Fourth Convention of the Workers party opened in Chicago on August 21, 1925. As soon as Foster was elected chairman over

Gitlow by a vote of 40 to 21, it was clear that he had won, by fair means or foul, a majority of the delegates.[29]

At last Foster stood on the verge of his second and greatest victory in two successive conventions. At the beginning of 1924 he had won control of the top leadership but had been forced to concede the secretaryship to Ruthenberg, to share control of the *Daily Worker*, and to forfeit several important districts to Ruthenberg's followers. Now his triumph appeared complete and he prepared to come forth as the undisputed leader of the party. He made no secret of his intention to remove Ruthenberg from the secretaryship and Lovestone from the C.E.C., to gain undisputed control of the *Daily Worker*, and to disperse the opposition leaders from the party center to the outlying districts. The two disputed resolutions were rammed through by the same majority, 40 to 21.

One of the parity commission's unanimous resolutions had barred Lore or any of his followers from the C.E.C. But at the convention itself Bedacht and Bittelman introduced a joint motion for the expulsion of Lore from the party, a step that went beyond anything that the Comintern had demanded. The motion was overwhelmingly adopted. Only one person, Juliet Stuart Poyntz, spoke up on Lore's behalf. Not only did Foster have his decisive majority, but now he owed none of it to his former ally, Lore.

Gusev watched the convention drag on, the enmities flame, the wrangling verge on open violence. In anticipation of a possible split, Dunne, Shachtman, and a few of their co-factionalists, armed with pistols, barricaded themselves in the *Daily Worker* building for thirty-six hours and refused to permit any factional opponent, including the co-editor, Engdahl, to enter.[30] Within Ruthenberg's group, a revolt against the convention's pro-Foster majority, even to the point of staging a walk-out, was barely put down.[31] On the evening of the eighth hot and grueling day, August 28, Gusev called together the parity commission and pulled a piece of paper out of his pocket. There had been many cables from Moscow, and there would be many more, but this one was never equaled in its melodrama or in its consequences.

It read:

Communist International decided under no circumstances should be allowed that Majority suppresses Ruthenberg Group because:

FIRSTLY—It has finally become clear that the Ruthenberg Group is more loyal to decisions of the Communist International and stands closer to its views.

SECONDLY—Because it has received in most important districts, the majority or an important minority.

THIRDLY—Because Foster Group employs excessively mechanical and ultra-factional methods.

Demand as minimum:

FIRSTLY—Ruthenberg group must get not less than 40 percent of Central Executive Committee.

SECONDLY—Demand as ultimatum from majority that Ruthenberg retains post of secretary.

THIRDLY—Categorically insist upon Lovestone's Central Executive Committee membership.

FOURTHLY—Demand as ultimatum from majority refraining removals, replacements, dispersions against factional opponents.

FIFTHLY—Demand retention by Ruthenberg group of co-editorship on central organ.

SIXTHLY—Demand maximum application of parity on all executive organs of Party.

If majority does not accept these demands then declare that, in view of circumstances of elections, unclear who has real majority and that methods of majority raise danger of split and therefore Communist International proposes that now only a temporary Parity Central Executive Committee be elected with neutral chairman to call new convention after passions have died down. Those who refuse to submit will be expelled.[32]

Foster, Bittelman, and Cannon sat dumfounded. When the Comintern delivered ultimatums and ordered expulsions, they knew that they could only obey or rebel. The cable was so detailed and precise that it had clearly originated with Gusev himself: Gusev had cabled Moscow and then Moscow had cabled Gusev.

Instinctively Foster rebelled. The cable offered him a 60-40 majority but in such a way that he could not accept. The damning part of the cable was buried in the political verdict that "the Ruthenberg Group is more loyal to decisions of the Communist International and stands closer to its views." Control of the party by a narrow margin without the Comintern's confidence was not merely foolhardy, it was useless, because the majority's own supporters were sure to go over to the side politically favored by the Comintern.

Foster could not master his emotions. He exploded with rage. He refused to accept a majority under such humiliating conditions or even to sit on the new committee, since the Comintern had cast doubt on his loyalty. He told Gusev, whom he blamed for his sudden misfortune, to carry out the reorganization alone and not to expect the Fosterite majority to do it for him.

Foster, Cannon, and Bittelman went straight to a caucus of their own followers. For once the three did not consult and reach agreement in advance. Foster walked out still determined to fight. But Cannon had already made up his mind to go along with Gusev.

Foster broke the bad news about the cable to the stunned group. He launched into another tirade against the injustice of it all and reiterated his opposition to the Comintern's cable. Cannon immediately disassociated himself from Foster. He held out the specter of a split in which the Fosterites would find themselves the prisoners of the Right-Wing Finns and in active rebellion against the Comintern. He appealed for uncompromising loyalty to the Comintern and unwavering faith in its Russian leadership.

Cannon and Dunne proposed settling for a fifty-fifty division; Foster and Bittelman held out for giving the majority to the Ruthenberg faction. As one by one the delegates rose and chose sides, the caucus split wide open, and formed two clearly defined factions—the Fosterites and the Cannonites.

Foster later claimed that his refusal to participate in the next Central Executive Committee had lasted no more than an hour. In any case the debate in the caucus lasted all through the night and the next day. In the end the majority of the caucus voted with Cannon and Dunne, or rather, to support the Comintern which they had made the decisive issue. To assuage Foster's wounded feelings, however, the caucus designated him and Bittelman as its candidates for the Political Committee.[33]

Cannon's victory in the caucus enabled Gusev to get a "unanimous" vote in the parity commission. The deal was worked out in fine detail and duly incorporated in the published proceedings of the convention. In its final form, it read:

RESOLUTION OF PARITY COMMISSION
ON INCOMING CENTRAL EXECUTIVE COMMITTEE
(Minutes of the Parity Commission, August 29)

Motion that the Central Executive Committee be constructed on the basis of an equal number from each group, with a neutral chairman.

Motion that the number be ten from each side including two proletarians from each side.

Motion that each side elect three candidates for the C.E.C. who participate with a voice but no vote in all plenary sessions of the C.E.C.

Motion that the District Executive Committees of New York, Philadelphia, and Cleveland be constructed on the basis of an equal number from each group.

Motion that the C.E.C. member elected by the Y.W.L. [Young Workers League] National Executive Committee shall not disturb the parity character of the C.E.C. If the group which now has the Y.W.L. representative be in a minority in the Y.W.L. convention, it will add an alternate to the C.E.C. to balance the Y.W.L. member

Motion that a control commission be elected consisting of two members from each side. This control commission to act as grievance committee as well as auditing committee.

Motion that the representative of the C.I. shall be given power by a resolution of the convention to participate in the C.E.C. meetings and to cast a deciding vote and to act as chairman.

All motions accepted unanimously.

P. Green
Wm. Z. Foster
J. P. Cannon
Alex. Bittelman
C. E. Ruthenberg
Max Bedacht
Jay Lovestone [34]

Rarely has the name of a Comintern representative, even pseudonymously, appeared publicly, as it did in this resolution. To show that his was not an ordinary name, even among the top party leaders, the signatures were printed in such a way that he stood out by himself. Since the resolution explicitly mentioned the power of "the representative of the C.I." to cast the deciding vote, the authority behind the strange name was not hard to guess. After "P. Green" came the American names, headed by Foster, visible evidence of the capitulation required of the one who had fought the hardest and lost the most.

This pact enabled the convention to wind up its work. The leading committees were chosen by the caucuses and rubber-stamped by the convention.[35]

At the last session, Foster acted out another ritual ceremony of submission. "We are Communists," he said, "and realize that when the Communist International speaks it is our duty to obey." [36] But he was not yet ready for unconditional obedience, because he also served notice of his intention to appeal the decision at the next opportunity in Moscow.

Even so, Foster had not yet drunk to the dregs his cup of woe.

The disparity of parity

Gusev had another surprise in store for the Americans.

When the Fourth Convention closed, the division of spoils in the party leadership was still left in a somewhat ambiguous state. Ostensibly it was equally divided between the two major factions, with the balance of power in the hands of the "neutral chairman," Gusev. But the question in everyone's mind was: how neutral would he be?

It was soon answered. At the first meeting of the new C.E.C. on September 1, Gusev calmly announced:

> Of course we now have a parity C.E.C. but it is not exactly a parity C.E.C. With the decision of the Communist International on the question of the groups in the American party there goes parallel instructions to the C.I. representative to support that group which was the former minority. If the C.I. continues this policy, that will always be the case, that is, the C.I. representative will be supporting that group and therefore although we have a nearly parity C.E.C., we have a majority and a minority in the C.E.C.[37]

The Comintern, in effect, had sent two sets of instructions, one for the convention's benefit, proposing a 60-40 split in favor of Foster's group, and the other for Gusev's private benefit, ordering support of Ruthenberg's group. A parity C.E.C. which was not exactly a parity C.E.C. had become a nearly parity C.E.C. with a majority and a minority. This was more than even Cannon had bargained for but again he took the line of least resistance and agreed.[38]

Gusev's vote enabled Ruthenberg's group to take over the party's leading committees. Not only were the Fosterites reduced to a minority in the key Political Committee and Secretariat but Gusev barred Bittelman, who had been chosen by the Foster-Cannon caucus for the Political Committee in the last hours of the convention. Gusev interpreted Bittelman's nomination as indirect punishment for Cannon, whom he wished to reward for splitting the former majority's caucus, and insisted on substituting Cannon for Bittelman.[39] The new Political Committee was made up of Ruthenberg, Lovestone, Bedacht, Cannon, and Foster. The smaller Secretariat was composed of Ruthenberg, Lovestone, and Cannon. Ruthenberg remained as General Secretary, Lovestone came in as Organization Secretary, and Bedacht as Director of Agit-Prop. Foster went back to his old role as head of the "Industrial Department." [40] A member of the Ruthenberg group, Herbert Zam, took over as the new National Secretary of the Young Workers League.[41]

Lore's influence in the German section was liquidated by strong-arm measures. When the motion to oust Lore from the German Bureau, of which he was secretary, failed by a vote of 7 to 3, the C.E.C. suspended the pro-Lore members, substituted "loyal" ones, and reversed the decision.[42]

The spark of rebellion still left in Foster and his remaining supporters continued to flicker vainly. Foster had no reason to believe that he could do better in Moscow than he had done in Chicago, but he refused to back down on his formal right to appeal to the Comintern. Again Cannon thwarted him. When Foster tried to get local party organizations to endorse his appeal, Cannon objected on the ground that endorsement was tantamount to considering the Comintern's decision wrong. He argued against the appeal: "This in itself has an inevitable tendency to discredit the Communist International before the party comrades, to break down faith in the Communist International decisions. It is a step away from the Communist International." While Cannon questioned the implications of Foster's appeal, Stachel went so far as to deny Foster even the right to appeal.[43] In a perverted way Cannon had a point: Foster had a right to appeal, but it was impossible to appeal to the Comintern against its own decision without implying that the Comintern had made a mistake—and that was forbidden.[44]

This contradiction almost trapped the Fosterites. At a meeting in New York on September 25, some of Foster's more extreme partisans, Zack, Krumbein, and Aronberg, openly attacked the Comintern's intervention. The news reached Gusev in Montreal, and he seized the opportunity to crack down on the hard core of Fosterite resistance. His reprisal took the form of an article in the *Daily Worker* in which he reviewed the inner-party struggle before, during, and after the recent convention. When he came to the meeting in New York at which the three bitter-end Fosterites had dared to defy the Comintern's decrees, he aimed the finishing stroke:

> Foster and Bittelman are actually following a line against the Comintern although they declare that they are for the Comintern. (Such declarations are very cheap.) They are gathering the right wing of the party around them.[45]

Foster realized that his henchmen had gone too far and speedily declared:

> I am for the Comintern from start to finish. I want to work with the Comintern, and if the Comintern finds itself criss-cross with my opinions, there is only one thing to do and that is to change my opinions to fit the policy of the Comintern.[46]

Despite Foster's decision to conform, he had wavered and had to pay for it. The combination of Ruthenberg, Cannon, and Gusev had cut him down from the victorious leader of a decisive majority to the defeated leader of an isolated minority. Membership meetings all over the country overwhelmingly endorsed the Comintern's intervention, and Foster paid lip-service to his own disgrace.[47] A "Unity Resolution" aimed directly at him was voted 17 to 5 by the C.E.C., a reduction of his influence in the top leadership to less than one-third.[48] Cannon and Lovestone made a joint tour of the country to put across the new line and leadership.[49] For a time the enmity between the Fosterites and the Cannonites exceeded the rivalry between the Fosterites and the Ruthenberg-Lovestone group.

Where was Foster to go? A lifelong rebel against the existing order, he could not bring himself to make peace with it. Small and weak as American Communism was, other movements were even less encouraging. The Socialist Labor party vegetated hopelessly. The I.W.W. was no more than a shell of its old self and only eleven delegates attended its 1925 convention.[50] The Socialist party, its historian says, "came out of the LaFollette campaign weaker than ever" and for the rest of the decade "did very little to attract the attention of the general public." [51] The A.F. of L. had sunk into a decade-long torpor, its leaders blissfully oblivious to a dwindling membership and far more interested in imitating capitalism than in organizing against it.[52] For Foster, at the age of forty-four, the prospect of starting all over again outside the Communist movement was not inviting. Instead of rebelling against the indignities heaped on him by the Comintern, he chose to write them off as experience.

The experience of 1925 showed that the way to win a majority in the party was to win the confidence of the Comintern. This lesson was never forgotten by either the victors or the losers. It was not the first time the Comintern had played a crucial role in American Communist affairs. But it was the first time the Comintern had stepped in to break and make an American Communist leadership. It was the first time a cable from Moscow had overridden the majority decision of a party convention. This situation was sufficiently new to take Foster by surprise and throw him into confusion. After this experience he took his Comintern lickings quietly and nursed his wounds in private.

The new American ruling group, headed by Ruthenberg and Lovestone, repaid the Comintern's favor with a gratitude bordering on idolatry. The Comintern had previously enjoyed the most exalted status in the Communist world. But there had never been anything in the American party like the official campaign of Comintern-worship inaugurated late in 1925. In order to justify themselves, Ruthenberg, Lovestone, and their followers glorified the Comintern, which had restored them to power in the American party. In self-interest, they assailed anyone who suggested that the Comintern could possibly make a mistake, or questioned the Comintern's authority to determine national leaderships, or hinted that a cable from Moscow might be something less than holy writ.

The fullest rationale for the Comintern's omniscience was provided by Lovestone:

> The Communist International is the outward, the real form of the international unity of our Communist movement. Decisions of the Communist International are the expressions of one international experience on the problems of the different national parties. The value of this experience lies not only in the fact that, in the form of Comintern decisions, it corrects wrong policies, but also, and most important of all, it conveys this international experience in the form of theoretical and practical lessons to the Party concerned. When a Comintern decision reverses a policy of a national party it is done on the basis of an experience that was not at the disposal of the body which decided the original policy. The decision of the Communist International makes available such international experience to the leadership of the national party. And this leadership, in turn, must be instrumental in making this experience available to the whole membership.[53]

This theory effectively deprived each national party of any real power of decision. By internationalizing every national decision, even the choice of a national leadership, it removed in advance the basis for an appeal against a Comintern decision. For, by definition, no national party possessed enough international experience to make the international decisions which now took precedence over national decisions. This theory also assumed that the international leadership could not make mistakes in international decisions. It empowered the

Comintern to correct national mistakes, but it cut off the national parties from correcting the Comintern's mistakes. This Communist version of "Papa knows best"—for it was little more than that—had, of course, innumerable local variations, which made the national leaders immune from criticism and control by their own rank and file.

It provided, in short, an airtight rationale for political captivity and personal irresponsibility. Lovestone gave it the most extreme expression when it suited his immediate purpose against Foster. In so doing he taught his enemies to avenge themselves by following his example.

7

Bolshevization

THE time has come to turn our attention to the organizational structure of the American Communist movement. There is much to learn not only from the party's structure but from the way it came into existence.

The Fourth Convention in the summer of 1925 was an organizational as well as a political dividing line. Gusev did more than settle the factional struggle; he also supervised the party's total reorganization.

Important as these organizational changes were, the magic word "Bolshevization" gave them a special aura of reflected glory. Everything that Gusev did, and everything that was henceforth done in the name of the Comintern, was invested with the glamour of Bolshevization. It was the chief over-all slogan of the second half of the decade, dinned into the consciousness of every party member, the goal of every true and loyal Communist.

The term Bolshevization was loose enough to mean anything the Comintern wanted it to mean, and is therefore best understood in practical rather than abstract terms. Zinoviev had theoretically warned against confusing Bolshevization with Russification. At the same time the Comintern had distinguished among three groups of parties in three stages of Bolshevization: those parties which were still predominantly propagandist in nature, those which had won considerable mass support, and those which had already conquered political power. The American party was still in the first stage; parties like the German and French belonged in the second stage; and only the Russian party had reached the third and final stage.[1] In practice, there was only one truly Bolshevized party, the Russian, and the other parties had no other example to follow in Bolshevizing themselves.

It took six years for the American party to go from Bolshevism in theory to Bolshevization in practice. We can trace the steps by comparing the organizational development of the American party, the Russian party, and the Comintern.

Units and fractions

Organizationally as well as politically the American Communist movement had grown out of the American Socialist movement.

In the Socialist party, the territorial or neighborhood branch was the basic local unit and the Organizer was its chief officer. Above the branch there were borough, city, county, and state representative bodies. On the national level, the Socialists elected a National Executive Committee; the permanent staff was headed by an Executive Secretary; and an International Secretary was charged with conducting the party's relations with the international Socialist movement. Affiliated to the party were foreign-language federations, which had arisen independently among the various immigrant nationalities and continued to function virtually autonomously side by side with the English-speaking party. The first of these foreign-language federations, the Finnish, was set up in 1904. By 1917, they numbered fourteen and accounted for about 40 per cent of the total Socialist membership. The influx into these federations following the Bolshevik revolution raised the figure to over 50 per cent in 1919 and gave the newly formed Communist movement its overwhelmingly foreign-language mass basis.[2]

The Russian form of organization differed markedly. At the base of the Russian Communist party structure were local units or "cells," the great majority of them industrial rather than territorial in make-up. These industrial cells brought party members together where they worked instead of where they lived and voted. This type of economic rather than political organization antedated the Bolshevik revolution and constituted a traditional difference between Russian and Western practice; open political activity rated low in Czarist Russia, and factory organization made illegal activity easier and safer. At the top of the Russian hierarchy in 1917 were a Central Committee of twenty-one members and four candidates and a Political Bureau (Politburo) of seven members. Below the Central Committee was the district (*oblast*) committee, followed by other committees of smaller geographical divisions. In March 1919 the three top executive organs were: a five-member Politburo, a five-member Organization Bureau (Orgburo), and a Secretariat, at first headed by one secretary but in 1922 reorganized with a General Secretary—Stalin—and two assistants. The Politburo was empowered to make decisions between meetings of the Central Committee, the Orgburo to take charge of all organizational activity, and the Secretariat to attend to routine technical matters. In addition, the party exercised control over innumerable "non-party" organizations, such as soviets, trade unions, schools, and the like. A party statute, adopted in December 1919, gave formal status to the technique of control by providing for party "fractions" in every non-party organization. These fractions were made up exclusively of party members to carry out the party's policies, but independent authority was withheld from them and they were formally subordinate to higher party committees.[3]

When the first American Communist parties were organized in 1919, they were largely modeled after the Socialist party. Yet even at this early date some differences betrayed the beginning of Russian influence. The Communists took over bodily the Socialist set-up of territorial branches, branch organizers, city central committees, executive secretaries, international secretaries, and foreign-language federations. But after the first two months, the Communist party strongly recommended "shop branches" in addition to the regular neighborhood or territorial branches. This work was "fundamental," it stated, in order to reach the mass of workers most easily and protect members against repression.[4] Instead of a National Executive Committee, the Communist party named a Central Executive Committee. It also introduced into its organizational structure the "district," at the head of which the C.E.C. appointed District Organizers. The Communist party's constitution of 1919 defined districts as following "the lines of industrial rather than state divisions." The Communist Labor party, however, made no changes in the Socialist set-up.[5]

The Comintern also developed by tentative, makeshift stages. It started in 1919 with an Executive Committee (E.C.C.I.), then a small "bureau" of five, a president, and a secretary. After some tinkering, it was reorganized in 1922 with an E.C.C.I. of twenty-five members, headed by a chairman (Zinoviev); a Presidium of nine to eleven members, recognized as the equivalent of a Politburo; and an administrative Secretariat with a general secretary and two assistants. In addition, other executive bodies were set up: four main departments—Organization, Agitation and Propaganda (Agit-Prop), Statistics and Information, and Eastern; an International Control Commission to audit finances and administer discipline; and a Technical Information Bureau.[6] Modifications and additions were made later, but this basic structure remained. The first three congresses were held annually, but two years intervened between the Fourth in 1922 and the Fifth in 1924, four years before the Sixth in 1928, and seven years before the Seventh in 1935—in violation of the Comintern's own statutes requiring one every two years. Beginning in 1921 the E.C.C.I. also held "enlarged sessions," known as "plenums," which enjoyed the same power or authority as congresses but were attended by far fewer delegates. From 1921 until 1933 plenums took place once a year, except for two in 1926—in violation of the Comintern's own decision to hold them every four or six months.[7]

The underground Communist party of America, formed in 1921, was organizationally a mixture of old and new elements. Its basic unit was the "group" of approximately ten members; not more than ten groups within the same city or locality formed a branch; two or more branches within a locality made up a section; subdistricts of not more than ten sections and districts of two or more subdistricts were set up "within industrial sections regardless of political boundaries." The Central Executive Committee and Executive Secretary remained, but three new top committees appeared: Political Committee (Polcom), Organization Committee (Orgcom), and Industrial Committee, the first two corresponding to the Politburo and Orgburo. In addition, a system of "party nuclei," the equivalent of Russian-style fractions, was instituted for party members "in the shops, in the unions, and in other workers' organizations; within the army and navy, and ex-soldiers' organizations." [8]

The next step was a throwback to 1919. The Workers party was set up at the end of 1921 with territorial branches, city central committees, districts, Central Executive Committee, executive secretary, chairman, and foreign-language federations, and without shop branches or party nuclei. Gradually, however, the specifically new Communist forms of organization were grafted on. When the underground Communist party went out of existence in April 1923, leaving the Workers party alone in the field, the latter added to its top committees an Executive Council, Polcom, Orgcom, Industrial Committee, and Secretariat—without making any provision for them in its constitution. But it did little or nothing about shop units or fractions.[9]

From the viewpoint of the Comintern's Orgburo, this left much to be desired.

Piatnitsky's Orgburo

The American party was one of the Comintern's most troublesome sections. For a relatively small party, it occupied an inordinate amount of the Comintern's time. In the two-year period between the Fourth and Fifth Congresses, 1922–24, the American party ranked fourth in the number of times its affairs were discussed by the Comintern's leading bodies, surpassed only by the far more important German, Italian, and French parties.[10] In the first five years, much was said and little done about the American party's problems.

The Comintern's Orgburo, headed by Ossip Piatnitsky, a veteran

Russian Bolshevik, began to function in January 1924.[11] A dedicated organizer, Piatnitsky immediately stepped up the Comintern's pressure for far-reaching structural changes in all the Western parties. From the American party, he mainly demanded three things—more "factory nuclei," more fractions, and the abolition of the foreign-language federations.

The Comintern inaugurated this campaign in 1924 without getting much encouragement from the Americans. Its Presidium adopted a lengthy resolution on factory nuclei on January 21 and another on Communist fractions in February. A declaration of the American party in March dutifully echoed that "the Party organization must be gradually and systematically transformed from its present territorial basis to that of shop and factory units."

At the Comintern's Fifth Congress in July, Piatnitsky called on all parties to reorganize on the basis of the Russian party's factory nuclei. The American and Canadian delegates woefully recounted their difficulties. One American accused the foreign-language groups of being the greatest obstacles to building factory nuclei, inasmuch as workers speaking different languages refused to belong to the same party unit. Another American explained that practically all the organizers favored, and the rank and file opposed, factory nuclei. The Canadian delegate cited two extenuating circumstances—80 per cent of his party could not speak English, and few worked in large factories or heavy industry.

Piatnitsky refused to give them much comfort. He insisted that neither "in America nor in Canada can we renounce the creation of factory nuclei," and bade them to "commence activity amongst the native English-speaking workers in the big factories, mines, etc." The American and Canadian delegates humbly promised to carry out his orders. The American party subsequently adopted a "program of action" to "proceed directly to the formation of shop nuclei."[12]

The next big push came at the Comintern's Fifth Plenum, the Bolshevization plenum, in the spring of 1925. At the Orgburo's first Organization Conference, held in conjunction with this plenum, one misguided delegate asked why the Russian party, unlike the others, had made no report. Piatnitsky gave him the answer: "Because all our organizational experience in connection with the organization of the party on the basis of factory nuclei has been taken from the Russian Communist Party." [13] In effect, the Russian party did not have to report to other parties, which were required to emulate it. Piatnitsky singled out the American party as a particularly horrible example of organizational "chaos," and allotted most of the blame to the foreign-language federations. The American delegate, Foster, did not have much to show in the way of progress—only seven factory nuclei in Chicago, and fraction work that was "not very advanced." He complained, "There is great resistance within the Party against reorganization." [14]

Piatnitsky gave the Americans a bad mark. As long as the foreign-language federations persisted, he said glumly, the American party was "not yet ripe for reorganization." He warned ominously: "The Organizing Department of the E.C.C.I. will devote very serious attention to the reorganization of the Workers Party." [15]

The Orgburo left nothing to chance. It told all the parties to adopt new constitutions embodying the organizational principles of Bolshevization; and to make sure that there would be no slips, it drew up "model statutes" which left little for the national parties to do but fill in blanks, thus:

1. Name of the Party

1. The Communist Party . . . . is a Section of the Communist International and is called: Communist Party . . . . , Section of the Communist International.[16]

To set the stage for the American party's Bolshevization, the Comintern sent it a long letter of instructions, spelling out in detail the changes to be made and the way to make them.[17] This letter was converted into one of the parity commission's unanimous resolutions and unanimously adopted by the Fourth Convention in August 1925. The reorganization of the party was, therefore, much less dramatic than Gusev's upset of the party leadership, but its consequences were in the long run far more lasting and pervasive. Whether Foster or

Ruthenberg headed the party was far less important than the kind of party either of them would head.

From top to bottom

The Fourth Convention's "Resolution on Bolshevization of the Party" and the new constitution based on it adopted in September 1925 gave the American Communists for the first time a typically Communist form of organization. Later changes did not affect the fundamental structure, and therefore we can now get acquainted with the long-term Communist set-up.

The resolution set itself the aim of achieving "not the modification of the existing forms, but the *complete* reorganization of the Party from top to bottom on the basis of shop nuclei, international branches (street nuclei) and a centralized apparatus." To symbolize the change, the party's name was officially changed from the Workers Party of America to the Workers (Communist) Party of America, though the shorter form persisted in ordinary usage. The next change of name, Communist Party of the U.S.A., was made in 1929.

The top leadership was reorganized as follows:

Central Executive Committee. Formally the highest authority of the party between conventions (increased from 13 members and 7 alternates to 21 members and 6 candidates).

General Secretary. The highest political and executive officer (replacing the Executive Secretary). The Chairmanship was eliminated.

Political Committee (Polcom). To conduct the work of the C.E.C. between full sessions (5 members and 2 candidates). The Executive Council was eliminated.

Secretariat. To conduct permanent current work (3 members).

Departments. Agitation-Propaganda (Agit-Prop), Organization, Trade Union, Research, Women's Work, Agrarian, Negro, and Sport.

Central Control Commission. Financial supervision and disciplinary control (4 members).

Organizers headed the intermediate divisions of the party as follows:

Districts. One or more states (except two in New York state).
Subdistricts. A combination of several cities.
Sections. Subdivisions of larger cities.
Subsections. Subdivisions of larger sections.
City Organizations. In small cities with not more than 200 members.

The lowest party organizations were defined as follows:

Shop (or Factory) Nucleus. The basic unit consisting of not less than three members at a place of employment.
Street Nucleus (or International Branch). A residential unit for all members unattached to shop nuclei.*

Fractions were defined in general terms and more specifically for the foreign-language groups:

Fractions. Organs of the party within non-party organizations.
Language Fractions. All members of the party speaking the same language within a subsection, section or city organization.[18]

The reorganization of 1925 brought the American party for the first time formally into line with the Russian party. The few remaining differences were purely nominal—Central Executive Committee instead of Central Committee, and Political Committee instead of Political Bureau, though even in this period the latter two were used interchangeably. The final change to Central Committee and Political Bureau was made by the American party in 1929.

Another formal change, relating to the Comintern, was made in 1925. The first American Communist parties of 1919 were officially affiliated to the Comintern, but when the Workers party was formed in 1921, it was given the status of a "fraternal" party, because an official underground American Communist party still existed. After the underground party merged with the Workers party in 1923, the fraternal designation continued, though the Workers party functioned as a Communist party in every other way.[19] Nevertheless, the dis-

* The 1925 constitution used the term "nucleus," but "cell" and "unit" were also used interchangeably, and "unit" eventually became the most common expression. The term "branch" came back into vogue in the late nineteen-thirties.

tinction rankled, and in 1925 the party seized the opportunity to go back to the original, official affiliation. Article 1, Section 1, of the new constitution proclaimed the Workers (Communist) party of America as "the American section of the Communist International." Ruthenberg made a point of emphasizing the significance of the change: "With the adoption of the constitution which follows our party becomes openly 'the American Section of the Communist International,' and takes its rightful place with the other Communist parties of the world as an organic part of the Communist International." [20]

There would be no need to belabor this point if American Communist leaders had not gone to so much trouble in later years to deny the change. At the end of the nineteen-thirties, they created the myth that the American party had never been closer to the Comintern than a "fraternal" affiliation and therefore had not been subject to the organizational rules then applied to the European Communist parties.[21] The truth was otherwise. Not only was the American party subject to the same rules, but its 1925 constitution closely followed the Orgburo's "model statutes" prescribed for all Communist parties. Entire passages were copied almost word for word, and the only differences were nominal or immaterial.[22]

A small but revealing change turned up in the party's new membership application card. The card of 1919 had mentioned the party before the Comintern:

> The undersigned, after having read the constitution and program of the Communist Party, declares his adherence to the principles and tactics of the party and the Communist International: agrees to submit to the discipline of the party as stated in its constitution and pledges to engage actively in its work.[23]

The card of 1925 put the Comintern before the party:

> The undersigned declares his adherence to the program and statutes of the Communist International and of the Workers (Communist) Party and agrees to submit to the discipline of the Party and to engage actively in its work.[24]

Bolshevization was not the sharp, total break with the past that it claimed to be. Whether a title was General Secretary or Executive Secretary or whether the party or the Comintern came first in the application card made little practical difference. The introduction of shop units and the abolition of the foreign-language federations hardly merited all the fanfare, and in any case it was easier to do something about them in words than in deeds. Bolshevization was a culmination rather than an initiation; it climaxed six years of gradual development toward the Russian organizational model, and changes in terminology took on a psychological significance out of all proportion to their practical consequences. In practice Bolshevization and Russification were synonymous, and the identification with the Russians was so vital to the American Communists that they would not have had it any other way.

The world party

The American and other parties were also directly affected by the Comintern's Bolshevization. Here too the principles were not new but the ways of carrying them out were.

The Comintern had never conceded any independent existence to the individual parties. Its statutes, adopted at the Second Congress in 1920, read: "The Communist International must, in fact and in deed, be a single communist party of the entire world. The parties working in the various countries are but its separate sections."

The statutes gave the E.C.C.I. the right to issue obligatory instructions to all constituent parties and organizations; to expel groups of members from individual parties and even entire parties; to establish in various countries its own "technical and auxiliary bureaus" responsible only to itself; and to send out "representatives" to carry out its wishes.[25] The Third Congress in 1921 extended the Comintern's control to individual members, and made the party leaderships responsible to the Comintern as well as to the party congresses or conventions, thus depriving the latter of their traditional role as the undisputed highest source of authority within each party.[26]

The framework of the world party was fully formed at the Fourth Congress in 1922. The rules were stiffened to keep the party leaderships stringently controlled by the Comintern and responsible to it instead of to their own memberships. Some of the parties had sent delegates to the congress with instructions on how to vote. Since this procedure implied that these parties still regarded themselves as the ultimate source of the delegates' authority, the Comintern's chieftains met the challenge by prohibiting "binding mandates" because they "contradict the spirit of an international, centralized, proletarian world party."

The parties were also accustomed to choose their own representatives on the E.C.C.I., thereby retaining a measure of control over them. Now they were stripped of this prerogative, and provision was made for direct election to the E.C.C.I. at the Comintern's congresses. Members of the E.C.C.I. could, in effect, still represent their own parties but could not be removed by them.

Some party leaders were old-fashioned enough to believe that the thing to do if they disagreed strongly enough with the Comintern's policy was to resign, and some parties normally accepted resignations. This procedure was condemned "decisively" and the law laid down: "Every leading post in a Communist party belongs not to the bearer of the mandate, but to the Communist International as a whole." This somewhat peculiar wording was interpreted to mean that party leaders could resign, and their parties accept resignations, only with the consent of the Comintern. It gave rise to an even more extreme Communist tradition that outlawed resignations for any reason whatsoever—the only way to get out of the Communist party was to be expelled.[27]

The parties too had not been broken of the habit of holding their own congresses or conventions before the Comintern's congresses. This custom troubled the Comintern because it might enable the parties to discuss and determine policy without benefit of the Comintern's instructions, and it was even known to lead to awkward situations if the Comintern's congresses came to different conclusions.

Henceforth all party conferences were ordered to take place after the Comintern's congresses.

Finally, the Comintern was dissatisfied with the parties' laxity in sending communications and delegates to Moscow. It remedied this defect by deciding to make use of "representatives" with "the widest powers." [28]

For all practical purposes, the world party was governed by the E.C.C.I.; the E.C.C.I. was governed by its Presidium; the Presidium was governed by its Russian members; and the Russian members carried out the orders of the Russian party. Hence the real power was exercised in reverse order. The Russian Politburo made decisions binding on the Russian members of the Presidium and the Comintern's other executive organs, from which they were transmitted to the foreign parties or sections.

The world party put every Communist in the world at the disposal of the Russian party in the name of the Comintern. In return, weak parties or sections warmed themselves in the glow of the distant star. If Russian interests demanded the sacrifice of one or another section of the world party, the victims comforted themselves with the thought that, as in every great army, some soldiers and even some corps are expendable.

There was nothing about Russian superiority in the Comintern's statutes. The voting and representational arrangements made it appear that the Comintern had five co-equal parties in the first rank —German, French, Russian, Czechoslovak, and Italian; five in the second—British, Polish, American, Bulgarian, and Norwegian; and all others in the third.[29] But an unwritten law elevated the Russians to a position of lonely grandeur.

At the Fifth Congress in 1924, the German delegate, August Thalheimer, declared: "It is absolutely necessary, a historic necessity, for the Russian party to have the leadership of the Third International —of this there is no need to speak any further—and other parties will rank with it as equals only when they also take power, and know how to hold on to power and to make the transition to socialism." [30] The Japanese, Katayama, exclaimed: "I affirm that I am opposed to the statement of Bordiga that the leading position of the Russian Communist party in the Communist International can be called into question." [31]

At the Seventh Plenum, toward the end of 1926, the Italian, Palmiro Togliatti (Ercoli), brought the unwritten law into the open: "Of course, we have the statutes of the International which guarantee certain rights to certain comrades, but there is something else which is not contained in these statutes. That is the position of the Russian party in the International, its leading function—that goes beyond the limits of the statutes." [32]

But it took time for the Comintern's organizational apparatus to catch up with the increasing emphasis on centralization and uniformity. In 1919 the entire staff had occupied two or three rooms in the Kremlin. By 1921 the Comintern had taken over the aristocratic former German Embassy as its headquarters and a hotel in Moscow to house its staff and foreign delegates, and had established publishing enterprises in Russia, Germany, and England, and later in France.

The more control the Comintern sought to impose on its constituent parties or sections, the larger and more intricate its organizational structure became. One of the foremost effects of Bolshevization was the proliferation of Comintern departments, bureaus, secretariats, and schools. The whole machinery was geared to directing, controlling, instructing, advising, and checking the parties in matters large and small. The careers of numerous Communist officials in Europe and Asia after World War II date back to service in the Comintern in this earlier period of expansion.

The Orgburo held two organizational conferences in Moscow in 1925 and 1926 to direct the reorganization of the parties. It used three main methods to indoctrinate them: correspondence, instructors, and "attached workers." A stream of messages went to the Orgburo informing it of problems and progress, and another stream of messages went out from the Orgburo bearing criticism and suggestions. Instructors were sent to represent the Orgburo within the parties. Some party organizers were brought to Moscow and attached to the Orgburo for special training.[33]

An "Org instructor" named Victor Wachsoff became the subject of controversy in 1927. The American party received a cable from Moscow announcing his appointment, but Lovestone opposed him on the ground that he was "incompetent and factional" and requested another instructor, "either Edelman or Grolman." Foster preferred Wachsoff, but the Orgburo decided to send a pseudonymous "Jenkins" as the compromise candidate.[34] He arrived, shortened his name to "Jenks," and one of his contributions to American Communism was a little booklet entitled *The Communist Nucleus: What It Is—How It Works,* hitherto one of the American party's more mystifying publications.[35] A "Comrade Loaf" represented the Information Department in the United States in 1927.[36] There is also a record of a request in 1929 from the American party's Women's Department to the Comintern's International Women's Department for "an instructor for work among women to the U.S.A." [37]

Other activities were supervised by different Comintern departments. The Agit-Prop Department was divided into a Propaganda subdepartment—its main responsibility—and an Agitation and Press subdepartment. Its jurisdiction covered education, theory, and propaganda campaigns, and it relied mainly on circular letters and publications to broadcast its directives and instructions. The Information Department at its inception was headed by Pepper, who in 1925 presided over an Information Conference in Moscow to coordinate the Communist press all over the world. Besides the usual stream of letters, circulars, and telegrams, this department made use of a system of reporters or *Referenten* from each country to work in Moscow. The first American to fill this post in 1926 was A. G. Bosse (Alfred J. Brooks), a New York schoolteacher, who served in Moscow during extended leaves of absence.[38]

The Comintern's Secretariat was enlarged in the spring of 1926. Section or National Secretariats were set up to do the preparatory work for the higher bodies. Of the eleven new subsecretariats, No. 5 grouped together the United States, Canada, and Japan.[39] Later the English-speaking countries were amalgamated in an Anglo-American Secretariat, which was first headed by the former Indian Communist,

M. N. Roy. One of Roy's successors was a man of many countries and names, Goldfarb-Petrovsky-Bennet.

Dr. Max Goldfarb had been a member of the Jewish Bund and had emigrated from Russia to the United States before World War I. In New York he had been one of the leaders of the Jewish Socialist federation and labor editor of the Socialist Jewish *Daily Forward.* After the Bolshevik revolution of 1917 he returned to Russia, was speedily converted from social-democracy to communism, had found a niche for himself in the Comintern, and had adopted the pseudonym of "D. Petrovsky." In 1924 the Comintern sent him as its resident representative to Britain, whereupon he metamorphosed himself into "A. J. Bennet." Called back to Moscow in 1928, he assumed charge of the Anglo-American Secretariat, once more under the name of Petrovsky.[40]

At other periods the Anglo-American Secretariat was nominally headed by a British or an American Communist, but its executive functionary was usually a Russian, among others, I. Mingulin. Analogous to the Anglo-American Secretariat of the Comintern was the Anglo-American Section of the Profintern.

Another phase of the Comintern's expansion was a large-scale training program for party leaders. In 1921 a Communist University of Toilers of the East, usually called the Far Eastern University, had been founded, but it had been attached to the Soviet Government's Commissariat of Nationalities. Though intended for two groups of students, from the Soviet East and from colonial countries, in 1925 it admitted four American Negroes and one African Negro student then in the United States.[41]

That spring, Bela Kun, then head of Agit-Prop, reported plans for a Comintern school to train a maximum of sixty to seventy qualified "students" in both theoretical subjects and practical activities.[42] After some delay the Lenin School, serving Western Europe and North America, opened in Moscow in May 1926.[43] It offered a full course of three years and a short course of one year. The first American quota numbered seven, among whom were Clarence Hathaway, Charles Krumbein, and W. F. Kruse. American Negroes were normally assigned to the Far Eastern University, but a few attended the Lenin School, which ranked higher in prestige and influence.[44] Some Americans were also sent to another Comintern institution, the Central European School, which was primarily set up for the Balkan and Baltic countries. According to Zack, from 1927 to 1929 there were eleven Americans at the Lenin School, eight at the Far Eastern University, and four at the Central European School.[45]

These students, generally of district- or section-organizer caliber, were chosen as much for their dispensability as for their ability. A top leader could not afford to spend so much time in Moscow; he preferred to send those of his lieutenants who could be spared. At least until 1929, the majority of students were selected by the factions on a *pro rata* basis, but these leaves of absence did not take them out of the factional struggle. Each faction expected its members to act as its wire-pullers and listening posts in Moscow, in addition to taking theoretical courses in Marxism-Leninism and engaging in such practical activities as observing a Soviet trade union or collective farm at work. In the end, however, the Comintern's schools imbued their students with loyalty to the Comintern above everything else and thereby gave the Comintern a most important weapon at a crucial moment of the factional struggle in 1929.

A sizable group of Americans, therefore, was required in Moscow to represent the party in the Comintern's and Profintern's departments, bureaus, sections, secretariats, and schools. One of them, however, formally took precedence over all the others—the official party representative to the Comintern. He wrote reports for the Comintern about the party and for the party about the Comintern, contributed articles to the Comintern's publications and the Soviet press, and in general acted as the party's chief trouble-shooter and "ambassador" in Moscow.

Among the American representatives to the Comintern were Bedacht (1920–21 and 1926), Minor (1921 and 1926), Katterfeld (1922), Amter (1923), William F. Dunne (1924–25), Engdahl (1927–28), and Wolfe (1929). Among the American representatives to the Profintern, with analogous duties, were Charles E. Scott

(1924–25), Browder (1926), Harrison George (1927), and Wicks (1928–29).[46]

After Bolshevization, the Comintern stationed representatives in the United States for various periods. Before 1925, it had sent three delegations for special purposes: Scott, Fraina, and Katayama in 1921; Valetski, Reinstein, and Pepper in 1922; and Gusev in 1925. But after Gusev's departure, there arrived at the end of 1925 a resident Comintern representative, Yrjo Sirola, whose American pseudonym was "Frank Miller." [47] Sirola was a Finnish Communist who had spent some time in the United States during the First World War and had served as Foreign Minister of the short-lived, revolutionary "People's Republic" of Finland in 1918. Thereafter one of the Comintern's leading functionaries, he stayed in the United States as its representative for over a year. He was followed for a short time in 1927 by a German Communist, Arthur Ewert, whose pseudonym in Moscow was "Braun" and in the United States "Grey." [48] A third Comintern representative in 1929–30 was the Russian Boris Mikhailov (Williams). At various times the Profintern and the Young Communist International also sent representatives to the United States. Among the Y.C.I. representatives in the nineteen-twenties were a Swiss, Sigi Bamatter, a Russian who called himself "Bob Katz," another Russian, Nasanov, and the Englishman, William Rust. In turn the American youth league sent representatives to the Y.C.I. in Moscow.

Americans were also used by the Comintern and Profitern for missions to other countries. Among the earliest of these American Comintern agents were Dr. Maximilian Cohen, a dentist by profession, who was sent on an ill-fated expedition to Brazil in 1920, and Louis C. Fraina, who went to Mexico in 1921. Two Americans, Manuel Gomez, a non-Latin-American Communist who used that pseudonym, and Bertram D. Wolfe, lived in Mexico and worked in the Mexican Communist party in the early years; Wolfe represented the Mexican Communist party at the Comintern's Fifth Congress in 1924.[49] Later, other Comintern missions were entrusted to Jack Johnstone in Mexico and India, S. A. Darcy in the Philippines, Wicks in Australia and elsewhere, Zack in Venezuela, and Bittelman in India. Browder worked for the Profintern in the Far East in 1927–28.

The total effect of these comings and goings was to bind the American Communists ever closer to the Comintern and to make them more responsive to its wishes. For the top leaders, the Comintern was not a faraway abstraction; it was an immediate, living presence.

Belts and cogwheels

Thus far we have been looking at American Communism from the inside. But the party was only the controlling center, the hard core, of a much larger and more complex system of organizations and individuals. Outside the party, yet within its orbit, rotated a constellation of "auxiliary organizations," "mass organizations," "transmission belts," "fronts," fellow-travelers, sympathizers, money-givers and name-lenders. For this reason, it is best to think of Communism as a movement rather than merely a party, a movement of which the party constitutes only a part. To envisage the full strength and complete structure of this movement, we must look beyond the card-carrying, dues-paying membership.

The old Socialist and syndicalist movements had been, in this respect, relatively innocent and straightforward. A pre-Communist revolutionary had usually spurned anything but revolutionary means, openly avowed and loudly proclaimed, and had made no attempt to dominate other groups. The American radical tradition had generally ruled out the practice of a revolutionary party setting up and controlling other organizations to achieve its ends indirectly and deviously. The De Leon-inspired Socialist Trade and Labor Alliance had aroused such stormy opposition that it had split the Socialist Labor party, and in any case had never amounted to much.

Lenin had originally conceived of the Communist system of auxiliaries or fronts in purely Russian terms. Like much of Communist doctrine, what had once been considered Russian exceptionalism was converted into a general rule for all countries.

The "bible of Bolshevism," as Zinoviev called it, was a booklet,

What Is to Be Done? written by Lenin in 1902.[50] In it he had demanded a small, highly centralized party made up wholly of professional revolutionaries. All that was needed, he argued, to set the backward Russian workers into action was this "small, compact core," this "vanguard" type of party. But an illegal, conspiratorial party faced the problem of cutting itself off from the broad masses in order to evade the Czarist secret police. To reach the Russian masses, Lenin also advocated "a large number of other organizations intended for wide membership and which, therefore, can be as loose and as public as possible." He suggested "trade unions, workers' circles for self-education and the reading of illegal literature, and socialist and also democratic circles for *all other sections of the population,* etc., etc." Out of this distinction between the party and "other organizations" came the prototype of the future Communist "fronts."

A careful reading of this famous booklet makes it clear that Lenin conceived of this organizational plan as a purely Russian expedient demanded by special Russian conditions. He specifically cautioned that "I have only autocratic Russia in mind" and "we base our argument on the concrete conditions prevailing in Russia at the present time." By these concrete conditions, he meant principally the weakness of the Russian working class and the strength of the Czarist secret police. The original Leninist argument for organization by conspiracy and absence of party democracy in Russia rested chiefly on the ubiquity of the Ochrana.[51]

After the revolution, however, Lenin found another use for his old tactic of revolutionary subterfuge. The new starting point was the Leninist theory of the party.

The older Western conception of a socialist party had provided a home for different tendencies and had aimed at a broad base within the working class. The Leninist "vanguard" party had room in it for only a relatively small portion of the working class. The vanguard, according to Lenin, could not operate the dictatorship of the proletariat by itself and needed to work through other institutions containing a majority of the working class. In the Bolshevik regime, Lenin held, the Soviets and trade unions pre-eminently fulfilled these functions as intermediary institutions theoretically situated between the party and the state. Lenin tried to describe this system of indirect control by using such images as "a complicated system of cogwheels" and "the complicated system of transmission belts." For the exigencies of avoiding persecution, he substituted the exigencies of wielding power.

Lenin also gave transmission belts another function: to protect the workers from the Bolshevik state's "bureaucratic distortions." [52] He never explained how the Soviets or the trade unions could protect the masses against the state if the party ruled all three. By charging them to do something without providing them with the power to do it, Lenin cut the ground from under one of his better intentions. Without living a life of their own, the Soviets and trade unions could not protect anyone or anything, including themselves, and inevitably deteriorated into puppets of the all-powerful, all-embracing party bureaucracy.

In 1920 the transmission-belt theory traveled from the Russian party to the Comintern. At the Comintern's Second Congress, Zinoviev made the most direct application of the Russian practice to other parties. He held up to them the example of the "so-called 'non-party' workers' and peasants' conferences" in Russia and suggested that other parties could get the same results with "associations of disabled ex-servicemen in various countries, the 'Hands Off Russia' committees in England, proletarian tenants' leagues, etc." [53] The theory of the united front, which Zinoviev introduced at the end of 1921, amounted to little more than a refinement of the theory of transmission belts. As long as the united front, by definition, required Communist leadership, it could not fail to serve the interests of, and act as a transmission belt for, the party.

In time the Comintern spawned a family of international fronts, among others, the International Workers' Relief in 1921, the Workers' or Red Sport International in 1921, the International Red Aid (M.O.P.R.) in 1922, and the Peasants' International or Krestintern in 1923. Each of these international fronts begat a family of national fronts for which the respective parties assumed responsibility.

Traditionally the main American Communist fronts have operated in the fields of legal aid, unemployment, support for the Soviet Union, workers' relief, women, protection of foreign-born, anti-imperialism, antifascism, farmers, and Negroes. The term "transmission belt" was apparently first used in the American party by Bittelman in reference to the Workers party which, at its inception in 1921, was only the legal front of the illegal Communist party. In the debate on its formation, Bittelman came out in favor of the Workers party "as a sensitive transmission apparatus between the revolutionary vanguard of the proletariat and its less conscious and as yet non-revolutionary masses." [54]

The first fronts

In general, the American fronts may be divided into two classes: letterhead and membership.

All that a letterhead organization needed to go into business was what it put on its stationery. The basic equipment consisted of a name, address, executive secretary, and executive committee. The name represented an objective capable of winning outside support; the address was usually a party-controlled building reserved for just such tenants; the executive secretary was chosen by the party for his special qualifications or temporary availability; and the executive committee was composed of party members, sympathizers, and, if possible, a sprinkling of "non-political" name-lenders who wanted to be bothered as little as possible.

Membership fronts had all this and more. They accepted both group and individual affiliations, established local branches, held conventions, published house organs, and maintained larger staffs. Letterhead fronts might consist of little more than their Communist fractions. In membership fronts, the fractions usually constituted a numerical minority, and the Communists maintained control by their monopoly of key positions, particularly the position of secretary or secretary-treasurer, and the selectively pro-Communist character of the membership.

Each of these classes was represented in the early years.

The Society for Technical Aid to Soviet Russia was formed in New York in the summer of 1919 at the initiative of Ludwig C. A. K. Martens, head of the Russian Soviet Government Bureau, the first official Soviet agency in the United States. He sought to further Russia's reconstruction by inducing Russian immigrants in the United States who had the necessary technical and political qualifications to return to Russia, bringing, if possible, tools and machinery. Similar groups soon sprang up in other cities, and a national organization was formed in July 1921. It claimed credit for sending tractor-equipped units to thirty large-scale model Russian farms, most of which proved disappointing failures.[55] This society was less a party front than an auxiliary of an official Soviet agency to which the party gave its aid and from which it obtained indirect benefits.

Another early predecessor was the National Defense Committee, formed in 1920 to fight the official persecution of the Palmer raids period. It was primarily a letterhead organization, and all five members of the committee were well-known Communists. It functioned virtually as an integral part of the party, though it obtained some outside support.[56]

This committee gave way in the fall of 1922 to a broader legal-aid front, the Labor Defense Council, to defend the Communist leaders arrested in the raids on the Bridgman convention of the underground Communist party. Its Executive Committee included such Socialist and trade-union figures as Eugene V. Debs and Max S. Hayes, but its secretary was a trusted Communist. The Council, also largely a letterhead front, reported raising over $100,000.[57]

One of the first real membership fronts came out of the depression of 1921. An Unemployment Conference of Greater New York was held in March of that year, at which thirty-four A.F. of L., I.W.W., and independent unions were represented. It established the Unemployed Council of Greater New York with the Communist leader, Israel Amter, as secretary. By the end of the year, it tried to spread out nationally as the Workers Unemployment Council of America. Its program of "immediate demands" included unemployment relief, public works, and low-cost housing. The Unemployed Council held conferences and demonstrations in 1921–22, but failed to survive the economic revival that started in the fall of 1922.[58]

The famine that struck Russia in 1921 provided the setting for the largest of the early membership fronts—Friends of Soviet Russia. It was formally launched in August 1921 at a conference in New York which elected an executive committee of seven, of whom at least five were Communists, including the chairman, Caleb Harrison. In the darkest hours of the underground period, the F.S.R. did most to rescue the party from isolation; the humanitarian appeal of starving Russia reached far beyond the party's narrow confines and won for Alfred Wagenknecht, the F.S.R.'s secretary, a lasting reputation as the party's champion money-raiser.

"Hardly a city or factory town but what had its efficient and vigorous F.S.R. group or united front," Wagenknecht recalled nostalgically. He claimed that the F.S.R. had sent a million dollars in money and an equal amount in clothing, medicines, tools, and other equipment to Russia. It also maintained a goodly number of party functionaries on its payroll. Even children were organized in groups called Famine Scout Cubs. But the F.S.R., which was affiliated with the International Workers' Relief, was born of the Russian famine and died with it. Wagenknecht lamented: "We failed to guide the hundreds of thousands of workers and sympathizers, the thousands of organizations we had won for famine relief, into channels of other forms of proletarian aid." [59]

In an attempt to pump new life into the Friends of Soviet Russia, the American party took advantage of the Ruhr crisis in Germany in 1923 to rename it the Friends of Soviet Russia and Workers Germany. After the German crisis had passed, the name was changed again in 1924 to Workers International Relief. Two years later, it re-emerged as the International Workers Aid with another Communist, Fred Biedenkapp, as secretary, and the former Episcopal bishop, William Montgomery Brown, as chairman. Toward the end of 1927 Biedenkapp asked permission of the Political Committee to revert to the previous name of Workers International Relief, and his request was granted. It continued to exist into the nineteen-thirties as a weak letterhead organization which came to life sporadically during strikes and other emergencies.[60]

The original Friends of Soviet Russia was resurrected in 1929 as Friends of the Soviet Union, later amended to American Friends of the Soviet Union. The various changes of name, sponsorship, and activities reflected the periodic changes in the Communist line. As this genealogy shows, one front sometimes led to another, and some fronts tried to do business under different names.

One of the Comintern's auxiliary organs, the International Women's Secretariat, formed in October 1920, was responsible for another American front. It held Communist Women's Conferences in Moscow in 1920 and 1921; the second, attended by Ella Reeve Bloor for the Americans, asked the parties to form special women's departments. The American party set up a Women's Bureau in January 1922, and the Women's Bureau in turn set up the United Council of Working Class Women (or Wives, as it was also called) at a conference in New York City in December 1923. Its secretary was Kate Gitlow, mother of Benjamin Gitlow. Similar organizations, the Mothers League of Boston and the Detroit Proletarian Women, were formed elsewhere; they were local membership fronts that never seem to have attracted many members, and none lasted beyond the nineteen-twenties.[61]

The large percentage of foreign-born among Communist party members and sympathizers and the periodic threats of antialien legislation spurred the party to organize the National Council for Protection of Foreign Born. Beginning in December 1922, local groups were formed, but they suffered a high rate of mortality, and the National Council was not established until May 1926 at a conference in Washington, D.C. A total of 110 delegates claimed to represent 700,000 to 800,000 members, including the Polish Catholic Union of 150,000 members. Though this turn-out was impressive for a conference so patently Communist-organized, the basis of the National Council in delegated bodies rather than individual memberships gave it much less effective backing than the numbers indicated. A Communist served as its secretary and Communists dominated its national executive committee of twelve. Despite its ups and downs over the years, this organization proved to be one of the most long-lived in the galaxy of American Communist fronts.[62]

A succession of trips to Mexico by Lovestone, Johnstone, and Gomez in 1924 and 1925 preceded the formation of the All-American Anti-Imperialist League in 1925. Gomez was appointed secretary of the United States section, with headquarters in Chicago. A Central American secretariat was set up and a Spanish organ, *El Libertador,* edited for a time by Bertram D. Wolfe, was published monthly, in Mexico. The A.A.A.I.L. claimed national sections in eleven countries, as well as individual memberships. In Puerto Rico and elsewhere the Anti-Imperialist League, as it was generally called, prepared the way for the emergence of local Communist parties. In 1926 Gomez received the first request from Puerto Rico for a charter as a branch of the party in the United States "until such time as the movement is strong enough in Puerto Rico to establish a separate party." The Norteamericanos, however, decided to tell the Puerto Rican Communists to form a "Communist circle" directed from the United States "until such time as it can function by itself." In the United States, the Anti-Imperialist League never amounted to much more than a letterhead front with a small membership, and it gave way in 1933 to the American League Against War and Fascism.[63]

At the time that the Comintern's agrarian front, the Peasants' International, was formed in the fall of 1923, the American Communist line called for working through existing farm organizations, such as the I.W.W.'s Agricultural Workers' Industrial Union, the Farmers' Union, and the Western Progressive Farmers. Two years later, however, the party's Agricultural Committee decided to go ahead with plans for an American farmers' front affiliated to the Peasants' International, and as a result the United Farmers' Educational League was set up in the spring of 1926. Its program ranged from "compulsory state hail insurance" to a "Workers' and Farmers' Government." A subscription to its organ, *The United Farmer,* included membership in the League. With a circulation of about 6000, the paper could build little more than a narrow membership front, limited chiefly to the state of North Dakota. The League's secretary, Alfred Knutson, doubled as the party's Agricultural Organizer.[64]

The Anti-Fascist Alliance of North America was one of those fronts captured, not made, by the Communists. Originally organized in 1923 to counteract the influence of Mussolini's profascist sympathizers in Italian groups in the United States, it had welcomed Socialists, Communists, anarchists, and others, and its secretary, the radical poet Arturo Giovannitti, had enjoyed the confidence of all factions. Three years later, the Communists seized control; the Socialists and others stormed out and formed their own Anti-Fascist League for the Freedom of Italy; and the Alliance, that rare political phenomenon, a genuine united front, was transformed into a common variety of Communist front.[65]

The new secretary of the Anti-Fascist Alliance was a mysterious character who then called himself Enea Sormenti. A native of Trieste, he had been forced into exile by Mussolini's regime, and soon after arriving in the United States had been appointed secretary of the Workers party's Italian Bureau and editor of its official organ, *Il Lavoratore*. Shortly after he had engineered the coup in the Anti-Fascist Alliance, the United States government took steps to deport him to the Soviet Union. Subsequently he was sent to Mexico as the Comintern's representative, and still later, as Carlos Contreras, he was active in the Spanish civil war. After it ended, he returned to Mexico and was allegedly implicated in the assassination of Leon Trotsky. When World War II came to a close, he went back to his native Trieste and under his real name, Vittorio Vidali, headed the Stalinist wing of the local Communist party in a split caused by the Titoist defection in Yugoslavia.[66]

Another case of united front into Communist front took place in the field of workers' sports. A Labor Sports Union of America was organized at a conference in Detroit, January 1927. The twenty-five delegates, most of them representing Finnish clubs, included Communists, Socialists, and I.W.W.'s. The following year, however, the Communists expelled the Socialists and I.W.W.'s, and the purged L.S.U. affiliated with the Red Sports International in August 1929. This front never gathered much momentum, but survived, small and ingrown, into the nineteen-thirties.[67]

Finally, and most important, there was the International Labor Defense. Its story is worth relating in somewhat greater detail to illustrate a relationship to the Comintern and the party common to other important fronts. Though it never rose to the spectacular heights of the earlier Friends of Soviet Russia, the I.L.D. outclassed all the other early fronts in staying power, widespread activity, and far-reaching influence. Internationally it derived from the International Red Aid (M.O.P.R.), a Comintern front set up in Moscow in September 1922 at the initiative of the Society of Old Bolsheviks and Former Political Exiles and Prisoners. It owed its immediate inception to a discussion in Moscow in 1925 between William D. Haywood and James P. Cannon, who decided that something more than the Labor Defense Council was needed to wage campaigns and provide relief for political prisoners.[68]

Before this plan could be carried out, some delicate negotiations took place in Moscow. The line between the International Red Aid and the International Workers' Relief (previously mentioned in connection with the Friends of Soviet Russia) was not always clear. The American delegates in Moscow negotiated an agreement with these two international fronts, each jealous of its jurisdiction all over the world, to demarcate their respective spheres of influence. The eight-point agreement worked out in detail the procedure for organizing the International Labor Defense, its relationship to the existing American branch of the International Workers' Relief, and the American party's responsibility for the whole operation.[69]

Then the American party's top leadership came together to put the finishing touches on the plan. Cannon submitted a slate of candidates for the I.L.D.'s National Committee, thirteen of whom he listed as "Non-Party" and sixteen "Party." Lovestone tried unsuccessfully to strengthen his faction's representation. Cannon also submitted a slate of seven for the I.L.D.'s executive committee. After more factional bickering, Cannon's amended motion for six "Party" and three "Non-Party" members carried unanimously.[70]

The party's decisions enabled the new front's founding conference to proceed smoothly in Chicago the next day, June 28, 1925. With some slight last-minute changes, the I.L.D. came into existence for the legal defense and support of "class-war prisoners." By the end of 1926, it claimed 156 branches with 20,000 individual and 75,000 collective memberships.[71]

The I.L.D. represented the most mature expression of a front thus far achieved by the American Communists. Its first national committee was decorated with such respected non-Communist figures as the Socialist, Eugene V. Debs, nearing the end of his long career; a California liberal churchman, Robert Whitaker; the mine leader Alexander Howat; the feminist Alice Stone Blackwell; and the "Wobbly" poet Ralph Chaplin. The operational control was tightly held by Communists, headed by the National Secretary, Cannon. The national headquarters, the official organ, and the regional offices gave jobs to many more deserving Communists.

In a faction-ridden party, however, party control assumed the form of factional control. Cannon converted the I.L.D. into his personal political fortress. He surrounded himself with his closest adherents, Martin Abern as Assistant National Secretary, and Max Shachtman as editor of the official organ, *The Labor Defender*. The first issue of *The Labor Defender* announced that the I.L.D. aimed at 200,000 dues-paying members. Had it come anywhere near that mark, Cannon could have used it to enormous advantage in the factional struggle for control of the party. By making the I.L.D. into a mass organization, he would have put himself in a position to make good his claim that he could do the same for the party.

During Cannon's reign, the I.L.D. did not limit itself to Communist causes. It waged campaigns to save the anarchists Nicola Sacco and Bartolomeo Vanzetti, and to gain the release of the trade-unionists Tom Mooney and Warren Billings, the labor leader J. B. McNamara, and various Communist defendants here and abroad.[72] It devoted most of its legal defense activity to I.W.W. and Communist cases, and sent $5 a month to 106 "class-war prisoners" in the United States, most of them I.W.W.'s.[73]

Communist fronts for Negroes are treated in connection with the discussion of the Negro question in Chapter 15.

Party and front

What did the party gain from these fronts? Where did they fit into the party's grand design?

The fronts tried to do for the party what the party could not do for itself. The party demanded complete, unconditional adherence to its full program from its members. Relatively few gave it this total commitment in theory and fewer still in practice. Had the party persisted in demanding all or nothing, it would have risked becoming a political sect.

But Communism has never accepted this lilliputian role for itself. Its self-image as a mass movement has repeatedly led it to use all possible means to break out of its self-imposed isolation or its enemies' *cordons sanitaires*. At a very early date, the front became the most institutionalized of these means of mediating between the politically pure sect and the politically impure mass movement.

The front acted both as transmission belt from the party to the masses and as recruiting ground of the party among the masses. It served as a halfway house between the disciplined inner party and the undisciplined outside world. To accept Communist leadership for a "partial demand" within a front was often equivalent to taking the first step on the road to acceptance of the full Communist program. Experience has taught the Communists that anyone who accepts their leadership in one field may eventually extend this acceptance to other fields. The most intensive Communist recruiting, therefore, has taken place inside the party's own fronts.

In penetrating new and particularly difficult territory, the party sometimes used its fronts as entering wedges. For example, a discussion took place in the Secretariat in 1927 on the appointment of a

Southern organizer. Lovestone proposed testing the ground by arranging some public meetings and basing the final decision on the results obtained. But Foster added, "That the first meetings should be held by auxiliary organizations." [74]

"Auxiliary organizations" was the favorite Communist term for fronts, and the most accurate. It appears repeatedly in the Minutes of the top committees, which treated the fronts as if they were merely one more type of party organization.

Among the duties of the Secretariat, as adopted by the Political Committee in September 1927, the following was listed:

> Organization of financial control of the finances of the Party and of the auxiliary organizations.[75]

This provision was implemented the following month by another motion in the Secretariat, which was carried unanimously:

> That every Auxiliary organization of the Party be instructed to send monthly reports indicating its income, source of income and expenditures for the month.

The Comintern representative, Sirola, present at the meeting, added this proviso:

> That these reports should not be addressed to the Party but simply sent to the office.[76]

The Political Committee unanimously accepted this recommendation a week later:

> Recommended that every Party auxiliary and every fraction bureau and Party paper submit financial monthly reports regularly to the National Office for the purpose of getting a line on the budget and perhaps come to some agreement as to a general party budget.[77]

An even more elaborate accounting system was introduced in the spring of 1928 and a method of transferring some of the party's financial burden to the fronts proposed:

> All auxiliary organizations, language papers, *Daily Worker*, language bureaus, District Committees, should within one week after the receipt of these instructions, supply the National Office with a list of employees,

their functions, their salaries and should also indicate whether they are Party members or not. This shall include technical workers as well as political workers.

On the basis of these returns, the Polbureau [Political Committee] should later consider the proposal to have some of the auxiliaries assume the salaries of some of the National Office employees.[78]

Most of the fronts could not support themselves and received party subsidies. When the secretary of the National Council for Protection of Foreign Born reported that the organization could not afford to pay her salary, the Political Committee voted to guarantee half of it until the council could afford more.[79] On the other hand, the Political Committee ordered the International Labor Defense, one of the more solvent fronts, to make a loan of $3000 to Communist needle-trades strikers in 1928.[80]

The Comintern's international fronts also entered into some of the financial arrangements. The Peasants' International sent a letter to the American party in 1927 inquiring about the cost of an anti-war campaign among American "peasants." The Americans replied by wire that $9000 would be needed for a special campaign and to put out a weekly paper.[81]

Fronts also provided a form of organization for Communist sympathizers and fellow travelers, who might, depending on time, place, and circumstance, outnumber party members by ten to one, or even more. At the end of 1925 the party reported a membership of about 16,000. At the same time, it issued twenty-seven publications in nineteen languages with a total circulation of 177,250.[82] Sympathizers undoubtedly made up a substantial portion of this circulation. Three years later, when the membership hovered around 10,000, Foster estimated the sympathizers "in a general way" at "a couple of hundreds of thousands," or about twenty to one.[83] Among these sympathizers were ex-party members who, for one reason or another, wished to free themselves from the party's direct organizational control but were willing to serve the party in front organizations.

This amorphous, floating body of sympathizers constituted the party's main reserve force. Second only to the party's own membership, it entered into the party leadership's calculations. In effect, fronts gave sympathizers and fellow travelers the luxury of pro-Communist activities without forcing them to pay the price of Communist discipline. Thus sympathizers enormously complicate the problem of estimating Communist strength and influence, because some "active sympathizers" might just as well be free-lance or part-time party members.

To what extent was it possible, at least in the nineteen-twenties, to belong to a Communist front without being a Communist sympathizer? Only the most naïve could have belonged to a front for any considerable length of time without realizing its political coloration. The top leaders of the early fronts were not merely Communists; they were top-ranking Communists, most of them members of the Central Executive Committee, and one, Cannon, of the Political Committee. In this respect, the fronts of the nineteen-twenties differed somewhat from those of the Popular Front period in the next decade, when the Communists maintained their control in a much more surreptitious manner.

Finally fronts paid off most dramatically in battles for control of nonfront organizations. The party itself was usually allotted only a few delegates and needed many more to take over a conference or meeting by sheer weight of numbers. Such was the case of the Farmer-Labor conference of July 3, 1923, in Chicago. By mobilizing every front and near-front at its disposal, the party increased the number of Communist delegates from ten to about two hundred. Thus the more organizations the Communists controlled, the easier it became for them to seize control of other organizations.

8

Party Life

DID the American Communists gain or lose from Bolshevization?

Did the membership figures rise or fall?

Was the new type of party able to retain its members any better than the old one?

Did the party change its foreign-language character by wiping out the foreign-language federations?

To what extent did shop nuclei and fractions succeed in winning over the American working class?

How many party members belonged to trade unions?

What was party life like for the rank and file? For the top and middle leadership?

The answers to these questions should enable us to take stock of the social make-up of American Communism in its first decade. There are available enough facts and figures from official party sources to do away with much of the obscurity that has surrounded this aspect of the subject. But can these facts and figures be trusted? Several factors must be considered. It should be remembered that it was in the interest of every leadership to make the best possible showing in the growth and composition of membership. Thus the official figures represent the maximum rather than the minimum, and it is usually safer to discount them than to exaggerate them. The continuous factional warfare must also be taken into consideration. It was not in the interest of the minority faction to permit the majority to make extravagant claims; therefore, a partial check existed on the statistical contents of official reports. And the Comintern took a keen interest in the party's progress and in its own interest discouraged false or misleading factual information.

In any case, the official figures are the only ones we have. If they are handled with sufficient care and regarded mainly as a basis for broad outlines and general trends, no harm can come from scrutinizing them. Indeed, the student can only wish that the party had chosen to provide him with more figures about more things. Fortunately the American Communists were less secretive about themselves in the nineteen-twenties than ever again, and there seems to be little doubt about the basic answers to the main questions.

Membership

The American party reported an increase in average membership from 12,058 in 1922 to 16,325 for the first six months of 1925.[1] After Bolshevization, the total dropped from 14,037 in September to 7213 in October 1925.[2] Then it slowly rose again to about 9500 in 1927, and hovered around that figure for the rest of the decade.[3]

Thus the immediate effect of Bolshevization was a decline in membership of almost 50 per cent. It took the party seven years to climb back to the pre-Bolshevization figure, and that achievement in 1932 owed far more to the economic depression than to Bolshevization.[4]

One reason for the seemingly precipitous loss of membership was the abolition in 1925 of the "dual-stamp system," which had permitted husbands and wives to buy a single dues stamp. As a result, the rolls of the party had contained many housewives who were members in name only. About 4000 were estimated to be in this category;[5] but another 3000 members, representing about 20 per cent of the total, dropped out for other reasons, most of them foreign-language members who could not fit into the new set-up. If Bolshevization had attracted many more "American" workers, as promised, this loss might have been shrugged off. But it did not work out that way. For every seven members that went out, only two came in, and the new members were not very different socially from the old ones.

Soon the high cost of Bolshevization in membership was officially recognized and deplored. One leading organizer wrote: "The [Bolshevization] reorganization, however, cost our party a large number of members, and no comrade should shrug his shoulders and say there is no loss to the party, if the members who left should not rejoin." [6] By 1927 even Lovestone, who was chiefly responsible for carrying out the reorganization, admitted that the party had lost "a too great number of members." [7]

If the Workers party membership is revised to compensate for the distortion created by the dual-stamp system, the figures would be closer to 8000 in 1922, 11,000 in 1923, 13,000 in 1924, 12,000 for the first six months of 1925, 7250 for the last six months of 1925, 7500 in 1926, and 9500 in 1927–29. The upward trend between 1922 and 1924 coincided with the party's activity in the Farmer-Labor movement; a sharp drop was caused by Bolshevization, though it was less drastic than it seems, because the foreign-language members who dropped out were the most inactive group in the party; and a small recovery was staged toward the end of the decade.

Fluctuation

The pre-Bolshevization party had a much greater power of attracting members than of holding them.

From the beginning of 1922 to the middle of 1925, about 20,000 new members were admitted. Of them, about 6000 stayed and 14,000 left. For every member gained, two were lost, or, to put it another way, two ex-Communists were made for every Communist. This "fluctuation," as it was called, was greatest among English-speaking members. Of the 12,742 admitted in the three-and-a-half-year period, only about 1000 remained. The turnover for English-speaking members was about six times that of the party as a whole.[8]

The post-Bolshevization party attracted fewer members but retained a larger percentage. In 1923–24, about 10,000 of the 15,000 new members dropped out. In 1925–27, about 2000 of the 5000 new members dropped out. For the entire period, 1923–27, it appears that about 18,000 of the 23,000 new members were lost.

By 1927, then, there were three distinct categories of members: old-timers who went back to the original parties of 1919; those who entered between 1919 and 1923; and those who joined after 1923. Of 9542 members reported in 1927, about a quarter probably belonged to the first, another quarter to the second, and a half to the third.[9]

We do not have enough information to compare the fluctuation in English-speaking members before and after Bolshevization. But since, as late as 1929, two-thirds of the party was still registered in foreign languages, the difference could not have been very great.[10]

We may estimate, then, that about 100,000 people entered the party in the decade 1919–29, of whom only about 10,000 stayed in long enough to represent a basic membership.[11]

What were the reasons for this phenomenon?

One was undoubtedly economic. With the exception of the depression of 1920–22 and the short-term recessions in 1925 and 1927, the decade was one of improving economic conditions, rising wages, advancing living standards, minimum unemployment, and increased social mobility. Communist propaganda of capitalist decay made relatively little headway in a social atmosphere of easy money and high profits.

Yet it would be erroneous to imagine that there was any simple correlation between the party's fortunes and the economic situation. In the depression of 1920, the Palmer raids reduced the party to a small fraction of its original membership. The party's upsurge in 1923–24 coincided with a period of economic recovery. The recessions of 1925 and 1927 benefited the party little or not at all.

The prosperity of the nineteen-twenties was sufficiently checkered and uneven to leave large pockets of suffering and want. The general trend worked against the party, but the specific condition of individual industries, such as the garment trades, worked for it.

More potent was the political factor. A much closer correlation existed between the party's fluctuation in membership and the party's political line than between the fluctuation and the economic situation. Its underground sectarianism, combined with the government's persecution, drove out most of its original members. The only important influx of new members came during the T.U.E.L.–Progressive trade-union bloc, the Farmer-Labor campaign, and the Third Party alliance. The downhill slide began with the Farmer-Labor and trade-union split, and the infusion of sectarian Bolshevization did nothing to turn the tide. The economic situation in itself might not have prevented a sizable American Communist movement from developing even in the nineteen-twenties. There was enough dissatisfaction and distress to give the party a basis of substantial growth, if it could have held on to all or most of the members that it temporarily attracted. The party's political line primarily determined to what extent it could realize its limited but not negligible objective possibilities.

Nationalities

Bolshevization wiped out the foreign-language federations without wiping out the foreign-language problem.

In the original Communist party of 1919, the Russians made up the single largest national group with almost 25 per cent of the total, the East-Europeans as a whole represented over 75 per cent, and the English-speaking members only 7 per cent. By the end of 1921, when the Workers party was formed, most of the Slavic membership had either returned to Russia or had drifted out of the organization.

From 1922 to 1925, the Finnish section accounted for 40 to 50 per cent of the total membership. The East Europeans were second with 27 to 34 per cent; within this group the South Slavs (Yugoslavs and Bulgarians) ranked first. Only about 10 per cent were English-speaking, and about 8 per cent came from the Jewish section. These four groups made up about 90 per cent of the party; the rest were German, Greek, Hungarian, Italian, Rumanian, and Scandinavian.[12]

Thus not much had changed in six years except for the preponderance of Finns instead of Russians. Though there were not as many Jews in the party as some people supposed, the Jewish influence was greater than the numbers indicated. An indeterminate number of Jews were counted in the English-speaking and other groups. Most of the Jewish members were concentrated in New York and were therefore most noticeable where the party was strongest. The party's influence was also greatest in the largely Jewish garment trade unions in New York. Of the nine daily papers published by the party in 1925, the Jewish daily *Freiheit* reported the largest circulation, with 22,000 against the *Daily Worker*'s 17,000. In the nineteen-twenties perhaps as much as 15 per cent of the party membership was Jewish, but only a minute percentage of the 4,000,000 Jews in the United States were Communists.

Soon the new set-up gave the party almost as much trouble as the old one had. The foreign-language members, forced into the shop and street nuclei, either abandoned them or swamped them. "It is often difficult to secure a nucleus secretary because of the lack of ability to write English," one organizer complained almost a year after Bolshevization.[13] "Now (almost three years after the reorganization) there still are Language Federations in our Party," another revealed with some surprise. "They only carry other names, e.g. 'fractions' in the Party, language 'sections' of the Party, etc." [14] Five years later the party was still taking its first "decisive step" to Bolshevize the non-English-speaking language groups which had somehow mysteriously survived in the party's largest district.[15]

The foreign-language branches were immediately reconstituted as foreign-language Workers' Clubs for which both party members and nonmembers were formally eligible. The party members in these clubs formed themselves into "fractions," as in other non-party organizations; all the fractions of the same language were coordinated by district and national fraction bureaus; the old foreign-language federations were replaced by foreign-language sections under the direction of the Central Executive Committee. These sections were stripped of the power to collect dues or to make final decisions, but in their personnel and manner of functioning, the change was more superficial.

Thus Bolshevization rid the party of a symptom, not a cause. It drove out many foreign-language members without replacing them with the native-born. It was not until the depression in the first half of the nineteen-thirties and the Popular Front in the second half that the native-born entered the party in large numbers.

Social composition

It may be estimated from an "industrial registration" taken in 1924–25 that about 75 per cent of the membership belonged to the working class, about 15 per cent were housewives, and no more than 10 per cent came from the middle-class and professional ranks. Of the workers, about 25 per cent were employed in such heavy industries as the metal trades (including auto workers) and mines, and about 50 per cent in the relatively small-scale or distributive industries such as the needle and food trades.[16]

The Comintern tirelessly berated the American party for its weakness in the heavy, mass, basic industries. Its recipe for overcoming this weakness was the substitution of shop or factory nuclei for street units. Ironically, however, the post-Bolshevization party was far less proletarian than the pre-Bolshevization party had been. Such strength as the pre-Bolshevization American party had in these industries it owed mainly to its foreign-language members. Since they contributed most to the exodus from the party after the reorganization of 1925, the party's existing strength in the basic industries immediately suffered a noticeable drop. The ratio of metal workers declined from 15 per cent in 1925 to 10.7 per cent in 1928, while that of the needle-trades workers jumped from 9 per cent to 21 per cent, a shift directly attributed to the reorganization.[17]

Four years after Bolshevization an official report stated that the party's industrial workers were restricted to one or two basic industries. Minnesota was cited as a good district from the point of view of "social composition"—of a total of 850 registered members, 250 were industrial workers, 150 farmers, 150 clerks and office employees, 250 housewives, 10 "petty-bourgeois elements," and 40 intellectuals.[18] Since most districts were much weaker in industrial workers, these figures indicated a sharp and steady deproletarianization in the years after Bolshevization.

Theoretically the shop nuclei should have proletarianized the party, but party organizers discovered that American workers, even Communists, did not take to shop nuclei. Generally these units were too small to operate successfully. Members speaking different languages lacked cultural homogeneity. Employers and foremen could victimize Communist workers more easily in shop nuclei. American workers were accustomed to think of the factory as a place to work and the home as the place for political activity. Shop nuclei could not create Communists in the basic industries; there first had to be enough Communists in the basic industries to create shop nuclei.

One frustrated organizer made a revealing analogy between Russianizing American workers and Americanizing Russian peasants. He accused the Americans of "standing aghast" before the "latest and most improved model, the product of many years of revolutionary experience in the Russian Communist Party," namely, the shop nuclei machinery, "somewhat like the Russian *muzhik* on his first contact with the American tractor." [19]

But shop nuclei were set up. The constitutional minimum of three members was so hard to satisfy that, in desperation, wherever two members could be found in a single shop, a third was sent in from elsewhere to patch together a so-called shop nucleus. After a year of heaving and straining, only thirty to forty effectively functioning shop nuclei were formed. Two years after Bolshevization, no more than 15 per cent of the membership belonged to shop nuclei, and the number fell from 10 per cent in 1928 to only 4 per cent by 1933.[20] For years the party leadership continued to pay lip-service to the primacy of shop nuclei, but nothing could make them come alive. It was not until the nineteen-thirties that the party succeeded in gaining a mass basis in the basic industries—and then it went back to bigger and better neighborhood branches and, at least officially, banned trade-union fractions altogether.

For much the same reasons, Bolshevization did not score any notable success in luring the party members into trade unions. Part of the trouble was a hold-over from the formative revolutionary-or-nothing "syndicalist" period of American communism. But even with the change of line after 1921 favoring work in "reactionary" trade unions, getting members to join was an uphill battle. The 1924–25 registration showed that only 32 per cent belonged to trade unions, of whom a small number were really active, though at least 90 per cent were eligible to join unions.[21] The Bolshevization campaign increased the union membership to between 45 and 50 per cent, of which a maximum of half participated in systematic union work.[22]

Thus the Bolshevization of the American party registered generally unsatisfactory results:

A loss of membership of about 33 per cent.
A decline in the party's power to attract new members of about 33 per cent.
The problems of language sections instead of language federations.
A partial deproletarianization of the party in the basic industries.
An increase of unionized party members from about 33 per cent to about 50 per cent.

Clearly Bolshevization solved none of the party's problems and exchanged some for worse ones. For years afterward, the party leaders bemoaned the failure of the long-suffering rank and file to build enough shop nuclei, recruit new members, improve the national composition, and increase union activity. But no one dared to question the fundamental aims and methods of Bolshevization.

The rank and file

There was no place for part-time rank-and-filers in the revolutionary party originally conceived by Lenin. He demanded a party of revolutionaries who would devote "not only their spare evenings, but the whole of their lives," though he had in mind a relatively small, conspiratorial group of dedicated revolutionists.[23]

The Comintern's preference for mass parties made this ideal impossible of attainment. In 1921, the Third Congress recognized that the rank and file could not be expected to work for the party full-time and introduced a somewhat more flexible standard:

> A Communist Party must strive to have only really active members, and to demand from every rank and file party worker, that he should place his whole strength and time, in so far as he can himself dispose of it [them], under existing conditions, at the disposal of his Party and devote his best forces to these services.[24]

Mass parties could not expect all their members to be full-fledged, politically conscious Communists. If they were to make the mastery of Communist doctrine a condition of membership, relatively few, in or out of the party, could have passed the test. As a result, less restrictive conditions came to be accepted for the admission of new members. Joining the party was no longer the culminating act in becoming a true Communist; it was mainly a declaration of intention to become one; Communists were made after joining the party, not before. Eventually Stalin made a basic distinction between *accepting* the party program and *mastering* it; only the first, he said, was necessary for party membership.[25] Cannon touched on the problem in this observation of trade-union Communists: "As a rule they do not go through a course of study before admission and do not inquire very deeply into the fundamental theory upon which the party's whole life and activity is founded." [26]

These considerations imply that an important distinction must be made between those who go *into* the Communist party and those who go *through* it. Even if we take into account the ex-party members who have taken refuge in the more comfortable status of fellow-travelerdom, relatively few joined and stayed; many more joined and left.

It is sometimes ignored or forgotten that much more has been involved in becoming a Communist than getting a party card.

The fluctuation has always been greatest in the first year of membership. One of the chief reasons which the party leadership has traditionally offered for its difficulty in keeping new members has been the disappointing party life at the local level of the rank and file. Olgin once gave a vivid description of a typical early party meeting:

> What is the life of a branch of the Workers Party? In an overwhelming majority of cases it is a chain of humdrum questions. A collection for the F.S.R. [Friends of Soviet Russia]. A collection for the Technical Aid. A collection for the Jewish Workers Relief (or a similar other organization). A collection for the Labor Defense. A collection for the party press. Tickets for the party picnic. Tickets for the excursion of the C.C.C. Tickets for a picnic of our branch. Dues. Special assessments. Sale of literature. Preparations for a party meeting. Preparations for a celebration. Local quarrels between members. Elections of delegates to a city conference or other party gathering. This takes 75 per cent of branch sessions. This is the regular work of a branch. Seldom do the members hear a report of the party's work (press service is of no avail where live contact is required). Seldom do they partake in a discussion of the tasks before the party. Almost never have they been permitted to vote upon one or the other policy of the Workers Party. The result is that the rank and filer understands under the word "party" the C.E.C. [Central Executive Committee] or some other body which to him appears shrouded in mystery and far beyond reach. The average member does not think he is the party, that his opinion is forming the opinion of the party, that his error may be injurious to the party. He does not think so because he has not been made an organic element of the party.[27]

Three years later, Wolfe complained:

> Hitherto we have had a few experienced propagandists who did all the speaking and lecturing, a few experienced editors who did all the writing, a few in each branch who made all the motions and did all the arguing on them, and a few devoted Jimmie Higginses who did most of the technical and organizational work that was to be done. The bulk of the party membership sold tickets, put money into collection baskets, made up the audiences at mass meetings, made up the bulk of the readers of what the few editors wrote, of the listeners to what the few speakers said, paid dues and came to vote when the faction strife ran high.[28]

So permanent was this state of affairs that the same sad little vignettes were written a dozen years later.[29] The party's excessive fluctuation was the rank-and-filers' revenge for incessant boredom and inordinate pressure. Newcomers expecting exciting and romantic history-making meetings faced endless hours of humdrum detail and tedious bickering. The least rewarding part of rank-and-file Communist lives was usually spent within the party, the most rewarding outside the party. In the party they were passive objects of their leaders' plans and directives; outside the party, they became active agents for carrying them out. A rank-and-filer who hardly ever uttered a word at a party meeting was often transformed into a loquacious political authority handing down the party line to non-party shopmates and acquaintances. Thus the Communist rank-and-filer tasted outside the party the joys of superiority denied him inside the party.

This study is primarily concerned with the Communist leadership rather than the rank and file, because the leadership was the decisive factor within the movement. Yet the leadership could do little by itself; the rank and file was its lifeline to the masses outside the party; hence the leadership pressed heavily on the rank and file to get results in every phase of its activity.

The cadre

The original Leninist ideal of the professional revolutionary still applies to the Communist movement, but to a part only—the cadre. The meaning of this word of military origin indicates the distance between the Communist leadership and the rank and file. An army cadre constitutes the permanent staff which trains and commands the shifting mass of common soldiers. It constitutes an army within an army, proud of its own professional standards and morale. An able and reliable cadre cannot be quickly improvised; years of instruction, discipline, and molding must be invested in commissioned and noncommissioned officers. With a good cadre, new recruits can be processed in a few months or even weeks. In Communist usage it is best for most practical purposes to draw an objective line between those who work full-time *in* the party and those who work part-time *for* the party.

In this respect the Communist movement again represented a sharp break with the Socialist tradition. The Socialist officialdom, at least in the United States, enjoyed relatively little power or prestige. It merely attended to the indispensable day-by-day drudgery of running the national or local offices. The National Executive Secretary was usually a devoted, hard-working, underpaid, secondary figure. The major Socialist policy-makers and public spokesmen, such as Morris Hillquit and Victor Berger, were more interested in setting policy than in running the party. They limited themselves to seats on the National Executive Committee which met only once in three months, earned their livelihoods at private occupations, and owed their influence over the rank and file to platform eloquence or literary ability rather than to status in the organizational hierarchy. Debs set an extreme example of shunning organizational responsibility by attending only one national convention in twenty-four years. He once explained why he refused to act like a Moses leading the masses out of the capitalist wilderness: "I would not lead you into the promised land if I could, because if I could lead you in someone else could lead you out." [30]

For such old-time Socialist self-restraint, the new generation of Communist functionaries had nothing but contempt and derision. The Leninist ideal of the professional revolutionary captured their imaginations and made them devotees of the cult of the party to which they willingly, and even exultantly, gave "the whole of their lives." By working exclusively in and for the party, they committed themselves to it totally—politically, materially, and emotionally. Cannon has vividly contrasted the Socialist and Communist traditions of leadership:

> As for the [Socialist] party functionaries, the people who devoted all their time to the daily work and routine of the party, they were simply regarded as flunkeys to be loaded with the disagreeable tasks, poorly paid and blamed if anything went wrong. A prejudice was cultivated against the professional party workers. The real honors and the decisive influence went to the leaders who had professional occupations outside the party and who, for the most part, lived typical petty-bourgeois lives which were far removed from the lives of the workers they were presumably "leading."

> When we organized the Communist Party in this country in 1919, under the inspiration of the Russian revolution, we put a stop to all this nonsense. We had the opinion that leadership of the revolutionary movement was a serious matter, a profession in itself, and the highest and most honorable of all professions. We deemed it unworthy of the dignity of a revolutionary leader to waste his time on some piddling occupation in the bourgeois world and wrong for the party to permit it. We decreed that no one could be a member of the Central Committee of the party unless he was a full time professional party worker, or willing to become such at the call of the party.[31]

The revolutionary profession of the professional revolutionary developed its own peculiar rules and risks. There was only one possible employer—the party. Unemployment meant loss of job, profession, and even reason for existence. Communist party workers have usually disliked thinking of themselves as members of a distinct profession; they prefer to recall the professions of their youth, to hide behind a profession like journalism, which all of them practice to some extent, or to consider themselves without a profession.[32] But an ex-machinist who became a full-time professional Communist organizer was no more a machinist than an ex-machinist who became a life-time trade-union official or a corporation executive.

The difference between the Communist cadre and the rank and file took many forms. The cadre's party life was vastly more exciting and rewarding. Politics, friendships, and work fused into one another, and little or nothing existed outside party life. The professional Communist was perhaps the political animal *par excellence,* who led a life fully integrated in a party which politicalized everything. A social evening became an informal political discussion with the same kind of people, if not the very same people, who participated in formal discussions. Party work provided a constant, feverish round of activities. (Some ex-Communists suddenly find life outside the party empty and dull because they miss the automatic, incessant activity, even after it has lost all meaning and direction.) For the party worker, a break with the party represented a total personal crisis; he lost all at once his faith, friends, and profession.

Hence there are two types of party crises—a crisis of the rank and file, endangering the party's influence; and a crisis of the cadre, endangering its very existence.

Within the cadre itself, three main levels may be distinguished—the top leadership in the national office, the middle leadership in the districts, and the lower leadership in the sections. Because Communist policy is made at the top, the middle and lower ranks primarily devote themselves to the application of the line. A District Organizer who has too many original ideas must go up or down. Yet a little of Stalin rubs off at every step of the hierarchy; the lowliest branch, nuclei, or unit organizer can taste the keen and subtle pleasure of handing down the line to those below.

At the top, and to a lesser extent farther down, different leaders specialize in different functions—policy-making, organizing, propaganda, theory, trade-unionism. Ruthenberg was primarily an office executive and policy-maker, Bedacht a mass agitator, Foster a trade-union organizer, Bittelman a theoretical propagandist, Lovestone a tactician. Some can serve as public figures, notably a Ruthenberg or a Foster; others, such as a Bittelman or a Stachel, cannot. It would not be too hard to imagine one Communist leader as a highly successful garment manufacturer, and another as the mayor of a medium-sized town. Yet most Communist leaders, whatever their personal aptitudes or specialities, must be Jacks-of-all-trades. They organize, write, make speeches, edit papers, lecture intellectuals, and go from one job to another at different phases of their careers. The top leaders spent about half their time in party work and half in factional activity. Most of them were men of unusual energy or they could not have survived both the grueling pace of the party and the factional demands upon them.

Only once has a representative group of Communist leaders volunteered information about its background. *The American Labor Who's Who,* published in 1925 and edited by a party member, contained biographical data for over forty leading or representative Communists and provided enough vital statistics to draw a composite picture of the main features of the Communist leadership.[33] This composite picture of the first decade did not change materially for another two decades, because the same men, with relatively few exceptions, continued to lead the party.

The data varies, with the result that we have fuller information about some things than about others.

Age. As of 1925, six years after the party's foundation, only one out of 43 had reached his early fifties, 15 were in their forties, 15 in their thirties, and 12 in their twenties.

Birthplace. Of the 43, 23 were born in the United States and 20 in Europe. Of the latter, 12 came from Eastern Europe, including 7 from Russia and 8 from Western Europe.

Sex and color. It was a white man's world—in a total of 43, there were one woman and one Negro.[34]

Education. Of 29 replies, 4 reported spending less than five years in elementary school, 8 had never gone beyond elementary school, 6 had attended high school, 2 business school, 6 college; and 3 reported postgraduate work. About 40 per cent, then, had received an elementary-school education or less, and about 30 per cent a college education or better.

Occupations. Of 38 replies, a majority of 25 reported a white-collar working-class background, including 10 professionals. Only 13 disclosed a non-white-collar working-class occupation, including 6 skilled industrial workers.[35]

Former political affiliations. Of 28 replies, 20 reported the Socialist party; 2 Socialist Labor party; 1 I.W.W.; 3 S.P.–I.W.W.; 1 S.L.P.–I.W.W.; and 1 S.P.–I.W.W.–Syndicalist League. Almost 80 per cent of those with former political ties, then, had once belonged to the Socialist party.

It may be concluded from this limited survey that the great majority of Communist leaders were male, white, and in their thirties or forties. About half were born in the United States and about half in Europe; more than half of the latter came from Eastern Europe. More had received an elementary-school than a college education, and more had gone to college than only to high school. There were about two former white-collar workers for every non-white-collar worker. And the great majority were former Socialists.

Finances

There are few more closely guarded secrets in the Communist movement than its finances, especially its sources of income, here and abroad. Yet so important a subject cannot be entirely ignored, even if we must take more risks than usual in assessing the information at our disposal.

In the early days of the Communist movement, there was very little squeamishness about admitting, or rather boasting, about Russian financial help to weaker parties. In December 1918, A. A. Joffe, the Soviet Ambassador in Berlin, was expelled from Germany for interfering in internal German affairs and answered the charges by publishing in *Izvestia,* the official organ of the Soviet government, an accounting of all the marks and rubles he had presented to German revolutionists.[36] At its first meeting, the Executive Committee of the Communist International decided to ask the Russian party to assume the chief financial burden for its support, and Zinoviev soon reported that some activities of the Italian party had been made possible only because the Comintern had supplied the money.[37] Louis C. Fraina was given about $50,000 in Moscow in December 1920 for himself and others to use in Great Britain, Mexico, and the United States.[38]

But the lack of currency in Russia soon after the revolution made it necessary for the Comintern to sell diamonds and jewelry abroad to raise cash subsidies. Sailors brought these valuables to the United States where they were turned over to an American Communist businessman who sold them for the party.[39] One of those who unsuccessfully tried to smuggle jewels into the United States was Michael Borodin, later famous for his exploits in China. Borodin tried also unsuccessfully to use the poet Carl Sandburg, then returning from Norway to the United States, as a courier for $10,000 and propaganda material. Jewels were unquestionably used by Ludwig Martens, the first official Soviet agent, as security for a loan of $20,000 from the Irish Republican delegation in New York.[40] In 1922, Gitlow says, the American Communists received a Russian subsidy in dollars and tried to improve on them by speculating in the wildly fluctuating German currency market, but the operation resulted in a loss of several thousand dollars.[41]

The underground American party's membership dues and other revenues certainly could not have accounted for its relatively large expenditures. A membership at maximum of 10,000 was assessed 60 cents monthly dues, and under underground conditions probably no more than half paid it regularly.[42] Yet documents seized during the Bridgman raid in 1922 and subsequently confirmed in court by the party's current secretary revealed expenditures of $185,715.09 from July 1921 to July 1922.[43]

There are available public financial statements by the national office of the Workers party from November 1922 to June 30, 1925. These statements show receipts and expenditures of about $115,000 annually, of which dues accounted for about 40 per cent.[44] There is also a record of the financial statement for one month, December 1927, privately entrusted to members of the Central Executive Committee.[45] It reported cash receipts of $6507.36, and cash expenditures of $7110.25, which, if typical of the year, indicates an annual expenditure of about $85,000, of which dues accounted for less than a third. Gitlow has estimated the expenses of the national office in the late nineteen-twenties at approximately $100,000 a year. He also says that the Secretariat once estimated the total expenditures of the party and subsidiary organizations at $1,250,000 a year.[46]

There is no doubt, however, that the party was almost always in financial distress despite the help that it received. The Minutes of the top committees are full of financial crises, last-minute loans from party auxiliaries and individuals, and special assessments to stave off imminent disaster. The biggest drain on the party's finances was the *Daily Worker,* which always ran up heavy deficits. Special fund-raising campaigns were always saving it from catastrophe. Its crises were not imaginary. The Minutes of the Political Committee of September 2, 1925, tell the story of a typical emergency. The business manager reported that "the Daily is on the verge of suspension and $2000 is needed immediately." Ruthenberg answered that "all possible resources have been exhausted" and proposed another special campaign, which was duly voted. Two years later, the *Daily Worker* could not meet its payroll of non-party workers; two auxiliaries, the International Labor Defense and International Workers' Aid, were instructed to provide $150 and $100 within twenty-four hours.[47]

Most of the party's other publications, twenty-six in number, could not support themselves and needed frequent or occasional financial assistance from the national office. The majority of auxiliaries and trade-union committees also depended on the party financially.

Where did all the money come from? Apart from dues and initiation fees, which probably brought in no more than a quarter to a third of the necessary funds, the party depended on special assessments, fund-raising drives, meetings, bazaars, picnics, donations, literature sales, and the like. While most of the auxiliaries and foreign-language federations or sections were not self-supporting, some of them, such as the Friends of Soviet Russia and the Finnish organization, were able at times to help out the party. The American Fund for Public Service, set up by Charles Garland in 1922, included the party and some of its auxiliaries, as well as other radical and liberal organizations, among the beneficiaries of its largesse.[48] The Communist publishing house, International Publishers, was founded in 1924 and subsidized during the next fifteen years to the amount of $115,000 by a millionaire Communist, A. A. Heller, owner of an oxygen company and one-time holder of economic concessions in the Soviet Union.[49] Two Minneapolis sympathizers, Bertha and Samuel Rubin, donated $2000 in 1927 to help establish the party's official Workers Library Publishers.[50] The party took a percentage of the profits from special group tours to the Soviet Union and some Soviet films shown in the United States.[51]

Yet the party's greatest financial mainstay was undoubtedly the devotion and sacrifice of its paid officers and organizers. Whatever their political and psychological compensations were, money was not one of them. An early wage scale of the underground Communist Party of America in 1922 provided weekly salaries of $25 to $35 for single persons, $30 to $40 for those with one dependent, and $40 to

$45 for those with more than one dependent.[52] In October 1927, the complete payroll of the national office amounted to $507.50 weekly, allotted as follows:

Executive Secretary: Lovestone, $40; stenographer, $25.
Agit-Prop: Wolfe [$40], paid by New York Workers School; Bedacht, $40; Bittelman, $40; stenographer, $25.
Organization: Stachel, $30; stenographer, $25.
Industrial: Johnstone, $35; Foster, $40; Gitlow, $40; stenographer, $25.
Anti-Imperialist: Gomez, $30.
Agricultural: Knutson, $25.
Negro: Moore, $40.
Accounts and Supplies: A. Thompson, $25.
Students (Lenin School): Hathaway, $12.50; Bell, $10 (for dependents).[53]

But Gitlow once wryly remarked, "When I got paid, I got paid $40 a week." [54] Party salaries were notoriously erratic and deferable. Non-party workers in the *Daily Worker* printing plant were paid, even if loans were necessary, but party members were the first to be told that there was no money for them that week—or month.

The party's financial structure was peculiarly rickety and yet it never toppled over. In the privacy of the Political Committee in January 1927, Foster proposed organizing a New York Port Bureau, to which Ruthenberg answered that "the Party did not have funds for even its most pressing work under way at the present time" and therefore could not engage in new ventures.[55] A few months later, the Union Press asked the party to settle the accounts of certain party organizations, and Lovestone told the Secretariat that the Union Press should take up the matter with the organizations directly "because the Party is absolutely broke." [56]

But the party was not an ordinary business enterprise that could go "absolutely broke"; every financial crisis was merely a prelude for raising more funds by frantic appeals to its members, sympathizers, and other benefactors. For a relatively small organization, it was capable of raising a great deal of money, far more than any other radical organization. But it habitually spent more than its current income; it stretched its available resources far beyond the safety point; it made extreme, even outrageous, demands on its full-time workers. Its financial difficulties were largely caused by its overexpansion and overextension and they in turn nerved it to greater efforts in raising more funds.

The question again arises to what extent in the nineteen-twenties the American Communists supported themselves and to what extent they depended on subsidies from the Comintern. This is not a question to which many people have volunteered answers, for one reason because very few Communists or ex-Communists were ever in a position to know about these highly secretive transactions.

One of the few who knew and one who has volunteered voluminous answers is Benjamin Gitlow. He has written and testified about these alleged subsidies by the Comintern and Profintern to the American Communists:

> The Profintern gave Foster $25,000 in 1921 to promote the Trade Union Educational League.
> The Comintern supplied "a large portion" of the money for the Communist activity in the Farmer-Labor movement.
> The Comintern donated $35,000 to start the *Daily Worker* in 1924.
> The Comintern provided $50,000 for the presidential campaign in 1924.
> The Comintern contributed $100,000 in two installments of $50,000 for the campaign against John L. Lewis in the mine union.
> Gitlow personally received $3,500 in Moscow as the first installment of $35,000 for the presidential campaign in 1928.[57]

On only two occasions, however, was Gitlow personally implicated. In addition to receiving $3500 in 1928, he says that he temporarily replaced Foster, who went to Moscow for the Sixth World Congress later that year, as custodian of the anti-Lewis mine-union fund, and received about $27,000 or $29,000 for that purpose.[58] Though Gitlow produced some corroborative evidence for the disbursement of some of these last funds, the reliability of his testimony rests essentially on his personal credibility.

Lovestone was once questioned about the Comintern's subsidies and answered in general terms that partially confirmed and partially contradicted Gitlow's statements. He verified the fact that money was frequently brought by American Communists from Moscow, generally by delegates returning to the United States. "I occasionally brought some funds with me, others did the same," he declared.[59] But he denied that the sums were anywhere nearly as large as Gitlow had alleged.

To make matters more complicated, Gitlow was responsible for varying figures. In his testimony before the Special Committee on Un-American Activities of the House of Representatives in September 1939, he stated that the sum had fluctuated between $100,000 and $150,000 a year from 1922 to 1929.[60] In his book, *I Confess,* published later that year, one page specifically gives the sum as $250,000 a year and another page might be interpreted to mean that it was almost twice as large.[61] Lovestone dismissed such figures as "romantic" and testified that "in general it was no more than about twenty or twenty-five thousand dollars a year."[62]

It is difficult to reconcile such widely varying estimates as $25,000 and $250,000 from two witnesses whose careers in the Communist movement were so similar. There is no doubt that Gitlow was in a position to know a great deal, but he often raises doubts about his credibility by telling the same story in different ways or by failing to distinguish between personal knowledge and hearsay.*

In 1927, British police raided Soviet House, headquarters of Arcos, the Soviet trading corporation in London, and seized incriminating documents. One of them, found in the possession of a Russian courier, listed names and addresses, some of them American, which revealed how the American Communists had been receiving secret messages and funds from abroad. Four categories were covered in these instructions: "half legal cables," letters, "cipher-telegrams" and "money, per Bank." Among the confidential recipients were Lydia Gibson, wife of Robert Minor (for "half legal cables"), Anna E. David, better known as Anna Damon (letters), and the party's lawyer, Joseph R. Brodsky ("money, per Bank").[63] The American

* I have been informed by Earl Browder that in a later period, 1930–35, the Comintern provided about 10 per cent of the American Communist funds.

Communists made little effort to deny the allegations. A statement by the Central Executive Committee blandly asserted: "We have neither the desire nor the means of ascertaining whether all of these addresses are genuine. But let us assume that they are." [64]

In any case, Comintern funds were handled by the Budget Commission, whose indefatigable watchdog was Piatnitsky. Profintern funds were apparently sent directly to Foster.[65] The Comintern paid the bill for all delegates, representatives, and students in Moscow, including living quarters, food, cigarettes, and allotments of Russian currency. Since the American Communists resident in Moscow might number as many as fifty at one time, the total cost was not negligible. In general, all activities directly connected with the Comintern were charged to the Comintern, which paid the expenses in advance or refunded them if the party had laid out its own money. Piatnitsky was notorious for guarding the Comintern's funds jealously and demanding a strict accounting.

Those determined to ignore the evidence can still believe that the American Communists did not receive substantial subsidies from the Comintern, and, in effect, from the Russian Communist party. It was inherent in the very concept of a world party that the weaker sections should receive financial and other support from the stronger ones, and any American Communist leader who refused Russian money would have committed a serious political indiscretion. Lovestone says that Stalin suspected his motives for trying to reduce the Comintern's subsidy in 1926–27.[66]

There is little doubt that American Communism received considerable outside financial aid in the first fifteen years of its existence. At minimum, this aid in all its ramifications probably totaled half a million dollars, at maximum as much as five million dollars. This money was generally allotted for special purposes rather than as a means of existence. The American Communist leadership was certainly enabled to do some things which it could not otherwise have done; it benefited enormously from the assurance that it could run to Moscow for money in time of necessity. But the importance of "Moscow gold" should not be exaggerated. It occupied a relatively minor place in the total American Communist outlay. It was never large enough to save the American Communist movement from an almost permanent financial crisis or to lessen the sacrifices made by the full-time party workers. The financial and political ties between the Comintern and the American Communist movement were intimately related to each other, but it would not have made much difference if the Comintern had called the tune without having paid the piper.

Dozenberg's assignment

Among the passengers of the *Norge,* a small Norwegian boat crossing the Atlantic in 1904, was a tall young man named Nicholas Dozenberg, a native of Riga, then capital of the Russian province of Lettland, later known as Latvia. With only a grammar-school education and the high hopes of one who had just passed the age of twenty-one, he had set out alone from the old world to the new.

Dozenberg went straight to Boston, where a colony of Lettish immigrants flourished. Two years later, he went to work for the New York, New Haven and Hartford Railroad as a locomotive machinist, his job for the next fourteen years. He joined the International Association of Machinists and married a Lettish girl of similar background. He drifted into Left Wing politics through the Lettish Workers Society of Boston, the mainstay of the Lettish Federation which was admitted into the Socialist party in 1908. At one time he served as secretary of the Malden branch of the Socialist party and as an officer of his machinists' local.[67]

The Lettish Left Wing was the training ground for a special type of revolutionary. In Russia, during the Bolshevik revolution, the Lettish regiments of "sharpshooters" were given the most difficult and dangerous missions. In the United States, the Socialist Propaganda League of 1915–19, the first organized form of the pro-Bolshevik Left Wing, was largely dependent on the Letts in Massachusetts for its existence and support. The Lettish element in the American Communist movement, though relatively small in numbers, contributed an unusual group of activists who could be trusted with work of the most delicate and secret nature. One of these Letts was Carl Jansen or Johnson of Roxbury, Massachusetts, who carried out assignments in various countries for the Profintern and Comintern under the name of Charles E. Scott. Another was the long-time head of the Central Control Commission of the American party, Charles Dirba. A third was Nicholas Dozenberg.

Dozenberg did not take part in the foundation of the American Communist movement in 1919 because he happened to be working in Canada at that time. When he returned to New York in 1920 or 1921, he joined the Communists. Through Scott, who came to the United States in 1921 on a mission for the Profintern, he received an offer to become business manager of the unofficial Communist organ, *Voice of Labor,* in Chicago. Dozenberg jumped at the chance, and his active Communist career began.[68]

For the next seven years, Dozenberg served the party faithfully as one of its leading technical workers. He was no writer, intellectual, or political leader. He was the kind of party militant who asked no questions and did what he was told to do. After managing the business end of the *Voice of Labor* and then of the *Worker* through 1923, he took over the party's Literature Department. In 1925 he ran for alderman of the Twenty-eighth Ward in Chicago on the Communist ticket, and the *Daily Worker* headed the story of his campaign: "Not Graduate of Harvard But Militant Working Class Fighter."[69] The following year he headed the "Accounts and Supplies Dept." of the national office. When the national office moved from Chicago to New York in 1927, he took charge of the physical details; after the move, he was appointed manager of the party's small publishing house.

Then Dozenberg fell sick and received a leave of absence from party work. He had been dissatisfied with his job, which paid him $20 a week—when it paid him at all. As he put it: "I was a married man and then the wages were so uncertain—one week you did get it, and the next one not, and then two weeks not, and then you might get wages back for one week back and then forget about the rest of it, and all that sort of stuff. The economic situation was simply rotten."

Dozenberg made known that he wanted a new job. The Secretariat took steps to get him one.[70]

In a restaurant on Lenox Avenue in New York, Dozenberg made contact with a man whom he first knew as "Alfred," and later as "Joseph Paquett" and "Alfred Martin." A year or two later, however, Dozenberg learned in Moscow that he was Alfred Tilton, a member of the Fourth Department of the Red Army, the Soviet Military Intelligence. Tilton was also a Lett, and he and Dozenberg talked in their native tongue.[71]

Tilton asked Dozenberg for assistance in "technical matters." According to Dozenberg, his first assignment seemed innocent enough —to interview people who could be sent to Soviet Russia for various purposes and to report on them to Tilton. The salary was $35 a week, more than Dozenberg had received from the party, and the pay promised to be more regular. Dozenberg readily agreed to one condition for his employment—to drop out of the party and "simply disappear from the scene altogether."

Late in 1927 or early in 1928, Nicholas Dozenberg disappeared and "Nicholas L. Dallant" took his place.[72] As far as is known he was the first American Communist to make the transition to Soviet military intelligence. Tilton, however, was probably not the first Soviet intelligence agent in the United States.[73]

What we know of Dozenberg's career as a Soviet agent comes largely from himself, and there is reason to believe that he did not tell much more than he thought his interrogators already knew.

In 1928 Tilton was called to Moscow, and Dozenberg soon followed him. Dozenberg met the chief of the Fourth Department, Jan Berzin, also a Lett, and by this time he knew, if he did not know before, for whom he was working and what his role was. Later Dozenberg refused to admit that he ever did any spying himself. He claimed that he had specialized in setting up commercial enterprises to provide a "cover" for other Soviet agents—a dried-fruit enterprise in New York, a motion-picture company in Rumania, a photographic equipment business in China and the Philippines. He was mixed up in a bizarre plot to finance his Rumanian venture with counterfeit dollars, a fiasco that sent one of his associates to jail for fifteen years.[74] He admittedly tried to recruit a dozen others for service as Soviet agents and succeeded in recruiting two.[75]

Why did he do it? He was asked: "You did it through conviction largely because you believed in the Soviet Union, didn't you?"

Dozenberg answered: "Partly convictions, and partly once you run into a game of that sort, well, it becomes so regular that you don't pay any attention to it, except in the later years I grew away from it. I was sick and tired of it and in a certain sense I felt more than glad that I was through, although the economic side was rather —very desperate because after all you must realize that I had been away from friends, relatives, and associates for so many years all of a sudden to be left out in the open field is no joke." [76]

Dozenberg's desperation gradually outdistanced his conviction.

In March 1939, he was called to Moscow and asked to operate in the United States. He allegedly refused and, nevertheless, was permitted to leave Moscow. He returned to the United States in June and settled in Washington, D.C. Still camouflaged as "Nicholas L. Dallant," he lived quietly and waited.

On September 9 Benjamin Gitlow, a former member of the Communist party's Secretariat, named Dozenberg as a Soviet agent in hearings before the House of Representatives' Special Committee on Un-American Activities. Later that month the *Saturday Evening Post* appeared with an article by the former Soviet military intelligence official who had adopted the name of Walter G. Krivitsky, identifying Dozenberg as a Soviet agent. In October Earl Browder, then General Secretary of the American Communist party, was indicted on a charge of having used fraudulent passports.

After Browder's indictment, Dozenberg fled from Washington. He was traced and discovered to be running a grocery store in the town of Bend, Oregon. The *Daily Worker* of December 11 hastily reported him to be the victim of a "trumped-up charge" of passport violation.

He was accompanied to court by the Communist party's lawyer, Joseph R. Brodsky, who, however, decided not to represent him.

Dozenberg pleaded guilty at his trial in January 1940. When the news leaked out that he planned to testify against Browder, an editorial in the *Daily Worker* of January 11, exactly one month after its first sympathetic report of his plight, screamed at him as a "Van der Lubbe" (the half-witted witness in the famous Nazi trial of the Bulgarian Communist, Georgi Dimitroff), a "discredited unknown," "stool-pigeon," and "scum of the earth." The Communist organ carefully avoided telling its readers of Dozenberg's past record in the party.

A few days later Dozenberg testified that Browder's first trip to Moscow in 1921 had been made on his passport. After giving information to the FBI, Dozenberg received a jail sentence of a year and a day. He testified for the Special Committee on Un-American Activities, served his sentence, and disappeared.[77]

He was a true conspirator. It would help in understanding the Communist movement if the terms "conspirator" and "conspiracy" were reserved for actual Soviet agents. Except for a tiny minority, the Communist membership has devoted its efforts to gaining mass influence with means that have been blatantly nonconspiratorial. If the Communist movement is regarded as merely or even primarily a conspiracy, it is paradoxically the most public and self-publicized conspiracy of all time.

But a certain type of politically motivated spy is more likely to be found by Soviet espionage agencies in the Communist movement than anywhere else. This simple fact is sometimes absurdly exaggerated and oversimplified to mean that every non-Russian Communist should be regarded as at least a "potential" Russian spy. This caricature is based on a theoretical abstraction, not on the real people who for a multitude of reasons and in different periods of social stress have gone in and out of the Communist movement.

The recruitment of individual non-Russian Communists as Soviet agents was a gradual process. Trotsky seems to have opposed the efforts of Russian intelligence agencies to avail themselves of the services of non-Russian Communists.[78] According to the Canadian Royal Commission, there was "an organization at work in Canada directed from Russia and operating with Communist sympathizers in Canada" as early as 1924.[79] This "organization" was first set up in Canada because secret work throughout North America was then most conveniently carried out from Canada.

The Russians could have had no illusions about the political risks that they imposed on non-Russian Communist parties by tying them into the Russian espionage networks. They recognized the dangers by taking special precautions to withdraw their agents from party work and by maintaining liaison with a single member of the Secretariat at the very top of the party hierarchy. Increasingly they faced the problem of balancing the benefits that might accrue to Soviet intelligence agencies from recruiting a few foreign Communists against the harm that might befall an entire party if the tie-up were to leak out.

At first the harm far outweighed the benefits in the Russian estimation. But as the foreign parties lost caste in Moscow, as the Russian security and intelligence agencies entrenched themselves in power, and as Stalin felt more sure of himself, the balance shifted in favor of the benefits that would accrue to the Soviets' secret agencies.

Thus Dozenberg's assignment was a landmark. Further than that, subordination could not go.

9

Politics and Trade-Unionism

We can now pick up the thread of the story as it unfolded after the Comintern representative, Sergei Ivanovich Gusev, turned the Workers party over to Ruthenberg's faction at the Fourth Convention in the summer of 1925.

In October Foster, accompanied by his liege, Bittelman, set off for Moscow to contest Gusev's decision. But by the time they arrived in the Russian capital, they were confronted with an even more ominous threat to their dwindling power.

Ruthenberg was not content with depriving Foster of his hard-won political leadership. He soon moved to strip Foster of his hitherto unchallenged trade-union leadership and even to do away with his personal base, the Trade Union Educational League. Thus the next round in the factional struggle was fought most fiercely in the trade-union field.

Much had happened to Foster and the T.U.E.L. to make both of them vulnerable to this line of attack.

Three periods

Before Bolshevization three periods of American Communist trade-union policy can be clearly distinguished.

The first, from 1919 to 1921, was based on revolutionary dual unionism. The Communists considered the A.F. of L. a "bulwark of capitalism" and aimed at its destruction. Their own activity and influence in the trade unions was minimal; most of their strength was concentrated in a few small, independent unions in New York with a total membership of about 25,000. These independent unions, which formed the United Labor Council of New York and Vicinity in January 1922, were sympathetic to the Profintern but refused to follow its advice about working in the A.F. of L.[1]

The second, from 1921 to 1923, was based on a bloc with the Progressive group within the A.F. of L. It began with the adoption of the T.U.E.L. as the Communists' chosen instrument in the trade-union field and ended with the break with Fitzpatrick. In these two years the Communists succeeded in making considerable headway among the garment workers, railwaymen, miners, and metal workers.[2]

The third, from 1923 to 1925, was based on the split with the Progressives. It resulted in the precipitous decline of the T.U.E.L. and, except for the New York garment trades, the general collapse of Communist hopes in the unions. The A.F. of L.'s expulsion campaign drove the T.U.E.L. underground, and the T.U.E.L. soon resorted to the desperate expedient of ordering its members to deny their affiliation.[3] By 1925 Foster admitted that the T.U.E.L. "consisted practically only of Communists" and of the one-third of the party membership that belonged to unions, "only a very small portion are really active in the trade unions." [4]

There was not much left in the T.U.E.L., therefore, for Foster's enemies to destroy. Foster himself had deprived the T.U.E.L. of its *raison d'être* by making a sharp turn to the left after the split with Fitzpatrick. The turn was demonstratively marked by the inclusion of the dictatorship of the proletariat in the program of the T.U.E.L.,[5] and by the amalgamation of the official organs of the T.U.E.L., the Friends of Soviet Russia, and the Workers party into a single, all-inclusive official organ, *The Workers Monthly*.[6] As its membership, program, and publication became identical with the party's, the T.U.E.L.'s independent existence dwindled to the vanishing point. As long as Foster controlled both the party and the T.U.E.L., he could compensate for trade-union losses with political gains. When he lost control of the party, all he had left were the gutted remains of the T.U.E.L.

The trade-union problem, to be sure, was not a simple one. Foster's personal background and trade-union philosophy committed him unconditionally to a policy of working exclusively with organized labor in the A.F. of L. But organized labor in the nineteen-twenties constituted only a small portion of the labor force; the A.F. of L. was aggressively uninterested in organizing the vast unorganized majority; and the T.U.E.L. had been rendered impotent as a lever to move the A.F. of L. or even its Progressive section into action. Everyone agreed that the only hope was to organize the unorganized. But how? Foster's panacea of boring from within the A.F. of L. had reached a dead-end, and he had nothing more to offer than more denunciations of the A.F. of L.'s "reactionary bureaucracy" and the Progressives' "betrayal." Dual unionism was still a dirty word to good Communists, but every effort to find a way out of the impasse of boring from within led in its direction. Thus the T.U.E.L. was not only organizationally defunct, it also seemed intellectually bankrupt; and Foster's enemies were not slow to take advantage of his plight.

From T.U.E.L. to "Left bloc"

The trade-union dilemma of the American Communists did not go unnoticed in Moscow.

As the T.U.E.L. faded away, the Profintern looked around for other ways to challenge the A.F. of L. At its Third Congress in July 1924, it proposed three methods of organizing the unorganized in the United States: through the A.F. of L., through independent mass unions, and through the Workers party's shop nuclei. But it left the choice up to the party: "All must be used as expediency dictates." [7]

In the spring of 1925, the Comintern went a step farther and came up with a recommendation "to convert the T.U.E.L. into a great opposition movement of the Left bloc." [8] On the eve of the Workers party's Fourth Convention that summer, the new line was spelled out in greater detail.

A joint letter on trade-union work signed by both the Comintern and Profintern declared: "In those places and industries where no labor unions exist the Communists must take the initiative and organize unions." For the T.U.E.L. it enjoined: "The party must strive to convert the League into an extensive Left Bloc Organization, lining up all the revolutionary and progressive elements in the labor unions against the reactionary bureaucracy." It added that such unity must come "through the medium of the Trade Union Educational League." [9]

These instructions shifted the emphasis away from working in the A.F. of L. to organizing new unions and replacing the existing T.U.E.L. with something else. But they left some vital questions unanswered. Should the Communists organize new unions directly through the T.U.E.L. or through the party's shop nuclei? Should the T.U.E.L. be "converted" into a wholly new organization or a revised version of the old one?

Foster's enemies in the party pounced on those passages of the Comintern-Profintern documents that lent themselves to an interpretation of by-passing the T.U.E.L. The stress on working within new unions instead of the A.F. of L. and through shop nuclei instead of the T.U.E.L. gave them the rudiments of a new trade-union policy, halfway between boring from within the A.F. of L. and old-style dual unionism.

As long as Foster had controlled the party, these threats to his trade-union policy had remained on paper. But when Gusev handed Ruthenberg's faction the majority at the Fourth Convention, the threats came to life. Already, at the convention, Dunne had accused Ruthenberg of trying to supplant the T.U.E.L. with the party as the trade-union organizing body.[10] The convention's trade-union resolution had blurred the issue sufficiently to leave the answer in doubt.[11] But it did not remain so for long.

The party's trade-union department, in which the Fosterites were entrenched, found itself with less and less to do. Organizers in the field stopped sending it their reports and proposals, and the

Ruthenberg-dominated Political Committee developed the habit of taking up trade-union questions before the trade-union department had a chance to consider them. The new majority pushed Gitlow forward as Foster's successor in charge of the trade-union field. These moves so alarmed Foster's former allies, Cannon and Dunne, that they protested to the Political Committee: "A continuation of these practices will have the inevitable result of practically liquidating the trade-union department." [12]

Lozovsky to the rescue

While Foster and Bittelman were off in Moscow wrangling over party control, their successors in the leadership aimed a death-blow at the T.U.E.L. Armed with the mandate from the Comintern and Profintern, the Ruthenberg group worked out a plan for "converting" the T.U.E.L. into a broad Left bloc organization, and presented it to a plenum held at the end of December 1925, the first held in the post-Bolshevized American party in imitation of the Comintern's practice.

The trade-union resolution introduced at this plenum "converted" the T.U.E.L. all the way. It proposed expanding the party's industrial national committees, of which only one, for the needle trades, was connected with the T.U.E.L., into broad Left bloc organizations. Then it provided for local Left bloc conferences, a national conference, a national committee and program, a provisional national organizing board, and a new Left Wing trade-union organ. Thereafter, it directed the T.U.E.L. to be "absorbed" into the new set-up.[13]

In the absence of Foster and Bittelman, their lieutenants, Browder and Johnstone, bore the brunt of the anti-T.U.E.L. attack. They protested that the new trade-union line amounted to liquidation of the T.U.E.L., to incipient dual unionism, to a factional pogrom. But they pleaded and shouted in vain. With Gusev's bestowal of power still fresh in everyone's memory, Ruthenberg commanded a steamroller, and the resolution won by a Central Executive Committee vote of 18 to 4. The Browder-Johnstone opposition gained only one concession —the new line would not go into effect until the Comintern and Profintern had given it their approval.

This proviso put the final decision up to the Comintern's next plenum in February 1926, two months off. Fearing that Foster and Bittelman might not be able to hold their own owing to their unfamiliarity with the new developments at home, Browder moved to send them a reinforcement to bring them up to date. Ruthenberg's majority blocked this proposal, whereupon another anguished appeal went off to the Comintern.[14]

Meanwhile, Foster fought back from Moscow as best he could. His protector in the Profintern, Lozovsky, cabled the Political Committee to stave off the T.U.E.L.'s abandonment:

> TELEGRAPH IMMEDIATELY TEXT RESOLUTION REGARDING LEAGUE BEFORE CONSIDERATION QUESTION HERE STOP LEAGUE IS PART OF PROFINTERN STOP ON NO ACCOUNT TAKE ANY DECISIONS AGAINST LEAGUE WHATEVER OR WEAKENING LEAGUE WORK STOP

Ruthenberg's cabled reply refused to retreat. It merely summarized the plan, boasted of the huge majorities in its favor, and reiterated that it needed Comintern-Profintern approval to be put into effect.[15] But Lozovsky sided with Foster's faction so openly that Ruthenberg hit back at him with another and sharper cable to the Comintern:

> WE ARE COMPELLED TO POINT OUT TO THE PRESIDIUM THAT THE EFFECT OF THIS CABLE WILL BE TO ENCOURAGE FOSTER CAUCUS TO INTENSIFY DESTRUCTIVE FACTIONAL FIGHT THEY HAVE BEEN WAGING SINCE THE CONVENTION [16]

In Moscow, Foster and Bittelman pulled strings and composed long, accusing documents. One of them complained of their enemies' plot to liquidate the T.U.E.L.:

> Although stating that the proposed policy will not be put into effect until the Comintern and Profintern have passed upon it, the CEC is actually applying it at the present time. The first phase of the policy is an active campaign to discredit all the leading figures in the TUEL as disloyal to

the Comintern. This is accompanied by the removal of leading TUEL comrades from responsible positions and the hamstringing and isolation of others who are not actually removed, in an attempt to cripple their activities. Finally the TUEL organization itself is being dismantled by the substitution of fractions for the TUEL machinery, by the refusal to permit the TUEL to send delegates to various important conventions, by refusing to support the activities of the TUEL, and by carrying on a widespread propaganda that the TUEL must be dissolved.[17]

When Foster and Bittelman complained that their foes were applying the new trade-union line before the Comintern and Profintern had passed on it, their factional outcry was not without foundation.

Party and unions

The new trade-union line was tried out for the first time during the anthracite coal strike in the fall of 1925. Communist organizers under Gitlow's direction invaded the mine fields with orders to work in the name of the party rather than of the T.U.E.L. They succeeded mainly in getting themselves arrested, after which the party retreated hastily from the scene. This fiasco enabled Lozovsky later to use the anthracite strike to denounce the Ruthenberg leadership's "ultra-Left" trade-union policy and to make Gitlow the special butt of his attack.[18]

Ruthenberg's regime almost scored a major victory in the Fur Workers Union. An unusual coalition of Communists and Progressives had resulted in the election of Ben Gold, a Communist, as manager of the New York Joint Board in May 1925. It was the first union in the United States to come under outright Communist control, although it had only 50 Communists in a membership of about 10,000.[19] At the end of the year, however, a memorable *faux pas* prevented the Communists from taking over the international union. A telegram from Ruthenberg to Weinstone, the party representative at the Fur Workers Convention, giving him instructions on how to gain control of the incoming executive board, fell into the wrong hands and to their embarrassment the Communists heard it read aloud from the platform. Ruthenberg refused to admit or deny its authenticity, but the Communists' allies were sufficiently disturbed to prevent his instructions from being carried out.[20]

The party also intervened in the International Ladies' Garment Workers' Union with mixed results. The Communist influence in this union sprang from the Shop Delegates League of 1919 in which two future Communist leaders, Charles S. Zimmerman and Rose Wortis, had served their trade-union apprenticeships. In 1923 a victory for the T.U.E.L. in the dressmakers' Local 22 of the I.L.G.W.U. was nullified by expulsions and other repressive measures, but the Left Wing soon bounced back and gained control of the three largest locals—2, 9, and 22. The I.L.G.W.U.'s Communists were repeatedly hampered by the party's inconsistent policies. The Right and Left Wings in the union finally sought to negotiate a truce, and the party leadership stepped in to veto it. Then the Left Wing, which was admittedly supported by a majority of the union, attempted to stage a walkout from the I.L.G.W.U.'s convention late in 1925, and the party leaders turned around and forbade it. When the Left Wing withdrew, and its spokesman, Louis Hyman, refused to go back, the party's representative, William F. Dunne, ordered him to return to the convention with the words: "Then you'll crawl back on your belly!" [21] Thus Ruthenberg's ruling group backed away from the full implications of dual unionism in the one major needle-trades union the main body of which the Communists and their allies could have taken over. Of the 110 Left Wing delegates to the convention, 52 were Communists; of the approximately 65,000 I.L.G.W.U. members in New York, only 455 were Communists.[22]

The Communists also fought hard for the milliners' union. They took charge of the largest local—24—of the United Cloth Hat, Cap and Millinery Workers International Union in 1921 and made a strong bid for the entire union in 1925. But most of the union's energies were dissipated in a merciless and indecisive struggle for control that lasted for the next four years.[23]

Despite the T.U.E.L.'s general decline, therefore, the Communists always remained a significant and even dominant factor in a limited sector of the trade-union movement. While the T.U.E.L. weakened in the country at large, the Workers party's direct trade-union activity rose in specific industries and localities. In fact, the greatest Communist strikes of the decade coincided with the T.U.E.L.'s most extreme retrogression. But they took place in and around New York in the needle-trades which were in Ruthenberg's rather than Foster's sphere of influence.

For our present purpose, which is essentially that of exploring the political implications of Communist trade-union activity and policy, the first great Communist strike in the United States—the Passaic textile strike—offers the most concentrated and many-sided lesson in early Communist trade-unionism.

The Passaic story

One September day in 1925, calamity struck thousands of textile workers in Passaic, New Jersey. The Botany Mills put up a notice of a 10-per-cent wage cut, and other mills soon followed suit. Half the workers were women, most of them Polish, Italian, and Hungarian immigrants, earning less than $15 a week.[24]

Half desperate, half resigned, the Passaic workers did not know where to turn for help. The I.W.W. had tried to unionize them in 1912, and the Amalgamated Textile Workers had repeated the attempt in 1919 and 1920, without tangible or lasting results. The United Textile Workers, the A.F. of L.'s union in the field, had never tried at all. Its historian says that an estimate of less than 3 per cent for its organizational achievement in this period in the entire field of textile labor "is probably flattering to the strength of the U.T.W." [25]

In Passaic itself, the Workers party had some members from the former foreign-language federations. A small shop nucleus had been organized and sent into the mills to organize a few mill committees.[26] In textile centers in Massachusetts, the Communists had been making some headway through so-called United Front Committees, six of which were operating on a local scale by the spring of 1925.[27] Originally they were given the task of bringing together the existing unions in the textile field, of which there were no less than sixteen, but they also lent themselves as bases for independent Communist organizing activity as dictated by the new trade-union line of the dominant Ruthenberg group. Though these committees had not yet gained much ground, they gave the Communists a springboard from which to fling themselves into the Passaic situation.

The United Front Committee was brought to Passaic by a young and relatively recent Communist, Albert Weisbord.[28]

Weisbord's father was a Russian-Jewish immigrant who had climbed from poverty into the middle class by manufacturing accessories for men's coats. His son went from New York's City College, where he was a Phi Beta Kappa student, to a scholarship in the Harvard Law School. Unlike most of the young revolutionary idealists of his generation, he chose at first to identify himself with the Socialists instead of the Communists. He joined the Socialist party in 1920 and became National Secretary of the Young People's Socialist League two years later.

In his last year at Harvard in 1924, he came to communism through the study of Lenin's writings. Toward the end of that year, he resigned from the Socialist party, walked into the Communist headquarters in Boston, and offered himself to the cause. But the new convert had ideas of his own about the true faith. He soon submitted to the party leadership the thesis that the American Communists should shift their emphasis from the big cities to the "industrial villages" or factory towns. He gave up his legal career and spent the next year working in textile mills. He attached himself to Ruthenberg's faction and fervently believed in the new line of direct Communist organization of the unorganized as applied to the textile workers who were largely forsaken by the regular unions.

When the wage cuts hit the Passaic mills, Weisbord was working as a silk weaver in Paterson, New Jersey, and in his spare time organizing a United Front Committee strike in a silk mill at West New York, on the New Jersey side of the Hudson River.[29] He was then shifted over to Passaic and rapidly set up another United Front Committee, which issued membership books and dues stamps as if it were a regular union.

On the eve of the party's December 1925 plenum, at which the new trade-union line made its appearance, the Passaic policy assumed far-reaching significance. Johnstone, Foster's deputy, attacked the United Front Committee's issuance of membership books and dues stamps as a perversion of the united front and the equivalent of dual unionism. Ruthenberg at first refused to back down, but Johnstone pressed the attack and the ruling faction was sufficiently unsure of itself finally to give way. Johnstone also insisted on affiliating the United Front Committee with one of the existing textile unions, and here again he eventually won out.[30]

After three months of feverish preparation, the Passaic strike was called on January 25, 1926. The 5000 Botany Mills employees walked out immediately, followed by some 11,000 from other mills in the next few weeks. The mill owners, accustomed to dealing with defenseless workers, demanded unconditional surrender. To break the strike, city officials resurrected a Riot Act from the Civil War; police carried out mass arrests, including Weisbord, and clubbed newspapermen, press photographers, and strikers indiscriminately. So great was the national scandal that the strikers, despite their Communist leadership, won the sympathy of outstanding political and religious figures, among them ex-Secretary of State Bainbridge Colby, Rabbi Stephen S. Wise, the local Catholic Associated Societies and Parishes, and the Socialist leader, Norman Thomas, who was arrested as he sought to hold a meeting to test the constitutionality of the Riot Act.

The Passaic strike showed that, in a decade of "prosperity," cruelly exploited and violently downtrodden workers, abandoned by everyone else, would accept Communist leadership. The combination of underpaid immigrant workers, a moribund A.F. of L. union, and antediluvian employers created a vacuum which the Communists for a time filled with great success against tremendous odds. Selig Perlman and Philip Taft have written: "So far as public awareness was concerned, the Passaic strike was the outstanding labor conflict of the Coolidge era." [31] And the Communists were responsible for it.

The leader of the strike, Weisbord, was then only twenty-five years old. He had been in the Communist party less than two years. For him the strike was more than a trade-union struggle; it was a bid for Communist leadership against the older, established factional chieftains. He barely concealed his contempt for the party's office generals, and they paid him back by muttering about his "Napoleonic complex" and "illusions of grandeur." Among the striking workers, he was a revered and romantic figure, almost daemonic in his energy and charismatic in his appeal. Once the strike had started, the party and its auxiliaries gave it full support, but it is hard to imagine the Passaic upheaval without him.

Unknown to the Passaic strikers and to Weisbord himself, however, their fates were partially entangled in another American struggle in Moscow.

From Passaic to Moscow

When the strike broke out in Passaic in January 1925, the Comintern's American Commission was holding its first sessions in Moscow. The American delegates were Ruthenberg and Pepper for the existing majority, Foster and Bittelman for the former one. The party's chief executive and its most famous trade-union leader had battles to fight abroad more important than the first great American Communist strike at home.

The previous October Foster and Bittelman had set out for Moscow with only one fight on their hands—to recapture the control of the party which Gusev had filched from them. But two months later they were faced with a second fight—to save the T.U.E.L. from "absorption." Foster was prepared for the first fight, but not for the second. Already absent from the American scene for three months, he could not pretend to speak about the trade-union situation with the same authority as the freshly arrived Ruthenberg. To overcome this disadvantage, Foster obtained permission to call for a reinforcement, Browder, who had previously tried without success to send him help.

Browder arrived in Moscow as the Passaic strike ended its second week early in February 1926. He immediately received an advanced lesson in Comintern politics from Bittelman, who broke the big news to him—the Comintern had changed its line and the "ultra-Left" was now the main danger. The chief target of this turn was the former Maslow-Fischer leadership of the German party and the Bordiga group in the Italian party.[32] But the new line was sure to be translated into American terms, and it contained embarrassing implications for both Foster and Ruthenberg.

For almost two years, the Fosterites had tried to live down their earlier reputation as the American "ultra-Right." They had gone over to the "ultra-Left" during the presidential election of 1924, and had worked hard at pinning the label of "ultra-Right" on the Ruthenbergites for holding on to some semblance of the old Farmer-Labor policy. Now this maneuver threatened to backfire and link Foster with the doomed Maslow-Fischer group. On the other hand, the Ruthenberg group was responsible for the "ultra-Left" trade-union policy of working through the party instead of through an established union in the anthracite and Passaic strikes.

Browder still had much to learn in Moscow. A few minutes after he made his appearance in the American Commission, a Russian voice suggested that "the commission should hear from the American comrade who had just arrived." Browder, still unsure of himself, replied to the effect that "having just arrived, I found the situation somewhat difficult to understand and therefore was not prepared to speak." [33]

Stalin, to whom the Russian voice belonged, never again asked him to speak, and afterward, in all his years of power in the American party, Browder never dealt with Stalin directly.

As the American Commission came to an end, Ruthenberg suggested its comradely atmosphere in a letter to Lovestone:

> Our opponents (Bittelman, Browder, Foster) have submitted at least 150 pages of documents against us. . . . They are shining examples of Foster's methods—continuous, shameless lying. If one needs to be convinced that there can be no peace while Foster's methods continue, one need only read a score of pages of his brazen lies.[34]

One of Foster's documents attacked the Ruthenberg group for perverting the united front and reverting to "ultra-Leftist dual unionism" in the Passaic textile strike. The Fosterites insisted on getting the textile policy back on the track of the existing unions instead of bringing in a party-operated new union.[35]

After a month of such preliminaries, the Comintern's Sixth Plenum opened in the middle of February 1926. Its American Commission was considered important enough for the leading Russians, Zinoviev, Bukharin, and Stalin, to attend.[36]

For once, the Americans could agree on something—the appalling danger of ultra-Leftism. All those who for almost two years had been utterly blind to it at home rose to pronounce anathemas against it in Moscow. Foster made his personal contribution to the auto-da-fé of the Maslow-Fischer group in Germany, and Pepper congratulated him for the performance "with much pleasure and full unanimity," a rare tribute from such a source.[37]

On the more practical matter of who was to control the American party, and especially its trade-union activities, there was somewhat less pleasure and unanimity. To regain control of the party, Foster had asked the Comintern to reshuffle the Central Executive Committee to give him a majority of 13 to 8. The Comintern replied sanctimoniously that "there can be no question of a change in the composition of the present Central Committee of the American Communist Party; the Party itself determines the composition of the C.C. at its Party Congress"—as if Gusev had not already done what Foster asked the Comintern to do.

But this rebuff to Foster was part of a larger deal. In the six months since Gusev had drummed him out of the party leadership, Foster had been thrown on the defensive in the trade-union field, where he could not afford to admit defeat without suffering a total loss of face. Here the Comintern gave him full satisfaction. The leadership of the central committee ordinarily implied the leadership of all subordinate committees in order to ensure a single source of authority in the party. It was most unusual for the Comintern to give the majority of the central committee to one faction and the majority of the important trade-union committee to another faction. Yet this is exactly what the Comintern decided to do on this occasion.

It ordered the Fosterites to get a majority on the Trade-Union Committee, and advised Ruthenberg's majority on the Central Executive Committee not to exercise "petty control." It rescued Bittelman from the cloud that Gusev had put him under by ordering him back on the Political Committee, and maintained the balance on the committee by adding Gitlow, a Ruthenbergite. It abolished the Secretariat of three on which the Fosterites were not represented. It stipulated that Foster should remain head of the T.U.E.L., shorn of its purely Communist program and again given the trappings of a united front. Browder was permitted to remain in Moscow as the T.U.E.L.'s representative to the Profintern.

As for future ventures like the Passaic textile strike, it strictly enjoined: "Secessional movements and the formation of parallel trade unions should not be instigated or encouraged in any form." [38]

For Foster and Bittelman, the Russian trip was not all politics. One of its rewards was a tourist journey with their wives. This tour enabled Foster to produce another pamphlet on Russia, and gave the Soviet regime a morale-builder for Russian workers to whom the American Communist leaders were presented as tangible evidence that foreign workers looked to them for inspiration and swore to aid their cause. In his report of the latest Russian trip, Foster told how, as they were about to leave Leningrad, Ugaroff, the local secretary of the Central Labor Council, asked them what the American unions could teach the Russian unions:

> We were utterly stumped. It was such an unexpected question. We cudgeled our brains, trying to conjure up a single feature of the American unions that the Russian unions could profitably pattern after. But in vain. We could think of nothing, and we said so.

Still the question haunted him:

> All the way back to Moscow, in fact all the way back to the United States, we pondered over Ugaroff's leading question. And our final conclusion is that our answer to him was absolutely correct. The American

trade unions have nothing whatever to teach the Russian workers, except how not to build a labor movement; whereas the Russian workers have innumerable precious lessons for the American workers on the way to construct a real labor organization.[39]

The leader of the great 1919 steel strike was unable to remember that American workers could strike and Russian workers could not.

From Moscow to Passaic

The Passaic strike was still going strong in its third month when Foster returned to the United States in April 1926.

For the Foster group, the Passaic strike had always borne the stigma of incipient dual unionism. During Foster's absence, his spokesman, Jack Johnstone, had waged a hard, dogged campaign against the United Front Committee, first to stop it from behaving like a union, and then to hand over the strikers to one of the existing textile unions. For the Ruthenberg group, the strike represented a policy rendered obsolete by the Sixth Plenum's prohibition of Communist-inspired secessional movements and parallel trade unions.

After Foster returned from Moscow, therefore, both major groups had lost their former factional interest in the strike. But Weisbord, the country ringing with his name and the strikers solidly behind him, had other plans. He demanded that the strike should be expanded to take in other nearby textile centers and called on the party to mobilize all its forces for this purpose. The party leaders, worried about the ability of the strikers to hold out much longer and about the soundness of Weisbord's judgment, redoubled their efforts to unload the strike on the A.F. of L. One stumbling block was the A.F. of L.'s refusal to deal with the Communists of the United Front Committee in charge of the strike.

In August Weisbord was prevailed on to step out in the interest of inducing the A.F. of L.'s United Textile Workers to take over the strike and settle it on more favorable terms than he could. Behind the scenes, however, Weisbord put up one last show of resistance by voting against the motion in the party committee.[40]

Weisbord's withdrawal took the heart out of the strike and the strikers without making any noticeable difference in the attitude of the mill owners or the police force. It took four more months for the U.T.W. to settle the strike on terms which gave the strikers little more than the right to be rehired without discrimination. The strikers and Communists then proceeded to go back where they had started from. In 1928 the U.T.W. expelled the Passaic local; by 1929 the Communist party's Passaic unit contained only fifteen members.[41]

In time, the Communists rewrote the story of the Passaic strike. The T.U.E.L.'s role, or lack of it, particularly embarrassed Foster. During the year of the Passaic strike, none of the Communist writings mentioned the T.U.E.L., for the reason that the strike was not only non-T.U.E.L. but, in its implications, anti-T.U.E.L. Gitlow and Weisbord wrote articles on the strike in the official organ, the central committee issued a long statement, and Ruthenberg summed up the trade-union achievements of the party for the period without mentioning the T.U.E.L. and pointedly giving all credit to the party. Minor wrote a long report in the Comintern's theoretical organ on "The Party on the Trade Union Front in the United States," dealing with the strikes of 1926, without once mentioning the T.U.E.L.[42] For another ten years, the party's literature similarly ignored the T.U.E.L. at Passaic.

But in 1937, Foster's book, *From Bryan to Stalin,* suddenly discovered that the Passaic strike was "the first big T.U.E.L. mass movement among the textile workers" and the United Front Committee a new name for the T.U.E.L. In 1952, Foster's *History of the Communist Party of the United States* claimed that the Passaic strike was "initiated by the Party and conducted directly by the T.U.E.L.," at best a half truth, and made the United Front Committee a "form" of the T.U.E.L. One wonders whether, with the passage of years and repetition, Foster himself has come to believe this myth.[43]

Another troublesome aspect of the Passaic strike for the Communists was Weisbord's personal role. During the strike, the party had made the most of his achievement and had helped to glorify him. The officially inspired pamphlet on the strike portrayed him rhapsodically: "His unalterable faith in his workers has kept alive their enthusiasm. His tireless courage had kept the workers alight with his own flame. With a concentrated will, with a tirelessness which sometimes seemed to his fellow-workers inhuman, he has been a true leader of the workers. They trust him and they love him." [44] Even Foster wrote at the time: "But when the unorganized go on strike, untrained and inexperienced, they look especially for inspiration and guidance not so much to their weak union nucleus as to the personalities at the head of their movement. Usually they dramatize their hopes, aspirations, and fighting spirit in the personality of one man. The case of Weisbord in Passaic is typical." [45]

But Weisbord the hero was to become Weisbord the villain. In 1937 Foster dismissed him as "a good mass speaker but a mediocre strategist." [46] By 1952 even this was too kind, and he sneered at him as "a weakling." [47] For once, Gitlow agrees with Foster. Gitlow disparages Weisbord as a "leader in name only" and "this fortuitous nominal leader." According to Gitlow, the chief leader of the Passaic strike was Gitlow.[48] More recent non-Communist writers have credulously called Weisbord a "figurehead." [49] Other sources have been more generous.[50]

Although the Passaic strike came to a sad end, it set the example for two other important Communist-led strikes in 1926. The New York fur workers, led by Ben Gold, tied up the entire fur market in February. After seventeen weeks, the union won a 10-per-cent pay increase and a 40-hour week, the first 40-hour, 5-day week in the garment industry. The following year, the A.F. of L. tried to break the Communists' power among the fur workers by officially dissolving the Communist-controlled Joint Board and expelling its leaders, but in the shop-and-street war that followed, the A.F. of L. came off second best.[51]

The Communist-led New York ladies' garment workers union called a general strike on July 1. The strike might have been settled on favorable terms, but the party's Needle Trades Committee refused to approve. The strike dragged on for six months; the employers regained the advantage; the anti-Communist national office of the union stepped in to settle the strike, and expelled the New York leadership, charging it with being a tool of the Communist party and ruining the union. This time, in the ensuing shop-and-street war, the Communists came off second best.[52]

Thus 1926 was a year of great Communist strike struggles. Of the three, the furriers, the textile workers, and the ladies' garment workers, they scored a victory and obtained a permanent foothold only in the first and smallest union. In the former areas of T.U.E.L. influence, the machinists, carpenters, and miners, the existing administrations put down the Communist oppositions with ease in the first two and after another sharp struggle in the third.

The Communists' earlier trade-union offensive of 1922–23 differed markedly from the later one of 1925–26. The former, conducted by the T.U.E.L. directed by the Foster group, had penetrated the basic industries in the Midwest by boring from within the A.F. of L. The latter, largely managed by the party itself controlled by the Ruthenberg group, was confined to a single group of garment trades around New York.

And so, after five tumultuous years, Foster was back where he had started from—the party's official trade-union leader and no more. The Comintern's refusal to upset Gusev's verdict had left him with only the choice of rebelling or submitting. By submitting, he had suppressed his outraged sense of justice and had compromised his principles, but he had survived in the Communist movement to fight for political power another day.

Yet he still had one flag flying—his opposition to dual unionism. The Comintern's decision, however disappointing in other respects, permitted him to keep his self-respect in the field with which he was most intimately identified. But even as the Comintern gave him this consolation prize, an inner voice must have asked—for how long?

10

Ruthenberg's Last Wish

AFTER the Comintern's verdict in favor of Ruthenberg as party leader, the factional storm gradually subsided. Membership meetings throughout the country "unanimously endorsed" the new leadership and its policies. At the Seventh Plenum at the end of 1926, the Comintern, for the first time in five years, found it unnecessary to appoint an American Commission to deal with an American factional struggle.[1]

The men around Ruthenberg were seasoned veterans, who had never accepted Foster as a "real Communist" and never intended to let power slip out of their hands again. The "big three" in the Chicago national office—the General Secretary, Ruthenberg; the Organization Secretary, Lovestone; and the Director of Agit-Prop, Bedacht—had fought side by side since the formation of the Workers party. In the key New York district, Weinstone went back to his old job as District Organizer, which he decided to rename "General Secretary," as more befitting to his sense of self-importance. The New York Agit-Prop director, Bertram D. Wolfe, was an old-timer who had helped to form the party in 1919 and had recently returned after three and a half years in Mexico. Jack Stachel, head of the New York organization department, was a fast-rising newcomer.

Stachel was born of East-European Jewish parents who had emigrated to New York's East Side when he was still a child. After leaving school at an early age, he had worked at odd jobs and had once belonged to the millinery workers union. Like Weisbord and at exactly the same age, twenty-four, he had switched from the Socialists to the Communists in 1924 and quickly became an organizer for the Communist youth league in New York. The younger members of Ruthenberg's group welcomed him to their ranks, and he soon attracted Lovestone's attention as a hard-working organizer and hard-hitting factionalist. When Lovestone took over the national organization department, he recommended Stachel for the New York organization post. Stachel's unusually rapid rise—within two years—to the second most important post in the most important district indicated a big party career ahead for the dark, saturnine, ambitious young man.[2]

Ruthenberg's machine worked so smoothly and efficiently that it made those outside his inner circle increasingly restless. Beneath the surface of the factional lull, another rebellion smoldered, with the helpful encouragement of Cannon, who had touched off the anti-Ruthenberg rebellion three years earlier. After Cannon broke with Foster over Gusev's intervention in 1925, he and Ruthenberg suspended hostilities. Soon, however, Cannon began to feel neglected, and the strange bedfellows parted company. By the middle of 1926, Cannon went back to his old habit of voting with Foster and Bittelman in the Political Committee, the three of them consistently outvoted by Ruthenberg's four.

Unable to win by the factional system, Cannon declared war on it. His group was far more personal than Ruthenberg's or Foster's; it was based on a portion of the cadre rather than on the rank and file. His International Labor Defense was no match for Ruthenberg's party machine or Foster's trade-union base. As a result, Cannon was compelled to maneuver between the two larger factions or to make alliances with other discontented elements. While Ruthenberg claimed credit for reducing factionalism, Cannon charged that it was worse than ever before, with the ruling faction passing itself off as the party. Cannon professed to be tired of the game and launched a campaign for a nonfactional collective leadership, or, as it came to be known, a faction to end all factions.

Cannon started out with the basic ingredients of his former combination, Foster and himself. With Lore gone, however, he needed an ally from within Ruthenberg's own forces. In the Political Committee, Ruthenberg's majority could not be budged. But the larger Central Executive Committee was so equally divided between Ruthenberg's followers and those of Cannon and Foster that one or two defections could make the difference between victory or defeat.[3]

Cannon broke through Ruthenberg's front in the strategic New York district. For reasons of his own, its secretary, Weinstone, decided to make common cause with Cannon and Foster for the ostensible purpose of breaking down the existing factional barriers and establishing collective leadership. Weinstone brought along with him John J. Ballam, another C.E.C. member originally elected on the Ruthenberg slate. In the New York set-up, Stachel went along with Weinstone, and they were backed by the youth leader Sam Donchin, later better known as Sam Don.[4]

Meanwhile, Ruthenberg's majority and Comintern support made opposition futile. How the combination worked was shown by the lengthy negotiations which preceded the transfer of the national office and the *Daily Worker* from Chicago to New York. They had been moved in 1923 from New York, Ruthenberg's stronghold, to Chicago, Foster's stronghold, in the days of the Federated Farmer-Labor party's grand illusion. In the middle of 1926, Ruthenberg raised the issue of taking them back to New York. He maintained that the *Daily Worker* was losing too much money in Chicago and could be saved only by gaining the greater financial support possible in New York. Foster, Cannon, Dunne, and Bittelman opposed and held up the move. A poll of the entire C.E.C. resulted in an 11-to-11 tie.

In due course, the question went to the Comintern for decision. After three months of wrangling, a cable from Kuusinen advised the Americans that the move of the national office required unanimous consent of the next American convention, whereas the move of the *Daily Worker* merely needed a decision of the Political Committee.[5]

At the same time, however, Ruthenberg received a cable from his "unofficial ambassador" in Moscow, William F. Kruse, a Lenin

School student. Kruse advised him that the Comintern really wanted the *Daily Worker* to move to New York immediately, and the national office to follow eventually—without authorization by a convention. Kruse's cable, which gives the flavor of these confidential exchanges, reads:

LAST CLAUSE OF CONTRACT MUST BE ACTED ON IMMEDIATELY STOP SEEMING SEPARATION OF TWO BUSINESSES IS ONLY TO ACCOMPLISH PURPOSE WITHOUT TOO MUCH MECHANICS FROM DISTANCE STOP CONTRACT MAKERS SAY BOTH BUSINESSES MUST GO TO NEW YORK AND THEY EXPECT YOU TO ACT IMMEDIATELY ON LAST CLAUSE AFTER WHICH OTHER BUSINESS CAN BE ACCOMPLISHED AMICABLY WITHOUT STOCKHOLDERS MEET.[6]

Ruthenberg needed no more urging. He rammed through a 4-to-3 vote in the Political Committee to move the *Daily Worker* to New York in time for its third anniversary in January 1927.[7] The next convention in September of that year voted to move the national office to New York.

As long as Ruthenberg headed the party, Cannon's new antifactional faction rumbled underground and bided its time. The "contract makers" in Moscow had more important problems on their minds.

Zinoviev's downfall

Ruthenberg's period in the American party almost coincided with Zinoviev's regime in the Comintern.

The repercussions of Zinoviev's break with Stalin reached the Comintern in 1926. The struggle came to a head in July at a plenum of the Russian party which voted to withdraw Zinoviev from his position in the Comintern. In some parties, such as the German, the leadership was so closely linked with Zinoviev that it could not survive without him. But there were no real Zinovievites in the American party. All the Americans were pro-Zinoviev as long as he represented the power of the Russian party; not a single one came to his defense when he lost that power. This attitude, prevalent throughout the Comintern, doomed Zinoviev in the Communist world as soon as word of his defeat in the Russian party spread.

It was hard to feel sorry for Zinoviev. The pudgy little man with the high, squeaky voice had been an arrogant, capricious, and unlucky master. His system of court favorites, his unstable character and erratic policies, had endeared him to few of those who had fawned on him. He was, in the end, a victim of his own methods; he could not suppress freedom of discussion or groupings in order to destroy Trotsky and then revive them to save himself. He could not defend "socialism in one country" in 1925 and attack it in 1926 without revealing an utter lack of principle on a fundamental article of doctrine.[8] After he had successfully indoctrinated the entire Communist movement with the abominable depravity of Trotskyism, he formed a bloc with Trotsky. Yet, in desperation, Zinoviev and his associates, Kamenev, Krupskaya, and others, tried to defend themselves against Stalin by going back to the *status quo ante*. Willy-nilly, Zinoviev's break with Stalin represented the last hopeless gasp of an era.

The hopelessness of Zinoviev's cause in the Comintern may be partially explained by the behavior of his protégé, John Pepper. At the beginning of 1926, with the return of his ally Ruthenberg to power, Pepper re-emerged as a major force in the American party. He remained in Moscow, but his articles again appeared regularly in the American Communist press. In January, he began to contribute a regular column to the *Daily Worker* and leading articles to *The Workers Monthly*. He served as Zinoviev's spokesman and at the Comintern's Sixth Plenum that spring spoke most respectfully of Zinoviev's wisdom.[9] But when Zinoviev was withdrawn from the Comintern by the Russian plenum that summer, Pepper reported the event for the *Daily Worker* with fulsome approval.[10]

After Pepper's signals from Moscow, the American party hastily joined the anti-Zinoviev stampede. It was one of the ten parties privileged to follow the Russian party's lead and, in a declaration signed by Minor, Browder, and Pepper, it demanded Zinoviev's removal as head of the Comintern.[11] Just before the Comintern's Seventh Plenum in the late fall of 1926, Pepper, always a step ahead, sent the *Daily Worker* articles with an unmistakable pro-Stalin slant.[12] At the plenum, Pepper turned on his former patron, Zinoviev, and successfully attached himself to the entourage of Zinoviev's successor, Bukharin.[13] To an American writer at the plenum, Pepper bitterly complained of his disenchantment with Zinoviev.*

Bittelman was also taken by surprise. He had invested much time and effort in a translation of Zinoviev's *History of the Russian Communist Party*. Several installments of this work were published in *The Workers Monthly* before Bittelman and the editors learned of Zinoviev's downfall, and the series was abruptly cut short.[14]

The Seventh Plenum was the scene of the great debate in the Comintern on "socialism in one country." For the first and last time, Stalin went before the delegates to defend his position, which he did in a speech lasting three hours. The following day Zinoviev, now allied with Trotsky, tried to tear down Stalin's arguments in a speech of almost two hours. The day after that, Trotsky demanded two hours to answer Stalin, and received only one. He delivered one of his greatest virtuoso performances, in Russian, German, and French successively, acting as his own translator. In the small hours of the morning, Bukharin made another long speech to counteract the effect of Trotsky's oratory. On subsequent days, Kamenev spoke in support of Zinoviev, and then Rykov, Bukharin's associate, was sent in to refute Kamenev. To close the discussion, Stalin spoke again for more hours. The discussion lasted six days and almost fifty speakers participated in it.

The defeat of Trotsky, Zinoviev, and Kamenev was a foregone conclusion. The overwhelming majority of delegates had made up their minds in advance. Only two other speakers supported Trotsky and Zinoviev, a margin which certainly failed to reflect the sympathy for Trotsky's position in the International. Nevertheless, it would be short-sighted to imagine that Stalin owed his one-sided victory wholly to organizational manipulation. His name and fame were still comparatively new; he was opposed by Zinoviev whose orders the delegates had been accustomed to take; and the non-Russian leaders

* His exact words were: *"Joe! Joe! Eben habe ich entdeckt, dass ich sieben Jahre lang den falschen Arsch geküsst habe!"*

were obliged to think of their followers back home over whom Stalin had no direct control.

Superficially it might appear that Trotsky's position should have been more congenial than Stalin's to the non-Russian Communists. Trotsky assigned the starring role to the West, Stalin to Russia. But by the middle of the nineteen-twenties the Western Communists could not carry out the role that Trotsky had allotted to them. He had more faith in, or perhaps illusions about, their revolution than they had. After the German fiascoes of 1921 and 1923, a miasma of failure and frustration had settled over them. While Trotsky reminded them that they lived in the Leninist "epoch of wars and revolutions," practical policy could not be made in terms of an epoch. From month to month and week to week, they were confronted with less catastrophic and spectacular conditions. If they could not find enough to boast about and lift up their spirits at home, they could seek comfort and make political capital out of world-shaking revolutionary achievements, real or imaginary, in Russia.

Trotsky's revolutionary perspective dismayed the Westerners more than it inspired them. He could not translate it into living circumstances or practical policy. The revolutionary romantics and those congenitally indisposed to taking dictation from the Russians had already been purged out of the Comintern by Zinoviev, who had accomplished this task too well for his own good. The remainder needed Stalin as much as he needed them. They could identify themselves with Stalin far more easily than with Trotsky; they could, without difficulty, imagine themselves telling their own people what Stalin told the Russian people; and in the process they could rid themselves of the guilt of having left the Russians in the lurch.

While Trotsky cried out despairingly that "socialism in one country" betrayed the world revolution, the "betrayed" battalions of the world revolution desperately wanted socialism to succeed, with or without them, in at least one country. The Russian revolution was their reason for existence, bastion of faith, source of power. They were like shareholders safeguarding an investment in a common property.

These motives clearly emerged in the debate at the Seventh Plenum. Some of the up-and-coming young Stalinist leaders in the Western parties came close to the nub of the problem. They identified the attack on "socialism in one country" with an attack on the successful development of the Russian revolution and their own stake in it.

A German Communist, Heinz Neumann, envisaged Stalin's perspective for the Soviet Union as applicable everywhere:

> Therefore, it is necessary to settle accounts sharply with this [Trotskyist] theory at this plenum not only for reasons of solidarity with the Communist Party of the Soviet Union but also in the name of the revolutionary perspective for Western Europe and in the whole world. Just as the question poses itself for the Soviet Union, so does it arise for Germany and in the last analysis also on an international scale.[15]

The young Italian candidate for leadership, Palmiro Togliatti (Ercoli), made an exceptionally revealing case against his former master:

> Zinoviev said: If you raise the perspective of the possibility of building socialism in a single country, in Russia, you are sowing pessimism and defeatism in the ranks of the parties and proletariat of the West. When Lenin stated that the revolution could be victorious in a single country, did he thereby wish to found a defeatist theory? No, certainly not. The problem must be considered from a different point of view. It must be considered from the standpoint of the influence which the Russian Revolution and the action of the Russian Communist Party has on the revolutionary forces in the world. When we consider this problem from this point of view, we must recognize that the achievement of the Russian party, the Russian Revolution, has been in the postwar period the strongest organizational factor, the strongest stimulus for the revolutionary forces of the world.
>
> But is this fact still effective in the working class of the whole world? Obviously, it is still effective. But to be effective, another element must be effective in the consciousness of the working class of the world—that is the conviction that the proletariat in Russia, after seizing power, can build socialism, and that today it is actually building socialism. (Applause). The Russian Revolution has an influence to the extent that this element is ideologically and politically effective in the working class of all countries.[16]

The American spokesman, Jay Lovestone, applied and extended the same line of reasoning to the United States and the American party:

Comrades, the Soviet Union plays an extraordinary role for us in America. The objective conditions are far more favorable in Germany, in France, in England: there the working class is far more developed, the revolutionary interests are far more advanced. The lack of these forces, the absence of these elements for the revolutionizing of the American working class, presents us with a situation in which precisely the example, the role and the experience of the Soviet Union are revolutionary factors.[17]

And he read a declaration by the entire American delegation, including Bittelman, Browder, and others, that claimed for the American party the honor of needing Russian "socialism in one country" more than any other party:

The shining example of the Communist Party of the Soviet Union is one of the most important sources of inspiration for the will-to-fight for our Party as well as for the class-conscious section of the American working class. The Communist Party was founded in America when a mighty wave of enthusiasm was brought forth by the outbreak of the Russian Revolution. In America (with its limited number of other revolutionary factors)—where capitalism is still on the upgrade, in the country of the strongest imperialism and the most reactionary labor aristocracy, where so few independent mass actions of the working class occur, where the working class does not yet have a political mass party—the existence of the Soviet Union and the successful building of socialism within it plays a relatively more important role as the revolutionary stimulus of the working class than in other countries where capitalism is declining or in countries which possess a revolutionary tradition.[18]

Zinoviev made pointed reference to the attitude in the Comintern that worked for Stalin and against himself:

We have noticed the following attitude among individual foreign Communists: the proletarian revolution is not yet coming for us (in Germany or Czechoslovakia)—so at least let the Russians build socialism for themselves, even if without our assistance.[19]

It was no accident, therefore, that American Communists like Browder have dated their allegiance to Stalin's leadership from this plenum.[20] They candidly recognized their dependence on the Russian party and drew the full implications from it. Having put all their revolutionary eggs in the Russian basket, they wanted that basket to be as large and strong and beautiful as possible. They embraced "socialism in one country" not merely in Stalin's interest but in what they considered to be their own.

Ruthenberg's apotheosis

Charles Emil Ruthenberg died suddenly in Chicago on March 2, 1927, three days after an emergency operation for appendicitis which had developed into peritonitis. He was in the prime of life, not yet forty-five years old. His death took the entire party by surprise.

Across the front page of the *Daily Worker* swept a heavy black headline: RUTHENBERG IS DEAD. For two days the body lay in state in Chicago flanked by a guard of honor, as long lines of mourners passed by. Then a mass procession accompanied it to a crematorium. A special delegation greeted the train that brought the ashes to New York. Inscribed to "Our Leader, Comrade Ruthenberg," the urn containing the ashes went on display in a bronze case in the main auditorium of the Manhattan Lyceum, "guarded continually by a corps of devoted workers," after which a special guard wearing red shirts with black arm bands carried it to a memorial meeting in Carnegie Hall. Nation-wide Ruthenberg memorial meetings and a Ruthenberg Recruiting Drive went on for weeks.[21]

At a meeting of the Political Committee a few hours after Ruthenberg's death, Lovestone reported his last wish to be cremated and to have his ashes sent to Moscow. "Tell the comrades to close their ranks, to build the Party," Ruthenberg had allegedly said. "The American workers, under the leadership of our Party and the Comintern, will win. Let's fight on!" [22] Cynics cast some doubt on the authenticity of these last words, but a cable was sent to the Comintern with Ruthenberg's last request.[23] The Russian party wired back: "His ashes will rest beneath Kremlin wall together with those of heroes of November Revolution."[24] Since Ruthenberg's original request and the Political Committee's cable to the Comintern were never publicly revealed, the party was led to believe that the idea of burying his ashes in Moscow had originated with the Russians.[25]

Ruthenberg's ashes were devoutly carried to Moscow by J. Louis Engdahl. The urn was duly buried with revolutionary pomp and ceremony in a niche in the Red Wall of the Kremlin. Red Army infantry stationed atop the Kremlin wall fired three volleys that reverberated through the vast square; a military band played the "Internationale"; regiments of Red Army soldiers stood stiffly at attention. Nikolai Bukharin, the new head of the Comintern, paid homage to the dead American Communist leader in a speech from Lenin's mausoleum. Of the Comintern leaders whom Ruthenberg had known, only one was missing, the one under whom he had served, Zinoviev.[26]

John Reed was the first and Ruthenberg the last American Communist leader to receive the honor of being buried in the Kremlin wall. Ruthenberg's request showed where he felt he truly belonged, and the Russian party's consent showed that it accepted him as one of its own or at least felt that it could not refuse the American request. In a few years, such ceremonies for a non-Russian Communist leader would become unthinkable. The occasion was celebrated in a poetical beatification in the *Daily Worker:*

> Under the walls of the Kremlin the bed will be soft.
> Lenin and Jack Reed will be waiting to welcome you, Charlie.[27]

But no one had ever called Ruthenberg "Charlie" while he was alive. Foster was "Bill" and Cannon was "Jim" to almost everyone who knew them, but Ruthenberg had been "Comrade Ruthenberg" to all but an intimate handful, including his wife, who were permitted to call him "C.E."

American Communism owed much to Ruthenberg. As its titular leader since 1919, he had done more than anyone else to rid it of its underground mentality and to hold it together. At crucial periods, however, he had yielded the real leadership to others, particularly to

Pepper. Yet a stronger or a weaker man in his position might have split the party. He assumed the role of one too proud, too dignified, too sure of himself to stoop to the petty vices of his rivals and supporters. This attitude struck some as merely an exasperating pose. But, on the whole, it had served Ruthenberg's ambitions well by partially disarming the opposition, which could never work up as much animus against him as it could against Pepper or Lovestone. In Moscow, he had always been trusted to lead the party, but not to lead it too much.

In a faction-ridden party, Ruthenberg continued to serve the interests of his faction, dead or alive. His glorification subtly glorified those who had been wise enough to choose him as their leader. If he had deserved the leadership, one of his lieutenants obviously deserved the succession. Lovestone bewailed Ruthenberg's passing with apostolic fervor: "Yes, farewell, Comrade Ruthenberg, farewell, our leader." [28]

But Ruthenberg's apotheosis never really got off the ground. For many years he remained a dim figure from the past and the factional seesaw did strange things to his memory. Ruthenberg's first memorialist was Lovestone, whose works, including those canonizing Ruthenberg, were soon proscribed.[29] The chief Communist historian of the next period, Bittelman, attempted to get around the problem of honoring his old foe by giving the impression that Ruthenberg had been allied with Foster:

> The coming together of these two revolutionists [Ruthenberg and Foster] and their followers into one working class Party marked a historic event of the first magnitude. The meaning of this event was that, for the first time in the history of the American working class, there came to an end the traditional separation between the advanced revolutionary elements of the trade unions, on the one hand, and the revolutionary elements of the Socialist (political-parliamentary) Party, on the other.[30]

This is exactly what did *not* happen. Ruthenberg and Foster came together only in the most formal sense; they could not fuse their forces and traditions. By covering up the fierce, ceaseless feud between Ruthenberg and Foster, Bittelman made it impossible for the new generation of Communists to understand the great misfortune of the party's early years—that the political and trade-union trends represented by Ruthenberg and Foster had not been able to end their separation and work in harmony within the party.

A biographical sketch of Ruthenberg by Elizabeth Gurley Flynn presents "Lenin and Stalin" as Ruthenberg's "chosen models," thereby depriving Ruthenberg of the good fortune of having led the party before the standardization of the Stalinist model of Communist leaders.[31]

Ruthenberg's latest official Communist biographer, in a full-length study, has simply surrendered without a struggle. He decided to side-step the whole embarrassing problem by devoting fully six-sevenths of his book to Ruthenberg's *pre*-Communist career and then referring the reader for most of the rest to Foster's frequently apocryphal *History of the Communist Party of the United States*. The least that can be said of Ruthenberg's role in the Communist movement is that he deserved a far better and braver hagiologist.[32]

The caliber of Foster's treatment may be judged from the statement:

> During the factional fight Ruthenberg enjoyed the confidence of both warring groups, so that even during its bitterest phases he remained general secretary.[33]

Unluckily for Ruthenberg, Foster chose to show his confidence in peculiar ways; and luckily for Ruthenberg, he enjoyed the Comintern's confidence in addition to Foster's. Foster's strange desire to pay homage to Ruthenberg's memory probably arises less from a guilty conscience than from the need to find at least one past general secretary of the party of whom some good may be said. Yet Foster has never faced up to the basic contradiction in his latter-day apotheosis of Ruthenberg—that Ruthenberg was the party's first great, good leader but that the two men who worked with him so closely and so long, Pepper and Lovestone, were, according to Foster, the party's greatest, most sinister misleaders. How could Ruthenberg have remained so blameless if he preferred them to Foster?

Ruthenberg's era of Communist leadership in large part paralleled the postwar upswing of American capitalism as well as Zinoviev's reign in the Comintern. Neither was propitious for the emergence of a truly successful and creative American Communist leader. The economic tide beat back every movement of reform as well as of revolution, and Zinoviev's Comintern prized obedience far above originality. No great practical achievement and no significant theoretical contribution was linked with Ruthenberg's name. He gave American Communism an efficient, respected, colorless office manager; he did not give it an authoritative, inspiring, path-finding leader.

11

Lovestone in Power

WITHIN a few hours of Ruthenberg's death, the struggle for the succession broke out.

The contest narrowed down to two members of Ruthenberg's old faction, Lovestone and Weinstone. As Ruthenberg's right-hand man in the national office and field commander of their faction, Lovestone was his natural successor. Weinstone came forward to challenge him as the choice of Ruthenberg's former rivals, Foster and Cannon. Cannon had not been able to get his new team into action against Ruthenberg, but he was ready for Ruthenberg's successor.

In less than forty-eight hours after Ruthenberg's death, Foster, Cannon, and Weinstone came together and decided to back Weinstone as the new General Secretary.[1] Among them, they controlled a majority of the Central Executive Committee, which was constitutionally empowered to elect the General Secretary.[2]

Foster made the first move. At a meeting of the Political Committee three days after Ruthenberg's death, he proposed that a plenum of the C.E.C. for the purpose of filling the vacant post should be held in conjunction with the Ruthenberg memorial meeting in New York, only five days off. Lovestone and his backers knew that the combination behind Weinstone could not be headed off in so short a time. They righteously protested that they would not permit "mechanical arrangements" in the C.E.C.—by which they meant the triumvirate's private understanding—to thwart the will of the membership. They were determined to use their pro-Lovestone majority in the Political Committee to sidetrack the "artificial" pro-Weinstone majority in the C.E.C.

To checkmate Foster, Gitlow immediately nominated Lovestone as "Acting Secretary." Lovestone followed with a proposal to defer the plenum for later consideration. In rapid succession, the Political Committee voted to defer the plenum and to name Lovestone as Acting Secretary.[3]

And so began the Lovestone period of American Communism in the spring of 1927. The new style of leadership was evident from the outset.

Enfants terribles

Of all the major leaders, Jay Lovestone was the youngest. He was only twenty-nine years old in 1927, seventeen years younger than Foster, sixteen than Ruthenberg, eight than Cannon and Bittelman, seven than Browder and Gitlow. Yet he was already a veteran of over a decade of training and service in the Socialist and Communist movements.

Lovestone was born in Lithuania, then part of Russia, and came to the United States at the age of nine. His boyhood was typical of that in poor Russian-Jewish immigrant families whose talented, ambitious sons were thrown at an early age into the uphill battle for livelihood and recognition. In New York, his father obtained a job as the sexton of a synagogue, but the family needed the extra money earned by the children to scrape along. Socialist street-corner speakers did not have a hard time convincing young Lovestone of the evils of capitalism. He was first attracted in his early teens to the De Leonite Socialist Labor party from which he soon moved on to the Socialist party. After the usual public-school education in New York, he attended the College of the City of New York, where a Socialist Study Club, affiliated with the Intercollegiate Socialist Society, flourished. In 1917 the C.C.N.Y. chapter of the I.S.S. was headed by Lovestone as president and his later Communist ally, rival, and enemy, Weinstone, as secretary. As the split in the Socialist party widened in 1918–19, Lovestone and Weinstone represented the student contingent in the pro-Communist Left Wing.[4]

For about three years after his graduation from City College in 1918, Lovestone shifted from job to job and school to school. He spent six months at the City College School of Accounting, a year at the New York University Law School, and some time at Columbia University. He worked, among other things, as a statistician, social worker, and drugstore manager. Early in 1919, when he was barely twenty, he helped to organize the Left Wing Section of the pro-Communists in New York; later that year he was one of the New York delegates to the founding convention of the Communist party, which elected him to both the Program Committee and the first Central Executive Committee. The official account of the convention singled him out as "one of the youngest of this Convention of young men, [who] proved himself one of the most aggressive and ablest." [5]

Lovestone received his first full-time paid position in the party in 1921 as editor of the official underground organ, *The Communist.* Four months later he was the underground party's Assistant Secretary and for most of 1922 its National Secretary. The following year, he produced a full-length book, *The Government—Strikebreaker,* a study of government intervention in the strike wave of 1921–22. The first large-scale intellectual effort of its kind by an American Communist, it was largely based on Lovestone's favorite source for Communist propaganda, the "capitalist press." Next came a phase as the party's first anti-imperialist expert, during which he wrote a pamphlet, *American Imperialism,* again full of facts and figures.[6] A prolific propagandist, with a stream of articles and pamphlets as well as the book to his credit, he belonged in part to the small group of college-bred Communist intellectuals, and in part to the larger group of party functionaries.

From the outset, Lovestone had cast his lot with Ruthenberg. He followed him in all the early splits and sought recognition only as his trusted aide. When Gusev presented Ruthenberg in 1925 with the political leadership, Ruthenberg chose Lovestone as his organizational lieutenant. The young intellectual merged into the organization secretary and carried out the Bolshevization of the party.

Lovestone respected Ruthenberg, but Lovestone had been charmed by Pepper. For almost two years, from 1922 to 1924, the old Hungarian master had conducted informal classes—teaching by example—in the theory and practice of getting ahead in the Communist movement. When Foster had demanded Pepper's removal from the American party, Lovestone had sent the Comintern one of several protests against the proposed "exile." In it, he wrote feelingly: "My opponents will throw it up to me that I am only a young 'intellectual.' The truth is, however, that I have spent practically my whole life in the revolutionary and Communist movement. I can say that if today I am a Bolshevik in the Leninist sense of the word, I have a great debt to pay to Comrade Pepper and to his work and his teachings." [7]

After Pepper's "deportation," the Pepper-Ruthenberg faction rapidly became the Ruthenberg-Lovestone faction. While Ruthenberg made a show of leading the party, Lovestone relieved him of the grimier task of leading the faction. Lovestone fought by fair means or foul; he gave no quarter and asked none. Ruthenberg's grave demeanor tended to have a soothing effect on the opposition; Lovestone could not resist the wounding phrase and cutting epithet. Some Fosterites were tempted from time to time to toy with the idea of making peace with Ruthenberg; they could think only of destroying or being destroyed by Lovestone. Like Pepper, Lovestone tended to overplay his hand; he collected enemies faster than he could make friends.

The older Communists had layers of other movements beneath their Communist consciousness; Lovestone's pre-Communist experiences had been far more superficial and adolescent. He had grown up within the Communist movement and had taken part in every stage of its development. No one else his age had started at the top and had stayed so close to the centers of power. No one had enjoyed greater opportunities to observe the inner workings of the Communist apparatus from the inside—as a member of every Central Executive Committee, as right-hand man of the perennial leader, Ruthenberg, and as the favorite of yesterday's *éminence grise* and today's Comintern oligarch, Pepper.

Like many another idealistic young man, he had made the discovery that practical politics did not stop at the door of revolutionary movements and that those who refused to play the game did not get very far. Lovestone differed from the others not by playing the game but by playing it more ferociously and indefatigably than anyone else.

Lovestone's rival as Ruthenberg's successor, William Wolf Weinstone, was strikingly similar in background but not in temperament. He too was born in Lithuania, a year before Lovestone, and was brought to the United States as a child. He too attended the College of the City of New York, succeeding Lovestone as president of the C.C.N.Y. chapter of the Intercollegiate Socialist Society. He took part in the early development of the pro-Communist Left Wing in New York and formation of the Communist party. He had preceded Lovestone as National Secretary for a short period in 1921–22, and then had served as New York organizer. Except for the Foster-dominated period in 1924–25, when he marked time as secretary of the International Workers' Aid, he was the Ruthenberg faction's choice as District Organizer in New York, a post which made it possible for him to build up a personal following and gave him a springboard for higher office. A more effective mass speaker than Lovestone, Weinstone did not have Lovestone's superabundant energy and daring; his indecisiveness and frequent changes of mind had earned him the name of William "Wobbly" Weinstone.[8]

The third of the "City College boys," Bertram D. Wolfe, American born of German-Jewish parentage, was graduated before Lovestone and Weinstone. He taught high school for a year, attended law school for a year in company with Lovestone, and acted as publicity director for the Rand School of Social Science, then the intellectual center of socialism in New York. Wolfe's interest in socialism arose after his graduation from City College during Morris Hillquit's campaign for mayor in 1917, and he was soon caught up in the upsurge of the pro-Communist Left Wing in 1918–19. Wolfe was far more the innate student than Lovestone or Weinstone, and his absence of almost six years in California and Mexico had removed him from the centers of party factionalism from late 1919 to the middle of 1925. He returned to New York in time for the Ruthenberg-favored upset at the Fourth Convention in August 1925, and shortly thereafter took his place with the Ruthenberg-Lovestone forces as Director of Agit-Prop in the New York District and head of the New York Workers School.[9]

In the party's factional wars, Lovestone, Weinstone, and Wolfe labored under the handicap of a college education. The most damaging thing that Lovestone could think of saying of Foster was that he had been and would always be a "trade-union syndicalist," and the most contemptuous thing that Foster could think of saying of Lovestone was that he would never get over being a "City College intellectual."

To "Mecca" again

Lovestone's enemies did not expect him to stay long as Acting General Secretary. Cannon, Foster, and Weinstone, with a majority of the Central Executive Committee behind them, gave him a few days or at most a few weeks.

Lovestone, however, had other plans. With Bedacht and Gitlow, his top confederates in the Political Committee, he hatched a scheme for limiting the plenum to questions of policy and proposing a later convention to determine the leadership. To get Weinstone's backing for the convention, the Lovestoneites held out to him the same bait that the opposition had offered—the general secretaryship. But Weinstone, fearing a trap to isolate him and make his position appear completely unprincipled, refused the offer.[10]

At the next meeting of the Political Committee, Lovestone first tried to postpone the plenum for six weeks. Cannon and Foster countered with two weeks. Weinstone held out for one week only, and in addition proposed sending a delegation to settle the entire question of the succession in Moscow. Just when the opposition seemed to have a plenum, sooner or later, in its grasp, the Lovestoneites sprang their surprise play, the convention, in order to prevent the C.E.C. from making the decision. Bedacht picked up Weinstone's reference to the Comintern and gave it another twist—to request the Comintern's permission to call an American convention, and to ask the Comintern to send a representative for the purpose. Lovestone took over from Bedacht and demanded an "immediate convention" to permit the leadership to be determined by the entire membership, instead of by factional "alignments" and "mechanical arrangements" in the C.E.C.

Then came the votes. Cannon and Foster quickly swung over to Weinstone's proposals. Bedacht's motion for a convention and a Comintern representative won by a straight factional 4-to-3 vote. Cannon, Weinstone, and Foster immediately served notice of their intention to appeal to the Comintern.[11]

One way or the other the Comintern would decide.

By this time the old factional machines were going full blast. The leaders kept their followers across the country alerted with regular letters and bulletins. Neither side could suppress a natural curiosity about the other's activities. Foster's first lieutenant, Jack Johnstone, came to the Political Committee with a complaint that won everyone's sympathy. He protested that his files had been rifled; the culprit had pilfered a carefully selected portion of his correspondence and a complete collection of the Foster faction's bulletins. He accused no one, but pointed out: "The fact that whoever was guilty had a key to the office, that they knew where my file was located, that no other file or matter was touched in the office, shows that it was done by, or with the knowledge of, someone in the office." Indignantly he demanded an immediate investigation by the Acting General Secretary. The Acting General Secretary gave him full satisfaction and named himself and Johnstone's co-factionalist, Bittelman, to investigate the knavery. Years later, Gitlow closed the case: "Our group had of course arranged for the rifling of his files." [12]

Meanwhile five cables sped to the Comintern in Moscow.

Three of them, sent separately by the Cannon, Foster, and Weinstone groups, demanded the same things: immediate intervention by the Comintern to summon an American delegation to Moscow as the only way out of a destructive factional fight at the proposed convention. The Lovestoneite cable requested the Comintern's permission to call a convention with a Comintern representative in attendance, and attacked the Opposition's proposed delegation to "Mecca" (the code-name actually used for "Moscow" in this and other messages).* As an afterthought, Weinstone and Ballam sent another cable demanding the Comintern's "speedy action" and insisting that they belonged to the new opposition as part of the old Ruthenberg, not the Foster, group.[13]

To these petitions, the Comintern cabled back that it did not want a delegation to come to Moscow and instead invited the warring groups to send written arguments. The Comintern's reply went on:

WE CATEGORICALLY INSIST THERE BE NO CHANGES IN POLITICAL BUREAU OR OTHER LEADING POSITIONS OF THE PARTY UNTIL THE PARTY CONVENTION AND ON OTHER HAND WE ARE AGAINST ORGANIZATIONAL MEASURES AGAINST MINORITY STOP DISPUTE RE PARTY CONVENTION WILL BE DECIDED ON RECEIPT OF RESPECTIVE WRITTEN STATEMENTS STOP WE INSIST UPON THE LAYING ASIDE OF FACTIONAL FIGHTING IN ORDER TO CONCENTRATE THE FORCES OF THE PARTY UPON THE PRESENT EXTRAORDINARILY IMPORTANT TASKS STOP PLENUM OF THE CENTRAL SHOULD BE CALLED AS QUICKLY AS POSSIBLE IN ORDER TO CONSIDER FIRST OF ALL THE QUESTION OF THE STRUGGLE AGAINST IMPERIALISM AND THE CAPITALIST OFFENSIVE STOP [14]

Great was the jubilation in Lovestone's camp. The Comintern's cable gave it everything and the Opposition nothing. The delegation to Moscow had been denied, the convention had been granted, the plenum had been restricted to nonorganizational questions.

In the Political Committee, the Lovestoneites hastened to wring the maximum advantage from their stunning victory in Moscow. Lovestone solemnly pledged "loyal execution of the decision without any reservations." Gitlow proposed a letter to the districts which began with a paean of thanksgiving: "Comrades: Close your ranks! We must

* "OPPOSITION APPEAL INCLUDES REQUEST LARGE DELEGATION PARTY LEADERS MINIMUM FOUR GO MECCA IMMEDIATELY STOP" (part of cable).

have full faith in the C.I. The Comintern will guide us well in our difficult moments."

For the moment, Foster, Cannon, and Weinstone sat crushed. Despite their outrage, the Comintern's rules of correct behavior required them to "accept the decision," and so they did.[15]

But all was not lost for the Opposition. While the Americans had not yet straightened out the tangle of their own plenum and convention, word arrived from Moscow of another plenum, the Comintern's Eighth, which had been set for the middle of May 1927.[16] Though the Comintern had turned down the Opposition's bid to send an American delegation to Moscow, a cable from the Comintern some two weeks later directed the Americans to send a delegation to Moscow for the Comintern's plenum. This cable named five American delegates. Three of them—Lovestone, Gitlow, and Foster—were obligatory; two—Cannon and Weinstone—could come at the discretion of the Political Committee. The Lovestone-controlled Political Committee vetoed Cannon and Weinstone, but they appealed to the Comintern and finally obtained permission to go.[17]

With one plenum opening in Chicago on May 4, another in Moscow several days later, and an American convention to follow, a series of pitched battles loomed for the American groups. Of the three meetings, the first counted the least. As the first American plenum without Ruthenberg, however, it gave Lovestone a chance to flaunt his new style of leadership.

For Lovestone the Chicago plenum no longer held a threat. It was merely a nuisance because the Comintern had forbidden it to change the leadership. For the Opposition it took on some importance as the first opportunity to demonstrate the new Cannon-Foster-Weinstone majority in the Central Executive Committee. As soon as the plenum opened, the Opposition achieved this purpose by forcing Lovestone to share the chairmanship with Foster and Weinstone. That same night the Lovestoneite high command gathered to assess the damage and strike back.

The next day, Lovestone and Gitlow were not at the plenum. They were not even in Chicago. They were on their way to New York en route to Moscow. When the Opposition learned of their flight, pandemonium broke loose in Chicago. Lovestone's enemies roared with rage and threatened physical revenge on his remaining cohorts. Foster, Cannon, and Weinstone, ready to believe anything of Lovestone, credited him with a deep-laid plot to trick them into staying in Chicago while he and Gitlow slipped off to Moscow without them. All they could do was to rant and rave, bring the plenum to an abrupt end, and head for Moscow themselves.[18]

It is doubtful whether Ruthenberg would have engaged in such a grandstand play. It is also doubtful whether Lovestone gained much by making his enemies look foolish and by driving them to work all the harder for his destruction.

Meanwhile fortune smiled and "Mecca" beckoned.

Favorite son

At the Eighth Plenum, which opened on May 18, 1927, the American imbroglio was one of the Comintern's lesser problems.

A war scare had gripped Moscow. In China the three-year-old Communist-Kuomintang alliance had exploded bloodily. The Nationalist commander, Chiang Kai-shek, had crushed the Chinese Communists in Shanghai and Nanking. In England British police had raided Soviet House, headquarters of Arcos, Ltd., the Russian trading corporation, and the British government had followed up by breaking off diplomatic relations with Soviet Russia.

In the Comintern the Chinese debacle overshadowed the British crisis. For the last time Trotsky rose in a plenum of the Comintern to accuse Stalin of betrayal for having sponsored the Communist-Kuomintang alliance, and Stalin accused Trotsky of having formed "something in the nature of a united front" with the British Foreign Secretary, Sir Austen Chamberlain. Organizationally the debate was superfluous. With Bukharin's assistance, Stalin swept through the plenum with the loss of only one vote.[19]

The Americans were not content merely to cast their votes against Trotsky. They sought and obtained the privilege of being one of the five parties to present the resolution demanding Trotsky's expulsion from the Comintern's Executive Committee.[20] By now all the American delegates, from Lovestone and Gitlow to Foster and Cannon, were experienced enough to know that anti-Trotskyism was *de rigueur* in Comintern circles. But the next step, pro-Stalinism, required a higher degree of sophistication. Not all the American delegates as yet possessed this in equal measure. Lovestone's delegation put the Opposition to shame by obtaining the first personal interview granted by Stalin to a group of American Communists.

Stalin received a delegation of seven, including Lovestone, Pepper, Gitlow, Kruse, Minor, and Engdahl, in his office in the Kremlin. The Americans heard that he had postponed a trip to the Caucasus to receive them. For over three hours he asked questions about American conditions, compared wages and social benefits in Russia and the United States, and offered advice on building the American party. More important than anything said at the interview, however, was the fact that it took place at all. By extending his invitation solely to the Lovestoneites and treating them with marked cordiality. Stalin had visibly bestowed on them his benediction.[21]

In Moscow, at least, Lovestone seemed to live a charmed life. Having walked out of a plenum in contemptuous disregard of the accepted amenities, he might well have risen in Stalin's estimation as the kind of leader who handled his opposition the way Stalin himself could have done. But whereas Stalin merely deigned to receive Lovestone, Bukharin admitted him into his intimate circle. They had met for the first time during a mission by Lovestone to Berlin in 1922. Lovestone's increasingly frequent trips to Moscow had forged a bond of personal friendship and political sympathy between them. Other Americans noticed that Lovestone had begun to displace Pepper as Bukharin's chief adviser on American affairs. As long as Stalin needed Bukharin, however, Lovestone's close ties with Bukharin did not hurt him with Stalin.

Toward the end of the plenum, an American Commission was appointed to settle the differences in the American party. The first step toward getting a favorable decision from a commission was, if possible, to get a friendly chairman at the head of it. In such matters the Lovestoneites excelled. The friendly head of this American Commission was Arthur Ewert, a German Communist close to Bukharin, who then used the name of "A. Braun." [22] Under his direction the commission proceeded to go through the usual formalities: long speeches, statements, memoranda, documents, acrimonious debates, and wire-pulling.

To strengthen their position, Cannon, Foster, and Weinstone decided to band together more formally and announced the organization of an "Opposition Bloc." By calling themselves a "bloc," they implied that they had not fused their forces into a single faction but still maintained separate identities.[23] A faction might have favored Foster, whose backing outnumbered Cannon's and Weinstone's; a bloc protected each of them by forcing all three to act by unanimous agreement rather than by majority vote.

After sessions lasting a full month beyond the plenum, the American Commission produced a "Resolution of the Comintern on the American Question," and the Comintern's Presidium gave it final endorsement on July 1, 1927. This resolution was divided into four sections, each of which attempted to answer fundamental questions that had been troubling the American party.

The first section dealt with the problem of America's place in "The Struggle Against Imperialism and the War Danger." The problem arose because the war scare in the Soviet Union had been set off by British threats, despite the fact that the United States, not Britain, was considered "the mightiest imperialist power." Did the United States, then, represent a lesser danger? The resolution decided that American imperialism was no less dangerously aggressive than Britism imperialism, though American aggressiveness sometimes assumed different forms.

The second section discussed the problem, closer to home, of "The Development of the Revolutionary Movement in America." In the flood tide of American prosperity, what were the prospects of American Communism? For the first time Bukharin's regime in the Comintern attempted to face this question frankly. Objectively it based itself on the premise that "American capitalism is still on the upward grade of development." It immediately cautioned, however, that "the time is approaching when the crises of world capitalism will also extend to the United States of America." Meanwhile, it admitted, American imperialism could provide "a comparatively high standard of living" for "a large section of the working class." Subjectively, therefore, the result of this position for "very considerable sections" of the American working class was described as "ideological bourgeoisification." The prognosis for American Communism was not very encouraging: "A great rise is not to be expected in the nearest future."

Third, the much-debated problem of "Trade Union Work" came up. Over it still hung the shadow of Ruthenberg's ill-fated attempt to sidetrack the T.U.E.L. and the A.F. of L. with independent, Communist-organized unions. On the role of the T.U.E.L., the resolution gave Foster everything he demanded. It ordered the party to "do everything in its power to help build up" the T.U.E.L. "on a broad basis." But it refused to limit the Communists in the T.U.E.L. solely to working within the A.F. of L., as Foster had originally intended. To organize the unorganized, it adopted a two-fold approach: to act through the existing trade unions, but also through new unions in fields where none existed or where the existing organizations refused to enter. In the second case, however, it added the significant proviso of making very effort to "link" up the new unions with the existing ones. On trade-union policy, therefore, the resolution veered away from Foster's traditional policy without going as far as the Ruthenberg group's previous "Passaic policy."

Finally, the resolution reached "The Inner Party Situation," the distribution of power. In its usual fashion, the Comintern began by denouncing the factional struggle and demanding its unconditional liquidation. Before presenting its practical decisions, it carefully distributed blame to both sides. After this show of impartiality, it proceeded to set forth the conditions for the American party's convention at the end of August. The convention's preparation was handed over to a "commission," composed of both sides equally, headed by a "neutral" chairman, with Lovestone and Foster as deputy chairmen. To set an example of collaboration until the convention, Lovestone and Foster were advised to function jointly as the party's secretaries, and Foster and Gitlow as secretaries of the Trade Union Department. After the convention, it recommended a "collective secretariat of three," including Lovestone and Foster. Meanwhile, it rejected immediate changes in the top leadership as "inexpedient" and left the future leadership to the convention.[24]

This decision was implemented by an agreement signed by all the American representatives, plus "A. Braun." It worked out the preparations for the convention in detail, decided the majority and minority proportions of the next Central Executive Committee, and named Pepper the American representative to the Comintern until he could be replaced immediately after the convention.[25]

The Comintern's document appeared to walk a tightrope between the factions. As such, it ostensibly represented a setback, or at least no victory, for Lovestone, who was ordered to share the secretaryship with Foster. A week later, however, the new Opposition Bloc of Cannon, Foster, and Weinstone unexpectedly played into Lovestone's hands.

On July 1, the very day that the decision was issued in Moscow, a mimeographed circular signed "National Committee of the Opposition Bloc" was distributed in the American party. This circular was sent throughout the United States by Bittelman and a few others close to the bloc's leaders then in Moscow. It boasted, somewhat overoptimistically, that the Comintern had endorsed the bloc's political line on everything from the war danger to the internal situation, and it called upon all fellow-factionalists to organize local committees of the Opposition Bloc. A more unfortunate name could hardly have been chosen for the bloc. For the Russians it was sure to evoke the image of the United Opposition Bloc of Trotsky and Zinoviev, the worst possible recommendation for an American faction in the Stalin–Bukharin-dominated Comintern.

When this circular fell into the hands of the Lovestoneites, it threw them into an uproar of confusion and indignation. Lovestone's stand-in as Acting General Secretary, Max Bedacht, shot off a lengthy cable of protest to the Comintern. He gave the Comintern his version of the offending circular and demanded action to restrain the Opposition from claiming the Comintern's intention to change the leadership.[26]

Bedacht's cable created a furor among the Lovestoneites in Moscow. It alerted them to the danger of a Comintern resolution which did not make the Comintern's political preferences clear. When Gusev had dispossessed Foster of the leadership two years earlier, he had based his investiture of Ruthenberg on political grounds. Now Lovestone used Bedacht's cable to convince Ewert that the only way to prevent the Opposition from claiming the Comintern's political support was to give that support openly to the former Ruthenberg group under Lovestone's leadership.

And so the readers of the *Daily Worker* on July 8, 1927, found a large box on the front page headed: "Comintern Demands Immediate Liquidation of the National Committee Opposition Bloc." A short editorial note announced that a cablegram had been received the day before from the Comintern rebuking the Foster-Cannon-Weinstone Opposition for its circular letter calling for local Opposition committees.

Then, in type twice as large as the news on the rest of the page, came the cablegram in full:

THE CABLEGRAM OF THE COMINTERN

MOSCOW, U.S.S.R., July 7, 1927

You should publish the following cable of the Executive Committee of the Communist International in the Party Press:

> The Comintern is categorically against the sharpening of the factional struggle and under no circumstances supports the statement of the "National Committee of the Opposition Bloc." The Comintern recognizes that in many political questions the Ruthenberg group followed a more correct line in the past than the Foster group. On the other hand the Executive is of the opinion that the Ruthenberg group had not understood how

to estimate sufficiently the full significance of the trade union forces in the Party and that Foster at that time was more correct on many trade union questions. The line of the Comintern has been: On the whole for the political support of the Ruthenberg group and for bringing Foster nearer to the general political line of the Ruthenberg group, at the same time, however, following the course towards the correction of the trade union tactic of the Ruthenberg group on the line of Foster through cooperation in the Party leadership. Now the previous political and trade union differences have almost disappeared. The Comintern condemns most categorically every attempt towards the sharpening of the situation in the party, especially in the present objective situation as exemplified by the formation of a National Committee of the Opposition bloc. The Comintern considers factionalism without political differences as the worst offense against the Party.

(Signed) PRESIDIUM OF THE EXECUTIVE COMMITTEE OF THE COMMUNIST INTERNATIONAL

To make matters worse for the Opposition Bloc, Ewert was persuaded to incorporate the substance of this cable into the American delegates' agreement as the Comintern's statement of policy.[27]

The National Committee of the Opposition Bloc did not survive this cable. Bittelman hastened to inform the Political Committee that it had been dissolved. Then, fighting back, the Opposition leaders sent three cables to Moscow protesting the charges against them. Four days later, June 12, another box appeared on the front page of the *Daily Worker* with another Comintern cable which tried to soften the effect of the first one by denying any intention to "support the hegemony of one group."

Meanwhile tempers flared in the Political Committee. Bedacht, Lovestone's lieutenant, stormed at Johnstone, Foster's lieutenant: "The methods you bring into the factional struggle are the methods of a pure and simple labor faker. You deliberately lie to the C.I. and deliberately misrepresent C.I. decisions to the membership." Johnstone's group thereupon issued another factional circular charging Bedacht's group with harboring "petty bourgeois intellectuals" and "clique leadership." This broadside gave Bedacht's group another chance to complain to Moscow, and a third cable from the Comintern, again on the front page of the *Daily Worker* of July 30, censured these expressions as "impermissible." [28]

Soon after the American delegation returned from Moscow, Foster received a lesson in Comintern diplomacy. The Moscow agreement had provided for two party secretaries, Lovestone and Foster, but the Lovestoneites refused to permit Foster to function as Lovestone's equal or even to give him a desk in the national office. To his dismay, Foster discovered that Lovestone had sent a cable to the Comintern appointing himself the first party secretary and Foster the second, with Foster the first trade-union secretary and Gitlow the second.

When Foster protested in the Political Committee that this arrangement violated the Comintern's decision, Lovestone came back with surprising news. At one conference with top Comintern officials in Moscow, which had been limited to the Lovestoneites and about which Foster had known nothing, Kuusinen had stated that the Lovestoneites could make the concession of two secretaries "because Comrade Lovestone was first secretary." In return for this the Lovestoneites had asked for and had been granted the second trade-union secretaryship for Gitlow.

Thus what had seemed like a demotion for Lovestone from a single "Acting General Secretary" to one of two "secretaries" was now transformed into a promotion which enabled him to sign party documents as General Secretary, without the "Acting," and without consulting the second secretary.[29] Within six weeks of the Comintern's latest resolution on the American question, the Opposition was driven to lament that the Lovestone group had not changed its factional course "in the slightest degree" and that it completely disregarded the Opposition groups "without manifesting the slightest intention of coming to any agreement with them." [30]

Lovestone appeared capable of political sleight of hand. He outtalked, outwitted, and outfought his opponents at every turn. From the disdainful walkout from the Chicago plenum to the first American interview granted by Stalin and the feat of snatching victory from near-setback in the American Commission, his instinct for striking at the political jugular seemed infallible.

More important than the entire Comintern resolution, which filled almost two pages of the *Daily Worker,* was the single paragraph in the Comintern's cable of July 7 reminding the American party members of the Comintern's long-standing political support of the Ruthenberg group, which Lovestone had inherited. The clear implication in the cable that the Comintern preferred Lovestone as the party's political leader and Foster as its trade-union leader, combined with the private understanding that two secretaries meant a first and second secretary, enabled Lovestone to return from Moscow in triumph.

Lovestone triumphant

One more step stood between Lovestone and full realization of his ambition to become Ruthenberg's successor—the Workers party's Fifth Convention. Only the convention could legitimatize his *de facto* position and give him a "constitutional" status as head of the party.

The campaign for delegates inevitably degenerated into a factional free-for-all. Opposing speakers and resolutions clashed by prearrangement at all membership meetings, and whatever its limitations a more "democratic" election never took place in the American party. The votes at the ten largest membership meetings quickly showed that the Lovestoneites were running ahead by a 3-to-2 popular majority. They captured the lead in nine of the ten largest Communist centers, including Weinstone's stronghold, New York, and Foster's stronghold, Chicago.[31]

Despite the decisiveness of Lovestone's victory, Lovestone had not won the party for the Comintern; the Comintern had won it for him. Lovestone skillfully succeeded in making loyalty to the Comintern the issue and making loyalty to his group the test of loyalty to the Comintern.

In Zinoviev's time, Comintern cables had determined the course of the Workers party and its leadership, but they had never been published on the front page of the *Daily Worker*. In the Bukharin-Stalin period, the Comintern flaunted its power openly; it boldly ordered its cables printed in the party press. Instead of controlling the party through the top leaders, as in the past, it went over the heads of the leaders to control the party. The cables spoke directly to every party member and made the rank and file conscious as never before of the Comintern's constant supervision.

As a result the Fifth Convention, which met in New York from August 31 to September 7, 1927, turned out to be the least eventful in the party's history to date. Ewert, the Comintern's representative to this convention, who changed his pseudonym from "Braun" in Moscow to "Grey" in New York, faced none of the delicate problems of overriding a majority that had confronted Gusev, his predecessor at the previous convention in 1925.

His victory assured, a new, more benign Lovestone made his appearance. When the Opposition wanted to reopen old wounds, he tried to turn away their wrath with soft words. He refused to be lured into defending himself against accusations of "trickery, clever words, maneuvering, manipulations and insincerity," and piously rebuked Cannon for perpetuating the "spirit of quarrels and insults." He made a special effort to win over Foster and praised Foster's T.U.E.L. In return, Foster praised the Passaic strike, which the Fosterites had not so long ago considered the entering wedge to dual unionism, as "in many respects a model of the way to organize the unorganized." Most of the other oppositionists remained as obstreperously non-cooperative as ever, but Lovestone assured the party that it had entered a new era, marked by the "last gasp of factionalism," political differences reduced to a minimum, a beginning of the merger of the two main groups, and the achievement of bases for establishing the broadest collective leadership.[32]

Nevertheless, Lovestone took no chances. He commanded majorities of 25 to 13 in the new Central Executive Committee, 8 to 3 in the Political Committee, and 2 to 1 in the revived Secretariat.[33] Resistance seemed so futile that Weinstone and Ballam crept back into the Lovestone majority after the convention. For deserting the Opposition, Weinstone, though permitted to remain head of the New York district, was cut down to size by being forbidden to use the title of "General Secretary" of the district.[34] At Ewert's suggestion, Lovestone assumed the title of Executive Secretary (instead of General Secretary) and Foster became Secretary of the Trade-Union Department.[35]

In the party's national office, a new team came in with Lovestone. He chose Stachel to replace himself as head of the Organization Department, and Wolfe to replace Bedacht as head of the Agit-Prop Department. These three young New Yorkers—Lovestone, twenty-nine; Stachel, twenty-seven; and Wolfe, thirty—took over the key organizational posts just as the national headquarters moved from Chicago to 33 East 125th Street, New York City.

Lovestone's partisans were also put in charge of the chief party publications. Minor was appointed editor of the *Daily Worker,* and William F. Dunne was demoted to assistant editor; Dunne had previously shared the editorship with J. Louis Engdahl, who was named American representative to the Comintern in Moscow. Wolfe assumed the editorship of the monthly magazine, the name of which had been changed from *The Workers Monthly* to *The Communist;* he replaced Bedacht, who was sent to Chicago as District Organizer, ousting Arne Swabeck, a Cannonite.

So many shifts were made among the District Organizers that soon all but two of the twelve belonged to Lovestone's group. Only in the trade-union field were the Fosterites permitted to retain their foothold in the leadership.[36]

Never had Ruthenberg or Foster been able to wield such power as Lovestone did in 1927. Never had Foster and Cannon suffered so disastrous a defeat or seemed so far from a comeback.

12

American Exceptionalism

WAS all this only a cynical struggle for power? There was more to it than that, if only because in the Communist movement personal differences legitimately express themselves in terms of political differences. What might otherwise be an open clash of personalities for power often takes the form of a grave doctrinal conflict.

Lovestone's victory precipitated a doctrinal conflict peculiar in its virulence, obstinacy, and significance. It was, indeed, the last great open conflict in the American party for more than fifteen years over the old and ever-new issue of doctrine versus reality.

The party that Lovestone took over claimed somewhat less than 10,000 members and was predominantly foreign-language in character.[1] Even in its stronghold, New York City, where one-third of the membership was concentrated, it scraped together less than 5000 votes in 1926 and about 10,000 in 1927.[2] Its youth movement reported only 700 members in good standing in 1927.[3] Even if all the necessary adjustments are made—the party had many more sympathizers than members, its foreign-born members were least represented in elections, and it held some strategic positions in the garment unions—American Communism in the mid-twenties still remained a weak and isolated body, battering itself hopelessly against the richest, strongest, and most confident social system in the world.

As long as this reality prevailed, it obviously jeopardized Lovestone's leadership—unless he could establish in advance that the fault was elsewhere. Motivated by more than scientific curiosity, then, Lovestone and his opponents entered into an intense and prolonged debate on the perspectives of American capitalism and communism.

Questions and answers

Two questions haunted American Communism: Why was it so weak and unsuccessful? When would it become strong and successful?

In the first half of the nineteen-twenties it gave purely doctrinal answers to these questions and promised, almost from month to month, a devastating American depression and millions of unemployed. These calculations had influenced the Communists during the Farmer-Labor movement of 1923–24 and despite the disappointing outcome they had lingered on.

In the spring of 1925, for example, Browder still wrote as if economic catastrophe were just around the corner. Capitalism, he maintained, was "just one crisis after another" for the working class, only small sections of which received any benefits from prosperity. Besides this permanent crisis for the working class, he gave assurances of a more exceptional crisis, which he defined as "that breakdown of the capitalist system of production that closes the factories on a mass scale and halts production or brings on a war." He forecast this crisis "definitely in the near future for the United States." [4] That same summer Bittelman detected a "quiet depression" in the United States. He expected "a long period of hesitating development on a downward scale with occasional severe disturbances." [5] At the end of the year, Lovestone saw "multiplying signs that the end of our present period of so-called prosperity is fast approaching." [6] In the spring of 1926 he also developed a theory that the "upper stratum" of the American working class would be revolutionized as a result of increasing conflict between American and European capitalism.[7]

Was American capitalism going up or down?

The Comintern's answers came haltingly. In 1924 its chief economist, Eugen Varga, emphasized the downward path and saw the beginning of "one of the most serious crises in the United States." [8] The following year when the Comintern officially recognized the "partial stabilization" of world capitalism, he hastened to change his mind. "American capitalism is still healthy," he admitted. "As opposed to European capitalism, it is certainly on the upgrade." But he still held out hope that the American upswing would "come to a quick end." [9] The Comintern's 1925 resolution on the American question took the same line. It declared that American finance capital was "now more powerful than ever" but would "get ever more deeply entangled in the contradictions and crises of European capitalism." [10]

The emphasis on the strength of American capitalism caught some American Communists unprepared.

At the Comintern's Sixth Plenum in the spring of 1926, Varga repeated the formula that American capitalism was "on the upgrade," and Foster echoed him.[11] Browder, a victim of overenthusiasm for the previous line of American capitalist breakdown, spoke for those who refused to accept this "one-sided estimation"; he continued to stress the negative, revolutionizing factors in the American economy.[12] Pepper, then at the height of his influence in the Comintern, pronounced judgment for the key Political Commission. He scoffed at the idea that the American working class was then undergoing a process of radicalization or that its real wages were moving downward.[13] The plenum's thesis referred to the "upswing of American capitalism," but softened the blow by conceding that it was not proceeding smoothly and that a general economic crisis was not ruled out.[14]

In the fall of 1926 Ruthenberg attempted to combat the deeply ingrained doctrinal assumption that the party could grow only in a period of downswing and depression. He accused "some sections of the party" of "a tendency toward pessimism" because they lacked faith in the willingness of the workers to struggle and the ability of the party to make headway in a period of high prosperity and general employment. Instead of denying the existence of prosperity or predicting imminent depression, he took the position that the party could grow in periods of prosperity as well as in periods of crisis; prosperity, he held, encouraged demands for higher wages and better working conditions.[15]

So urgent had this problem become that the American plenum at the end of 1926 made it the chief subject of discussion and temporarily pointed to a positive solution by adopting Ruthenberg's general line.[16] But just before his death early in 1927, Ruthenberg went back to forecasting a depression "in the offing" and consequently a "sharpening of the struggle" against reduced wages and less favorable working conditions.[17]

How was the American capitalist upswing related to the rest of the capitalist world?

This question agitated the Comintern's Seventh Plenum in the winter of 1926, the scene of the great debate on "socialism in one country." The official position, set forth by Bukharin when he made his debut as Zinoviev's successor as head of the Comintern, divided the world economy into six groups. Of these only the United States, and to a lesser extent Japan and some of the British Dominions, ranked as countries of upward capitalist development.[18] A somewhat different emphasis, however, was voiced by the Indian Communist, M. N. Roy, then head of the Comintern's newly formed Anglo-American Secretariat. He was disturbed that "some of our American comrades" believed that American imperialism had not yet reached its "zenith," a view which, he contended, made the American situation seem too "bright." He preferred to put American imperialism at "just the zenith of its power," which implied that it had nowhere to go but down.[19] Bittelman accepted the premise that American capitalism was still going upward, but complained that the Comintern and the American party had not until then "formulated the perspectives lying before us." [20]

After 1926, then, it was officially orthodox to consider American capitalism to be "on the upgrade." But the practical implications for the American Communists' strength and growth depended largely on the interpretation of "upgrade." Bukharin, for whom the end of the upgrade was still some way off, observed: "Our party in America is quite small. American capitalism is the stronghold of the entire capitalist system, the most powerful capitalism in the world. Our tasks in this country are for the present still very modest." [21] Roy, for whom the peak of the upgrade had already been reached, protested: "I must declare before the plenum of the Communist International that the general view prevailing in the Communist International regarding the strength of the American party is absolutely incorrect. The American party is not a negligible factor." [22] But Roy was then a lonely voice.

All this took place before Ruthenberg's death. By the time that Lovestone, Gitlow, Foster, Cannon, and Weinstone came to Moscow in the spring of 1927 to fight for the succession, Bukharin's line had hardened into Comintern dogma. The "Resolution on the American Question," following the Comintern's Eighth Plenum, spelled out the "upward grade of development" of American capitalism and expected no great rise of the revolutionary labor movement "in the nearest future."

Later the ideas that American capitalism was "on the upgrade" and that the United States was an exception to the rule of capitalist decline were stigmatized as peculiar Lovestoneite aberrations. Forgotten or suppressed were their Muscovite origins in official Comintern doctrine which Bittelman as well as Lovestone had unquestioningly accepted.

Americanization

American Communists have periodically ventured to engage in "reconsiderations" and "re-evaluations." Despite great differences, these occasions have had some things in common—they have required a favorable conjuncture of national and international Communist policy; they have been easier to start than to stop; and they have led to a re-examination of the American past as well as the present.

The first Communist effort to re-examine the American past came in 1926. Until then the Communists had shared the traditional radical attitude of debunking American history and its heroes. The works of Socialist writers, notably A. M. Simons's *Social Forces in American History* and James Oneal's *The Workers in American History,* had served them in lieu of their own efforts. Communist writers rarely bothered to pay any attention to the American past. When H. M. Wicks did so in 1923, he dismissed George Washington as "a rich landowner," the John D. Rockefeller of his day, and described Abraham Lincoln as "the personification of the class interests of the industrial capitalist class of the North." [23]

But in 1926, the 150th anniversary of the American Revolution, a change took place. At first, the Communists held on to the old historical line. Bittelman belabored the Founding Fathers for having "deserved the eternal gratitude of every capitalist, of every exploiter and enemy of the toiling masses of the United States." Ruthenberg attacked the Constitutional Convention of 1787 as a "counter-revolution" and the Constitution itself as "not the product of the American revolution, but the product of the counter-revolution." Wicks insisted that there was not one fact in Lincoln's whole life "to support the fiction" that he was the "great emancipator." [24]

For the Fourth of July, however, a new Communist interpretation of the American Revolution, much of it borrowed from Charles A. Beard, appeared. It was heralded by a front-page editorial in the *Daily Worker,* written by a co-editor, William F. Dunne, who claimed the "revolutionary tradition" for the American working class and the Fourth of July as its holiday. But Dunne could not bring himself to say a good word for the Founding Fathers, whom he accused of stealing the fruits of the revolution from the workers and farmers who had fought for it.[25] The work of elaborating the new historical attitude was taken up by two others, Wolfe and Lovestone.

For *The Workers' Monthly* of July 1926, Wolfe wrote a full-length article, "Whose Revolution Is It?" In it he broke sharply with the tradition of Oneal, who had dismissed the American Revolutionary leaders as "smugglers" and "land speculators." Throughout, Wolfe attempted to show the similarities between the American, French, and Russian revolutions, and he urged that "it is time that the American working-class began to 'discover America' and its body of native revolutionary traditions." [26]

Lovestone joined the campaign with two articles in the *Daily Worker*. Like Wolfe, he emphasized that the American Revolution had been made by a minority, which used force and violence, employed the methods of "dictatorship," and accepted "foreign" money. Over a decade before Browder's Popular Front period, Lovestone chose Jefferson as the Communist favorite among the Founding Fathers. And like the later Browder, Lovestone recognized that the American historical tradition was linked with the "Americanization" of the American Communists, though he never went as far as Browder and warned against an "Americanization craze." [27]

Not all American Communists accepted the Wolfe-Lovestone historical approach. In 1927 Washington's birthday was commemorated in the *Daily Worker* by articles that went back to the debunking tradition of Simons and Oneal. Dunne himself returned to the older fashion of abusing Washington as an exponent of capitalist "robbery." When the next Fourth of July came around, however, William F. Kruse went to the defense of Wolfe and Lovestone with another long historical article that characterized the American struggle for independence as "a skillfully managed revolution from which there are lessons to be learned by Communists." On the Fourth of July in 1928 a *Daily Worker* editorial tried to identify American Communism with the revolutionary tradition in this way: "Join the proletarian 'Minute Men' of today, the fighters of the revolution in the present—the Communist Party." [28]

Paradoxically Lovestone made himself the foremost exponent of both Bolshevization and Americanization. One looked toward, the other away from, Russia. In practice, however, the process was more complex. Lovestone, Wolfe, and Kruse saw the American Revolution afresh through Leninist lenses; instead of being merely a bourgeois revolution, it was now a "bourgeois national liberation struggle." They embraced only those aspects of the American Revolution which lent themselves to Communist coloration. Nevertheless this first reinterpretation of the American past coincided with the equally unprecedented recognition of the United States's exceptional place in the contemporary capitalist world. For the time being, the Russians encouraged both trends, and Lovestone was not compelled to choose between Bolshevization and Americanization.

But when the time did come to choose, the Fourth of July of 1926 assumed a significance in the development of Lovestone and Wolfe which they had never contemplated. In retrospect, it began the confused and contradictory process whereby they partially liberated themselves from the Russian revolutionary tradition by identifying themselves with the American revolutionary tradition.

"Bourgeoisification"

The next item for reconsideration was the state of the American working class. What was this working class like in the only capitalist country that was still on the upgrade? What was it like in this period of unprecedented prosperity?

The Communists were not the only ones to occupy themselves with these questions. In some of the theories spawned by the economic boom, the working class had practically disappeared or was disappearing. In a fashionable book, *The Present Economic Revolution in the United States,* published in 1925, Professor Thomas Nixon Carver of Harvard declared that "Laborers are becoming capitalists." He based his conclusion on the rapid growth of savings deposits, the investment of workers in corporate stocks, and the increase of labor banks.[29] As production, profits, and wages soared, despite temporary fluctuations, a literature of the "new capitalism" sprang up, and the new capitalism invariably assumed or implied a new working class or a vanishing working class. Professor Rexford Guy Tugwell of Columbia, the future New Deal brain-truster, wrote *Industry's Coming of Age,* in which he confidently looked forward to the diffusion of private ownership and the transformation of private into "socialized" industry.[30] When Lincoln Steffens came home from Europe in 1927 with his young English wife, Ella Winter, they thought, as she put it, that American capitalism had given the workers what the European Socialists "have always said they wanted, and more." [31]

The "new capitalism" also played havoc with the trade-union movement by attempting to substitute "company unionism" for trade-unionism, and voluntary welfare services for union-contract working conditions. Company-dominated unions, restricted to the workers of a single plant or the plants of a single company, mushroomed after the war to embrace about 1,500,000 workers, or to about half the size of the A.F. of L. The concept of "welfare capitalism," which flourished during the Coolidge administration, included company unionism, employee stock ownership, insurance and pension plans, and various types of personnel, welfare, and service activities. It constituted the capitalist alternative to trade-unionism, even the complaisant, lackadaisical trade-unionism of the boom.[32]

Within the trade unions themselves, an even newer and cruder imitation of capitalism took hold. This "trade-union capitalism" was based on the idea that labor banks could beat capitalism at its own game. After the first bank was set up by the machinists' union in 1920, huge sums were sunk by unions in investment corporations, real-estate speculations, and industrial enterprises, especially by the Brotherhood of Locomotive Engineers. By 1926 the number of labor banks had reached an all-time high of thirty-six, and the A.F. of L. had set up a Union Labor Life Insurance Company to outfinance the financiers. The total collapse of the Locomotive Engineers' financial empire in 1927 punctured the bubble of "trade-union capitalism." By 1932 only seven labor banks remained.[33]

For a while, however, even Foster was tremendously impressed with the possibilities of "trade-union capitalism." When the Union Labor Life Insurance Company was formed in 1926, he viewed it with alarm because it enabled "the controlling bureaucrats in the unions" to maintain themselves in power. In an unguarded outburst of pessimism, he warned that "once they get the resources of a whole series of trade union capitalistic institutions behind them, they will become virtually invincible." As a remedy he proposed investing American workers' funds "in the industries of the Soviet Union." [34]

Foster's enemies in the party jumped on him for overestimating "the power of the trade union bureaucracy and labor aristocracy." [35] But what was that power? And on what did it rest? The pressure from both the "new" and "trade union" capitalism forced the Communists to turn their attention to these questions, and a subcommittee of the Central Executive Committee was set up in the spring of 1927 to analyze the American workers' "bourgeoisification," as the problem was known in Communist circles.[36]

At first, there was little disagreement over the main factors—the upward trend of American capitalism, the "super-profits" of imperialism which enabled the capitalists to "bribe" the skilled workers with high wages and other advantages, and the whole system's future collapse in economic crisis and imperialist rivalries. What differences there were among the American Communists amounted to matters of emphasis and caused no great controversy.

In the heyday of "trade-union capitalism," Foster stressed the "material bourgeoisification" of the American working class, particularly the tremendous financial resources at the disposal of the trade-union bureaucracy.[37] Lovestone distinguished more sharply between ideological and material bourgeoisification. Ideologically, he regarded the entire American working class, except for a very small section, as "bourgeoisified." Materially, he limited bourgeoisification to "only a small section" of the "upper layer, the highly skilled, the labor aristocracy." He estimated this segment at the not so small figure of "several millions." But, like all the others, Lovestone ruled out the principle of the "new capitalism" and ridiculed "this illusion that the bourgeoisie is spreading, the fraud that in America there is no basis for a class struggle, that in America the workers are becoming capitalist." [38]

At the American party's 1927 convention, Charles Krumbein, a Fosterite, complained that Lovestone's report had overemphasized the unfavorable objective conditions for American Communism and underestimated the favorable ones. In what was perhaps the clearest statement of his position, Lovestone replied:

> We maintain that the objective conditions prevailing today in the United States are not favorable for the development of a mass Communist Party and it would be a crime against the Party to develop such illusions among the members if we were to say that the conditions of a mass Communist Party are favorable. Where we differ from the enemies of our Party and from those who have pessimistic ideas regarding the development of the class struggle in the United States is in this: we say that these unfavorable conditions are temporary and passing.[39]

Nevertheless, in its immediate effect, Lovestone's position was pessimistic. He and his closest associates based themselves essentially on a necessary relationship between the up-curve of American capitalism and the down-curve of American Communism. In a lecture at the New York Workers School, Wolfe explained:

> What effect will this upward trend have on the American working class? This tactic of corrupting parts of the working class will continue and will drive parts of the working class to the right. This situation will continue as long as American capitalism is on the up-grade and continues its briberies.[40]

No one looked askance at these words when they appeared. Foster wrote essentially the same thing at about the same time. At most a difference in emphasis might have been detected, a stress on the negative side of the present instead of the more roseate promise of the future.[41] Among the American Communists there was not enough ammunition in this issue to warrant a full-scale factional war at the height of Lovestone's power.

But, once again, a greater power intervened unexpectedly.

Stalin versus Bukharin

In 1927 Stalin stamped out the Russian Opposition of Trotsky and Zinoviev. They were formally expelled at the Russian party's Fifteenth Congress in December. Zinoviev and his group capitulated and crawled back into the party; Trotsky, unrepentant, was exiled to Alma-Ata in Central Asia.

In the Russian party and in the Comintern, only one other leader threatened Stalin's power—his ally, Bukharin. But Bukharin was even less of a match for Stalin than Trotsky or Zinoviev had been. If the struggle for power had been a popularity contest, Bukharin's wit and affability might have won him an easy victory. But his influence was largely personal and intellectual; he lacked a machine in the Russian party; and he never dominated even the Comintern as Zinoviev had once done.

The alliance between Stalin and Bukharin began to come apart as soon as it had ensured the downfall of Trotsky and Zinoviev. The next stage of the struggle for power abruptly changed the factional spectrum in the Russian party. Formerly, Trotsky and Zinoviev had represented the "Left," Stalin the "Center," and Bukharin the "Right," as these terms were then understood in Russian Communist circles. With the elimination of Trotsky and Zinoviev, Stalin moved into their old position by launching a campaign against the "Right." The campaign, a Stalinist classic, proceeded by stages, first ideological, then organizational.

On the eve of the Fifteenth Congress, Stalin struck a new, more ominous note on the subject of capitalist "stabilization." Early in November 1927 he received a "foreign workers' delegation" for a highly publicized interview. One of its questions was: "How do you estimate the situation in Western Europe? Are revolutionary events to be expected within the next few years?" Giving the Sacco-Vanzetti demonstrations all over the world as evidence, he answered, "We are on the threshold of new revolutionary events." Early in December, at the Fifteenth Congress, he spoke of the "collapsing stabilization" and "the eve of a new revolutionary upsurge." [42]

The reasons Stalin gave for believing in an imminent "revolutionary upsurge" at the end of 1927 might more correctly have proven the opposite. He pointed to "facts" like the Chinese Communist debacle of 1927, the British general strike of 1926, the Viennese uprising of 1927, and, above all, the Sacco-Vanzetti demonstrations—all of them actually followed by periods of decline and retreat.[43]

Bukharin attempted to avoid a clash with Stalin by going along part of the way. At the Fifteenth Congress he agreed on the beginning of a "new period" but defined it as merely one of "active struggle," a far cry from Stalin's "revolutionary upsurge." More incautiously, Bukharin observed: "I do not wish to say that we are now on the eve of an immediate revolutionary situation in Europe," though Stalin had wished to say it. The United States, Bukharin implied, was in a class by itself because the real wages of the American working class exceeded those of the average European worker fourfold. Despite the American Communists' prominence in the Sacco-Vanzetti movement, he cautioned against overestimating their influence.[44]

Bukharin was headed for trouble. That was clear at the Fifteenth Congress, at which Stalin's henchmen dared to snipe at him. One of them, Dimitri Z. Manuilsky, a top Comintern official, particularly criticized Bukharin's references to the United States. "In listening to Comrade Bukharin's report," he objected, "many comrades may have drawn pessimistic conclusions as regards the prospects of a Communist movement in America." For Manuilsky, the prospect before the American labor movement was "revolutionization." His more optimistic conclusion rested on two things—a Pacific war in the distant future, and an industrial crisis for the more immediate future. He was right on both counts, but wrong about the "revolutionization" they would bring about.[45]

This change of line was immediately felt in the Comintern. Even before the Fifteenth Congress, a circular letter to all Communist parties dated November 30, 1927, had instructed them to shift over, in the "overwhelming majority of cases," to the "united front FROM BELOW," the invariable sign of a "Left turn." A previous letter had already advised them "that the masses in the West are swinging to the Left."

When Lovestone read this letter to the Political Committee, the top leaders of each faction reacted to it immediately; they wanted something done to show that the American party had jumped to attention. But the full import of the new line sank in slowly.[46]

For no other American leader was it as important to adapt to the new line as it was for Lovestone. The Russian party's Fifteenth Congress, at which Stalin had committed himself to the end of capitalist stabilization, met only about three months after the American party's Fifth Convention, at which Lovestone had committed himself to the extreme American version of capitalist stabilization. As yet Stalin had merely delivered himself of a generalization without direct application to the United States. But that was the customary procedure —the general line first, then the specific application.

Thus Stalin's pronunciamento raised questions which cast a shadow on Lovestone's power: Was the end of the capitalist stabilization also to be the end of America's upward development? And if American capitalism was now to be considered on the downgrade, was its decline to be accompanied by a revolutionary period throughout the West, including the United States?

For Lovestone, as for every Communist leader in the world, a falling out between Stalin and Bukharin posed the same problems as those which the Stalin-Trotsky conflict had presented. Who was going to win in the new Russian struggle for power? And what was it necessary to say to be permitted on the victor's bandwagon?

Against Trotsky, Lovestone had come out at the head of the class. He had pitched in early and had said all the right things. Against Bukharin, Lovestone faced a more difficult and delicate problem. There existed between Lovestone and Bukharin a close personal relationship that had never existed between Lovestone and Trotsky. Bukharin's policies in the Comintern propped up Lovestone's policies in the American party.

At the end of 1927, as Stalin moved to outflank Bukharin by making a "Left turn," the prop under Lovestone began to crumble.

13

The Turning Point

As 1928 OPENED, Lovestone appeared to be firmly in command. His opponents, still dazed by his smashing victory the year before, held their fire, not knowing where he was vulnerable to attack. Early in February he completely dominated an American party plenum, and the Opposition permitted him to present a unanimous report for the Political Committee. When he said that "the party was never as homogeneous and unified in principle as it is today," it did not seem like an idle boast.[1]

Stalin's new line apparently did not hold any terrors for him. The American economy was even making an effort to bear it out. From the middle of 1927 to the middle of 1928 industrial production and factory employment fell off; some industries suffered sharply. The *Daily Worker* saluted the new year jubilantly: "The prosperity bubble has been pricked," and assured its readers that "all signs point to a rapid increase in the intensity of the class struggle." [2]

Much depended, however, on the exact estimate of the next stage. Was it a temporary recession or an ever-deepening depression? If a depression, what would it do to the Comintern's old line which was predicated on America's upward development? Would America remain an exception to the rule in the capitalist world?

For the next year and a half, Lovestone's fate was bound up with these questions, and his first attempt to answer them showed him poised to leap in whatever direction events might dictate. The United

States, he held, was not facing "an immediate, deep-going crisis"—but it was coming soon, inevitably. The bottom of the "present depression" had not been reached—but there might be an end to the depression "in a short time." The developing crisis was of a "fundamental," not merely of a "temporary, cyclical," character. "But we should not develop a disease with which we once suffered in America, where we expected the final crisis, the collapse, to be around the corner, every time unemployment increased in volume," he said. American capitalism "still has tremendous resources and reserve powers to stay this crisis, to counteract certain effects of the crisis on the economy"—yet "it would be very dangerous to overestimate the basic, the fundamental strength of American capitalism." [3]

Thus Lovestone did not start out in 1928 with any clearly defined position. He reflected the dilemma of a Communist leader caught between two lines without a clear directive from Moscow. His political conclusion at the time clearly edged over to Stalin's new line: "The class struggle in the United States is today at a turning point. The period of retreat we are leaving behind us. A period of sharp fights is ahead of us." [4]

What did the Comintern think of all this? For the time being, the Comintern was thinking mostly of other things. Its own Ninth Plenum also took place in February 1928. Since there was no "American question" on the agenda, none of the top American leaders bothered to make the trip to Moscow, and Americans already there were named as delegates.

On the main point of the agenda, Lovestone ran no risks. Bukharin's main report was devoted to justifying Trotsky's exile in Central Asia. The Lovestoneites needed little encouragement here, and the Agit-Prop Director, Wolfe, soon produced the first official anti-Trotskyist pamphlet written by an American Communist.[5] The plenum's instructions to the European parties provided the Americans with far more food for thought. The British Communists were told to declare war on the Labor party and Trade Union Congress leaders; the French Communists to attack the Socialists, the reformist trade-union federation (C.G.T.), and "Left petty-bourgeoisie"

(*Cartel des Gauches*); the German Communists to fight the Social-Democrats and trade-union leadership. Electoral alliances were prohibited and the united front from below decreed. From this plenum flowed the suicidal Communist policies which heavily contributed to Hitler's victory five years later.[6]

For Europe, then, the Ninth Plenum signified a sharp, general "turn to the Left." But were European conditions and policies to be transplanted mechanically to the United States? Should the American Communists give up their goal of a Labor party, the American equivalent of European Communist alliances with reformists?

The nearest thing to an answer came from the old oracle, John Pepper, who was one of the "American" delegates to the plenum. It appeared in an article, which seemed to bear the Comintern's official imprimatur, in the American party's theoretical organ. According to Pepper, the answer was an unequivocal no. European policies, he said, could not be mechanically applied to the United States, because European and American conditions were basically different. He enumerated five "fundamental differences": American capitalism was still on the upgrade; American imperialism was still increasing in power; the American working class was more privileged than the European; it did not have its own mass political party; and it showed no marked tendency of a Left trend on a national scale. Pepper admitted that other counteracting factors were operating to make the period a transitional one, but concluded that American conditions still demanded a Labor party.[7]

If Pepper was right, "American exceptionalism" was still orthodox Comintern doctrine. But could Lovestone trust Pepper to be his eyes and ears in Moscow in the period of Stalin's ascendancy as he had been in the heyday of Zinoviev and Bukharin? That remained to be seen.

Lozovsky's warning

Solomon Abramovich Dridzo, better known as A. Lozovsky, was a dangerous enemy to have in Moscow. In his years of exile before the Russian Bolshevik Revolution, he had headed a small trade union of Jewish hatmakers in Paris, had collaborated with Trotsky on a Russian émigré paper, and had associated himself with protests against Lenin's high-handed methods. After the revolution, he had made peace with the victorious Bolsheviks, who, lacking trade-union leaders with non-Russian experience, had rewarded him with the leadership of the Profintern. Without power of his own, he became an expert at adapting himself to the dominant powers in the Russian party and guessing what their next move would be. He was in a far better position than were the American Communists to pick the winner in the emerging struggle between Stalin and Bukharin.

Stalin's "Left turn" was peculiarly compatible with Lozovsky's own interests. The Profintern's old line of boring from within the established unions had not succeeded elsewhere much better than it had in the United States, and a shift on an international scale from boring from within to dual unionism held out the promise of reviving the Profintern as an independent factor in the trade-union world. For both personal and organizational reasons, and no doubt with Stalin's blessing, Lozovsky hastened to apply Stalin's new line to the Profintern and international Communist trade-union policy.

Unfortunately for Lovestone, Lozovsky had always been the chief protector and mentor in Moscow of Foster's faction. Lozovsky considered the Profintern's affiliate in the United States, the T.U.E.L., his sphere of influence and its leaders his wards and agents. In Zinoviev's time Lozovsky had never been able to swing enough influence in the Comintern to intimidate Ruthenberg and Lovestone. They had been accustomed to trading punches with him, and with Pepper's help had bested him so often that they had lost all fear of him. By now Lovestone underestimated the danger from Lozovsky and returned the next blow from the Profintern's chieftain as if he could still be defied with impunity.

The blow from Lozovsky fell at the trade-union commission of the Ninth Plenum. He struck at the American Communists' general trade-union policy. He accused them of taking a "waiting position," of advancing "meaningless slogans" like "Save the Union," and of appealing to the trade-union bureaucracy to organize the unorganized. He specifically pointed to the decline of John L. Lewis's United Mine Workers of America and called for the creation of new miners' unions. Engdahl and Pepper, Lovestone's representatives at the plenum, fought back gamely. They denied that the American Communists had appealed to the trade-union bureaucracy; they held out for continuing to build a Left Wing in the A.F. of L., and they opposed leaving the United Mine Workers.[8]

A cable from Engdahl and Pepper rushed to New York the ominous news of the clash in the plenum's trade-union commission. The top leadership immediately divided three ways. Lovestone backed Engdahl and Pepper and rejected Lozovsky's proposal for a new miners' union as "too precipitate." Bittelman agreed with Lozovsky on creating new unions but disagreed about entirely giving up the "Save the Union" slogan. Foster played for time by suggesting a cable to Moscow proposing that the decisions on the American mining situation be held up pending the arrival of American representatives for further discussion. Later, however, Foster joined forces with Lovestone against Lozovsky and Bittelman.[9]

In Moscow, the Ninth Plenum adopted a seemingly peculiar trade-union resolution. In general, it did not depart from the old line of "working in reactionary unions." The main report by Humbert-Droz, one of Bukharin's close associates, indignantly denied that the Comintern contemplated any change in its opposition "to the establishment of separate revolutionary trade union organizations." But the section devoted to the United States went off in a somewhat different direction; it was sufficiently ambiguous and contradictory to mean anything that the Comintern might later choose to make it mean. The American party was exhorted "on its own accord" to organize trade unions "in those branches of industry where workers are not organized at all or very inadequately organized (the steel, automobile, rubber, boot and textile industries, water-transport service, etc.)." It was also told to form a strong Left Wing in the A.F. of L. and to take the initiative in forming new mine locals without leaving the mine union.[10]

This resolution was obviously transitional and partially reflected different tendencies within the Comintern. The American section was not wholly new, but something new had been added—the Communist-organized mine locals. Lozovsky did not get all he wanted, but he did get an entering wedge.

In these circumstances, what was an American Communist leader to do? Something new and strange was going on in Moscow, and it was for the time being expressing itself in the trade-union field. But what was it? How far would Lozovsky go? What power in the Russian party or the Comintern was behind him?

It did not take long for the Americans to learn a little more about what Lozovsky wanted and how far he would go to get it. After the Comintern's Ninth Plenum in February came the Profintern's Fourth Congress in March. The Big Three of the American party, Lovestone, Foster, and Cannon, did not attend, although in the Communist world a Profintern Congress was no small event, and this was the first one in four years. Despite a cable from Lozovsky expressly asking for his presence, Foster refused to go, on the ground that the miners' campaign required his personal attention, a pretext that had not prevented him from staying in Moscow for months during other campaigns.[11] Instead, the leaders sent their lieutenants, Gitlow, Johnstone, and Dunne, with a large delegation, twenty-two in all.

On his home grounds, Lozovsky fired away again. He accused the American Communists of suffering from an "illness"—the "fear of 'dual unionism.'" He sneered at the "Save the Union" movement: "Should we save the American trade unions? We must rather save the workers from the gang that stands at the head of the American unions."[12]

These salvoes did not bring the Americans to their knees at once. The American delegation chose Bill Dunne as its spokesman to answer Lozovsky. He criticized the Russian leader's position as "one-sided," and complained that Lozovsky had put too much emphasis on building new unions, and not enough against abandoning the A.F. of L. to the "reactionary bureaucracy."[13] Gitlow made an even stronger attack on Lozovsky's proposals for new unions. Such an "error," he said, would "divorce us from the masses in the trade unions," and had already proved itself "truly catastrophic." [14] Only Foster's deputy, Johnstone, tried to appease Lozovsky, and even he cautioned against "dualism." [15]

Most of the American delegates were appalled by Lozovsky's demand for new unions. They put up a strong show of resistance but, as the sessions dragged on, the pressure on the Americans to fall into line increased relentlessly. One of the few exceptions was Albert Weisbord, who had never reconciled himself to the decision to turn over the Communist-organized textile workers in Passaic to the A.F. of L. To Weisbord's delight, Lozovsky raked up the two-year-old Passaic strike as a horrible example of surrendering to the "corrupt bureaucrats." Because Lovestone had praised the Passaic policy as a "model way" of bringing unorganized workers into the mainstream of the labor movement—the A.F. of L.—Lozovsky singled him out for special abuse. Lozovsky also fell upon Gitlow for differing with him about how much the American Communists had done to organize the Negro workers.[16]

After ten days of Lozovsky's battering, the Americans were much less belligerent. The chairman of the American delegation, Johnstone, attempted to reconcile the differences by offering three ways of organizing the unorganized—by building up the "reactionary unions," by forming new locals of old unions, and by founding entirely new unions.[17] In the end, the resolution on the "tasks" of the Americans adopted the same approach. On paper, it combined working in the old unions with building new unions and gave the T.U.E.L. a double role: "The T.U.E.L. must now become the genuine organizational center of the unorganized workers, as well as being the center of the Left wing in the reformist unions." In addition, the "Save the Union" policy was condemned as "no longer correct," and "further hope in the so-called Progressives" was ruled out as "useless and false."

One paragraph in the resolution was never published. It read:

The organization of the Left Wing in the UMW and amongst the unorganized miners must prepare to become the basis of a new union (NOT FOR PUBLICATION).[18]

This may be considered the breakthrough for Communist dual unionism. Once the principle was decreed for one union, and precisely the one in which the Communist-Progressive alliance was most promising, it was established and inexorably extended to all others.

Superficially this resolution coupled the old line of boring from within with the new line of dual unionism. The American Communists could not yet admit, even to themselves, that their "new" unions were fatally headed toward dual unionism. Lozovsky was not so squeamish. He had given away what he had in mind by twitting the Americans about their diseased fear of dual unionism, and had carefully hedged a tie-up between the new unions and the A.F. of L. with impossible conditions. Lozovsky knew, and Dunne had pointed out, that the very existence of new Communist unions would be the kiss of death to their Left Wing in the A.F. of L., and in any event the Communists did not have the resources to pursue both policies at once. Even if the policies could have been made compatible and the Communists had been stronger, the repudiation of the "Save the Union" movement and the required break with the Progressives foredoomed the Left Wing.

Although the congress represented a historic turning point in Communist trade-union policy, it received a very peculiar treatment in the American Communist press. For weeks, the most careful reader of the *Daily Worker,* the party's theoretical organ *The Communist,* and even the T.U.E.L.'s monthly, now called *Labor Unity,* could not have discovered what had happened to the American delegation at the congress.[19] But if some Americans thought that they could give Lozovsky's congress the silent treatment, they soon learned better.

In due time, the March 15, 1928 issue of *The Communist International,* then published in England, arrived in the United States. It contained an article written by Lozovsky prior to the Profintern congress. In it the Americans were told to stop "dancing a quadrille the whole time around the A.F. of L. and its various unions," and the "Save the Union" slogan was taken to task for "overevaluation of the importance of the Fascist A.F. of L." [20] Lozovsky's article, rather than the Profintern congress, created a furore in American Communist ranks. Without warning, it brought into the open an unsuspected clash between one of the highest Russian leaders and the American party's trade-union policy. Lozovsky's colorful phrase, "dancing a quadrille," buzzed through the American party and broke through its curtain of silence around the Profintern's congress.

Lozovsky's intervention could not have come at a more inconvenient moment for the Americans. For years the Communists had accused John L. Lewis of wrecking the United Mine Workers and had based their campaign to oust him on the "Save the Union" slogan. In 1926 a "Save the Union Committee," with Communist support, had nominated John Brophy, a Progressive, to oppose Lewis for the U.M.W.'s presidency. Amid charges of foul play, Brophy's challenge was beaten back, but the "Save the Union" campaign went on, feeding on the precipitous decline of the U.M.W. in the mine fields.

After months of endless preparations and concentration of all their forces, the Communists had succeeded in getting a committee of three, Brophy, Powers Hapgood, and Pat Toohey, the latter a well-known Communist, to call a "National Save the Miners Union Conference" in Pittsburgh on April 1, 1928. More than 1100 delegates from all over the country came together and a mine strike was called for April 16.

Lozovsky chose this very period to assail the "Save the Union" movement. There was no sense in "saving" the U.M.W. if, as he demanded, the Communists shifted over to building a new miners' union in opposition to it. The Communists dutifully lost interest in the "Save the Union" movement; the strike fizzled; the alliance between Brophy's Progressives and the Communists fell apart.[21] Though John L. Lewis did not know it, Lozovsky had come to his aid.

The new line-up

Suddenly John Pepper turned up in New York for his second American incarnation. Again his fortunes had sunk in Moscow and he came to the United States to outwait the storm. Pepper had been in China in 1927 during the Communist debacle, and had returned to Moscow full of criticism for the activities of the two principal Comintern representatives, Heinz Neumann of the German party and Besso Lominadze of the Russian party. Lominadze and Pepper had enlivened the Comintern's Ninth Plenum with blasts of mutual recrimination, and Pepper had more than held his own.[22] But Pepper could not hurt Neumann and Lominadze without hurting himself; they had merely carried out Stalin's orders in China. It seems that the Comintern had ordered Pepper to go to Korea, considered the graveyard of Comintern representatives. Somehow he had changed his destination to New York.

Pepper went right back into the top leadership of the American party. During his second stay in the United States, he adopted the name of "Swift" for his party activities but retained "Pepper" for his published articles. In the factional struggle, however, he decided to cast himself in a new and unfamiliar role—that of the great conciliator. "If I have come back now," he announced to the Political Committee in the middle of March 1928, soon after his arrival, "it will not, on my part, mean a continuation of any factional fight, just the opposite. I do not feel myself as a member of any group in the American Party. All the old differences have been liquidated and the Party now needs real team work." For real team work, he implied, it needed John Pepper.[23]

In the next few months, Pepper took upon himself the seemingly hopeless task of wooing his most rancorous enemy, William Z. Foster. First incredulously, then more and more sympathetically, Foster listened to Pepper's siren song. Soon a concrete issue bound them together, and to everyone's amazement, a Pepper-Lovestone-Foster community of interest began to take shape.

The concrete issue was Lozovsky's assault on the American Communists' trade-union policy. Though Lovestone and Foster knew that Lozovsky had aimed at them, neither rushed forward to engage in battle with the Profintern head. Pepper, however, was a peculiar combination of opportunism and temerity. As soon as he had sized up the American situation, he jumped into the arena against Lozovsky. Pepper playfully chided the Profintern chief for accusing the Americans of dancing an old-fashioned quadrille around the A.F. of L. instead of "the newer fancy dances in vogue like the Charleston or Black Bottom." More seriously, he foresaw "many dangers" inherent in Lozovsky's policy, leading to complete neglect of work in the A.F. of L. Instead, Pepper proposed a dual policy of putting the main emphasis on organizing the unorganized while at the same time strengthening the Left Wing within the A.F. of L. His major heresy consisted in advancing the possibility, in the event of an economic crisis, of "a new mass development" of the A.F. of L., which Lozovsky considered moribund and beyond hope.[24]

Foster and Lovestone soon agreed in principle with Pepper. Foster recommended a three-phase trade-union policy—new unions in the unorganized and semiorganized industries, a Left Wing in the old unions, and a combination of new and old unions in special circumstances. He hit back at many of Lozovsky's criticisms as "manifestly incorrect" and accused the Russian leader of failure to give a sufficient analysis of the "American situation." [25] Lovestone also dared to tilt at Lozovsky: "Is there any value in Comrade Lozovsky's line? Of course there is some, but I am convinced that there is plenty of harm in it. It puts us in danger of our weaker and more confused comrades leaving the trade unions." [26]

Pepper, Foster, and Lovestone did not go all out in their opposition to Lozovsky. They tried to meet him halfway by admitting, as Foster did, the need for greater stress on new unions on condition that the old ones were not to be abandoned. There was, on the surface, a large area of agreement: they did not openly oppose forming new unions and Lozovsky did not openly oppose working in the old unions.

Yet both sides knew that there was far more to the dispute than a matter of emphasis in trade-union policy. Each side suspected the other of something less than candor—and not without reason.

The strange alliance

It was bound to become more than a trade-union dispute if only because the American Communists had not created the problem themselves. An incident the year before showed how far the Americans had been from thinking of a change in their trade-union policy.

In 1927 Joseph Zack, a trade-union specialist in Foster's group, had been punished for advocating what proved to be premature Lozovskyism. On his own, Zack had rashly criticized the party's "chief orientation" of working inside the A.F. of L. and had proposed shifting the emphasis to organizing the unorganized outside the A.F. of L. There was little in Lozovsky's argument that Zack had not thought of first. But Zack's timing had been unlucky by a few short months. The editor of *The Communist* had devoted an article denouncing his "attitude of a blind man," and had triumphantly quoted Lenin against him. The Comintern had taken the trouble to reject some of his ideas as "completely false." Zack had sent an anguished appeal to the Comintern, explaining that he had been misunderstood and complaining that the Lovestoneites were aiming at his "political assassination." No one came to his defense, and he was shipped off to the Lenin School in Moscow.[27]

When Lozovsky leveled the same criticisms and made essentially the same proposals, a new dimension was given to the same problem. A disagreement with Lozovsky brought into play the higher forces behind Lozovsky in the Comintern, and ultimately in the Russian party. In Zinoviev's time, Lozovsky could be overruled. Now the supreme arbiter of the Communist world, Stalin, found Lozovsky a useful tool in the struggle against Bukharin. From the trade-union problem, therefore, it was just a short step to a much more profound and far-reaching problem—the relationship between the Russian and the American Communists.

And from there it was only another short step to the factional warfare in the American party. For almost a year, the furies of American factionalism had been held in leash by Lovestone's one-sided victory in 1927. The Opposition had lacked a good issue with which to upset the balance of power and early in 1928 had even stopped trying. A few weeks later, Lozovsky had providentially created an issue. Lozovsky's intervention suddenly injected new hope and militancy into the beaten and dejected Oppositionists.

With the exception of Zack, not a single Fosterite or Cannonite had ever contemplated what Lozovsky now proposed. In 1926 Johnstone, Browder, and Bittelman had waged a bitter campaign against the Passaic policy—only a pale approximation of the dual unionism that Lozovsky now had in mind. Besides Zack, Weisbord had come closest to Lozovsky's position, but he had been a Ruthenbergite and the Fosterites could not claim credit for him.

In fact, the factional line-up on the trade-union issue in 1928 was topsy-turvy. Logically the Lovestoneites should have embraced Lozovsky's new line as a continuation and justification of their former Passaic policy. But the Comintern had then slapped them down for it, and had later permitted new unions on condition that they were "linked up" with existing ones. To this edict, the Lovestoneites now remained true. The Opposition, on the other hand, had never favored any kind of new unions and had always based its trade-union policy on the organized rather than on the unorganized workers. Lozovsky's new line required the Opposition to jump over the Lovestoneites in a headlong leap from one extreme to the other.

One thing spoiled the pleasant prospect that had suddenly opened before the Opposition—the mutiny of its leader, William Z. Foster. Forced to choose between Lozovsky and Lovestone on trade-union policy, he chose—to the consternation of his co-factionalists—to side with Lovestone.

This strange alliance emerged at a plenum of the American party in May 1928. The old factional demons again seemed to possess the party. Armed with Lozovsky's criticisms, the Opposition broke loose and hurled charges of pessimism and opportunism at Lovestone's leadership in the trade-union field.

Luckily for Lovestone, the Opposition could not fling brickbats at him without hitting its own leader, Foster. For once Lovestone sidestepped in favor of Foster and let him write the trade-union resolution, adopted by the plenum with Lovestoneite votes. Despite Foster's refusal to be stampeded by Lozovsky, the resolution tried to appease the Russian leader by authorizing the Americans to organize new textile and mine unions.[28]

In the melee, Foster's old ally Cannon jumped into the breach left by Foster and led the charge of the Fosterites against Foster. History seemed to be repeating itself. The last time Foster had been put in the position of defying a Russian—Gusev—Cannon had also parted company with him.

Like Lozovsky, Cannon did not come out for leaving the old unions. He agreed that the real question was "one of emphasis," and objected to making it "either one or the other"—new unions or old. But he insisted that the "old faker-ridden unions" had failed to organize the unorganized in the period of prosperity and "will serve even less" in the period ahead. Cannon declared that the hopelessly reactionary impotence of the A.F. of L. was the real issue: "No two opinions on this question can be allowed." [29]

This presupposition that the A.F. of L. was an enemy organization without the power of growth or even survival doomed the new Communist unionism to drift, in fact if not in name, into dual unionism. It gave the Communists theoretical justification for overwhelmingly transferring their limited trade-union forces and energies outside the A.F. of L. It made such work as the Communists continued to do in the A.F. of L. a wrecking operation to get rid of an obstacle to their own unions. It compelled the Communists to split with the A.F. of L.–oriented trade-union Progressives, the only basis for a broad Left Wing in the existing unions.

When Lovestone and Foster emphasized the importance of work in the old unions, Lozovsky and Cannon rightly suspected them of sabotaging new unions. When Lozovsky and Cannon emphasized new unions, Lovestone and Foster rightly suspected them of heading toward dual unions. At this stage neither side could afford to make a clean breast of its intentions and ulterior motives.

Yet when the unorganized were organized in the next decade, it did not happen the way anyone had foreseen. The Communists' new unions organized only a tiny fraction of the unorganized. Then came what Pepper had foreseen as a possibility, "a new mass development of the American Federation of Labor unions." Finally the big push of industrial unionism by the C.I.O. took the form of a peculiar coalition between ex-A.F. of L. officials and Communists, headed by the man of whom the leader of American Communism had said in 1927 that there was "no worse gangster in the entire A.F. of L." and "no worse parasite in the labor movement"—John L. Lewis [30]—and aided by an American government which the Communists then considered near-Fascist.

The new Opposition

Was Lovestone slipping?

Halfway through 1928, he was certainly not the same lucky, cocky leader he had been at the beginning of the year. The trade-union issue first betrayed the fact that Lovestone could no longer fully control the situation. Pressure from within the American party did not make him change his mind or his policy. He still had a firm grip on the party machine, and without Foster the Opposition was too divided on this issue to force his hand.

The pressure that he was unable to resist came from Moscow. Back in February the Comintern, and in March the Profintern, had demanded a policy of new American unions. Lovestone could not defy this policy but for some time he did not apply it. Later he admitted that he had been "somewhat pessimistic for a short time about building new unions." [31] He had never reconciled himself to them and had delayed as long as he dared. Even after the decision at the American plenum in May 1928 to organize new textile and mine unions, no steps were taken immediately.

Then a reckoning in Moscow approached. The Sixth Congress of the Comintern, held in the summer of 1928, made some action imperative. The day before it opened in Moscow, a call for a new American textile union appeared. A week later, another call for a new mine union was issued.[32]

The Communists' call for a new mine union completely finished the "Save the Union" movement—"the greatest upheaval ever known in the American labor movement," as Foster had called it just before its collapse.[33] In April 1928, the month of the Pittsburgh "Save the Union" conference, Foster had solemnly warned against the danger of dual unionism among the miners.[34] Yet the following month Foster himself wrote and introduced the resolution which committed the Communists to a new mine union.

Brophy and Hapgood refused to go along, and Hapgood went to see Foster for an explanation. Hapgood recalled saying:

> Now look here, Bill, you wrote a book about the bankruptcy of the American labor movement. I think that book is a hell of a good book. In that same book you denounced dual unionism and I agreed with you one hundred per cent. I still feel the same way. Now I am told that you and the Communist party have come out for dual unionism, and frankly, Bill, I just don't understand it.

Foster looked away momentarily and answered quietly:

> Powers, the Communist party decided that policy. As a good Communist I just have to go along.[35]

In a moment of personal humiliation Foster revealed the secret of his longevity in the Communist movement.

Before leaving for the Comintern Congress the American leaders also set up a presidential campaign committee in April, and Pepper, back in the country less than a month, was put in charge of it.[36]

The tenor of the Communist campaign was determined by a resolution of the Comintern dealing with the Labor party and other current political questions in the United States.[37] It permitted the American Communists to continue their campaign for a Labor party on condition that they carried it on "from below" and in a subordinate role. It sternly upbraided them for having committed Right-Wing mistakes vis-à-vis the Socialist party, particularly in their confused support of Judge Jacob Panken in the New York municipal elections in 1927.[38] A national Communist nominating convention met in New York, May 25–27, 1928, and nominated William Z. Foster for President of the United States and Benjamin Gitlow for Vice-President.

The Stalinist Left turn was clearly reflected in the Communist election platform of 1928 for which Pepper wrote the basic draft. It went down the line for new unions, soviets, and the dictatorship of the proletariat—the latter for the last time in a Communist presidential platform.[39] In his acceptance speech, Foster fell back on the old gospel: "When a Communist heads a government in the United States—and that day will come just as surely as the sun rises (Applause)—that government will not be a capitalistic government but a Soviet government and behind this government will stand the Red Army to enforce the Dictatorship of the Proletariat (Applause)." In a sudden outburst of realism at the very end, however, Foster blurted out: "In this period the American working class is relatively apathetic." He promised its awakening, its radicalization, and its revolutionization "one day, sooner perhaps than we realize." [40]

After the nominating convention, Foster went east instead of west; the Comintern congress was more important to him than the presidential campaign. For the next three months, the Communist candidate for President ran for power in Russia rather than the United States. His running mate, Gitlow, stayed home and campaigned alone throughout the summer.

On the eve of the Comintern's Sixth Congress the factional forces in the American party were not what they had been the year before. Lovestone's enemies had seized the initiative on two fronts—they charged that he was underestimating the economic crisis and accompanying mass radicalization in the United States, and that he opposed or at least did not enthusiastically favor new unions.

Both these fighting issues had emanated directly from Moscow, the first from Stalin himself, the second doubtless from Stalin via Lozovsky. In the long run, these changes of line were only episodes in American Communist history. Far more important and enduring was what they did to the people who identified themselves with them. Armed with these issues, the Opposition succeeded in flinging the challenge at Lovestone: who was more quickly, correctly, and zealously applying the Comintern's line to the United States—Lovestone or the Opposition? The Opposition was no larger than before; it was made up of the same old names—Bittelman, Johnstone, Browder, Cannon, Dunne, and their immediate followers. It was even superficially weaker because it could not count on Foster in the crucial trade-union issue.

Nevertheless, it was suddenly imbued with a fervor and self-assurance that Lovestone lacked. It was at last able to demonstrate that it could beat Pepper and Lovestone at their own game. On all such previous occasions, when it was necessary to choose the correct—or winning—side in the Comintern and the Russian party, the Pepper-Lovestone combination had made all the correct moves. But, through their victories, Pepper and Lovestone had taught their rivals how to win. The Cominternists of Stalin's day needed only to follow in the footsteps of the Cominternists of Zinoviev's and Bukharin's day.

At the penultimate moment, however, one Oppositionist lagged behind the rest. Foster acted as front man in the creation of the new mine union which the party decreed, but he could not throw himself into the fight for the new line with the frenzy of his lieutenants. The opposition to dual unionism was his last shred of principle, and he could not give it up without a struggle.

14

The Sixth World Congress

For the first time in four years, two years late by its own statutes, the highest body in the Communist world, a World Congress of the Communist International, the Sixth, convened in the Palace of Labor of the Soviet trade unions in Moscow from July 17 to September 1, 1928. Of the 515 delegates from 58 parties or sections, 29 came from the United States, including 20 voting and 9 advisory delegates. With few exceptions, the American party was denuded of its top leadership for the duration of the congress.

The congress itself was held in the shadow of the rupture between Stalin and Bukharin. Their falling out had started with purely Russian policy. At the end of 1927, in line with his Left turn, Stalin had begun to press for a speed-up of Russian industrial development and agricultural collectivization. The first Five Year Plan, decided in principle in December 1927 but not put in operation until the following year, had precipitated a prolonged debate on the tempo and scope of the new economic program. The Stalinist "Left" had urged the most extreme objectives and methods. A "Rightist" group, headed by Bukharin, Mikhail P. Tomsky, head of the Soviet trade unions, and Alexis I. Rykov, chairman of the Council of People's Commissars, had advocated more limited goals and more moderate methods. This disagreement had crystallized prior to a plenum of the Russian party in July 1928, just before the Comintern congress; the differences had been hushed up, a unanimous resolution had been adopted, and a statement was issued denying any discord within the Russian top leadership.[1]

Actually the split had become so wide and bitter that, a week before the congress, a repentant Bukharin had secretly come to see Zinoviev's associate, Kamenev, whom he had helped to crush, to tell him of his own desperation. In a letter to Zinoviev, then banished from Moscow, Kamenev related the substance of the conversation, and quoted Bukharin as having said of Stalin: "He is an unprincipled adventurer who subordinates everything to his appetite for power. At any given moment he will change his theories in order to get rid of someone." Later this letter fell into the hands of the Trotskyists, who made it public, and Stalin used the incident to make Bukharin's situation even more disagreeable. At the time of the congress, only rumors of Bukharin's contact with Kamenev circulated among the delegates, and few knew what to believe.[2]

Those skilled in reading the telltale signs of a shakeup in the Soviet leadership could also ponder the suspicious fate of Bukharin's booklet, *Building Up Socialism.* At the end of 1926, when Bukharin replaced Zinoviev at the head of the Comintern, its theoretical organ, *The Communist International,* had begun to feature an advertisement of the booklet with these words: "Nikolai Bukharin is now acknowledged as the most outstanding theorist of the Communist International." Until the issue of April 1, 1928, or for over a year, this advertisement appeared regularly; then the booklet was relegated to a brief listing with other works. In the issue of May 15, 1928, the magazine began to feature an advertisement for a new book, *Leninism,* by J. Stalin, in these terms: "A complete, up-to-date, and authoritative book on the Communist Theory and Practice." Two months later, just before the Sixth World Congress, all mention of Bukharin's booklet disappeared.[3]

Had his booklet outlived its usefulness? Or was Bukharin no longer "acknowledged as the most outstanding theorist of the Communist International"?

A year later the mystery of the advertisements was cleared up. Stalin assailed Bukharin's booklet for its "incorrect, non-Marxist approach to the question of the class struggle in our country," its "nonsense" and "absolutely non-Marxist approach," none of which he had deemed worthy of notice for the many months it had circulated throughout the world as the latest and ripest wisdom from Soviet Russia.[4]

In the twilight period before and during the congress, the foreign Communist leaders were put to the supreme test of their ability to navigate in the treacherous waters of the Russian struggle for power without receiving official storm warnings from Moscow. Most of them came to the congress dimly aware of a crisis which only later became clear to them.

The third period

Formally the chief task of the Sixth World Congress was the adoption of a full program, which the Comintern had hitherto lacked. In fact, the delegates were far more interested in other things than fine points of doctrine. The congress reverberated with rumors of another great power struggle within the Russian party and its inevitable repercussions in the Comintern. While Bukharin and others made long speeches in the main hall, delegates promenaded up and down the large outside corridor, gossiping, speculating, and plotting.

One incident partially lifted the lid of the Russian caldron. The first item on the agenda was Bukharin's report on "The International Situation and the Tasks of the Comintern." He divided the postwar development into three periods. The first, beginning with the Russian revolutions of 1917 and ending with the German defeat of 1923, was the period of "acute revolutionary crisis." Then followed the second period, characterized by the "partial stabilization of capitalism." He defined the third and current period as one of "capitalist reconstruction." [5]

The first period was clear enough, but the second and third created trouble for Bukharin. He significantly failed to specify when the second had ended and the third had begun; and he made the third a continuation and intensification of the second rather than a disjunction and reversal. He stressed the "technical revolution" in some countries and primarily in the United States, the growth of international trusts, and a general increase of production no longer limited to one or two countries. Not only was the United States still "marching ahead," he said, but German capitalism was also "developing rather rapidly," France was "becoming transformed into a substantial industrial country," and even declining Britain was increasing its forces of production "on certain sectors." Though he held out the assurance that capitalist stabilization was "decaying," he explained it in the most general terms—the development of capitalism along new lines inevitably intensified the "contradictions of capitalism," and this, in turn, led to "the great collapse, the final catastrophe." [6]

The same words did not mean the same thing to Bukharin and Stalin. To Bukharin, the third period meant a greater and more general development of capitalist production in the present, leading to a catastrophic collapse in the indefinite future. To Stalin, it meant a collapsing stabilization in the present, leading to a "revolutionary upsurge" in the immediate future.

After Bukharin's report, the two interpretations provoked a clash within the Russian delegation. Instead of submitting his report to the Russian delegation first, Bukharin had sent copies to it and to the foreign delegations at the same time. Until then the Russian delegation had been accustomed to dictate to the Russian head of the Comintern by passing on all such documents in advance.

The Russian delegation, controlled by Stalin, hit back at Bukharin by finding fault with his "theses" in about twenty places, including the definition of the "third period." The delegation obliged Bukharin to present an amendment which gave more emphasis to the intensification of the contradictions of capitalism. The final version contained elements of both interpretations without fusing them into a single, unified whole. This incident created, as Stalin later put it, not without relish, "a rather awkward situation" for Bukharin.[7]

There was fire as well as smoke, then, in the gossip, speculation, and intrigue about Bukharin. Hints and innuendoes assailed the foreign delegates, who had no means of assessing the facts. The

Stalinist hatchetmen, Neumann and Lominadze, went around whispering about Bukharin's contagious "political syphilis." [8] To a favored few in each delegation, they dangled offers of private interviews in the Kremlin with the real power, Stalin. Delegates from afar, who had come to Moscow without the slightest doubt of Bukharin's greatness, wondered whether they had been worshiping the wrong idol.[9] Yet they could hardly believe their senses. It was Bukharin and not Stalin who occupied the limelight at the congress, and it was Bukharin who lent his enormous intellectual prestige to the theoretical justification of every controversial proposition.

Only once did Bukharin drop his guard and indicate that he knew what was going on. He did so, most delicately, by quoting an unpublished letter from Lenin to Zinoviev and himself, containing the following advice: "If you are going to expel all the not very obedient but clever people, and retain only the obedient fools, you will most assuredly ruin the party." [10]

As in a Greek tragedy, Bukharin himself said and did the things which paved the way for his own destruction. He identified the Right Wing as the "greatest danger" in the Comintern, so that Stalin had only to identify Bukharin himself as the Right Wing in the Russian party. He compromised himself by accepting Stalin's premise of a third period, but redefined it in such a way that it seemed like a continuation of the second one. He permitted himself to be so disarmed by the Stalin-controlled discipline of the party that he made no effort to clarify the issues and thoroughly confused his own well-wishers. He assumed responsibility for a policy which he did not believe in, and which doomed him to political annihilation, just as ten years later in the purge trials he assumed responsibility for a confession which he did not believe in and which doomed him to physical annihilation.

Yet the full Stalinization of the Comintern awaited Bukharin's departure. The Sixth World Congress fell somewhere between the positions of Bukharin and Stalin and therefore assumed a basically transitional character. This can be seen most clearly in the patchwork definition of the third period, but there were other indications as well. The demand for the "united front from below" still distinguished between Social-Democratic workers and leaders, a distinction soon to be wiped out. The trade-union directive still combined forming "revolutionary industrial" unions with winning over the "reformist" unions. The theory of social-fascism presented itself, not for the first time, in embryo.[11]

The timing of Stalin's Left turn showed that it had little to do with the state of capitalism. At the end of 1927 capitalism showed no signs of collapse. The American crash was still two years away. Even when capitalist stabilization gave way to capitalist crisis, the Stalinist third-period policies of extremism and isolation provided the conditions for a fascist rather than a revolutionary upsurge.

The other theoretical underpinning of the third period—the change that had allegedly taken place in Social-Democracy—was hardly more tenable. Nothing had happened in the Social-Democratic parties between 1926 and 1928 to make them the justification for a major upheaval in Communist policy; in any case the Social-Democrats could not get any worse than the Communists had already painted them.

The explanation for the Stalinist third period must be sought in Russia and not in the outside world. By 1927, the Soviet regime faced a serious deficit in the supply of grain made available by the peasant villages to the industrialized cities. The peasants held back their produce because they could not exchange it for sufficient industrial goods, and industry suffered for want of adequate provisions to satisfy the minimum needs of its workers. Stalin's solution—to speed up the collectivization of agriculture and the productivity of industry—was not novel; Trotsky had urged it earlier against Stalin's opposition. But the means used by Stalin were unprecedented in the magnitude of their brutality. The forced collectivization of agriculture and the speed-up of industrialization at the cost of millions of lives and the total suppression of all freedom of criticism inside as well as outside the party transformed the abstraction of "socialism in one country" into the reality of a vast police state and an unrestrained personal despotism.

After Trotsky's downfall, only Stalin's allies, Bukharin, Rykov, and

Tomsky, stood in the way of his Left turn—and of Stalin's absolute rule in the Soviet state, the Russian Communist party, and the world Communist movement. In this way policy and power were intermingled. The Left turn served Stalin's tactical ends in the Russian struggle by signifying the ideological equivalent of a declaration of war on the Bukharinite "Right Wing." It also outflanked the Trotskyist Left Opposition, which was confused and divided by the maneuver.

Through the Comintern, the Russian struggle was internationalized. Every little Stalin in the world needed his little Bukharin, his Left turn, and his "conciliators with the Right danger." And the American party was no exception.

The Right danger

The Americans at the congress lapped up all the rumors but did not know which of them to swallow.

"There was a great deal of speculation as to what was really going on in the Russian party," Cannon recalls, "but no one seemed to know." He personally received inside information from his factional ally, Clarence Hathaway, who spoke with the authority of one who had just finished a full three-year course at the Lenin School. The provincial Minnesota trade-unionist, transformed into an international Muscovite politician, briefed him on the mounting campaign against the Right Wing of Rykov and Tomsky but apparently stopped short of implicating Bukharin himself.

Cannon, like the other Americans, could only feel his way through this fog of hearsay and gossip. Stalin's system of playing his cards close to the vest and forcing everyone, outside his own narrow circle, to guess at his intentions, did not make it easy to become a Stalinist. Cannon has described the method of selecting would-be Stalinists through their reaction to Stalin's action:

> They were required to "guess" what it meant and to adapt themselves in time. Selections of people and promotions were made by the accuracy of their guesses at each stage of development in the factional struggle. Those who guessed wrong or didn't guess at all were discarded. This guess-

ing game was played to perfection in the period of Stalin's preparation to dump Bukharin. I don't think many people knew what was really going on and what was already planned at the time of the Sixth Congress.[12]

It was not yet safe for any American to attack Bukharin openly, and no one did. But it was perfectly safe to attack the Right Wing, which Bukharin himself in his opening report had designated the greatest danger in the Comintern. The only question was which Americans could successfully pin the Right Wing label on which other Americans.

The first move was made on the day Bukharin's opening report was distributed. A document entitled "The Right Danger in the American Party" was submitted to the Anglo-American Secretariat of the Comintern. It was signed by J. W. Johnstone, M. Gomez, W. F. Dunne, J. P. Cannon, Wm. Z. Foster, A. Bittelman, and G. Siskind. Bittelman was chiefly responsible for it, and all seven signers were Foster-Cannon factionalists in high standing. The document summed up the case against Lovestone which the Opposition had been developing for the past six months. In essence, it accused him of overestimating the strength of American capitalism and underestimating the extent of American radicalization. On the first count, it took the position that "American capitalism is about to reach the apex of growth," thereby contributing what came to be known as Bittelman's "apex theory." On the second, it made the discovery of a "general growth of discontent, militancy, and readiness to struggle" among the American semiskilled and unskilled workers, and a "widespread and general radicalization" in all industries among the most exploited workers.[13]

The title of this document, more than anything else, packed political dynamite. At the psychological moment, as the Comintern gave the signal for a witch hunt of the Right Wing, it pinned the fatal label on the Lovestoneites. Henceforth, who was Right Wing mattered far more than who was right or wrong.

For the Americans, the congress quickly degenerated into an orgy of denunciation. There was no struggle of principle between clearly defined, consciously articulated Left and Right wings. Each faction strove desperately to force the other into the position of being the Right Wing, a mutual need which left little room for consistency or convictions on either side.

Dunne and Foster deplored and decried the resistance to the new unions—despite their own records. Lovestone repressed his own misgivings so thoroughly that he boasted of new unions which did not yet exist. Pepper went all the way back to the 1924 elections for conclusive evidence of the Opposition's incurable Right Wing disease. Bittelman triumphantly cited the 1928 Communist election platform to prove that the faction in power wanted to "reform" the capitalist state—by abolishing the Senate, the Supreme Court, and the President's veto power.[14]

If the congress had awarded a prize to the most attacked delegate, Pepper would have won it easily. The American Oppositionists, Dunne, Bittelman, Cannon, and Foster, made him their favorite personal target. Lominadze used the congress to settle accounts with Pepper in revenge for the latter's criticism of his role in China; incidentally he also rallied to the support of the American Opposition on the state of American capitalism and the perspective for American radicalization.

In the running battle between himself and Pepper throughout the congress, Lominadze scored some damaging hits. "Comrade Pepper is a capable and experienced man," he said, "but his demeanor —petty intrigues and quarrelsomeness—makes it impossible to treat him with the consideration due to a serious politician." In another wounding thrust, he accused Pepper of changing his position "in the course of a day or an hour" to avoid disagreement with "some authoritative comrade" in the Comintern. Lominadze concluded: "By such tactics Pepper has shown once more that he fully deserves the position which he has created for himself in the Communist International."

Neumann struck a blow at Pepper's "unprincipled manner." Lozovsky delighted all of Pepper's enemies by calling Pepper "the muddler of two hemispheres." The head of the Anglo-American Secretariat,

Petrovsky, engaged in a bitter dispute with Pepper on the nature of the economy of India. Pepper took on all comers and gave as much punishment as he received, but he could not go on collecting enemies forever without paying for it.[15]

Lovestone also enjoyed battles more than he could afford them. He made Lozovsky the butt of his most scathing remarks. Echoing Lozovsky's own words against Pepper, he referred to "Comrade Lozovsky, who has been making a muddle of nearly everything he has touched." [16] Behind the scenes in committee sessions, Lovestone and Lozovsky staged some of the most riotous brawls of the congress. Never before had an American Communist dared to make such insolent attacks on a high Russian leader.[17]

Even more daringly, Lovestone took the lead in defending Bukharin. At the last meeting of the "Senioren Konvent," a so-called Council of Elders made up of delegation heads, Lovestone hotly denounced what he called the "Corridor Congress" against Bukharin. A special meeting was called, with Bukharin as chairman, at which, on behalf of the Russian delegation, Stalin made a formal denial of the rumors of differences within the Russian leadership. Since the differences existed, as Stalin later admitted, Lovestone's action hardly helped to endear him to Stalin.[18]

Foster stood to benefit most from Pepper's and Lovestone's difficulties. But hard luck always dogged Foster whenever he approached close to power. Comintern representatives had frustrated him in 1925 and 1927. Now he blocked his own way.

Foster's embarrassment at the congress arose from the fact that Lozovsky and others could not attack Lovestone on the trade-union issue without implicating him. Lovestone did not fail to point out that he had merely voted for Foster's trade-union resolution at the American party's most recent plenum. Thereupon Foster's associates called on him to repudiate his previous position and promise to repent.

Foster's conscience permitted him to join in attacking Lovestone for resisting the new unions, but he boggled at donning sackcloth and ashes himself. This intramural crisis blew up in Foster's face at a private meeting of the joint Foster-Cannon caucus. The entire Fosterite faction rose against its leader and savagely flayed him for betraying its interests. Bittelman, Johnstone, and Browder, his principal co-workers, stepped forth as his chief inquisitors. Cannon has described one scene:

> Foster stood over Johnstone threateningly, with his fist clenched, and tried his old trick of intimidation with the snarling remark: "You're getting pretty bold!" Johnstone, almost hysterical, answered: "You have been trampling on me for years, but you're not going to trample on me any more." Johnstone and Browder gave the impression at this meeting of people who had broken out of long confinement and were running wild.[19]

As a result of this fracas, Foster lost control of his own faction and Bittelman took over. Because of Foster's refusal to admit his "mistakes," Bittelman delivered the minority report in the American Commission. For the next few months, he replaced Foster as the acknowledged leader of their faction.[20]

Browder's role at the congress differed somewhat from those of the other Oppositionists. After serving a year as the American party's Profintern representative in Moscow, he had been sent to China in 1927 with the Englishman Tom Mann and the Frenchman Jacques Doriot, in a so-called International Workers Delegation, sponsored by the Comintern. Browder then spent most of the next two years in the Far East as secretary of the Profintern-sponsored Pan-Pacific Secretariat and editor of its organ, the *Pan-Pacific Monthly*.

During this long tour of foreign duty, a significant change came over Browder. He recognized Stalin as the strong man in the Russian party and guided himself accordingly; he obtained an intimate knowledge of the inner workings of the international Communist movement and increasingly saw the world through the eyes of a working Comintemist. Moreover, he gradually rebelled at being considered a subordinate member of Foster's entourage and saw himself as an independent factor in the American factional struggle. On a trip to Moscow in January 1928, six months before the Sixth World Congress, he had spoken against the "developing Right Wing line" in the American party and had disassociated himself from all former party groupings. At the congress, he continued to hold himself aloof to the extent of refusing to sign the Foster-Cannon declaration against the Right danger, but publicly identified himself with its political position. While this show of independence was to the other factionalists little more than an empty gesture, it laid the basis for his emergence as a candidate in his own right for the leadership of the American party.[21]

Throughout the congress, the Opposition carried the fight to Lovestone. It tried to get the congress to send the American party an open letter instructing it to effect a change of policy. When that failed, Foster scored a personal triumph—a private interview with Stalin.

Foster and Johnstone hastened to send their co-factionalists at home a letter boasting of Stalin's encouragement to their cause. In due time, Gitlow, who was holding the fort for Lovestone, got wind of the letter and commissioned one of his henchmen to filch it. The mission successfully accomplished, Gitlow promptly reported its contents in a long cable to Lovestone who vainly tried to get Stalin to repudiate it. The Lovestoneites subsequently published part of this letter.

Foster reported:

> On the inner Party situation, he [Stalin] said he was opposed to our proposal for the removal of the Lovestone group from power at one blow, that this cannot be done from the top—meaning from here—leaving the implication that it must be done from below—at home. We very soon told him that we were not making such a proposal, but that our proposition was that the Communist International send an Open Letter to our Party criticizing the Right line of the Central Committee and the Lovestone group, and that a convention of the Party be held two months after the presidential elections. He stated that no good could come out of the Lovestone group, that they simply liked to play with policies and mass work. Although he did not commit himself to any particular program, we feel that in him we have a very good friend and supporter. We drew to his attention the fact that Bukharin had not criticized the Right-wing danger in the American Party and he said he would have to read the uncorrected stenogram of the Bukharin speech and that he would have a talk with him the following morning before going on his

vacation for a month. We were very satisfied with the interview. How much he will actually intervene in our behalf here is an open question. . . .

Our conclusions from these meetings were about the following lines: *That Stalin was decidedly against the Lovestone group and in favor of us,* that he will have little influence in the present struggle now, *but that the main support will come after we show him in the next few months that we are a fighting group and are fighting in the Party for our position.* [Italics in original.] [22]

Months later, Stalin gave his version of the interview. According to Stalin, Foster complained to him of the "factionalism and unprincipledness" of Lovestone's group; Stalin agreed but added that Foster's group was guilty of the "same sins." Stalin also expressed surprise that Foster should have drawn the "singular conclusion" that his group could count on Stalin's support.[23] Whichever version may be believed, the decisive role that Stalin had assumed in the American factional struggle is common to both accounts, and the only matter in dispute is the extent to which he committed himself to one side. The future bore out Foster's expectations with singular accuracy, and it is not hard to believe that Foster had shrewdly estimated the practical effect of Stalin's attitude.

Bittelman and Gomez also had an interview with Molotov during the congress. Bittelman did most of the talking about the differences in the American Party. He accomplished his main purpose by assuring Molotov that Lovestone "was speculating on Bukharin" in the rumored division within the Russian party. Molotov listened impassively and made no commitment. But the two Americans left highly satisfied with the result; they had succeeded in getting across the message linking Lovestone with Bukharin.[24]

Just before the congress closed, Johnstone went to greater lengths than any American Oppositionist had ever dared to go at a Comintern congress. In the name of five others, including Dunne and Bittelman, he read a statement expressing their disagreement with the section of the political theses dealing with the American party. It scored the section on eight counts for insufficiently emphasizing the "growing contradictions confronting American imperialism," the "increasing radicalization" of the American masses, and the Right danger in various aspects of the party's work. Three names were significantly missing from Johnstone's group—Foster, Cannon, and Browder.[25]

Johnstone's bombshell, in defiance of the Comintern's code of discipline, failed to shake Lovestone's confidence. In reply, Lovestone made the most of the opportunity to demonstrate his superior loyalty to the Comintern and its Russian leadership. He pointedly offered his own group's "full acceptance and the hearty endorsement of the theses on the political situation as presented by the Russian Delegation," and read into Johnstone's failure to get the congress to send an open letter to the American party "a vote of confidence" in his leadership.[26] He saw no cause for alarm in the American section of the theses, which gave the American party credit for "more lively activity," especially among the miners and in the Sacco-Vanzetti case, and took it to task for some "Right mistakes" in connection with the Socialist party, Negro work, and anti-imperialist propaganda. On the whole, the American party's report card compared favorably with that of most other parties.[27]

The top committees appointed by the congress also lulled Lovestone's normally acute sense of danger. The new Executive Committee of the Communist International included three Americans, Lovestone, Foster, and Gomez, as full members, and two others, Gitlow and Otto E. Huiswoud, as candidates. One American, Weinstone, was put on the International Control Commission. The extreme Oppositionists, now commanded by Bittelman and Johnstone, failed to receive any recognition.[28]

It is clear in retrospect that the Sixth World Congress should have warned Lovestone that his fences in Moscow needed mending desperately and without delay. It is equally clear that he failed to take the warning signals seriously. He based his optimistic judgment of the congress on Bukharin's retention of nominal leadership, the official denial of disagreement among the Russians, the rejection of the American Opposition's demand for a critical open letter, the mildly worded American section of the theses, and the appointments to the Comintern's highest top committees. The congress, after all, was the Comintern's highest body and its decisions were presumably binding on all Communists until the next congress. In the next few months, the Opposition thought of no new charges against Lovestone that had not been brought up at the congress. Formally, Lovestone emerged the victor from the congress. But the struggle for power in the Russian party and in the Comintern was not governed by formalities.

The Sixth World Congress in Moscow also contributed two new features to the American radical scene—a unique Communist policy for American Negroes and the birth of American Trotskyism. Both of these repay careful re-examination, for their own intrinsic interest and for the light they cast on the basic forces at work before, during, and after the Sixth World Congress. After considering these two aspects of the American scene, we shall return to the struggle for power and its climax.

15

The Negro Question

THE most obscure and puzzling chapter in the story of American Communism has long been its one-time policy for Negroes in the South—"the right of self-determination of the Negroes in the Black Belt." For many years this policy was exclusively associated with the Communists and, more than any other theoretical and practical program, distinguished them from other American radical movements.

To trace the development of the Communist position on the Negro question, we must roam far afield in both the Negro and Communist past. Long as the trail may be, it will take us to many forgotten phases of American Negro history and to many of the most closely guarded secrets of American Communism.

In the older Socialist tradition, no special Negro program existed, and no need for one was recognized. The Socialist views ranged from the equality militantly espoused by William English Walling, a founder of the National Association for the Advancement of Colored People, to the racial inequality argued by Victor Berger. Segregation prevailed in the Socialist party's southern branches. The Socialist *Appeal to Reason* once envisioned the separation of Negroes and whites in a Socialist America with Negro cities, plantations, and shops, "black cities," as "beautiful as those the whites live in." The Socialist party, David A. Shannon wrote, "made no special effort to attract Negro members, and the party was generally disinterested in, if not actually hostile to, the effort of Negroes to improve their position in American capitalist society." In the main, the Socialist and Socialist Labor parties avoided dealing with the Negro problem as such; they equated it with the general social problem and told the Negroes that they would have to wait for socialism to achieve complete social equality. Eugene Victor Debs expressed this position uncompromisingly: "We have nothing special to offer the Negro, and we cannot make separate appeals to all the races. The Socialist party is the party of the whole working class, regardless of color—the whole working class of the whole world." [1]

The earliest American unions excluded Negroes more often than they admitted them, or else they organized Negroes separately. The first important national trade-union federation, the National Labor Union of 1866–72, recognized the need for breaking down the barriers between Negro and white workers but accomplished little against the separatist tendencies on both sides. The next dominant labor organization, the Knights of Labor, for the first time made a real effort to organize Negro workers and reported at its high point in 1885 that "Negroes were flocking" into it. In this field as in others, however, the collapse of the Knights after the formation of the American Federation of Labor in 1886 reversed the trend.

In its first years, the A.F. of L. professed to uphold the same principles of labor solidarity, irrespective of race or color, but the autonomous craft unions soon made this portion of the A.F. of L.'s creed a dead letter. The affiliated unions usually made a practice of excluding Negroes, and the A.F. of L.'s leaders lacked power to intervene. As early as 1900 the A.F. of L. resorted to the futile and tainted device of issuing its own charters to separate Negro locals. As a result, the A.F. of L for half a century largely evaded the problem of, or blocked the way to, organizing Negroes. The I.W.W., on the other hand, tried to live up to its constitutional provision that "no working man or woman shall be excluded from membership in unions because of creed or color." It issued thousands of membership books to Negroes, but its organizational instability lost them as easily as they came in.[2]

The rejected strain

In American Negro history, the central aim of the struggle for Negro liberation has always been the achievement of full social, economic, and political equality. But some who have despaired of ever achieving equality in the United States have sought other means, notably migration to new territory, inside or outside the United States. These emigration schemes have traditionally been linked with Negro separatism and national consciousness.

Isolated examples of Negro references to the American Negroes as a "nation" have come down from the late eighteenth and early nineteenth centuries, but even the Communist student who has assiduously collected them has emphasized their "purely verbal character." [3] Before the Civil War, Martin R. Delany, an associate of the Negro abolitionist, Frederick Douglass, gave clear expression to the conjuncture of Negro emigration and nationhood. In 1852 he advocated a Negro nation on the eastern coast of Africa in which "colored adventurers from the United States and elsewhere" could settle. "We are a nation within a nation," he wrote; "as the Poles in Russia, the Hungarians in Austria; the Welsh, Irish, and Scotch in the British dominions." Douglass did not share Delany's view. After the Civil War and the disillusionment following the collapse of Reconstruction, migration sentiment again rose. A "Negro Exodus" took place in 1879 and 1881, mainly from Louisiana and South Carolina to Kansas. An African Emigration Association, established in 1881, aimed at a "United States in Africa, modeled after this government, and under the protecting care of the same." Fifteen years later another "Back-to-Africa" prophet, Bishop Henry M. Turner, called on two or three million American Negroes to "return to the land of our ancestors, and establish our own nation, civilization, laws, customs, style of manufacture." At about the same time, attention in some Negro circles turned to the sparsely settled territory of Oklahoma or parts of Texas as the most suitable place for an independent Negro republic or predominantly Negro state.[4]

These early American Negro intimations of "nationhood," however, were not known to the Communists when they adopted their own position on the American Negro problem as a "national question." Long after the American Communist movement had come to it by another path, a Communist student dug them out of long-buried historical archives to provide the Communist position with native antecedents.[5]

In any case, these "ideological forerunners" claimed by the Communists suggest two things.

First, they indicate that there has been an offshoot of American Negro life which has sought some form of separate political existence to escape from the subjection and rejection suffered by the Negroes in American society. These counsels of desperation long antedated the Communists and rose out of totally different influences. Nevertheless, they should caution against the easy assumption that the Communists, whatever the derivation of their policy, totally lacked an indigenous basis for making converts to a "national" interpretation of the Negro question.

Second, this aspect of American Negro history has been remarkably weak and spasmodic. Martin R. Delany viewed the Negroes as a "nation within a nation" in 1852, but he utterly failed to strike a responsive chord in the Negro people; these "forerunners" constituted a rejected strain in American Negro life and were consigned to historical oblivion long before the Communists discovered them. In view of the American Negroes' travail, it is less surprising that such a strain has existed than that it has not been far more influential and insistent.

Of all nationalistic, "Back-to-Africa" movements, the greatest was Marcus Garvey's Universal Negro Improvement Association. Garvey, a native of Jamaica, brought his U.N.I.A. to the United States in 1916 after two years of slight success in the West Indies. He preached "Africa for the Africans at home and abroad" by mass migration and independent business enterprises. Though his program was ostensibly African, he set up his "Empire" and "armed forces" in the United States—an imperial travesty with himself as Provisional President, assisted by a Supreme Potentate and a Supreme Deputy Potentate, and surrounded by such honorary orders as the Knights of the Nile, Dukes of Nigeria and Uganda, and Distinguished Service Order of Ethiopia. A Universal African Legion, Universal Black Cross Nurses, Universal African Motor Corps and Black Eagle Flying Corps hinted of a potential military reconquest of Africa.[6]

However much of a demagogue and charlatan Garvey may have been, the tens of thousands who flocked to his meetings and gave him money with which to buy ships for his ill-fated Black Star Line expressed through him genuine hopes and resentments. The U.N.I.A. was essentially an American Negro movement in the guise of an African fantasy. It showed that recently uprooted Negro migrants from the Southern states and recently arrived immigrants from the West Indies could respond in large numbers to the old appeal of nationalism and emigrationism—a spurious nationalism and an imaginary emigrationism.

Another type of "New Negro" also emerged toward the end of the First World War. With the publication of the *Messenger* in 1917, socialism gained its first American Negro organ. Its editors, Chandler Owen and A. Philip Randolph, defined their "New Negro" in terms of political and social equality, economic betterment, and radical methods. They cheered on the Communist revolutions in Europe but greeted the emergent American Communist movement much more circumspectly. They kept aloof from the Communist-Socialist battle in 1919, without leaving the Socialist camp.[7]

"For the first time in the Negro's history, he has a Left Wing or Radical group," a Negro writer noted in 1920. "It is socialistic to the core." [8] In this ferment, peculiarly, the Communists lagged far behind.

Reed's report

The first American Communists carried on in the Socialist tradition. They showed no special interest in the Negro problem and subordinated it wholly to the general social problem.

There is no record of Negro participation in the foundation of the American Communist movement in 1919. The Communist Party of America, however, devoted a paragraph to the Negro problem in its first program that year. "The Negro problem is a political and economic problem," it maintained. "The racial oppression of the Negro is simply the expression of his economic bondage and oppression, each intensifying the other. This complicates the Negro problem, but does not alter its proletarian character." The Communist Labor party's program ignored the subject. In the next two years, Communist programs treated it in one way or the other.[9]

Two of the earliest American Negro Communists came from the *Messenger* group. The first, Otto E. Huiswoud, a native of Dutch Guiana in South America and by profession a union printer in New York, had also been active in the Harlem branch of the Socialist party before he went over to the Communists, probably by 1920. The other, Lovett Fort-Whiteman, had served as the *Messenger*'s first drama critic and joined the Communists a year or two later.[10]

The first discussion on record of the Negro problem by an American Communist took place in Russia, not in the United States. One of the subjects on the agenda of the Comintern's Second Congress in 1920 was the "national and colonial question." When Lenin submitted a draft of his theses to the delegates, he asked them for opinions and suggestions, particularly on sixteen points. The fourteenth read: "The Negroes in America." [11] In the committee, which Lenin himself headed, the American Negroes were discussed at length. One of the American delegates, John Reed, delivered two reports on the American Negro problem, one to the committee and the other to the congress.[12]

Reed defined the American Negro problem as "that of a strong racial and social movement, and of a proletarian labor movement advancing very fast in class-consciousness." He alluded to the Garvey movement in terms that ruled out all Negro nationalism and separatism: "The Negroes have no demands for national independence. All movements aiming at a separate national existence for Negroes fail, as did the 'Back to Africa Movement' of a few years ago. They consider themselves first of all Americans at home in the United States. This makes it very much simpler for the Communists." The Communists should not stand aloof from Negro movements for social and political equality, Reed advised, but should use them to point out the futility of bourgeois equality and the necessity of the social revolution to free the Negroes as well as all other workers from servitude.[13]

After Reed's report, the Comintern decided to invite a "commission" of Negro "revolutionists" to come to Russia as guests of the Soviet Union.[14] Evidently as a result of this plan, which was never carried out in full, John Reed sent an invitation to the American Negro poet, Claude McKay, which resulted in his visit to Russia two years later.[15]

Also at the Second Congress, Lenin mentioned the American Negroes in the "Theses on the National and Colonial Question," but that is discussed later in connection with Lenin's other references to the subject.

Organizationally, it seems, Lenin was responsible for the American Communists' first activity among American Negroes. According to Joseph Zack, the American Communists received a letter from Lenin some time in 1921 expressing surprise that their reports to Moscow made no mention of party work among Negroes and urging that they should be recognized as a strategically important element in Communist activity. Zack, formerly the section organizer in Yorkville and Harlem, was thereupon put in charge of Negro work, the first to serve in this function in the American party.[16]

Toward the end of 1921, the first discussion articles on "The Party and the Negro Struggle" appeared in the Communist press. "The Negroes of America have hardly been touched by our propaganda," the first article, of which Zack was co-author, admitted. "Of all the races and nationalities of this country they are the farthest removed from class concepts and class organization. But they are dissatisfied and potentially rebellious. How can we give a class character to their dissatisfaction and protest? How can we draw the Negro masses into the struggle against the oppressors of all workers? What shall the Party do to win the Negroes for Communism?"

A second article attempted to give the answer: "Our task is not to oppose such aspirations as a free Africa, race equality, social equality, and better conditions, but rather to intensify those aspirations and help to direct them into effective channels. The most important point in our agitation must be to *fix responsibility for the Negro's sufferings where it rightly belongs: on the bourgeoisie and their Capitalist-Imperialist System!*" Summing up the Communist position, the article concluded: "Thus we see that the Negro struggle takes on the aspect of a racial as well as a class struggle. Fundamentally it is, of course, a struggle against Capitalism and Imperialism." [17]

The Workers party, formed in December 1921, devoted an entire section of its program to "The Race Problems." It promised to fight for the Negroes' economic, political, and social equality, to destroy the barrier of "race prejudice," and to "weld" black and white workers "into a solid union of revolutionary forces for the overthrow of their common enemy." [18]

This spurt of interest in the Negro problem in 1921 led, after the affiliation of Huiswoud and one or two others previously, to the first small influx of Negroes into the American party through a hitherto mysterious Negro organization, the African Blood Brotherhood, and its founder, Cyril V. Briggs.

Briggs and the Brotherhood

The American Communists have never given credit to the one real forerunner of "self-determination" in their own ranks—Cyril V. Briggs.

Briggs came to the United States in 1905 at the age of seventeen from the little island of Nevis in the British West Indies. He started working for the *Amsterdam News* in New York in 1912 and served as its chief active editor during the First World War. In its editorial columns, he opposed Negro participation in the war and proposed various schemes for Negro "self-determination." When pressure against his anti-war stand was brought to bear on the paper, he resigned in 1918 in protest against the publisher's attempt to censor his editorials. He soon received financial backing to start his own publication, a monthly magazine, *The Crusader,* the first issue of which was dated September 1918.[19]

In September 1917, just before the Bolshevik Revolution, Briggs wrote in the *Amsterdam News* a two-part editorial entitled, " 'Security of Life' for Poles and Serbs—Why Not for Colored Americans?" Departing from Garvey's plan for a Negro state in Africa, he advanced the idea that the "race problem" could be solved by setting up an independent Negro nation on American territory. "Considering that the more we are outnumbered, the weaker we will get, and the weaker we get the less respect, justice or opportunity we will obtain, is it not time to consider a separate political existence, with a government that will represent, consider, and advance us?" he argued. "As one-tenth of the population, backed with many generations of unrequited toil and half a century of contribution, as free men, to American prosperity, we can with reason and justice demand our portion for purposes of self-government and the pursuit of happiness, one-tenth of the territory of continental United States." Unlike the Communist self-determinationists who followed him, however, he suggested locating the "colored autonomous State" in the West, either in the states of Washington, Oregon, and Idaho or, as he thought preferable, in California and Nevada, then relatively sparsely settled, rather than in the Deep South.[20]

After President Woodrow Wilson had promulgated the Fourteen Points in January 1918, Briggs pushed his program by identifying the plight of the American Negroes with that of the European nations occupied by Germany. "With what moral authority or justice," Briggs demanded in the *Amsterdam News,* "can President Wilson demand that eight million Belgians be freed when for his entire first term and to the present moment of his second term he has not lifted a finger for justice and liberty for over TEN MILLION colored people, a nation within a nation, a nationality oppressed and jimcrowed, yet worthy as any other people of a square deal or failing that, a separate political existence?" [21]

By 1919 Briggs advocated in *The Crusader* a Negro state in Africa, South America, or the Caribbean to which American Negroes could emigrate. Two years later he speculated that such a state would not necessarily require "a wholesale exodus of American Negroes," but he thought that they might well prefer to build up their own state elsewhere "in preference to helping build up a state in which the vast majority are white and in which the rights of minorities would always be dependent upon the *state of mind* of the majority." [22]

At first *The Crusader* sympathized with the Socialists and in 1918 and 1919 it supported Socialist candidates. At the same time, however, it came out for an alliance with Bolshevism against "race prejudice." [23] Gradually it edged over to a combination of the national and the social, which it most clearly expressed in the spring of 1921: "The surest and quickest way, then, in our opinion, to achieve the salvation of the Negro is to combine the two most likely and feasible propositions, viz.: salvation for all Negroes through the establishment of a strong, stable, independent Negro State (along the lines of our own race genius) in Africa and elsewhere; and salvation for all Negroes (as well as other oppressed people) through the establishment of a Universal Socialist Co-operative commonwealth." [24]

Despite some of the similarity in their aims, Briggs attacked Garvey for running a one-man movement. Subsequently Garvey's rejection of an offer of cooperation brought another blast from Briggs against Garvey's "loose chatter and mock heroics." Garvey hit back at the light-complexioned Briggs by calling him a white man passing himself off as a Negro. Briggs sued for libel, and forced Garvey to apologize publicly.[25]

At the end of *The Crusader*'s first year, Briggs founded an organization around the magazine, called the African Blood Brotherhood. It was first mentioned in the issue of December 1919 as the African Blood Brotherhood "for African Liberation and Redemption," later changed to "for immediate protection and ultimate liberation of Negroes everywhere." [26] Since it was a romantic revolutionary secret organization, the Brotherhood discouraged familiarity and it is only now possible to clear up some of the mystery surrounding it.[27]

The name of the Brotherhood derived from an African rite of fraternization by mingling drops of blood.[28] Briggs started the organization with less than twenty members, all in Harlem and most of them West Indian in origin. It gradually spread to other sections of the United States and the West Indies but at its peak never exceeded 3000 members. It influenced many more, however, through its organ, *The Crusader,* which reached a circulation of 36,000, and the Crusader News Service, which provided some 200 Negro papers with a free weekly service. As Executive Head, Briggs presided over a Supreme Council; local "posts" were headed by Post Commanders. West Indians predominated in the Supreme Council and in the New York post, but American Negroes made up the bulk of the membership in the Chicago post and elsewhere in the United States.[29]

The Program and Aims of the Brotherhood contained eight points: "a liberated race; absolute race equality—political, economic, social; the fostering of race pride; organized and uncompromising opposition to Ku Kluxism; *rapprochement* and fellowship within the darker masses and with the class-conscious revolutionary white workers; industrial development; higher wages for Negro labor, lower rents; a united Negro front." The first point was elaborated as follows: "A liberated race—in the United States, Africa and elsewhere. Liberated not merely from political rule, but also from the crushing weight of capitalism, which keeps the many in degrading poverty that the few may wallow in stolen wealth." [30]

The African Blood Brotherhood was thus a small propagandist organization typical of the "New Negro" period. It attracted national attention once in 1921 when it was falsely charged with responsibility for starting the "race riots" in Tulsa, Oklahoma.[31] Alone, the Brotherhood fell far short of the Garvey and other Negro movements of the time in importance, but it earned a special niche for itself by virtue of its relation to American Communism.

Some time in 1921, evidently in response to pressure from Moscow, American Communists made the first serious attempt to attract Negro members. Zack says that he did not know a single Negro Communist when he was put in charge of Negro work. A Negro Socialist of his acquaintance advised him to get in touch with Briggs. Subsequently, some of the Brotherhood's top leaders, including Briggs and Richard B. Moore, went into the Communist party. A majority of the Supreme Council became Communists or Communist sympathizers who willingly cooperated in recruiting party members within the Brotherhood.[32] In return, Huiswoud, and perhaps a few others already in the party, came into the Brotherhood. Another group, including Fort-Whiteman, Otto Hall, and Harry Haywood, was later recruited into the party from the Brotherhood.[33]

The Communists subsequently propagated a legend that the African Blood Brotherhood had owed its existence to the Communist party. As we have seen, the Brotherhood was organized in 1919 in complete independence of the Communist party. About two years later, the Communists moved into the Brotherhood by winning over the top leaders. Historically this relatively small group was the core of the first American Negro Communist cadre.[34] The Communists at first influenced Briggs and his group to give up their original national bias in favor of American radicalism's traditional social egalitarianism. By the end of the decade, however, the former Brotherhood leaders rediscovered the "national question" by a totally different route.

From A.B.B. to A.N.L.C.

The American Negro problem sporadically arose for discussion in the Comintern and the American party. In the next few years, however, the Communist line took a number of different turns before arriving at the formula of "the right of self-determination of the Negroes in the Black Belt."

In 1921, at the Comintern's Third Congress, the South African delegation proposed for future study by the Executive Committee "the Negro question or the proletarian movement among the Negroes as an important aspect of the Eastern problem." Beyond agreement, nothing more was done.[35]

The next year, at the Fourth Congress, an extended discussion took place. For the first time, a Negro Communist, Otto Huiswoud, was one of the delegates of the American party. The Negro poet Claude McKay also attended as an unscheduled "special delegate." Huiswoud called the Negro question "another part of the race and colonial question." Though the Negro problem was essentially an economic problem, he explained, "the frictions between the white and black races aggravated and intensified it." In his description of conditions in the United States, he emphasized the exclusion of Negroes from the trade unions and the situation in the South—"when you come there, you imagine yourself to be in Dante's Inferno." [36]

McKay startled the delegates by accusing the American Communists themselves of discrimination—the first of many such complaints: "In relations with American comrades, I have found evidence of prejudice on various occasions when white and Negro comrades get together. The greatest difficulty that the Communists in America have to overcome is that they must first free themselves from their attitude towards the Negroes before they can succeed in reaching the Negroes with any kind of radical propaganda." [37]

The Negro Commission, the first appointed by a congress, brought in "Theses on the Negro Question," the Comintern's first real effort to state its position. These theses treated the Negro question as an aspect of the colonial question and therefore regarded the American Negroes in terms of what they could do for self-determination—in Africa. "The history of the Negro in America fits him for an important role in the liberation struggle of the entire African race," the document declared. It based this role on the conception of a single "world Negro movement," including the Negroes of Africa, South and Central America, the Caribbean, and the United States, in which the latter, by virtue of industrial development, had been placed "in the vanguard of the African struggle against oppression." [38] The Comintern, as yet lacking Negro delegates from Africa,[39] substituted American Negroes for African Negroes in the leadership of African liberation. A decision by the congress to hold a Negro World Congress in Moscow never materialized.

The Fourth Congress opened a period of Communist policy for

the American Negro in which the international and especially the African aspect of the question predominated. "The status of the American Negro cannot be raised without the awakening of Africa," a South African wrote in one Comintern organ. "But it is no less true that the European proletariat cannot obtain a real link with Africa except through the more advanced Negroes of America." [40] The American representative to the Comintern in 1923, Israel Amter, declared in another Comintern organ: "Africa, the home of the most exploited people, must be added to the battle line. The American Negro, by reason of his higher education and culture and his greater aptitude for leadership, and because of the urgency of the issues in America, will furnish the leadership for the Negro race." [41] Robert Minor and William F. Dunne, Zack's successors in charge of Negro work in the American party, made similar statements.[42]

Despite this new note, the American party's third convention at the end of 1923 viewed the Negro question in purely American terms: "The Workers Party will oppose among the Negroes all movements looking to the surrender of the Negroes' rights in this country, such as the 'Back to Africa' movement, which is only an evasion of the real struggle and an excuse to surrender the Negroes' rights in their native land, America. The United States is the home of the American Negro, and the Workers Party champions his full, free and equal partnership with his white brothers in the future society." [43]

The Negro problem came up again at the Fifth Congress in 1924 in connection with the first draft of the Comintern's program. The discussion in the Program Commission and at the congress directly concerned the applicability of the right of self-determination to the United States and particularly to the American Negro.

The German, August Thalheimer, reported for the commission: "It was pointed out that a number of national questions exist in countries like the United States with an extraordinary national mixture of populations where it cannot be said that the slogan of the right of self-determination is the solution for all national questions, in which the race question is also involved." He went on: "The Program Commission was of the opinion that the slogan of the right of self-determination must be supplemented by another slogan: 'National equality for all national groups and races.' " The commission also decided that it was "virtually impossible" to define the concept of nation to satisfy all requirements.[44]

Pepper made himself the spokesman for this anti-self-determination position. "In many countries the nationalities are such that we cannot in any way separate them," he said. "Let us take the Negro race of America for example. Why should they want to have anything to do with the slogan for the right of self-determination of the Negro? They do not want to establish any separate state within the United States. There exists a Negro-Zionist movement in America which wishes to go to Africa, but the thirteen million Negroes wish to remain in America and demand 'social equality.' We should change this slogan to the following: Complete Equality in Every Respect." [45]

No one disputed Pepper. Other American delegates made other contributions. The second American Negro delegate to come to Moscow, Lovett Fort-Whiteman, without specifying exactly what he wanted, emphasized the "racial" aspect of the Negro problem and appealed for a special Communist approach to the Negroes. Amter proposed a general conference of Negroes to demand admission to the regular unions and a systematic propaganda campaign to link the Negroes in Africa and America by various methods, such as pamphlets for Africa-bound sailors. In the end, the congress decided to set up a permanent commission on the national question with an American representative as chairman, but nothing more seems to have been heard of it.[46]

Fort-Whiteman stayed on in Moscow for further "training," the first American Negro Communist to enjoy this distinction.[47] His continued emphasis on "race" soon brought forth an answer from the Comintern. When he demanded that the American Communists make the racial factor their "starting basis" and "manipulate this racial revolutionary sentiment to the advantage of the class struggle," the Comintern's reply admitted that the American party could not go on evading "the ticklish question of race antagonism." But it offered advice which still subordinated race to class: "Our Party in America must sound the alarm with respect to the growing race antagonism. It must make clear that it is a product of a society divided into classes, that it serves the selfish interests of the ruling classes, and that it will only disappear when the proletariat is victorious." American Negroes were urged to support the movement for self-determination—of their "kinsmen" in Africa and elsewhere. For the Americans, however, the main task remained the fight for "full equality." [48]

At about the same time as the Fifth Congress, a new Communist approach to Garveyism was tried out, primarily by Robert Minor, the Ruthenberg group's white Texas-born Negro specialist. Despite the Garvey movement's determination to be a "submissive, docile, anti-Bolshevik, reactionary organization," Minor contended, its program rang with "the spontaneous, classic cry of the Black Spartacus." [49] An invitation to Garvey to attend the Comintern's Fifth Congress was even contemplated.[50] Editorials in the *Daily Worker* and a long official letter from the Communists greeted the fourth convention of the Garveyite U.N.I.A. in August 1924 with unusual warmth and benevolence.[51] But the flirtation soon soured. Minor accused Garvey of collusion with the Ku Klux Klan; a second long letter to the Garveyite convention warned it against betraying the "Negro Race." The *Daily Worker* finally exploded with disappointment: "The dramatics of Marcus Garvey, under cover of which he sabotages the struggle against the Ku Klux Klan, while he builds up a petty bourgeois circle of 'leaders' with a vested interest in subduing the class struggle in America with the opiate of emancipation through running away from this continent are another form of the exploitation of the Negro." [52]

Garveyism tempted and eluded the Communists. They could not find a way to make use of the discontent which Garveyism fed on. By 1925, when the American party went through the Bolshevization process, its Negro work clearly stood in need of a general overhauling. The African Blood Brotherhood could not make headway against the Garvey movement, which blocked the Communists off from access to the most rebellious Negro masses. The Comintern decided that what the American party needed in opposition to Negro middle-class organizations was a typical Communist front for Negro workers and farmers.

Instructions came from Moscow to replace the African Blood Brotherhood with an American Negro Labor Congress.[53] After months of preparatory work, including a two-week school for Negro Communists and sympathizers "on the national colonial question and party organization," the final plans went to the Political Committee. The Committee met on October 12, 1925, decided that the congress should take place on October 25, and ordered a subcommittee to submit the organization plan and resolutions for the congress to the committee on October 19.[54]

Over 40 delegates came together in Chicago the last week of October 1925 to launch the American Negro Labor Congress. Lovett Fort-Whiteman returned from his training in Moscow to become its national Organizer, and another Communist, H. V. Phillips, was named National Secretary. Despite its claim to represent the Negro working class, Minor admitted: "A hard-boiled organizer will have to say that there were only a very few thousand of organized Negro workers behind the delegates who sat in the American Negro Labor Congress." Only a small handful, he said, directly represented trade unions and none at all Negro farmers.[55]

In a Comintern organ, Fort-Whiteman defined the purpose of the congress with such candor that he produced one of the best official descriptions of a Communist front: "The fundamental aim in calling the American Negro Labor Congress is to establish in the life of the American Negro working class an organization which may serve as a medium through which the American Communist Party may reach and influence the Negro working class, and at the same time constitute something of a recruiting ground for the Party." [56]

The A.N.L.C. neither reached nor influenced much of the Negro working class and never constituted much of a recruiting ground for the party. A report for the first two months by John J. Ballam, the party's representative to the A.N.L.C., shows how dutifully the party carried out the Comintern's instructions with a minimum of human material. The A.N.L.C.'s total dues payments for November and December 1925 amounted to $96.45 for an average of 32½ dues-paying members in the entire country. Its income from all other sources was $87.35, its expenses $612.49, and its subsidy from the party $465.10. It owed the *Daily Worker* about $700 and required a minimum of $300 a month to operate. Its official organ, *The Negro Champion,* came out sporadically. "Organizationally the A.N.L.C. seems to have no active membership or functioning groups outside of Chicago, where there is a group of 50 members," Ballam reported sadly.[57]

The American Negro Labor Congress lasted five years. James W. Ford, one of the few Negro Communist leaders recruited from it into the party, wrote of it: "For the period of its existence it was almost completely isolated from the basic masses of the Negro people."[58] In this period, following Garvey's imprisonment and deportation for fraudulent use of the mails, Garvey's movement collapsed. But the A.N.L.C. could not pick up the pieces of the Garvey movement. This failure made inevitable another reconsideration of the Negro question in Moscow.

From Omaha to Moscow

Among the instructions on Negro work sent from Moscow in 1925, in addition to that concerning the American Negro Labor Congress, was one that seemed like a comparatively minor chore. It advised the American party to choose a Negro delegation to attend the Communist University of Toilers of the East, also known as the Far Eastern University.[59] The American central committee complied by sending a questionnaire to a number of Negro party members and other Negroes not in the party for the purpose of selecting a suitable group.[60]

Toward the end of 1925, this group, made up of four American Negroes and one Gold Coast (now Ghana) student at the Carnegie Institute of Technology, arrived in Moscow to begin their studies. Of the five, one continued to play an outstanding role in the American party's Negro work for many years. He was Otto Hall, then thirty-four years old. His brother, Haywood Hall, better known as Harry Haywood, eight years younger, came to Moscow the following year for the same purpose, and was destined to play a leading part in the development of the Communist doctrine of "self-determination" for the American Negro.[61]

Through the Hall brothers, we can trace the living threads of Negro history from the Civil War to American Communism.

Their grandfather, born a slave in Tennessee, had served in a Massachusetts regiment in the Civil War. He returned to Tennessee to claim his "forty acres and a mule," then with his wife, also a former slave, fled to Iowa to escape the revenge of the former slave-owners. Their son, father of the brothers, was brought from Tennessee to Iowa as a boy and worked for forty years as a porter and night watchman for the Cudahy Packing Company in Omaha, Nebraska. There his three children, Otto, Haywood, and a daughter, were born. The Halls owned a six-room cottage, and the children attended integrated schools long before "integration" became a fighting word. Later the family moved to Minneapolis, then to Chicago.

In Minneapolis, Otto Hall listened to Bill Haywood, Elizabeth Gurley Flynn, and other I.W.W. street speakers, and in his early twenties became an I.W.W. sympathizer. Both he and his younger brother served overseas in the United States Army in World War I. Like most Negro soldiers, they returned discontented and disillusioned with the democracy they were told to fight for in France but could not fully enjoy at home. Back in Chicago, Otto attended one of Garvey's spectacular meetings, was swept into the U.N.I.A., and signed up as an officer in the "Black Legion." When a friend gave him a copy of Cyril Briggs' new magazine, *The Crusader,* he liked its more "social" appeal even better and joined the first post of the African Blood Brotherhood organized in Chicago in 1919. Two years later, when Briggs went into the Communist movement, Hall did so too.

According to Hall, the little group of five Negroes had not been at the Far Eastern University in Moscow more than a week when Stalin sent for them. As the Russian party's specialist on the national and colonial question, Stalin considered this institution his ward, and it was unofficially called the "Stalin University of Peoples of the East." [62] The group was taken to the Kremlin in a car sent by Stalin. Karl Radek, who knew enough English to serve as interpreter, was present at the interview. They drank tea and talked informally for several hours.

Stalin held forth: The Negroes represented the most oppressed section of the American working class. Therefore, the American party should have more Negroes than whites. Why weren't there more Negroes in the American party?

Hall answered that prejudice and discrimination within the party were largely responsible for the shortage of Negro members. He told the Russians about the South Side branch of the Chicago party which had been formed in 1922 with about 75 Negro members, most of whom had soon drifted away in resentment against the patronizing attitude of the whites.

Hall remembers Stalin as saying: "The whole approach of the American party to the Negro question is wrong. You are a national minority with some of the characteristics of a nation." He asked them to write memoranda on the Negro question and promised to provide them with American Negro publications and books.

At this time, as far as can be determined, Stalin for the first time tentatively broached the idea of a Negro "national question" to American Negro Communists. To Hall and the others, "it sounded like Jim Crow" in a revolutionary guise, and among themselves they reacted to it unfavorably. Stalin told them that they could learn Leninist theory from the Russians and the Russians could learn the facts of Negro life and history from them. Resistance from American Communists, including Negro Communists, apparently came as no surprise to him. He was prepared to expose them to a lengthy period of indoctrination, based on Leninist theory as interpreted by him at the Far Eastern University and the Lenin School.[63]

Despite misgivings about some Russian ideas on the American Negro problem, Hall and the others looked to the Russian Communists to redress their grievances against the white American Communists. Before coming to Russia, the Negro Communists had often told themselves that, if only they could get to Moscow and tell the Russians about the conditions which displeased them in the American party, everything would be set right without delay. More than any other segment of the American party, most Negro Communists maintained a dual existence; they were Negroes first, Communists second. American Negro Communists nursed grievances against West Indian Negro Communists, and both groups harbored deep resentments against the whole dominant white American Communist world. The Russian Communists stood outside this disturbing American world and American Negro Communists could more easily accept them as the supreme arbiters over it.

And it was no small source of gratification for American Negro Communists to come to the home of the World Revolution and within a few days engage in intimate conversation with its most powerful leaders inside the Kremlin, of which Claude McKay had sung:

> And often now my nerves throb with the thrill
> When, in that gilded place, I felt and saw
> The simple voice and presence of Lenin.[64]

Lenin's voice

American Communists have claimed that Lenin spoke of American Negroes as a nation three times in his voluminous writings. Each of these citations fails on examination to bear out the extreme construction that has been placed on it.

In 1913, Lenin wrote a study of some one hundred pages on "Capitalism and Agriculture in the United States of America," based on the American census figures of 1900 and 1910. In one section, devoted to "The Formerly Slave-Owning South," he alluded to the condition of American Negroes:

Segregated, hidebound, a stifling atmosphere, a sort of prison for the "emancipated" Negroes—this is what the American South is like.

And:

There is a striking similarity between the economic position of the American Negroes and that of the *"former landlords' peasants"* [ex-serfs] of the central agricultural regions of Russia.[65]

There is nothing in this work to imply, as one American Communist has claimed, that Lenin considered the Negroes in the South an "oppressed nation." [66] He was obviously concerned here with feudalism, not nationalism. Of the three citations, this one is clearly the least convincing.

In the beginning of 1917, just before the downfall of the Czarist regime, Lenin worked on a large study, "Statistics and Sociology," with the intention of collecting factual data on national minorities and nationalities throughout the world. The February revolution interrupted the work and he never returned to it. A fragment of this unfinished manuscript contained a reference to the American Negroes:

In the United States, only 11.1 per cent of the population consists of Negroes (and also mulattoes and Indians) who must be considered an oppressed nation, insofar as the equality, won in the Civil War of 1861–65 and guaranteed by the constitution of the Republic, has in reality been more and more restricted in many respects in the main centers of the Negro population (in the South) with the transition from the progressive, pre-monopolistic capitalism of 1860–70 to the reactionary monopolistic capitalism (imperialism) of the latest epoch. . . .

But he added this important qualification:

As is known, especially in view of the favorable conditions for the development of capitalism in America and especially in view of the speed of this development, nowhere do the vast national differences shrink so fast and so radically as here into a single "American nation." [67]

It would appear, then, that there may be some foundation for the view that Lenin in some sense considered the American Negroes an "oppressed nation." But he also seemed to expect the Negroes' "national differences" to diminish as had those of other national groups within the evolving American nation. By quoting only the first portion of the reference and omitting the qualification two sentences away, an American Communist source has seriously distorted the sense of the entire passage.[68]

In any case, this citation could not have influenced the original formulation of Communist policy in 1928 because it was not published in Russian until 1935 and even then so completely escaped the attention of the American Communists that it did not appear in English until 1946.

The whole case for a Leninist interpretation of the American Negro problem as a "national question" rested on a third citation from 1920. In the "Theses on the National and Colonial Question" at the Comintern's Second Congress, for which Lenin had asked suggestions and criticisms from the other delegates, the ninth thesis made an incidental reference to the American Negroes:

> Communist parties must give direct support to the revolutionary movements among the dependent nations and those without equal rights (e.g., in Ireland, among the American Negroes, etc.) and in the colonies.*

A strange fate awaited these few words. American Communists, to whom they were most important, have known them in inaccurate English translations. In the official German and Russian texts of these theses, "without equal rights" appears as an adjective before "nations." Communist translations have changed "without equal rights" into "subject" or "subordinated" nations, or have omitted it alto-

* This translation is based on the final text in German and Russian. The key phrase, "among the dependent nations and those without equal rights," reads in German: "unter den abhängigen und nicht gleichberechtigten Nationen" (*Protokoll des II. Weltkongresses der Kommunistischen Internationale*, p. 228). It reads similarly in Russian: "zavicimykh ili neravnopravnikh natsiakh" (*Vtoroi Kongress Cominterna,* revised edition, 1934, p. 493 for resolution and p. 648 for draft). The adjectival use of "without equality" cannot be rendered literally in English.

gether. By accident or not, these mistranslations have oversimplified what Lenin may have had in mind for the American Negroes.*

What did Lenin mean by "dependent nations and those without equal rights"? Did he mean to class Ireland with "dependent nations" and the American Negroes with "those without equal rights"? Or did both attributes apply to Ireland and the American Negroes in equal measure?

We can only speculate. The passage was so loosely formulated that it lends itself to more than one interpretation. Lenin probably did not intend to equate Ireland with the American Negroes, the first a historic nation deprived of its national independence, the second never a nation and at best striving to become one. Only three years earlier he had stressed that even vast national differences tended to shrink rather than to expand in the process of Americanization. Yet we cannot be sure that he was clear in his own mind what he meant by alluding to Ireland and "among the American Negroes" as "dependent nations and those without equal rights." He may very well have toyed with the idea that the American Negroes had been or

* These English mistranslations go as far back as *The Communist International,* No. 11–12, June–July 1920, col. 2157, which gave the phrase in the preliminary draft as "dependent and subordinated nations." The translation of the final resolution in the very next issue shortened it to "subject nations," leaving out the second adjective altogether (ibid., Vol. II, no. 13, col. 2413). The authorized translation in Lenin, *Selected Works,* vol. x, p. 235, uses "dependent and subject nations." Foster's *The Negro People in American History,* p. 460, follows this translation. A reprint of the theses in *The Communist,* January 1931, p. 41, went back to "subject nations," as did James S. Allen (ibid., January 1934, p. 56). The only substantially accurate Communist translation that I have been able to find appeared in 1921 and gave the phrase as "subject nations and those deprived of equal rights" (*The Theses and Statutes of the Communist International,* issued by the Central Executive Committee of the Communist Party of America, 1921, p. 64), but it was never repeated.

Mrs. Jane Degras accurately translates "dependent nations and those without equal rights," but omits the "etc." (*The Communist International,* Documents, Vol. I, p. 142).

The editors of the revised Russian edition of the stenographic record of the Second Congress found that the Russian texts were most unreliable. Lenin's speech on the national and colonial question was made in German, not in Russian. And the additional theses on the national and colonial question, which had been translated into Russian from the German, turned out to have been English in the original! (*The Communist International,* June 5, 1934, pp. 381–82.)

could be considered to be a nation without ever having worked out to what extent and under what conditions the concept of nation applied to them.

The difficulties of interpretation increase if we take other factors into consideration.

This reference to American Negroes was not the only one at the Second Congress. As we have seen, John Reed made a lengthy report on the American Negroes. He said nothing that implied they were a nation and much that implied they were not. According to Reed, the Negroes considered themselves "first of all Americans at home in the United States." There is no indication that Lenin or anyone else disagreed with him, though we know that Lenin did not suffer deviationists gladly and that Reed in particular brought down on himself a storm of criticism on other questions.

Yet we must take into consideration the testimony of the Japanese Communist, Sen Katayama, a leading member of the national and colonial commission at the Second Congress, who had lived for many years in the United States and took a special interest in the Negro question. In 1928 Katayama stated that Lenin had fully discussed the Negro question with the American delegates at the Second Congress, had laid down "certain principles" for this work, and had "considered the American Negroes as a subject nation, placing them in the same category as Ireland." [69] The question arises why Katayama had waited eight years to make this disclosure, during which time Lenin's closest co-workers had frequently manifested a different understanding of the American Negro question.

After the Second Congress, the mystery deepens. For the next eight years, there is no record in the Comintern or in the American party of any reference to the American Negroes as a "nation" or any implications of Negro "self-determination." On the contrary, all the documents and discussions point in different directions. As we have seen, the Fourth Congress in 1922, during Lenin's lifetime, stressed the American Negroes' role in the liberation of Africa, not their own independent political existence. The Fifth Congress in 1924, soon after Lenin's death, arrived at a consensus that the right of self-determination did not apply to the United States. The American party's conventions in 1923, 1925, and 1927, all of them minutely scrutinized by Comintern commissions and representatives, did not give the slightest hint of an American Negro "national question." When Claude McKay asked Trotsky for his views in 1923, he was merely told that Negro work should be carried on in "a spirit of solidarity of all exploited without consideration of color." [70]

The explanation for this strange and unusual neglect of Lenin's view of the American Negro question may only be surmised. Even if we assume that Lenin considered the American Negroes in some sense a "nation," he expressed this idea so laconically, tangentially, and infrequently that it did not enjoy the same exalted status as other pronouncements by him. By common consent, it remained undisturbed for several years in a kind of theoretical limbo. Or it ran counter to the American radical and Negro tradition so drastically that the same words did not mean the same thing to different people. William F. Dunne hailed the Negro resolution of the American party's Fourth Convention in 1925 as giving "a practical expression to the theses of the [Comintern's] Second Congress," though it did not make the faintest allusion to the "national question." [71]

Whatever Lenin's voice may have told the Communists on the American Negro question, it was the voice of a man who had never had any direct experience with it. He was acquainted with the census reports of 1900 and 1910 before vast changes had taken place in the distribution of the American Negro population, and had left his followers a few words so cryptic that for years they had ignored or misunderstood them. More than Lenin's voice was needed to persuade the American Communists that the American Negro problem was a "national question."

Race and class

Meanwhile, as the Far Eastern University and the Lenin School poured Leninist theory into their students, the rising star in the American party, Jay Lovestone, turned his attention to the American Negro problem. The starting point for Lovestone's analysis was the migration of Negroes from South to North since the census of 1910. He noted that 10,000 to 12,000 Negroes had migrated northward annually before 1916 and about 200,000 annually after 1916. But since the Negro in the North also suffered from inequality and prejudice, he reasoned, migration did not solve the problem. For his conclusion, he went all the way back to the traditional Socialist position: "The rapidly advancing concentration of the Negro proletariat, the increasing political significance of the Negro workers, the efforts of the bourgeoisie to stimulate racial antagonism between the Negro and the white workers, and finally the growing racial consciousness of the Negro—all of these demand that the workers of the United States and their organizations should not allow racial prejudice to dominate in the least but should adhere only to the class principle." [72]

Though they offered no final solution, Lovestone saw the greatest hope in migrations from the South, not rebellion in the South, and in the end, he fell back on "class," not "race." He regarded the land-bound, economically backward Southern Negroes as "a reserve of capitalist reaction" that the forces of migration and industrialization were freeing to become an ally of the proletariat.[73] By implication, he placed the focus of Negro liberation in the North, not in the South, and on the Negro proletariat, not on the Negro share-cropper.

In addition to all his other accomplishments, John Pepper also considered himself an authority on the American Negro question. When he returned to the United States in the spring of 1928, he quickly assumed command in this field too. Lovestone, Bittelman, and Pepper made up a subcommittee in April 1928 to re-examine the American party's Negro policy, and Pepper wrote the resolution unanimously adopted by the Political Committee on May 30.[74]

Unlike Lovestone's articles, Pepper's resolution veered sharply to a racial emphasis. "The Negro question is a *race question,* and it is the task of the Communist Party to fight for the Negroes as an oppressed race," it stated. To the Communists, however, it assigned the special duty of being "the champion and organizer of the *Negro working class elements.*" Pepper's chief practical recommendation, a

"Negro Race Congress," to be called, as he put it, on "the initiative (not openly)" of the Communist party, was never carried out.[75]

Pepper's resolution invited factional attack in the Foster-Cannon platform, "The Right Danger in the American Party," submitted to the Sixth World Congress in July 1928. It was criticized for completely neglecting to mention work "among the Negro peasantry in the South" and the necessity for a campaign against "white chauvinism in the ranks of the Party." Not unlike Pepper, however, the opposition's platform offered this definition of the party's main task: "The development of a revolutionary Negro race movement led by the Negro proletariat." [76]

Thus we know what the leading American Communists thought, or considered it expedient to think, on the Negro question, literally to the day they arrived in Moscow for the Sixth World Congress. They still gravitated around the concepts of "class" and "race," with the latter uppermost on the eve of the congress. Both Pepper, who wrote the May resolution, and Bittelman, who wrote the Opposition's July platform, missed rare opportunities to make some allusion to the concept of "nation" that might have enabled them to gain some factional advantage and save the American delegates from the embarrassment of bringing home from Moscow a wholly unanticipated and unprepared new Negro line.

Stalin's voice

The man whose voice the American Communists really heeded on the American Negro question never made a public statement about it. For lack of other evidence, Stalin's decisive influence in this area has hitherto been deduced or surmised from his decisive influence in all areas and his special interest in the national question. It is now possible, however, to present more concrete and direct testimony of his involvement.

As we have noted, Otto Hall says that Stalin gave him and four other Negroes at the Far Eastern University their first intimations of a

Negro "national question" in 1925. One more direct and one indirect association with Stalin has come to light.

William F. Kruse recalls that, about two years later, he and other American students at the Lenin School were invited to attend a discussion on the American Negro question in the Anglo-American Secretariat of the Comintern. To their surprise, among those seated around a long table was Stalin, flanked by two young Russian members of the Institute of Red Professors. One of the Russian professors read a long "thesis" in support of the theory of self-determination as applied to the American Negro question. Stalin himself said nothing throughout the entire session, except for whispered consultations with the speaker. Kruse did most of the talking for the Americans and upheld the older position that equality rather than self-determination constituted the revolutionary solution. The discussion ended without reaching any conclusion.[77]

Finally, another American student at the Lenin School, Joseph Zack, says that he first heard of the doctrine of Negro self-determination in the United States from the head of the Profintern, Lozovsky, who told him that it came from Stalin himself. Like most Americans, Zack first reacted unfavorably. A week later, Lozovsky asked Zack to come to his apartment and showed him the outline of a thesis by Stalin on the subject, consisting of a few brief points.[78]

Cumulatively, the experiences of Hall, Kruse, and Zack go far to implicate Stalin in the derivation of the Communist theory of the right of self-determination of the Negroes in the Black Belt. In all three cases, the Americans held back; their reluctance confronted the Russians with a problem of getting Americans, especially American Negroes, to sponsor their view. An outstanding opportunity awaited the first Negro Communist willing to do so.

This key role was filled by Otto Hall's aggressive and articulate younger brother, Harry Haywood. He had joined the African Blood Brotherhood about 1922, the Communist youth league in 1923, and the Communist party in 1925. He was sent to the Far Eastern University in 1926 and transferred to the Lenin School the next year. Not yet thirty years old, he had never occupied a party post and, since he was sent to the Far Eastern University a year after joining the party, had spent most of his party life in Moscow. Until he came forward as the American Negro champion of self-determination, he was considered no more than a promising young Negro recruit serving his apprenticeship.

One of Haywood's closest friends in Moscow was N. Nasanov, a Russian Communist youth leader about his own age, who had once represented the Young Communist International in the United States and spoke English quite well. In 1927 and 1928 Nasanov frequently discussed the American Negro question with Haywood from the Russian point of view of self-determination. Since Nasanov was not sufficiently important politically to advance such a far-reaching innovation on his own, it may be assumed that he spoke with the approval of the Russian party's hierarchy.

In addition to acting, in all probability, as the *éminence grise* behind Nasanov and others, Stalin provided the theoretical foundation on which the entire discussion in this preparatory period was based. The starting point was the definition of a nation given in an essay by Stalin, "Marxism and the National Question," written at Lenin's suggestion in 1913:

> A nation is a historically evolved, stable community arising on the foundation of a common language, territory, economic life, and psychological make-up, manifested in a community of culture.[79]

Haywood and others made an intensive effort to apply this definition to American Negroes. The problem was broken down to the consideration of four criteria—language, territory, economy, and culture. The first criterion—a common language—was easily satisfied by making a distinction between a common language and a different one; the American Negroes, it was decided, had a common language, English, but not a different one. A common territory was staked out in the so-called Black Belt of the South by selecting counties with Negro majorities or large Negro minorities.[80] A common economic life was attributed to the Negro sharecroppers in the predominantly cotton-growing ante-bellum plantation region. A common psychological make-up and culture were deduced from the historic circumstances and social conditions peculiar to the Negro.

The derivation of the Communist theory of the right of self-determination of the Negroes in the Black Belt, therefore, may be divided into three phases: Lenin had supposedly called the American Negroes a nation; Stalin provided the definition of a nation; Haywood and other American Communists provided material which justified applying the definition to the American Negroes.

At the Sixth World Congress

As the Sixth World Congress approached, the Comintern's high command decided to bring to a head the new approach to the American Negro question.

Early in 1928 a subcommittee on the Negro question was formed within the Anglo-American Secretariat to prepare a resolution and other material for submission to the congress. In August, at the congress itself, a thirty-two-member Negro Commission was appointed to make the final recommendations. This commission included seven Americans—five Negroes, including Harry Haywood, Otto Hall, and James W. Ford, plus Lovestone and Bittelman. Among the others were Nasanov, representing the Young Communist International, Bunting of South Africa, and Andrew Rothstein of England. The commission's chairman was the Finnish Comintern official, Kuusinen; its vice-chairman, the secretary of the Anglo-American Secretariat, Petrovsky; and its secretary, the Russian Mikhailov (Williams).[81]

In the discussions, three viewpoints clashed. One held that the American Negroes represented a racial problem to be solved fundamentally by the achievement of full social and political equality. Another maintained that this was true in the North but not in the South, where the Negroes, constituting a majority of the population, had been developing the characteristics of a nation and therefore required the right of national self-determination. A third view went still further and advocated the slogan of a Negro Soviet Republic.[82]

One of the documents favoring the national viewpoint was submitted to the commission by Haywood and Nasanov jointly. They condemned Pepper's resolution of April 30 for completely overlooking the South, and attacked another statement of policy oriented toward the Northern Negroes by the American Negro Labor Congress leaders, Fort-Whiteman and Phillips. They criticized Lovestone for regarding the mass of Southern Negroes as a "reserve of capitalist reaction" instead of "natural allies of the revolutionary proletariat." They took to task another American Negro Communist leader, Richard B. Moore, for allegedly overemphasizing petty-bourgeois rather than working-class organizations in Negro work. At this stage Haywood and Nasanov formulated their own position, with some confusion between race and nation: "The Party must also bear in mind that in the South especially there are some prerequisites which *may* lead to the future development of a national (racial) revolutionary movement among the Negroes." [83]

The Comintern's theoretical organ, *The Communist International,* published four discussion articles on the American Negro question in 1928. The first, by A. Shiek, supported the position taken by John Reed in 1920 that the Negroes made no demands for national independence and considered the United States their home. Shiek wanted the Communists to demand complete political and social equality for the Negroes as a race and he rejected the proposed right of Negro national self-determination.

A second article, by James Ford and William Wilson, called for a "revolutionary racial movement" to bring together the Negro working and lower middle classes to fight for "the full political and social equality of the races." It contended that the American Negro Labor Congress was too narrow and proposed replacing it with a "League of Struggle Against Prejudice and Racial Inequality."

In the third article, John Pepper argued that the Black Belt of the South was not only a Negro nation but *"virtually a colony within the body of the United States of America."* Segregated housing strengthened the basis of a Negro national movement in the North and East. And while Negroes in general should make their own decision about the form their self-determination should take, *"Negro* Communists should emphasize in their propaganda *the establishment of a Negro Soviet Republic."*

The fourth article, by Harry Haywood, came closest to the official position adopted by the Sixth World Congress. For him, the American Negroes constituted a "national minority" and the Negro problem was rooted economically "in the agrarian question in the South." He ridiculed Communists like Lovestone who expected the migration northward to deprive the Negro masses in the South of their "compact unity" and the process of industrialization to free the Negro peasantry of its "half-feudal" bondage. While he urged the Communists to continue the struggle for full social and political equality, he advocated "a national-revolutionary movement" for the right of "national self-determination" to go as far as an "independent Negro state."

Pepper's article was destined to play a peculiar role in the immediate development of the new Negro policy. Owing to his influence in the American party, it was the only one of the four to be reprinted in *The Communist* and again as a pamphlet. To the consternation of Haywood and others in Moscow, the American membership heard of Negro self-determination for the first time in Pepper's version, without realizing that three other articles were entitled to at least the same consideration.[84] Haywood's more important article never appeared in English because the English edition of *The Communist International* suspended publication for four months at the end of 1928. Students of American Negro communism have perpetuated this misunderstanding by giving Pepper's article an importance that the Comintern never intended.[85] In actuality Pepper was already *persona non grata* in the Comintern, and this article further contributed to his undoing by going far beyond anything the Comintern contemplated.

The "Negro Soviet Republic" was a typical Pepperism. At the Fifth Congress in 1924 he had spoken up against the very idea of applying the principle of self-determination to the United States in general and to the American Negroes in particular. As recently as his resolution of April 30, 1928, he had not shown the slightest interest in anything smacking of self-determination or the Black Belt. But when he got to Moscow and saw the way the wind was blowing in the Negro Commission, he hastened to make up for lost time—and overreached himself.[86]

But Pepper was not the only one to jump on the self-determination bandwagon in Moscow. Bittelman, Hathaway, Foster, and Dunne also leaped aboard.[87] Lovestone made no effort to conceal his misgivings; both he and Wolfe privately regarded the whole idea of Negro self-determination as a pseudo-revolutionary form of Jim-Crowism which the American Negroes would never accept; but they made no effort to oppose it.

At the congress, not one of the three American Negro speakers supported the program. Fort-Whiteman ignored it in a brief message of greeting. James W. Ford hit out against it by stating unequivocally: "It seems that any nationalist movement on the part of the Negroes does nothing but play into the hands of the bourgeoisie by arresting the revolutionary class movement of the Negro masses and further widening the gulf between the white and similar oppressed groups." Otto Hall held out even more strongly, declaring unmistakably: "The historical development of the American Negro has tended to create in him the desire to be considered a part of the American nation. There are no tendencies to become a separate national minority within the American nation." [88]

The speeches at the congress in favor of the self-determination policy were delivered by the Japanese Communist, Sen Katayama, and the secretary of the Anglo-American Secretariat, Petrovsky.[89] The real battle was fought out behind the scenes in the Negro Commission.

The American Negro question was bound up with a related South African Negro question. The South African delegation, which contained no Negroes, was confronted in the Negro Commission with a proposal, which the American, Harry Haywood, had helped to work out, for an immediate demand for "an independent native South African Republic." Bunting, the South African spokesman, vainly protested that the majority of the South African party, "mainly for practical reasons," was opposed to it. The commission's secretary, Kuusinen, sternly insisted that "we must tell the majority of the leadership of the South African Party that they must unconditionally correct their attitude; their opposition in the question of the slogan of the Native Republic must be given up." And so the congress decided.[90]

The original draft of the "Theses on the Revolutionary Movement in the Colonies and Semi-Colonies" did not contain the new line on the American Negro question. It was added toward the end of the congress in the form worked out, under Kuusinen's direction, in the Negro Commission. The final paragraph represented the Comintern's first official announcement of the new Negro policy:

> In those regions of the South in which compact Negro masses are living, it is essential to put forward the slogan of the Right of Self-determination for Negroes. A radical transformation of the agrarian structure of the Southern States is one of the basic tasks of the revolution. Negro Communists must explain to non-Negro workers and peasants that only their close union with the white proletariat and joint struggle with them against the American bourgeoisie can lead to their liberation from barbarous exploitation, and that only the victorious proletarian revolution will completely and permanently solve the agrarian and national question of the Southern United States in the interests of the overwhelming majority of the Negro population of the country.[91]

Possibly because Kuusinen was chairman of the Negro Commission, some writers have given him credit for originating the theory of self-determination for the Black Belt. One of them is George Padmore, a former Negro Communist born in the British West Indies and educated in the United States, who served until his death as a leading adviser to the president of the African state of Ghana. Padmore called Kuusinen "the genius behind this scheme" and thereby put in circulation a legend on a par with the myth of Pepper's influence in this field. Kuusinen was no doubt entrusted with the management of this operation, but that he did not originate this theory, there can also be no doubt. If there was a "genius" in this scheme, it was undoubtedly Stalin, whose bidding Kuusinen unfailingly obeyed. Indeed, in addition to the experiences of Hall, Kruse, and Zack, the influence of Nasanov, and the key role played by Stalin's definition of a nation, the fact that Kuusinen headed the commission, flanked by two Russians, Petrovsky and Mikhailov, should make its Stalinist origins unmistakable.[92]

Made in Moscow

How the new Negro policy was decided was easily as important as what it decided.

There had never been a single word, written or spoken, in the American party, on the right of self-determination of the Negroes of the Black Belt, before the Sixth World Congress. The entire discussion was conducted and the decision was made in Moscow.

Discussion, and much of it, there had been in Moscow. All schools of thought had been given a hearing in the Commission and in the Comintern's theoretical organ. It cannot be said that the Comintern rushed into a decision impulsively or carelessly.

But the Comintern had completely ignored the American *party*. A few American Communists, mainly in the Lenin School, had participated in the discussion and decision. Back home, however, the party's leading bodies, the Political Committee and the Central Executive Committee, had never even considered it; the party press had never once hinted at it; the membership simply did not exist as a factor in the decision-making process.

At the Sixth World Congress, Katayama deplored the paucity of Negro party members—"only fifty or so."[93] Of this number, only Harry Haywood seems to have espoused the new Negro line actively. Huiswoud, Fort-Whiteman, Phillips, Ford, and Hall resisted and opposed it. Briggs and Moore had been left at home and knew nothing before they read about it as an accomplished fact.

The Comintern had imposed its will on the American party before, but never so absolutely and externally. The campaign to educate and win over the American party, including the bulk of Negro members, to the new line came after it went into effect. Then no one could argue against it without questioning a Comintern decision.

Even so, the questioning, particularly by Negro members, persisted for an unusually long time. About two years elapsed before the new Negro line could be put into effect.

In a report on the congress early in October 1928 to a general membership meeting in New York, Lovestone made a start by discovering signs of a "national movement" among Negroes. As we have seen, Pepper's article in *The Communist* that month appeared to be the first authorized commentary instead of the discussion article it really was. An editorial in the *Daily Worker* in November, "The Communists Are for a Black Republic," reflected Pepper's personal influence: "National self-determination for the Negro race can be realized only in the course of the proletarian revolution." [94]

Meanwhile, on October 26, 1928, the Political Secretariat of the Comintern issued the first official resolution defining the new Negro line at length, though it was not published in the *Daily Worker* until February of the following year. "While continuing and intensifying the struggle under the slogan of full social and political equality for the Negroes, which must remain the central slogan of our Party for work among the masses," this resolution stated, "the Party must come out openly and unreservedly for the right of Negroes to national self-determination in the southern states, where the Negroes form a majority of the population." It made no mention of Pepper's "Negro Soviet Republic," and explicitly took exception to Lovestone's former view, without mentioning his name, that the Southern Negroes constituted "reserves of capitalist reaction." [95]

But the Comintern's Negro resolution of October 1928 left too many questions unanswered, or answered ambiguously, to serve as a practical program of action. There were two more years of discussion and exegesis in Moscow before the Comintern issued a second and final resolution in October 1930.[96] The differences between the two resolutions reveal the questions that arose and the answers arrived at—and incidentally reveal the type of thinking that went into such major pronouncements of policy.

Was Pepper right in calling the Black Belt a "virtual colony" of the United States? The 1928 resolution said nothing. The 1930 resolution rejected Pepper's view as incorrect.

Was Pepper right in raising the slogan of a "Negro Soviet Republic"? The 1928 resolution did not say. The 1930 resolution said that he was wrong.

How were the national revolution in the Black Belt and the social revolution in the United States as a whole related? The 1928 resolution did not answer. The 1930 resolution took the position that the sequence could not be foretold. A Negro rebellion might be the outcome of a general revolutionary situation in the United States or it might be the prelude of a struggle for power by the American proletariat.

What was the relation of equality and self-determination as Negro demands? The 1928 resolution made full social and political equality the "central slogan." The 1930 resolution applied equal rights to all Negroes, North and South, but made self-determination the "main slogan" in the South.

Should self-determination be a slogan of action or only a concept of propaganda? The 1928 resolution did not answer. The 1930 resolution definitely made it a slogan of action in the South, and suggested demonstrations, strikes, and tax boycotts.

Did self-determination go so far as to include actual separation of the Negro republic from the United States? The 1928 resolution did not say. The 1930 resolution recognized the abstract right to separate only as long as capitalism prevailed in the United States. If the Communists came to power, they would oppose separation in favor of federation.

Could the Negro republic be achieved peacefully or only by force? The 1928 resolution gave no clear answer. The 1930 resolution clearly indicated the expectation of an "uprising" and "national rebellion."

Who was to lead this struggle—the Negro proletariat or the Negro "peasantry"? Both resolutions assigned the "hegemony" of the Negro national movement to the proletariat but in its economic aspect stressed the agrarian basis of the movement.

What, for American Negroes, was uppermost, race or nation? The 1928 resolution still referred to the "oppressed Negro race." The 1930 resolution sharpened the distinction by characterizing "racial distinctions" and "social antagonism" as factors peculiar to the "oppressed nation" which distinguished the American Negroes' national question from that of other oppressed peoples.

And, finally, how soon could a "revolutionary crisis" be expected in the Black Belt? The 1928 resolution did not venture to predict. The 1930 resolution expected a "rapid approach" of such a crisis and considered it "even probable" that separatist efforts to obtain complete state independence of the Black Belt would gain ground among the Negro masses of the South "in the near future." [97]

As late as February 1930 Huiswoud, the pioneer Negro Communist, wrote an article for *The Communist* which amounted to a refusal to accept the new Negro line. He held that the Negro question assumed a "National-colonial character" in Africa and the West Indies and a "racial character" in the United States.[98] Harry Haywood struck back scathingly at Negro Communists like Huiswoud: "The fact that there exists a 'practical' alliance between the chauvinist elements and some of our Negro comrades, should not be occasion for wonder." [99]

The Negro opponents of self-determination changed their minds or left the American scene. Huiswoud went back to Dutch Guiana. Fort-Whiteman stayed in Soviet Russia and died there. Hall, Ford, Briggs, and Moore embraced the new faith. Haywood shot ahead in the Negro Communist leadership as the first national secretary of the next American Negro front, the League of Struggle for Negro Rights, formed in November 1930, with the right of self-determination of the Negroes in the Black Belt included in its program.

The wasted effort

The theory of Negro self-determination in the South represented the boldest effort ever made by the Russian party and the Comintern to demonstrate that they understood the dynamics of American society better than the Americans did. They chose as their proving ground the most profound and painful problem in American life. The authors of the 1928 and 1930 resolutions flattered themselves with knowing what *would* as well as what *should* be the political destiny of the American Negroes. To justify the self-determination of the Black Belt, they took the position that the future of the great majority of the Negro people would continue to be in the Black Belt. They painted a picture of Negro slaves who could not escape from the Southern plantations. They predicted the "rapid approach" of a revolutionary crisis in the Black Belt. They foresaw the probability of separatist movements among the Negro masses of the South "in the near future."

None of these prophecies even remotely came to pass. The number of American Negro Communists multiplied a hundredfold in the nineteen-thirties,[100] but the great majority came into the party in the North, not the South, and in the South, few share-croppers were organized by the Communists even in a Share-Croppers Union.[101] The theory of the right of self-determination in the Black Belt never succeeded in breaking out of the narrow confines of the Communist party into the larger Negro world.[102] "Nearly all" non-Communist Negro leaders rejected the Communist theory, Haywood admitted.[103]

The material and social conditions of the American Negroes have changed—in exactly the opposite directions from those forecast by the Comintern. The long-term trends among American Negroes—migration, industrialization, and urbanization—have combined to break down the image of "compact masses" of enslaved Negro peasants in the Black Belt on which the concept of self-determination rested. As a result of migrations to the cities, North and South, only about one-third of the Negro people has been left in the plantation area of the Black Belt. The number of Southern counties with Negro majorities has been cut from 286 in 1900 to about half as many, and the latter are far less contiguous today. The percentage of Negroes in agriculture has decreased from 42 in 1940 to only 19 in 1952; the percentage of Negroes living in urban communities has increased from 20 in 1890 to 34 in 1920 and to 60 in 1950.[104]

The policy of Negro self-determination has lived twice and died twice. After overthrowing Lovestone's "revisionism," Browder made self-determination one of the cardinal articles of faith of his leadership. In November 1943, long after it had ceased to show any signs of life, he delivered a funeral oration over the corpse of self-determination; he explained that the Negro people had already exercised the historical right of self-determination—by rejecting it.[105] After overthrowing Browder's "revisionism," Foster made self-determination one of the cardinal articles of faith of his leadership. In 1946 self-determination was reincarnated in a slightly watered-down version—as a programmatic demand and not as an immediate slogan of action.[106]

In 1958, the Communist leadership again buried the corpse of the right of self-determination. It decided that the American Negro people were no longer a "stable community"; that the Negro national question was no longer "essentially a peasant question"; that the Negroes did not possess any distinctively "common psychological make-up"; that the main currents of Negro thought and leadership "historically, and universally at the present time" flowed toward equality with other Americans; that the American Negro people did not constitute a nation; and therefore that the right of self-determination did not apply to them.[107]

Harry Haywood and Cyril Briggs remained faithful to the bitter end to the Sixth World Congress' slogan of the "right of self-determination of the Negroes of the Black Belt." They rebelled against the second repudiation as they had rebelled against the first.[108]

On the other hand, James S. Allen, a white Communist who had spent a good part of his life propagandizing for the cause of Negro self-determination, came to the conclusion that it was as wrong in

1928 as in 1958. He admitted that the Communists had based the theory of Negro self-determination on the apex theory of American capitalism. The mistaken assumption, he explained, that "American capitalism had reached its apex and had fallen into a condition of permanent stagnation, had indeed entered upon a period of constant decline" had been responsible for the equally mistaken conclusion that the American economy would be incapable of assimilating the "mass Negro migrations from the Black Belt plantations into industry South, North and West." [109]

It would be hard to find a better example of the wasted effort that has gone into American Communism than this epitaph for the "apex theory" and the "Communist solution of the Negro question."

16

The Birth of American Trotskyism

FINALLY, and most curiously, American Trotskyism was born at the Sixth World Congress.

Trotsky needed help desperately from 1924 to 1927, when he was still able to put up a fight within the Russian Communist party. In those years he received least encouragement in the American party.

As we have seen, his first American sympathizer, Ludwig Lore, was driven out of the party in 1925. Lore's crushing defeat demonstrated that there was no future in Trotskyism for those caught up in the American factional struggle. Once the stigma of Trotskyism attached itself to Lore, his allies and associates fled from him as from a political leper.

In this period, however, Foster and Cannon focused their attention on American problems so wholeheartedly that the issue of Trotskyism annoyed them more as an extraneous nuisance than it disturbed them as an ideological heresy. Foster paid little more than lip service to the anti-Trotskyist campaign. At the Comintern's Fifth Plenum in 1925, Cannon was a member of the Political Commission that drew up a condemnation of Trotsky.[1] Foster and Cannon depended on Bittelman, their Russian expert, to defend them on their anti-Trotskyist flank, and he fell to with a zeal that was the envy of his factional opponents.[2]

Despite Foster's efforts not to repeat the mistake of consorting with Trotskyist sympathizers like Lore, Trotsky once had a kind word for Foster. Trotsky wrote of Foster that he "always seemed to me made of more trustworthy material than Lovestone and Pepper." Trotsky even suspected that Foster was not a genuine convert to Stalinism and had merely adopted its protective coloration "in order by this contraband route to move toward the leadership of the American party." But Trotsky underestimated Foster's staying power; he predicted that Pepper and Lovestone would beat Foster at the game of putting through "any zigzag whatever according to the administrative necessities of the Stalinist staff." [3]

Next to Pepper, Lovestone irked Trotsky more than did any other American Communist. A review by Lovestone of Trotsky's book *Whither England?* made Trotsky angry. Lovestone had given the book somewhat backhanded praise by congratulating Trotsky for changing his mind about a previous error in connection with Anglo-American relations, and Trotsky took the trouble to accuse Lovestone of having attributed "absurdities" to him.[4]

Yet it should not be imagined that Trotsky's once-irresistible magnetism could be switched on and off in the American party. To the top leadership, he was political poison. But Communist intellectuals could still pay homage to him as a writer and a thinker. When Trotsky's *Literature and Revolution* appeared in 1925, Michael Gold wrote: "Trotsky's book on literature is an amazing performance. This man is almost as universal as Leonardo da Vinci." Joseph Freeman has recalled: "The unbounded admiration for Trotsky was not confined to Mike Gold; it marked all the extreme radicals of this country, who followed Russian events at a distance in both space and time." Even in the official *Workers Monthly,* Moissaye J. Olgin contributed this rapturous appreciation: "But whatever emerged from under his pen is intense with thought, astir with theoretical passion, backed up by a broad and well-rounded knowledge, and ablaze with that peculiar brilliance of which even a sound translation of his writings into a foreign tongue can hardly give an idea." [5]

But, as Max Eastman found out, Trotsky himself did not make it easy for an American to take up his cause.

Eastman and Trotsky

An old-time Socialist, former editor of *The Masses* and its successor *The Liberator,* and ardent defender of the Bolshevik revolution, Max Eastman came to Soviet Russia in 1922 as a valued and trusted friend. He had never been there before and had known none of the Soviet leaders.

In the winter of 1923, totally innocent of the campaign building up against Trotsky inside the Russian party, Eastman decided to write a biography of Trotsky, and the latter agreed to cooperate. The complete life was never written, because Trotsky could not spare enough time, and Eastman was obliged to limit the work to Trotsky's youth. In this way, Eastman came to know Trotsky personally.[6]

In the following year, after spending a few months in the southern part of Russia, Eastman returned to Moscow to find the campaign against Trotsky in full blast. To Eastman it seemed that "a desperate war had been going on between the idealists and the machine politicians in the party." He associated the idealists with Trotsky, and himself with the idealists. But Eastman, now busy working on a critique of "dialectical materialism," made no effort to get into the battle.[7]

A confidence by Trotsky forced Eastman off the sidelines. At the Thirteenth Congress of the Russian party in May 1924, in a little nook behind the platform, Trotsky let Eastman in on the greatest secret of the Russian party—Lenin's "Testament." In this document of several parts, dictated on his sickbed at the end of December 1922, Lenin had warned of the danger of a split in the party, and in a postscript ten days later, at the beginning of January 1923, he had virtually called for Stalin's removal from the post of General Secretary. Known only to Lenin's wife and his secretary for more than a year, the testament was read at a meeting of party leaders the day before the opening of the Thirteenth Congress. Stalin, Zinoviev, and a majority voted against making it public, but Trotsky partially circumvented the decision by whispering key phrases from it to Eastman, who was leaving Russia the following day.[8]

By now Eastman had been sucked into the Russian party struggle and could not keep his mind on his critique of dialectical materialism. He left Russia with a mass of material on the internal Russian crisis, and in Paris, helped by two of Trotsky's sympathizers, Boris Souvarine and Alfred Rosmer, he produced an explosive little book, *Since Lenin Died,* published in the spring of 1925.[9]

Before publishing it, Eastman took the precaution of sending the manuscript to one of Trotsky's closest associates, Christian Rakovsky, the Soviet Ambassador in Paris, whose wife assured Eastman of their enthusiastic approval. Without knowing the full text of Lenin's testament, Eastman came close enough to the gist of it to break through the conspiracy of silence that had virtually suppressed it for a year. Far more detailed and authoritative than anything that had yet appeared on the Soviet struggle for power, filled with admiration for Trotsky and contempt for his enemies, the book created a world-wide sensation and immediately made Eastman one of Trotsky's outstanding defenders.

In Moscow the repercussions shook the top leadership. Despite his ever-growing power, Stalin could not yet afford to admit the existence of a document in which Lenin had recommended his removal from the office of General Secretary. As Trotsky's official biographer, Eastman could not be easily and effectively dismissed as a fabricator of anti-Soviet lies.

Unluckily for Eastman, Trotsky had started something which he was not able to carry through. In the privacy of the Russian party's Political Bureau, Stalin's henchmen demanded Trotsky's repudiation of Eastman's revelations. To avoid a showdown at an unpropitious moment, Trotsky's supporters prevailed on him to give way. In a telegram and article, reprinted by the Communist press throughout the world, Trotsky disowned Eastman's efforts on his behalf. Krupskaya, Lenin's widow, denounced Eastman's book as a "collection of petty gossip." [10]

With Trotsky and Krupskaya as expert witnesses against Eastman, the American Communists had little trouble believing the worst of their erstwhile comrade-in-arms. Minor assailed *Since Lenin Died* as a "veritable goulash of incoherent lies" and "bosh and melodrama of the bedchamber." The Central Executive Committee issued a special statement denouncing the book as "the product of an enemy of the Russian revolution and of the Comintern," scoring Trotsky's repudiation for not going far enough, and justifying Eastman's expulsion from the American party, which he had joined as a formality before leaving for Russia.[11]

The following year Trotsky's adherents in Paris seized an opportunity to make amends to Eastman. From Russia came news that the new Opposition bloc of Trotsky, Zinoviev, and Kamenev planned to go to the factories to make an open appeal for the support of the Russian workers. Again, Lenin's testament played a leading role in their calculations. A secret messenger brought the full text to Paris, and Eastman was chosen to make it public to the entire world.

Again Trotsky's supporters in Paris could not coordinate their plans with developments in Russia. The factory demonstrations proved disappointing, and the Stalin-controlled Central Committee demanded the Opposition's surrender. On October 16, 1926, Trotsky, Zinoviev, and Kamenev complied in part by issuing a declaration admitting violations of party discipline; they promised to abstain from them in the future; and they repudiated sympathetic foreign groups. On October 18, *The New York Times* published the text of Lenin's testament together with a page-long story by Eastman explaining its background.[12]

For the second time in two successive years, Eastman had gone out on a limb for Trotsky, and for the second time it had been cut off by the exigencies of the unequal struggle in Moscow. Eastman had expected the publication of the testament to coincide with news of Trotsky's offensive in Moscow; instead it had come out on the heels of Trotsky's retreat. Over a year later, after the need to deny the existence of the testament had passed, Stalin taunted Eastman as "this gentleman, who mixed with the Trotskyists in Moscow, picked up some rumors and gossip about Lenin's 'will.'"[13]

After five years abroad Eastman returned to the United States in the spring of 1927, a pariah to his former friends and associates. Yet Eastman was no more a reasonable facsimile of a terrible Trotskyist than Lore was. His admiration and sympathy for Trotsky had been sorely tried. He agreed more with Trotsky's criticisms of the existing Soviet regime than with the full range of Trotsky's own beliefs. Politics enticed him only partially and intermittently, in competition with half a dozen other interests. Between Trotsky and Eastman an uneasy tension always existed. They could not wholly accept each other and for years they could not do without each other.[14]

Spector and Cannon

In the entire Western hemisphere there was at this time only one real Trotskyist—Maurice Spector, a Canadian. At the precocious age of twenty-three, he, together with Jack MacDonald, Tim Buck, and Bill Moriarty, had been largely responsible for forming the Canadian Communist party in 1921. As editor of the official organ, Spector was recognized as the party's leading propagandist and ideologist.

Spector's Trotskyist sympathies had originated during a trip to Germany and Russia in 1923–24. The German Communists had made him conscious of Stalin's power drive and anti-Trotsky campaign long before most American Communists had sensed the seriousness of the struggle. His curiosity awakened, he had avidly followed the first stages of the open conflict at close range in Moscow, and Trotsky's ideas and style had won him over. On his return to Canada, he became chairman of the party in 1924.

The following year, the Canadian party gave a rare exhibition of independence on the issue of Trotskyism. The Canadian representative in Moscow, Moriarty, advised the Canadian leadership to send a message to the Comintern denouncing Trotsky. Spector wrote a reply to the effect that the Canadian party could not make a decision because it had never received adequate information an the matter.[15] At about the same time, it may be recalled, the American representative, Scott, had asked for a similar message and Ruthenberg had complied.

As Trotsky suffered one defeat after another in the Russian struggle, Spector maintained his position with increasingly greater caution. He was helped by the absence of a factional struggle of the United States type, by the relative Canadian lack of interest in such far-off issues, and by his own intellectual prestige. Yet his anomalous position in the Canadian top leadership could not go on indefinitely.

Spector came to New York in February 1928, soon after Trotsky's first exile to Alma-Ata, as the Canadian party's fraternal delegate to the plenum of the American party. Alone with his political views in the Canadian party, he was eager to find allies in the United States. During a visit to the International Labor Defense, he learned from Cannon's associates, Shachtman and Abern, that Cannon was depressed and disturbed. They told him that Cannon showed a tendency to withdraw from the factional struggle in the party to the "mass activity" of the I.L.D., as if he felt himself to be at a dead end in the party.

Of all the American leaders, Spector surmised, Cannon might be most willing to give him a sympathetic hearing. One evening, he managed to get together alone with Cannon, with whom he had never before talked at length. Before long, Cannon recalls, they were "frankly discussing our doubts and dissatisfactions with the way things were going in Russia." Spector spoke openly of Trotsky's great contributions and the Comintern's internal crisis. Beyond expressing his own dissatisfaction with Trotsky's exile, Cannon responded cautiously and made no commitment. Yet they understood each other and knew that some bond had brought them together.

The evening ended inconclusively. Neither knew what to do next. Cannon again bottled up his misgivings, and revealed the tenor of his discussion with Spector to no one. Repressed in the rough and tumble of factional warfare, his doubts and dissatisfactions had begun to seep out, but they still lacked any clear direction.

At the party plenum, Trotskyism was belabored for hours. A long report by Wolfe was followed by a succession of speakers from all groups anxious to put themselves on record against Trotsky. Cannon sat grimly silent. His best friend in the party, Bill Dunne, tried to get him to join the chorus.

Cannon recalls that Dunne said, "Jim, you have got to speak on this question. It is the Russian question. They will cut our faction to pieces if you don't say a few words for the record." [16]

Cannon refused to budge. Yet he did not consider himself a Trotskyist or even anticipate that he might become one. He was rather immobilized by a mood of depression and disquiet, which could not find an outlet within the party.

Cannon was not looking for trouble. He spent most of the next few months before the Sixth World Congress on a speaking trip for the I.L.D. He did not raise his voice for or against the expulsions of Trotsky and Zinoviev. When the time came to choose delegates to the Sixth World Congress in the summer of 1928, he was still totally preoccupied with American problems and had no intention of getting dragged into the labyrinthine depths of the "Russian question." He did not want to go to Moscow, and only the pressure of his faction forced him to change his mind.

The first disciples

The phenomenon of conversion is peculiarly inherent in revolutionary movements. At some point, the revolutionary crosses a threshold of belief, faith, and action. Some edge up to it slowly; some hurl themselves across impulsively. But for all, there is a moment of decision, a step from one world into another.

Rarely can we get so close to a moment of decision as in the case of the founder of American Trotskyism.

The Program Commission at the Sixth World Congress contained sixty members from forty different parties. Among those appointed to it were Bukharin and Stalin for the Russian party, Cannon and Weinstone for the American party, and Spector for the Canadian party.[17] It was not considered one of the more exciting and factionally profitable commissions. Cannon accepted the assignment apathetically.

A few weeks earlier, in the apple orchard of a little reed-thatched peasant house in far-off Alma-Ata, Leon Trotsky had dictated a short book to a young girl seated at an old typewriter. Originally conceived as a criticism of the proposed program of the Communist International, it grew into one of Trotsky's fundamental works and summed up his thought on the main questions that had arisen in the past five years.[18] This document was hurriedly sent off to the Sixth World Congress in Moscow. There the Russian leaders decided to go through the motions of submitting it to the congress, while preventing it from coming to the attention of the vast majority of the delegates. About two-thirds of the document was translated and distributed only to members of the Program Commission; a report was made on it to the Senioren Konvent, but it was never discussed even in these two bodies.[19]

One day, as Cannon and Spector looked into the folder of material provided for members of the Program Commission, they found in it Trotsky's document entitled *The Draft Program of the Communist International: A Criticism of Fundamentals.* The Comintern had unwittingly acted as the intermediary between him and his first American and Canadian disciples.[20]

For Cannon and Spector, once these pages came into their hands, nothing else mattered. Cannon relates: "We let the caucus meetings and the Congress sessions go to the devil while we read and studied this document. Then I knew what I had to do, and so did he. Our doubts had been resolved. It was as clear as daylight that Marxist truth was on the side of Trotsky. We made a compact there and then—Spector and I—that we would come back home and begin a struggle under the banner of Trotskyism." [21]

They made up their minds that they could not return without Trotsky's document. It had converted them, and they trusted it to convert others. But getting such a dangerous document out of Moscow was no easy task. They were held strictly accountable for their copies, which were marked "Return to Secretariat," and they were repeatedly asked to return them. They stalled for time by inventing excuses and they lived in fear of being searched.

Cannon almost exposed himself. He was so carried away by Trotsky's words that he incautiously showed the document to one of Lovestone's supporters, Harry M. Wicks, who proceeded to accuse Cannon publicly of using Trotsky's document as his source for some uncomplimentary references to John Pepper.[22] When the congress voted down Trotsky's appeal for reinstatement, Cannon conveniently absented himself.[23] Though Cannon may have drawn some suspicion on himself, he was not given any trouble, probably because no one took his incipient Trotskyism too seriously.[24]

Temptation also beset the two lonely Trotskyists. Cannon's prospects in the party had taken a sharp turn for the better at the Sixth World Congress. His two main rivals for the leadership, Foster and Lovestone, had fallen back, the first temporarily dethroned by his own followers, the second under ominous attack by powerful forces in the Comintern. As Cannon showed less and less interest in the proceedings of the congress, the group around him saw greater and greater possibilities of pushing him into the leadership of the combined opposition bloc and, as soon as Lovestone could be overthrown, of the entire party.

About a dozen of Cannon's personal backers, including congress delegates, Lenin School students, and Spector, came together to discuss the situation. They offered to go all-out in Cannon's support if he would stop dragging his feet and give himself over to the party fight. Cannon asked time to think it over.

Cannon and Spector went into a huddle for a couple of days. They had sworn to each other to serve Trotsky's cause, but it was still new and strange territory to them. Alone in Moscow, surrounded by potential enemies, they wrestled with their consciences to determine their attitude to the unexpected turn of events.

Should they take advantage of Cannon's opportunity in order to get into a strategic position for the ultimate purpose of winning over a larger and more important section of the American party? But would it not be necessary—the two secret disciples asked themselves—for Cannon to play for time and outwit the Comintern by feigning zeal in the fight against Trotskyism? Would he not then be breeding anti-Trotskyists without any guarantee that he could reconvert them? Might he not hopelessly compromise himself waiting for the opportunity to tear off his mask and proclaim his true allegiance?

Spector faced much the same problem. As chairman of the Canadian party and editor of its official organ, *The Worker,* he wielded relatively more power in Canada than Cannon did in the United States. A young and restless group, dissatisfied with the Canadian General Secretary, Jack MacDonald, who was then closely linked with the Lovestone regime in the United States, looked to Spector as its candidate to succeed MacDonald. Despite his past Trotskyist indiscretions, the Canadian delegation nominated Spector to the Executive Committee of the Communist International; he was duly elected at the congress, the only Canadian member of the nominally highest organ of power in the Comintern.[25]

Only thirty years old, eight years younger than Cannon, Spector struggled within himself against the temptation to reach even greater heights of influence and power in the Canadian party and in the International. He knew full well what his future career in the organization demanded—suppression of his quixotic fascination with the defeated outcast of Alma-Ata, and subservience to the interests of the Comintern's master in the Kremlin.

After some hesitation, Cannon and Spector decided to put these temptations behind them and dedicate themselves solely to the cause of Trotskyism. They gave themselves over to the task of saving the only political capital in their possession—Trotsky's document. In the end both managed to smuggle their copies out of Russia and headed homeward to certain, self-inflicted excommunication.[26]

The Communist League

Meanwhile, unknown to Cannon, others had been trying to plant the seed of Trotskyism in American soil.

One was a secret Trotskyist named Solntsev, a young Russian who worked for the Amtorg Trading Corporation, the official Soviet agency in New York. With the assistance of Ludwig Lore, still the editor of the influential *New Yorker Volkszeitung* and still a Trotskyist sympathizer, Solntsev in the winter of 1928 succeeded in bringing together a little group of five to form the nucleus of a Trotskyist party in the United States. Besides Solntsev and Lore, the group included the recently returned Max Eastman, his wife Eliena, and Dr. Antoinette Konikow of Boston.

"We talked about the miserable plight of the revolution in America," Eastman recalls, "my unwillingness to become an organizer being one of the most regrettable features, and then broke up and went home." [27]

Before they broke up, Solntsev approached Eastman about another matter. Solntsev had also smuggled documents out of Russia; his documents related to the period before Trotsky's exile to Alma-Ata and therefore antedated the document brought out by Cannon and Spector. This smuggling of purely political documents, largely about abstract points of doctrine, was necessitated by the ruthless suppression of all Trotskyist statements in Russia. Thus, from the outset, publication and propagation of Trotsky's literary works became one of the chief reasons for the existence of the Trotskyist movement.

Would Eastman, Solntsev asked—sheepishly, in view of Eastman's previous experiences with Trotskyist exposés—translate and publish his documents? These included Trotsky's last speech in Russia, the "platform" of the Opposition, and a letter on Stalin's falsifications of history. Again Eastman agreed. Out of this material he made a book by Trotsky called *The Real Situation in Russia,* which appeared just before the Sixth World Congress.[28]

Later that year, Trotsky retracted his previous disavowal of Eastman and call him "an absolutely irreproachable revolutionist." Trotsky explained that his statement against Eastman in 1925 had been concocted by the majority of the Russian Political Bureau and foisted on him with an ultimatum to sign it or enter into an open struggle for which he was then unprepared.[29]

But the Solntsev-Lore meeting was not completely wasted. One of the five, Dr. Antoinette Konikow, was an unusual woman, then nearing sixty, a physician, pioneer of the birth-control movement, and a veteran of both the Russian and American revolutionary movements. She went back to Boston and formed a small Trotskyist group which called itself the Independent Communist League of Boston, with herself as secretary. It published one issue of a little paper, entitled *Bulletin No. 1,* dated December 1928.[30]

When Cannon returned to the United States from the Sixth World Congress, he knew nothing of these first efforts on behalf of American Trotskyism. Because he had taken no one into his confidence since his first discussion with Spector, he could not be sure how even those closest to him would react to his incredible news.

The first one to whom he confided the secret was his wife, Rose Karsner, the assistant secretary of the International Labor Defense. After recovering from the shock, she decided to go along with him. His two long-time followers and co-workers in the I.L.D., Max Shachtman and Martin Abern, came next. They were also completely unprepared and somewhat appalled by the sudden revelation. To each in turn, Cannon entrusted his only copy of the Trotsky document to work on them the same wonder that it had worked on him. And the revelation of Trotskyism suddenly overwhelmed them, too. These men represented three basic types of leadership in radical movements—the agitator, Cannon; the intellectual propagandist, Shachtman; and the technical functionary, Abern.

For about a month it went this way. Cannon relates: "We had one copy of Trotsky's document, but didn't have any way of duplicating it; we didn't have a stenographer; we didn't have a typewriter; we didn't have a mimeograph machine; and we didn't have any money. The only way we could operate was to get hold of carefully selected individuals, arouse enough interest, and then persuade them to come to the house and read the document. A long and toilsome process. We got a few people together and they helped us to spread the gospel to wider circles." [31]

One day Cannon telephoned Eastman to arrange a secret meeting. "I thought there was a law against fraternizing with Trotskyists," said Eastman to Cannon. That night, in Eastman's home at Croton, one of communism's perennial little dramas was enacted—the reunion of a heretic of one period with a heretic of a later period. This reunion, however, cost Eastman something—his royalties on *The Real Situation in Russia,* which he turned over to Cannon for the purpose of bringing out the first issue of a new American Trotskyist organ.[32]

Meanwhile, the factional struggle went on as usual. The last thing that Cannon's allies, the Fosterites, now temporarily headed by Bittelman, wanted to find in their midst was a nest of Trotskyists. Despite their suspicions, they tried hard to look the other way as long as Cannon did nothing to embarrass them overtly. The two groups continued to meet and hatch plots against the common enemy, the Lovestoneites, who had not yet awakened to the good fortune that awaited them in Cannon's defection.

At a meeting of the Foster-Cannon caucus in New York on October 2, 1928, about a month after the Sixth World Congress, an effort was made to smoke Cannon out on the issue of Trotskyism. Though he refused to commit himself, the caucus unanimously elected him to act as its spokesman at an important New York membership meeting that evening.[33]

An indiscretion made further evasion in the caucus impossible. One of Cannon's overzealous converts made the mistake of showing Trotsky's forbidden document to the girl friend of an unsympathetic Fosterite, and he spread the alarm.

One of the caucus leaders was Clarence Hathaway, who had just returned from three years in the Lenin School, to which he had been sent on Cannon's recommendation. Hathaway now stepped out as Cannon's chief prosecutor. While the others hesitated to cause an open break with Cannon, Hathaway forced everyone to declare himself in the Moscow manner with a motion condemning Trotskyism. Cannon abstained, Shachtman voted no, and Abern, who opposed a premature split, voted yes. The caucus interpreted Abern's vote as part of a well-planned maneuver to enable the three to play different roles and expelled all of them from its ranks.

Foster and Bittelman happened to be elsewhere at this time. When they returned to New York, they decided to expose their old allies before Lovestone could do so, and on October 16 submitted a statement to the Political Committee charging Cannon, Shachtman, and Abern with organizing a Trotskyist faction.[34] The committee ordered an investigation into the charges and the immediate removal of the three culprits from their positions in the International Labor Defense, a supposedly independent organization accountable only to its own membership and elected officials.[35]

For about ten days, the committee conducted hearings at which a parade of witnesses testified to such things as Cannon's "growing pessimism, skepticism, and cynicism," his increasing lack of interest in party affairs, and his suspicious behavior at the Sixth World Congress in Moscow. The "trial" dragged on because Cannon, Shachtman, and Abern refused to "confess"; the Lovestone majority in the committee enjoyed what had become a fishing expedition into the confidential affairs of their rivals; and Cannon's former associates used the occasion to prove their own innocence of Trotskyism by turning on Cannon.

Finally Cannon had enough. He cut short the proceedings by reading a statement signed by himself, Abern, and Shachtman, avowing their support of Trotsky's Russian Opposition. The Political Committee unanimously expelled all three of them on October 27, 1928, with the right to appeal to the coming American plenum and to the Comintern. Announcement of the expulsions, however, was held up for three weeks until the end of the election campaign, by which time the three Trotskyists had time to bring out the first issue of a semimonthly organ, *The Militant,* dated November 15, 1928.[36]

Swift preventive and punitive action followed the expulsions. Meetings of every party organization were immediately called to ferret out real or potential—and sometimes imaginary—Trotskyists.

Individual members received letters giving them one week to state in writing their attitude toward Cannon and Trotskyism.[37] Since the little Trotskyist group in New York had lacked the time and resources to get in touch with most of their friends throughout the country, many of them heard of Cannon's expulsion for the first time through the demand that they approve it. When some of Cannon's friends in Minneapolis, who had never before given thought to Trotskyism, demurred and asked to hear what the expelled had to say before deciding, they were forthwith expelled—and promptly became Trotskyists.

In the next few weeks, Cannon gained the support of several small groups—Dr. Konikow's handful in Boston, about a dozen party members led by Arne Swabeck and Albert Glotzer in Chicago, about two dozen headed by Vincent R. Dunne and Karl Sköglund in Minneapolis, three or four in Kansas City, two in Philadelphia, and some previously expelled Italians and Hungarians in New York. The new movement contained one member of the top Political Committee, Cannon; two members of the C.E.C., Abern and Swabeck; and one alternate member of the C.E.C., Shachtman. It severed the closest of friendships between Cannon and William F. Dunne, and came between the latter and his three brothers—Vincent R., Grant, and Miles—all of whom went with Cannon. About one hundred members were expelled from the party on charges of Trotskyism.[38] Yet the party reacted as if it had far more to fear.

Cannon's home was ransacked by politically minded "burglars," exclusively interested in his letter file, manuscripts, subscription list, and the like. Photostats of some of the purloined letters soon turned up in the pages of the *Daily Worker*.[39] According to Gitlow, the raid on Cannon's apartment was carried out by Stachel and the business manager of the *Daily Worker,* Ravich, who brought Cannon's records to Stachel's home where they were examined by Lovestone, Pepper, and Stachel.[40] Trotskyist meetings were broken up by strong-arm squads.[41]

When Cannon's followers formally organized themselves as the

Communist League of America (Opposition) at their first National Conference in Chicago, May 17–19, 1929, they still numbered only about one hundred.[42] The total membership reported in 1931 was 156, of whom only 24 had belonged to Cannon's group before 1928.[43]

In Canada, Spector fared no better. Like Cannon, after his return from Moscow he tried to play for time while secretly proselytizing for Trotskyism. He first aroused suspicion as a result of a public speech in which he failed to give as glowing an account of Soviet economic development as custom demanded. One of those who took the lead in "exposing" Spector was another young alumnus of the Lenin School, Stewart Smith, who played much the same role against Spector in Canada as Hathaway had played against Cannon in the United States.

Spector's undoing came when the American party asked the Canadian party to endorse the expulsion of the American Trotskyists. In order to carry out his compact with Cannon to push ahead with Trotskyism, and being largely unsuccessful in his own proselytizing efforts, Spector abandoned the policy of evasion. After voting as a minority of one against the endorsement, he made a dramatic declaration of his Trotskyist program, and expulsion automatically followed. After the rifling of Cannon's apartment, Lovestone transmitted to the Canadian secretary, Jack MacDonald, copies of Spector's correspondence with Cannon, portions of which the Canadian Communist organ hastened to publish to prove that Spector and Cannon had been working together. The outlook for Trotskyism in Canada seemed so limited that Spector soon came to New York to assist the American Trotskyists.[44]

After a decade of Trotskyism, Spector, and later Shachtman, rebelled against it and returned to an older conception of democratic socialism. It fell to Cannon, supported by Vincent R. Dunne and Arne Swabeck, to carry on the Trotskyist tradition in the United States. Yet it is most unlikely that anyone, before 1928, would have chosen Cannon, of all the early American Communists, as the first and last American Trotskyist.

The appeal of Trotskyism

"It was the document that hit us like a thunderbolt," Cannon said, years later, of his conversion to Trotskyism. "It just knocked us completely over." [45]

"I will never want, or be able, to forget the absolutely shattering effect upon my inexcusable indifference to the fight in the Russian party, upon my smug ignorance about the issue involved, upon my sense of shame, that was produced by the first reading of Trotsky's classic *Critique of the Draft Program of the Comintern,*" Shachtman recalled.[46]

What was there in this singular document, Trotsky's criticism of the draft program of the Communist International, that made such an overwhelming impression on Cannon and Shachtman? Why did the thunderbolt miss so many other American and Canadian Communists?

The document that Cannon and Shachtman read was divided into two parts, the first on the question of socialism in one country, the second on the defeat of the Chinese Communists in 1927. Only a single page was devoted to American Communism; it repeated Trotsky's familiar criticism of Pepper's flirtation with the LaFollette movement in 1924.[47]

Thus Trotsky's appeal was primarily theoretical and international. It demanded an intense concern for the issues in the Russian struggle and for their repercussions on the Comintern's European and Far Eastern policies. Cannon, Shachtman, and Abern had previously revealed only the most superficial interest in such questions. They had blindly followed whatever line had officially emanated from Moscow. Ever since his successful campaign against the underground party in the early nineteen-twenties, Cannon had personified the "Americanizer" who stressed practical work rather than theory, which he had been content to leave to Bittelman and others. Much of his energies had been spent in purely factional maneuvers in which he had disposed of smaller forces than had either Lovestone or Foster. There seemed little in his past to prepare him for Trotskyism.

But Cannon's state of depression before the Sixth World Congress had made him receptive to a new cause that offered hope of escape from the personal and factional impasse. The new cause did not require a fundamental reconsideration or a painful breach with the past. Trotskyism called on all errant Communists to return to the true faith of Leninism, to the faith which had originally brought Cannon into the Communist movement. If Trotsky was right, the Soviet Union was heading toward an economic smash-up, the Comintern toward an inevitable breakdown. Trotsky confidently expected a series of world-wide disasters to wake up the mass of Communists and force them to sweep out the existing leadership to avoid the total destruction of their work and movement. This faith gave him and even his most isolated followers the strength to carry on what might have otherwise seemed a hopeless struggle against impossible odds.

In American terms, Cannon expected the Comintern to ensure the victory of the new "Right," represented by Lovestone, over the new "Left," represented by Foster and Bittelman.[48] He viewed Trotskyism as the most principled expression of the Left, which was bound to come into its own with the reaction against Lovestone's anticipated victory. As an old ally of the Fosterites, he saw Trotskyism in the best position to reap the fruits of their disillusionment.

Cannon was never able to test this theory, because his presupposition proved false. Instead of turning "Right," the Soviet and Comintern leadership turned "Left." This Left turn, inaugurated officially in 1928 and driven much further in 1929, succeeded in cutting the ground from under most of Cannon's potential support. Instead of a clear-cut fight against Bukharin and Lovestone, Trotsky and Cannon faced the far more dangerous enmity of Stalin and his emergent American adjutants, Foster, Bittelman, and Browder. The Stalinists were capable of outbidding the most extreme Leftists in one period and the most extreme Rightists in another. Quite a few American Communists who maintained contact with Cannon wavered for a time and then used Stalin's Left turn as a reason for deciding against Trotsky's Left Opposition.

Once having made his decision, Cannon never turned back. He thereby extricated himself, by means of Trotskyism, from the onrushing Stalinist tide. But Trotskyism could not give Cannon the means of finding a new revolutionary road; at best, it promised to lead back to an old one. In an anti-Stalinist form, it helped to perpetuate the dependence of all branches and offshoots of the American Communist movement on the Russian revolution and Russian revolutionaries.

17

The Runaway Convention

WE LEFT the Sixth World Congress of the Comintern as it came to a close in Moscow at the end of August 1928. Lovestone had received some hard blows, but had emerged from the congress seemingly unscathed. The Opposition had mounted several major offensives against him, but they had dwindled in action to little more than raiding operations. To make the outcome even more confusing, Foster, the Opposition's foremost leader, had wandered away from the main body of his troops into a strange no man's land between the warring camps.

To most American Communists Lovestone was still the Comintern's favorite American son. Any doubts about it were soon dispelled by a supplementary decision issued on September 7, 1928, only a week after the congress, by the Comintern's top command. It expressed the opinion that, despite some Right errors by both sides, "the charge against the majority of the Central Committee of the Party representing a Right line is unfounded." Since this was precisely the charge that the Opposition had made the crux of its case against Lovestone's majority, the Comintern's statement did not leave the Opposition much to shoot at.

The majority made this statement public and, lest anyone miss the point, added its own interpretation that "the Comintern is continuing its policy of supporting the present Party leadership." [1] Even if this claim went too far, the least that could be said was that the Comintern had not abandoned the present party leadership.

The Comintern also gained for Lovestone a two-month breathing spell from open factional warfare. It instructed the Americans to make a special effort to abstain from all factionalism and to postpone preparations for the next party convention until the end of the presidential election campaign in November 1928.[2]

The highlight of the Communist campaign was a sensational report in the *Daily Worker* that Gitlow, the candidate for Vice-President, had been kidnaped from a train at Phoenix, Arizona, and abandoned in the middle of a desert. This lurid tale was featured for several days in the Communist paper and then suddenly dropped without explanation. As Gitlow tells the story, the Communist organizer in Arizona had canceled his speaking dates in Phoenix owing to rumors that a vigilante committee was organizing to drive Gitlow out of the state and dump him in the desert. Forewarned, Gitlow had not stopped over in Phoenix while the kidnaping story was running on the front page of the *Daily Worker*. Later he spoke in Phoenix in a public square because no hall could be secured.[3]

The victorious Republican candidate in 1928, Herbert C. Hoover, received over 21,000,000 votes; the Democratic candidate, Alfred E. Smith, about 15,000,000; and the Socialist candidate, Norman Thomas, about 267,800. The Communist candidate, William Z. Foster, was credited with 48,228 votes in thirty-three states in 1928 compared with 33,076 votes in fourteen states in 1924. The gain was a modest one, considering the increased number of states. In New York State, the Socialists outdistanced the Communists by 107,332 to 10,876. For the first time, the Communists forged ahead of the Socialist Labor party nationally.[4]

The American Communist factions interpreted the 1928 vote in accordance with their basic political perspectives.

Lovestone and Pepper saw in it a confirmation of their more pessimistic analysis. Lovestone evaluated the 1928 result as "the smallest total vote, in years, of the electorate for the parties that were either frankly revolutionary, like the Workers (Communist) Party, or did not boast loudly about their petit-bourgeois character, like the Socialist Party." In passing, he advanced the possibility that the newly elected Governor of New York, Franklin D. Roosevelt, might "come forward as the leader of the Democratic Party." [5] Pepper interpreted the 1928 election as a "Republican landslide" and "a big victory for trustified capital, a big victory for capitalist reaction." [6]

Bittelman and Foster were required by their more optimistic political line to see the election as evidence of radicalization by the American proletariat. They recalled that Lenin had written of Theodore Roosevelt's vote in 1912 that it had signified that millions of Americans could "no longer live in the old way"; this was "doubly true," they maintained, of Smith's vote in 1928.[7] Not being able to make a case for radicalization on the basis of the Communist vote, they accomplished their purpose by substituting the Democratic vote.

Yet of this election a recent historian has written: "On every important issue, the Democratic platform of 1928 paralleled that of the Republicans." [8]

The mechanics of a factional dispute were well illustrated by the election issue. A Left turn in tactics required a Leftist interpretation of the objective situation in the United States to justify itself. In turn a Leftist interpretation of the objective situation required the election results to reflect the radicalization of broad masses of the American electorate. However mistaken the Leftist faction may have been about the objective situation in the United States in 1928, it benefited from the fact that it made the objective situation appear consistent with the Left turn in tactics; and no Communist could question the Left turn in tactics without defying the Russian leadership and the Comintern.

Because Lovestone and Pepper scoffed at the radicalization of the American electorate in 1928, Bittelman and Foster accused them of favoring a "fatalistic, Right Wing analysis" of the objective situation and of sabotaging the Left turn in tactics. Yet Lovestone and Pepper were vulnerable to attack because they took issue with the political implications of the Left turn but not with the Left turn itself. In effect, they went along with the Left turn but denied that the time was ripe for it.

The Leftist line of attack was typical of the reasoning that has chronically caused the American Communists to substitute doctrine for reality. It derived the objective situation from Communist tactics —not, as Communist theory itself demands, Communist tactics from the objective situation.

The hunt for the Right danger

Lovestone was no novice at this game. He could tell a Left turn from a Right turn as expertly as anyone. And if the Comintern's chieftains insisted on a Left turn, he was not going to stand in the way.

In his report on the Sixth World Congress to a general membership meeting in New York a month later, Lovestone showed full awareness of what was expected of him. "The feature of the World Congress was a thoroughgoing search for any Right deviations in all Communist Parties," he said. "The Sixth Congress examined and hunted for Right dangers with a microscope and telescope, and wherever it found these, it hunted them down with heavy artillery and machine-gun fire." [9]

The hunt in the American party started by stepping up the campaign for new unions. After the first calls had been issued in July 1928 for new textile and mine unions, similar steps were taken the following month in the needle trades.[10] The first new union, the National Miners' Union, was officially formed on September 10, 1928, with Pat Toohey as secretary-treasurer; the National Textile Workers Union was set up a few days later with Albert Weisbord as secretary-treasurer; and the Needle Trades Workers' Industrial Union, an amalgamation of the cloak, dress, and fur fields, came into existence on January 1, 1929, with Ben Gold as secretary-treasurer.[11]

The Left turn on the Negro question was executed with unseemly haste. The party's platform for the presidential elections, drawn up prior to the Sixth World Congress, had made no mention whatsoever of "the right of self-determination of the Negroes in the Black Belt." Before any explanation or even announcement of the new line was made to the membership, the national office sent out telegrams to the party candidates instructing them to add self-determination to their list of Negro demands.[12] The first published notice of the new Negro line appeared a few days after the election in an editorial in the *Daily Worker,* "The Communists Are for a Black Republic," which reflected Pepper's unauthorized version; the already proclaimed new line was so little understood that no one detected the difference.[13]

The California Communists gave the Lovestone-dominated Political Committee another chance to hunt the Right danger. The California District Organizer and Executive Committee came under fire for challenging the California Socialists to a pre-election debate in a letter addressed to "Dear Comrades." The Political Committee seized on the incident to reinstate in all its purity the "united front from below," always the sign of a Left turn. It severely condemned the "grave error" of sending a letter, "independent of its contents," to the ever "more fascist" Socialist leadership.[14]

Lovestone's agility in making the Left turn did not prevent his enemies from continuing to charge him with being the foremost exponent of the Right danger in all fields of party work. In order to push this line of attack, however, the Opposition was compelled to credit Lovestone with far more consistency than he could afford to exhibit. Yet there was some truth in the charge; both Lovestone and Foster gave the impression of accepting the new line against their inner feelings and better judgment.

Whenever the objective situation in the United States came into dispute, however, there was a more deeply rooted difference between the factions. After the elections, the present and future of the American economy became a factional issue.

In Communist mythology, Lovestone has been ridiculed for preaching that American capitalism was "exempt from that system's laws of growth and decay" and that "there was no prospect of an economic crisis in the United States." [15] This latter-day version has so little relation to the facts that it creates a difficulty in understanding why any Communist of the period should have taken Lovestone seriously.

In reality, the debate was primarily over the immediate condition, not the ultimate fate, of American capitalism. Lovestone, an avid reader of business magazines, was largely influenced by economic statistics. When they went down, as in the latter half of 1927, he spoke of a depression. But the index of industrial production took a decided jump from 97 to 102 in July–August 1928, and continued onward until the dizzying height of 116 was reached in September 1929.[16]

In the latter half of 1928, therefore, Lovestone emphasized the upward movement of American economic development. At the end of 1928, theses signed by Gitlow, Lovestone, and Pepper made this clear: "A powerful technical revolution is taking place in the United States, a tremendous rationalization, an increase in the forces of production, which in its effects can be compared to a second industrial revolution." [17]

At this time Lovestone's fondness for quoting business magazines backfired. In an article at the end of 1928, he sought to prove that "finance capital" had frankly boasted of its success in the 1928 election. He cited a eulogy of Hoover's victory in the *Magazine of Wall Street* which had ended with this rhetorical flourish: "As Rome had its Augustinian age and Britain its Victorian age, so we are about to enter upon an epoch of affluence and magnificence, of peace and prosperity, that history may well record as the Hooverian age." [18] On this Lovestone commented: "Translate 'we' into Wall Street and the truth is here." [19]

For years this comment on a quotation haunted Lovestone; it was exhibited as the most damning proof that he had believed in a "Hooverian age" of American capitalism corresponding to the "Victorian age" of British capitalism. The official history of the American Communist party even makes it part of the "whole body of revisionist theory" which Lovestone allegedly developed, as if he were the author of the analogy and it had represented a serious theoretical pronouncement on his part.[20]

In fact, Lovestone, as much as any other Communist of the period, took for granted the inevitability of an economic crisis. He merely contended that it had been delayed by the unexpected arrival of recovery in the middle of 1928. The theses of Gitlow, Lovestone, and Pepper stated: "The crisis which would put at least a temporary end to American prosperity has already been due for quite a long period. But it has been delayed, though by no means prevented as apologists of imperialism maintain." They gave three reasons for the delay: rapid industrialization of the South, intensified exploitation of Latin America, and increased foreign trade with Europe. Lovestone's formula in 1928 for getting around the boom was the same as Ruthenberg's had been in 1926—the Communists could take advantage of opportunities for mass struggles in good times as well as bad. Lovestone vainly tried to get the opposition to stop "confusing the immediate economic situation with the basic trend of American capitalism." [21]

For the Foster-Bittelman Opposition, the problem of distinguishing between the immediate and the basic was not so acute, because its members simply refused to recognize the existence of economic recovery in 1928–29. At the end of 1928, on the eve of the hectic, if unhealthy, last burst of the boom, their theses professed to see the end of the "slight upward turn" and the revival of "downward trends." They refused to admit that the upturn of 1928 had made any "notable improvement in the general depression"; the only concession they made was that the depression had been prevented from degenerating into an economic crisis.[22]

In this area, then, there were real differences between the factions in 1928–29. Lovestone tended to emphasize the strength of American capitalism, Bittelman its weakness. Lovestone projected the inevitable crisis into the indefinite future; Bittelman made it seem far more imminent and unavoidable.

The Opposition had, of course, the last laugh. When the crisis did break out at the end of 1929, the niceties of the discussion were easily forgotten. All that mattered was that the Opposition had long been clamoring about depression and crisis and the Lovestone regime had not. Leaving nothing to chance, the victors later rewrote the history of the controversy to make a caricature of Lovestone's position.

After the crash, Lovestone continued to insist that it had resulted from the strength, not the decline, of the American capitalist economy.[23] But by that time, the distinction was too abstruse for the average Communist to appreciate.

In the end, however, the apex of American capitalism was much further away than any Communist could then imagine. That it would survive the crisis of 1929–33 and go on after World War II to even greater heights of production and consumption was impossible for any pre-depression faction of the Communist movement to contemplate.

A small dark cloud

The fortunes of the Bittelman-led Opposition were never lower than they seemed to be at the end of 1928. The first test of strength after the Sixth World Congress came at a plenum of the American party, December 15–19, 1928. All the disputed questions were fully and freely debated in the party press and meetings. The Comintern made no overt effort to influence the plenum's decisions. The Gitlow-Lovestone-Pepper theses on the general situation scored a one-sided victory over the Foster-Bittelman theses by a vote of 28 to 7, with one abstention.[24] Membership meetings gave Lovestone's leadership a majority of 70 per cent in 1928 as compared with 58 per cent the year before. The majority rose to 75 per cent in the industrial areas of Pittsburgh, Cleveland, and Detroit.[25]

The Opposition's position seemed so hopeless that long-time supporters began to desert it. Ella Reeve Bloor, then active in California, wrote to Foster of her withdrawal from his group: "There would really be no 'Opposition' *without you.* No one through the country knows Aronberg or Bittelman. Out here, the Opposition is called the 'Foster group' and things are done in your name that would make you gasp for breath to behold." [26] With the two most popular figures of the old Opposition knocked out of commission—Foster temporarily for his trade-union deviation and Cannon permanently for his Trotskyism—Lovestone seemed to have less to worry about than ever before.

Then, from across the seas, a small dark cloud of trouble suddenly drifted into view on the far horizon.

The cloud was a letter from the Political Secretariat of the Comintern, dated November 21, 1928. In sharp contrast to its previous letter of September 7, 1928, absolving Lovestone's majority of representing the Right danger, this message was entirely critical and menacing in tenor. It raked up the seven-week-old self-congratulatory declaration which the Lovestone leadership had issued in response to the September 7 letter, and severely reprimanded it for too little self-criticism and too much self-praise. It specifically expressed displeasure with the declaration's claim that the Comintern was "continuing its policy of supporting politically the present Party leadership." The November 21 letter admonished: "This formulation could easily lead to the interpretation that the [Sixth World] Congress has expressly declared its confidence in the majority, in contrast to the minority. But this is not so." The letter ended by instructing the American leadership to postpone its next convention until February 1929.[27]

Lovestone kept this letter to himself for a week before turning it over to the top committee with his answer.[28] He knew that it was futile to argue with such a communication and proceeded to give it his humble endorsement.[29] But he also realized that its minatory note could not be ignored and that he could not delay strengthening his fences in Moscow. With this in mind, he immediately moved to replace J. Louis Engdahl, the American representative to the Comintern, who was considered a political lightweight. His choice for the post was his old City College schoolmate, Bertram D. Wolfe, with whom he worked in the party in closest rapport. At the same time, he took steps to send Harry M. Wicks, a member of his faction but a strange choice in an emergency, as the American representative to the Profintern.

The origin of Lovestone's crisis, therefore, can be quite precisely dated. It took shape in the Comintern between September 7 and November 21, 1928. Since nothing threatened Lovestone at home in these ten weeks, the key to the crisis must be sought in Moscow.

Lovestone and Bukharin

For the sequence of events, we must go back to the Sixth World Congress.

When it ended on September 1, 1928, Bukharin still nominally headed the Comintern and the existence of differences among the Russian leaders was officially denied. On September 30, the Russian Communist organ, *Pravda,* published Bukharin's article, "Notes of an Economist," in which he cautiously, but unmistakably, warned against the excesses of Stalin's Left turn in Russian economic policy.[30] Bukharin was never permitted to make another public protest. On October 19, Stalin declared war on the "Right danger" in the Russian party, but maintained the fiction that no one in the Political Bureau, to which Bukharin belonged, was a target of his attack.[31] On November 19, at a plenum of the Russian party, Stalin made the campaign against the "Right danger" the keynote of his address. This time he named close associates of Bukharin as the chief offenders but again pretended that the Political Bureau was "all united." [32]

Thus the Comintern's letter of November 21 to the American party came two days after Stalin's policy-making speech at the Russian plenum. As long as Stalin continued to play his cat-and-mouse game with Bukharin, however, the American leadership could not be absolutely sure of Bukharin's standing or gird itself for a shake-up in the Comintern.

Meanwhile, a case of special interest to Lovestone—and to Stalin—had flared up in the German Communist party. A scandal in the mishandling of party funds by Wittdorf, the Hamburg party chieftain, threatened to bring down the party's national leader, Ernst Thaelmann, Wittdorf's protector and brother-in-law. The Wittdorf affair was exploited by an opposition group headed by Arthur Ewert, the same "Braun" and "Grey" who had been largely instrumental in enabling Lovestone to win the American leadership in 1927. Without outside support, Thaelmann could not put down Ewert's bid for power. Ewert's principal lieutenant in this struggle was Gerhardt Eisler, then known by his first name and so designated in Comintern documents of the period. Thaelmann's faction fought back by accusing Ewert and Gerhardt of "conciliationism" toward the German Right Wing of Heinrich Brandler and August Thalheimer. In October 1928 the Comintern stepped in and prevented Ewert and Gerhardt from removing Thaelmann from the leadership.[33] In December Stalin gave his personal attention to the case in one of his rare appearances at a meeting of the Comintern's Presidium. Besides protecting Thaelmann, he assailed two other Comintern leaders close to Bukharin, the Swiss, Humbert-Droz, and the Italian, Serra.*

In his denunciation of Serra, Stalin made a significant reference to the United States:

> Therefore, a situation is quite conceivable in which it may be necessary to create parallel mass associations of the working class, against the will of the trade-union bosses who have sold themselves to the capitalists. We already have such a situation in America. It is quite possible that things are moving in the same direction in Germany too.[34]

Stalin's seemingly casual reference to the American situation is of more than passing interest. The "parallel mass associations of the working class"—or dual unions, in American trade-union terminology—had been conceived in Moscow and imposed on the American Communists despite their misgivings. Now the American example gave Stalin a precedent for beating down resistance to dual unionism among European Communists. This export and re-export of policies

* Forbidden to stay in Germany after his unsuccessful bid for power against Thaelmann, Ewert was appointed Comintern representative in Brazil, where he was imprisoned and tortured to death. Eisler made his way to the United States in the early nineteen-thirties and, like Pepper a decade earlier, acted the role of the putative Comintern representative.

from and to Moscow made it possible for the Comintern to use one party or another as pace-setter for the rest without always appearing to have taken the initiative.

It was not by chance, then, that Stalin happened to mention the American situation in connection with the new trade-union line or that he was soon willing to give so much of his time to the culmination of the American factional struggle. The intrinsic importance of this American struggle was slight by Comintern standards. But its relationship to the larger, fast-maturing struggle against Bukharin gave it a resonance on the international Communist stage that increasingly demanded and repaid Stalin's attention.

It was also no accident that Molotov attended this meeting of the Comintern's Presidium in December 1928 and Bukharin did not. After the Sixth World Congress, Molotov had moved into the Comintern as Stalin's deputy and Bukharin's *de facto* successor without fanfare or even announcement.[35]

Lovestone was not unwilling to join the chorus against the German Right Wing. Early in December 1928, the American leadership issued a declaration endorsing "wholeheartedly the expulsion of Brandler and Thalheimer," with whom Lovestone was destined to find himself allied in the not too distant future.[36] Of much greater interest in Moscow, however, was Lovestone's attitude toward Bukharin.

At this decisive moment, Lovestone made a public avowal of his attitude toward Bukharin. It occurred at the plenum of the American party in December 1928. During the dispute on the strength of American capitalism, Lovestone invoked Bukharin's authority:

> What did Comrade Bukharin say about this? I still quote Comrade Bukharin. For me he does not represent the Right wing of the Communist International; although for some he does. For me Comrade Bukharin represents the Communist line, the line of the C.E.C. of the C.P.S.U. Therefore Comrade Bukharin is an authority—of the C.I.[37]

Years later, Lovestone added some details not in the official record of the plenum and attributed his downfall to this meeting.

> Everybody was rallying to endorse Stalin. I was not only a personal friend of Bukharin, but I had fundamental agreement with him on international questions, though on Russian questions I had agreement with Stalin and not with him. In that meeting I objected to the American Communist Party lining up. I said, "We will wear no Stalin buttons, and we will wear no Bukharin buttons, and we will not engage in gangsterism against Stalin or Bukharin." I said that Stalin was my leader as leader of the Communist Party; that I respected him, had high regard for his opinion and caliber of thinking.
>
> . . . Saying that, a cable was sent to Moscow. That cable was passed around throughout the International, and that pretty much served as the blot on my political death certificate in my relations with the Stalin leadership.[38]

The facts were that Bukharin no longer represented the Communist line or the line of the C.P.S.U. and that he was no longer an authority of the C.I. Whatever Lovestone's motives may have been—and we will try to examine them more fully at a later stage—it is clear that he was suffering from a disastrous shortage of reliable information on the state of affairs in the Russian party and the Comintern. It is hard to believe that Lovestone would have made such an extraordinary blunder in public if he had known better.

This breakdown of Lovestone's lines of communication with Moscow showed how much his position had changed for the worse. As long as Zinoviev or Bukharin had headed the Comintern, he and Ruthenberg had always been a jump or two ahead of their rivals in adapting themselves to changes of line or winning support in the right quarters. But since Stalin had moved into the Comintern, Lovestone, without his being fully aware of it, was gradually cut off from the seats of power and the sources of inside information. The Anglo-American Secretariat had become the chief center of intrigue against him. His official representative in Moscow, Engdahl, knew little and cared not much more about the inner politics in the Comintern. Lozovsky was accurately calling the shots for Lovestone's enemies. And Pepper was no longer in Moscow to counteract Lozovsky.

The Anglo-American Secretariat was a particularly grievous source of the Lovestone group's tribulations. As the Comintern agency in direct charge of American affairs, it was responsible for most of the cabled instructions that made the American leadership merely an executive organ for carrying out the Comintern's wishes. There had always been a problem of balance in the powers exercised by the Comintern and those reserved for the party leaderships; this problem had been reduced to a minimum as long as the Comintern favored the existing American leadership. But after the Sixth World Congress the Anglo-American Secretariat's cables to the American party increased in both frequency and fault-finding. The Secretariat insisted more than ever upon flaunting its prerogative of overruling the American leadership even in relatively petty technical and organizational matters. A wit in the party summed up the situation picturesquely; he likened the party to the Brooklyn Bridge because both were "suspended on cables."

This condition was all the more galling because some American Communists remembered Goldfarb-Petrovsky-Bennet, head of the Secretariat, as a one-time Menshevik who had used his considerable gifts of invective against the pro-Bolshevik Left Wing in the columns of the Socialist Jewish *Daily Forward*. What the men around Lovestone said among themselves about the Anglo-American Secretariat and its top functionary may be gathered from portions of an indignant letter written by Bedacht to Wolfe early in 1929:

> . . . We are living in an almost impossible atmosphere. After we were told to fight it out, at the World Congress, and after we fought it out to live in constant expectation that some Goldfarbian cable will nullify the whole history of the last few months and will declare that the membership of our Party proposes and God Goldfarb disposes.
>
> I have told you in my last letter and I repeat here that the role played by the Goldfarbs creates a most impossible relation with the Comintern. No edict of any person or any body can establish confidence of our Party members in the face of the Comintern if this face is that of an old Menshevik whose outstanding contribution to American Party history is his alliance with Abe Cahan [editor of the *Forward*] and his right wing gangster tactics against the Left Wing. No matter how loud he hollers now about Bolshevism, he cannot drown the sound of his past tirades against the Left wing in the American SP and he cannot eradicate his history.

> It is bitter experience for us who have gone through the struggle against the Goldfarbs here, against his counter-revolutionary Menshevik conceptions and tactics, to be now treated like schoolboys by the same Goldfarb, posing as a schoolmaster of Bolshevism. That makes not only a cat laugh but also makes angels weep. . . .
>
> Deceit and hypocrisy are not yet recognized Bolshevik methods and we refuse to use them, as well as refuse to be made victims of them. Isn't there any sane person left in the Comintern to see that these tactics and policies lead to a crisis in our Party which can only end in disintegration and weakening of the Comintern itself? [39]

Meanwhile, to make matters worse, Pepper had become more a liability than an asset. After returning to the United States from the Sixth World Congress he was almost immediately called back to Moscow in September 1928.[40] Aware that his enemies in the Comintern were preparing no friendly reception for him, Pepper succeeded in staving off the evil day by protesting that he could not leave the United States, and the American leadership backed him up. In the next few months, Pepper resumed his old role as one of the American Communists' foremost leaders. With Gitlow and Lovestone, he put his name to the principal political resolution at the December 1928 plenum; he also delivered a report on "The Right Danger and Trotskyism," one of the three main reports to the plenum.[41]

This was the worst possible moment for Lovestone to make a public announcement of his unbroken record of solidarity with Pepper, but he was lured into it by a carefully planted rumor of differences between them. To deny the rumor, Lovestone and Pepper solemnly issued a statement affirming that they had "always been working together politically very closely" since 1922 and that they had "shared the same views" for the past six years.[42] With these declarations of esteem for Bukharin and Pepper, Lovestone was well on his way to becoming a champion of lost causes.

Thus, as 1929 opened, Lovestone's political fortunes were peculiarly divided. At home he was stronger than ever; in Moscow he was deeply in trouble and begging for more.

Wolfe's mission

Wolfe left for Russia late in December 1928 to replace Engdahl as the American representative to the Comintern.

Before leaving, he arranged with Lovestone a private code of communication for confidential messages. Lovestone directed him to assure the Comintern of the total loyalty of the American leadership, to explain that the leadership realized it had won the overwhelming majority of the party only through the Comintern's past support and could not hold its majority against the Comintern, and to protest that therefore it did not understand why the Comintern was harassing it. Lovestone asked Wolfe to try to find out what was behind the trouble and what could be done about it.

Wolfe and his wife arrived in Moscow in the first days of January 1929 after a painful journey. Mrs. Wolfe was recovering from an illness and he had been suffering from an abscessed ear. Wolfe immediately asked for interviews with Bukharin and Stalin, but was shunted off to lesser figures in the Comintern. Whenever Wolfe asked about Bukharin, he was told that Bukharin was too sick to be seen, that he was away on vacation, and similar evasions. Engdahl professed to know nothing of these mysterious happenings but showed Wolfe the draft of an Open Letter which the Comintern intended to send for the guidance of the American Communists' forthcoming Sixth Convention. This letter opened Wolfe's eyes for the first time to the seriousness of the situation; it clearly indicated that the Comintern had decided to withdraw its support from the Lovestone majority leadership.

Wolfe immediately demanded a meeting of the Executive Committee of the Comintern to reconsider the letter. He was put off with excuses that it was too late, that the letter was about to be cabled, that Engdahl had offered no objections to it. Everyone advised Wolfe to see Stalin, but Stalin refused to see him. Only when Wolfe threatened to send word to the United States that the Comintern had refused to give him a hearing was he finally informed that a special one-hour meeting of the Presidium had been called for that purpose the following day. He stayed up the whole night, with a temperature of 104, drinking coffee and vodka, and preparing his report.

At the meeting the next day, Wolfe spoke under great physical and emotional stress. After a few minutes, he was asked to stop for translation, and noticed that the largest group was clustered around the German translator. When he went over to this group, he was dismayed to learn that the translator was making little effort to interpret his words accurately. To overcome this handicap, Wolfe decided to change to German, which he had studied but had never spoken publicly. After another half hour, however, he suddenly collapsed, weak with fever, on the platform. There was a stir in the room, but only one person, Eliena D. Stassova, then head of the International Red Aid (M.O.P.R.), came forward. She gave him two aspirins and begged him to cease speaking. He insisted on finishing his speech unless the meeting were postponed, and he went on.

After Wolfe's speech, no action was taken. As he walked down the aisle, he felt that people he had known for years looked as if they feared contact with him and wanted to remove themselves from the danger of political contamination. Only the oldest veteran of the German Communist movement, Clara Zetkin, herself in political difficulties at the time, moved toward him, hobbling on her cane; she extended her gnarled hand to shake his hand warmly, and hoarsely uttered some words of encouragement.

After recovering from his illness, Wolfe noticed Bukharin arriving one afternoon in an automobile at the Hotel Lux, where the Comintern officials lived. Wolfe greeted him, and suggested that they should get together for a chat in a nearby tearoom after Bukharin had finished his business in the building. Bukharin, looking fit and healthy, accepted the invitation and soon joined him. When Wolfe told him that he was supposed to be ill, Bukharin calmly agreed.

"Well, are you well or ill?" Wolfe asked.

"By a vote of five to four, I am too ill to function as Chairman of the Communist International," Bukharin answered wryly.

Thus Wolfe learned the important distinction between the health of Bukharin and the health of the Chairman of the Communist International.[43]

The last shred of principle

Wolfe's experience confirmed that Lovestone and his closest associates had known little of what had been happening in Moscow. By the middle of January 1929 Wolfe knew the worst but could do little about it. The ruling Comintern circles kept him in ignorance of their plans as if he were a stranger in their midst.

Despite Wolfe's protest and while he was still confined to bed with his abscessed ear, the draft of the Comintern's letter to the American Communists arrived in New York. We know that it arrived some time before January 6, 1929, as a result of a peculiar embarrassment which it caused William Z. Foster.

After his humiliation at the Sixth World Congress the previous August, Foster had tried to make his peace with Bittelman by humbly recognizing the latter's political pre-eminence. At the plenum of December 1928, delegates had heard Foster declare that Bittelman was the greatest living Marxist on the American continent and that he, Foster, was only a simple worker in the vineyard of Bittelman.[44] Foster even related in the party organ that Bittelman had gone over what he had written in their theses for the plenum "with a double microscope." [45] But in the midst of these conciliatory gestures Foster again made a political misstep which brought down on him the wrath of Bittelman and his former subordinates.

In January 1929 Foster published an article in *The Communist* on the 48th annual convention of the A.F. of L. held the previous November. He used the occasion to dispute Pepper's theory that the A.F. of L. was capable of future growth, and instead offered the view that company unions rather than the A.F. of L. or the Socialists represented the "main reliance of the employers for propagating reformist illusions among the workers." In the same article he formally withdrew his resistance to new unions, recognized them as "our major task," and merely warned against completely abandoning work in the old unions.[46]

Foster's article drew fire from both party factions. Bedacht, the Lovestoneite editor, went Foster one better by coming out for new unions even if the old ones continued to grow and did not decline as Foster expected. Bedacht criticized Foster for underestimating the "social reformism" of the A.F. of L. and the Socialists.[47]

Far more embarrassing to Foster was the reaction of his own factional partners. Eight of the foremost members of his faction, headed by Bittelman and Browder, published a formal statement repudiating their former leader for having implied that the A.F. of L. was not the main enemy because it was declining anyway, and for having linked the A.F. of L.'s decline with the necessity for new unions. The eight went beyond the former demand for new unions; they now called for a new "revolutionary trade-union center," or full-fledged dual unionism.[48]

To defend himself, Foster had to tell tales out of school. He revealed that Bittelman and Hathaway had gone over his article with him in detail without objecting to anything in it. But between the time Foster's article was written and the time it was published, the draft of the Comintern's letter to the forthcoming American convention was received. According to Foster, it concentrated the attack on the A.F. of L. bureaucracy far more heavily than either faction had hitherto done. Benefiting from this advance notice of the Comintern's latest line on the A.F. of L., on January 6, 1929, Bittelman hastily wrote an article conforming to it and criticizing Foster for having committed a major deviation with his theory of the decline of the A.F. of L. To make this indignity by his former lieutenant even harder for Foster to swallow, Bittelman's article was not published until February 16, but the unpublished article was quoted against Foster by his eight fault-finding companions as if none of them had ever been guilty of Foster's heretical thoughts on the A.F. of L.

Not without restraint, Foster accused his co-factionalists of having perpetrated "one of the most outstanding instances of irresponsible diplomatizing in the life of our Party." [49]

These petty maneuvers owe their interest to the light they cast on the methods used to gain factional advantage by adapting to the wishes of the Comintern. The draft of a Comintern directive, ostensibly sent to permit the local leaders to express their opinions before its final adoption, was actually an advance notice for local leaders to change their views immediately in order to qualify as supporters of the Comintern's line before it was officially promulgated. The difference between Bittelman, Foster, and Lovestone was not so much in their ultimately accepting a new line—no Communist leader could last very long who did not do that—as in the speed and thoroughness with which they made it their own. In this race, Bittelman had no equal, and his superiority in this respect enabled this Communist scholastic, with far more of the Russian past than the American present in him, to give lessons in American trade-unionism to a veteran American trade-unionist like Foster. Comintern orthodoxy, interpreted in the narrowest and most rigid fashion, was Bittelman's weapon, and no one could stand up against it.

Foster cried foul and pleaded for justice but could not hold out. In the same articles in which he accused Bittelman of bad faith and double-dealing, he confessed his own errors and promised to abide by the Comintern's edict. And when Foster finally capitulated to the new trade-union line, he blurted out what no one else in either faction was yet willing to admit: "We are now entering upon a prolonged period of dual unionism." [50]

When he wrote his history of the American Communist party, published twenty-three years later, Foster could not bear the dreaded term and protested that the changed labor policy of 1929 "did not signify that the Communists were reversing themselves and going back to dual unionism." He also noted that Lovestone and his followers had generally opposed the new trade-union line; he could not bring himself to recall that this was one occasion on which he had agreed with Lovestone rather than with his own followers.[51]

With his formal acceptance of dual unionism, Foster surrendered the last shred of principle on the very issue that had brought him into the Communist movement. But he had held out for almost a year. In his faction, he was the only one who had exhibited any qualms about repudiating an article of faith in which they had all devoutly believed. Foster's former aides, Johnstone and Browder, had come out of the same anti-dual-union tradition and had fought any suggestion of dual unionism in the Communist movement just as vociferously as Foster. Browder, in particular, now emerged as an ardent proponent of the new trade-union line. After the Sixth World Congress, he went back to the Far East and did not return to the United States until January 1929, two months before the next party convention. As soon as he had taken stock of the situation, he began to vie with Bittelman as an uncompromising enemy of the "Right danger," "American exceptionalism," and any further alliance with Progressive trade-unionists like Brophy. At the same time he continued to support his old group, but with critical reservations about its past policies.[52]

Lovestone and Pepper had no intention of permitting Bittelman and Browder to out-maneuver them as partisans of the Comintern's line. The former presented an eleven-point program calling for the unconditional acceptance of the Comintern's estimation of American imperialism and radicalization; in addition, they demanded the dissolution of the opposition's factional apparatus and its "subordination" to the ruling majority.[53]

In the top Political Committee, the Opposition minority, then composed of Aronberg, Browder, Bittelman, and Foster, met this move with a counterproposal—to request the Comintern to "guide" the coming party convention in the final formulation of the party line and the choice of a "non-factional" leadership. This strategy entailed the postponement of the convention until the party could get the Comintern's "guidance and advice." The Lovestone-Pepper majority in the committee refused to be sidetracked and voted to go ahead with the convention as planned.[54]

Again the Opposition, defeated at home, showed peculiar prescience about developments abroad. For it had proposed the kind of "guidance and advice" that the Comintern had already decided to give the convention.

The Comintern proposes

The vote for delegates to the Sixth Convention of the American party was Lovestone's greatest triumph. Of the 104 delegates, his group won 95, or slightly over 90 per cent.[55] In the Comintern's official organ, Wolfe boasted that the voting for delegates had "completely wiped out the Opposition as a political force in all industrial centers." [56]

But there were two delegates to the convention who were more important than all the others combined and whom Lovestone could not win. They were the Comintern's special representatives—Philipp Dengel, a German Communist, and Harry Pollitt, a British Communist. The dominant figure was Dengel, an ultra-Leftist member of Thaelmann's group, who bore himself with the militaristic stiffness of a former German army officer. The American representative in Moscow, Wolfe, had not even been told that they were being sent to the American convention.[57]

With Dengel and Pollitt came two types of proposals from the Comintern: political and organizational. The political directive was embodied in the Comintern's Open Letter to the convention, the substance of which had been known to the leaders for two months but which was not made public until after the convention had opened.

This Open Letter made clear that the Comintern no longer supported the Lovestone regime; it did not make clear what other kind of regime the Comintern wished to support in its stead. The main emphasis was placed on "the absence of substantial differences on points of principle" between the two factions to justify a struggle of such length and intensity within the party—an ironic commentary on the subsequent charge that Lovestone had long represented a major Right Wing deviation. Every criticism of one faction was carefully balanced with a criticism of the other faction. The Open Letter concluded with a four-point program which called for liquidating factionalism and drawing workers into the leadership.[58]

The two Comintern representatives also brought with them confidential "organizational proposals." These, far more than the Open Letter, revealed the Comintern's real plans for the American party.

One of the organizational proposals advised the convention to appoint a new General Secretary—William Z. Foster. Another requested that the two chief factionalists, Lovestone and Bittelman, be withdrawn from work in the American party and put at the disposal of the Comintern in Moscow. Dengel, who did most of the talking, made no secret of his support for the Opposition and his intention of installing it in power.[59]

Thus, despite his mishaps in his own faction, Foster stood once again on the threshold of power. He had lost power four years earlier at the behest of one Comintern representative, Gusev, and it was now dangled before him as the gift of another, Dengel.

Lovestone, however, had won too massive a majority at the convention to give it up without a struggle. His numerical advantage emboldened him to defy the Comintern representatives and prevent them from awarding the prize to Foster.

At factional caucuses on the eve of the convention, Lovestone and his lieutenants succeeded in holding the immense majority of their followers in line. They were able to do so by making a distinction between the Comintern's political instructions, which they accepted, and the Comintern's organizational proposals, which they rejected. They whipped up a spirit of rebellion against handing over the party to the ruinous control of a hopelessly defeated minority. Apparently only one vote was cast in the Lovestone caucus against resisting the Comintern representatives.[60]

For the first—and last—time in the history of American Communism, a convention was deliberately organized to disobey the Comintern and to flout the wishes of its authorized representatives.

The convention disposes

The Sixth Convention, which took place in New York, March 1–9, 1929, was the most tumultuous in party history. At times the delegates even came to physical blows.[61]

In his opening remarks to the convention, Lovestone uttered the required formula of submission to the Comintern: "In our Party the first prerequisite of being worthy of the name Communist is unquestioned and unquestionable loyalty to the Communist International (Applause)." [62] But this loyalty did not extend as far as the organizational proposals.

On the third day of the convention, at a meeting of the Political Committee, the Comintern representatives demanded the immediate acceptance and endorsement of the Comintern's proposal to make Foster the General Secretary. Every member of the Lovestone majority, including Weinstone, voted against the proposal. Bedacht, Minor, Stachel, and Weinstone joined in the oratorical demolition of Foster's candidacy.[63]

Throughout the convention, the Lovestone group made Foster the chief target of criticism and abuse. Even the story of Foster's sale of Liberty Bonds in World War I was raked up to besmirch his record and block his road to the secretaryship.

The Opposition hammered away at what it considered Lovestone's weak point—his tie with the fallen Bukharin. It was not satisfied with Lovestone's seeming neutrality in the Russian party struggle, as expressed in his phrase "no Stalin buttons and no Bukharin buttons." [64] His rivals, recalling how it had been necessary to denounce Trotsky and Zinoviev by name, now demanded the same treatment for Bukharin.

The Opposition spokesman, Johnstone, declared that his group "would not permit this convention to get away with a mere declaration on policy but would force it to take an open vote on the condemnation of Comrade Bukharin by name." Nor was this all: Johnstone and his cofactionalists took one more step and proclaimed themselves the only true and faithful American supporters of Stalin by name.

Not to be outdone, the New York District Organizer, Weinstone, an in-and-out member of Lovestone's caucus who had again decided that the time had come to get out, also introduced a statement endorsing Stalin's leadership and questioning Bukharin's further usefulness in the Comintern.

The onslaught by Johnstone and Weinstone, both of whom were suspected of collusion with Dengel, set off a stampede in Lovestone's steering committee, which consisted of himself, Bedacht, Gitlow, Minor, and Stachel. At an all-night conference, the Comintern representatives confirmed the group's worst fears. Under questioning, they acknowledged that the Comintern considered Lovestone's group to be Bukharinite in character, and that it could not clear itself without naming names.

Faced with this near ultimatum, Minor pressed for a third anti-Bukharin resolution. All the others except Lovestone quickly fell into line. At first Lovestone assailed the maneuver as unprincipled and even threatened to resign from the group if it were carried through. His colleagues dissuaded him by pleading that they would lose control of the party machinery if he broke away.

In the end Lovestone and Gitlow introduced the resolution denouncing Bukharin and suggesting that he should be formally ousted from the leadership in the Comintern. A cable of congratulations to the Russian Communist party, proposed by Lovestone, dutifully mentioned "the Bolshevik leadership, headed by Comrade Stalin." [65]

Stalin's power was recognized in still another way. Taking their cue from the Comintern's Open Letter, which had stressed drawing workers into the leadership, the Lovestone strategists arranged for a group of "proletarian" delegates to send a cable to Stalin appealing to him to reverse the Comintern's organizational proposals and to permit the convention to make its own decisions, subject to the Comintern's approval.

Stalin's reply was a historically unique document—the only message ever sent by him personally to the American Communists. In his cable, he softened the blow by mixing praise—which Lovestone called "Flowers for those who are about to die"—with the blame. He relented sufficiently to permit the convention to choose its own Central Executive Committee, which in turn was empowered to elect the party's top leadership, but he insisted uncompromisingly on the banishment of Lovestone and Bittelman to Moscow, the immediate departure of Pepper, and a review of the convention's decisions by the Comintern.[66]

The most unhappy readers of Stalin's cable were Foster, Lovestone, and Pepper. By giving the convention permission to elect its own leadership, Stalin had, in effect, waived the Comintern's designation of Foster as the next General Secretary. Again Foster was compelled to stifle his disappointment and bide his time.

Stalin's cable seemed to offer a temporary respite to Lovestone's group but made no concession to him personally. Lovestone knew that exile in Moscow would virtually eliminate him as a factor in the American scene and open the way to new alignments without him and against him in the party. It would also expose him there to a campaign by the Russians to break his spirit, a fate suffered by other Comintern-condemned exiles from other countries. His bitterness spilled over in a reference during the convention to the "running sore" in the Comintern.[67] For months this unguarded phrase pursued him. He claimed afterward to have meant by the phrase the factional activities of Lozovsky, but that was not likely to be considered an extenuating circumstance by the man who stood behind Lozovsky.

The chief victim of Stalin's cable was the once resourceful Pepper, now a man on the run. After having ignored his recall to Moscow in September 1928, he had again been ordered by the Comintern to return at the beginning of February 1929. He had also been forbidden to attend the approaching Sixth Convention; the American leadership had appealed on his behalf to the Comintern without success. Pepper was not merely unhappy about leaving the United States; he was afraid to go back to Russia. He asked for two weeks to prepare for the journey and suddenly disappeared from his usual haunts. In the party the story was circulated that Pepper was leaving or had left for Mexico to board a Pacific-bound ship. It was later admitted that Pepper's trip to Mexico had been wholly imaginary and that he had met surreptitiously with one or another of the Lovestone steering committee all through the convention.

Meanwhile the Sixth Convention ground slowly and painfully to a close. With Stalin's permission, it elected a new Central Executive Committee of 44, the vast majority of them pro-Lovestone.[68] The new C.E.C. then elected a Political Committee of 14, with a pro-Lovestone majority of 10 to 4, and a Secretariat of three co-equal secretaries: Gitlow as head of the Executive Department, Bedacht in charge of Agit-Prop, and Foster the Trade-Union Secretary.[69] The convention also formally changed the name of the party from Workers (Communist) Party of America to the Communist Party of the U.S.A., Section of the Communist International.[70]

Lovestone could not be reappointed party secretary because the Comintern's organizational proposals and Stalin's cable had disbarred him. Yet the choice of Gitlow to replace him maintained the factional line-up intact. With a safe majority in the Central Executive Committee, Political Committee, and Secretariat, the victorious faction had nothing to fear except the review of the convention's decisions by the Comintern. This threat was undoubtedly real, but it put the onus of overthrowing the will of a majority on the Comintern, which had never hesitated to intimidate conventions but had never before been faced with a runaway convention that had so completely defied its "proposals."

It is hard to say what might have happened if Lovestone's group had decided to let well enough alone and had waited for the Comintern to make the next move. A policy of watchful waiting could not have been more disastrous than the one actually pursued.

Instead of waiting for the Comintern to react, the convention's managers decided to take the fight to the Comintern. The more aggressive strategy was apparently inspired by Wolfe, who cabled Lovestone a suggestion for an American delegation to come to Moscow to settle all outstanding problems with the Russian leadership on the spot.[71] Lovestone seized on this idea and developed it into a "proletarian delegation," headed by the three top leaders, Gitlow, Bedacht, and himself. Gitlow says that he welcomed the scheme because Stalin's cable empowering the convention to elect its own leadership had beguiled him into thinking that Stalin had experienced a change of heart. The only one, according to Gitlow, who opposed the plan and warned that it was "playing into Stalin's hand" was the doleful Pepper, whom they secretly consulted in a restaurant.[72] But the majority obtained at the convention had gone to the leaders' heads, and they ignored the Hungarian prophet of doom.

The convention appointed a delegation of ten, including William Miller, a Detroit machinist; Tom Myerscough, a mine organizer; William J. White, a steel organizer; Alex Noral, a farm expert; Ella Reeve Bloor, a woman organizer; Otto Huiswoud and Edward Welsh, Negroes; as well as Lovestone, Gitlow, and Bedacht. They were officially authorized by the convention to go to Moscow to appeal against the Comintern's decisions.

With this act, the runaway convention stopped running and prepared to come back home to the Comintern.

18

How to Lose a Majority

THE preparations for the delegation's trip to Moscow were no less extraordinary than the trip itself.

The simultaneous absence of three key leaders, Lovestone, Gitlow, and Bedacht, was clearly fraught with danger. They could not fight successfully abroad unless they could be sure of holding their forces intact at home. Before leaving, therefore, they were confronted with the problem of filling the vacuum in the top leadership during their absence.

They entrusted their power to two other leading figures of their group—Robert Minor, whom they made Acting General Secretary, replacing Gitlow in the highest executive post, and, as his right-hand man, Jack Stachel, the Organization Secretary.

The delegation went off to Moscow in high spirits. Its leaders exuded optimism that right was on their side, that the Russians could not disregard their overwhelming majority at the convention, and that Stalin was the kind of man with whom they could make a favorable deal. This optimism helps to explain why they decided to go at all.

But they did not wholly disregard the possibility that they might be in error and that the party might be taken away from them. Against this eventuality, they took the most extraordinary of precautions. They later revealed that Stachel and Minor had prepared a list of names of reliable members of their faction to whom all party property could be transferred in case the Comintern after all decided to turn the party over to the Opposition minority. They had also arranged with the party's lawyer, Joseph Brodsky, to sell the party buildings, especially the Workers Center in New York, which was held in trust by the District Organizer, Weinstone, who had wobbled over to the other side at the Sixth Convention. These preparations for a take-over included the fronts or auxiliaries as well as the party itself. They did not expect to use these desperate expedients, but they wanted to be ready for any eventuality.[1]

The delegation of ten left New York at the end of March 1929, traveling on the same ship as its implacable enemy, Bittelman, who had decided to carry out the Comintern's orders without a murmur of protest. Foster and Weinstone were also called to Moscow and sailed separately. This exodus assured the presence in the Russian capital of major leaders of all the American factions, in addition to the Comintern and Profintern representatives, Wolfe and Wicks, and the sizable group of American students at the Lenin School.

On a stopover in Berlin for the purpose of obtaining Russian visas, the leaders of the official delegation received a second portent of disaster. The Indian Communist, M. N. Roy, himself a refugee from the Comintern which had recently expelled him in the furor of anti-Bukharinism, warned them that they were heading into a trap and urged them to turn back. They ignored him, as they had previously ignored Pepper, and continued their journey to Moscow.[2]

In the Comintern the usual procedure was indicated—an American Commission to conduct hearings on the delegation's appeal, submission of documents, formal speeches and informal statements, cross-examination of witnesses, proposals from all the interested parties, a small subcommission to draft a decision, and a final vote by the entire Presidium of the Comintern.

But the make-up of the American Commission was unusual. Of the twelve members, eight were Russian: Stalin, Molotov, Lozovsky, Manuilsky, Gusev, Khitarov (representing the Young Communist International), Moireva, and Mikhailov (Williams), the secretary of the commission. The other four were Kuusinen of the Finnish party, chairman of the commission, Tom Bell of the British party, Bela Kun of the Hungarian, and Walther Ulbricht of the German.[8]

That Stalin himself decided to serve on this time-consuming commission indicated to the entire Comintern that more was at stake than the bickering of a relatively small, weak party. In the entire commission, there was not a single member from whom the Americans could expect any sympathy. The chairman, Kuusinen, had once served Bukharin with devotion but had saved himself by denouncing Bukharin with fervor; he could be trusted to show no mercy to those accused of Bukharinism.

With the delegation in Moscow, the commission appointed, the dossiers brought up to date, the eight Russians were ready for the ten Americans.

The American Commission

The American delegation arrived in Moscow on April 7, 1929, and the first session of the American Commission was held a week later. Over a hundred participants and spectators filled a large room in the Comintern's headquarters. Leaders from other parties put in regular appearances to see the spectacle and to assess its political implications.

Gitlow, the first speaker, presented the case for the delegation. For over two hours, in his best soapbox manner, he emphasized the achievements of the American Communists, the one-sided majority won by his group at the party's Sixth Convention, Lovestone's great contributions, and Foster's abysmal shortcomings.

Foster then spoke for the Opposition. He denounced Lovestone and Pepper as the chief American exponents of the Right danger, deplored the majority's rebellion against the Comintern's representatives at the convention, scored the Lovestone regime's failures in party work, and protested against the campaign to discredit his record before and after joining the party.

The next few sessions were devoted to cross-examination of the American delegates by members of the commission. All the charges and countercharges of the American factions for months and even years past were raked up and minutely examined. The weak points of each American were mercilessly probed and ridiculed. These early sessions dragged on slowly and the meetings were recessed for several days to enable the Russian members of the commission to attend a Russian party plenum. Unexpectedly the Americans were embroiled in the Russian plenum, with unpleasant consequences for them in the commission.[4]

The Russian plenum in April 1929 formally extinguished the last of Bukharin's influence in the Russian party and officially removed him from the Comintern. In the course of the plenum, Bukharin complained that a campaign had been conducted against him in the Comintern. As an example of this campaign, he cited the anti-Bukharin resolution at the recent American Communist convention.

The charge was sufficiently disturbing to bring forth a reply from Dengel, the Comintern representative to the American convention, who issued a statement protesting his innocence and blaming the resolution entirely on the convention's majority. Dengel's statement aroused so much indignation among the embattled American leaders that they decided to set the record straight by sending a letter to the Russian plenum, signed by Gitlow, relating the circumstances of the resolution and detailing the pressure from Dengel, Johnstone, and Weinstone to make them present an anti-Bukharin resolution of their own. According to Gitlow, who attended the Russian plenum, the American statement provoked Stalin to anger and the Russian plenum was never permitted to hear of it.[5]

The commission went on as before—the Americans accused one another, defended themselves, confessed errors, and promised repentance. Weinstone labored at length to explain why he had shifted sides. Bittelman tried to show that the American economy was already falling off. Lovestone heaped scorn and invective on Dengel, Foster, and Weinstone. Wolfe complained that the Comintern had not permitted him to attend meetings at which important decisions concerning the American party had been reached. Wicks, the most recent deserter from the Lovestone ranks, flayed about on all sides, giving the impression that he hoped to inherit the leadership by eliminating everyone else.

Then came the Comintern and Profintern officialdom—Lozovsky, Bell, Gusev, Kun, and Kolarov. The speeches by Stalin and Molotov were saved for the last working session of the commission on May 6, 1929.

This speech by Stalin, and two other speeches made by him eight days later, are of unusual interest for an understanding of the man and his movement. They show him in action as the operational head of world Communism rather than in his more familiar role as the spokesman of Russian Communism. Stalin had never before and would never again put himself on record at such length on the internal affairs of the American or any other party. This record exists thanks to the vicissitudes of the American factional struggle; the speeches have never been published in the original Russian and are available only in English.[6]

Stalin began his first speech with an important dictum on the relative weight to be given the general and specific features of American capitalism. He accused both American groups of exaggerating the specific features:

> It would be wrong to ignore the specific peculiarities of American capitalism. The Communist Party in its work must take them into account. But it would be still more wrong to base the activities of the Communist Party on these specific features, since the foundation of the activities of every Communist Party, including the American Communist Party, on which it must base itself, must be the general features of capitalism, which are the same for all countries, and not its specific features in any given country. It is on this that the internationalism of the Communist Party is founded. Specific features are only supplementary to the general features. The error of both groups is that they exaggerate the significance of specific features of American capitalism and thereby overlook the basic features of world capitalism as a whole.

This principle, enunciated by Stalin in its starkest form, explains much of the problem of American Communism. In theory, the specific features of American capitalism could never be the determining factor in arriving at American Communist policy; the specific features could modify the details of, but never go counter to, the direction of the general features; and the general features were primarily represented, from the perspective of Moscow, by European capitalism. The alleged dominance of the general features gave the Comintern a rationale for dictating to the individual parties; the American Communists might claim to know more about the specific features of American capitalism, but they could never pretend to know more than the Comintern officials about the general features of world, and particularly of European, capitalism.

Stalin's rule was not unlike the view that Lovestone had advanced at the end of 1925 to justify Gusev's decision in favor of Ruthenberg.[7] But now the tables were turned. At the beginning of 1928, when the Comintern had inaugurated its extreme Left turn, Pepper had taken the position that it applied to Europe but not to the United States, because European and American conditions were basically different.[8] According to Stalin's dictum, European and American conditions could differ, but they could never differ so much that a Left turn in Europe would not apply to the United States.

From "general observations" about American capitalism, Stalin went on to the "main defects" of American Communism. He summed them up as twofold: the leaders of both the majority and the minority, but particularly of the majority, were guilty of "unprincipled factionalism," and both groups, but particularly the majority, based their relations with the Comintern "not on a principle of confidence, but on a policy of rotten diplomacy, a policy of diplomatic intrigue." He cited the newly adopted practice of Foster and Bittelman of calling themselves "Stalinites"; the "even more disgraceful" behavior of the Lovestone group in demanding Bukharin's removal from the Comintern; Pepper's reluctance to return to Moscow; and the rumors spread by Foster and Lovestone concerning the interviews which he had given them. He denied having said anything to Foster implying that he sympathized with Foster's group. He told how Lovestone had recently promised to be "a loyal soldier of the Comintern" if the decision to withdraw him from America were rescinded, to which he had replied that such experiments had been going on for three years without any good coming from them.

In the course of this bill of particulars, Stalin made two comments of general interest. Of "Stalinites," he said:

> Foster and Bittelman see nothing reprehensible in declaring themselves "Stalinites" and thereby demonstrating their loyalty to the C.P.S.U. But, my dear comrades, that is disgraceful. Do you not know that there are no "Stalinites," that there must be no "Stalinites"?

And of speculating on the ups and downs in the Comintern, he declared:

> But, Comrades, the Comintern is not a stock market. The Comintern is the holy of holies of the working class.

The entire speech reeked with modesty and virtue. Only a few years later, it would be disgraceful for a Communist to deny being a "Stalinite," or at least a Marxist-Leninist-Stalinist. There was no one in Stalin's audience, least of all Stalin himself, who did not know that "rotten diplomacy" and "diplomatic intrigue" had become a law of survival in the "holy of holies of the working class." It was necessary for Foster to sit quietly and hear Stalin imply that he had deliberately distorted the tenor of their discussion, even as events were bearing out Foster's interpretation of Stalin's intentions. Stalin expressed outrage that the American Communists should have demanded Bukharin's removal, as if his own agents had not made them do it.

There was no madness in this method. Stalin seems to have made a habit of indicating his intentions by ascribing them to his victims.

Stalin ended his speech by presenting a six-point "solution" of the American Communist problem: approval of the actions and proposals of the Comintern's representatives, except for handing over control of the party to the Fosterites; a second Open Letter from the Comintern to the American party; condemnation of the action of the leaders of the majority, especially in the matter of Pepper; an end to the factional struggle; "reorganization" of the Secretariat; and the transfer of Lovestone and Bittelman from the American party to the Comintern. The last two clauses were the operative ones: the reorganization of the Secretariat implied a different type of control from that voted by the Sixth Convention, and the removal of Lovestone and Bittelman affirmed one of the most controversial points in the Comintern's organizational proposals to the convention. Molotov followed with a speech in a similar vein.[9]

Except for its formal decision, the work of the commission was over. The Americans knew what to expect.

Yes or no?

Normally, at this point in a crisis, the Americans should have capitulated. They had made a fight such as few Communist parties had ever dared to make; the highest Russian and Comintern authorities had decided against them; further resistance was obviously futile.

While the leaders of the American delegation had all but lost their battle in Moscow, they could console themselves with their American support. So great, however, was the distance between them and the American party that they were chiefly dependent on cables from the two caretakers, Minor and Stachel, for news of the home front.

As the weeks in Moscow stretched out, the estrangement of the delegates and the responsibilities of the caretakers increased. Early in May the cables from Minor and Stachel began to hint of trouble without suggesting real cause for alarm. A cable of May 3 denied "false rumors of any differences between Minor, Lovestone, and Stachel," but urged the "quickest return of the delegation including Lovestone" to combat the "sabotage" of Browder, Weisbord, and Johnstone. On May 9, three days after Stalin's first speech, another cable warned of "sharpening factionalism" and "spreading rumors" but again gave assurances of "unquestioned" rank-and-file support.[10]

Another warning came from the Organization Secretary of the New York District, Bert Miller, whose suspicions of Minor and Stachel were aroused by their sudden fraternization with factional enemies. In an effort to put the delegation on guard, he sent one of his friends in Moscow a cryptically worded cable signed "Liver and Onions," his favorite delicacy in the party cafeteria. But his friend could not decipher the signature and the cable failed of its purpose.[11]

Instead of waiting for the subcommission of Molotov, Kuusinen, and Gusev to bring in its verdict, the Americans again took matters into their own hands. After mulling over Stalin's speech and the cables that had been arriving from Minor and Stachel, the delegates on May 9 took the unusual step of issuing a statement anticipating an unfavorable decision. This statement warned that if the proposals of Stalin and Molotov were adopted, the American party membership would be forced to conclude that "the Executive Committee of the Communist International desires to destroy the [American] Central Committee and therefore follows the policy of legalizing the past factionalism of the opposition bloc and inviting its continuation in the future." [12]

After May 9 the atmosphere in the American Commission abruptly changed.[13] For almost a month, the work of the commission had not differed too much from that of previous commissions. There was nothing in the records of the American leaders to indicate that they were capable of rebelling against a Comintern decision once the formalities of giving them a hearing had been cleared out of the way. The Comintern's rulers saw nothing excessive or unprecedented about their own demands. They had upset many other national leaderships in the past; more important national leaders than Lovestone and Bittelman from far larger parties had been exiled to Moscow without protest from the Americans, who had known all about the practice; and the precedents had been established in the days of Zinoviev long before Stalin had taken over the Comintern.

Prior to the American statement of May 9, the Comintern had made demands but not threats, and it had been careful to place the blame on both American factions, with emphasis on the Lovestoneites' more serious transgressions. After May 9 the struggle between the American factions was transformed into a struggle by one American faction against the Comintern. All the past issues of the controversy were superseded by a new one—for or against the Comintern.

On the following day, according to Gitlow, the American delegates attended a farewell party by an American member of the Soviet intelligence service, who informed them that he was leaving for Berlin on May 12, the same day that the decision was scheduled to be handed down by the subcommission of the American Commission. In anticipation of a more desperate crisis, the Americans asked him to take a message out of Moscow for them, to be mailed in Berlin in order to evade the Soviet censorship. He promised to do so.[14] Thus, for two reasons, May 12 promised to become a day of decision.

Molotov, Kuusinen, and Gusev presented their findings at the last full meeting of the American Commission on May 12 in the guise of an "Address by the Executive Committee of the Communist International to All Members of the Communist party of the United States." The draft of this address had been distributed the day before, and the meeting was held to give the Americans an opportunity to accept or reject it.

The form of this document showed that the leaders of the Comintern had determined on a policy of no concessions and no compromises. It was directed over the heads of the American leadership to the party membership to make the issue as unmistakable as possible—loyalty to that leadership or loyalty to the Comintern.

In substance, the draft went much further in its denunciation of Lovestone's regime than either the Open Letter to the Sixth Convention or Stalin's first speech had done. For the first time in a Comintern document, Lovestone and Pepper were identified as the clearest exponents of the theory of American "exceptionalism." This was defined as the belief in a crisis of capitalism, a swing of the masses to the Left, and the necessity of accentuating the struggle against reformism and the Right danger—everywhere except in America. Though both factions were still blamed for the party's faults, the main responsibility was placed on the leaders of the majority and especially on Lovestone personally. They were accused, in language far more intemperate than had been used in the past, of "misleading honest proletarian Party members" and "playing an unprincipled game." Stalin's six points were reduced to five: immediate dissolution of all factions on pain of expulsion from the party; removal of Lovestone and Bittelman from work in the American party; rejection of the minority's demand for a special convention; reorganization and extension of the Secretariat; and commitment of Pepper's case to the International Control Commission.[15]

When the turn of the Americans to state their views came, the delegation tried to avoid answering yes or no, as the question was put, and postponed its statement until the following day.[16] Lovestone declared: "Whatever work is given me I will do. But we have a deep conviction that such an organizational proposal as the one aiming to take me away from our Party today is not a personal matter but a slap and slam in the face of the entire leadership." [17]

Kuusinen, the reporter for the commission, refused to be satisfied with Lovestone's "Yes, but" reply, and charged him with preparing to split the party. Kuusinen hinted broadly that the Comintern counted on wholesale desertions from the delegation's supporters at home. He cited Weinstone and Wicks among those in Moscow who had unreservedly accepted the Comintern's proposals, and added ominously: "In the United States there is a whole number of such comrades." He clearly confronted them with the shift in the nature of the struggle: "From your declaration we see plainly that it is no longer a question of factionalism of the leaders of the Majority of the CC against the Minority group, but it is already a factional attitude towards the Executive of the Comintern."

In conclusion, Kuusinen posed the question at issue in such a way that nothing remained but total capitulation or total defiance: "Will you take up a fight against the Executive upon this question, or will you submit unconditionally and without reservations? Will you urge your own supporters, the whole of the membership, to carry out unconditionally the decisions of the Comintern? Yes or no?" [18] In the same spirit, Molotov interpreted the American delegates' refusal to give an immediate answer as a sign that "they wanted to secede as a group" and "to unite first" before opposing the Comintern's line.[19] Thus, by May 12, the Comintern leaders spoke so openly of a split that they had undoubtedly begun to take measures against it.

Immediately after this inconclusive meeting, the four chief majority leaders, Lovestone, Gitlow, Bedacht, and Wolfe, met and drafted a cable to Minor and Stachel. The message was taken out of Moscow by the American agent of the Soviet intelligence service at whose farewell party the arrangements had been made two days before, and was cabled by him from Berlin to New York on May 15. This cable attempted to put into effect the preparations made a month earlier with Minor, Stachel, and Brodsky to take over the property and other assets of the party and its auxiliaries in the event of defeat in Moscow.

It opened on a note of utter despair:

> Draft decision means destruction Party unless firm solid front maintained. Take no action any proposals by anybody or cabled CI instruction cabling draft letter instructing publish same, until delegation arrives. Situation astounding, outrageous, can't be understood until arrival. Possibility entire delegation being forcibly detained, therefore, unless you hear from us within ten days that we are returning start wide movement units and press for return complete convention delegation inclusive Lovestone Wolfe to hear report our side case.

The cable went on to sound an alarm that the decision provided a basis for expelling thousands of party members, that it would create a "general CI crisis" by violating the will of the Sixth World Congress, and that the accompanying speeches by the Comintern leaders implied that they intended to promote Weinstone, Wicks, and Weisbord to the top leadership, with Weinstone as General Secretary.

Then came the practical instructions:

> Carefully check up all units all property all connections all mailing lists of auxiliaries, all sublists district lists removing same offices and unreliables. Check all checking accounts all organizations seeing that authorized signers are exclusively reliables appointing secretariat for auxiliaries and treasury disauthorizing present signature. Instantly finish preparations sell buildings especially eliminating W[einstone] trusteeship. Remove Mania Reiss.

And finally a warning:

> Absolutely don't cable acknowledgement or cognizance this cablegram but guide thereby.[20]

Were the men who sent this cable ready to accept the full implications of an unavoidable split in the party and their inevitable expulsions from the Comintern?

It would seem so. The seizure of party property and funds was so drastic a measure and the justification for it in the cable was so clearly directed against the Comintern itself that it is hard to see how they could have had any illusions about the fact that they were in effect declaring war on the Comintern.

Yet it should be remembered that they were supposedly communicating in greatest secrecy with their trusted confederates, and that as long as the cable remained a secret within their own family of top leaders they did not think that they were necessarily burning their bridges behind them. They also imagined that, by seizing control of the party's material assets, they could negotiate with the Comintern from a position of strength and that in the end the Comintern would recognize and accept them on more favorable terms.

Their position, therefore, was more confused and complex than this cable may indicate, and they were still far from having fully realized where they were going and how they would get there. At the moment, they were far more interested in preventing the Comintern from taking the party away from them than they were in taking the party away from the Comintern.

No longer wholly in and not yet wholly out of the Communist movement as they had known it, the beleaguered American delegates were summoned to their last meeting in Moscow.

The night of May 14

About 150 participants and spectators assembled on the evening of May 14 for a meeting of the Presidium, the permanent governing body of the Executive Committee of the Communist International, to decide the fate of the American Communist movement. Besides the ten American delegates, American Communists working in the Comintern and Profintern, as well as those studying at the Lenin School and Far Eastern University, were invited. Among the spectators were top leaders of many parties and ranking officials of the Comintern and Profintern. Only one American, Gitlow, was entitled to vote in the final decision by the Presidium. The meeting lasted for some six hours, until three or four o'clock the next morning. At about midnight tea and sandwiches were served.[21]

The chairman of the American Commission, Kuusinen, presided. He opened the meeting by reading the report of the commission, embodied in the proposed "Address" of the Executive Committee of the Comintern. Then Gitlow read a declaration in the name of the ten American delegates stating that they could not accept the Address because it would promote "demoralization, disintegration and chaos in the Party." This declaration warned that acceptance "would make it absolutely impossible for us to continue as effective workers in the Communist movement." [22]

One after another, leading members of other parties appealed to the Americans to remain faithful to the Comintern and give their approval to the commission's proposals. All the other Americans present, especially the large contingent from the Lenin School which had been efficiently mobilized for the occasion, rose and called upon the delegation to obey the will of the Comintern. As this long procession of hostile speakers dragged on, the isolation of the ten Americans increased steadily and the pressure on them mounted visibly.

Of all the speeches made before the Presidium voted, the most important was of course Stalin's. He devoted most of his speech to the evils of factionalism and the virtues of discipline. He conceded that Lovestone was "a capable and talented comrade," but immediately accused Lovestone of employing his capabilities "in factional scandalmongering, in factional intrigue," and he scoffed at the idea that Lovestone was so talented that the American party could not get along without him. Foster, he added, had not repudiated the "concealed Trotskyists" in his group in time, because "he behaved first and foremost as a factionalist."

Ever since its smashing victory at the Sixth Convention, only two months before, the Lovestone majority had contended that it was no longer a faction, that it was virtually the entire party. Stalin faced this objection boldly and answered it in such a way that the essential relationship of American Communism and the Comintern was forever illuminated.

> You declare you have a certain majority in the American Communist Party and that you will retain that majority under all circumstances. That is untrue, comrades of the American delegation, absolutely untrue. You had a majority because the American Communist Party until now regarded you as the determined supporters of the Communist International. And it was only because the Party regarded you as the friends of the Comintern that you had a majority in the ranks of the American Communist Party. But what will happen if the American workers learn that you intend to break the unity of the ranks of the Comintern and are thinking of conducting a fight against its executive bodies—that is the question, dear comrades? Do you think that the American workers will follow your lead against the Comintern, that they will prefer the interests of your factional group to the interests of the Comintern? There have been numerous cases in the history of the Comintern when its most popular leaders, who had greater authority than you, found themselves isolated as soon as they raised the banner against the Comintern. Do you think you will fare better than these leaders? A poor hope, comrades! At present you still have a formal majority. But tomorrow you will have no majority and you will find yourselves completely isolated if you attempt to start a fight against the decisions of the Presidium of the Executive Committee of the Comintern. You may be certain of that, dear comrades.[23]

It was fundamentally the same answer that had been given in the Comintern before Stalin's era to an earlier American delegate who had come to Moscow claiming to represent a majority. In 1922 the representative of the then Left Opposition, John J. Ballam, had written to his associates at home of his unfavorable reception by the Comintern leaders:

They care nothing for majorities. They will support a minority who will carry out their policies against a majority that is opposed to them. They consider the greatest crime against the International is splitting. They say, "You report 5,000 comrades in America, whose comrades are they? Dobin's, Moore's and Henry's? * or are they Lenin's, Trotsky's and Bucharin's? You must obey the discipline first." [24]

Seven years later Stalin again asked, in effect, "Whose comrades are they?" The formula which had once beaten down a Left Opposition was now turned against a Right Opposition. The principle that the comrades in America would be loyal not to their own leaders but to the Russian leaders, whoever they were, had been instituted by Zinoviev and given its most extreme expression by Stalin.

Long past midnight, the Presidium voted. The proposed Address was endorsed by all but one—Gitlow.

The vote immediately created a new situation for the totally isolated American delegation. Before, as Stalin admitted, it had been permissible to disagree with and oppose the proposals of the American Commission. Now, Stalin warned, the decision of the Presidium had made disagreement and opposition no longer possible.

Stalin himself moved to force the ten Americans to cross the last line of insubordination by demanding a poll of each individual American delegate.

Every member of the delegation was called to the platform and asked point-blank: Do you accept the decision?

With three exceptions, they answered that they still disagreed with the decision but would accept it as a matter of discipline until the next discussion period.

Two delegates, Bedacht and Noral, broke down.[25] Noral, a comparatively recent party member, was no great loss, but Bedacht's capitulation represented a major victory for the Comintern.

Until the last moment, Bedacht, one of the delegation's top command, had been most militant in holding out against the Comintern's demands, and, it is said, had even written, in consultation with Gitlow, Lovestone, and Wolfe, the cable of May 12 which had in-

* Pseudonyms of the period for the leaders of the Left Opposition, Dirba, Ballam, and Ashkenudzie.

structed Minor and Stachel to take over the party's property and assets. But, as the total break with the Comintern neared, Bedacht's nerves cracked, and he could not bear the thought of living outside the Comintern. Before the scornful eyes of his roommate, Gitlow, he had tossed on his bed, weeping all night, in anticipation of the Presidium's decision. In his last chance to repent and rehabilitate himself, he tearfully accepted the Presidium's decision and promised to carry it out faithfully.

Some weeks later, Bedacht gave an explanation for his change of mind:

> After we have argued the matter out with the Comintern and after the argument is settled by a definite decision, we not only accept the decision as a matter of discipline but we accept the correctness of the decision as a matter of recognizing the international and ideological superiority of the Comintern over ourselves. The formal acceptance of the decision must therefore in all cases be transformed into a political acceptance. The formal acceptance of a CI decision must be completed with a conscious analysis of the decision to which we submit in order to penetrate and absorb the political reasons of the Comintern for making the decision. Only thus can the political unity of the Comintern and the International uniformity of its struggle against capitalism be preserved.[26]

For long-time Communist leaders like Bedacht, discipline was not enough. Once the Comintern had spoken, it was necessary not only to accept the decision but also to accept its correctness. The Comintern was not satisfied merely with formal obedience; it required faith based on recognition of its superior wisdom.

It may be asked: Was it possible to press a button in one's mind and believe today what one had rejected for months past? For some it was impossible, and they could not stay long in the Communist movement. Others could make themselves believe because they were not prepared to pay the price of not believing, and after one or more personal crises, they learned not to believe or disbelieve in anything too strongly, in order to be able to change their "beliefs" with a minimum of personal and political discomfort. Still others pretended to believe, and secretly relieved their wounded egos by cultivating a private cynicism. And for many, there was no problem, because they considered themselves "activists" and "organizers" who looked to others to make policy.

The last American to speak was Gitlow, and he parted company with the other delegates for the opposite reason. As the recently appointed party Secretary, Gitlow had potentially more to lose by the new set-up demanded by the Comintern than anyone else. An irascible man, he could not bow his head with the heartsick resignation of Bedacht or contain his anger with the cold calculation of Lovestone. Instead Gitlow declared that not only did he oppose the Presidium's decision but that he would go back to the United States to fight against it.[27]

Gitlow's outburst brought Stalin to his feet. Usually Stalin spoke so softly that he forced his listeners to lean forward to hear him. Now he shouted in anger. The published version of this speech is comparatively mild and self-controlled, but witnesses agree that it hardly does justice to the fury in his voice and the violence of his language.

According to the official account, Stalin paid tribute to the "firmness and stubbornness" of the eight American hold-outs, but admonished them that "true Bolshevik courage" consisted in submitting to the will of the Comintern rather than in defying it. He assailed Lovestone, Gitlow, and Ella Reeve Bloor by name for acting like anarchists, individualists, and strike-breakers, and concluded by assuring them that the American Communist party would survive the downfall of their faction.[28]

But, according to Wolfe, Stalin also shouted:

> Who do you think you are? Trotsky defied me. Where is he? Zinoviev defied me. Where is he? Bukharin defied me. Where is he? And you? When you get back to America, nobody will stay with you except your wives.[29]

According to Lovestone, who later called it the "graveyard speech," Stalin warned the Americans that the Russians knew how to handle strike-breakers:

> There is plenty of room in our cemeteries.[30]

Stalin stepped down from the platform and strode out first. Guards and secretaries flocked after him. No one moved until he had walked down the aisle. But as he reached the Americans, he stopped and held out his hand to the Negro delegate, Edward Welsh, who stood next to Lovestone.

Welsh turned to Lovestone and asked loudly, "What the hell does this guy want?" and refused to shake Stalin's hand.[31]

The American delegates, totally shunned by everyone else, walked out into the gray dawn and bought oranges from a street peddler.[32]

Lovestone in flight

Lovestone still hoped that all was not lost. The cable to the two caretakers, Minor and Stachel, arrived in New York on May 15, the day after the Presidium's meeting. He counted on them, especially on Stachel, to carry out the plan to take over the party's property and other assets, and he wanted to get back to the United States quickly enough to bring the delegation's story to the party membership before the Comintern could mobilize all its forces against him.

The Comintern beat him to the punch. On May 17, even before the Comintern's Address could reach the United States, the Political Secretariat in Moscow decided to remove Lovestone, Gitlow, and Wolfe from all their leading positions, to purge the Political Committee of all members who refused to submit to the Comintern's decisions, and to warn Lovestone that it would be a gross violation of Comintern discipline to attempt to leave Russia.[33] The "loyal" American Communists—Bedacht, Foster, and Weinstone—were permitted to leave Russia immediately. Also dispatched to the United States was a special Comintern representative, the secretary of the American Commission, Mikhailov (Williams), sent secretly to take charge of the shake-up in the American party.

The Address reached the two caretakers in the United States on the following day, May 18.[34] According to Minor, the cable to take over the party had been discussed for two days previously, and they had realized that it implied a fight "not from within but from outside" the Comintern.[35] With the receipt of the Comintern's Address, the ten-man top caucus of the former majority faction, now headed by Minor and Stachel, was faced with choosing between the cable and the Address.

As soon as this choice appeared before them in all its nakedness and enormity, the decision was never in doubt. As if by reflex, they voted in favor of the Comintern's Address, the source of which embodied all that they had been taught for a decade to fear and to revere.[36] That same day the Central Committee unanimously accepted and endorsed the Address, called upon the American delegates in Moscow to withdraw all opposition to it, and instructed the Secretariat to proceed immediately to put its proposals into effect.[37]

The delegates in Moscow were not immediately informed of the full significance of the action in New York. On May 19, a cable from the caucus leaders stated reassuringly that they were "standing by" all the actions of the Sixth Convention, including the demand for Lovestone's return, and implied that the Comintern's decision was "antagonistic" to their personal views.[38] These sentiments were still so encouraging that Lovestone later believed his caretakers had been playing a double game by voting for the Comintern on May 18 and sending him a sympathetic cable on May 19.

As yet the vast majority of American Communists knew nothing of the disaster of their delegation in Moscow. The highest officer in the party, Gitlow, duly elected by the Central Committee after a convention only two months past, had been stripped of all his powers by a body containing only one American, Gitlow himself, but not a word of the proceedings had been permitted to appear in the American party organ, the *Daily Worker*. On May 18, however, the Russian party organ, *Pravda,* published four columns about the decisions of the American Commission and the Presidium. The Moscow correspondent of *The New York Times,* Walter Duranty, immediately used this information as the basis of a report to the *Times,* which published it the following day.[39] Twenty-four hours later, on May 20, the *Daily Worker* gave the party membership its first inkling of the downfall of Lovestone and Gitlow by publishing the Comintern's Address and the Central Committee's decisions of May 18.

The *Daily Worker*'s publication of these documents opened the floodgates of abandonment and submission. Forty-eight hours later, on May 22, the party organ was able to publish the first telegrams repudiating the fallen leaders in Moscow and pledging unconditional loyalty to the Comintern—from four District Organizers formerly identified with Lovestone and Gitlow.[40] For weeks thereafter, the paper devoted much of its space to messages of fidelity from party organizations and organizers, high and low; the closer they had been to the former leaders, the more zealous they were in denouncing them. On May 24, Noral, Huiswoud, and Ella Reeve Bloor joined Bedacht by issuing a statement in Moscow maintaining their disagreement with the Comintern's organizational proposal but disclaiming all intention to resist the Comintern's decisions.[41] Of the original ten, only six were left.

Of these six, the Comintern was determined to detain two, Lovestone and Gitlow, as well as the former American representative, Wolfe. The others, considered less important, were permitted to depart within a few days. All were subjected to a variety of bribes and threats to prevent them from returning in time to influence the "reorganization" of the party at home. Welsh was offered a vacation in the Crimea, followed by an extended stay in Russia to speak and write on American Negro problems.[42] Gitlow was asked to work for the OGPU, the Soviet intelligence agency, in Latin America.[43] Wolfe was given the choice of going to Korea as the Comintern representative, taking a long rest at Sochi, the vacation resort on the Black Sea, or being employed by the OGPU. Efforts were made by Gusev to induce Wolfe's wife to leave him.[44] Lovestone asked, "Where are you going to send me—to India?" He was told, "Nowhere where they speak English." [45]

But all three wanted more than anything else to go home. They knew of similar cases from other parties, men punished for their own or the Comintern's misdeeds with years of detention in Moscow, which ended in political destruction and spiritual demoralization. First Gitlow was permitted to go, then Wolfe. But since the Comintern had made a commitment to prevent Lovestone from returning to the United States, his problem was more complex.

On two occasions, May 22 and May 30, Lovestone tried to get back into the good graces of the Comintern by presenting statements withdrawing his previous resistance to the Comintern's decisions and proffering his submission to them, while maintaining his disagreement with the Comintern's previous organizational instructions to the Sixth Convention.[46] On May 31, the Comintern accepted Lovestone's second overture, which was similar in its wording to the formula used by Noral, Huiswoud, and Bloor, and sent the following cable to the caretakers in New York:

> Lovestone requests permission to go to America for personal affairs for two weeks in America beginning June 12th after which he consents to remain at the disposal of the ECCI for work in the CI. He withdrew his declaration made in the Presidium regarding insubordination as incorrect and impermissible in the Comintern. He declared that he submits to ECCI and in this connection he pledged not to interfere in the internal affairs of the CPUSA. The Political Secretariat permitted him to go for two weeks but date departure will be fixed if you don't object to his going America now. Communicate your opinion immediately.[47]

By this time the new American leadership, made up of Lovestone's former lieutenants allied with their former Fosterite enemies, was more anxious to get rid of Lovestone than the Comintern was. The flight from Lovestone by his own supporters had taken on such momentum that he could be ousted with impunity. Yet it was most inconvenient to have him back on the American scene even for two weeks and then to have him work in the Comintern with the possibility of a comeback.

The new leadership decided to take no chances and to discourage the Comintern from letting him out of Russia. The threat of Lovestone's imminent return so disturbed the caretakers that they considered it necessary to divulge the hitherto carefully guarded secret of the cable of May 15 which had instructed them to take over the party, though they prudently omitted all mention of their own part in its preparation.

On June 4 a cable informed the Comintern that the Secretariat doubted the validity of Lovestone's personal reasons for his trip home because it possessed a "factional cable dated Moscow May 15th giving detailed technical instructions preparing split Party," and asked the Comintern to demand from Lovestone a written political declaration for American publication accepting the decisions and condemning his "previous splitting tactics." The Secretariat added that, even if Lovestone made such a statement, it would consider Lovestone's visit possible only after the completion of its own "Enlightenment Campaign" and not before the beginning of July.[48] This campaign to enlighten the party of Lovestone's heresies had been announced on June 1 and party members were asked to send material for it to one of the caretakers, Jack Stachel.[49]

Meanwhile Lovestone had one last meeting with Stalin. As Lovestone recalled the incident, he told Stalin that he was determined to leave Russia and that he was not going to accept any responsibility for the new line forced on the American Communists. Stalin rose angrily, banged his fist on his desk, and declared, "Well, there is one request I want to make of you. When you go back to America see that your friends don't commit any stupidities." Lovestone replied, "Comrade Stalin, my friends, even I can't prevent their committing stupidities; and your friends, not even you can prevent them." Stalin banged on the desk again, turned about, and slammed the door.[50]

After the departure of Wolfe and Gitlow, Lovestone remained in Moscow alone. At a meeting of the Comintern's Political Secretariat on June 7, he was confronted with the demand for a stronger declaration of self-denunciation and unconditional submission. According to the Political Secretariat, he agreed to provide one for the party press recognizing his mistakes, condemning his factional activity, and promising to carry out the Comintern's decisions.[51] Two days later, he sent a cable to New York repeating the statement that he had given the Comintern on May 30, which had disagreed with the Comintern's proposals but had accepted its decisions. This peace offering, which the Comintern had previously accepted, was promptly rejected by the new American Secretariat as "inadequate" and unfit for publication in the party press.[52]

In Moscow, alone, depressed, and defenseless, Lovestone came to the end of the road. He had been cut off from his own party for almost two months; he felt trapped in the Russian capital while his political fate was being decided without him five thousand miles away; he was filled with the desperate need to escape and renew the unequal struggle on more familiar ground. The Comintern returned his passport but refused to give him an exit visa and other necessary papers on the ground that it was not asking him to leave and therefore he would have to get everything else himself. Russia in 1929 was not yet hermetically sealed, however, and he succeeded, with the help of friendly connections, in getting the visa and other papers. Instead of taking the train, as he was expected to do, to Poland, where he knew that the borders were closely watched and he might be halted, he left by plane on June 11 for Danzig. His absence was not known to the Comintern for several days.[53]

Lovestone's flight broke the last bonds that had tied him to the Comintern. On July 22 it cabled New York that he had left Moscow despite a decision of the Comintern's Political Secretariat and despite his promise to submit a political declaration for publication. The cable declared war on Lovestone and his remaining supporters by calling on all party members to condemn "these methods of intrigue, falsehood and disruptive activities." [54] According to Minor, Lovestone and Gitlow were twice summoned to meet with the American Secretariat and refused to appear, but Wolfe came to a meeting of the Political Committee and made such a defiant speech that the others were "absolutely astounded." [55]

The Secretariat sent out letters to Gitlow and Wolfe on June 21 giving them forty-eight hours to make written statements and telling them what to put in them—recognition of "the complete correctness of the Comintern Address and the related Comintern decisions on the American question" and denunciation of "the anti-Comintern conduct" of the American delegation to Moscow.[56] Gitlow replied that he was ready to accept any kind of assignment from the party and carry it out faithfully, but that he would not vote for or approve the Address.[57] Wolfe summed up his position formally as "one of disagreement with the recent address and related decisions and submission as a matter of discipline and loyalty." [58]

Lovestone's expulsion was announced in the *Daily Worker* of June 27, 1929. Then Wolfe, the only one who had voted against it in the Political Committee, was suspended from the Committee. He was requested to make a nation-wide tour in support of the Comintern's decisions, and when he replied, "I cannot persuade others to believe what I do not believe," he was expelled. By the end of the month Lovestone, Wolfe, and Gitlow were officially out of the party.[59] As a last resort, they sent an "Appeal to the Comintern" the following month requesting the approaching Tenth Plenum of the Comintern to overrule the decision of the Presidium of May 14 and to appoint a special commission to re-examine the situation in the American party.[60] The plenum answered that Lovestone's appeal would be heard if he returned to Moscow; otherwise, his expulsion would be considered final.[61]

And it was final.

Aftermath

The changes that took place in the American Communist movement were not what any of the Americans had expected.

Lovestone and Gitlow had gambled on the loyalty of the 90 per cent of the party that had supported them at the Sixth Convention in March 1929. Two months later, few party members would talk to them or even walk on the same side of the street with them. The same strong-arm methods that they had used against the Trotskyists in 1928 were employed against the Lovestoneites in 1929, and with equally effective results. Party meetings were called throughout the country to endorse the expulsions, and anyone who did not raise his hand to support the motion was summarily suspended or expelled. When Lovestone tried to rally his forces in midsummer, he found most of them away on vacation or so pessimistic that they saw no point in carrying on the struggle. It took him four months to organize a conference of forty supporters to publish an Opposition organ, *Revolutionary Age,* the first issue of which was dated November 1, 1929.[62]

In the end, the official party lost barely two hundred members to the pro-Lovestone group, which adopted the name of "Communist Party (Majority Group)" in memory of its former position in the party.[63] The 90 per cent had dwindled to 2 per cent in two months.[64] But it also appears that over 2000 members dropped out of the official party in the year following Lovestone's expulsion, an indication that many more showed their dissatisfaction by leaving the party than by joining Lovestone's group.[65] Besides Lovestone, Gitlow, and Wolfe, the new group included the trade-union leader, Charles S. Zimmerman, the former Organization Secretary of the New York District, Bert Miller, and the youth leaders, Herbert Zam and Will Herberg. The District Organizer in Chicago, William F. Kruse, was expelled for refusing to denounce Lovestone but declined to join him actively. After changing its name to the Communist Party of the U.S.A. (Opposition) and then to the Independent Labor League of America, reflecting changes in its policies and program, the group, which lost Gitlow in 1933, disbanded in 1940.[66] All its principal leaders became intransigent enemies of Communism. Since they were still relatively young men, they were able to spend far more of their lives opposing Communism than they had spent espousing it.

The post-Lovestone Secretariat of the official party was composed of Bedacht, Minor, Weinstone, and Foster.[67] On the motion of Mikhailov (Williams), the Comintern representative, Bedacht was appointed acting secretary.[68] In this way the members of the former majority group, of which Bedacht had been a part, were reassured that the party was not being handed over to the former minority.

Bedacht's appointment was clearly an interim measure; he was not strong enough to dominate the other contenders for power and lasted in office only a year. Browder superseded him in 1930, and Bedacht was forced out of the running completely in 1932 by being sent to head the International Workers Order, which he built into the party's largest and most prosperous auxiliary. In 1948 Bedacht was expelled from the party, after twenty-nine years of service, for criticizing the party's position on the "national question" and for maintaining that the party had not gone sufficiently far to the Left after the expulsion of Browder three years earlier.[69]

Minor remained a useful and prominent figurehead in the party until his death in 1952. Outwardly impressive, and the bearer of a rich radical tradition extending from anarchism to communism, he was always more important nominally than in reality. He carried little political weight in the party's inner circles and protected his position by cringing before whomever he recognized as the temporary power in the party. He later served Browder as slavishly as he had served Lovestone, and betrayed both of them in much the same fashion, because he never deviated from the rule that the supreme power was lodged, not in any American, but in the rulers of Soviet Russia and the Comintern.

Weinstone was added to the Secretariat in 1929 in order to give representation to all the chief groups in existence prior to Lovestone's expulsion. He fought hard for a while to become Lovestone's true successor, but his abilities were never equal to his ambitions. He was shunted off to Moscow as the American representative to the Comintern at the end of 1929, and returned two years later to find Browder far ahead of him in the race for leadership. Yet he was able to survive the party's vicissitudes for another three decades, without ever managing to regain the influence that he had possessed in the first one.

For Foster, membership in the Secretariat was little more than a consolation prize. He was hemmed in by three others who had long opposed him and who owed their position to the Comintern rather than to him. For one who had come so close to winning the first prize, the comedown was particularly galling. He became General Secretary of the Trade Union Unity League, successor to the Trade Union Educational League, at a convention in Cleveland, Ohio, August 31–September 1, 1929. For the next three years Foster devoted most of his energies to carrying out the dual-union policy which he had fought for the previous twenty years. A heart attack during the presidential election of 1932 eliminated him from party politics for three years. When he returned to active duty again, he found Browder firmly in the saddle and determined not to share his power with his former chief.

From 1935 to 1945, in the years of the party's greatest influence, Foster had least to do with its policies and direction. He wandered about in the top leadership uncertainly, spent most of his time in "literary work" rather than action, suffered mortification and humiliation, and assuaged his bitterness by criticizing the Browder regime from the sidelines with an increasing fixation on Leftist orthodoxy and sectarian extremism. When Browder was finally overthrown in 1945, Foster obtained his revenge not by virtue of his own powers of persuasion but as a result of another fiat from abroad. And then, for the next fifteen years, Foster at last towered above all other Communists in prestige and influence; he, in effect, presided over the virtual liquidation of the American Communist movement in the nineteen-fifties.

Besides these four front-runners, the other contenders for power after Lovestone's expulsion rose and fell as the years passed.

Bittelman dutifully served two years of exile in the Comintern, during which time he carried out a mission in India. When he returned to the American scene at the end of 1931, the party's extremism gave free play to his doctrinaire intelligence. The Popular Front policy of the last half of the decade made him more and more obnoxious to the new leader, Browder, who finally shunted him off to the Jewish Communist movement from which he had come two decades earlier.

After Browder's downfall, history played a cruel trick on Bittelman. After having served five years in prison for his Communist faith, he was freed in 1957 and, at the age of sixty-seven, made a painful effort to take a "fresh look" at the American Communist movement. He announced publicly that among the chief causes of its failure were a "dogmatic and sectarian trend," an inability to take adequate account of American "peculiarities," and the error of having gone "overboard" in the war against American "exceptionalism" after Lovestone and Browder were overthrown. These belated revelations brought down on Bittelman the wrath of his former apprentice in Communist theory, Foster, who denounced him mercilessly for underestimating the danger of revisionism and flirting with Lovestone's old "American exceptionalism." [70] After Bittelman's four decades of unbroken service to the cause, Foster drove him out of party activity.

Like Minor, Jack Stachel, the other caretaker, also benefited from his loyalty to the Comintern and his disloyalty to the leaders of the American delegation with whom he had conspired in 1929. Following Foster's heart attack in 1932, Stachel emerged as acting head of the T.U.E.L.; and after its official termination in 1935, he reassumed his old role as Organization Secretary in the heyday of the Browder regime's Popular Front period. For a decade, he was the party apparatus's kingpin, Browder's right-hand man as he had once been Lovestone's.

And then for a second time he faced the problem of disengaging himself from the disgrace of the leader with whom he had been most intimately linked. In 1945, however, Stachel betrayed more qualms about Browder's dethronement than he had had about Lovestone's; though, as always, he accepted the decision, he was soon demoted from the post he then held as trade-union director. But, after five years' imprisonment resulting from the anti-Communist trials of the early nineteen-fifties, Stachel proved that his hand had not lost its cunning by acting as hatchetman in the expulsion in 1957 of the neo-Browderite group headed by John Gates, then editor of the *Daily Worker*. It is safe to say that no one contributed more than Stachel in 1935–45 to the expansion of the party's influence and that no one has been more responsible in the long run for its misfortunes than this dour, cynical, opportunistic arch-functionary.

Two others who expected to profit from Lovestone's expulsion were sorely disappointed.

Weisbord had never been able to reconcile himself to the existing leadership or fit into the factional set-up after the Passaic strike and the death of Ruthenberg. He blamed Lovestone for an unhappy experience as District Organizer in Detroit, and his next assignment —as secretary of the newly formed National Textile Workers Union—had removed him even further from the center of party power. He was therefore delighted with Lovestone's downfall and supported the Comintern enthusiastically, but he was quickly disenchanted by the Comintern's choice of some of Lovestone's closest collaborators, whom he indiscreetly held to be just as guilty as their former chief, to succeed to the leadership. To make his political disagreements with the new leadership clear, Weisbord offered his resignation as the party representative in the textile field, as a result of which he fared even less well under the new order in the party than he had under the old one.

From Moscow, Lozovsky reviled him as "but a rag, an alien element to be banished from our ranks." He was removed at the end of 1929 from his position in the Communist-controlled textile union. The party soon expelled him on trumped-up charges ranging from "Lovestoneism" to "white chauvinism." Shortly thereafter, he was converted to Trotskyism, but he was soon divorced from the official American Trotskyists for the same tendency that had exasperated the official Communists—the recent convert claimed to be a more authentic exponent of the true faith than the founders. From 1931 to 1937 he headed his own minuscule organization, the Communist League of Struggle, edited its official organ, *Class Struggle,* and wrote a ponderous two-volume work, *The Conquest of Power,* published in 1937.[71]

Harry M. Wicks, the American representative to the Profintern in 1929, was briefly considered in Moscow as a possible addition to the Secretariat, but was passed over and instead sent to Australia and other countries for over a year as Comintern representative to purge the parties of their Right-Wing deviationists. In 1937 he was quietly expelled from the American Communist party on charges, for which no evidence appears to exist, that for all his eighteen years in the Communist movement, most of them as a member of the Central

Executive Committee, he had been the private agent of an anti-Communist organization.[72] He spent the last years of his life working as a typesetter in Chicago and writing a book on the Communist movement which sheds little light on his own role or the reasons for his expulsion.[73]

The winner of the struggle for power initiated by the upheaval of the top leadership in 1929 was a dark horse, Earl Browder. He had not been considered important enough to send to Moscow for the confrontation of the chief American leaders in the American Commission, and had been absent from the American scene during the summer of 1929 to attend the last congress of the Pan-Pacific Secretariat in Vladivostok. But on his return in the fall, the Secretariat was reorganized: Minor and Bedacht remained, Foster and Weinstone went off, and Browder came on. From this base of operations, he swiftly and steadily left all his rivals behind. By 1934 he enjoyed undisputed control, and for the next eleven years dominated the American Communist movement as no one had done before or could do afterward. Yet his past record had hardly suggested that he was capable of such a feat, the full account of which properly belongs in another volume.

Finally, the story of John Pepper came to an unhappy end. Ever since his mythical trip to Mexico to embark on a nonexistent boat en route to Russia, he had lived in fear of the Comintern's reprisals. His old confidence and ingenuity had completely deserted him; his streak of hard luck seemed inexhaustible. After the departure of the American delegation for Moscow, the caretakers took fright at his continued presence in the United States and voted to expel him from the party; then, frightened by their own temerity, they hastily reinstated him.[74] Without a country and almost without a party, Pepper surrendered to his fate. Overcome by despair, he left for Russia and arrived in Moscow in the midst of the deliberations in the American Commission, at which Stalin repeatedly held him up to scorn and derision as an evil influence. The International Control Commission decided to expel him, not only for having deceived the Comintern about his trip to Mexico in 1929 but for having handed in an expense account the year before for a trip to Korea that he had not made.[75]

But Pepper survived in Russia a few more years. The last American Communist to see him was Browder. In 1937, during a visit to Russia, the American Communist leader was referred to the Gosplan, or State General Planning Commission, for information on Soviet economic policy. To his astonishment, he recognized the expert assigned to answer his questions as his old bête noire, John Pepper. Instead of entering into a discussion, Pepper arranged a magnificent banquet, at which everyone ate so long and so much that no time or inclination was left for possibly troublesome economic problems.[76] The following year, it appears, Pepper was swallowed up in the great purge that engulfed Russia before the war.

The essence of the process

Why was Lovestone, once so skillful and successful in Communist factional politics, so inept and helpless in these last months of his Communist career?

In retrospect it is clear that he committed a number of costly tactical blunders. Every step of the delegation to Moscow seemed dogged by misfortune.

The purpose of the delegation was dangerously double-edged. It was never presented to the membership as an act of defiance. The implication was rather that the American Communists continued to recognize the Comintern as the court of last resort and intended to abide by its decisions, favorable or unfavorable. The American party's Sixth Convention would never have agreed to send a delegation to Moscow on any other terms. In this respect, the Communist tradition was undeniably rigid and clear, and neither Lovestone nor any of his lieutenants ever dared to challenge it.

Even if the delegation's leaders intended in the last extremity to defy the Comintern, that is not how their followers understood the mandate of the convention. For this reason the preparations to take over the party if the decision went against them had to be carried out with the greatest secrecy, and knowledge of the plan was restricted to a handful of top leaders. Yet these leaders were themselves fatally unclear in their intentions. If they had seriously foreseen the probability of a break with Moscow, they would have been better advised to stay at home and wait for the Comintern to make the next move. Instead they precipitated a showdown in the wrong way at the wrong time in the wrong place.

Whereas Lovestone's faction could have waited, Lovestone himself could not. Both the Comintern and Stalin had refused to compromise on one thing—his withdrawal from the American scene. This was essentially the principal issue on which Lovestone's faction was asked to stake its dominant position in the party. It was not wholly personal in character, because Lovestone's faction could not have remained the same without Lovestone. Yet Stalin's taunt that he was not indispensable could not be openly denied, and Lovestone was maneuvered into the embarrassing position of equating his own fate with that of his faction and the party.

For years the Comintern had punished Communist leaders by separating them from their parties and either detaining them in Moscow or scattering them on Comintern missions to distant lands. Lovestone had known enough victims of this treatment to resist it most vehemently for himself. On the other hand, he went to Moscow voluntarily and thereby presented the Comintern with the opportunity to separate him from his party long enough to sever the ties between him and the party. He did not want to stay in Moscow for as long as two years, as Bittelman was forced to do, but by remaining there for almost two months, he enabled the Comintern to achieve its purpose in an even shorter period of time.

Of all his tactical blunders, probably the most devastating was his choice of commanders to hold the fort in his absence. He had no illusions about the opportunism of Stachel and the weakness of Minor, but the qualities which had made them useful to him made them even more useful to the Comintern. If they had remained faithful to him, the ultimate result might have been the same, but they could undoubtedly have enabled him to put up a better show of resistance to the Comintern and chip off a larger segment of the official party. Their swift about-face closed the party against him before he could get home, and doomed him to defeat before he could begin to fight.

In Moscow, Lovestone's insubordination went against all precedent. He had no jurisdictional grounds for denying the Comintern the right to remove him from his party, to keep him in Moscow, or to send him on any mission wherever it pleased. He was unable to protest in principle against the Comintern's well-established practice of making and unmaking national leaderships. After all, he had risen to the top precisely because the Comintern had favored him in the past. Thus his protests and objections were peculiarly unconvincing, half-hearted, and contradictory. He resisted with reservations and he submitted with reservations.

Lovestone's dilemma was a familiar one. Many other leaders after him were destined to suffer from it. He had lived by the Communist code of discipline and loyalty for so long that he could not successfully rebel against it when it failed to work in his favor. He had served his own interests only by serving the Comintern's interests; he could not suddenly serve his own interests against the Comintern's interests. The whole machinery of his downfall had been used, with his knowledge and acquiescence, to destroy others, but now that he was its victim, Lovestone saw the Comintern's methods in a new light, and he could not degrade himself sufficiently to accept them. In any case, whatever the circumstances, it took considerable courage and determination for Lovestone, Gitlow, Wolfe, and the others to defy Stalin in Moscow, as it had taken courage and determination for Cannon and Spector to get out of Moscow with Trotsky's document in their possession.

The most self-defeating of all Lovestone's tactical moves was undoubtedly the cable ordering Stachel, Minor, and Brodsky to put into operation the plan to take over the party's material assets. When this became generally known, his own followers were shocked by its audacity and it gave them an alibi for disassociating themselves from their former leaders. The secrecy with which the takeover was plotted betrayed the inherent weakness of the plan; it could not be revealed in advance to the majority of Lovestone's own top caucus. To them it seemed like a palace revolution, not against their factional enemies, but against the Comintern. Some who might have defended Lovestone on other grounds could not bring themselves to justify the "treason cable," as it was called by Lovestone's enemies.

The Comintern also outsmarted Lovestone after his ouster in the division of the spoils. Its choice of his former associate, Bedacht, as the new acting secretary, and its reward to Stachel, Minor, and Weinstone for breaking with him, invalidated his chief charge that the Comintern intended to turn the party over to the Fosterites. Actually the Comintern was far more interested in welding together a monolithic party loyal only to itself than in using one of the old factions against the other.

Yet all these tactical blunders and miscalculations do not adequately explain Lovestone's sudden ineptitude and helplessness. A far more fundamental flaw in his strategy accounted for his downfall.

Lovestone went to Moscow convinced that he could deal with Stalin as the leader of one Communist party with another. He recognized Stalin's power and thought that Stalin would recognize his power. That is why Lovestone and his closest associates never missed an opportunity to stress their "majority" in the party. That is why, ten years after his expulsion, Lovestone was still able to say: "I was not only a personal friend of Bukharin, but I had fundamental agreement with him on international questions, though on Russian questions I had agreement with Stalin and not with him." [77] This statement implied that Lovestone, as the American Communist leader, enjoyed such an independent status that he could make separate "agreements" with the two Russian leaders even when they were at loggerheads with each other.

But Stalin knew his American Communists better than Lovestone knew them. When Stalin said, "You declare you have a certain majority in the American Communist Party and that you will retain that majority under all circumstances. That is untrue, comrades of the American delegation, absolutely untrue," Stalin was right. And when Stalin warned them, "At present you still have a formal majority. But tomorrow you will have no majority and you will find yourselves completely isolated if you attempt to start a fight against the decisions of the Presidium of the Executive Committee of the Comintern," Stalin was right again.[78] All Lovestone's tactical moves were based on the premise that he could keep his majority in a fight against the Russian leadership of the Comintern. Wrong in this, he was wrong in everything else.

In effect, Lovestone's position in 1929 represented an incipient form of what later came to be known as Titoism. Two decades later, the Yugoslav Communist leader succeeded in maintaining his "majority" against Stalin's wishes because he led a party which had won power virtually by itself, without the help of the Soviet army, because he headed a government backed by its own army and police, and because he benefited from a favorable international situation. Lovestone had tried to pit his strength against Stalin's with none of these advantages, and the odds were too much for him.

The lesson of Lovestone's defeat was burned into the consciousness of the founding generation of American Communist leaders. It taught them that resistance against the Russian leadership of the world Communist movement was futile and barren. This was the end of the molding process. After ten years, nothing and no one could alter the fact that the American Communist party had become an instrument of the Russian Communist party. This was the essence of the process.

Yet the sequel should not be oversimplified. The next generation of Communists, born of the economic depression, knew little or nothing of the experiences of the older party leaders. The Popular Front of the late nineteen-thirties and its concomitant, Americanization, seemed to turn away from the earlier tradition of Bolshevization and Russification. But the second generation gradually learned the same lesson as the first, some from the Hitler-Stalin pact and the outbreak of war in 1939, some from the downfall of Earl Browder in 1945, some from the valiant and tragic Hungarian uprising in 1956. Each generation had to discover for itself in its own way that, even at the price of virtually committing political suicide, American Communism would continue above all to serve the interests of Soviet Russia.

NOTES

ACKNOWLEDGMENTS

INDEX

Notes

In the following Notes, sources are usually given in full on their first appearance. Some government sources, however, are so cumbersome that it seemed best to list them here in full in order that the reader may be able to refer to them, if necessary, with greater ease.

Government Sources

Hearings Before the Subversive Activities Control Board: Official Report of Proceedings Before the Subversive Activities Control Board: Attorney-General of the United States versus Communist Party of the United States of America (Washington, D.C.: typewritten record, 1951–53).

References to this source are given as *Subversive Activities Control Board.* However, in addition to the testimony, I have been able to consult the *Exhibits,* which were not made part of the public record; these instances are indicated in the Notes. This source, minus the *Exhibits,* is available on microfilm in several large libraries throughout the country.

Hearings Regarding Communist Espionage: Hearings Before the Committee on Un-American Activities, House of Representatives, 81st Congress, 1st and 2nd Sessions (Washington, D.C.: Government Printing Office, 1951), one vol.

Investigation of Un-American Propaganda Activities in the United States: Hearings Before a Special Committee on Un-American Activities (Dies Committee), House of Representatives, 75th–76th Congresses (Washington, D.C.: Government Printing Office, 1939–1940).

References are given as *Investigation of Un-American Propaganda Activities.* Unless otherwise noted, all references are to the Hearings. In Chapter VIII, however, there are several references to the *Executive Hearings,* a series containing testimony originally given to the same committee in private sessions. And there are some references to a single volume, called *Appendix—Part I,* which contains documents only.

Organized Communism in the United States, issued by the Committee on Un-American Activities, House of Representatives (Washington, D.C.: Government Printing Office, 1954), one vol.

Revolutionary Radicalism: Report of the Joint Legislative Committee Investigating Seditious Activities, filed April 24, 1920, in the Senate of the State of New York (Albany: J. B. Lyon Co.), 4 vols.

Subversion in Racial Unrest: Public Hearings of the State of Louisiana, Joint Legislative Committee (Baton Rouge, 1957), 2 vols.

Chapter 1: The New Day

1. *Manifesto and Program, Constitution, Report to the Communist International* (Chicago: Communist Party of America, 1919), p. 1.
2. I have dealt with these forerunners in some detail in *The Roots of American Communism* (New York: Viking, 1957), Chapter 1.
3. This paragraph is mainly based on the first Communist manifestoes and programs, of which the most convenient compilation may be found in *Organized Communism in the United States.* The most explicit references to force and violence appeared in the 1921 program and constitution of the Communist Party of America, pp. 55–56.
4. See *The Roots of American Communism,* Chapter 4, for fuller information about these foreign influences. Subsequently I was able to obtain an article by S. J. Rutgers, "Meetings with Lenin," in the Russian magazine, *Istorik Marksist,* Nos. 2–3, 1935, pp. 85–98, which is partially a memoir of his American experiences and fully confirms the intimate relationship between these émigré groups.
5. C. E. Ruthenberg, "The Bolsheviks: Grave-Diggers of Capitalism," *The Ohio Socialist* (Cleveland), January 29, 1919, p. 4, and "After the War—What?", ibid., February 12, 1919, p. 1.
6. Fraina's full story was told in *The Roots of American Communism.* Since then, new documents published in the Soviet monthly, *Inostrannaya Literatura,* No. 11, 1957, pp. 5–27, contain material of great interest dealing with John Reed and Louis C. Fraina. The documents clearly reveal Lenin's high regard for Fraina and imply his somewhat less serious interest in Reed. Two articles describing these hitherto unpublished documents have appeared: Esther (Mrs. Lewis) Corey, "Footnote on Lenin and Some American Writers," *The Antioch Review,* Winter 1958, pp. 510–15; and Leo Gruliow, "Lenin and Lewis Corey (Louis Fraina)," *Columbia Library Columns* (Columbia University), February 1959, pp. 12–15. The same issue of the latter publication also contains an interesting appreciation,

"Lewis Corey: A Portrait of an American Radical," by David E. Apter.

7. C. E. Ruthenberg, *The Ohio Socialist,* April 23, 1919, p. 4.
8. William E. Leuchtenberg, *The Perils of Prosperity* (Chicago: University of Chicago Press, 1958), p. 76.
9. *Manifesto and Program,* p. 8.
10. C. E. Ruthenberg, "Communism in the Open Again," *The Liberator,* February 1923, p. 12.
11. "No social order ever disappears before all the productive forces, for which there is room in it, have been developed" (Karl Marx, Introduction to *A Contribution to the Critique of Political Economy,* Chicago: Kerr, 1904, p. 12).
12. "We know that revolutions cannot be made to order, or by agreement; they break out when tens of millions of people come to the conclusion that it is impossible to live in the old way any longer" (V. I. Lenin, *Selected Works,* New York: International, 1937, Vol. VII, p. 414).
13. *The Communist* (published by the National Organization Committee), July 19, 1919, p. 3.
14. *The Communist,* May 1, 1920, p. 8 (italics in original).
15. The first National Secretary of the Workers party was Caleb Harrison (*The Toiler,* Cleveland, August 6, 1921, p. 1). Harrison was replaced by Elmer Allison (ibid., November 19, 1921, p. 13), and Allison by Ruthenberg (*The Worker,* May 20, 1922).
16. *The Worker,* November 4, 1922.
17. *The Worker,* November 3, 1923, p. 4.
18. *The Communist,* August 1, 1920, p. 8.
19. *Daily Worker,* March 5, 1924, magazine supplement, p. 2.

CHAPTER 2: THE FARMER-LABOR UNITED FRONT

1. The Farmer-Labor movement of 1919–24 still awaits its historian. Nathan Fine, *Labor and Farmer Parties in the United States* (New York: Rand School of Social Science, 1928), and Selig Perlman and Philip Taft, *History of Labor in the United States, 1896–1932* (New York: Macmillan, 1935) contain single chapters dealing with the basic facts. Stuart A. Rice, *Farmers and Workers in American Politics* (New York: Columbia University Press, 1924), and James H. Shideler, *Farm Crisis 1919–1923* (Berkeley: University of California Press, 1957), provide useful background material.
2. *Manifesto and Program,* pp. 8–9.
3. *Organized Communism in the United States,* p. 44.
4. The first program of the United Communist party in 1920 made the following differentiation: "It is to be remembered at all times that the Communist proposals for the socialization of industry have noth-

ing in common with the proposals for the nationalization and government ownership which abounds in the Socialist, Labor and Non-Partisan Leagues programs. These are plans for the extension of the public service under the capitalist rule" (*The Communist* [U.C.P.], June 12, 1920, p. 4). The program adopted by the Communist party at its second convention in 1920 prohibited cooperation with groups or parties "not committed to the principles and policies of the Communist International" (*The Communist* [C.P.], August 1, 1920, p. 7). The program of May 1921 of the Communist party of America ignores the Farmer-Labor movement.

5. *Lenin on Britain* (New York: International, 1934), p. 261.
6. *The Roots of American Communism,* p. 253.
7. *Lenin on Britain,* p. 269.
8. Bedacht to Draper, letter dated January 20, 1955. Bedacht was one of the American delegates to the Third Congress.
9. *New York Times,* December 1, 1921. According to Ludwig E. Katterfeld, then the American representative to the Comintern, Christensen asked for the interview with Lenin, and Katterfeld helped him to obtain it (interview with Katterfeld, September 8, 1956). Browder says that the Farmer-Labor leaders asked Christensen to make the trip to Moscow to interest Lenin in their movement (interview with Browder, October 22, 1954). But this must have been an incidental mission, since Christensen spent over two years on the trip (*The New Majority,* Chicago, June 2, 1923).
10. Alexander Bittelman, *The Workers Monthly,* December 24, 1924, p. 86.
11. V. I. Lenin, *"Left-Wing" Communism: An Infantile Disorder* (rev. ed.; New York: International, 1934), p. 68.
12. Zinoviev, *Protokoll der Konferenz der Erweiterten Exekutive der Kommunistischen Internationale,* 12–23 Juni 1923 (Verlag Carl Hoym, 1923), pp. 9–10.
13. *Resolutions and Theses of the Fourth Congress of the Communist International* (London: Communist Party of Great Britain, 1923), p. 30.
14. *Protokoll des V. Kongresses* (Verlag Carl Hoym, 1924), Vol. I, p. 81.
15. Ibid., Vol. I, p. 173.
16. *Die Taktik der Kommunistischen Internationale gegen die Offensive des Kapitals:* Bericht über die Konferenz der Erweiterten Exekutive der Kommunistische Internationale, Moskau, vom 24 Februar bis 4 März 1922 (Verlag der Kommunistischen Internationale, 1922), p. 35.
17. *Protokoll des Vierten Kongresses der Kommunistischen Internationale,* 5 November bis 5 Dezember 1922 (Verlag der Kommunistischen Internationale, 1923), p. 421.
18. *The Communist International* (London), June 28, 1929, p. 666.
19. Ruthenberg, in *The Liberator,* February 1923, p. 13, and Bittelman,

in *The Workers Monthly,* December 1924, p. 88, refer to the May 1922 thesis.

20. *For a Labor Party:* A Statement by the Workers Party (New York: Workers Party of America, 1st ed., October 15, 1922).
21. *The Second Year of the Workers Party of America,* Report of the Central Executive Committee to the Third National Convention, December 30, 31, 1923, and January 1, 1924 (Chicago: Literature Department, Workers Party of America, 1924), p. 15.
22. *The Liberator,* January 1923, p. 11.
23. Alexander Bittelman, *The Workers Monthly,* December 1924, p. 88 (italics in original).
24. The circumstances of Pepper's election at the Bridgman convention and his subsequent appointment as secretary of the Political Committee are mentioned in Ruthenberg's letter to the Executive Committee of the Communist International, dated April 11, 1924. This letter is further explained in Note 44, Chapter 5. *The Worker,* January 6, 1923, reported Pepper's election to the C.E.C. "from San Francisco."
25. The first edition of this pamphlet was unsigned; the second, third, and fourth editions, all published in 1923, were credited to John Pepper.
26. *The Autobiography of Lincoln Steffens* (New York: Harcourt Brace, 1931, one-vol. ed., p. 695); Hutchins Hapgood, *A Victorian in the Modern World* (New York: Harcourt, Brace, 1939, pp. 189, 210). Hapgood wrote Johannsen's biography in *The Spirit of Labor* (New York: Duffield & Co., 1907).
27. See *The Worker,* May 12 and 19, 1923, for the material in this paragraph.
28. Browder to Draper, February 24, 1959.
29. Swabeck to Draper, May 14, 1956. According to Browder, Fitzpatrick "merely reminded us politely that we should not consider ourselves the bosses" and did not use the expression that the Communists should occupy a "back seat" (Browder to Draper, February 24, 1959). On the main point—that Fitzpatrick issued a warning to the Chicago committee—there is agreement.
30. Browder, "A Political Autobiography" (in manuscript), pp. 184–85.
31. *The Second Year,* p. 23, refers to Cannon's letter; the circumstances surrounding it were further described in Browder to Draper, February 20, 1956.
32. *The Second Year,* p. 24. According to Bedacht and Lovestone, Swabeck reported on June 10, 1923, that the Chicago committee had pursued a policy of "as much as possible following the lead of the national officers of the Farmer-Labor Party" (*Daily Worker,* December 24, 1924, p. 4).
33. Swabeck to Draper, May 14, 1956. Ruthenberg's appearance in Chicago to confer with Jay G. Brown is mentioned in *The Second Year,* p. 23.

34. Ruthenberg's letter to the E.C.C.I., April 11, 1924.
35. *The Second Year,* pp. 17–18.
36. *The Labor Herald,* January 1924, p. 8.
37. *The American Labor Year Book,* 1923–24 (New York: Rand School of Social Science, 1924), p. 143. Pepper claimed representation from 50,000 miners, 10,000 machinists, 60,000 clothing workers, 7000 food workers, West Virginia Federation of Labor (87,000 members), central labor bodies of Buffalo, Detroit, Minneapolis, and Butte (112,000 members) in *For a Labor Party,* 3rd ed., p. 71.
38. Estimates of the total number of delegates vary widely. The lowest seems to be "some 440" by Robert Morss Lovett (*The New Republic,* July 18, 1923, p. 198). Ruthenberg offered three figures: 539 (*The Federated Farmer Labor and the Workers Party* [see below], p. 4); "about 540" (*The Second Year,* p. 19); and 550 (*From the Third Through the Fourth Convention* [see below], p. 7). Pepper gave 650 (*For a Labor Party,* 3rd ed., p. 75) and 740 (*The Worker,* July 21, 1923, p. 2). Foster says the estimates ranged from 600 to 800 (*The Labor Herald,* August 1923, p. 5).

    Pepper gave the number of Communist delegates as 180 (*The Worker,* July 21, 1923, p. 2) and as almost 200 (*For a Labor Party,* 3rd ed., p. 75). Ruthenberg reported 200 Communist delegates in *From the Third Through the Fourth Convention of the Workers (Communist) Party of America* (Chicago: Daily Worker Publishing Co. [1925], p. 7) and 190 in *The Federated Farmer Labor Party and the Workers Party:* A Statement and Instructions to the Membership by the Central Executive Committee (mimeographed, 6 pp., signed by C. E. Ruthenberg, issued end of 1923), p. 4.
39. In later years this fact became so inconvenient that Foster has twice insisted on the very opposite. In *From Bryan to Stalin* (New York: International, 1937), he pretended that "only a very small minority" of the delegates were Communists (p. 179). Fifteen years later, in his *History of the Communist Party of the United States* (1952), he again tried to make it appear that the Communists made up "but a very small minority," as if the only Communist delegates were ten official ones from the party. Foster himself attended as a delegate of the Brotherhood of Railway Carmen of Chicago (*The New Majority,* July 14, 1923, p. 2).
40. *The 4th National Convention* (Chicago: Daily Worker Publishing Co., 1925), p. 29, for the Workers party figure. Foster says "at least 600,000" (*The Labor Herald,* August 1923, p. 5) and Pepper says 616,000 (*For a Labor Party,* 3rd ed., p. 71) were represented at the Chicago convention.
41. *The Second Year,* p. 18; *The Federated Farmer Labor Party and the Workers Party,* p. 3.
42. This portion of the story appears in Communist sources only: *The Second Year,* p. 18; *The Federated Farmer Labor Party and the*

Workers Party, p. 4; *The Labor Herald,* August 1923, p. 5; *For a Labor Party,* 3rd ed., p. 79. All substantially agree on the main point but express it in varying ways.

43. Ludwig Lore, *Daily Worker,* December 29, 1924, p. 5. The other members of the steering committee were Manley, Lovestone, and Lore.
44. Charles Woll, Chicago *Herald and Examiner,* July 7, 1923. Also Swabeck to Draper, June 25, 1957: "Delegates who were members of the W.P. were organized into groups of ten with a captain in charge of each group and placed in positions most favorable for winning friends and influencing people."
45. Lore, *Daily Worker,* December 29, 1924.
46. *The Voice of Labor* (Chicago), July 14, 1923, carried the full speeches of Fitzpatrick, Foster, and Ruthenberg.
47. *The New Majority,* July 14, 1923, p. 2.
48. *The Federated Farmer Labor Party and the Workers Party* (p. 5) says "not more than 50" supported the Farmer-Labor proposal; *The Second Year* (p. 19) says "about 40"; and *For a Labor Party* (p. 82) says 50.
49. *The New Majority,* July 14, 1923, p. 2, admitted only the defection of the Washington state organization, but added that the dozen or so other F.-L.P. delegates who went over to the Communists represented only themselves. Ruthenberg claimed that the state organizations of Washington, Ohio, Kentucky, and part of Illinois affiliated with the F.F.-L.P. (*The Federated Farmer Labor Party and the Workers Party,* p. 5). Pepper added California and Wisconsin to the Communist claims (*For a Labor Party,* 3rd ed., p. 71). James Oneal, *American Communism* (New York: The Rand Book Store, 1927), mentions Washington state only (p. 170).
50. Robert Morss Lovett, *The New Republic,* July 18, 1923, p. 199.
51. Joseph Manley, *Daily Worker,* January 7, 1925, p. 3, for his avowal as a Pepperite in 1923.
52. Oneal, op. cit., p. 169.
53. *The Federated Farmer Labor Party and the Workers Party,* p. 6.
54. Manley, *Daily Worker,* January 7, 1925, p. 3.
55. "Statement of Principles and Organization Rules of the Federated Farmer-Labor Party," *The Voice of Labor,* July 14, 1923, p. 6.
56. *The New Republic,* July 18, 1923, p. 199.
57. Interview with Charles N. Wheeler, Chicago *Herald and Examiner,* July 7, 1923, p. 2.
58. *The New Majority,* July 21, 1923, p. 5.
59. *The Second Year,* p. 19.
60. *For a Labor Party,* 3rd ed., p. 75.
61. *The Labor Herald,* January 1924, p. 8.
62. *Daily Worker,* January 16, 1931, p. 4.
63. *The Worker,* May 19, 1923, p. 1.

64. Foster, *The Labor Herald,* January 1924, p. 8; *The Second Year,* p. 16.
65. According to Ruthenberg, this agreement provided for the formation of a Federated Farmer-Labor party if half a million workers were represented by July 3; a National Executive Committee of the F.F.-L.P. to replace the existing National Committee of the F.-L.P.; the structure of the F.F.-L.P. to follow that of the F.-L.P.; resolutions containing a general statement of principles; and support for recognition of Soviet Russia (*The Second Year,* pp. 17–18, and *The Federated Farmer Labor Party and the Workers Party,* p. 3).
66. Ruthenberg said that Fitzpatrick, "it appeared, was opposing the plan which the Farmer Labor Party representatives had agreed to" (*The Second Year,* pp. 17–18). There is no evidence of any such agreement in Farmer-Labor sources.

CHAPTER 3: ROADS TO CHICAGO

1. Oakley C. Johnson, *The Day Is Coming: Life and Work of Charles E. Ruthenberg* (New York: International, 1957), p. 117. This is the official Communist biography. Ruthenberg related the details of his background in testimony at his various trials. Johnson's book, despite its gross political distortions, is useful for Ruthenberg's early years.
2. *The Autobiography of Lincoln Steffens,* pp. 470–81, contains a short, sympathetic portrait of Tom Johnson.
3. *Cleveland Press,* October 18, 1912, p. 13.
4. Johnson, op. cit., p. 25.
5. *New York Call,* July 30, 1912, p. 4.
6. *The Workers Monthly,* October 1925, p. 531.
7. *Daily Worker,* April 9, 1930, p. 4. The rest of the passage complained about Lovestone's agitated manner as compared with Ruthenberg's own calm.
8. David Damon [C. E. Ruthenberg], "The Communist Party and Its Tasks," *The Communist,* July 1921, pp. 25–26. "David Damon" was Ruthenberg's pseudonym in the underground period.
9. Damon [Ruthenberg], "Make the Party a 'Party of Action,'" *The Communist,* April 25, 1920, p. 4.
10. Damon and Marshall [Ruthenberg and Bedacht], "Problem of Communist Organization in the U.S.," *The Communist,* July 1922, p. 24.
11. Max Bedacht, interview, June 1, 1954, and letter, Bedacht to Draper, December 13, 1954.
12. Baron Albert Kaas and Fedor de Lazarovics, *Bolshevism in Hungary* (London: Grant Richards, 1931), p. 74, says that before it was Pogany or Pepper, his name had been Schwarcz.
13. Ladislaus Rudas, *Abenteurer und Liquidatorentum* (Vienna: Verlag "Vörös Ujsag," 1922), pp. 30–33; Henrik Ungar, *Die magyarische Pest in Moskau* (Leipzig: Veritas Verlag, 1921), pp. 16–17.

14. Bela Szanto, *Klassenkämpfe und Diktatur in Ungarn* (Petrograd: Verlag der Kommunistischen Internationale, 1920), p. 61.
15. Dr. J. Mrose, *Räterepublik Ungarn* (Leipzig: Staatsbürgerlicher Verlag, 1919), p. 8; Elemér Málusz, *The Fugitive Bolsheviks* (London: Grant Richards, 1931), pp. 17, 340; Oscar Jaszi, *Revolution and Counter-Revolution in Hungary* (London: P.S. King & Son, 1924), pp. 46, 89, 96; Wilhelm Böhm, *Im Kreuzfeuer zweier Revolutionen* (Munich: Verlag für Kulturpolitik, 1924), pp. 294, 321.
16. Ossip K. Flechtheim, *Die KPD in der Weimarer Republik* (Offenbach: Bollwerk-Verlag Karl Drott, 1948), p. 73; Edward Hallett Carr, *The Bolshevik Revolution 1917–1923* (New York: Oxford Press, 1953), Vol. III, p. 335; Ypsilon [pseudonym of two former Comintern officials], *Pattern for World Revolution* (Chicago: Ziff-Davis, 1947), p. 39.
17. *Die Taktik der Kommunistischen Internationale gegen die Offensive des Kapitals* (Moscow: Verlag der Kommunistischen Internationale, 1922), p. 233; *International Press Correspondence,* April 28, 1922, p. 233.
18. Ludwig E. Katterfeld, then American representative to the Comintern in Moscow, recalls that Pepper bothered him about the possibilities of coming to the United States (interview with Katterfeld, September 7, 1956).
19. Trotsky says that Pepper was supposed to work on the Hungarian paper (*The Militant,* October 1, 1929, p. 8). Cannon, who was in Moscow at the time of Pepper's departure, states: "In other writings, I have seen various references to Pepper as a 'representative of the Comintern.' Was this really the case? What was Pepper's real status in the American movement, and what, if any, authority did he have as a representative of the Comintern? Strange as it may seem, that was never completely clear. I, at least, never knew for sure; and up till the present no one has ever explained it to me. I don't think anyone in the American party ever really knew. . . . We were told in Moscow that he had been shipped to America in one of the moves to break up the raging faction fight in the émigré leadership of the defeated Hungarian Communist Party, and that his assignment was to work with the Bureau of the Hungarian Federation of the party in the U.S. As far as I know, that's all the official authorization he ever had" (Cannon to Draper, May 19, 1954).
20. Michael Gold, "American Intellectuals and Communism," *The Worker,* December 1, 1923, p. 5.
21. Karl Reeve, *International Press Correspondence,* December 31, 1925, p. 1368.
22. *The Worker,* May 26 and August 25, 1923.
23. Foster has written two autobiographical works, *From Bryan to Stalin* (1937) and *Pages from a Worker's Life* (New York: International, 1939), the second more personal.

24. Ira Kipnis, *The American Socialist Movement 1897–1912* (New York: Columbia University Press, 1952), pp. 176–78, refers to Titus's program.
25. Earl C. Ford and William Z. Foster, *Syndicalism* (Chicago: William Z. Foster, 1912), expresses this early stage of Foster's view.
26. William Z. Foster, *The Great Steel Strike and Its Lessons* (New York: Huebsch, 1920), p. 259.
27. *Investigation of Strike in Steel Industries:* Hearing Before the Committee on Education and Labor, U.S. Senate, 66th Congress, 1st Session (Washington, D.C.: Government Printing Office, 1919), pp. 76, 423.
28. Wm. Z. Foster, *The Railroaders' Next Step* (Chicago: Trade Union Educational League, 1921), pp. 11, 18, 26.
29. Jay Fox, *Amalgamation* (Chicago: Trade Union Educational League, 1923), p. 36.
30. *The Railroaders' Next Step,* p. 48. Also see Foster, *Trade Unionism: The Road to Freedom* (Chicago: Trade Union Educational League, 1921), pp. 12, 19, 21, 28.
31. David J. Saposs, *Left Wing Unionism* (New York: International, 1926), p. 97.
32. J. B. S. Hardman, *American Labor Dynamics* (New York: Harcourt, Brace, 1928), p. 20.
33. Wm. Z. Foster, *The Bankruptcy of the American Labor Movement* (Chicago: Trade Union Educational League, 1922), pp. 23, 32, 41.
34. Fox, op. cit., p. 44.
35. *The Communist,* September 27, 1919, p. 2.
36. *Investigation of Strike in Steel Industries,* p. 399.
37. *The Militant,* August 15, 1929, p. 3. Cannon says he visited Foster in company with Ralph Chaplin, the Wobbly poet.
38. The backgrounds of Cannon and Browder are largely based on letters from Cannon to Draper, April 21 and August 4, 1954, and interview, September 23, 1955; letters from Browder to Draper, January 24 and February 29, 1956.
39. Joseph Zack [Kornfeder] testified that he came to the United States in 1917, worked as a tailor, and helped to organize the Communist party in 1919 (*Subversion in Racial Unrest,* Part 1, pp. 17–18).
40. See *The Roots of American Communism,* pp. 315–19, for a fuller account of the first Profintern congress and the American delegation.
41. Wm. Z. Foster, *The Russian Revolution* (Chicago: Trade Union Educational League, 1922) contains the articles he sent from Russia to the Federated Press.
42. *The Bankruptcy of the American Labor Movement,* p. 51.
43. *Pages from a Worker's Life,* p. 295.
44. *The Bankruptcy of the American Labor Movement,* p. 45; for a similar statement, see Foster's foreword to A. Lozovsky, *Lenin and the*

Trade Union Movement (Chicago: Trade Union Educational League, 1924), p. 5.
45. *The Bankruptcy of the American Labor Movement,* p. 38.
46. Charles Krumbein, *The Labor Herald,* February 1923, p. 3. The T.U.E.L.'s National Committee reported that active work "practically began in February, 1922" (*The Labor Herald,* September 1922, p. 7).
47. *The Second Year,* p. 68.
48. Swabeck to Draper, June 25, 1957. The vote on the amalgamation resolution was 114 to 37 (*The Labor Herald,* May 1922, p. 16).
49. The figures differ, probably because they were made at different times: Browder, *Trade Unions in America* (Chicago: Trade Union Educational League, 1924), p. 26; Edward B. Mittelman, "Basis for American Labor Opposition to Amalgamation and Politics at Portland," *Journal of Political Economy,* February 1924, p. 90; Johnstone, *The Worker,* October 20, 1923; Swabeck, ibid., November 17, 1923.
50. *Trade Unions in America,* p. 26.
51. *The Labor Herald,* September 1922, p. 7.
52. Wm. Z. Foster, *International Press Correspondence,* February 8, 1923, pp. 75–76.
53. Browder, *The Labor Herald,* May 1922, p. 31.
54. Philip Taft, *The A.F. of L. in the Time of Gompers* (New York: Harper, 1957), p. 454.
55. *The Labor Herald,* September 1922, p. 7.
56. Browder, *International Press Correspondence,* June 23, 1922, p. 392. See David M. Schneider, *The Workers' (Communist) Party and American Trade Unions* (Baltimore: Johns Hopkins Press, 1928), for a chapter (pp. 8–25) on the machinists' union in this period.
57. Schneider, op. cit., pp. 38–59.
58. *The Labor Herald,* September 1922, p. 7.
59. S. T. Hammersmark, ibid., October 1922, p. 25.
60. Charles Krumbein, *International Press Correspondence,* February 15, 1923, p. 89.
61. *The Labor Herald,* December 1922, p. 6.
62. *The Worker,* April 22, 1922, p. 2.
63. *The Voice of Labor,* February 16, 1923, p. 4.
64. Jeannette D. Pearl, ibid., September 15, 1922, p. 12.
65. John Pepper, "Wm. Z. Foster—Revolutionary Leader," *The Worker,* April 14, 1923, p. 2.
66. Dorsey [Foster], speech at session of the American Commission of the Comintern, May 6, 1924 (emphasis in original). Photocopy of the typewritten stenogram is in my possession.
67. *History of the Communist Party of the United States,* p. 222. But instead of wholly assuming the responsibility, Foster foists it off on the "Bittelman-Foster group," which did not then exist.

Chapter 4: The Parting of the Ways

1. Manley, *Daily Worker,* December 30, 1924; *Farmer-Labor Voice,* August 1, 1924, p. 1; *Daily Worker,* January 14, 1924, p. 4.
2. Manley, *Daily Worker,* December 5, 1924.
3. Wagenknecht, ibid., December 26, 1924.
4. *International Press Correspondence,* August 30, 1923, pp. 633–34.
5. Ibid., September 20, 1923, p. 677.
6. Foster, *The Labor Herald,* November 1923, pp. 6–7.
7. Fitzpatrick gave up independent politics locally by supporting Democratic and Republican candidates in the Chicago judicial elections in November 1923, and adopted the "nonpartisan" policy nationally the following year (*The New Majority,* May 24, 1924, p. 1).
8. Mittelman, *Journal of Political Economy,* op. cit., p. 91.
9. *The Workers Monthly,* June 1925, p. 351.
10. *Proceedings: 16th National Convention, Communist Party, U.S.A.,* February 9–12, 1957 (New York: New Century, 1957), p. 137.
11. Browder to Draper, February 24, 1959.
12. The Chicago delegates were Foster, Canon, Krumbein, Johnstone, Aronberg, and Swabeck (*The Worker,* January 5, 1924). Yet when the Foster-Cannon caucus won control of the convention, Browder was rewarded by being put on the new C.E.C. and the last four were not.
13. *Trade Unions in America,* p. 25.
14. *Daily Worker,* December 11, 1924.
15. Claude McKay, *A Long Way from Home* (New York: Furman, 1937), p. 178.
16. Cannon to Draper, May 28, 1954.
17. *The Worker,* July 21, 1923; *The Liberator,* August 1923, p. 10.
18. *The Worker,* October 20, 1923, p. 2.
19. "Theses on Our Labor Party Policy," Workers Party of America Press Service, mimeographed, with covering letter signed by C. E. Ruthenberg, dated September 10, 1923. It does not seem that this document was otherwise published; the copy in my possession is the only one I have been able to locate.
20. Cannon, *Daily Worker,* December 11, 1924. The Executive Council was made up at this time of Bittelman, Cannon, William F. Dunne, Marian Emerson, Engdahl, Lindgren, Lore, Theodore Maki, Olgin, Ruthenberg, Wicks, and Foster (*The Worker,* January 20, 1923; except for Foster who had not yet admitted his membership in the party).
21. *The Worker,* August 25, 1923.
22. Ibid., September 1, 1923.
23. Ibid., September 8, 1923.
24. Ibid., September 8, 1923.

25. Ibid., September 15, 1923.
26. Cannon to Draper, May 28, 1954.
27. *The Worker,* September 8, 1923.
28. *The Liberator,* September 1923, pp. 9, 12.
29. Ibid., October 1923, p. 9. The Kerensky analogy was also used by Cannon six months later (*Daily Worker,* April 22, 1924, p. 2).
30. *Daily Worker,* January 19, 1924. Zinoviev partially encouraged this line of reasoning (ibid., January 21, 1924).
31. Cannon to Draper, May 28, 1954.
32. Minutes of the Political Committee, September 10, 1923.
33. I am indebted to Mr. Charles S. Zimmerman for a copy of the seventeen-page mimeographed "Statement on Our Labor Party Policy, submitted by Coms. Foster and Cannon," the only complete one I have been able to locate.
34. The original, entitled, "Thesis on the Present Economic and Political Situation and the Policy of the Workers Party," submitted by Comrades John Pepper and C. E. Ruthenberg, was first mimeographed, and later published, with short excisions, in *The Second Year,* pp. 47–56, omitting the names of its sponsors, Pepper and Ruthenberg.
35. *The Worker,* May 26, 1923; Gitlow, *I Confess,* pp. 160–62.
36. Lore had been closely associated with the Workers' Council group in 1921 and with it went into the Workers party, but Bittelman later revealed, with some puzzlement, that Lore had been a member of the Communist party of America at the time of its negotiations with the Workers' Council leading to the Workers party (*Daily Worker,* August 29, 1924).
37. Lore, *Daily Worker,* December 29, 1924, and Cannon, ibid., December 11, 1924.
38. *The 4th National Convention,* pp. 45–46.
39. *The American Labor Who's Who,* edited by Solon De Leon (New York: Hanford Press, 1925), p. 33, contains a short biography of Burman.
40. See Melech Epstein, *The Jew and Communism* (New York: Trade Union Sponsoring Committee, 1959), pp. 398–403, for an intimate sketch of Bittelman.
41. *Daily Worker,* February 12, 1929, p. 3.
42. *The Worker,* May 26, July 1, and August 11, 1923.
43. Ruthenberg mentions 53 delegates (*Daily Worker,* January 13, 1924, p. 7), but *The Second Year,* p. 9, lists only 52, probably because Pepper's name was omitted for security reasons.
44. *The Second Year,* pp. 56–61.
45. Ruthenberg, *Daily Worker,* January 13, 1924, p. 7
46. Lore, ibid., December 30, 1924.
47. Ruthenberg, ibid., January 13, 1924, p. 7.
48. *The Second Year,* pp. 61–72, 87–100.
49. The C.E.C. elected at the Third Convention was made up as follows

—*Majority:* Alexander Bittelman, Earl Browder, Fahle Burman, James P. Cannon, William F. Dunne, William Z. Foster, Ludwig Lore, and Y.W.L. representative; *Minority:* J. Louis Engdahl, Benjamin Gitlow, Jay Lovestone, John Pepper, and Charles E. Ruthenberg.

The Political Bureau (also called Committee)—*Majority:* Foster, Browder, Cannon, and Dunne; *Minority:* Ruthenberg, Pepper and Lovestone. (*Daily Worker,* January 12, 1924, p. 1.)

50. *Daily Worker,* May 5, 1924, p. 5.
51. Ibid., April 3, 1924, p. 3.
52. Ibid., January 12, 1924, p. 5.
53. Ibid., January 12, 1924, p. 2.
54. Ibid., January 19, 1924, magazine supplement, p. 1.

Chapter 5: The LaFollette Fiasco

1. *The Worker,* December 22, 1923, and *Daily Worker,* March 13, 1924.
2. *Daily Worker,* March 7, 1924.
3. Ibid., March 8, 1924, magazine supplement.
4. Ibid., April 10, 1924.
5. "Present Economic and Political Situation and Our Immediate Tasks," Memorandum to the E.C.C.I., submitted by Foster, Cannon, and Bittelman, adopted by the C.E.C. of the Workers party on March 16, 1924 (*Daily Worker,* March 22, 1924, magazine supplement).
6. Ibid., April 12, 1924, p. 4.
7. Ibid., April 10, 1924.
8. *The Worker,* July 28, 1923, p. 2.
9. Wicks, *Daily Worker,* December 15, 1924, p. 4.
10. *Daily Worker,* May 30, 1938; *The Worker,* September 21, 1958; *American Labor Who's Who,* p. 99.
11. Ruthenberg, *Daily Worker,* December 15, 1924, p. 4.

    Arthur Naftalin, "A History of the Farmer-Labor Party of Minnesota" (a doctoral thesis, typewritten, University of Minnesota, 1948), deals in detail with the story of 1923–24 but unfortunately utilizes almost no contemporary Communist source material.

    Governor Floyd B. Olson's biographer seems squeamish about admitting the Communists' role in forming the Farmer-Labor Federation and apparently ignored Communist sources completely (George H. Mayer, *The Political Career of Floyd B. Olson,* Minneapolis: University of Minnesota Press, 1951, p. 31).
12. Ruthenberg, *Daily Worker,* December 8, 1924.
13. *Daily Worker,* March 7, 1924.
14. Minutes of the Executive Council, January 28, 1924.
15. Minutes of the Central Executive Committee, February 15–16, 1924.

16. Minutes of the Executive Council, February 26 and March 7, 1924.
17. Bittelman, *Daily Worker,* March 22, 1924; Ruthenberg, ibid., April 12, 1924; ibid., March 12, 1924, p. 2.
18. Foster, ibid., December 13, 1924, magazine supplement.
19. *Daily Worker,* May 14, 1924, p. 5, for the text; and Foster, ibid., December 13, 1924, magazine supplement for explanation.
20. Foster, ibid., December 13, 1924, magazine supplement.
21. *The Toiler* (Cleveland), August 27, 1921.
22. Wm. Z. Foster, *The Russian Revolution* (Chicago: Trade Union Educational League, 1921), pp. 107–12.
23. Boris Souvarine, *Stalin* (New York: Alliance Book Corp., 1939), p. 367, says that Stalin "took part for the first time in the proceedings of the International" in 1924 at the Fifth Congress. This seems mistaken. Stalin is listed as one of the Russian delegates to the Comintern's First Congress in 1919 (*Der I. Kongress der Kommunistischen Internationale,* Verlag der Kommunistischen Internationale, 1921, p. 4) and again at the Second Plenum in June 1922 (*Bericht über die Tätigkeit des Präsidiums und der Exekutive der Kommunistische Internationale,* Verlag der Kommunistischen Internationale, 1922, p. 360). It does seem true that he did not make his influence felt until the Fifth Congress (cf. Ruth Fischer, *Stalin and German Communism,* Cambridge: Harvard University Press, 1948, pp. 404–405).
24. *Hearst's International,* April 1924, p. 64. Miss Strong seems to have trusted to her memory and quoted somewhat different words when she boasted of this prophecy thirty-two years later (*The Stalin Era,* New York: Mainstream, 1956, p. 117). She recalled that she had been told about Stalin "by Russian Communists" but the "words sank into a well in America; nobody cared." And curiously, Miss Strong's article in *Hearst's International* was introduced by a note by the editor Norman Hapgood: "When I was in Russia and Lenin was still living, I was talking with an American who had done business there for many years, and who was a friend of Lenin. I asked him who, in his opinion, was likely to come nearest to filling Lenin's place, and he mentioned Stalin. . . ."
25. *Protokoll des III. Kongresses der Kommunistischen Internationale* (Verlag der Kommunistischen Internationale, 1921), pp. 106–12 (Pogany) and pp. 129–32 (Trotsky). Pepper later apologized for this indiscretion (*International Press Correspondence,* November 8, 1928, p. 1476).
26. *The Militant* (New York), August 15, 1929, p. 4.
27. *New Yorker Volkszeitung,* March 5, 1924.
28. Ruthenberg, *Daily Worker,* December 6, 1924, magazine supplement. However, Lovestone seems to date this incident March 7, 1924, or perhaps it occurred twice (*Daily Worker,* December 13, 1924, magazine supplement).

29. Minutes of the Executive Council, March 7, 1924. Foster, Browder, Abern, and Burman voted against Pepper, Ruthenberg, Lovestone, and Engdahl.
30. Ruthenberg, *Daily Worker,* December 6, 1924, and August 29, 1925; Lovestone, ibid., December 13, 1924, magazine supplement.
31. Ruthenberg, ibid., December 6, 1924, and August 29, 1925; Lovestone, ibid., December 13, 1924, magazine supplement. The "discussion" ran in the *Daily Worker* from the end of February to the middle of April 1924 and merely constituted a reprint of material in *International Press Correspondence* (January 29–March 14, 1924), which was under Zinoviev's control.
32. *Daily Worker,* May 24, 1924, p. 1, for the text; and Ruthenberg, ibid., December 6, 1924, magazine supplement, for the background.
33. Trotsky's criticism of the Third Party alliance appears in his 1924 introduction to *The First Five Years of the Communist International* (New York: Pioneer, 1945), Vol. I, pp. 12–14.
34. *Daily Worker,* December 13, 1924, magazine supplement.
35. Foster, *Daily Worker,* December 9, 1924, p. 4.
36. Lovestone, ibid., December 26, 1924, p. 4.
37. Amter, ibid., January 7, 1925, p. 4.
38. "Workers Party Issues Declaration of Policy," *Daily Worker,* August 20, 1924 (see Note 57 for explanation).
39. Olgin, ibid., December 6, 1924, magazine supplement.
40. Ibid., December 6, 13, and 20, 1924, magazine supplement.
41. Moissaye J. Olgin, *The Soul of the Russian Revolution* (New York: Holt, 1917), p. 376; "Lenin and the Bolsheviki," *Asia,* December 1917.
42. M. J. Olgin, *Trotskyism: Counter-Revolution in Disguise* (New York: Workers Library, 1935).
43. Foster, *Daily Worker,* December 30, 1924, p. 4.
44. These four letters to the Comintern have come into my possession, but there may have been others. Ruthenberg's letter, dated April 11, 1924, is particularly rich in details of secret party history and has been previously cited.
45. Lovestone, *Daily Worker,* December 18, 1924, p. 3.
46. Gitlow, ibid., December 30, 1924, p. 4.
47. *Protokoll des V. Kongresses,* Vol. II, p. 1004.
48. *International Press Correspondence,* May 6, 1925, p. 1.
49. Foster, *Daily Worker,* December 30, 1924, p. 4.
50. Lovestone, ibid., December 26, 1924, p. 4.
51. Ruthenberg, ibid., December 6, 1924, magazine supplement.
52. *Protokoll des V. Kongresses,* Vol. II, p. 583.
53. *Daily Worker,* December 13, 1924, magazine supplement.
54. A previous cablegram from the Comintern had been published in the *Daily Worker* on May 16, 1924: "Communist International considers

June 17th Convention momentous importance for Workers Party. Urges C.E.C. not to slacken activities preparation June 17th. Utilize every available force to make St. Paul convention great representative gathering labor and left wing."

55. Manley, *Daily Worker,* January 7, 1925.
56. Bittelman, ibid., August 29, 1925, magazine supplement.
57. "Workers Party Issues Declaration of Policy," op. cit., p. 40. This "declaration" was signed by "The Central Executive Committee of the Workers Party of America, Wm. Z. Foster, Chairman, C. E. Ruthenberg, Executive Secretary." Actually, it was the text of the Comintern's decision for the American party. This may be demonstrated by the excerpts from the Comintern's decision, cited by Foster, *Daily Worker,* December 9 and 13, 1924; and Olgin, ibid., December 20, 1924. In effect, the C.E.C. of the Workers party adopted the Comintern's decision and passed it off as its own.
58. Kenneth Campbell MacKay, *The Progressive Movement of 1924* (New York: Columbia University Press, 1947), pp. 86–88. The *Daily Worker,* May 29, 1924, also published the full text of LaFollette's letter to Ekern.
59. Trotsky, writing immediately after this sequence of events, on June 4, 1924, confirmed that LaFollette's letter came out "a few days following" the Comintern's decision (*The First Five Years of the Comintern,* Vol. I, p. 14 note). Earl Browder has speculated that LaFollette may have known of the Comintern's decision in advance "and that if the Communists had been going to really support him he would not have taken up the issue." Browder's chief reason is that LaFollette waited so long to denounce the Communists, though he had been urged to do so for two years (Browder to Draper, February 24, 1959).
60. *Minnesota Union Advocate,* May 29, 1924 (quoted by Bittelman, *Daily Worker,* June 5, 1924).
61. Cannon, *Daily Worker,* December 8, 1924, p. 3.
62. Ruthenberg, ibid., June 7, 1924, p. 4.
63. Manley, ibid., December 5, 1924; Swabeck, ibid., December 17, 1924; Hathaway, ibid., December 22, 1924; Manley, ibid., December 5, 1924.

    On the last item, Ruthenberg claimed that the Communists had spent only $19,491.50, but Manley came back at him with such detailed evidence that Ruthenberg dropped the subject (ibid., December 30, 1924).
64. "Report of the National Farmer-Labor Progressive Convention," official mimeographed minutes, including platform and organization report, 15 pages. Hathaway reported 522 delegates in his report, but *The New Leader,* June 21, 1924, reported only 377, and *The American Labor Year Book, 1925,* p. 146, "nearly 400 delegates." Mahoney

told Naftalin that hundreds of cancellations came in after LaFollette's letter to Ekern: "We had expected 5000 to attend. As it turned out, there were about 500 who came" (Naftalin, op. cit., p. 107).

65. Bittelman, *Daily Worker,* August 29, 1925, magazine supplement.
66. The official "Report of the National Farmer-Labor Progressive Convention," p. 9, states that Mahoney "said that the proper thing for us to do would be to leave the matter open." But the *Daily Worker,* June 21, 1924, p. 3, gave a fuller version of Mahoney's position: "Mahoney held that the national committee of this convention will negotiate with the Cleveland gathering of the candidates, inferring that if LaFollette became the candidate at Cleveland, instead of McAdoo, as is anticipated, that LaFollette would become acceptable to the forces gathered here, would thereupon, through their national committee, withdraw their candidates."
67. The exact wording of Foster's statement was given in the *Daily Worker,* June 21, 1924, p. 3. The official "Report" states that Foster said "the only way this organization could accept Sen. LaFollette is that he will subscribe to principles and program of the Farmer-Labor Party and be under the control of this organization" (p. 10).
68. *New York Times,* July 13, 1924, p. 2.
69. Foster, *Daily Worker,* June 27, 1924, p. 3.
70. Bittelman, ibid., August 29, 1925, magazine supplement.
71. The preceding two paragraphs are mainly based on Manley, *Daily Worker,* December 5, 1924, p. 3.
72. Cannon, ibid., December 3, 1924, p. 4; Manley, op. cit.
73. Bittelman, ibid., August 29, 1925, magazine supplement.
74. The National Executive Committee consisted of Alexander Howat (chairman), C. A. Hathaway (secretary), Scott Wilkins, Alfred Knutson, Joseph Manley, William Mahoney, and Alice Lorraine Daly. The first five issued the statement; Hathaway, Knutson, and Manley were known as Communists.
75. "We can understand how our decision to put Foster and Gitlow in the field may have taken some of the Labor Party leaders in the west by surprise. We were obliged to move quickly" (Cannon, *Daily Worker,* July 29, 1924).
76. Browder, ibid., January 31, 1925, p. 4.
77. Naftalin, op. cit., p. 121.
78. *Daily Worker,* front-page headline, June 5, 1924; editorial, July 7, 1924; Bittelman, July 12, 1924; Lovestone, August 13, 1924; editorial, September 16, 1924; Engdahl, October 14, 1924; Trachtenberg, October 15, 1924.
79. *The Liberator,* September 1924, p. 11.
80. *Daily Worker,* August 30 and October 10, 1924. Foster predicted: "And in America we can confidently predict, with the full knowledge that the class interests controlling LaFollette will have their way with him, that in any great struggle of the workers that may arise when

the LaFollette movement comes to power, the governmental powers will here also be turned against the workers or turned over to the Fascist elements in the United States" (*The Workers Monthly*, November 1924, p. 10).

81. Foster, *Daily Worker*, October 24, 1924, p. 6.
82. *New York Times*, September 7, 1924.
83. Alexander Bittelman, *Parties and Issues in the Election Campaign* (Chicago: Literature Department, Workers Party of America, 1924), p. 5.
84. Bittelman, *Daily Worker*, November 15, 1924, magazine supplement.
85. Foster, ibid.
86. Bittelman, ibid., December 4, 1924, p. 3.
87. *The Worker*, February 15, 1924 (Pepper); *Daily Worker*, February 2, 1924 (Lovestone); *The Liberator*, July 1924, p. 11 (Lovestone); Earl R. Browder, *Unemployment* (Chicago: Literature Department, Workers Party, 1924), p. 3; *Daily Worker*, October 24, 1924 (Gitlow); *The Labor Herald*, February 1924, p. 3 (Foster).
88. *International Press Correspondence*, March 12, 1925, p. 277.
89. "Scott Nearing and Party Policy," *Daily Worker*, May 10, 1924, magazine supplement.
90. "Foster's Reply to Nearing," ibid., May 17, 1924, magazine supplement.
91. Foster's first letter to Debs, *Daily Worker*, July 16, 1924, p. 1; Debs' reply and Foster's second letter, ibid., July 31, 1924.
92. Foster, ibid., October 8, 1925.
93. *The Workers Monthly*, November 1924, p. 34.
94. This remark by Zinoviev was included in the full text of his speech as published in the *Daily Worker*, July 29, 1924, p. 4, and in *Protokoll des V. Kongresses*, Vol. I, p. 77, but it is omitted from the English version, *Fifth Congress of the Communist International*, where it should have appeared on p. 26.
95. *The Worker*, September 8, 1923, p. 2, and January 12, 1924, p. 2.

Chapter 6: How to Win a Majority

1. "The Results of the Elections," *Daily Worker*, November 7, 1924, pp. 1–2.
2. Ruthenberg, *Daily Worker*, December 1, 1924, p. 4; Lovestone, ibid., December 9, 1924, p. 4.
3. Ballam, ibid., December 29, 1924, p. 4.
4. Foster, ibid., p. 4.
5. "Statement on the Results of the Elections," ibid., November 17, 1924, p. 4, and "Statement of Minority of Central Executive Committee," ibid., May 19, 1925, p. 3, both submitted by Ruthenberg, Lovestone, Bedacht, Engdahl, and Gitlow.
6. *Protokoll des V. Kongresses*, Vol. I, pp. 58, 64, 97, 130.

7. Stalin, *Works,* Vol. IX, p. 125.
8. In February 1926, in a work known to English readers as *Problems of Leninism,* Stalin admitted the difference between the April and December 1924 versions. Subsequently, he substituted the December version for the corresponding paragraph in the April version, thereby effacing the difference. Yet this literary juggling sometimes created peculiar problems. The two-volume set of Stalin's writings, entitled *Leninism,* published in the nineteen-thirties, reprinted the doctored version of *Foundations of Leninism* (Vol. I, pp. 40–41), and represented it purely and simply as "Lectures Delivered at the Sverdlov University in the Beginning of April 1924." But the same volume also reprints *Problems of Leninism,* which goes into the change in some detail and even includes a note to the effect that the new formulation has been substituted for the old one (Vol. I, pp. 296–98). Thus a reader of pp. 40–41 of one work could correct the misrepresentation by reading pp. 296–98 of an entirely different work in the same collection. The same thing is true of Stalin's *Works* (Vol. VI, pp. 110–11, and Vol. VIII, pp. 64–67). The innumerable pamphlet editions of *Foundations of Leninism* for mass consumption circulated the doctored version throughout the world without explanation of the change.
9. Trotsky's classical criticism of "socialism in one country" appears in *The Third International after Lenin,* pp. 1–73.
10. All the relevant texts from Lenin were brought out in the debate at the Seventh Plenum in November–December 1926. Stalin's speech appears in *Works,* Vol. IX, pp. 1–155. The citation from 1915 obviously refers to the "victory of socialism in a single country" in terms of the seizure of power by a dictatorship of the proletariat. The following sentence goes on to the next stage of "raising revolts" in other capitalist countries (ibid., p. 117).
11. The complete record is in German, *Protokoll der Erweiterten Exekutive der Kommunistischen Internationale,* 21 März–6 April, 1925 (Hamburg: Verlag Carl Hoym Nachf., 1925). The English version, *Bolshevising the Communist International* (London: Communist Party of Great Britain, 1925) is abridged and often carelessly translated.
12. The *Protokoll* lists nine commissions, not including an American Commission (pp. 18–19), but the latter is later mentioned in Kuusinen's report (p. 355).
13. *Protokoll der Erweiterten Exekutive,* März–April, 1925, p. 23.
14. Ibid., p. 46. The term "Bolshevization" was first introduced by Zinoviev at the Fifth Congress in the summer of 1924, but it was not made the basis of a campaign until the Fifth Plenum the following year.
15. Ibid., pp. 290–311.
16. Ibid., p. 147.

17. Ibid., p. 157.
18. Cannon to Draper, March 31, 1955 (published in the *Fourth International,* Winter 1956, p. 28).
19. *Daily Worker,* March 28, 1925, p. 4.
20. Ibid.
21. The English text of the Comintern's decision appeared in the *Daily Worker,* May 19, 1925, and in *Bolshevising the Communist International,* pp. 185–91.
22. Foster, *Daily Worker,* October 8, 1925.
23. Lovestone states that Ruthenberg got fed up with the maneuvers in Moscow before the tide turned in his favor. On one occasion, Lovestone says, Ruthenberg told him: "We shouldn't stay here. They don't want an American movement." Lovestone then talked him out of breaking away: "No, this is not the time. We don't control the party yet" (interview with Lovestone, June 21, 1954). Lovestone apparently referred to this incident in his testimony (*Investigation of Un-American Propaganda Activities,* Vol. XI, p. 7146). I have not come across any other evidence that Ruthenberg ever entertained any thought of breaking away from the Comintern. However, Melech Epstein also offers this opinion: "If not for his death in March 1927, in his middle forties, Ruthenberg would undoubtedly have been expelled by the Comintern," a conclusion evidently based in part on Ruthenberg's behavior in Moscow in 1925 (*Jewish Labor in U.S.A., 1914–1952,* New York: Trade Union Sponsoring Committee, 1953, p. 116).
24. *Daily Worker,* May 27, 1925, and *Bolshevising the Communist International,* p. 133.
25. *Daily Worker,* May 27, 1925, and *Bolshevising the Communist International,* p. 191.
26. Minutes of the Executive Council, June 11, 1925
27. Some of the personal details of Gusev's career have been taken from his obituaries in *The Communist International,* June 22, 1933, and the *Daily Worker,* June 12, 1933. The dispute on military doctrine is authoritatively treated by D. Fedotoff White, *The Growth of the Red Army* (Princeton, N.J.: Princeton University Press, 1944). Trotsky touches on Gusev's role in the dispute with Stalin over the southern front in *Stalin* (New York: Harper, 1946), pp. 313–23. Gusev's manual on civil war was *Die Lehren des Bürgerkrieges* (Verlag der Kommunistischen Internationale, 1921). Gitlow says that Gusev "despised Trotsky and so worshipped Stalin because, as he told us, during one of the Civil War campaigns Trotsky had threatened him and a number of other officers of the Red Army with death for insubordination and due to Stalin's intervention not only were their lives spared but they were rehabilitated as military commanders and as Bolsheviks" (*I Confess,* p. 259). Gusev reported on the German dispute at the Fifth Plenum for the Russian Central Control Com-

mission (*Protokoll der Erweiterten Exekutive,* März–April 1925, pp. 312–13). Gusev's name was originally Yakov Davidovich Drabkin.

28. P. Green [Gusev], *Daily Worker,* October 3, 1925. Gitlow attributes to Gusev the pressure on Ruthenberg's group for this behind-the-scenes arrangement, and implies that he and Lovestone decided to rebel and fight against it to a finish (*I Confess,* pp. 265–70). Gusev gives the impression that the deal was accepted on both sides.
29. *Daily Worker,* August 26, 1925. Only 54 delegates were originally supposed to have been seated, but the credentials committee controlled by the Fosterites decided to seat additional delegates in the contested districts for a total of 61. Gitlow incorrectly gives the division as 40-23 (*I Confess,* p. 273).
30. Information from Max Shachtman, October 26, 1959.
31. According to Foster's *History,* at a meeting of Ruthenberg's caucus a motion by Lovestone against returning to the convention was defeated by one vote (p. 223).
32. Slight variations occur in different versions of this famous cable. I have chosen to use the one given by Ruthenberg himself (*The Workers Monthly,* October 1925, pp. 236–37), reprinted in his pamphlet, *From the Third Through the Fourth Convention of the Workers (Communist) Party of America* (Chicago: Daily Worker Publishing Co., 1925, pp. 18–19). This version, however, reads less like an actual cablegram than does the one given by Gitlow (*I Confess,* pp. 176–77). There is also a version in the *Exhibits, Subversive Activities Control Board,* which is textually closer to Ruthenberg's version. An example of the differences, all slight, may be found in the opening lines which read in Gitlow's version: "Under no circumstances must majority suppress Ruthenberg group. . . ."
33. The details of this incident are based on P. Green [Gusev], *Daily Worker,* October 3, 1925; Cannon and Foster, ibid., October 8, 1825; Cannon to Draper, March 31, 1955; Gitlow, *I Confess,* pp. 277–78. Gitlow says that Foster asked for time to confer with Cannon and Bittelman in another room after the cable had been read by Ruthenberg, and then Foster spoke. Cannon recalls that he and Bittelman remained silent, and Foster spoke out alone. The main facts can be established on the basis of the contemporary accounts by Gusev, Cannon, and Foster. Foster named Dunne, Abern, Bell, Hathaway, Shachtman, and Williamson as the main Cannonites. Bittelman, Browder, Krumbein, and Johnstone supported Foster.
34. *The 4th National Convention of the Workers (Communist) Party of America,* Report of the Central Executive Committee to the 4th National Convention Held in Chicago, Illinois, August 21st to 30th, 1925 (Chicago: Daily Worker Publishing Co., 1925), p. 165.
35. Central Executive Committee—*Majority:* Abern, Bittelman, Burman, Cannon, Dunne, Browder, Foster, Reynolds, Aronberg, with one to be elected by the Y.W.L.; *Minority:* Ruthenberg, Gitlow, Bedacht,

Engdahl, Lovestone, Ballam, Weinstone, Minor, White, and Schmies. Candidates—*Majority:* Krumbein, Hathaway, and Johnstone; *Minority:* Puro, Amter, and Wolfe. Alternates—*Majority:* Manley, Swabeck, Olgin, Sullivan. Owens, Wagenknecht, Gomez, O'Flaherty, and Loeb; *Minority:* Jakira, Kruse, Novak, Lifshitz, Bimba, Ashkenudse, Knutson, Henry, and Kuzinich.

Control Commission—*Majority:* Harrison George and Niels Kjar; *Minority:* D. J. Bentall and Felix Hensel.

(*The 4th National Convention,* pp. 165–66.)

36. *Daily Worker,* September 1, 1925, p. 1.
37. Ibid., September 3, 1925. Gitlow's version is slightly different (*I Confess,* pp. 279–80).
38. Gitlow says that Gusev had won over Cannon by "clever intriguing" in advance of the Comintern's cables (*I Confess,* p. 275). Cannon later explained: "I was then a convinced 'Cominternist.' I had faith in the wisdom and also in the fairness of the Russian leaders. I thought they had made a mistake through false information and that the mistake could later be rectified. I did not even suspect that this monstrous violation of the democratic rights of our party was one of the moves in the Moscow chess game, in which our party, like all the other parties in the Comintern, was to be a mere pawn" (Cannon to Draper, March 31, 1955). Wolfe has informed me that Gusev confidentially expressed the opinion that Cannon could be won away from Foster.
39. Green [Gusev], *Daily Worker,* October 3, 1925.
40. *Daily Worker,* September 3, 1925, p. 3.
41. Ibid., October 22, 1925.
42. Ibid., September 12, 1925, magazine supplement.
43. Cannon, ibid., October 8, 1925.
44. In his *History* Foster commits one of his monumental distortions to cover up the real source of his downfall. He writes: "At this [Fourth] convention the Bittelman-Foster group gave up its majority on the Central Executive Committee (a mistake) because of criticism from Zinoviev, head of the Comintern. For making this criticism, which was flatly against the thoroughly democratic procedure of the Comintern, Zinoviev was later severely condemned" (p. 223). Thus, Gusev's manipulation is completely blamed on Zinoviev, who, ironically, had attempted to ensure Foster's majority at this convention. Gusev is never even mentioned in Foster's book. On the same page, Foster refers indignantly to an alleged act of resistance by Lovestone in Ruthenberg's caucus, without a single word about his much more important rebellion in his own caucus. That Foster's group "gave up" its majority and that Zinoviev's so-called criticism tarnished the Comintern's "thoroughly democratic procedure" reads like an unconscious satire of these events.
45. P. Green [Gusev], *Daily Worker,* October 3, 1925.

46. Foster, ibid., October 8, 1925.
47. Foster supported Ruthenberg's resolution in Chicago, his former stronghold (ibid., October 12, 1925, p. 4).
48. Ibid., November 16 and December 15, 1925.
49. Ibid., December 3, 1925.
50. David J. Saposs, *Left Wing Unionism,* p. 174.
51. David A. Shannon, *The Socialist Party of America* (New York: Macmillan, 1955), pp. 181–82.
52. The membership of the A.F. of L. fell from 4,078,740 in 1920 to 2,879,000 in 1926.
53. Lovestone, *The Workers Monthly,* December 1925, p. 79.

Chapter 7: Bolshevization

1. *Thesen und Resolutionen der Erweiterten Exekutive,* März–April 1925 (Hamburg: Verlag Carl Hoym Nachf. 1925), p. 12.
2. *Revolutionary Radicalism,* Vol. I, pp. 563–613, contains the National Constitution, New York State Constitution, and By-Laws of Local New York of the Socialist party.
3. This paragraph is mainly based on Leonard Schapiro, *The Communist Party of the Soviet Union* (New York: Oxford University Press, 1960), Chapter 9, and Carr, *The Bolshevik Revolution,* Vol. I, Chapter 8.
4. *The Communist,* November 29, 1919, p. 6.
5. *Revolutionary Radicalism,* Vol. I, pp. 776–98, 809–17, contains the Communist and Communist Labor parties' programs and constitutions.
6. The early organizational development of the Comintern may be traced in the following:

   Der Zweite Kongress der Kommunistischen Internationale (Vienna: Verlag der Arbeiter Buchhandlung, 1920), pp. 12–14.

   The Theses and Statutes of the Communist International, as adopted at the Second World Congress (issued by the Central Executive Committee of the Communist Party of America, 1921), pp. 5–9.

   Resolutions and Theses of the Fourth Congress of the Communist International (London: Communist Party of Great Britain, n.d.), pp. 92–96.
7. *Der Zweite Kongress der Kommunistischen Internationale: Protokoll der Verhandlungen* (Verlag der Kommunistischen Internationale, 1921), p. 603, for the annual congress; *Protokoll des V. Kongresses,* Vol. II, p. 985, for the semiannual plenums; *Resolutions and Theses of the Fourth Congress of the Communist International,* op. cit., p. 93, for the plenums every four months. At the Fifth Congress a change was made to congresses every two years (*Protokoll des V. Kongresses,* Vol. II, p. 984).
8. *Investigation of Un-American Propaganda Activities, Appendix—*

Part I, pp. 225–31, contains the constitution of the Communist Party of America of 1921. The three top committees appear in the Minutes of 1922 in my possession.

9. See ibid., pp. 239–45, for the constitution of the Workers party of America of 1921. The Minutes in my possession reveal that the Executive Council, Polcom, Orgcom, and Secretariat existed by the end of 1923.
10. *From the Fourth to the Fifth World Congress:* Report of the Executive Committee of the Communist International (London: Communist Party of Great Britain, 1924), pp. 117–18. The score stood at 75 for the German, 61 for the Italian, 43 for the French, and 41 for the American. Of the latter, 17 were political questions, 19 organizational, and 5 "various." American questions came up in the full E.C.C.I. twice, Presidium nine times, Secretariat twenty-eight times, and Orgburo twice.
11. O. Piatnitsky, *Memoirs of a Bolshevik* (New York: International, n.d.) tells the story of his life up to the Bolshevik Revolution.
12. See *How to Organize the Communist Party* (London: Communist Party of Great Britain, 1924), pp. 16, 35–36, 39–40, 43, 90–109, for the Presidium's resolutions on factory nuclei and fractions, and the discussion in the Organization Committee at the Fifth Congress, July 1, 1924. The American delegates assumed the names of "Edwards" and "Johnson." The Canadian delegate was Tim Buck. See *Daily Worker,* March 22, 1924, for the American declaration; and *Our Immediate Work:* Program Adopted by the Central Executive Committee of the Workers party of America (Chicago: Literature Department, 1924), pp. 17–19, for the section on "shop nuclei" in the program of action.
13. *International Press Correspondence,* April 6, 1925, p. 357.
14. Foster (Dorsey), ibid., March 18, 1925, p. 322, and April 6, 1925, p. 360. At this time, Foster excepted the trade unions from the general shortage of fractions, but later that same year, he included the trade unions in describing fraction work in the United States as "so to speak making its first steps" (ibid., December 21, 1925, p. 1332).
15. Piatnitsky, ibid., April 6, 1925, p. 358; June 9, 1925, p. 652.
16. "Model Statutes for the Sections of the CI," ibid., June 9, 1925, pp. 660–63. This same issue contains the "Theses on the Organizational Structure of the Party," defining the exact function of each unit from the lowest to the highest. Both documents are indispensable for a student of Communist organization.
17. *Daily Worker,* August 17–18, 1925 (also reprinted in the pamphlet, *The Party Organization,* pp. 10–25).
18. The post-Bolshevization organization is based on the constitution of the Workers (Communist) party, adopted in September 1925 (*The Party Organization,* pp. 26–40) and the committee assignments (*Daily Worker,* September 3, 1925, p. 3). I have tried as far as possible to

use the original language of the constitution or other official party documents in the definitions or descriptions. The four charts in *The Party Organization,* pp. 41–43, should be helpful for further study, except that the important Central Control Commission has been omitted from the first one, and the fractions find no place in any of them.

19. Message signed by Bukharin, *The Worker,* January 27, 1923, p. 2.
20. *The Party Organization,* pp. 26–27.
21. In 1939 Browder wrote that the Workers party had "established the first American affiliation to the Communist International as a 'fraternal' affiliate not subject to the organizational rules then being applied in the Communist parties in Europe. (The 'underground' parties had declared their adhesion to the Communist International but had not been accepted, due to their splits and immaturity.) There has never been any formal change between the American Party and the Communist International, the close relationships between which have not been based upon formal statutes and rules" (*The Communist,* September 1939, p. 795).

    "Until 1938 the C.P.U.S.A. was fraternally affiliated with the Communist International" (John Williamson, ibid., January 1944, p. 66).
22. For example, Section 15 of the "model statutes" and Article 5, Section 4, of the American party's constitution, dealing with the nature of the "nucleus."
23. *Manifesto and Program,* p. 19.
24. *The Party Organization,* p. 27.
25. *Der Zweite Kongress der Kommunistischen Internationale: Protokoll der Verhandlungen,* pp. 602–606.
26. "Directives and decisions of the International are binding on the party and of course on every individual party member" and "The central leadership of the party is responsible to the party congress and to the leadership of the Communist International" (*The Communist International,* Documents, edited by Jane Degras, Vol. I, p. 267.)
27. The tradition against resignation was evidently brought on by the resignation of Schlapnykov from the Russian party (Leonard Schapiro, *The Origin of the Communist Autocracy,* New York: Oxford University Press, 1955, p. 319), and that of Clara Zetkin from the German party (*Protokoll des III. Kongresses,* p. 66).
28. The official English version of the "Resolution on Reorganization of the Communist International towards an International Communist Party" was published in the *Resolutions and Theses of the Fourth Congress of the Communist International,* pp. 92–96. I have preferred to use this version instead of the more convenient one in Degras, op. cit., pp. 436–42, because the former was used at the time. Degras translates "representative" as "delegate." To get the full import of

the resolution, it is necessary to consult the report on it by Eberlein in *Protokoll des V. Kongresses,* pp. 803–13.

29. The Fourth Congress of 1922 allocated additional representatives to the plenums on the basis of three to the first group, two to the second, and one to all others (*Resolutions and Theses, Fourth Congress,* p. 93).
30. *Protokoll des V. Kongresses,* Vol. I, pp. 240–41.
31. Ibid., Vol. I, p. 381.
32. *Protokoll der Erweiterten Exekutive,* November–Dezember 1926, p. 626.
33. *The Communist International Between the Fifth and the Sixth World Congresses, 1924–8,* pp. 31–34.
34. Minutes of the Secretariat, October 6, 1927, p. 1, and Minutes of the Political Committee, October 12, 1927, pp. 5–6, and January 11, 1928, p. 4. Wachsoff's name was also spelled "Waksoff" and "Voxof."
35. M. Jenks, *The Communist Nucleus: What It Is—How It Works* (New York: Workers Library, 1928).
36. Minutes of the Political Committee, May 19, 1927.
37. Minutes of the Political Committee, November 20, 1929.
38. Minutes of the Political Committee, June 15, 1926, for the decision to send Bosse to the Information Department. Bosse (or Brooks) was dismissed from the school system in 1942.
39. See *Thesen und Resolutionen, Erweiterte Exekutive,* February–März 1926, p. 187, for the decision to form these "Ländersekretariate," and *International Press Correspondence,* April 15, 1926, p. 446, for the list of eleven.
40. Dr. Max Goldfarb is mentioned by Melech Epstein, *Jewish Labor in U.S.A.,* p. 63. Henry Pelling, in *The British Communist Party* (London: Black, 1958, p. 28), writes about Petrovsky-Bennet.
41. Carr, *The Bolshevik Revolution,* Vol. III, pp. 268–69; Stalin, *Works,* Vol. VII, p. 135.
42. *Protokoll der Erweiterten Exekutive,* März–April 1925, p. 134.
43. J. T. Murphy, "The First Year of the Lenin School," *The Communist International* (London), September 30, 1927, pp. 267–69.
44. Minutes of the Political Committee, September 15, 1927, p. 6. The American party was informed that it was entitled to send seven students to the Lenin School, and ten Negro students to the Far Eastern University, but the Secretariat considered it difficult to get ten qualified Negroes and suggested three or four.
45. *Subversion in Racial Unrest,* Part I, p. 21.
46. The names of these American representatives and their dates of tenure in Moscow have been obtained from the Minutes of the Political Committee and personal interviews, but some of the dates may be approximate.
47. "Frank Miller," or Sirola, is first mentioned in the Minutes of the

Political Committee, December 23, 1925, and probably arrived shortly before this meeting. He appears for the last time in the Minutes of January 20, 1927.

48. "Grey" or Ewert is first mentioned in the Minutes of the Central Executive Committee, September 8, 1927. Gitlow says that he represented the Comintern in the U.S. "in 1927" (*I Confess,* p. 534). Evidently he stayed only two or three months.
49. *Protokoll des V. Kongresses,* Vol. I, p. 390.
50. *Protokoll der Erweiterten Exekutive,* März–April 1925, p. 48.
51. Lenin, *Selected Works,* Vol. II, pp. 53, 90, 98, 99, 127, 138–41, 147, 150–55.
52. Ibid., Vol. IX, pp. 4–9; *"Left-Wing" Communism,* pp. 31–33.
53. *The Communist International,* Documents, Vol. I, p. 131. Zinoviev's suggestions came in the "Theses on the Role of the Communist Party in the Proletarian Revolution." Other theses contained implications or intimations of similar tactics. In the "Theses on the Agrarian Question," drafted by Lenin, the Communist parties were advised to form small-peasant councils (p. 161). Two of the Twenty-One Points of admission to the Comintern, drafted by Lenin, dealt with a somewhat similar question, but not exactly in the same way. Number 3 instructed legal Communist parties to form parallel illegal organizations, and partially illegal parties to combine legal and illegal work. Number 9 ordered the parties to "carry on systematic and persistent communist activity inside the trade unions, the workers' councils and factory committees, the cooperatives, and other mass workers' organizations," which implied boring from within as well as transmission belts. Number 6, Part II, of the "Theses on the Trade-Union Movement, Factory Committees, and the Communist International," introduced by Radek, provided for the subordination, in practice, of the factory committees and unions to the Communist parties (omitted by Degras).
54. A. Raphael [Bittelman], "The Task of the Hour," *The Communist,* October 1921, p. 4.
55. Ludwig Martens, *Soviet Russia* (magazine), October 1921, pp. 156–57. See *Daily Worker,* August 15, 1924, p. 4, for the model farms; and *The Worker,* March 17, 1923, p. 5, for the S.T.A.S.R.'s admission of failure.
56. The committee was originally composed of Max Bedacht, L. E. Katterfeld, Charles E. Ruthenberg, I. E. Ferguson, treasurer, and Edgar Owens, secretary (*The Toiler,* September 24, 1920, p. 16). Early in 1922, the party decided to take it over officially and make it subordinate to the C.E.C. (*The Worker,* April 29, 1922, p. 5).
57. Moritz J. Loeb was appointed secretary of the Labor Defense Council (*The Worker,* October 14, 1922). The Bridgman defense fund was reported in the *Daily Worker,* August 30, 1924, p. 4. Communists were also active in the Workers' Defense Union, organized by Eliza-

beth Gurley Flynn in December 1918 and dissolved in 1923 (Elizabeth Gurley Flynn, *I Speak My Own Piece*, New York: Masses & Mainstream, 1955, pp. 233–35).

58. The conference of March 5, 1921, was reported in *The Toiler*, March 21, 1921, p. 1, and the program appeared, ibid., December 31, 1921, p. 11.
59. *The Toiler*, August 20, 1921, p. 1, reported the founding conference of the F.S.R.; see ibid., July 29, 1922, p. 4, for mention of the Famine Scout Cubs; Wagenknecht's reminiscences of the F.S.R. appeared in the *Daily Worker*, August 24, 1931, p. 4.
60. *Daily Worker*, November 1, 1924 and June 14, 1926; Minutes of the Political Committee, December 21, 1927, and March 19, 1928.
61. A. Kollontai, "The Work of the International Women's Secretariat," *The Communist International*, No. 19, 1921; *Protokoll des III. Kongresses*, pp. 914–17 and 932–33; Bloor, *We Are Many*, pp. 176–77; Lovestone, *Daily Worker*, February 25, 1924, p. 3; *The 4th National Convention*, pp. 124–27. The first Women's Bureau was composed of Mary Heaton Vorse, Ray Ragozin, Margaret Undjus, Jeannette D. Pearl, Elmer T. Allison, and J. Anderson (*The Toiler*, February 2, 1922, p. 6). The United Council of Working Class Wives seems to be a later name (*Daily Worker*, May 1, 1927, p. 5).
62. *Second National Convention*, pp. 23–24; *The Worker*, January 6, 1923, p. 2; *Daily Worker*, March 25, 1924; *The Second Year*, p. 14; Ruthenberg, *Daily Worker*, January 4, 1926, p. 4; *Daily Worker*, May 11, 15, and 18, 1926. The first secretary was Horacek, soon succeeded by Nina Samarodin.
63. Minutes of the Executive Council, May 14, 1924, pp. 3–4; *The 4th National Convention*, pp. 19–21; Gomez, *The Workers Monthly*, May 1925, pp. 310–11. The name was originally Pan-American Anti-Imperialist League, but it was changed to avoid confusion with the Pan-American Union and the Pan-American Federation of Labor (*Daily Worker*, June 2, 1925, p. 5).
64. *The 4th National Convention*, pp. 17, 109–14; Minutes of the Political Bureau, October 10, 1925; *The Communist International Between the Fifth and Sixth World Congresses*, p. 346. *The United Farmer*, Vol. I, No. 1, is dated March 1, 1926, and the "Farm Relief Program" appeared in the issue of December 14, 1927, p. 4.
65. References to the Anti-Fascist Alliance appear in the *Daily Worker*, July 1, 1924, September 5, 1926, October 29, 1926, and March 4, 1927. The Communist seizure and Socialist walk-out were described in *The New Leader*, July 31 and September 4, 1926.
66. Max Shachtman, "Enea Sormenti," *The Labor Defender*, January 1927, p. 2, provides some of the earliest biographical material. Vidali's alleged implication in the conspiracy against Trotsky is touched on in Leandro A. Sánchez Salazar and Julian Gorkin, *Mord in Mexico* (Frankfurt am Main: Parma-Edition, 1952), pp. 324–26,

and in Isaac Don Levine, *The Mind of an Assassin* (New York: Farrar, Straus, and Cudahy, 1959), p. 71. His postwar activity in Trieste is reported in *The New York Times,* August 23, 1948, p. 2; August 24, 1948, p. 1; September 9, 1949, p. 9; and by G. E. R. Gedye in *The New Leader,* June 18, 1951, p. 14.

67. Si Gerson, *International Press Correspondence,* January 19, 1933; *From the Fourth to the Fifth World Congresses,* pp. 100–102; *The Communist International Between the Fifth and Sixth World Congresses,* p. 347.
68. Sasha Small, *Ten Years of Labor Defense* (New York: International Labor Defense, 1935), p. 23; "A Message from Bill Haywood," *The Labor Defender,* June 1926, p. 86.
69. The eight-point agreement, entitled "Resolution on the Organization of the International Red Aid and the International Workers' Relief," is appended to the Minutes of the Executive Council, June 27, 1925.
70. Minutes of the Executive Council, June 27, 1925.
71. The *Daily Worker,* June 29–30, 1925, reported the first conference of the I.L.D. In final form, the National Committee numbered 35 and the Executive Committee 9 (*Labor Defense: Manifesto, Resolutions, Constitution,* Chicago: International Labor Defense, 1925). The membership claim appeared in *The Labor Defender,* October 1926, p. 167.
72. According to Foster, Mooney was a "warm sympathizer" of the Communist party, and McNamara, who served a twenty-nine-year prison sentence for the dynamiting of the *Los Angeles Times* in 1910, joined the Communist party several years before his death in 1941 (*History of the Communist Party of the United States,* pp. 110, 380).
73. *The Labor Defender,* September 1926, p. 156.
74. Minutes of the Secretariat, September 21, 1927.
75. Minutes of the Political Committee, September 15, 1927.
76. Minutes of the Secretariat, October 6, 1927.
77. Minutes of the Political Committee, October 12, 1927.
78. Minutes of the Political Committee, April 11, 1928. The paragraphs quoted constitute points 8 and 9 of a 23-point motion, carried unanimously. It does not appear whether the proposal for the fronts to pay some of the party salaries was put into effect.
79. Minutes of the Political Committee, March 22, 1927.
80. Minutes of the Political Committee, January 11, 1928.
81. Minutes of the Secretariat, September 21, 1927. The available minutes do not indicate what action followed.
82. *The 4th National Convention,* p. 41.
83. *Daily Worker,* June 23, 1928, p. 6.

Chapter 8: Party Life

1. *The 4th National Convention,* pp. 27–37. An earlier and slightly different set of figures for 1922–23 appears in *The Second Year,* pp. 29–30, but I have chosen to use the former because they came later and make it possible to establish conformity with figures over a longer period. Still different estimates can also be found. Ruthenberg once estimated that the membership rose to about 20,000 in December 1922 (*The Liberator,* February 1923, p. 12). He also gave the membership in 1923 as 20,000, of which 18,000 were dues-paying (*Daily Worker,* April 2, 1924).
2. Lovestone, *Daily Worker,* May 24, 1927.
3. Here again, different sources give different figures. Lovestone gave about 9500 for 1927 (*Daily Worker,* September 13, 1927), but *The Communist International Between the Fifth and Sixth World Congresses* lists 17,000 for 1924; 14,000 for 1925; 11,990 for 1926; and 12,000 for 1927 (p. 30). Stachel reported 14,000 for 1925; 7599 for 1926; 8200 for 1927; 9300 for 1928 and 1929 (*The Communist,* April 1929, pp. 180–81). The Lovestone-Stachel figures may be considered the most reliable, and I have tried to strike a balance between them.
4. Earl Browder, *Report to the 8th Convention* (New York: Communist Party, 1934, p. 81), gives 14,474 in 1932.
5. Lovestone estimated 3000 to 4000 (*Daily Worker,* May 24, 1927) and 4000 to 4500 (ibid., September 13, 1927).
6. Amter, ibid., July 7, 1926.
7. Lovestone, ibid., September 14, 1927.
8. The pre-Bolshevization fluctuation in membership is based on *The 4th National Convention,* pp. 28, 31, 35, 38, 40. The party started in 1922 with an estimated 10,000 members, of whom about 1500 were English-speaking.
9. This and the preceding paragraph are based on the following official figures: 6532 new members were admitted in 1923; 8456 in 1924; and 2899 in the first six months of 1925, for a total of 17,887 (*The 4th National Convention,* pp. 31, 35, 38). Then 5080 new members were admitted from September 1925 to September 1927 (Lovestone, *Daily Worker,* September 13, 1927). The total membership reported in September 1927 was 9542 (ibid.). The organizer of the New York District, William W. Weinstone, stated: "It is not far-fetched to say that one-half of our Party membership since 1923 are new members" (ibid., September 3, 1927). I have estimated the three categories from this starting point.
10. Stachel, *The Communist,* May 1929, p. 241.
11. This figure is based on the following: an initial paper membership in 1919 of 60,000 to 70,000, of whom only 30,000 to 40,000 signed

up after the conventions; 4271 new members in 1922; 6532 in 1923; 8456 in 1924; 2899 in January–June 1925; 5080 from September 1925 to September 1927; and an assumption of approximately the same figure for 1928–29 (for full sources, see Note 9, this chapter).

12. Based on *The 4th National Convention,* pp. 27, 29, 33, 37. The East European sections included the Armenian, Czechoslovak, Estonian, Hungarian, Lettish, Lithuanian, Polish, Rumanian, Russian, South Slav, and Ukrainian. The English-speaking percentage may have been considerably smaller, inasmuch as Stachel later admitted that "the so-called English branches included many elements that could hardly speak English" (*The Communist,* April 1929, p. 1851).
13. William Simons, *Daily Worker,* April 5, 1927, p. 4.
14. Ellis Peterson, *The Party Organizer,* May–June 1928, p. 22.
15. *The Party Organizer,* February 1930, pp. 2, 10.
16. This registration of occupations and union affiliation covered about four-fifths of the total membership. The five leading classifications were: metal trades, 2080 (15%); housewives and domestic workers, 2065 (15%); building trades, 1581 (11%); needle trades, 1242 (9%); and miners, 1165 (7%). I have added the percentages and compensated for those who failed to register, but the figures can be considered as estimates only (for the complete results, see *The 4th National Convention,* pp. 40–41).
17. *The Communist International Between the Fifth and Sixth World Congresses,* p. 351. Line 10 on this page, which is garbled, should refer to housewives and domestic workers. It is correctly given in the German version, *Die Komintern vor dem 6. Weltkongress,* p. 378.
18. Stachel, *The Communist,* April 1929, p. 183.
19. Bert Miller, *Daily Worker,* April 14, 1926.
20. Ruthenberg, *Daily Worker,* December 3, 1926. *The Party Organizer,* December 1927, p. 15, gave the figure of 1646 out of 10,538 for August 1927. Stachel (*The Party Organizer,* May–June 1928, p. 5, and *The Communist,* April 1929, p. 186) reported 10 per cent. On the other hand, Lovestone tried to make the picture look better in 1927 by claiming 35 per cent, though he admitted that "the shop nucleus which functions well is an exception" (*Daily Worker,* September 13, 1927). It is hard to take Lovestone's figure seriously when, at almost the same time, *The Party Organizer* (December 1927) gave a detailed breakdown of these shop nuclei for a total of 15 per cent. The 1933 figure derives from Browder (*The Communist,* August 1933, p. 717). It rose to 9 per cent, the majority in small shops, in 1934 (Browder, *Report to the 8th Convention,* p. 82).
21. *The 4th National Convention,* pp. 40–41; Foster, *Daily Worker,* December 5, 1925.
22. Ruthenberg, *Daily Worker,* November 30, 1926, gave the ratio as approximately 50 per cent and "probably less than half of these members actually carry on systematic work in their unions." Three

years later, the percentage was given as 46 (Stachel, *The Communist,* May 1929, p. 240).

23. Lenin, *Collected Works,* Vol. IV, Book 1, p. 57 (December 1900). The last phrase was used by Benjamin Gitlow as the title of a book.
24. *Decisions of the Third Congress of the Communist International* (London: 1921), p. 32.
25. "We have the Leninist formula about Party membership which is verified, has stood all tests. According to this formula, a Party member is one who *accepts* the Party program, pays membership dues and works in one of its organizations. Note that Lenin's formula does not speak about *mastering* the program, but of *accepting* the program. These are two entirely different things" (Stalin, *Mastering Bolshevism,* New York: Workers Library, 1937, p. 61).
26. *The Workers Monthly,* November 1924, p. 36.
27. Olgin, *The Worker,* July 28, 1923, p. 5.
28. Bertram D. Wolfe, *The Workers Monthly,* June 1926, p. 374.
29. See *The Party Organizer,* March–April 1933, pp. 22–23, and Ann Rollins, ibid., March 1938, pp. 36–37.
30. Ray Ginger, *The Bending Cross* (New Brunswick, N.J.: Rutgers University Press, 1949), pp. 213, 244.
31. James P. Cannon, *The Struggle for a Proletarian Party* (New York: Pioneer, 1943), p. 24.
32. In 1925, 19 out of 43 representative Communist leaders were listed as "journalists and writers" in *The American Labor Who's Who,* pp. 355–57. Testifying before the Joint Legislative (McNaboe) Committee of New York State in 1939, Earl Browder named his job as General Secretary of the Communist party of the United States and continued: "My profession is journalist" (*Report of the Joint Legislative Committee to Investigate the Administration and Enforcement of the Law,* Albany: J. B. Lyons, 1939, p. 1429). When Leon Trotsky was asked about the legend that he had worked as a tailor in New York, he replied, "Unfortunately I did not learn any productive trade in my life. I regret that very much" (*The Case of Leon Trotsky,* New York: Harper, 1937, p. 18). Oddly, Trotsky did earn a living from journalism most of his life; apparently he did not consider it a productive trade.
33. *The American Labor Who's Who.* The index lists 43 names for the Workers party (p. 354). These include almost all the important Communist leaders plus a few lesser-known figures. According to Max Shachtman, the number of Communists listed in *The American Labor Who's Who* was 61, indicating 18 more than the index for the Workers party acknowledges (*The New International,* Winter 1958, p. 55). I have decided to base my tabulation on the 43 names without change, in order to minimize the personal factor as much as possible, even though a few may be questioned as representative leaders. Except for a change in the nationality of William F. Dunne

(who was born in the United States, not Canada), the biographies were used without any alteration. The book contains biographies of Joseph Freeman, Juliet Stuart Poyntz, Michael Gold, and Yrjo (George) Halonen but for some reason does not include them in the Workers party list in the index; I have therefore omitted them from my calculations. I decided to use the list as the most objective basis, despite some sins of omission and commission, because a few different names more or less would not change any essential point.

The list of 43 reads: Martin Abern, Max Bedacht, Alexander Bittelman, Earl R. Browder, Fahle Burman, James P. Cannon, Ellis Chryssos, Solon De Leon, Nicholas Dozenberg, John L. Engdahl, William Z. Foster, Harrison George, Benjamin Gitlow, Sam T. Hammersmark, C. A. Hathaway, Nat Kaplan, Alfred Knutson, Charles Krumbein, Cyril Lambkin, Edward I. Lindgren, Moritz Loeb, Ludwig Lore, Jay Lovestone, Joseph Manley, Robert Minor, Moissaye J. Olgin, Edgar Owens, Gordon W. Owens, Joseph Podulski, Karl M. Reeve, Morris Rosen, Charles E. Ruthenberg, Max Shachtman, Rose P. Stokes, Arne Swabeck, Alexander Trachtenberg, Abraham Vaclav, Alfred Wagenknecht, William W. Weinstone, Albert Weisbord, H. M. Wicks, John Williamson, Harry M. Winitsky.

34. The book includes two biographies of Communist women, Juliet Stuart Poyntz and Rose Pastor Stokes, but only the latter appears in the list of 43. The only Negro on the list, Gordon W. Owens, was then organizer of the English branch on Chicago's South Side.
35. I have used my own judgment in classifying the replies under this heading. In the white-collar group, I have placed such occupations as clerk, journalist, teacher, and statistician. I have classified steamfitter, machinist, and electrician with the skilled industrial workers. There is a possible margin of error or difference of opinion in this category, but I feel that it could not be large enough to change the broad classifications significantly.
36. *Izvestia,* December 17, 1918 (translated in *Soviet Documents on Foreign Policy,* pp. 127–28).
37. *Der Zweite Kongress der Kommunistischen Internationale,* 1920, p. 28.
38. I have told this story in detail in *The Roots of American Communism,* p. 294. Since its publication, John T. Murphy, the former British Communist, has denied one part of Fraina's statement. Murphy says that Fraina did not give him $20,000 or $25,000, but at the same time confirms "the flow of cash from the Comintern to its subsidiaries in the early years" (*The New Reasoner,* London, Winter 1958–59, p. 120).
39. Testimony by Gitlow, *Investigation of Un-American Propaganda Activities,* Vol. VII, p. 4687.
40. *The Roots of American Communism,* pp. 240–41.
41. Gitlow blames Lovestone for the loss and says that he was brought

up on charges in 1922 without any action taken (*Investigation of Un-American Propaganda Activities,* Vol. VII, p. 4540, and *I Confess,* p. 388).

42. *Constitution and Program of Communist Party of America,* 1921.
43. *People vs. Ruthenberg:* Transcript of Record, Supreme Court of the United States, October Term, 1925 (containing a portion of the original record of the trial in St. Joseph, Michigan, 1923), p. 175. This testimony was given by Lovestone, secretary at the time of the Bridgman convention.
44. *The Second Year,* pp. 32–42, and *The 4th National Convention,* pp. 52–61.
45. *Exhibit, Subversive Activities Control Board.*
46. Testimony by Gitlow, *Investigation of Un-American Propaganda Activities,* Vol. VII, p. 4568.
47. Minutes of the Political Committee, April 25, 1927.
48. The Garland Fund held the mortgage on the *Daily Worker*'s plant in Chicago and the minutes tell the story of lengthy negotiations to pay off the debt when the building was sold in 1927 (Minutes of the Secretariat, September 13 and October 6, 1927).
49. Testimony by Alexander Trachtenberg, *Investigation of Un-American Propaganda Activities,* Vol. VII, pp. 4880–81. Trachtenberg stated that Heller had been the sole investor in International Publishers. However, Gitlow testified that Heller had originally owned 51 per cent and the Comintern 49 per cent of the stock, and the percentages had been reversed in favor of the Comintern on Gitlow's suggestion in 1928 (ibid., p. 4558).
50. Minutes of the Political Committee, September 12, 1927; Minutes of the Secretariat, September 21, 1927. Lovestone parlayed the $2000 into a fund of $10,000.
51. Minutes of the Political Committee, February 24 and March 22, 1927.
52. *The Communist,* January 1922, p. 15. A proposal had been made in 1921 to reduce salaries to $25 weekly for those without dependents, $35 for those with a wife or parents to support, and $40 for married members with children (*Official Bulletin No. 2,* issued by the Central Executive Committee of the Communist party of America, undated, probably August 1921, pp. 4–7).
53. Minutes of the Secretariat, October 6, 1927. The amount of Wolfe's salary was omitted in the original.
54. *Subversive Activities Control Board,* p. 974.
55. Minutes of the Political Committee, January 14, 1927.
56. Minutes of the Secretariat, September 21, 1927.
57. This list is based on Gitlow's testimony in *Investigation of Un-American Propaganda Activities,* Vol. VII, pp. 4547–59; *Subversive Activities Control Board,* pp. 732, 754, 851, 1175–77; and on *I Confess,* pp. 387–88 and 496. In *I Confess,* p. 496, he mentions the sum of $5000 as the first installment personally received by him in Moscow

in 1928, but the other two sources give the figure as $3500 and he subsequently agreed that the book had erred (*Subversive Activities Control Board,* p. 1175).

Gitlow's second book, *The Whole of Their Lives* (New York: Scribner, 1948), introduces, without explanation, some new figures. Charles E. Scott is supposed to have brought $250,000 in 1920 (p. 46); the T.U.E.L. now received "several hundred thousand dollars" (p. 104); and Moscow supplied $100,000 for the Farmer-Labor movement (p. 113). It seems strange that Gitlow should have omitted these large sums from his earlier testimony and writings. Scott came to the United States not in 1920 but in 1921, when Gitlow was in prison and therefore hardly in a position to know of such a matter firsthand. Manley had caused quite a scandal in the party by accusing it of having spent only $50,000 on the Farmer-Labor movement. The subsidies that Gitlow had previously attributed to Foster and the T.U.E.L. had fallen far short of "several hundred thousand dollars." It is hard to believe that the party leaders, including Gitlow himself, would not have benefited more if the Comintern and the Profintern had poured so many "hundreds of thousands of dollars" into the United States.

58. Gitlow gave the sum as $27,902 in *Subversive Activities Control Board,* p. 749, and $29,329.46 in *I Confess,* p. 387.
59. Lovestone's testimony, *Investigation of Un-American Propaganda Activities,* Vol. XI, p. 7149.
60. Gitlow's testimony, ibid., Vol. VII, p. 4568.
61. *I Confess,* p. 496 ($250,000), and the following: "Moscow was a generous donor, but far from all of our activities were paid for by the Russians. With a membership never exceeding sixteen thousand in those days, we spent an average of a million dollars a year, of which the better half was raised right in the United States" (p. 470).
62. Lovestone's testimony, *Investigation of Un-American Propaganda Activities,* Vol. XI, p. 7149.
63. *Documents Illustrating the Hostile Activities of the Soviet Government and Third International against Great Britain* (London: His Majesty's Stationery Office, 1927), pp. 20–21, 25. According to Gitlow, the Comintern funds to the United States and Canada were transmitted through Arcos, but an office in Berlin took over the transactions after the raid (*I Confess,* pp. 388–89).
64. *Daily Worker,* May 28, 1927, p. 1.
65. Lovestone's testimony, *Investigation of Un-American Propaganda Activities,* Vol. XI, p. 7149.
66. Ibid., p. 7148.
67. Dozenberg's background is mainly based on his own testimony in *Investigation of Un-American Propaganda Activities,* Vol. XIII, pp. 8137–61. There is also biographical data in *The American Labor Who's Who,* p. 62; *Daily Worker,* February 5, 1925, p. 4; and Osvald

Akmentins, *Amerikas Latviesi 1888–1948* (Vaidava, 1958), pp. 121–123.

68. In his 1940 testimony, Dozenberg said that he went to work on the *Voice of Labor* in 1920, but it was probably 1921, as stated in *The American Labor Who's Who,* p. 62.
69. *Daily Worker,* February 5, 1925, p. 4. A photograph of Dozenberg accompanies the story.
70. Dozenberg's career as a Soviet agent is mainly based on his own testimony before the Dies committee, published in its series of *Executive Hearings,* Vol. II, pp. 563–653, and on his affidavit in *Hearings Regarding Communist Espionage,* pp. 3540–42. Gitlow confirmed that the Secretariat made the decision to assign Dozenberg "as a liaison officer between the Ogpu and the secretariat of the American Party" (*Investigation of Un-American Propaganda Activities,* Vol. VII, p. 4675). Gitlow also mentions Dozenberg's case in *The Whole of Their Lives,* pp. 141–44. Dozenberg himself never made clear how the original approach was made to him and tells a disconnected story about receiving a letter in Chicago from "Alfred" (*Executive Hearings,* Vol. II, p. 569). Lovestone made several references in his testimony to the American Communist tie-up with Soviet intelligence agencies, but his published testimony does not go very far in this area (*Investigation of Un-American Propaganda Activities,* Vol. XI, pp. 7147, 7167, 7175).
71. The name is given as Alfred Tilton in Dozenberg's affidavit, *Hearings Regarding Communist Espionage,* p. 3540, but as Alfred Tiltin in the *Executive Hearings,* Vol. II, and as Alfred Tilden by W. G. Krivitsky, *In Stalin's Secret Service* (New York: Harper, 1939), pp. 127–31.
72. Dozenberg's affidavit (op. cit., p. 3540) gives the date as "in the latter part of 1927 or the early part of 1928" (p. 3540), and this is also the date he gave in the *Executive Hearings* (Vol. II, p. 564). Gitlow said (op. cit., Note 70) that the Secretariat assigned Dozenberg to work as a Soviet agent at the end of 1927.
73. The problem of Tilton's predecessors is confused. A publication of the House Committee on Un-American Activities, *The Shameful Years: Thirty Years of Soviet Espionage in the United States* (Washington, D.C.: Government Printing Office, 1952, p. 5), goes as far back as Ludwig C. A. K. Martens, the first official representative of the Soviet Government in the United States, who was deported in 1921. A former OGPU agent, Georges Agabeekov, referred to one Tschatsky as the first OGPU "resident" agent in the United States some time before 1928 (*OGPU,* New York: Brentano's, 1931, p. 198). Krivitsky testified that a German Communist, Felix Wolf, was chief of Soviet military intelligence in the United States from approximately 1924 to 1929 before Tilton, but the latter date contradicts that of 1927 for Tilton or Tilden in Krivitsky's book (*Investigation of Un-American Propaganda Activities,* Vol. IX, p. 5742).

A former Soviet diplomat, Grigory Bessedovsky, named one Filin, alias Semen, as chief of Soviet military intelligence in the United States in 1926 or thereabouts (*Revelations of a Soviet Diplomat,* London: William & Norgate, 1931, p. 114). Since these sources are contradictory, and most of them are suspect, the identity of Soviet agents prior to Tilton is still questionable.

74. The story of the counterfeit dollars has many versions: Dozenberg (*Executive Hearings,* Vol. II, pp. 585–92, 619–25); William Gregory Burtan, the associate who was sentenced to serve fifteen years in prison in 1934 (*Hearings Regarding Communist Espionage,* 1951, pp. 3556–61); Krivitsky (op. cit., pp. 135–58); Gitlow (*The Whole of Their Lives,* pp. 139–44); David J. Dallin (*Soviet Espionage,* New Haven: Yale University Press, 1955, pp. 393–96).
75. Dozenberg testified that he had recruited Albert Feierabend and Robert Zelms (*Executive Hearings,* Vol. II, p. 611). Feierabend was arrested in 1933 on a charge of illegal use of a passport. At the time of his arrest, he was carrying a small white ribbon with an inscription, dated July 18, 1930, reading: "The bearer of this credential is thoroughly trustworthy and should be given all possible support so that he may effectively accomplish the mission he is engaged in." It was signed by Max Bedacht for the Secretariat of the Communist party. Bedacht later confirmed that he used to sign such credentials for party members going abroad, but he could not remember Feierabend (*Hearings Regarding Communist Espionage,* pp. 3547–48).
76. *Executive Hearings,* Vol. II, p. 643.
77. The arrest and trials of Dozenberg and Browder were reported in *The New York Times,* December 10, 19, and 28, 1939; January 11 and 19, 1940; and March 29, 1940. Krivitsky's article appeared in the *Saturday Evening Post,* September 30, 1939, and constitutes the chapter, "When Stalin Counterfeited Dollars," in his book, *In Stalin's Secret Service.*
78. *Report of the Royal Commission* (Ottawa: Edmond Cloutier, 1946), p. 14.
79. Dallin, *Soviet Espionage,* pp. 16–17, 27–28.

Chapter 9: Politics and Trade-Unionism

1. Arne Swabeck, "The Left Wing Movement in the American Labor Unions," *International Press Correspondence,* September 15, 1922, pp. 591–92; *The Red Labor Union International* (organ of the Profintern), Moscow, December 15, 1921, pp. 547–48.
2. *International Press Correspondence,* November 2, 1922, p. 720.
3. Minutes of the National Committee of the T.U.E.L., November 14 and December 4, 1923.

4. Foster, *International Press Correspondence,* March 18, 1925, p. 322; *Daily Worker,* August 14 and December 5, 1925.
5. *The Labor Herald,* October 1923, p. 30, and July 1924, pp. 151–54. Later the Profintern rebuked the T.U.E.L. for putting the dictatorship of the proletariat in its program, despite the fact that the Profintern itself had ordered the T.U.E.L. to do so in 1924 (*Resolutions and Decisions: Third World Congress of the Red International of Labor Unions,* Chicago: Trade Union Educational League, 1924, p. 49).
6. *The Workers Monthly* superseded *The Liberator, The Labor Herald,* and *Soviet Russia Pictorial* in November 1924.
7. *Resolutions and Decisions: Third World Congress of the Red International of Labor Unions,* p. 50.
8. *Bolshevizing the Communist International,* p. 190.
9. "A Letter from the Comintern and the Profintern on Trade Union Work," *Daily Worker,* August 14, 1925.
10. *Daily Worker,* August 31, 1925.
11. *The 4th National Convention,* pp. 99–108.
12. Minutes of the Politbureau (Political Committee), October 10, 1925.
13. This paragraph is based on the text of the cable to Lozovsky appended to the Minutes of the Political Committee, January 4, 1926. The resolution itself was apparently never published. The plenum resolution published in the *Daily Worker,* January 6, 1926, p. 4, concerned other matters. This plenum took place December 26–28, 1925. Ruthenberg's report to the plenum for the Political Committee appeared in the *Daily Worker,* January 4, 1926, p. 4.
14. Browder's proposal appears in the Minutes of the Political Committee, December 30, 1925. Johnstone nominated Browder to go to Moscow (Minutes of the Political Committee, January 4, 1926).
15. The texts of Lozovsky's cable and the reply appear in the Minutes of the Political Committee, January 4, 1926. Johnstone protested that the reply did not comply with Lozovsky's request, but Ruthenberg stood pat. Since the American plenum had terminated less than a week previously, the speed of Lozovsky's intervention indicates that Browder and Johnstone had immediately wired to alert Lozovsky or Foster or both to the T.U.E.L.'s peril.
16. *Revolutionary Age,* March 1, 1930, p. 2.
17. Foster-Bittelman Statement to the Comintern on the Situation in the Communist Party of America, dated January 18, 1926, p. 15 (appended to the Minutes for 1926).
18. Lozovsky, *International Press Correspondence,* March 25, 1926, p. 349. Gitlow's version appears in *The Workers Monthly,* November 1925, pp. 15–18, and *I Confess,* pp. 383–86.
19. Stachel, *Daily Worker,* January 29, 1926, p. 4. This ratio was not unusual. Stachel also reported that the Communists, with 25 mem-

bers, elected an organizer of the hotel workers branch of the Amalgamated Food Workers Union by a vote of 7 to 1.

20. Joel Seidman, *The Needle Trades* (New York: Farrar & Rinehart, 1942), pp. 170–71. Philip S. Foner, *The Fur and Leather Workers Union* (Newark: Nordan Press, 1950), pp. 173–74, a Communist-line work, distorts the substance of the telegram and calls it a "forged message." The Minutes of the Political Committee, October 27, 1925, contain an amendment by Johnstone, carried unanimously: "That we demand the majority on the joint executive board for the left wing." The convention finally elected a General Executive Board of four Progressives, two Communists, four Right-Wingers, and two unattached members.
21. This is the version in Epstein, *Jewish Labor in U.S.A.*, p. 142. Benjamin Stolberg, *Tailor's Progress* (New York: Doubleday, 1944), p. 134, tells the same story in somewhat different words. Charles S. Zimmerman confirmed the incident in an interview with me, May 21, 1957.
22. The Minutes of the Political Committee, October 10 and 12, 1925, deal with the party's veto of any negotiations or alliance with the Sigman administration in the I.L.G.W.U. The Minutes of October 24, 1925, include texts of telegrams exchanged between Ruthenberg and Gitlow, one of the party's representatives to the I.L.G.W.U. convention, and suggest the likelihood that similar telegrams were exchanged between Ruthenberg and Weinstone at the Fur Workers convention a few days earlier. The 1925 I.L.G.W.U. convention is dealt with in Seidman, op. cit., p. 163, and Epstein, *Jewish Labor in U.S.A.*, pp. 142–43. Dunne, *The Workers Monthly*, February 1926, pp. 173–75, disclosed the Communist strength among the Left Wing delegates, and Stachel, *Daily Worker*, January 29, 1926, gave the Communist strength among the membership.
23. Epstein, *Jewish Labor in U.S.A.*, pp. 180–83. The Communist version appears in Jack Hardy, *The Clothing Workers* (New York: International, 1935), pp. 76–78.
24. The most ambitious study of the Passaic strike is Morton Siegel's "The Passaic Strike of 1926," an unpublished doctoral dissertation at Columbia University, 1953.
25. Robert R. R. Brooks, "The United Textile Workers of America," an unpublished doctoral dissertation, Yale University, 1935, p. 54.
26. A. G. Bosse, *International Press Correspondence*, January 6, 1927, p. 56.
27. The Minutes of the T.U.E.L. National Committee, March 26, 1925, mention the six local United Front Committees. Fred Beals, *Proletarian Journey* (New York: Hillman, Curl, 1937), pp. 84–85, claims that he first formed a Rank and File Committee of Textile Workers in Lawrence, Mass., which the Communists took over and changed to United Front Committee of Textile Workers.

28. I am indebted for these personal and other details to Albert Weisbord (interview, April 25, 1958, and letter of August 26, 1959).
29. Gitlow gives the impression that Weisbord went from Harvard Law School to the Passaic strike (*I Confess,* pp. 365–66). Actually, Weisbord went to the Passaic strike from the West New York strike, which he also led. Weisbord served as secretary of the United Front Committee of Textile Workers set up for the West New York strike (*Daily Worker,* October 29, 1925, p. 2).
30. The Minutes of the Trade Union Committee of the C.E.C., November 20, 1925, contain Johnstone's attack on the Passaic policy; the Minutes of January 3, 1926, the order to discontinue issuing membership books and dues stamps; the Minutes of January 15 and February 10, 1926, Johnstone's proposals for affiliating with existing textile unions.
31. Perlman and Taft, *History of Labor in the United States,* Vol. IV, p. 557.
32. Ruth Fischer tells her side of the story in *Stalin and German Communism,* pp. 432–55, 491–514, 541–55.
33. Browder, "A Political Autobiography" (in manuscript), Part II, Chapter XI, p. 10.
34. Ruthenberg to Lovestone, letter dated February 13, 1926, cited in *The Revolutionary Age,* March 1, 1930, p. 2.
35. Jay Lovestone, *Pages from Party History* (New York: Workers Library, 1929), pp. 15–16.
36. *International Press Correspondence,* March 4, 1926, pp. 255–56. The names were listed in this order.
37. Ibid., April 22, 1926, pp. 475–76. Foster used the name "Dorsey" at this plenum.
38. "Report of the American Commission," ibid., April 22, 1926, pp. 487–89, and "Resolution on the American Question," ibid., May 13, 1926, pp. 645–46. The "Resolution on the American Question," however, was not published in its entirety. Its concluding section, "Organizational Changes," appears only in the confidential mimeographed version sent out by Ruthenberg "to all District, City, Section Committees and Language Propaganda Bureaus," dated April 15, 1926 (in my possession).

    The new Trade Union Committee was composed of Foster, Dunne, Browder, Gitlow, and Johnstone, with Overgaard and one other as alternates during Browder's absence in Moscow. The enlarged Political Committee was composed of Ruthenberg, Lovestone, Bedacht, Cannon, Foster, Bittelman, and Gitlow.
39. Wm. Z. Foster, *Russian Workers and Workshops in 1926* (Chicago: Trade Union Educational League, 1926), pp. 50–51.
40. *Class Struggle,* June 1931, p. 5; Albert Weisbord, *The Conquest of Power* (New York: Covici-Friede, 1937), Vol. II, p. 1115 note.
41. John Williamson, *Daily Worker,* October 28, 1929.

42. Ben Gitlow, "The Passaic Textile Workers Strike," *The Workers Monthly,* June 1926, pp. 347–51; Albert Weisbord, "Lessons from Passaic," ibid., December 1926, pp. 636–40; "Passaic—A Challenge to the A.F.L. Leadership," Statement of C.C. of W.P., *Daily Worker,* October 18, 1926, p. 2; Ruthenberg, "The Achievements of the Party," ibid., November 29, 1926, p. 6; Robert Minor, *The Communist International,* February 28, 1927, pp. 39–42.
43. The Communist *History of the American Working Class* by Anthony Bimba (New York: International, 1927) put it this way: "For the first time in the history of this country a strike was conducted on a large scale under communist leadership" (p. 308). In *Labor and Textiles* (New York: International, 1931), Robert W. Dunn and Jack Hardy refer to "the United Front Committee, organized under Communist auspices" (p. 222). Foster's versions appear in *From Bryan to Stalin,* p. 201, and *History of the Communist Party of the United States,* p. 250. On the other hand, Ella Reeve Bloor's autobiography, *We Are Many* (1940), calls it "the first mass strike under Communist leadership" without mentioning the T.U.E.L. (p. 201).
44. Mary Heaton Vorse, *Passaic* (Chicago: International Labor Defense, 1926), p. 10.
45. Wm. Z. Foster, *Strike Strategy* (Chicago: Trade Union Educational League, 1926), p. 23.
46. Foster, *From Bryan to Stalin,* p. 202.
47. *History of the Communist Party of the United States,* p. 250.
48. *I Confess,* pp. 369–70.
49. Irving Howe and Lewis Coser, *The American Communist Party* (Boston: Beacon, 1957), pp. 239–43.
50. The historian of the Passaic strike, Morton Siegel (op. cit., p. 234), summed up: "Doubtless the United Front Committee's program as a whole, and the U.F.C. itself, helped to create and maintain the unity, but to Albert Weisbord as leader must go most of the credit for the singular success of the U.F.C. in retaining the support of the workers." Siegel cites numerous contemporary tributes to Weisbord's leadership from neutral and hostile sources. James P. Cannon has also written: "It is true that he [Weisbord] worked under close supervision and direction of a party committee in New York appointed by the national party leadership in Chicago. But it's a long way from committee meetings in a closed room, off the scene, to the actual leadership of a strike on the ground. The full credit for that belongs to Weisbord" (Cannon to Draper, June 9, 1955, published in the *Fourth International,* Spring 1956, p. 50).
51. Seidman, op. cit., pp. 171–73; Epstein, *Jewish Labor in U.S.A.*, pp. 171–73; Gitlow, *I Confess,* pp. 343–56; Foner, op. cit., pp. 179–312; Hardy, op. cit., pp. 120–34.
52. Epstein, *Jewish Labor in U.S.A.*, pp. 143–55; Seidman, op. cit., pp.

164–68; Stolberg, op. cit., pp. 135–44; Schneider, *The Workers' (Communist) Party and American Trade Unions,* pp. 99–104; Hardy, op. cit., pp. 38–52.

CHAPTER 10: RUTHENBERG'S LAST WISH

1. Ruthenberg, *Daily Worker,* July 1, 1926, p. 4, and December 26, 1926, p. 1.
2. Elizabeth Gurley Flynn (ibid., January 21, 1954), wrote a column on Stachel's background. His birthplace was originally in Austria-Hungary, then became part of Poland, and now belongs to the U.S.S.R.
3. It should be recalled that the C.E.C., elected at the Fourth Convention in August 1925, was equally divided between the Foster-Cannon and Ruthenberg factions before Gusev intervened to give the latter control of the Political Committee.
4. Cannon to Draper, July 22 and July 26, 1955. Gitlow gives his interpretation in *I Confess,* pp. 404–406. A letter from Weinstone to Cannon, dated September 14, 1926, replying to a letter from Cannon to Weinstone, August 19, 1926, expresses interest in Cannon's views and asks for more information (photo-copy in my possession). The future alliance began to take shape at this time, six months before Ruthenberg's death.
5. Minutes of the Political Committee, June 29, 1926. Kuusinen's cable was appended to the Minutes of the Political Committee, October 13, 1926, and was published, together with three other cables, including the one signed by Kruse mentioned in the next paragraph, in *Investigation of Un-American Propaganda Activities* (1939), Vol. VII, pp. 4599–4600.
6. This is half the cable; the other half is repetitious.
7. Minutes of the Political Committee, October 13, 1926. The vote was Ruthenberg, Lovestone, Bedacht, and Gitlow *versus* Foster, Bittelman, and Cannon.
8. See *International Press Correspondence,* May 30, 1925, p. 603, for Zinoviev's defense of "socialism in one country." He attacked it at the Seventh Plenum in November–December 1926.
9. Pepper served as reporter for the key Political Commission at the Sixth Plenum and praised Zinoviev's attack on the "ultra-Leftists" (*International Press Correspondence,* April 22, 1926, p. 477).
10. *Daily Worker,* July 28–31, 1926.
11. The C.E.C. published an anti-Zinoviev statement in the *Daily Worker,* July 31, 1926, the last day of Pepper's reports on the Russian plenum. Two cables by Pepper against the Trotsky-Zinoviev Opposition were followed by another C.E.C. statement, signed by Ruthenberg, in the *Daily Worker,* October 6, 1926, p. 6. Another cable from Pepper

reported the ten-party demand for Zinoviev's removal, signed by "Duncan" (Minor), Browder and Pepper (ibid., October 27, 1926, p. 1).

12. *Daily Worker,* November 4, 10, and 18, 1926.
13. *Protokoll der Erweiterten Exekutive,* 22 November–16 Dezember 1926 (Seventh Plenum), p. 570.
14. Bittelman's translation of Zinoviev's *History of the Russian Communist Party* started publication in *The Workers Monthly* of January 1925, and installments were published until May 1926. A note at the end of the last installment promised another one in the issue of June 1926, but it never appeared, nor did any others.
15. *Protokoll* (Seventh Plenum), p. 653.
16. Ibid., p. 628.
17. Ibid., p. 698.
18. Ibid., pp. 699–700.
19. Ibid., p. 560.
20. Information from Earl Browder.
21. *Daily Worker,* March 3–10, 1927. Gitlow, in *I Confess* (pp. 410–416), gives a colorful description of the rituals.
22. Minutes of the Political Committee, March 2, 1927. The version in the *Daily Worker,* March 3, 1927, changed "workers" to "working class."
23. Minutes of the Political Committee, March 2, 1927. Apparently Ruthenberg's latest biographer belongs among the cynics. He cites a last dictaphone recording made by Ruthenberg for International Woman's Day, but omits the famous last words (Johnson, *The Day Is Coming,* p. 179).
24. *Daily Worker,* March 4, 1927.
25. This myth is perpetuated in Johnson's biography: "now the Communist Party of the Soviet Union requested that his ashes be sent there for burial, and this was done" (op. cit., p. 179).
26. *Daily Worker,* May 18, 1927.
27. A. B. Magil, "Go To Sleep, Charlie," ibid., March 9, 1927.
28. Ibid., March 11, 1927.
29. Jay Lovestone, *Ruthenberg: Communist Fighter and Leader* (New York: Workers Library, 1927).
30. Alex Bittelman, *Milestones in the History of the Communist Party* (New York: Workers Library, 1937), p. 91.
31. Elizabeth Gurley Flynn, *Debs, Haywood, Ruthenberg* (New York: Workers Library, 1939), pp. 37, 39. "Lenin and Stalin were his chosen models."
32. Johnson, op. cit.
33. Foster, *History of the Communist Party of the United States,* p. 265.

Chapter 11: Lovestone in Power

1. Before Ruthenberg's death, according to Gitlow, Cannon proposed himself as Chairman, Weinstone as General Secretary, and Foster as trade-union specialist, but Foster was dissatisfied. Gitlow also implies that Foster intended to take over the leadership after Ruthenberg's death (*I Confess,* pp. 405–406, 412). The only firsthand account comes from Cannon, who denies that he discussed party offices before Ruthenberg's death and asserts that only the general secretaryship was discussed afterward. Cannon affirms: "Weinstone and I had come to agreement with Foster that Weinstone should become the new party secretary," which is the main point, obscured in Gitlow's rambling story (Cannon to Draper, July 22 and 26, 1955, published in *International Socialist Review,* Summer and Fall 1956).
2. Article 12, Section 3, *The Party Organization,* p. 35.
3. Minutes of the Political Committee, March 5, 1927. Gitlow tells of Foster's move to hold a plenum but neglects to mention his own nomination of Lovestone (*I Confess,* p. 412). A straight factional 4-to-3 vote carried Lovestone's amendment to defer the plenum. There is some confusion about Cannon's vote. The Minutes show that he voted against deferring the plenum, but, when he was defeated on this score, voted for Lovestone as "Acting Secretary." On this latter point, Cannon writes: "I haven't the slightest recollection of this. It is completely inconsistent with the context of this chapter which shows that I was supporting Weinstone for Secretary" (Cannon to Draper, May 28, 1959).
4. This paragraph is partially based on Lovestone's testimony in two trials: *The People of the State of New York against Harry M. Winitsky,* Supreme Court, Appellate Division—First Department, Judgment on March 29, 1920, pp. 375–445; and *People* vs. *Ruthenberg,* transcript of record, Supreme Court of the United States, October term, 1925, pp. 133–34, 147–48. There are minor discrepancies in the two testimonies. In the first, Lovestone said that he came to the United States in 1907, which would have been at the age of eight or nine, since he was born December 15, 1898; in the second, that he came at the age of ten.

   In his letter to the E.C.C.I. in 1924 on behalf of Pepper, Lovestone identified himself as having entered the Socialist movement "as a follower of Daniel De Leon after his death" and having later belonged to "that group of New York comrades who founded the Socialist Propaganda League and the 'Class Struggle,' and to which Comrades Trotsky and Bukharin, among others, belonged." There is no other evidence of Lovestone's connection with the S.P.L. A letter by Jacob Liebstein (Jay Lovestone) to *The Call,* July 8, 1917, defended Socialist Congressman Meyer Berger, then attacked by the S.P.L. as a hopeless Right-Winger.

In the Winitsky trial, Lovestone testified that he had joined the Socialist party at the end of 1916 or early in 1917 (p. 376). There is a letter by Jacob Liebstein in *The Call,* September 30, 1916, alluding to his political activity.

The C.C.N.Y. chapter of the Intercollegiate Socialist Society was called the Socialist Study Club in 1916 and had 115 dues-paying members. The club's troubles with the school authorities are related by James Henle (*The Call,* March 5, 1916, p. 7). *The Intercollegiate Socialist* (organ of the Intercollegiate Socialist Society), October–November 1916, lists Jacob Liebstein as secretary of the C.C.N.Y. chapter, and the October–November 1917 issue lists him as president with William Winestein (Weinstone) as secretary (pp. 22, 31). In an exchange of angry letters between Lovestone and Julius Gerber in 1919, the former replied to the accusation that he was using a pseudonym by stating that Jay Lovestone was his legal name, evidently adopted in 1918 or 1919 (*The Call,* February 6, 7, 11, 1919).

5. I. E. Ferguson, "The Communist Party Convention," *The Communist,* September 27, 1919, p. 5.
6. In the first three years of its existence, the American Communist movement published a pamphlet, *Manifesto and Program,* and translated works by Russian Communists. Foster produced three pamphlets and a booklet in 1921–22, but they were published by the T.U.E.L. before he acknowledged being a Communist. The pioneer official American Communist publication was Pepper's pamphlet, *For a Labor Party* (first edition, 1922). In 1923, a more ambitious Workers Party Library of cloth-bound books was undertaken and two volumes were published: Trotsky's *Dictatorship* vs. *Democracy* (better known as *In Defence of Terrorism*) and Lovestone's *The Government-Strikebreaker.* In the next year or two Lovestone wrote several pamphlets, *American Imperialism, The Labor Lieutenants of American Imperialism, Blood and Steel,* and *What's What About Coolidge,* outnumbering any other American Communist's pamphleteering record to date.
7. This is one of the letters of protest sent by Ruthenberg, Bedacht, Minor, and Lovestone in 1924, previously mentioned in Note 44, Chapter 5 (copies in my possession).
8. *The American Labor Who's Who,* p. 245. Weinstone's use of "General Secretary" appears for the first time in the *Daily Worker,* October 31, 1925, p. 1, and for the last time, March 3, 1927, p. 2.
9. Interview with Bertram D. Wolfe, June 16, 1956.
10. The story is told by Gitlow, *I Confess,* p. 416.
11. Minutes of the Political Committee, March 22–23, 1927.
12. Minutes of the Political Committee, April 8, 1927; *I Confess,* p. 416.

13. The Cannonite cable was signed by Cannon, Dunne, Swabeck, Abern, and Reynolds; the Fosterite by Aronberg, Bittelman, Foster, Johnstone, and Krumbein; the Weinstoneite by Weinstone, Ballam, Kaplan, Don, and Toohey (the last three from the youth league); and the Lovestoneite in the name of the majority of the Political Committee (texts in Minutes of the Political Committee, April 8, 1927).
14. Minutes of the Political Committee, April 8, 1927.
15. Ibid.
16. The Comintern's letter, as given in the Minutes of the Political Committee, April 25, 1927, set the date of the Eighth Plenum for May 10, 1927, but it actually took place May 18–30, 1927 (*International Press Correspondence,* June 9, 1927, p. 706).
17. Minutes of the Political Committee, April 25, 1927. The cable is reprinted in *I Confess,* p. 417.
18. Interview with Lovestone, June 21, 1954; *I Confess,* pp. 418–20.
19. Ostensibly owing to the war scare, the Eighth Plenum was conducted with unusual secrecy and only a small portion of its proceedings was published, namely, the verbatim debate on the Chinese question (*Die Chinesiche Frage,* Carl Hoym, 1928), and Stalin's speech, which appeared in a Comintern organ (*The Communist International,* June 30, 1927, pp. 200–207). Trotsky's only official supporter was Vuyovitch (*International Press Correspondece,* June 9, 1927, p. 707). Ruth Fischer claims that some other delegates spoke against Trotsky's expulsion (*Stalin and German Communism,* p. 582).
20. *International Press Correspondence,* June 16, 1927, pp. 735–37. The other four were the German, British, French, and Czechoslovak parties.
21. Interview with Lovestone, June 23, 1954; interview with Kruse, April 27, 1958; *I Confess,* pp. 429–31. Gitlow says that Stalin carried his arm in a sling because he was suffering from a severe attack of hardening of the arteries; Lovestone said that Stalin was heavily bundled up because he was suffering from arthritis; Kruse could recall no such details. Gitlow and Lovestone remember that Stalin asked one of his secretaries to bring him a folder and then shouted at him for getting the wrong one. The seventh member of the delegation was a former American Communist who had moved to Russia, George Ashkenudzi.
22. Ruth Fischer refers to Ewert in *Stalin and German Communism,* pp. 230, 583, 603.
23. Gitlow claims that Cannon, Foster, and Weinstone formed the bloc before leaving for Moscow (*I Confess,* p. 420). Cannon recalls that the bloc was formed in Moscow (Cannon to Draper, July 26, 1955).
24. "The Resolution of the Comintern on the American Question," En-

dorsed by the Presidium of the Executive Committee of the Communist International, July 1, 1927 (*Daily Worker,* August 3, 1927; also reprinted in *Investigation of Un-American Propaganda Activities,* Vol. VII, pp. 4635–42).

25. "Agreement for the Carrying Out of the Resolution on the American Question Adopted by the Presidium of the Executive Committee of the Comintern" (original in *Exhibits, Subversive Activities Control Board;* reprinted in *Investigation of Un-American Propaganda Activities,* Vol. VII, pp. 4642–44). This agreement was sent out to the party units but never published in the party press.
26. The first half of this cable was published in the *Daily Worker,* July 9, 1927, but the entire cable appears only in the Minutes of the Political Committee, July 7, 1927. Bedacht, a former barber, actually signed this cable "Barber," and again used "Mecca" as the code word for Moscow.
27. Original in *Exhibits, Subversive Activities Control Board,* reprinted in *Investigation of Un-American Propaganda Activities,* Vol. VII, p. 4644. The additional paragraph in the agreement consisted of the second, third, and fourth sentences of the cable, slightly rephrased and enlarged.
28. This paragraph is based on the Minutes of the Political Committee, July 7 and 11, 1927, and the *Daily Worker,* July 8, 9, 12, and 30, 1927. The third cable was dated July 27, 1927.
29. Minutes of the Political Committee, July 28, 1927. As Lovestone told the story, the conference was held with "Comrades B, K, and B," in all probability, Bukharin, Kuusinen, and "Braun." He attributed the statement to "K."
30. *Daily Worker,* August 6, 1927.
31. The cities with the largest membership meetings were New York, Chicago, Cleveland, Detroit, Philadelphia, Pittsburgh, Boston, Minneapolis, and New Haven (*Daily Worker,* August 5, 1927). The total vote was 1615 against 1103 with the Opposition ahead only in New Haven, the smallest (ibid., August 8 and 9, 1927). But the attendance at these mass meetings did not necessarily correspond with the number of delegates for every 200 members in good standing earlier in 1927 (ibid., August 11, 1927). Nevertheless, it is highly suggestive that less than 3000 members took the trouble to attend these key meetings in the largest Communist centers.
32. Lovestone's report to the Fifth Convention appeared in the *Daily Worker,* September 5–22, 1927; his reply to the discussion, ibid., September 26–October 4, 1927; and Foster's trade-union report in summary, ibid., September 5, 1927.
33. Central Executive Committee—*Majority:* Israel Amter, John J. Ballam, Max Bedacht, Benjamin Gitlow, J. Louis Engdahl, K. H. Heikkinen, Abram Jakira, Alfred Knutson, William F. Kruse, Benjamin

Lifschitz, Jay Lovestone, Robert Mahoney, Bert Miller, Robert Minor, M. J. Olgin, John Pepper, Henry Puro, Jack Stachel, John Schmies, Norman H. Tallentire, Alexander Trachtenberg, A. Fred, William W. Weinstone, William H. White, Bertram D. Wolfe; *Minority:* Martin Abern, Philip Aronberg, Alexander Bittelman, Earl R. Browder, James P. Cannon, William F. Dunne, William Z. Foster, John W. (Jack) Johnstone, Charles Krumbein, Bud Reynolds, Arne Swabeck, Alfred Wagenknecht, Joseph Zack. Candidates—*Majority:* Alex Bail, Ellis Peterson, H. M. Wicks, Anna David, Anthony Bimba, Herbert Benjamin; *Minority:* Rudolph Baker, H. Costrell, Manuel Gomez, C. A. Hathaway. Alternates—*Majority:* Biedenkapp, Bradon, Borich, Borisoff, Canter, M. Epstein, Fislerman, Peters, Poyntz, Shklar, Walker, Weisbord; *Minority:* S. Epstein, Halonen, Otis, Shachtman, Cowl, Bloomfield, Kerr, Gebert, Grecht.

Control Commission: Jacob Mindel, K. Radzi, Joe Brand, Max Lerner, M. Loonin. (*Daily Worker,* September 8, 1927.)

It should be noted that Weinstone and Ballam were originally included with the minority of the C.E.C. and Miller was accidentally omitted from the first published list (ibid., September 9, 1927).

Political Committee: Bedacht, Bittelman, Cannon, Engdahl, Foster, Gitlow, Lovestone, Minor, Puro, Weinstone, Wolfe.

Candidates: Browder, Dunne, Lifshitz, Stachel, Trachtenberg.

Secretariat: Lovestone, Foster, Gitlow (ibid., September 9, 1927).

34. Minutes of the Political Committee, September 16, 1927. Lovestone made the motion to abolish the title of "General Secretary" in the districts, and Gitlow moved to make "District Organizer" obligatory.
35. The distribution of titles was arranged in two stages: first, Ewert made the motion, adopted unanimously, in the Secretariat (Minutes of September 15, 1927), and then the Secretariat recommended it to the Political Committee, where it was also adopted unanimously (Minutes of September 15, 1927).
36. The move to New York, authorized by the Fifth Convention, was made at the end of September 1927. *The Communist* replaced *The Workers Monthly* with the issue of March 1927; Wolfe edited it from November 1927 to December 1928. The District Organizers at the end of 1927 were: Boston (1), Alex Bail; New York (2), William W. Weinstone; Philadelphia (3), Herbert Benjamin; Buffalo (4), James Saunders; Pittsburgh (5), Abram Jakira; Cleveland (6), Israel Amter; Detroit (7), Albert Weisbord; Chicago (8), Max Bedacht; Minneapolis (9), Norman H. Tallentire; Kansas City (10), Hugo Oehler; [no (11)]; Seattle (12), Aaron Fislerman; San Francisco (13), Emanuel Levine (*Daily Worker,* November 23, 1927).

Chapter 12: American Exceptionalism

1. Lovestone reported that the average dues-paying membership was 9367 in the last four months of 1925, 7597 in 1926, and 9642 at the Fifth Convention in September 1927 (*Daily Worker,* September 13, 1927).
2. The Communist vote for governor in New York City in 1926 was 4691 and about 10,000 votes were claimed in the municipal elections in 1927 (ibid., November 10, 1927).
3. Herbert Zam reported an average membership in good standing of the Young Workers (Communist) League of 500 in 1926, 700 in 1927 and 2000 in 1928 (ibid., April 8, 1929).
4. Browder, *International Press Correspondence,* March 12, 1925, p. 278.
5. Bittelman, *Daily Worker,* August 29, 1925.
6. Lovestone, ibid., December 21, 1925.
7. Lovestone, *The Workers Monthly,* March 1926, p. 205.
8. Varga, *Protokoll des V. Kongresses,* Vol. I, p. 21.
9. *Protokoll der Erweiterten Exekutive,* 21 März–6 April 1925, pp. 139–40. (The English version in *Bolshevising the Communist International,* p. 35, is unreliable.)
10. *Thesen und Resolutionen, Erweiterte Exekutive,* März–April 1925, p. 82.
11. Varga, *International Press Correspondence,* March 10, 1926, p. 282; Foster (Dorsey), ibid., March 25, 1926, p. 365.
12. Browder, ibid., March 17, 1926, pp. 302–303.
13. Pepper, ibid., April 8, 1926, pp. 399–400.
14. *Thesen und Resolutionen, Erweiterte Exekutive,* Februar–März 1926, p. 9.
15. Ruthenberg, "Do We Believe in the Theory of Misery?", *Daily Worker,* September 3, 1926, p. 6.
16. Ibid., November 27, 1926.
17. Ibid., February 5, 1927.
18. *Protokoll der Erweiterten Exekutive,* November–Dezember 1926, p. 60.
19. Ibid., p. 380.
20. Ibid., p. 211.
21. Ibid., p. 34.
22. Ibid., p. 280.
23. Wicks, *The Worker,* February 24, 1923.
24. *Daily Worker,* June 21, 1926 (Bittelman); July 3, 1926 (Ruthenberg); February 12, 1926 (Wicks).
25. "Uphold the Revolutionary Tradition," ibid., July 3, 1926, p. 1.
26. *The Workers Monthly,* July 1926, pp. 387–92. This article by Wolfe, one of Lovestone's articles discussed in the next paragraph, and a

truncated version of Dunne's editorial were reprinted in a pamphlet, *Our Heritage from 1776* (New York: The Workers School, 1926).

27. Lovestone's first two articles appeared in the *Daily Worker,* July 3 and 10, 1926. Of Jefferson he wrote: "Jefferson, it must be remembered, was the spokesman of the workers and poorer farmers." Eleven years later, Browder also discovered that Jefferson had fought "against vested interests and monopoly, and against financial control of government, for opening up the continent to the masses, and the fullest development of the economic life of the people as a whole, not merely the rich and privileged" (*The Communist,* September 1927, p. 803). Lovestone returned to the subject with reviews of *The Spirit of the Revolution* by John C. Fitzpatrick and *Letters on the American Revolution* by Margaret W. Wheeler (*The Workers Monthly,* November 1926, pp. 614–17 and January 1927, pp. 713–15).
28. *Daily Worker,* February 22, 1927 (Oliver Carlson); February 25, 1927 (William F. Dunne); July 4, 1927 (William F. Kruse); July 4, 1928 (editorial).
29. Thomas Nixon Carver, *The Present Economic Revolution in the United States* (Boston: Little, Brown, 1925), p. 11.
30. Rexford G. Tugwell, *Industry's Coming of Age* (New York: Harcourt, Brace, 1927), p. 231.
31. *The Autobiography of Lincoln Steffens,* p. 855.
32. Robert W. Dunn, *The Americanization of Labor* (New York: International, 1927) and *Company Unions* (New York: Vanguard, 1927); Wm. Z. Foster, "Capitalist Efficiency 'Socialism,'" *The Communist,* February 1928, pp. 90–104, and March 1928, pp. 169–74.
33. Foster devoted a chapter to "trade-union capitalism" in *Misleaders of Labor* (Chicago: Trade Union Educational League, 1927) and a booklet to the Locomotive Engineers' financial operations, *Wrecking the Labor Banks* (Chicago: Labor Herald Library, 1927). Perlman and Taft, op. cit., use the expression "Labor in Imitation of Business" as the title of a chapter (pp. 572–79). Still outstanding as a source for the entire period is *American Labor Dynamics,* edited by J. B. S. Hardman (New York: Harcourt, Brace, 1928).
34. Wm. Z. Foster, "Trade Union Insurance," *The Workers Monthly,* July 1926, pp. 413–15, 430.
35. Jay Lovestone, *Pages from Party History* (New York: Workers Library, 1929), pp. 13–14.
36. Bittelman's report for this subcommittee appears in the Minutes of the Political Committee, April 25, 1927.
37. This came out most clearly in Foster's article "Trade Union Insurance." Bittelman later admitted the Fosterite emphasis on bourgeoisification (*International Press Correspondence,* August 11, 1928, p. 845).
38. *Daily Worker,* September 15, 1927.

39. Ibid., September 26, 1927.
40. Ibid., May 17, 1927.
41. I see little essential difference between the Lovestone-Wolfe analysis and Foster's position as stated in *Misleaders of Labor* (1927), pp. 9–13, 334–36.
42. Stalin, *Works,* Vol. X, pp. 222, 291, 297.
43. Ibid., pp. 290–91.
44. *Report of the XV Congress of the Communist Party of the Soviet Union* (London: Communist Party of Great Britain, 1928), pp. 212–13, 262. How garbled American reports could become in Moscow is well illustrated by the revolutionary significance given to the Sacco-Vanzetti demonstrations. Not only did Bukharin give the American Communists sole credit for heading the Sacco-Vanzetti movement, but he gave the mistaken impression that the American Communists had organized the demonstration against the opposition of liberals and anarchists.
45. Ibid., p. 297. Manuilsky also hedged by cautioning that the "radicalization of the [American] proletariat" was "not a prospect of the immediate future" (pp. 297–98). But his emphasis was mainly on revolutionization and a catastrophic economic crisis. Lominadze also criticized Bukharin (ibid., pp. 285–86).
46. The full text of this letter, addressed to "The Central Committees of the Communist Parties," is appended to the Minutes of the Political Committee, November 30, 1927 (caps. in original). This letter referred to a previous letter, which is not available. In the Political Committee, Lovestone called for a letter to the districts applying the Comintern's instructions to American conditions; Bittelman proposed a subcommittee to review the party's experience in the light of the Comintern's letter; and Weinstone, Stachel, and Cannon made similar proposals.

Chapter 13: The Turning Point

1. Lovestone's report appeared in the *Daily Worker,* February 7–17, 1928. The plenum was held February 4–7, 1928.
2. *Daily Worker,* January 3, 1928.
3. This paragraph is based on Lovestone's report, ibid., February 7 and 9, 1928.
4. Ibid., February 17, 1928.
5. Bertram D. Wolfe, *The Trotsky Opposition* (New York: Workers Library, 1928).
6. Engdahl, Pepper, Browder, and Harrison George were appointed the American delegation (Minutes of the Political Committee, January 11, 1928), but Browder, then in China, could not attend. The official material on the Ninth Plenum is relatively scanty: *Resolutionen und Beschlüsse* (Hamburg, 1928); *International Press Correspondence,*

February 25, March 1 and 15, 1928; P. Braun, *At the Parting of the Ways: The Results of the Ninth Plenum of the Comintern* (London: Communist Party of Great Britain, 1928). This "Braun" was not Ewert, but the pseudonym of another German Communist.

7. John Pepper, "America and the Tactics of the Communist International," *The Communist,* April 1928, pp. 219–27.
8. Lozovsky's proposals and the Engdahl-Pepper substitute motion are contained in a cable from Engdahl and Pepper in the Minutes of the Political Committee, February 20, 1928.
9. Minutes of the Political Committee, February 21 and 22, 1928.
10. The main report on the trade-union resolution by Humbert-Droz and an English version of the "Resolution on the Trade Union Question" appear in *International Press Correspondence,* March 15, 1928, pp. 311–15, 318–20.
11. Minutes of the Political Committee, February 21, 1928.
12. *Protokoll über den Vierten Kongress der Roten Gewerkschafts Internationale,* Moskau, 17 März bis 3 April 1928 (Verlag der Roten Gewerkschafts-Internationale, 1928), pp. 77–78. There is no adequate version of the Profintern's Fourth Congress in English. Only a short summary of the proceedings was published in *International Press Correspondence,* March 22 and 29, April 5 and 12, 1928, and Lozovsky's remarks on the Americans were omitted.
13. *Protokoll über den Vierten Kongress,* p. 149. The English summary of Dunne's speech in *International Press Correspondence,* March 29, 1928, p. 402, actually falsifies its purport. These "editorial" changes in translation or abridgement occurred frequently and make many of the English versions of Comintern and Profintern documents untrustworthy.
14. *Protokoll über den Vierten Kongress,* p. 201. The English version in *International Press Correspondence,* March 29, 1928, p. 402, simply omits this portion of Gitlow's speech. Gitlow devotes ten pages to the congress without telling what he himself said (*I Confess,* pp. 453–63). Gitlow mistakenly calls himself "head of the American delegation" (ibid., p. 458); the chairman of the American delegation was Jack Johnstone (Minutes of the Political Committee, February 29, 1928, and *Labor Unity,* July 1928, p. 22).
15. *Protokoll über den Vierten Kongress,* pp. 224–27.
16. Ibid., pp. 274–75. The quotation from Lovestone seems to be a distortion of a passage in *The Communist,* November 1927, p. 432.
17. *Protokoll über den Vierten Kongress,* p. 354.
18. Ibid., pp. 617–23. The English version of this resolution in *Report of the Fourth Congress of the R.I.L.U.* (London: National Minority Movement, 1928, pp. 135–42) is such an obviously inferior translation from the German that I have retranslated some of the key passages that had been garbled, but the sense remains the same. Both the German and English versions omitted the passage calling for a

new miners' union, which appears only in the complete mimeographed version attached to the Minutes of the Political Committee, May 16, 1928.

19. Neither Lozovsky's criticisms of the American party, the American resistance to his pressure, nor the final American resolution ever appeared in the *Daily Worker*'s reports of the congress. Falsely, however, the paper gave the impression that William F. Dunne had spoken up in favor of new, revolutionary unions (*Daily Worker*, March 24, 1928, p. 1). *The Communist* never devoted an article or as much as a page to the congress. The T.U.E.L.'s *Labor Unity* never published the American resolution. Its first article on the congress by Morris Yusem, later known as George Morris, gave no idea whatever of the American delegation's experiences (June 1928, pp. 26–27). A second article by Jack Johnstone appeared three months after the congress and disclosed for the first time "sharp criticism" of the Americans "to focus their attention on this new emphasis on the building of new unions," which, it claimed falsely, "has always been a part of the T.U.E.L. program" and did not mean "an endorsement of the dual union philosophy of the I.W.W." (*Labor Unity*, July 1928, pp. 22–25). By this time, the American Communists had adjusted themselves to the congress's decisions. The English version of the American resolution in the *Report of the Fourth Congress of the R.I.L.U.* was published in London in July 1928 and became available in the United States some time later. To date, the only source that contains the story of the American delegation is the German *Protokoll*, a relatively rare publication.
20. A. Lozovsky, "Results and Prospects of the United Front," *The Communist International*, March 15, 1928, p. 146.
21. The "Save-the-Miners' Union Call" appears in *The Communist*, March 1928, pp. 175–80. An enthusiastic Communist report of the April 1 conference appeared in *Labor Unity*, May 1928, pp. 3–6, 21–22.
22. *International Press Correspondence*, August 23, 1928, pp. 932–33; August 25, 1928, pp. 971–72; October 30, 1928, pp. 1397–1400, 1420; November 8, 1908, pp. 1477; Ypsilon, *Pattern for World Revolution*, pp. 121, 191–92; H. M. Wicks, *Eclipse of October* (Chicago: Challenge, 1957), pp. 203–208.
23. Minutes of the Political Committee, March 19, 1928. Gitlow relates his surprise at learning of Pepper's return to the U.S. (*I Confess*, p. 459).
24. *The Communist*, May 1928, pp. 297–306.
25. After the May 1928 plenum, Foster, Cannon, and Lovestone stated their respective positions in *The Communist*, July 1928, which also contains the plenum's trade-union resolution, originally drafted by Foster.
26. *The Communist*, July 1928, p. 433.

27. Zack's articles appeared in the *Daily Worker,* May 14 and 28, and June 10, 1927; the Comintern's rejection of his position, ibid., August 3, 1927; the anti-Zack article by Max Bedacht, *The Communist,* July–August 1927, pp. 266–74. Zack's appeal, dated July 30, 1927, addressed to Kuusinen, is attached to the Minutes of the Political Committee for August 4, 1927.
28. *The Communist,* July 1928, p. 392.
29. Ibid., p. 409.
30. Jay Lovestone, *The Communist,* November 1927, p. 428.
31. *The Communist,* January–February 1929, p. 78.
32. *Daily Worker,* July 16, 1928 (textile) and July 23, 1928 (mine).
33. *Acceptance Speeches: William Z. Foster and Benjamin Gitlow* (New York: Workers Library, 1928), p. 24.
34. *The Communist,* April 1928, p. 198.
35. Saul Alinsky, *John L. Lewis* (New York: Putnam, 1949), p. 58. The author added this note: "A letter containing this excerpt was sent to William Z. Foster, chairman of the Communist Party of America, on August 23, 1949, requesting his comment for publication. It was unacknowledged."

    Nine years later, Foster passed up another opportunity to deny the authenticity of this quotation. In a review of *The American Communist Party* by Irving Howe and Lewis Coser, he devoted seven paragraphs to denying that the Communists had betrayed the "Save the Union" movement in the mine union, but he did not challenge their citation of his answer to Powers Hapgood (*The Worker,* December 14, 1958, p. 11).
36. Minutes of the Political Committee, April 11 and 20, and May 25, 1928.
37. "Resolution on Decisions of February Session of CEC of Workers (Communist) Party of America, Passed at Political Secretariat of ECCI on April 13, 1928," attached to the Minutes of the Political Committee, May 16, 1928.
38. The Panken incident probably hurt both sides. The New York Communists proposed a united Labor Ticket to the New York Socialists and offered to back Judge Jacob Panken, a Socialist, for re-election in the Second District Municipal Court of Manhattan. Panken immediately denounced the Communist offer; the Communists then repudiated him but asked their members and followers to vote for him in the absence of a Communist candidate. Panken was defeated by a close vote (*New Leader,* October 15, 1927; *Daily Worker,* October 10, 12, 13, 1928).
39. *The Platform of the Class Struggle: National Platform of the Workers (Communist) Party* (New York: Workers Library, 1928). The 1924 platform had also come out for "a Soviet Government and the Dictatorship of the Proletariat" (*Daily Worker,* August 6, 1924). But the 1932 platform, though Leftist in tendency for the period, limited

itself to "a revolutionary workers' and farmers' government" and "United States of Soviet America," but, significantly, omitted the "Dictatorship of the Proletariat" (*Communist Election Platform*, New York: Workers Library, 1932).

40. *Acceptance Speeches*, 1928, pp. 12, 47.

CHAPTER 14: THE SIXTH WORLD CONGRESS

1. Stalin, *Works*, Vol. XI, p. 334.
2. Boris Souvarine, *Stalin* (New York: Alliance Book Corp., 1939), pp. 482–85; Stalin, *Works*, Vol. XI, p. 333.
3. The advertisement for Bukharin's *Building Up Socialism* (London: Communist Party of Great Britain, 1926) appeared for the first time in *The Communist International* (London ed.), November 30, 1926, and for the last time, April 1, 1928, after which it was briefly listed with other works from May 1 to July 15, 1928, and then dropped.
4. Stalin, *Works*, Vol. XII, pp. 30–1, 38.
5. *International Press Correspondence*, July 30, 1928, pp. 725–26.
6. Ibid., p. 728.
7. The story was first told by Stalin the following year (*Works*, Vol. XII, pp. 21–25). According to Stalin, there were three more principal differences between the original theses of Bukharin and those of the Russian delegation: Bukharin had merely stated that it was necessary to fight against Social-Democracy, instead of emphasizing the fight against "Left" Social-Democracy; he had spoken of fighting against the "Right deviation," but not against "conciliation towards the Right deviation"; and he had omitted mentioning the necessity for "iron discipline" in the Communist parties. Bukharin's presentation of the amendment on the third period took place at the sixteenth session (*International Press Correspondence*, August 13, 1928, p. 864).
8. Interview with Lovestone, June 23, 1954.
9. The atmosphere at the congress has been described by those present:

   "Neumann and Lominadze were given the task of preparing things in the Comintern. From each delegation they selected a few who seemed to them worthy of confidence, and whispered in their ears: 'Bukharin is finished. He is a dangerous opportunist. If he isn't eliminated soon from the Russian leadership, there will be famine in the cities. In the Comintern he works hand in glove with all the renegades.'" (Ypsilon, *Pattern for World Revolution*, p. 120.)

   Stalinist lobbyists in the corridors, hotels, restaurants, and elsewhere "would cautiously observe that everything at the congress was not as it appeared on the surface, and that it was necessary to be alert to the 'right danger'; and if the delegate with whom one of the 'visitors' had managed to engage in conversation seemed interested he would usually be solemnly and confidentially permitted to share secret information 'from a high source' that many who were prominent in that convention never would attend another" (Wicks, *Eclipse of October*, p. 197).

10. *International Press Correspondence*, August 13, 1928, p. 874.
11. Ibid., November 23, 1928, p. 1573 (united front from below and trade-union line) and p. 1571 ("The ideology of class cooperation—the official ideology of Social Democracy—has many points of contact with fascism"). The idea was first broached by Zinoviev and Stalin in 1924.
12. Cannon to Draper, February 1, 1956 (published in *International Socialist Review*, Spring 1957, p. 62).
13. "The Right Danger in the American Party" first appeared in *The Militant*, November 15, 1928, and then in the *Daily Worker*, December 11, 1928.
14. *International Press Correspondence*, August 3, 1928, p. 781 (Dunne) and p. 788 (Pepper); August 13, 1928, p. 845 (Bittelman); August 18, 1928, p. 921 (Foster); August 23, 1928, p. 937 (Lovestone). Other American speakers, excluding those on the Negro question, were: Cannon, Weinstone, Browder [Dixon], Engdahl, Darcy, Gomez, Johnstone, and Wolfe.
15. Ibid., August 3, 1928, p. 781 (Dunne); August 13, 1928, p. 841 (Cannon) and pp. 845–46 (Bittelman); August 18, 1928, p. 914 (Lozovsky) and p. 921 (Foster); August 23, 1928, pp. 932–33 (Lominadze); August 25, 1928, p. 972 (Lominadze); October 30, 1928, p. 1420 (Neumann) and pp. 1425–26 (Petrovsky-Bennet); November 8, 1928, p. 1462 (Lominadze).
16. Ibid., August 23, 1928, p. 938.
17. There is a cable by Lovestone from Moscow which apparently relates among other things to his feud with Lozovsky at the congress (*Investigation of Un-American Propaganda Activities*, Vol. VII, p. 4599). But some of the references, especially to Stalin, seem dubious. However, Cannon has confirmed "the particularly impudent attacks which Lovestone and others made on Lozovsky" in the American Commission (Cannon to Draper, May 31, 1955). According to a Lovestoneite source, Lozovsky once proposed an amendment attacking the Lovestone leadership at a subcommittee of the Political Committee and stormed out when it was voted down (*Revolutionary Age*, December 15, 1929, p. 13).
18. *Revolutionary Age*, December 15, 1929, p. 12. This Lovestoneite source also states: "After this session of the Senioren Konvent Comrade Lovestone reported to the American delegation on what had happened there. Then Lovestone presented a motion condemning speculation and the rumors about differences, etc., in fact repeating the unanimous declaration of the Russian Polburo almost word for word. This motion was adopted—but *Browder, Foster, Bittelman, Cannon, Gomez, Siskind and Johnstone* (*the minority of the delega-*

tion) voted against it!" ("The Truth about the 'Corridor Congress,' " *Revolutionary Age,* December 15, 1929, p. 13.)

19. Cannon to Draper, February 1, 1956 (published in *International Socialist Review,* Spring 1957, pp. 64–65).
20. Bittelman's report is mentioned in the Lovestone-Pepper statement, *Daily Worker,* December 28, 1928.
21. *International Press Correspondence,* August 16, 1928, p. 876.
22. *Appeal to the Comintern* (1919) (see Note 60, Chapter 18) clearly states that the letter was sent by Foster and Johnstone but refers to the interview as Foster's alone. I have been told that the interview was arranged so hurriedly that Foster could not get one of the more important members of his faction to accompany him. According to another Lovestoneite source, Gitlow's cable about the Foster-Johnstone letter "was brought to the attention of the leaders of the Russian delegation. The matter was referred to the International Control Commission and was taken up in a special session of the Russian delegation. On the morning after this session, the meeting day of the last Senioren Konvent, Comrade Manuilsky came to Comrade Lovestone and said: 'What kind of stupidities did this man Foster again commit? He should be a little more careful at any rate' " ("The Truth About the 'Corridor Congress,' " *Revolutionary Age,* December 15, 1929, p. 13). Gitlow tells the story of the pilfered letter in *I Confess,* pp. 501–504. Cannon recalls that Foster reported on the interview to their factions (Cannon to Draper, May 31, 1955). But this is one historic occasion that Foster himself has never written about!
23. *Stalin's Speeches on the American Communist Party* (New York: Central Committee, Communist Party, U.S.A., 1929), p. 16.
24. Interview with Manuel Gomez, October 5, 1959.
25. *International Press Correspondence,* November 21, 1928, pp. 1538–39. Johnstone referred to the disputed section as paragraph 49 of the theses, "The International Situation and the Tasks of the Communist International," but it was later renumbered and appears as No. 52 in the published version.
26. Ibid., November 21, 1928, p. 1539.
27. Ibid., November 23, 1928, p. 1576.
28. Ibid., December 12, 1928, p. 1676.

Chapter 15: The Negro Question

1. Shannon, *The Socialist Party of America,* pp. 50–53; Kipnis, *The American Socialist Movement 1897–1912,* pp. 130–34; Ginger, *The Bending Cross,* p. 260; Sterling D. Spero and Abram L. Harris, *The Black Worker* (New York: Columbia University Press, 1931), pp. 402–14.
2. John R. Commons and Associates, *History of Labour in the United*

States, Vol. II, pp. 134–38; Spero and Harris, op. cit., pp. 16–115, 328–36; Paul Frederick Brissenden, *The I.W.W.* (New York: Columbia University, 1920), pp. 84, 208.

3. Herbert Aptheker, "Consciousness of Negro Nationality: An Historical Survey," *Political Affairs,* June 1949, pp. 89–95. The first example cited by Aptheker is the remark of the Negro poetess Phillis Wheatley in 1772, on learning that many Negroes were embracing Christianity: "It gives me very great pleasure to hear of so many of my nation seeking with eagerness the way of true felicity."
4. *A Documentary History of the Negro People in the United States,* edited by Herbert Aptheker (New York: Citadel, 1951), Vol. I, pp. 326–29 (Delany); Vol. II, pp. 646, 147–48 (African Emigration Association); pp. 713–27 (exodus); pp. 757–58 (Bishop Turner); pp. 648–49 notes (Negro state). Despite the tendentious nature of his editorial comment, Aptheker's documentary history contains long-neglected and richly rewarding material and represents one of the few noteworthy historical contributions by an American Communist.
5. The pioneer work in this field was done by Herbert Aptheker in the article previously cited in *Political Affairs,* June 1949, and the two-volume *Documentary History* (1951). Communist works on the subject before 1949 never mentioned these American Negro antecedents. But they play an important part in William Z. Foster's *The Negro People in American History* (New York: International, 1954).
6. E. D. Cronon, *Black Moses* (Madison, Wis.: University of Wisconsin Press, 1955); John Hope Franklin, *From Slavery to Freedom* (New York: Knopf, 1947), pp. 481–83.
7. "The New Negro—What Is He?" (*Messenger,* August 1920, pp. 73–74). "Soviet government proceeds apace. It bids fair to sweep over the whole world. The sooner the better. On with the dance!" (ibid., May–June 1919, p. 8). But the same issue betrayed mixed feelings, as shown a few pages later, about the American Left Wing Manifesto (ibid., pp. 21–22).
8. Harry H. Jones, "The Crisis in Negro Leadership," *The Crisis,* March 1920, p. 256.
9. *Manifesto and Program,* p. 18. The program of the United Communist Party of 1920 contained a similar paragraph (*The Communist,* June 12, 1920, p. 14). The program adopted by the Second Convention of the Communist Party of America dropped out all reference to the Negro problem (*The Communist,* August 1, 1920). Also without mention of the Negro problem was the program of the Communist Party of America of May 1921, representing the unification of the former Communist and United Communist parties (*The Communist,* July 1921, pp. 19–23).
10. It has not been possible to determine the exact dates of their en-

trance into the Communist movement. According to Cyril Briggs, there were only two Negro Communists, Huiswoud and one Hendricks, unidentified, when Briggs joined the party in 1921 (Briggs to Draper, June 4, 1958). *Revolutionary Radicalism* mistakenly listed the future Communists, Richard B. Moore and Cyril V. Briggs, as contributing editors of the *Messenger* (Vol. II, p. 1483). This apparently led Spero and Harris into making the same mistake (op. cit., p. 389) and evidently misled Wilson Record (*The Negro and the Communist Party,* Chapel Hill, N.C.: University of North Carolina Press, 1951, p. 44) as well as William Z. Foster (*The Negro People in American History,* p. 431). I have been assured by both Moore and Briggs that they were never associated with the *Messenger* and did not leave the Socialist party for the Communist. Fort-Whiteman was listed as the *Messenger*'s drama critic (November 1917) and Huiswoud contributed an article on Dutch Guiana (December 1919, pp. 22–23). Huiswoud's name is frequently spelled Huiswood. Foster's histories of both the Communist party and the Negro people do not even mention him.

11. Lenin, *Selected Works,* Vol. X, p. 231.
12. John Reed, "The World Congress of the Communist International," *The Communist* [U.C.P.], No. 10 (1920), pp. 2–3.
13. *Der Zweite Kongress der Kommunistischen Internationale: Protokoll der Verhandlungen,* pp. 152–57.
14. *The Communist* [U.C.P.], No. 10 (1920), p. 3.
15. Claude McKay, *A Long Way From Home,* p. 206.
16. Joseph Zack's testimony, *Subversion in Racial Unrest,* Part I, p. 37. On inquiry for further details about the letter, Zack wrote: "It had no bearing on self-determination, but did raise some of the issues of social justice, equality, etc." (Zack to Draper, April 18, 1958). I have not been able to find any other evidence of this letter, but there is no doubt that Zack, whether as a result of this letter or not, was the first to be put in charge of Negro work. He had been section organizer in Yorkville and Harlem in 1919–20 (*Subversive Activities Control Board,* p. 1412).
17. J. P. Collins [Joseph Zack] and John Bruce [Israel Amter?], "The Party and the Negro Struggle," *The Communist,* October 1921, p. 20, and November 1921, pp. 15–16. Zack says that Amter used to edit his articles; therefore Amter was most likely his collaborator, "John Bruce" (Zack to Draper, April 11, 1958). Amter's article on "The Black Victims of Imperialism" in *The Communist International,* Nos. 26–27 (1923), under his own name, strengthens the likelihood that he was "John Bruce."
18. *The Toiler,* January 7, 1922. Foster attempts to give this program the distinction of being "a long step ahead" of the 1919 program by singling out the Negro question as a "special one." He attributes

it to the fact that the American Communists were "by then more familiar with Lenin's historic writings" (*The Negro People in American History,* p. 455). The wording of the 1921 program is far more attributable to the fact that, in line with the Workers party's general approach at its inception, it was more loosely and more popularly written to appeal to a broader audience than the then underground Communist party.

19. I am indebted for this personal information to Mr. Briggs with whom I engaged in an extended correspondence in 1958. James H. Anderson, founder and publisher of the *Amsterdam News,* also held the nominal title of editor, but Mr. Briggs has informed me: "For several years up to my resignation from the paper I was editor in all but name."
20. *Amsterdam News,* September 5 and 19, 1917.
21. "Liberty for All!" *Amsterdam News,* 1918 (caps. in original). I have seen this clipping, in Mr. Briggs' possession, but it had been marked only with the year and not the exact date. Similar passages from other editorials in the *Amsterdam News* were cited by Briggs in an article, "The Negro Press as a Class Weapon," *The Communist,* August 1929, pp. 453–60, but the originals are not available. Foster's *History of the Negro People* cites Aptheker's article in *Political Affairs,* June 1949, as authority for the statement that "the *Amsterdam News* declared that the Negro people had as much right to self-determination as the Hungarians and Czechs" in 1919 (p. 478). Aptheker's article does not mention the *Amsterdam News;* "Hungarians and Czechs" should be Poles and Serbs; and the date could not have been 1919.
22. *The Crusader,* September 1919, pp. 11–12, and April 1921, p. 8 (italics in original). I am indebted to Mrs. Dorothy Porter, supervisor of the Moorland Foundation, for locating fourteen issues of *The Crusader* for me in the Howard University library, and to Mrs. Jean Blackwell, curator of the Schomburg Collection, for finding four copies in the Harlem branch of the New York Public Library (three of them duplicates of those at Howard).
23. *The Crusader,* November 1918, p. 6; October 1919, p. 11; December 1919, pp. 9–10.
24. Ibid., April 1921, p. 9. An earlier statement in this direction reads: "The Negro must also cooperate with the forces that are fighting his enemies: capitalism, bourbonism and reaction" (ibid., January 1920, p. 5). A later statement tied up a Negro state in Africa with equal rights in the United States in the following way: "Just as the Negro in the United States can never hope to win equal rights with his white neighbors until Africa is liberated and a strong Negro state (or states) erected on that continent, so, too, we can never liberate Africa unless, and until, the American Section of the Negro Race is

made strong enough to play the part for a free Africa that the Irish in America now play for a free Ireland" (ibid., November 1921, p. 15).

25. Ibid., April 1920, p. 5, and November 1921, pp. 3, 17; Cronon, op. cit., p. 75.
26. *The Crusader,* December 1919, p. 32, and November 1921, p. 32. Earlier, *The Crusader* had advertised itself as the "Publicity Organ of the Hamitic League of the World" (June 1919, p. 1). This so-called Hamitic League, with headquarters in Omaha, Nebraska, set itself the task of uniting the so-called Hamitic peoples, the chief ethnic group of North Africa. One of its leaders, George Wells Parker, made contact with Briggs and they agreed to support each other (Briggs to Draper, April 14, 1958). The reference to the Hamitic League was removed from *The Crusader* in the issue of January 1921.
27. Wilson Record merely mentions its existence (op. cit., p. 43). William A. Nolan refers briefly to it as "consisting mainly of West Indian Negroes living in the United States," which was rather true of New York (*Communism Versus the Negro,* Chicago: Regnery, 1951, p. 29). Foster's *The Negro People in American History* never mentions it. His *History of the Communist Party in the United States* refers to it once erroneously (p. 268). Harry Haywood's *Negro Liberation* (New York: International, 1948) also refers to it once, partially incorrectly (p. 204).
28. Theodore Burrell, *The Crusader,* November 1921, p. 6.
29. Briggs to Draper, March 17, 1958. *The Crusader*'s circulation was put at 33,000 in Frederick G. Detweiler's *The Negro Press in the United States* (Chicago: University of Chicago Press, 1922), p. 77. There were seven degrees of Brotherhood "as per the ancient Egyptian rule," of which the first went automatically to anyone who joined and the second to those who performed some service for the organization, with none in any higher degree "so far" (*The Crusader,* November 1921, p. 23).
30. The A.B.B.'s program presents a problem. None of fifteen available issues of *The Crusader* contains one. The only existing program appears in a dubious source, R. M. Whitney, *Reds in America* (New York: The Beckwith Press, 1924), pp. 190–93. It was one of the documents seized in the Bridgman raid of the underground Communist convention in 1922. Though this book is largely unbalanced and irresponsible, the documents reproduced are authentic and verifiable. In reply to an inquiry, Mr. Briggs wrote: "The quotation from Whitney's book on the Brotherhood's program strikes me as trustworthy" (Briggs to Draper, May 1, 1958). Nevertheless, the tenor of this version of the Brotherhood's Program and Aims indicates that it was probably not the original one but rather a later one influenced by the tie-up with the Communists in 1921. To compli-

cate the problem, there exists a typewritten interview with Cyril Briggs by Carl Offord, dated July 27, 1939, in the files of the Federal Writers Project deposited in the Schomburg Collection of the New York Public Library. Much of this interview, beginning with the first assertion that the African Blood Brotherhood was formed in the fall of 1917, has proven untrustworthy in the light of further research. In it, however, Briggs told Offord about a 6-point program in which point 2 reads: "Self-determination for the Negro in states where he constituted a majority." The major difficulty with this version is that no such programmatic demand was ever reflected in the pages of *The Crusader,* and the wording raises the suspicion that Mr. Briggs' memory in 1939 was partially influenced by the later Communist program. It is unfortunate that no first-hand copy of the A.B.B.'s program, especially the original one, has yet turned up.

31. *New York Times,* June 4 and 5, 1921. One story reported that the A.B.B. claimed a membership of 50,000!
32. *Subversion in Racial Unrest,* Part I, p. 37. Briggs says that his first contacts with the Communists came through Robert Minor and Rose Pastor Stokes, not Zack, but he agrees that Zack worked with him personally "as CP liaison" (Briggs to Draper, March 17, 1958).
33. Fort-Whiteman and Moore were connected at different times with the Socialist movement, the African Blood Brotherhood, and then the Communist party, but the exact sequence remains obscure. Briggs writes: "Huiswoud, Haywood and Fort-Whiteman were not among the founders of the Brotherhood. All three came in later. The last two were recruited into the party from the Brotherhood. The Supreme Council approved and aided such recruitment. Its majority, that is" (Briggs to Draper, March 17, 1958).
34. This legend goes as far back as 1922. Without naming the African Blood Brotherhood, James Carr (L. E. Katterfeld), then the American representative to the Comintern, wrote that the party had formed a group for agitation among Negroes (*International Press Correspondence,* March 8, 1922, p. 135). Harry Haywood gave it currency in *Negro Liberation* (1948): "The organization of the African Blood Brotherhood, with its organ, *The Crusader,* brought together left-wing split-offs of the Garvey movement and the Negro Communists" (p. 204). But the Brotherhood was organized before there were Negro Communists. Foster departed even further from the facts: "Among the earliest organized expressions of this Communist policy was the formation of the African Blood Brotherhood, with its paper, *The Crusader*" (*History of the Communist Party of the United States,* p. 268).
35. *Protokoll des III. Kongresses,* p. 1036.
36. Billings [Huiswoud], *Protokoll des Vierten Kongresses,* pp. 692–697.
37. Ibid., pp. 698–99. Despite the text of his speech in the *Protokoll,*

McKay later gave the impression that he had refused Zinoviev's invitation to speak at the congress (*A Long Way From Home*, pp. 172–73).

38. *Resolutions and Theses of the Fourth Congress*, pp. 84–87.
39. J. Steklov, "The Awakening of a Race," *International Press Correspondence*, November 24, 1922, pp. 825–26.
40. Ivon Jones, "Africa's Awakening," ibid., June 14, 1923, p. 422.
41. I. Amter, "The Black Victims of Imperialism," *The Communist International*, Nos. 26–27 [1923], p. 119.
42. "America, as the cultural center of the Negro world, must be called upon to furnish the intellectual leaders of the Negro people of the entire world" (Robert Minor, *The Liberator*, August 1924, p. 25).

    "The American Communist Negroes are the historical leaders of their comrades in Africa" (William F. Dunne, *The Workers Monthly*, April 1925, p. 260).
43. "Resolution on Negro Question," *The Second Year*, pp. 125–27.
44. *Protokoll des V. Kongresses*, Vol. II, pp. 580–81.
45. Ibid., Vol. II, p. 699.
46. Ibid., pp. 666–69 ("Jackson," the pseudonym of Fort-Whiteman); p. 707 (Amter), and p. 1031 (Commission).
47. *The Fourth National Convention*, p. 17. Fort-Whiteman was the "Negro comrade" in question.
48. James Jackson [Lovett Fort-Whiteman], "The Negro in America," and "Editorial Comment on 'The Negro Question,' " *The Communist International*, February 1925, pp. 50–54.
49. Robert Minor, "The Black Ten Millions," *The Liberator*, March 1924, pp. 15–17. The first part of this article appeared in the February 1924 issue.
50. Minutes of the Executive Council, May 14, 1924, p. 9.
51. *Daily Worker*, July 29 and 30, 1924 (editorials), and August 5, 1924 (first letter). When a reader complained that these editorials were too friendly to Garveyism, the editors explained that the Communists were not trying to win over Garvey but the masses behind him (August 9, 1924).
52. *Daily Worker*, August 9, 1924 (Minor), August 14, 1924 (second letter), and August 21, 1924 (editorial).
53. "In accord with the instructions of the Communist International, most of our work has been carried on in connection with the American Negro Labor Congress," *The 4th National Convention*, p. 18.
54. Minutes of the Political Committee [in this case, the minutes are headed "Politbureau"], October 12, 1925. The minutes for October 19, 1925, are missing from my collection.
55. Robert Minor, "The First Negro Workers' Congress," *The Workers Monthly*, December 1925, p. 69. The congress was reported in the *Daily Worker*, October 26–31, 1925.
56. Lovett Fort-Whiteman, "American Negro Labor Congress," *Inter-*

national Press Correspondence, August 27, 1925, p. 983. Also see, M. Rabinovitch, "The American Negro Labor Congress," ibid., December 10, 1925, pp. 1305–306.

57. "Preliminary Report on Negro Labor Congress by John J. Ballam, CEC Representative," attached to Minutes of the Political Committee, January 4, 1926. Ballam's report contains this recommendation: "Immediate request through our representatives in X for substantial bequest of not less than $1000."
58. James W. Ford, *The Negro and the Democratic Front* (New York: International, 1938), p. 82.
59. Carr, *The Bolshevik Revolution,* Vol. III, pp. 268–69. In 1925, it contained two groups of students—one from the Soviet East and the other from colonial and dependent countries (Stalin, *Works,* Vol. VII, p. 135).
60. *The 4th National Convention,* p. 18.
61. I am indebted to both Otto Hall and Harry Haywood for interviews. Mr. Hall also wrote for me a memorandum on his family background and early political activity.
62. It is so called, for example, in the report of Otto Hall's return to the United States in 1928 (*Daily Worker,* November 19, 1928).
63. Interviews with Otto Hall, November 28 and 29, 1958.
64. *A Long Way from Home,* p. 158.
65. Lenin, *Selected Works,* Vol. XII, pp. 198–201 (italics in original). There is another reference to "oppressed and downtrodden Negroes" in the South on p. 267.
66. Harry Haywood once cited these passages as the "basis" used by the Comintern's Second Congress to place the American Negro question "as a problem of an oppressed nation" (*The Communist,* September 1933, p. 891).
67. It was first published in the Russian magazine *Bolshevik,* January 31, 1935, p. 46 (editor's note) and p. 49. It appears in Lenin's works, *Leninskiisbornik* (1937), Vol. XXX, pp. 306–307, and *Sochineniia* (1949), Vol. XXIII, pp. 296–97. I am indebted to Mrs. Arline Paul of The Hoover Institution, Stanford, California, for careful checking of these references, to Mrs. Esther Corey for checking the translation, and to Bertram D. Wolfe for pointing out the relevance of the second passage.
68. The first passage appeared for the first time in English in an article by Claudia Jones in *Political Affairs,* January 1946, p. 71, but one word, "only," was omitted, and the date mistakenly given as 1913. I have been assured by Harry Haywood that this quotation was not available in the discussion in Moscow in the nineteen-twenties.
69. Sen Katayama, *International Press Correspondence,* August 13, 1928, p. 856. But it should be considered also that Katayama suddenly remembered Lenin's view of the Negroes as a "subject nation" just when it was needed to bolster the new line at the Sixth

World Congress. For Katayama's interest in the Negro question, see Claude McKay, *The Crisis,* December 1923, p. 64.

70. "Trotsky on the Negro Question," *International Press Correspondence,* March 15, 1923, pp. 158–59. Sixteen years later, however, Trotsky conditionally accepted the policy of Negro self-determination. He advised his American followers: "I do not propose for the party to advocate, I do not propose to inject, but only to proclaim our obligation to support the struggle for self-determination if the Negroes themselves want it" (*Internal Bulletin No. 9,* Socialist Workers party, June 1939, p. 14).
71. William F. Dunne, "Our Party and the Negro Masses," *Daily Worker,* August 13, 1925.
72. Jay Lovestone, "The Great Negro Migration," *The Workers Monthly,* February 1926, pp. 179–84.
73. "The migration of Negroes from the South to the North is another means of proletarianization, consequently the existence of this group as a reserve of capitalist reaction is likewise being undermined" (Lovestone, *Daily Worker,* September 22, 1927). "The great migration and industrialization of these Negro masses further robs the bourgeoisie of a tremendous reserve force of social reaction" (Lovestone, ibid., February 17, 1928).
74. Minutes of the Political Committee, April 11, 1928 (subcommittee) and May 30, 1928 (vote). Only Minor abstained on the ground that he had not had enough time to study it thoroughly.
75. "Policies on Negro Work, Submitted by J. Swift," attached to the Minutes of the Political Committee, May 30, 1928. "J. Swift" was Pepper's party pseudonym in this period. The resolution in *The Communist,* July 1928, pp. 418–19, was based on the resolution of May 30, 1928.
76. *Daily Worker,* December 11, 1928. This document, incidentally, confirms Pepper's authorship of the May 30, 1928, resolution.
77. Kruse to Draper, April 27, 1958 (interview) and May 19, 1958 (letter). Mr. Kruse placed this discussion toward the end of 1927 or beginning of 1928. Otto Hall thought that he had also attended this meeting.
78. Zack to Draper, April 18, 1958 (letter) and Zack's testimony, *Subversion in Racial Unrest,* Part I, pp. 34–35.
79. Richard Pipes, *The Formation of the Soviet Union* (Cambridge: Harvard University Press, 1954, pp. 37–38) points out that the official English translation incorrectly renders the words "stable community arising on the foundation of a common language" as "stable community of language" (J. Stalin, *Marxism and the National Question,* New York: International, 1942, p. 12).
80. Various maps of this Black Belt were later drawn on the basis of the 1930 census: J. S. Allen, *The American Negro* (New York: International, 1932), p. 5; James S. Allen, *Negro Liberation* (New

York: International, 1932), cover; *The Communist Position on the Negro Question* (New York: Workers Library, 1932), cover. According to the 1920 census, over 3,000,000 Negroes constituted the majority in 219 contiguous counties in the Black Belt.

81. *International Press Correspondence,* September 19, 1928, p. 1156. I have not been able to identify two of the five American Negro members, "Farmer" and "Carlstone." Haywood and Ford used their own names, but Hall is listed as "Jones." The rest of the commission represented France, South America, Italy, Spain, Belgium, Palestine, Syria, Turkey, Indonesia, India, and the Profintern. Haywood called it the Negro Sub-Commission of the Colonial Commission (*Die Kommunistische Internationale,* September 5, 1928, p. 2253).
82. The discussion is summarized, in somewhat different terms, by Jones [Hall], *International Press Correspondence,* October 30, 1928, p. 1393.
83. Haywood and Nassanoff, "The Tasks of the American Communist Party Regarding Negro Work" (italics in original). This document was contained in a file of material consisting of original copies (on Russian-style tissue paper) of discussion articles and speeches at the Negro Commission in 1928, now in the possession of a former American Communist who attended the Sixth World Congress as a delegate. I understand that the Haywood-Nassanoff document was one of two or three on which Haywood worked and that a later document was submitted by Haywood and Hathaway. The file also contains the text of a speech by Bittelman, a resolution signed by "N. Nasonov," and a pro-Negro Soviet Republic resolution, unsigned but probably by Pepper. I have adopted Nasanov as the uniform spelling, but the name appears in various transliterations from the Russian.
84. The only one to appear in the English edition was the first article by A. Shiek, "The Comintern Programme and the Racial Problem," *The Communist International* (London), August 15, 1928, pp. 407–11. Owing to the suspension of the English edition for four months, September–December 1928, the other three appeared in the German and Russian editions: James Ford–William Wilson, "Zur Frage der Arbeit der amerikanischen Kommunistischen Partei unter den Negern," *Die Kommunistische Internationale* (Berlin), August 29, 1928, pp. 2132–46; John Pepper, "Amerikanische Negerprobleme," ibid., September 5, 1928, pp. 2245–52; Harry Haywood, "Das Negerproblem und die Aufgaben der K.P. der Vereinigten Staaten," ibid., September 5, 1928, pp. 2253–62. Pepper's article, "American Negro Problems," was reprinted in *The Communist,* October 1928, pp. 628–38, and as a pamphlet with the same title (New York: Workers Library, 1928).
85. Wilson Record has made Pepper assume the "principal responsibility" for reinterpreting the Negro problem; Record was misled into

believing that Pepper's "statements reflected the official position of the Communist International" (*The Negro and the Communist Party,* pp. 58–59, and article in *The Phylon Quarterly,* Fall 1958, p. 324). William A. Nolan has mistakenly written: "There can be little doubt that Pepper was correctly expressing the mind of the Comintern, since the demand for a Negro Soviet Republic was explicitly repeated in the 1930 Resolution" (op. cit., p. 47). The 1930 resolution explicitly states: "Moreover, the Party cannot make its stand for this slogan dependent upon any conditions, even the condition that the proletariat has the hegemony in the national revolutionary Negro movement or that the majority of the Negro population in the Black Belt adopts the Soviet form (as Pepper demanded), etc." (*The Communist Position on the Negro Question,* p. 50).

86. Gitlow, *I Confess,* p. 481.
87. Nasanov mentioned Haywood, Hathaway, William F. Dunne, and himself as proponents of the new line ("Against Liberalism in the American Negro Question," *The Communist,* April 1930, p. 308). Bittelman appears in the file of material mentioned in Note 83, and I have been informed by a member of the commission that Foster also spoke in favor. I understand that one of those who openly opposed it was Samuel A. Darcy, then a delegate of the youth league.
88. *International Press Correspondence,* July 25, 1928, p. 708 (Fort-Whiteman); October 25, 1928, p. 1346 (Ford); October 30, 1928, p. 1393 (Hall, listed as "Jones").

    In view of these published declarations and other available indications of opposition, Wilson Record went far astray: "And yet the members of the American delegation to the Sixth World Congress gave their approval to the draft resolution without exception" (*The Negro and the Communist Party,* p. 57, and article in *The Phylon Quarterly,* p. 322). In this instance, Nolan came much closer to the truth (op. cit., p. 46). Haywood worked in the commission but did not speak at the congress.
89. *International Press Correspondence,* August 13, 1928, p. 856 (Katayama); and October 17, 1928, p. 1322 (Bennet). Dunne once touched on the subject without openly referring to self-determination (ibid., August 3, 1928, p. 781).
90. Ibid., November 8, 1928, p. 1451 (Bunting); November 21, 1928, p. 1528 (Kuusinen); December 12, 1928, p. 1674 (theses).
91. Ibid., December 12, 1928, p. 1674.
92. Padmore seems to have started the Kuusinen legend in his book, *How Russia Transformed Her Colonial Empire* (London: Dobson, 1946), p. 85. It was apparently picked up, without attribution, by Herbert Hill in an article in *The Crisis,* June–July 1951, and reprinted in a pamphlet, *The Communist Party—Enemy of Negro Equality* (New York: N.A.A.C.P., 1951), p. 2. William A. Nolan

refers to Padmore, but says more cautiously that "Stalin chose Otto Kuusinen for the task of elaborating this thesis" (op. cit., p. 46). Padmore repeated himself in *Pan-Africanism or Communism?* (London: Dobson, 1956), p. 306. But, in this latter book, he shows that his memory of American Negro movements can hardly be trusted; he makes the African Blood Brotherhood compete with the Communists for support of the Negro masses *after* the downfall of the American Negro Labor Congress (p. 305). Howe and Coser, without giving any evidence or sources, fall into the same trap by having the theory "manufactured" by Kuusinen (*The American Communist Party,* p. 206).

Gitlow was undoubtedly right when he wrote of Kuusinen: "Never was he the father of an original idea. He always phonographed the official tune of the time" (*I Confess,* p. 441).

93. *International Press Correspondence,* October 17, 1928, p. 1313. This figure was confirmed by Ford (ibid., August 3, 1928), though Briggs once wrote that "one could almost count the Negro membership on the fingers of one's hand" prior to the Sixth World Congress (*The Communist,* September 1929, p. 494). The figures for Negro membership at the time of the Sixth Convention in March 1929 vary. Stachel claimed between 150 and 200 (*The Communist,* April 1929, p. 184), but Browder later reduced it to "hardly 50 Negro members" (ibid., August 1930, p. 688).
94. *Daily Worker,* October 3, 1928 (Lovestone's report); *The Communist,* October 1928, pp. 628–38 (Pepper's article); *Daily Worker,* November 12, 1928 (editorial).
95. This first Comintern resolution on the Negro question was published in the *Daily Worker,* February 12, 1929, and reprinted in *The Communist Position on the Negro Question,* pp. 56–63.
96. This second Comintern resolution on the Negro question of October 1930 was published in *The Communist,* February 1931, pp. 153–67, and reprinted in *The Communist Position on the Negro Question,* pp. 41–56.
97. The two chief American Communist writers on Negro self-determination, James S. Allen and Harry Haywood, sometimes departed from a strict interpretation of some portions of the 1930 resolution but it is not within the province of this chapter to trace all the refinements of this policy in the next decade.
98. Otto E. Huiswoud, "World Aspects of the Negro Question," *The Communist,* February 1930, pp. 132–47.
99. Haywood, *The Communist,* August 1930, pp. 694–712.
100. The first Communist breakthrough among the Negroes came in 1930 when about 1000 were recruited (Browder, *The Communist,* August 1930, p. 689). The claimed Negro membership was about 2700 in 1935 (Stachel, ibid., July 1935, p. 627) and 5005 in 1939

(*The Party Builder,* mimeographed, July 1939, p. 12). After 1939, the Negro membership declined gradually to a small fraction of the high point.

101. The highest membership claimed for this Communist-organized "union" was 8000 (John Barnett, *The Communist,* February 1935, p. 178).
102. *Negro Liberation,* p. 216.
103. The most notable exception ever claimed by the Communists was Dr. W. E. B. DuBois, but this claim proved to be ill founded. In February 1947, DuBois wrote an introduction to an appeal to the United Nations submitted by the National Association for the Advancement of Colored People, which the Communists once chose to interpret as his endorsement of the concept of the American Negroes as a nation (*The Communist,* June 1949, p. 89). Dr. DuBois subsequently set the record straight by writing: "When we compare American Negroes with other groups, we are not comparing nations, nor even cultural groups; since American Negroes do not form a nation and are not likely to if their present fight for political integration succeeds" (*Freedom,* January 1953, p. 7).
104. These figures forced themselves on the attention of the Communists in the mid-nineteen-fifties: see John Swift, "Population Changes and Negro-White Unity," *The Communist,* August 1954, pp. 50–64; and William Z. Foster, "Notes on the Struggle for Negro Rights," ibid., pp. 20–42.
105. *The Communist,* January 1944, p. 84.
106. *The Communist Position on the Negro Question* (New York: New Century, 1947), pp. 9–13.
107. *Political Affairs,* January 1959, pp. 42–46. The major document on the change of line in 1958 on the Negro question was a 39-page supplement to *Party Affairs,* February 1959, entitled *Theoretical Aspects of the Negro Question in the United States* (issued by National Committee, Communist Party, U.S.A.). After James E. Jackson, the secretary for Southern and Negro Affairs, returned from a trip to Moscow, the international Communist organ, *World Marxist Review,* July 1959, pp. 16–24, published an article, "Some Aspects of the Negro Question in the United States," based on his report in *Theoretical Aspects of the Negro Question.*
108. Haywood was briefly associated with a small, Leftist splinter group, formed in 1958, called the "Provisional Organizing Committee for a Marxist-Leninist Communist Party" and wrote for it a defense of the old line on self-determination, *For a Revolutionary Position on the Negro Question* (mimeographed). Briggs criticized the change of line in a letter to *Political Affairs,* March 1959, pp. 58–62.
109. *Theoretical Aspects of the Negro Question,* p. 26.

Chapter 16: The Birth of American Trotskyism

1. *Protokoll der Erweiterten Exekutive,* März 1925, p. 18. Pepper was the other American member of this commission.
2. Bittelman paid his respects to Trotsky in "Lenin, Leader and Comrade," *The Workers Monthly,* January 1925, pp. 99–101. Bittelman also wrote the preface to the first American anti-Trotskyist pamphlet, *Leninism or Trotskyism* (Chicago: Workers Party of America, 1925), which contained articles and speeches by Zinoviev, Stalin, and Kamenev, but nothing by Trotsky.
3. "Tasks of the American Opposition," A Letter from Trotsky, *The Militant,* June 1, 1929. When this letter was written, Pepper and Lovestone had already lost the game to Foster, but Trotsky in exile did not yet know it.
4. *The Workers Monthly,* November 1925, pp. 37–41 (Lovestone's review); "Europe and America," a speech by Trotsky, delivered February 15, 1926 (*The Fourth International,* April 1943, pp. 125–26).
5. Michael Gold, "America Needs a Critic," *New Masses,* October 1926, pp. 7–9; Joseph Freeman, *An American Testament* (New York: Farrar and Rinehart, 1936), p. 384; Moissaye J. Olgin, *The Workers Monthly,* January 1926, p. 138.
6. Max Eastman, *Leon Trotsky: The Portrait of a Youth* (New York: Greenberg, 1925).
7. This critique was later published as *Marx and Lenin, the Science of Revolution* (New York: Boni, 1927).
8. Max Eastman, *Heroes I Have Known* (New York: Simon and Schuster, 1942), p. 256.
9. Max Eastman, *Since Lenin Died* (London: Labour Publishing Co., 1925). An American edition, published by Horace Liveright, as well as French and other translations, soon followed. Eastman's version in this book of how he came to obtain knowledge of the testament was deliberately distorted to protect Trotsky (p. 26, note, and pp. 30–31, note). Trotsky was apparently not the only one who had leaked information about the document. Only two months after the Thirteenth Congress, in July 1924, the Menshevik organ published in Berlin, *Sotsialisticheskii Vestnik,* had published a partially accurate summary, but it had not attracted much attention.
10. Stalin later told of the pressure that had been put on Trotsky (*Works,* Vol. X, pp. 178–79). Trotsky's telegram and article appeared in the *Daily Worker,* August 8, 1925. Krupskaya's repudiation appeared in *The Workers Monthly,* September 1925, p. 516.
11. *Daily Worker,* June 6, 1925 (Minor) and August 15, 1925 (C.E.C.).
12. *International Press Correspondence,* October 21, 1926, pp. 1171–73. The mood in Trotsky's group in this period is movingly conveyed by

Victor Serge, *Mémoires d'un Révolutionnaire* (Paris: Editions du Seuil, 1951), pp. 212–63. For many years, the version published by Eastman was thought to be the entire Testament. But in 1956, the Khrushchev regime released the text of the testament for the first time in Russian and two new parts were revealed, one dated December 23, 1922 and the other December 26, 1922. The authorized Russian version may be found in English in a pamphlet, V. I. Lenin, *Letter to the Congress* (Moscow: Foreign Languages Publishing House, n.d. [prob. 1957]), pp. 9–14.

13. Stalin, *Works,* Vol. X, pp. 178–82.
14. This section is largely based on the unpublished manuscript of the second volume of Max Eastman's autobiography, provisionally entitled, "Journey Through an Epoch," a sequel to his previously published *Enjoyment of Living* (New York: Harper, 1948).
15. Tim Buck mentions, without giving any details, that Spector first revealed his Trotskyist tendencies in 1925 (*30 Years: The Story of the Communist Movement in Canada,* Toronto: Progress Books, 1952, p. 67). The incident is also mentioned in *The Militant,* May 28, 1932, p. 1.
16. James P. Cannon, *The History of American Trotskyism* (New York: Pioneer, 1944).
17. *International Press Correspondence,* August 1, 1928, p. 750.
18. Leon Trotsky, *My Life,* pp. 548 and 554; *The Draft Program of the Communist International,* p. 1.
19. Introduction by Cannon, *The Draft Program of the Communist International,* p. x.
20. Cannon has suggested that Trotsky's document was translated and distributed through "some slip-up in the apparatus in Moscow" (*The History of American Trotskyism,* p. 49), but all the circumstances clearly imply a deliberate decision. A "slip-up" could easily have been rectified by withdrawal of the document at any point, and there was no necessity for a report to the Senioren Konvent as well as distribution to the Program Commission. The document was marked "Return to Secretariat," another indication of deliberate planning.
21. *The History of American Trotskyism,* pp. 49–50.
22. Wicks, *International Press Correspondence,* August 13, 1928, p. 850.
23. "The Struggle Against Trotskyism and the Right Danger," *Daily Worker,* November 16, 1928.
24. Gitlow says that Bukharin showed Lovestone a G.P.U. report of Cannon's "strong Trotskyist leanings" (*I Confess,* p. 508). Cannon accepts this evidence that he was suspected, and suggests that nothing was done about it because "they thought that maybe they could straighten me out and that this would be much better than to have an open scandal" (*The History of American Trotskyism,* pp. 50–51). He also has conjectured that "they could not bring themselves to

believe that I would do anything foolishly impractical about it. They didn't care what anyone's secret thoughts might be as long as they were not compromised by some overt action" (Cannon to Draper, February 1, 1956).

25. *International Press Correspondence,* November 21, 1928, p. 1547.
26. This section is largely based on Cannon's letter to Draper, February 1, 1956 (published in *International Socialist Review,* Spring 1957, pp. 61–65) and Cannon, *The History of American Trotskyism,* pp. 48–51. The information in Cannon's letter has been confirmed by Maurice Spector (interview, February 11, 1959).
27. Eastman's unpublished manuscript, "Journey Through an Epoch."
28. Leon Trotsky, *The Real Situation in Russia,* translated by Max Eastman (New York: Harcourt, Brace, 1928).
29. "Trotsky on Max Eastman," letter to N. I. Muralov, dated September 2, 1928, *The New International,* November 1934, pp. 125–26.
30. *The Militant,* July 13, 1946, commemorated Dr. Konikow's death with tributes containing much biographical material and a reproduction of the first page of *Bulletin No. 1.* Born in Russia, she studied in Switzerland, where, at nineteen, she was attracted to the first Russian Marxist group founded by George Plekhanov in 1888; emigrated to the United States ten years later and took an active part in both the Socialist Labor and Socialist parties; joined the Communist party at its inception in 1919; raised a family and practiced medicine.
31. *The History of American Trotskyism,* p. 52.
32. Eastman's unpublished manuscript, "Journey Through an Epoch."
33. "The Struggle Against Trotskyism and the Right Danger," *Daily Worker,* November 16, 1928. This meeting on October 2, 1928, was reported in the *Daily Worker,* October 4, 1928.
34. This statement of October 16, 1928, also signed by Aronberg, is reproduced in "The Struggle Against Trotskyism and the Right Danger," *Daily Worker,* November 16, 1928.
35. Their removal from the I.L.D. is mentioned in "The Struggle Against Trotskyism and the Right Danger" and in the Cannon-Abern-Shachtman statement, both in the *Daily Worker,* November 16, 1928.
36. The expulsions were announced in the Central Committee's declaration, "The Struggle Against Trotskyism and the Right Danger," in the *Daily Worker,* November 16, 1928, followed by the statement to the Political Committee signed by Cannon, Abern, and Shachtman.
37. Minutes of the Political Committee, Nov. 14, 1928.
38. Foster, *History of the Communist Party of the United States,* p. 270. Gitlow gives the figure as about 50 (*I Confess,* p. 571).
39. The burglary took place on December 23, 1928 (*The Militant,* January 1, 1929). An allusion was made to it in the *Daily Worker,* December 27, 1928, and the photostats appeared in the issue of Jan-

uary 8, 1929. A former Lovestoneite, William Abrams, clearly implied that the C.P was responsible for the burglary in the Jewish *Freiheit,* September 1, 1929.

40. *I Confess,* p. 491.
41. *The Militant,* February 15, 1929.
42. This conference was reported in *The Militant,* June 1, 1929.
43. Martin Abern, Albert Glotzer, and Max Shachtman, "The Situation in the American Opposition: Prospect & Retrospect," mimeographed, dated June 4, 1932, p. 2.
44. Interview with Maurice Spector, November 25, 1957; *The Worker* (Toronto), December 1, 1928, and January 19, 1929. Spector was expelled November 11, 1928. Cannon says a "substantial Canadian group was formed" (*History of American Trotskyism,* p. 62).
45. Interview with Cannon, June 4, 1957.
46. Max Shachtman, "25 Years of American Trotskyism," *The New International,* January–February 1954, p. 16.
47. It should be remembered that Cannon and Spector read only the first and third sections of the document, and this truncated version was published first (L. D. Trotsky, *The Draft Program of the Communist International: A Criticism of Fundamentals,* New York: *The Militant,* 1929).

    The second section contained a longer reference to the American party's Farmer-Labor policy, but it was not made available until the following year (*The Strategy of the World Revolution,* New York: Communist League of American, 1930). The complete text was published seven years later (Leon Trotsky, *The Third International After Lenin,* New York, Pioneer, 1936).
48. This expectation was clearly expressed by the Cannonites on the eve of Lovestone's downfall: "Foster and Bittelman are fooling the proletarian fighters in the Party with all kinds of rumors, illusions and false hopes. They are waiting for a 'cable'; a new secretarial decision; a new 'concession' from Moscow. This 'concession' will come but its whole import will be to further entrench the Lovestone faction and disarm its opponents. The present leadership of the E.C.C.I. is primarily responsible for the chaos of disruption in our Party. It is responsible for the domination of the faction of callous adventurers which ruins and discredits the Party. Help from 'Moscow' for the proletarian tendency in our Party will come only when the purifying principle struggle of the Opposition against the present leadership of the C.P.S.U. and the Comintern has been crowned with success" ("On the Eve of the Party Convention," *The Militant,* February 1, 1929, p. 3).

Chapter 17: The Runaway Convention

1. *Daily Worker,* October 2, 1928.
2. "Comintern Decision on American Question," *Daily Worker,* October 2, 1928.
3. Gitlow, *I Confess,* pp. 505–506.
4. *American Labor Year Book,* 1929, p. 144, gives 48,228. Foster's *History,* p. 263, gives 48,228 in 32 states. The figures vary because the Workers (Communist) Party appeared on the ballot in some states as the Independent party (Arkansas, Kansas, and Oregon) and as the Independent Workers party in Wisconsin.
5. Lovestone, *The Communist,* December 1928, pp. 746 and 749.
6. Pepper, *Daily Worker,* November 10, 1928, p. 6. A recent study, "The Communist Party in the Presidential Election of 1928," by Vaughn Davis Bornet (*Western Political Quarterly,* September 1958, pp. 514–38), mistakenly asserts: "If the election campaign had not been a total success from a party standpoint, Communist literature of the day does not reflect the fact" (p. 536). Bornet completely neglects the factional dispute that was whipped up by the optimistic and pessimistic interpretations of the election results.
7. "Theses of the Foster-Bittelman Minority," *Daily Worker,* December 25, 1928.
8. Leuchtenberg, *The Perils of Prosperity,* p. 234.
9. *Daily Worker,* October 3, 1928, p. 2.
10. Ibid., August 9 and 16, 1928.
11. Ibid., September 11, 1928, p. 1 (miners); September 24, 1928, p. 3 (textiles); January 2, 1929, p. 1 (needle trades).
12. Gitlow, *I Confess,* pp. 480–81. Gitlow says that he refused to carry out the telegram's orders. When he protested to Pepper against the new Negro line, he relates that Pepper answered: "Comrade Gitlow, there is much truth in what you say; but we could not help ourselves in Moscow. The Russians on the Commission could only see the American Negro question in the light of the minorities question which existed in Russia before the Revolution. Had we not fallen in line, we would have been severely condemned as deviators and khvostists [tailists] who neglect work among the Negro masses." This Pepperism rings true. The *Daily Worker* editorial of November 12, 1928, confirmed that the party came out for "the right of national self-determination for the Negroes" in the election campaign.
13. *Daily Worker,* November 12, 1928.
14. Ibid., November 29, 1928, p. 6.
15. Foster, *History of the Communist Party of the United States,* pp. 271–72.
16. *Historical Statistics of the U.S.,* p. 330 (unadjusted data). Lovestone once referred to the fact that the news of the economic upsurge

came during the Sixth World Congress (*The Communist,* January–February 1929, p. 68).

17. "Theses of C.E.C. of Workers (Communist) Party," submitted by Gitlow, Lovestone, and Pepper, *Daily Worker,* December 26, 1928.
18. *Magazine of Wall Street,* November 17, 1928, p. 101.
19. Lovestone, "The 1928 Elections," *The Communist,* December 1928, pp. 745–46.
20. Foster, *History of the Communist Party of the United States,* p. 271.
21. This paragraph is largely based on Lovestone, "Some Issues in the Party Discussion," *The Communist,* January–February 1929, pp. 64–72, and "Theses of C.E.C. of Workers (Communist) Party," submitted by Gitlow, Lovestone, and Pepper, *Daily Worker,* December 26, 1928.
22. This paragraph is largely based on the "Theses of the Foster-Bittelman Minority," *Daily Worker,* December 25, 1928.
23. "The panic in Wall Street did *not* come as a result of the decline of American capitalist economy. It came as a result of the very strength of American capitalist economy magnifying and sharpening the contradictions of world capitalism" (*The Revolutionary Age,* November 15, 1929, p. 1).
24. *Daily Worker,* December 25, 1928.
25. Ibid., January 8, 1929, p. 2.
26. Ibid., February 12, 1929, p. 3.
27. "Letter of Executive of the Comintern to the American Party," ibid., December 26, 1928.
28. Interview with Lovestone, June 28, 1954.
29. "Declaration of Central Executive Committee on the Comintern Letter of Nov. 21, to the C.E.C.," *Daily Worker,* December 26, 1928.
30. This article appeared in English in *International Press Correspondence,* October 19 and 26 and November 2, 1928. A revised translation appears in Bertram D. Wolfe, *Khrushchev and Stalin's Ghost* (New York: Praeger, 1957), pp. 295–315.
31. Stalin, *Works,* Vol. XI, p. 245.
32. Ibid., Vol. XI, p. 302.
33. *International Press Correspondence,* October 12, 1928, pp. 1293–94; Flechtheim, *Die KPD in der Weimarer Republik,* pp. 152–54.
34. Stalin, *Works,* Vol. XI, p. 315.
35. *International Press Correspondence,* December 27, 1928, pp. 1725–28.
36. "Strengthen and Deepen the Struggle Against Right Danger and Trotskyism," *Daily Worker,* December 3, 1928, p. 1.
37. Lovestone, *The Communist,* January–February 1929, p. 61. The "C.E.C. of the C.P.S.U." was a slip on Lovestone's part; it should have been "C.C." (Central Committee) of the C.P.S.U. (Communist Party of the Soviet Union).
38. Lovestone's testimony, *Investigation of Un-American Propaganda Activities,* Vol. XI, p. 7105.

39. These and other excerpts were published in the *Appeal to the Comintern* (see Note 60, Chapter 18), p. 4. The letter is dated February 20, 1929.
40. It is mentioned by Kuusinen, *Investigation of Un-American Propaganda Activities,* Vol. XI, p. 7127.
41. *Daily Worker,* December 25, 1928, p. 2.
42. The charge of Pepper-Lovestone differences was made in the Foster-Bittelman statement, "The Minority on the Results of the Plenum," and rebutted by Lovestone and Pepper in "One Line in the C.E.C. Majority," *Daily Worker,* December 28, 1928.
43. This section is largely based on an interview with Wolfe, October 6, 1953.
44. These statements were cited by Lovestone and Pepper in the *Daily Worker,* December 28, 1928, and in the statement of the C.E.C., "Foster's Right Wing Opportunism and Bittelman Opposition's Right Sectarianism," ibid., February 26, 1929. Foster never disavowed these statements publicly attributed to him twicc in the party organ, and they have been more recently confirmed to me by one who personally heard them. The next admission by Foster himself of Bittelman's ascendancy over him in this period substantiates the general tenor of their relationship at this time.
45. Foster, "As to New Lines and Old Lines," *Daily Worker,* February 12, 1929.
46. Foster, "The Decline of the American Federation of Labor," *The Communist,* January 1929, pp. 55–58.
47. Bedacht, ibid., pp. 43–46.
48. "The Opposition's Declaration Against Comrade Foster," *Daily Worker,* February 11, 1929. The eight were Bittelman, Browder, Aronberg, Hathaway, Wagenknecht, Costrell, Gomez, and Grecht.
49. Foster, "As to New Lines and Old Lines," ibid., February 12, 1929. "The Opposition's Declaration Against Comrade Foster," ibid., February 11, 1929, quotes from the article written by Bittelman on January 6, 1929, with an editorial note that it is to be printed in the paper in a few days. The quotation is identical with a portion of Bittelman's article, "Lessons of the Party Discussion," published February 16, 1929.
50. Foster, "Bourgeois Reformism and Social Reformism," ibid., February 22, 1929.
51. Foster, *History of the Communist Party of the United States,* p. 258.
52. Earl Browder and Joseph Zack, "The Right Danger and Trotskyism in America," *Daily Worker,* January 29, 1929; Earl Browder, "The New 'Progressives' in the American Federation of Labor," ibid., February 25 and 27, 1929
53. "Opposition Again Rejects Party Unity," ibid., January 21, 1929.
54. "For Party Unity on Basis of Line of Sixth World Congress," ibid., January 21, 1929.

55. This figure was given by Molotov (*Investigation of Un-American Propaganda Activities,* Vol. XI, p. 7133) and by Pollitt (*Daily Worker,* London, March 27, 1934, p. 4). Minor stated that the Lovestoneite majority was 85 per cent (*International Press Correspondence,* September 17, 1929, p. 1111). Wolfe reported only 99 delegates elected to the convention (ibid., February 15, 1929, p. 129).
56. Wolfe, "Results of Election to 6th American Party Congress," *International Press Correspondence,* February 15, 1929, p. 129.
57. Interview with Wolfe, January 22, 1954.
58. The full text of the "Open Letter of the E.C.C.I. to the Convention of the Workers (Communist) Party of America," was published in the *Daily Worker,* March 4, 1929, p. 3, and reprinted in the pamphlet *On the Road to Bolshevism* (New York: Workers Library, 1929, pp. 21–34).
59. Molotov confirmed the Comintern's decision, later withdrawn, to make Foster the new General Secretary (*Investigation of Un-American Propaganda Activities,* Vol. XI, p. 7131). Pollitt stated that one of the proposals was that "two leading members of each faction should be called to the Communist International" (*Daily Worker,* London, March 27, 1934). Stalin admitted that Dengel and Pollitt had favored the Fosterite minority (*Stalin's Speeches on the American Communist Party,* New York: Central Committee Communist Party, U.S.A., 1929, p. 18).
60. Carl Wall, *Daily Worker,* June 18, 1929.
61. Gitlow writes: "Often fights took place" (*I Confess,* p. 517). Pollitt also reported witnessing "actual physical force" (*Daily Worker,* London, March 27, 1934).
62. *Daily Worker,* March 5, 1929.
63. "The Traditional Right Wing in the American Party and Our Fight Against It," a typewritten pro-Lovestone document, dated August 17, 1929, p. 3. It is based on the Minutes of the Political Committee, March 3, 1929.
64. As previously indicated (Note 37), Lovestone placed this statement at the December 1928 plenum, but Gitlow mentions it in connection with the Sixth Convention (*I Confess,* p. 517). In any case, it represented Lovestone's position at this time.
65. This paragraph is largely based on the *Appeal to the Comintern,* pp. 2–3, because it was closest to the event and carried the endorsement of both Lovestone and Gitlow. Subsequently Gitlow gave slightly different versions, though the substance is similar, in *I Confess,* pp. 517–20, and *The Whole of Their Lives,* pp. 158–59. The Lovestone-Gitlow resolution and the cable to the Russian party appeared in the *Daily Worker,* March 11, 1929, p. 1. For some reason, Gitlow has Minor introducing the resolution and Lovestone endorsing it, instead of himself (*I Confess,* p. 520).
66. We know about Stalin's cable from Lovestone (*Investigation of Un-

American Propaganda Activities, Vol. XI, pp. 7139–40) and Gitlow (*I Confess,* p. 521; *The Whole of Their Lives,* p. 159; and *Subversive Activities Control Board,* pp. 808–809). According to Lovestone, the Stalin cable was overwhelmingly rejected by the delegates to the convention, but Gitlow records no such action. The cable from Stalin has never been published, and I have mainly relied on Gitlow's versions, which are the most detailed. Since the cable is unique, it would be an important contribution to the subject if the exact text or substance could be established with certitude.

67. Lovestone's testimony, *Investigation of Un-American Propaganda Activities,* Vol. XI, p. 1752. Lovestone here claims that he "wrote" the phrase, but this seems mistaken. He apparently uttered it at a caucus meeting of his faction. Stalin refers to it in his *Speeches on the American Communist Party,* pp. 32–33.
68. The major committees elected on March 9, 1929 were: Central Executive Committee—I. Amter, John J. Ballam, Max Bedacht, Chester W. Bixby, Bradley, Cyril Briggs, Earl Browder, J. Morris, Lena Chernenko, Anna David, Ellen Dawson, J. Louis Engdahl, Wm. Z. Foster, Tony Gerlach, Ben Gitlow, Otto Hall, John Henry, Leo Hofbauer, O. E. Huiswoud, Niels Kjar, E. Koppel, John Kamp, Krutis, Wm. F. Kruse, Benj. Lifshitz, Jay Lovestone, Lupin, Wm. Miller, N. Minutella, Robt. Minor, M. J. Olgin, H. Puro, John Schmies, Frank Sepich, Dan H. Slinger, Jack Stachel, Norman Tallentire, Patrick, Frank Vrataric, Albert Weisbord, W. J. White, Wm. W. Weinstone, Bertram D. Wolfe, Chas. S. Zimmerman. Candidates of C.E.C.: Alexander Trachtenberg, H. M. Wicks, K. E. Heikkinen, Pat Devine, A. Jakira, Juliet Stuart Poyntz, Bert Miller, Alex Bail, Anthony Bimba, Herbert Benjamin, Alfred Knutson, Ella Reeve Bloor, Chas. Novak, Ed. Welsh, Herbert Zam, J. Sorenson, F. G. Biedenkapp, I. Wofsey, Oscar Corgan, Dora Lifshitz, J. Johnstone.

    Central Control Commission—J. Mindel, K. Radzie, Chas. Dirba, A. Severino, J. O. Bentall, J. Lowrie, O. Held, A. Finkelberg, M. Ziebel, M. Nemser, S. Herman.

    (*Daily Worker,* March 11, 1929, p. 1.)
69. Ibid., March 16, 1929, p. 1. The names of the new Political Committee were not listed. A fifteenth member was slated to be added from the Young Communist League.
70. "Draft Statutes of Workers (Communist) Party of America," ibid., February 21, 1929, and editorial, March 20, 1929, p. 6.
71. Interviews with Wolfe, October 6, 1953, and Lovestone, June 28, 1954. The recollections of Wolfe and Lovestone differed somewhat on the exact nature of Wolfe's proposal, but they agreed that the basic idea of a delegation to Moscow had come from Wolfe.
72. Gitlow, *I Confess,* p. 521.

Chapter 18: How to Lose a Majority

1. *Appeal to the Comintern* (see Note 60), p. 3: Text of the cable of May 15, 1929, *Daily Worker,* June 27, 1929; Gitlow, *I Confess,* p. 522; Interview with Lovestone, July 2, 1954.
2. Interview with Lovestone, July 2, 1954; Gitlow, *I Confess,* pp. 527–28.
3. Eleven of the twelve names were listed in *The Communist,* June 1929, p. 293. The twelfth, Mikhailov (Williams), is mentioned as secretary in the speech before the Commission by H. M. Wicks (original in my possession). Gitlow is apparently mistaken in assigning the chairmanship of the Commission to Molotov (*I Confess,* p. 529).
4. A blow-by-blow account of the sessions of the American Commission was sent to an American confidant by the representative to the Profintern, H. M. Wicks. This letter, addressed to "Dear Louis," dated May 9, 1929, was mailed from Helsingfors, Finland, because Wicks was sent on a mission to Finland a few days before the commsion came to an end. After filling eleven double-length pages with a report of the commission's work, including long summaries of many speeches, Wicks demanded that the letter be returned to him whenever he came back to the United States. After Wicks' death I obtained the original of this letter, the stenogram of Wicks' speech of April 21, 1929, before the American Commission, and a copy of the memorandum submitted by Wicks to the commission, dated April 15, 1929, as well as much other valuable source material of a varied nature (see Note 72, this chapter). Though Wicks' letter is highly colored by bias and self-interest, it nevertheless provides a unique guide to the proceedings of the commission from one who took part in it and wrote down his impressions while they were still fresh. Gitlow has given his recollections of the commission in *I Confess,* pp. 548–67, and Lovestone in *Investigation of Un-American Propaganda Activities,* Vol. XI, pp. 7109–11, 7135–41.
5. The text of Gitlow's letter to the Russian plenum is given in *Appeal to the Comintern,* pp. 2–3, and the background in Gitlow, *I Confess,* p. 546.
6. There are two different English translations of Stalin's speeches. One was published in 1929 in a pamphlet now relatively rare, *Stalin's Speeches on the American Communist Party.* The other derives from the original English translation in mimeographed form made available to the participants in Moscow. These 26 mimeographed pages include speeches by Molotov and Kuusinen as well as the three by Stalin (copy in my possession). This mimeograph translation was subsequently published in *Investigation of Un-American Propaganda Activities,* Vol. XI, pp. 7112–33, and *Appendix—Part I,* pp. 876–97. However, page 2 of the mimeograph version is missing

in Vol. XI, p. 7113, and *Appendix—Part I,* p. 877, where material from a different document was mistakenly inserted from p. 7113, line 11, to p. 7114, line 7, and correspondingly in the Appendix. Both translations of the three Stalin speeches are similar in substance but differ in form. I have chosen to cite the pamphlet, *Stalin's Speeches on the American Communist Party,* because its validity cannot be disputed, and it is, in fact, cited by Foster, *History of the Communist Party of the United States,* p. 273.

7. See note 53, Chapter 6.
8. See note 7, Chapter 13.
9. *Stalin's Speeches on the American Communist Party,* pp. 11–20. Molotov's speech on May 6, 1929, is apparently not available, but it is summarized by Wicks in the letter of May 9, 1929.
10. *Appeal to the Comintern,* p. 3.
11. Interview with Benjamin Mandel [Bert Miller], December 2, 1958.
12. "Introduction to Documents," *Daily Worker,* June 12, 1929, p. 3. There is a slightly different translation in *On the Road to Bolshevization,* p. 41.
13. *Appeal to the Comintern,* p. 3. The effect of the statement is confirmed in *Stalin's Speeches on the American Communist Party,* p. 21.
14. Gitlow, *I Confess,* p. 555.
15. The draft was essentially the same as the published version of the "Address," but additions must have been made, since the latter refers to events after May 12 (*On the Road to Bolshevization,* pp. 35–45).
16. *The Communist,* June 1929, p. 294.
17. Lovestone's statement was cited by Kuusinen, but it is not clear whether it was made on May 12 or earlier (*Investigation of Un-American Propaganda Activities,* Vol. XI, p. 7129).
18. Kuusinen's speech is clearly dated May 12, 1929 (ibid., pp. 7124–30)
19. The only existing text of a speech by Molotov places it in the American Commission but omits the date. Internal evidence clearly indicates that it was made on May 12 (ibid., pp. 7130–33). Gitlow states that both Molotov and Stalin spoke on May 12 (*I Confess,* p. 556), but there is no evidence for a speech by Stalin at this meeting. After May 6, according to available sources, Stalin did not speak again until May 14.
20. This cable, with apparently one excision, was printed in the *Daily Worker,* June 27, 1929.
21. According to Lovestone, the meeting started about 9 p.m. and lasted until between 2 and 3 the next morning; tea and sandwiches were served at midnight (interview of June 28, 1954). Gitlow says on one page that the meeting lasted until 3 a.m. and on the next page until 4 a.m. (*I Confess,* pp. 557–58).
22. The text of this declaration appears in the *Appeal to the Comintern,* p. 1.
23. *Stalin's Speeches on the American Communist Party,* pp. 21–35.

24. *The Communist* (published by the United Toilers), June 1922, p. 8. The circumstances are related in *The Roots of American Communism,* Chapter 21.
25. There is some confusion about the delegates who accepted the Comintern's decision at this point. Stalin's third speech clearly states that only eight of the ten delegates held out after the Presidium's vote (*Stalin's Speeches on the American Communist Party,* p. 36). The two exceptions were named as Noral and Bedacht in *The Communist,* June 1929, p. 295, and in the *Daily Worker,* June 12, 1929, p. 3. Gitlow also identified the exceptions as Noral and Bedacht in his testimony, *Subversive Activities Control Board,* p. 821, but he omits Noral in *I Confess,* p. 559. In any case, Noral certainly signed a statement of submission ten days later.
26. Max Bedacht, "The Comintern Address to Our Party," *Daily Worker,* July 3, 1929, p. 4.
27. Gitlow, *I Confess,* p. 560.
28. *Stalin's Speeches on the American Communist Party,* pp. 36–39.
29. Interview with Wolfe, October 6, 1953. Gitlow says that Stalin ended his tirade with the words: "The only ones who will follow you will be your sweethearts and wives" (*I Confess,* p. 561). According to Wolfe, Stalin made three, not two, speeches at this meeting of the Presidium, but I have not been able to confirm this, and there does not seem to have been any occasion for more than two speeches. Gitlow implies only two.
30. Interview with Lovestone, October 6, 1953.
31. Interview with Edward Welsh, May 20, 1958. The incident was confirmed by Lovestone and Wolfe.
32. Gitlow, *I Confess,* p. 562.
33. The text and date of these decisions appeared in the *Daily Worker,* June 12, 1929, p. 3. But Gitlow gives the date as May 18, 1929, and says that the Political Secretariat also decided to send a committee of three to the United States, under the chairmanship of a Russian who was given absolute power of decision (*I Confess,* pp. 565–66).
34. Weinstone, *International Press Correspondence,* August 9, 1929, p. 817.
35. Minor, ibid., September 17, 1929, p. 1111.
36. The top caucus of the majority faction was then composed of Minor, Stachel, Engdahl, Puro, Ballam, Mindel, Olgin, Briggs, Radzi, and Miller (*Appeal to the Comintern,* p. 3).
37. *On the Road to Bolshevization,* p. 46, ascribes the decisions of May 18, 1929, to the Central Committee, and the *Appeal to the Comintern,* p. 3, attributes them to the Political Committee. It is most likely that the latter met first, and then acted in the name of the former.
38. *Appeal to the Comintern,* p. 3.
39. *New York Times,* May 19, 1929. Gitlow's story about Duranty's role is obviously untrustworthy. He says that he was told by Dr.

Julius Hammer on May 15, the day after the meeting of the Presidium, that Duranty had informed Hammer's son, Armand, that Stalin had requested him to send the news of the Presidium's decision to the United States immediately (*I Confess,* p. 563). Be this as it may, Duranty waited three days to send the story and then based it entirely on the long account in *Pravda,* with attribution.

40. The four were Abram Jakira (Pittsburgh), Alex Bail (Boston), Herbert Benjamin (Philadelphia), and Norman Tallentire (Detroit).
41. *Appeal to the Comintern,* p. 4. In *We Are Many,* Ella Reeve Bloor gives no hint of her own part in these events (p. 229).
42. Interview with Welsh, May 20, 1958.
43. *I Confess,* p. 568.
44. Interview with Wolfe, October 6, 1953. When Wolfe asked Piatnitsky, who made the offers, why he thought him fit for work in the OGPU, Piatnitsky replied: "We know you are fit for the job because we have been trying to crack the code you use in your cables and we have had no success whatsoever." The "code" was based on expressions likely to be known only to those born and bred in New York City.
45. Interview with Lovestone, July 2, 1954. This was the basis for the story that the Comintern wanted to send Lovestone as its representative to India (*Revolutionary Age,* January 15, 1930, p. 11). The impression that Lovestone would be sent to India was also behind the question asked by Wolfe of Piatnitsky in Moscow: "You are sending me to Korea because I can speak Spanish; you are sending Gitlow to Mexico because he can speak Yiddish; but why are you sending Lovestone to India?" Piatnitsky was amazed at Wolfe's levity (interview with Wolfe, October 6, 1953).
46. *Appeal to the Comintern,* p. 4, gives the dates of Lovestone's statements as May 22 and May 30 but infers that Lovestone prepared the second statement for the meeting of the Political Secretariat on May 31. Lovestone's second statement read:

    "While still maintaining my disagreement with the Open Letter and its organizational instructions and my conviction that they will not prove helpful to the Party, I hereby condemn all resistance to Comintern decisions and call upon the Party membership to take no steps to resist or hinder the execution of the decisions of the ECCI. In this connection, I, therefore, withdraw my previous declaration of non-submission in the Presidium as incorrect and impermissible in the Comintern and offer this statement of my submission to the decisions of the ECCI as supplanting my previous declaration.

    "I strongly urge all comrades to drop factionalism and to dissolve the groups."

    This statement was also published in the *Daily Worker,* June 27, 1929, p. 3, where it is described as a cable sent by Lovestone from Moscow, dated June 9, 1929.
47. *Appeal to the Comintern,* p. 4. The decision of the Political Secre-

tariat of the Comintern of May 31, 1929, on which this cable was based, reads: "Decision: Not to object to the trip of Comrade Lovestone to the United States for two weeks relative to personal matters. The question when Comrade Lovestone can begin this two weeks stay depends on the opinion of the ECCI delegation and on the ICC investigating the Pepper case in which Comrade Lovestone is involved."

48. See *Appeal to the Comintern,* p. 4, for the complete text.
49. "For a Broad Enlightenment Campaign," *Daily Worker,* June 1, 1929.
50. Lovestone's testimony, *Investigation of Un-American Propaganda Activities,* Vol. XI, p. 7137.
51. "A Cablegram from Communist International," *Daily Worker,* June 27, 1929, p. 4. In his testimony in 1939, Lovestone gave a somewhat different version. He related that an Italian member of the Secretariat had made a motion that he should be instructed to endorse the Comintern's new policy in the United States. Lovestone declared that he was prepared to issue the following statement: "Under instructions of the secretariat of the Communist International I hereby endorse the new decision." His proposal was almost accepted, but Molotov intervened: "No, we can't accept that, because the first part of it would indict us for resorting to questionable practices," and the proposal was rejected. Lovestone refused to endorse the Comintern's decisions "in their own official, formal way" and "that was the end" (*Investigation of Un-American Propaganda Activities,* Vol. XI, p. 7140).
52. "Material for Enlightenment of Party Membership on the C.I. Address to Our Party," *Daily Worker,* June 27, 1929, p. 4. Lovestone's cable of June 9 was published on June 27 in connection with his expulsion but not at the time it was received, when it might still have swayed some party members.
53. Interview with Lovestone, July 2, 1954.
54. "A Cablegram from Communist International," *Daily Worker,* June 27, 1929, p. 4. But Lovestone, probably for tactical reasons, claimed that he had returned to the United States "with full knowledge of the Comintern" (*Appeal to the Comintern,* p. 4).
55. Minor, *International Press Correspondence,* September 17, 1929, p. 1112.
56. Wolfe's reply cites this information, *Daily Worker,* June 27, 1929, p. 4.
57. Gitlow, *I Confess,* p. 568; *Subversive Activities Control Board,* pp. 832–33.
58. "Material for Enlightenment of Party Membership on the C. I. Address to Our Party," *Daily Worker,* June 27, 1929, p. 4, contains the text of Wolfe's reply.
59. Curiously, the exact dates of the expulsions never seem to have been

published. The announcement of Lovestone's expulsion probably followed the decision by four or five days.

60. This *Appeal to the Comintern* originally occupied 38 mimeographed pages but was later published as 4 printed pages of newspaper size, for which reason it was also known as the "Bedsheet." It was signed by William Miller, Tom Myerscough, Edward Welsh, and Wm. J. White, as well as by Gitlow, Lovestone, and Wolfe, and dated July 10, 1929. It contains much valuable information not available elsewhere, and its reliability may be judged from the fact that the official reply left its factual statements virtually unchallenged ("Statement of the Central Committee of the Communist Party of the U.S.A. on the Appeal of Jay Lovestone and Others to the Communist International," *Daily Worker,* July 23 and 25, 1929).
61. *Daily Worker,* July 29, 1929, p. 3.
62. *Revolutionary Age,* November 1, 1929, p. 18.
63. Gitlow stated in *I Confess,* p. 571, that the Lovestone group started with 150 members; in *The Whole of Their Lives,* p. 161, with 200 members. A mimeographed factional document entitled "A Letter to the Plenum of the Communist Party USA (Majority)," signed by 14 members, including D. Benjamin and Bert Miller, and dated November 27, 1930, stated that the group began with "less than 200 members" (in my possession). On the other hand, the pamphlet, *The Crisis in the Communist Party, U.S.A.: Statement of Principles of the Communist Party (Majority Group)* (New York: Revolutionary Age, 1930), stated that over 400 "leading functionaries" had been expelled, without explicitly claiming that they had joined the new group. The official party reported that "some two hundred" of Lovestone's "personal following" were expelled in 1929 (Browder, *The Communist,* September 1929, p. 797). The exact figure was given as 202 in *International Press Correspondence,* July 17, 1930, p. 603.
64. Gitlow estimated the figure at only 1 per cent (*I Confess,* p. 571), but I have been more magnanimous by assuming 200 for the Lovestone group and 90 per cent of 9300 for the pre-expulsion support.
65. Stachel gave the figure of 9300 for the membership in March 1929 (*The Communist,* April 1929, p. 180), and Browder the figure of 7545 for the membership in June 1930 (*Communism in the United States,* 1935, p. 66).
66. The stages of this group may be followed in the pamphlets: *The Crisis in the Communist Party, U.S.A.;* Bertram D. Wolfe, *What Is the Communist Opposition?* (New York: Workers Age Publishing Ass'n., 1933); Jay Lovestone, *The People's Front Illusion: From "Social Fascism" to the "People's Front"* (New York: Workers Age, 1937).
67. Foster, *History of the Communist Party of the United States,* p. 274.
68. Interview with Bedacht, June 18, 1954.

69. Bedacht gave the background of his expulsion in an article, "Our Party and Its Problems," published in the mimeographed bulletin, *Toward Socialism,* edited by Francis Franklin, dated May 1, 1949. In 1946–48, Bedacht especially attacked the party's policy toward the Negroes and Jews, which he considered too "nationalistic" and lacking in "socialist content."
70. Alexander Bittelman, "I Take a Fresh Look," *Daily Worker,* October 1–16, 1957, especially October 3–4, 1957; Foster, "The Party Crisis and the Way Out," *Political Affairs,* December 1957, pp. 47–61, and January 1958, pp. 49–65; Bittelman, "Key Problems of Party Program," ibid., February 1958, pp. 36–44.
71. Albert Weisbord, "My Expulsion from the Communist Party," *Class Struggle,* August–September 1931, p. 3, and December 1, 1931, pp. 7–9; Lozovsky, *International Press Correspondence,* October 4, 1929, p. 1197; Weisbord, *The Conquest of Power;* Cannon, *The History of American Trotskyism,* pp. 87–90.
72. Wicks had been a delegate to the first convention of the Communist party in 1919 but had soon dropped out. He joined the Proletarian Party in 1921; edited the organ of the United Toilers, *Workers Challenge,* in 1922; and returned to the official Communist party late in 1922. In 1923 he was accused of having been an anti-Communist spy in Gary, Indiana, and a party committee composed of Ashkenudzie, Browder, and Bedacht examined the charges, but he was exonerated and subsequently held many high positions in the party (documents of the Wicks examination of 1923 in my possession). Rumors in Left-Wing circles that there was an *"agent provocateur"* in the Central Executive Committee of the Workers party had cropped up in the nineteen-twenties (Benjamin Stolberg, *The New Leader,* January 7, 1928, p. 4). According to Browder, Wicks's expulsion in 1937 was based on documents originating in the Chicago Federation of Labor and made available to Jack Johnstone who carried out the expulsion during Browder's absence in Europe (interview with Browder, October 22, 1954). After Wicks's death, I was permitted in 1958 by his widow, Mrs. Ruth Wicks, whom he had met and married long after his break with Communism, to examine his private papers, which had not been touched, and I obtained all those that interested me. I found nothing in these papers to confirm the old charges.
73. This book, *Eclipse of October* (1957), was published posthumously by Mrs. Wicks. It is mainly a history of the rise of world Communism from 1914 to 1956, with little reference to personal experiences or activities. The last personal reference mentions Wicks's missions for the Comintern, beginning late in 1929 (p. 258), but he then goes on for another 170 pages without once reverting to his own role. The book is written from the point of view that "a Kremlin tyranny arose that was able to obliterate the achievements of the

Russian Bolshevik revolution of October, 1917, and to turn to its own designs the various parties in other countries that comprised the Communist International" (p. v).

74. It is mentioned in *Stalin's Speeches on the American Communist Party*, p. 14, and *Appeal to the Comintern*, p. 3.
75. *International Press Correspondence*, September 13, 1929, p. 1067.
76. Information from Earl Browder.
77. See note 38, Chapter 17.
78. See note 23, Chapter 18.

Acknowledgments

This volume, like its predecessor, *The Roots of American Communism,* was written as part of a project on Communism in American Life, sponsored by the Fund for the Republic and directed by Clinton Rossiter. I am grateful to the Fund for the Republic and to Professor Rossiter for making the work possible under conditions of complete freedom and independence.

I have tried to give credit in the Notes for the information and material obtained from personal sources. I have spent many hours, and sometimes days, interviewing and corresponding with the following: Max Bedacht, Earl Browder, James P. Cannon, Samuel A. Darcy, Joseph Freeman, Manuel Gomez, Otto Hall, Harry Haywood, Ludwig E. Katterfeld, William F. Kruse, Jay Lovestone, Benjamin Mandel, Max Shachtman, Maurice Spector, Albert Weisbord, Edward Welsh, and Bertram D. Wolfe. I corresponded with or obtained unpublished material from Cyril V. Briggs, Max Eastman, Joseph Zack Kornfeder, Arne Swabeck, Mrs. Ruth Wicks, and Charles S. Zimmerman. Some of the interviews and correspondence covered a larger period, and only a portion of this material has been used in this volume. All answered questions or provided material without any strings attached, and none can be held responsible for views expressed in this book or for the way the information has been used.

The onerous and delicate task of criticizing various stages of the entire manuscript was inflicted on Daniel Bell, Earl Browder, James P. Cannon, Joseph Carter, Joseph Freeman, Philip J. Jaffe, Murray J.

Rossant, Clinton Rossiter, Max Shachtman, and Bertram D. Wolfe. I owe to each of them an immeasurable debt of gratitude, and I have enormously benefited from their knowledge, counsel, and encouragement.

I am especially grateful for the devoted technical assistance of Frances Alexander and Kathleen Schwarzschild, made possible at various stages by the grant from the Fund for the Republic.

Above all, I owe to my wife, Evelyn Manacher Draper, more than I can express. She has been my true collaborator, gentle critic, and constant inspiration.

Index

A.A.A.I.L., *see* All-American Anti-Imperialist League
Abern, Martin, 92, 181, 363, 369, 371–372, 374
Accounts and Supplies Dept., 210
"Address by the Executive Committee of the Communist International to All Members of the Communist party of the United States," 414, 418, 420, 423–25, 428
Africa, 317–19, 322, 324–25, 327–30, 353; and American Negro nationalism, 317; liberation of, 327–28
African Blood Brotherhood, 322-26, 330–31, 333, 343; Program and Aims of, 325
African Emigration Association, 317
A.F. of L., *see* American Federation of Labor
Agents, Soviet, 211–14, 414, 416, 481–482 *n.* 73; *see also* Soviet intelligence service, Soviet Military Intelligence
Agitation and Press subdepartment, 167
Agitation and Propaganda (Agit-Prop), 148, 234, 253, 267, 283, 403; Department of Comintern, 156, 167–68; Department set up by Fourth Convention, 160
Agrarian Department, 160
Agrarian question in the South, 347
Agricultural Committee of Communist party, 178
Agricultural Workers' Industrial Union, 178
Agriculture, and American capitalism, 84; collectivization of, 305
"Alfred," *see* Tilton, Alfred
All-American Anti-Imperialist League, 178, 473 *n.* 63
Allen, James S., 338, 355–56
Alma-Ata, 279, 363, 365, 367–68
Amalgamated Clothing Workers, 43
Amalgamated Textile Workers, 223
Amalgamation campaign, 64–65, 70–71, 76
America, *see* United States
American Commission of the Comintern, 110, 134, 216, 226–28, 258-61, 264, 310, 406–15, 418–20, 423–24, 435, 485 *n.* 38
American Communism, *see* Communism, American
American Communist–Soviet Russian relations, 5
American Federation of Labor, 13–14, 25, 30, 36, 40–41, 50, 63–67, 71, 76, 80, 98, 150, 175, 215–18, 223, 225, 230, 232–33, 260, 276, 286–90, 292–93, 295–96, 316, 394–95
American Friends of the Soviet Union, 177
American Fund for Public Service, 204
American heresy, the, 82, 272; *see also* Exceptionalism, American

American Imperialism, 250
American Labor Alliance, 22
American Labor Party of Greater New York, 29
American Labor Who's Who, The, 200–201
American League Against War and Fascism, 178
American Negro Labor Congress, 331–332, 346
American party, *see* Communist party, Workers party
American question, 113, 428; *see also* American Commission of the Comintern
American Revolution (1776), 273–75
American Secretariat, *see* Leadership, American Communist; Secretariat, American
American situation and European patterns, 124–25, 280–81, 292
Americanization, 272–75, 338, 440
Amsterdam News, 322–23
Amter, Israel, 23, 61, 110, 169, 175, 328–29
Amtorg Trading Corporation, 368
Anarchism, 9, 431
Anarchists, 12, 179, 422
Anglo-American Secretariat of Comintern, 168, 271, 307–308, 343, 345, 389–90
Anglo-American Section of Profintern, 168
A.N.L.C., *see* American Negro Labor Congress
Anti-Fascist Alliance of North America, 179
Anti-Fascist League for the Freedom of Italy, 179
Anti-Imperialist League, *see* All-American Anti-Imperialist League
Anti-imperialist propaganda, 313
Anti-Lore campaign, 107, 110–11
Anti-Trotskyism, American, 106–107, 110–11, 113, 258, 283, 357
Anti-war campaign, 184
Apex theory of American capitalism, 307, 356, 384
"Appeal to the Comintern," 429
Appeal to Reason, 315
Application cards (membership), 162
Arcos, Ltd., 207, 257
Aronberg, Philip, 149, 384, 397
Ashkenudzie, George (pseud., "Henry"), 420
"August theses" (1923), 80–81, 87
Australia, 171, 434
Auto industry, Communists in, 192
Auxiliaries, Communist system of, 171–173; *see also* Fronts
Auxiliary organizations, *see* Fronts

"Back to Africa Movement," 317–18, 320, 328
Balkan countries, 169
Ballam, John J., 128, 236, 255, 266, 331, 419–20; pseud., "Moore," 420
Baltic countries, 169
Bamatter, Sigi, 170
Beard, Charles A., 273
Bedacht, Max, 19, 26, 56, 111, 142–143, 148, 169, 200, 205, 234, 253–254, 262–63, 267, 390–91, 395, 400–401, 403–405, 416, 420–23, 425, 430–31, 435, 439
Bell, Tom, 407, 409
Bennet, A. J., *see* Goldfarb, Dr. Max
Berger, Victor, 198, 315
Berzin, Jan, 211
Biedenkapp, Fred, 176
Billings, Warren, 181
Bittelman, Alexander, 19, 24, 32, 81, 87–89, 113, 116–18, 120–21, 125, 128, 140, 142–45, 148–49, 171, 174, 200, 205, 219–21, 226–27, 229, 235–236, 239, 242, 245, 249, 263, 269, 271–73, 286, 294, 299, 307–308, 310, 312, 341–42, 345, 348, 357, 370–71, 374–75, 379–80, 383–84, 394–97, 399, 401, 406, 408, 410–413, 415, 432–33, 437
Black Belt, self-determination of Negroes in, 6, 315, 326, 343–49, 352–54
Black Eagle Flying Corps, 319
Black Legion, *see* Universal African Legion
Black Star Line, 319
Blackwell, Alice Stone, 181
Bloor, Ella Reeve, 19, 68, 89, 177, 384, 404, 422, 425–26

Bolshevik party, *see* Communist Party of the Soviet Union
Bolshevik revolution, *see* Revolution, Communist, in Russia
Bolsheviks, American, 83, 251; Russian, 15, 18, 35, 57, 110, 113, 129–130, 158, 285; *see also* Old Bolsheviks, Old Guard Bolsheviks
Bolshevism, 15, 21, 83–84, 154, 324, 390–91
Bolshevization, 464 *n.* 14; of the American party, 152–67, 172, 182, 186–209, 251, 274, 330, 440; results of, 186–200; and Russification, 135, 153, 163; significance of, 163; slogan of Fifth Plenum, 134; three stages of, 153–54
Bolshevization plenum, *see* Comintern, Fifth Plenum of
Bookkeepers, Stenographers, and Accountants Union in Kansas City, 68
Bordiga, 166; group of, 227
Borodin, Michael, 202
Bosse, A. G. (Alfred J. Brooks), 167
Boston police strike, 16
Bouck, William, 48, 116–18
Boudin, Louis B., 15
"Bourgeoisification," 260, 275–78
Brandler, Heinrich, 387–88
Braun, A., *see* Ewert, Arthur
Bridgeport, Connecticut, labor party in, 29; machinists' strike in, 29
Bridgman (Michigan) convention, 26, 38, 61, 175, 203
Briggs, Cyril V., 322–26, 333, 350, 353, 355
British general strike, 279
British Labour party, 29, 31–33, 109, 284
British police, 207, 257
Brodsky, Joseph R., 207, 213, 406, 416, 438
Brooks, Alfred J., *see* Bosse, A. G.
Brophy, John, 290, 297, 397
Brotherhood, *see* African Blood Brotherhood
Brotherhood of Locomotive Engineers, 276
Brotherhood of Railway Carmen of America, 63
Browder, Earl, 3, 39, 41, 71, 73, 76–78, 103, 117–18, 122, 207, 212–13, 219–20, 238, 242, 249, 274, 294, 299, 310–11, 313, 353, 375, 395, 397, 412; and American capitalism, 269–70; background of, 67–69; and Foster, 67–69, 77–78, 310; in leadership, 430–33, 435–36; and Profintern, 69, 170–71, 229, 310
Brown, Jay G., 39–40, 63
Brown, William Montgomery, 176
Buck, Robert M., 40, 45
Buck, Tim, 362
Budget Commission of Comintern, 208
Building Up Socialism, 301–302
Bukharin, Nikolai, 14, 105, 129, 133, 135, 228, 239, 244, 257–59, 261, 271–72, 284–86, 293, 299, 301, 312, 364, 375, 386, 400–401, 407–408, 410–11, 439; and capitalist stabilization, 279–80; and Sixth World Congress, 300–307, 313; and Stalin, 278–281, 386–89, 391–94, 422; and three postwar periods, 302–303
Bulgarians, 190
Bulletin No. 1, 369
Bunting (of South Africa), 345, 349
Burman, Fahle, 88
Butte (Montana), mine strike, 16

Cadre, 197–201, 235; Negro, 326
Cahan, Abe, 390
Canada, 71, 158, 167, 210, 214; Communist delegates from, 158; Communist party in, 362–63, 367; Trotskyism in, 373
Canadian Royal Commission, 214
Candidates, Communist, 110, 114, 117–19; *see also* Election
Cannon, James, 7, 22, 24, 26, 41, 85–86, 97, 103, 107, 124–25, 148–50, 185, 195, 219, 244, 248–49, 253–54, 256–59, 261, 266–67, 272, 287, 295–296, 299, 306–308, 313, 366, 385, 438; background of, 67–69; alliances of (1923–24), 86–89, 90–95; and Draft Program of the Comintern, 364–67; at Fifth Plenum, 133–39; at Fourth Convention, 142–46, 148–

Cannon, James (*continued*)
150; and International Labor Defense, 180, 235, 363; and Opposition to Lovestone (1928), 235–37; and Pepper, 78–82; and Spector, 362–67; and Trotsky, 357, 362–76
Cannon-Foster-Weinstone majority, 256; in Opposition Bloc, 259
Cannonites, 145, 294
Capital levy, as slogan, 35
Capitalism, 16, 92, 99, 130, 242, 249
American: and agriculture, 84; and Communist policy, 260, 410; interpretations of, 269–72, 381–82; and the Negro question, 322, 336, 352, 356; Stalin on, 409–410; strength of, 11, 16, 247, 260, 283–84, 303, 307–308, 388
end of, 9, 13, 22, 65, 122, 269–70; European, 16–17, 33, 130, 269–70, 276, 410; German, 303; and Left turn, 305; new, 275–78; trade-union, 276–78; welfare, 276–78; Western, 130, 132; world, 35, 129, 260, 270, 409; *see also* Stabilization
"Capitalism and Agriculture in the United States of America," 335
Cartel des Gauches, 283–84
Carver, Thomas Nixon, 275
Catholic Associated Societies and Parishes, 225
C.C.N.Y., *see* College of the City of New York
"C.E.," *see* Ruthenberg, Charles Emil
C.E.C., *see* Central Executive Committee
Cell, *see* Nuclei
Central Committee, American, 139, 161, 199, 311, 332, 377, 413, 424–425; Russian, 155, 361, 388
Central Control Commission of the American party, 160, 210; of the Russian party, 141
Central European School, 169
Central Executive Committee, American, 32, 38, 42, 61, 73, 77, 81, 91, 94–95, 107–108, 111–13, 117, 128, 136, 142–48, 150, 156–57, 160–61, 185, 191, 196, 203, 208, 219–20, 228–29, 236, 248, 250–51, 253–56, 261, 266, 277, 338, 350, 361, 372, 401, 403, 434–35; Russian, 107
C.G.T., 283
Chamberlain, Sir Austen, 257
Changes in line, *see* Line
Chaplin, Ralph, 181
Chiang Kai-shek, 257
Chicago, 12, 18–21, 30, 41, 43, 57, 63, 69–78, 82, 85, 90–92, 99, 101, 112, 136, 142, 148, 178, 181, 210, 236, 243, 256–57, 266–67, 325, 331–33, 372–73, 430, 435
Chicago convention of 1923, Farmer-Labor party, 41–47, 52–53, 61, 78–79, 85, 99, 115, 185
Chicago Farmer-Labor party, 29, 36–37, 39–40, 49, 76
Chicago Federation of Labor, 29, 37–41, 49, 63, 71, 76, 79
China, 202, 212, 257, 279, 291, 308, 310, 374
Christensen, Parley Parker, 30, 32
C.I.O., 77, 296
Civil war, in Spain, 179; in Russia, 141; in United States, 317, 333, 336, Riot Act in, 225
Class struggle, 12–13, 31, 62, 93, 277–278, 282–83, 329–30, 434
Class Struggle, The, 15, 434
Cleveland, Ohio, 35–36, 53–54, 68, 102, 142, 146, 384, 431; convention in, 37, 46, 102, 105, 116
Coal strike of 1925, 221, 227
Cohen, Dr. Maximilian, 170
Colby, Bainbridge, 225
College of the City of New York, 224, 249–50, 252, 385
Columbia University, 250, 275
Comintern (Communist International), 20, 27, 47, 58, 74, 87, 89, 105–107, 109, 113, 122–26, 129–31, 153, 166, 236, 243–44, 246–47, 251, 265, 279–281, 285, 287, 293–94, 296–97, 301, 306–308, 329–30, 354, 361, 371, 379, 388, 392–94, 397–98, 410–12, 431–32, 435–40; American Commission of, 110, 134, 216, 226–28, 258–61, 264, 310, 406–415, 423–424, 435, 485 *n.* 38; Commission on Hungarians of, 58, 60

Congresses of: 156; Second, 25, 31–32, 163, 173, 320–31, 337, 339–40; Third, 32–35, 106, 163, 195, 215–233; Fourth, 25–26, 35, 157, 164, 326–28, 339; Fifth, 112–13, 124, 130, 157–58, 165, 170, 328–30, 339–340; Sixth, 206, 297–98, 300–314, 341, 342, 345–52, 355, 364–71, 375, 377, 380, 384, 386, 390–91, 394, 397, 416
control by, 12, 157, 159, 161–166, 187; and death of Lenin, 105; decisions on American questions, 90, 104, 110–16, 119, 121, 127, 130, 134, 137–38, 140–41, 143–45, 147–152, 164, 260–63, 297–98, 311–13, 385–86, 398–404, 406, 414–29; delegations of, to United States, 25–26, 38, 67, 108, 170; fifth anniversary of, 106; Information Department of, 112, 167; "model statutes" of, 159, 162; monolithic character of, 25, 125; Negro Commission of, 327, 348–50; Negro revolutionists invited to Russia by, 321; Open Letters of, 311–13, 398–99, 411; organic relation of to non-Russian parties, 25, 125, 159–62, 470 *n.* 21, *n.* 26; organizational development of, 154–56; parties' position in, 163–66
Plenums of: Fifth (Bolshevization), 129–30, 133–34, 143, 158–59, 357; Sixth, 220, 226–30, 238, 270; Seventh, 166, 234, 238–43, 271–72; Eighth, 256–61, 272; Ninth, 283–88, 291–93, 496 *n.* 6; Tenth, 429
proliferation of, 166; reference of American policy to, 85, 103, 128–129, 148–49, 236–37, 253–56, 429; representatives of, 59–60, 141, 146–148, 163–65, 167–68, 170, 210, 215, 266, 291, 387, 398, 400, 408, 411, 423, 425, 434; representatives to, 164–65, 169–71, 261, 267, 328, 385–86, 398, 406, 431; schools set up by, 166, 168–69; Stalinization of, 141, 304; subsidization of American party by, 206–209; three periods of, 135; trade-union policies of, 25, 67, 70, 126, 215–33, 285–93, 396; Twenty-one Points of, 25, 125; *see also* Executive Committee of the Communist International
Commissariat of Nationalities, 168
Communism, 9–10, 20, 23, 27, 80, 111, 114, 118, 168, 182, 224, 370, 409, 430–31
Communism, American, 9, 11, 15, 17, 20, 24–25, 28, 87, 124, 150, 167, 171, 186, 208, 244–47, 259–60, 268–69, 274, 296, 374, 410, 441; and Comintern, 419; history of, 12, 76–77, 299; Lovestone period of, 249; and Negroes, 315, 321–22, 325, 333, 347, 356; and Soviet Russia, 5; underground, 21–22
Communist, The, 15, 250, 267, 289, 293, 347, 351, 353, 394
Communist–Farmer-Labor alliance, 51, 91
Communist influence, cause of, 51; in unions, 71; *see also* Mass influence
Communist International, *see* Comintern
Communist International, The, 289, 301, 338, 346–47
Communist-Kuomintang alliance, 257
Communist Labor party, 19–21, 31, 155–56, 320; *see also* Communist party, American
Communist League of America (Opposition), 373
Communist League of Struggle, 434
Communist Nucleus: What It Is—How It Works, The, 167
Communist parties, 33, 134, 280; in Bulgaria, 165; in Canada, 362–63, 373; in Central America, 178; in China, 257, 279, 374; and Comintern, 25, 33, 159, 165; in Czechoslovakia, 165; in England, 31–33, 154, 165, 407; European, 162, 283; in Finland, 406–407; in France, 154, 157, 165; in Germany, 141, 154, 157, 165, 202, 237, 291, 362, 386–387, 407; in Hungary, 57, 407; in Italy, 157, 165, 202; in Mexico, 170; non-Russian, 214; in Norway, 165; in Poland, 165; in Puerto Rico,

Communist parties (*continued*) 178; in Trieste, 179; Western, 158, 241
Communist party, American, 4, 6–7, 12, 17–18, 23, 40–41, 54–56, 70, 73–74, 78, 92–93, 108–109, 111–112, 124, 136, 138, 151, 167, 210, 212, 238, 242–43, 274, 281, 284, 290–91, 294, 296–98, 300, 306, 310–13, 358, 380–81, 386, 389–90, 408–409, 412, 416–19, 422–27, 429–35, 437–40; and Comintern, 25–26, 161–65, 167, 259–60, 262–263, 399; constitutions of, 156, 162; history of, 382, 396; and Krestintern, 178, 184; and Lovestone, 416–417; and Negroes, 326–27, 330–35, 341–42, 349–51; in post-Lovestone period, 429–35; structure of, 154–156; and Trotsky, 357–58, 370–73; *see also* Comintern, Communist Labor party, Illegal party, Legal party, Workers party
Communist Party of America, of September 1919, 19–20, 31, 55, 189, 252, 320; of May 1921, 21, 25–26; Manifesto of, 9, 16; merger with United Communist party, 26
Communist Party (Majority Group), 430
Communist Party of the Soviet Union, 12, 69, 105, 107–108, 113, 141, 154, 158, 161, 165–66, 173, 193, 202, 208, 238, 241–44, 285, 287, 291, 293, 304, 306, 310, 334, 354, 388–389, 400–401, 408, 440; delegation of at Sixth Congress, 303, 309, 313; factional struggle in, 107–109, 113, 130, 302, 312, 314; Fifteenth Congress of, 378–81; Left, Right, and Center in, 279; Right danger in, 386; structure of, 154–55; Thirteenth Congress of, 107–108, 359; and Trotsky, 357, 359–60, 374; *see also* Comintern, Leadership, Plenum
Communist Party of the U.S.A. (Opposition), 430, 529 *n.* 63
Communist Party, U.S.A., name change in 1929, 160, 403
Communist-Progressive alliance, 85, 289; in United Mine Workers, 289
Communist–United Toilers opposition, 26
Communist University of the Toilers of the East, *see* Far Eastern University
Communist Women's Conference, 177
Communists, 34–35
American: 12–14, 16, 24, 29, 32, 52–53, 58–60, 66–67, 69–72, 75–78, 83, 85, 92, 109–110, 120–23, 126–127, 129, 137, 163, 170–71, 181, 191, 206–208, 258, 270, 272, 274–275, 277–78, 280, 283, 285–86, 288–289, 293, 298, 361–62, 376, 380, 383–84, 387, 401, 407, 410–11, 418, 424, 427, 434, 436, 439; American Negro, 320, 322, 325–26, 331–35, 343, 349, 351; in California, 381; in Chicago, 41, 43; and Farmer-Labor party, 30–31, 35–51, 114–16; and LaFollette, 117–19; in Minnesota, 99–100; and Negro policy, 318–21, 327, 329, 334–38, 340–42, 345, 350; in New York, 41, 89, 95
British, 31–33, 109, 113, 283; Chinese, 257, 279, 374; early, 10, 13, 24; European, 36, 387–88; French, 109, 113, 283; German, 109, 113, 283; Hungarian, 57; Russian, 129, 133, 141, 335
Communist-Workers party, 22
"Communists Are for a Black Republic, The," 351, 381
Company unionism, 276
"Comrade Loaf," 167
Conference for Progressive Political Action, 30, 36–37, 46, 50, 102–103, 116
Congress, party, *see* Convention
Connecticut, labor party in, 29
Conquest of Power, The, 434
Conspiracy, Communist, 213
Constitution, 156; adopted by Workers party, 160–62; model, for Communist parties, 159
Constitutional Convention of 1787, 273
Contreras, Carlos, *see* Vidali, Vittorio

Control Commission, *see* International Control Commission
Conventions, Communist, 20, 76, 129, 138–39, 144, 150, 163–65, 236–37, 254–55, 260–61, 311, 340, 378, 385, 431; *see also* Bridgman convention, Workers party, conventions of
Coolidge, Calvin, 118–20; administration of, 276; era of, 225
Cooperatives, 101; Danish, 83–84; Finnish, 88
Corey, Lewis, *see* Fraina, Louis C.
Corridor Congress, 309
Council of Elders, 309
Council of People's Commissars, 300
Councils of workers, in United States, 16
C.P.P.A., *see* Conference for Progressive Political Action
Craft unionism, 64–66
Crisis, economic, 280, 299, 382–84; financial, 209; party, 199–200; *see also* Depression
Critique of the Draft Program of the Comintern, see Draft Program of the Communist International: A Criticism of Fundamentals, The
Crusader, The, 323–25, 333
Crusader News Service, 325
Cudahy Packing Company, 333

Daily Forward, 168, 390
Daily Worker, 81, 108, 111, 118, 136, 143, 149, 183, 191, 206, 210, 212–213, 236–38, 243–44, 262–67, 273–274, 282, 289, 330, 332, 351, 372, 378, 381, 424–25, 429, 433; finances of, 203–205
Dallant, Nicholas L., *see* Dozenberg, Nicholas
Damon, Anna (Anna E. David), 207
Darcy, S. A., 170
David, Anna E., *see* Damon, Anna
Davis, John W., 118, 120
Dawes Plan, 130
Debs, Eugene Victor, 72–73, 123, 175, 181, 198, 316
"Decision of the Communist International on the American Question," 137
Degras, Jane, 338
Delany, Martin R., 317–18
De Leon, Daniel, 13, 15, 73, 171
Dell, Floyd, 15
Democratic party, 96, 379
Dengel, Philipp, 398–99, 401, 408
Department of Justice, 26
Depression, 3, 29, 382–83; in Communist theory, 121–22, 269–72; in factional differences, 121–22, 269–272, 282–83, 381–84; and party membership, 187, 189, 192, 270; *see also* Capitalism
Detroit Proletarian Women, 177
Dezettel, Max, 68
Dictatorship of the proletariat, 15, 20, 22, 40, 70, 172, 216, 298
Dimitroff, Georgi, 213
Dirba, Charles, 210, 420; pseud., "Dobin," 420
Direct action, *see* Mass action
Discrimination in Communist party, 334–35
Distinguished Service Order of Ethiopia, 319
Dobin, *see* Dirba, Charles
Doctrine, Communist, 12–13, 17, 19, 46–47, 96, 268, 380, 384
Donchin, Sam (Sam Don), 236
Doriot, Jacques, 310
Dorsey, *see* Foster, William Z.
Douglass, Frederick, 317
Dozenberg, Nicholas (Nicholas L. Dallant), 209–13
Draft Program of the Communist International: A Criticism of Fundamentals, The, 365–67, 369–70, 374
Dridzo, Solomon Abramovich, *see* Lozovsky, A.
Dual-stamp system, 187–88
Dual unionism, 13, 26, 70, 215, 217–219, 222, 225, 229–30, 233, 394–97; disavowed, 26, 229; and Foster, 63, 65–66, 68, 70, 266, 294–97, 299, 394–97; and Left turn, 285–90, 380; and Lozovsky, 285–90; and Stalin, 387–88; *see also* Unions, new
Dukes of Nigeria and Uganda, 319
Dunne, Grant, 372
Dunne, Miles, 372

Dunne, Vincent R., 372
Dunne, William F., 19, 23, 76–77, 80, 103, 143, 145, 169, 218–19, 222, 236, 267, 273–74, 287, 289, 299, 307, 312, 328, 340, 348, 364, 497 *n.* 13
Duranty, Walter, 424
Dutch Left Wing, 14–15

East Europeans, membership in 1919, 19–20; in 1925, 190
Eastern Department of Comintern, 156
Eastern University, *see* Far Eastern University
Eastman, Eliena, 368
Eastman, Max, 15, 60, 359–62, 368, 370
E.C.C.I., *see* Executive Committee of the Communist International
Edelman, 167
Eisler, Gerhardt, 387
Ekern, Herman L., 114
Election, of 1920, 29; of 1924, 86, 101, 117–20, 128, 206, 227; of 1928, 206, 297–98, 308, 378–79; of 1932, 432; *see also* Farmer-Labor party, LaFollette
Emigration, of Negroes, 317; from United States to Russia, 175
Engdahl, J. Louis, 21, 117, 143, 244, 258, 267, 286, 385, 389, 392
Engels, Frederick, 10–11
English-speaking membership, 18–20, 27, 101, 188–91; National Council, 19; workers, 84, 158
"Enlightenment Campaign," 427
Ercoli, *see* Togliatti, Palmiro
Europe, 9, 15–17, 33, 58, 65, 82, 109, 125, 130, 166, 201, 276, 280, 319, 383, 410; Eastern, 33, 201; situation in, contrasted with United States, 17, 82, 124–25, 130; trade with, 383; Western, 26, 168, 201, 241, 279
European patterns and American situation, 124–25, 280–81, 292
Ewert, Arthur (A. Braun, Grey), 170, 259, 261–62, 266–67, 387
Exceptionalism, American, 268–81, 284, 397, 414, 432; Russian, 171
Executive Committee of the Communist International, 105, 139, 156, 159, 163–65, 202, 258, 262, 313, 326, 367, 392, 413–15, 417–19, 426, 440
Executive Council, 87, 102, 107, 140, 157, 160, 456 *n.* 20

Factionalism, American, 116, 127, 169, 235, 262–63, 278, 294–96, 298, 310, 312, 378, 381, 388, 398, 410, 418–19
Famine in Russia, 176
Famine Scout Cubs, 176
Far Eastern University, 168–69, 332, 334, 340, 344, 418
Farmer-Labor Association, 118
Farmer-Labor–Communist alliance, 51; *see also* Federated Farmer-Labor party, Third party
Farmer-Labor convention, 43–47, 86, 450 *n.* 37–39, 451 *n.* 49
Farmer-Labor Federation of Minnesota, 101, 105, 118
Farmer-Labor movement, 29–32, 36, 38–39, 42–44, 52, 56, 76, 85, 95, 99, 109, 114–16, 118–21, 127–29, 134, 137–38, 206, 269
Farmer-Labor party, 23, 30, 37–39, 43–49, 63, 76, 85, 96–97, 103, 110, 114–19, 128; of Illinois, 115; of Minneapolis, 101; of North Dakota, 115; *see also* Federated Farmer-Labor party, LaFollette, Third party
Farmer-labor policy, 92, 136, 227; question, 128; revolution, 83
Farmer-Labor United Front, 29–32, 35, 38, 98, 101; *see also* Third party
Farmer-Labor Voice, 75
Farmer-Laborism, 116, 122, 128
Farmer-Laborites, 31, 37, 41, 44, 49–51, 103, 118; in Minnesota, 99–100
Farmers, 29, 43, 84, 99, 122, 135, 193
Farmers' Union, 178
FBI, 213; *see also* Department of Justice
February revolution, 336
Federated Farmer-Labor party, 45, 47–48, 75–81, 85–86, 90–91, 93,

96, 236, 452 *n.* 65; platform of, 48
Fellow travelers, 171, 184–85, 195
F.F.-L.P., *see* Federated Farmer-Labor party
Finance, 202–209; crises in, 205–206; and front organizations, 183–84, 203–204, 332; sources of, 204; and subsidies, 202, 206–209, 480 *n.* 57
Finnish foreign-language federation, 22, 24, 88, 95, 101, 145, 154, 190–191
Finns, *see* Finnish foreign-language federation
Fitzpatrick, John, 29, 37, 39–47, 49–52, 61–63, 72–74, 76–78, 87, 91–92, 95–96, 99, 104, 114, 118, 124, 126, 138, 216; break of, with Communist party, 46–51
Five Year Plan, 300
F.-L.P., *see* Farmer-Labor party
Flynn, Elizabeth Gurley, 246, 333
Food trades, and Workers party, 192
For a Labor Party, 36, 38, 60
Ford, James W., 345–46, 348, 350; and American Negro Labor Congress, 332, 353
Foreign-language federations of Communist parties, 18–19, 21, 155, 159, 163, 186, 190–92, 223; abolition of, by Comintern, 155, 190; and character of the party, 268; and control of the party, 55; *see also* Membership
Foreign-language federations of Socialist party, 18, 22, 154
Foreign-language sections, 190–92
Foreign-language Workers Clubs, 191
Fort-Whiteman, Lovett, 320, 326, 329, 331, 346, 348, 350, 353
Foster, William Z., 21, 24, 38–39, 43, 45–46, 60, 67–69, 72–74, 78–79, 81–82, 85–95, 105, 107–113, 122–23, 143, 148, 152, 159, 167, 183–84, 200, 205–206, 208, 234–36, 244–246, 248–49, 251–54, 256–58, 260–261, 264–67, 270, 272, 276–77, 307–311, 313, 348, 355, 357–58, 366, 371, 373, 377, 381, 384–85, 394–95, 399–400, 402–403, 406–408, 410–411, 418, 423, 430–33, 435, 466 *n.* 33; background of, 61–66; and Comintern, 125–26, 133–39, 144, 147–49, 215, 228–29, 308–309, 311–13, 407; "Dorsey," 134; and dual unionism, 63, 65–66, 68, 70, 266, 294–97, 299, 394–97, 432; "E.Z.," 66; and Federated Farmer-Labor party, 75–78; group of, 230, 233, 255, 262–63, 293; and LaFollette, 97, 102, 109–110, 114–16, 120–21; majority of, 108, 112, 127–128, 135, 138, 140, 142, 145–50; as presidential candidate, 117–19, 297–298, 378–79, 432; and trade-union policy, 63, 69–70, 215–20, 223, 226–33, 285–88, 291–92, 308–309, 431–32
Foster-Bittelman Opposition, 383–85
Foster-Cannon caucus, 90–95, 148, 310–311, 370
Foster-Cannon Opposition, 79, 81–82, 85–88, 307, 342
Foster-Cannon-Weinstone Opposition, 259, 262
Foster-Gitlow campaign, in 1924, 118; in 1928, 378
Foster-Ruthenberg, power struggle of, 128
Fosterites, 112, 145–46, 148–50, 218, 227, 229, 251, 266–67, 294–95, 370, 411, 426, 439
Founders of American Communism, 9, 440; *see also* Communists, early
Fourteen Points, 323
Fourth Department of the Red Army, 211
Fox, Jay, 64
Fraction bureaus, 183, 191
Fractions, 154–55, 157–58, 161, 186, 191, 194; defined, 161; and fronts, 174; and Russian party structure, 155
Fraina, Louis C. (Lewis Corey), 15, 19, 25, 27, 32, 67, 170, 202
Freeman, Joseph, 358
Freiheit, 87, 191
Friends of Soviet Russia, 176–77, 180, 196, 204, 216
Friends of Soviet Russia and Workers Germany, 176

Friends of the Soviet Union, 177
From Bryan to Stalin, 231
Fronts, 171–73, 203–204, 406, 416, 431; American, 174–82; finance and, 183–84; letterhead and membership types of, 174–75; Negro, 331; relation of to party, 182–85
Frunze, 141
Functionaries, 250; *see* Cadre, Professional revolutionaries
Fund-raising, 203–204
Fur Workers Union, 221, 232–33

Garland, Charles, 204
Garment trades, *see* Needle trades
Garvey, Marcus, 318–20, 324–25, 330, 332–33
Garveyism, 330
Gates, John, 433
"Geese," 22–23, 61
George, Harrison, 170
George, Henry, 53
Gerhardt, *see* Eisler, Gerhardt
German Bureau, 148
German Embassy, 166
German foreign-language federation, 87–88, 148, 190
Germany, 56, 59, 63, 87, 129–30, 166, 202, 228, 240–42, 303, 323, 362, 387; uprising in, 33, 58–59
Ghana, 332, 349
Gibson, Lydia, 207
Giovannitti, Arturo, 179
Gitlow, Benjamin, 6 *n.*, 19–20, 61, 87, 112, 122, 143, 205, 212, 219, 221, 229, 231–32, 249, 253–58, 261, 264, 272, 287–88, 311, 313, 372, 382, 391, 401, 403–405, 407–408, 414, 416, 418, 420–30, 438; and subsidization, 202–203, 206–207; as vice-presidential candidate, 117–18, 298, 378
Gitlow, Kate, 177
Gitlow-Lovestone-Pepper theses, 384
Glotzer, Albert, 372
Gold, Ben, 221, 232, 380
Gold Coast, 332
Gold, Michael, 60, 358
Goldfarb, Dr. Max (Petrovsky, Bennet), 168, 390
Gomez, Manuel, 170, 178, 205, 307, 312–13
Gompers, Samuel, 49, 64–65, 71, 76, 90, 120
Goose caucus, *see* "Geese"
Gosplan (State General Planning Commission), 436
Government—Strikebreaker, The, 250
Gradualism, peaceful, 13; *see also* Reformism
Green, P., *see* Gusev, Sergei Ivanovich
Grey, *see* Ewert, Arthur
Grolman, 167
Guralsky, 58
Gusev, Sergei Ivanovich, 140–42, 146–49, 153, 159, 170, 215, 218–219, 228–29, 233, 235, 250, 262, 266, 295, 399, 406, 409–10, 413–414, 425, 465 *n.* 27; pseud., "P. Green," 141

Hall, Haywood, *see* Haywood, Harry
Hall, Otto, 326, 333–35, 342–43, 345, 348, 350, 353
Hamburg, 386
"Hands Off Russia" committees, 173
Hapgood, Hutchins, 40
Hapgood, Powers, 290, 297
Hapsburg monarchy, 57
Harding, Warren Gamaliel, 29
Harlem, 320–31
Harrison, Caleb, 22, 176
Harvard, 24, 275; Harvard Law School, 224
Hathaway, Clarence A., 100, 103, 115, 168, 306, 347, 370, 373, 395
Hays, Max S., 175
Haywood, Harry, 326, 333, 343–48, 350, 353–55
Haywood, William D., 54, 73, 180, 333
Headquarters, American party, 90, 267
Hearst's International, 106
Heller, A. A., 204
Helman, B., 37
Henry, *see* Ashkenudzie, George
Herberg, Will, 430
Heresy, American, 82; *see also* Exceptionalism, American
Herriot, Édouard, 109

Hillquit, Morris, 198, 252
History of the Communist Party of the United States, 74, 231, 246, 467 *n.* 44
History of the Russian Communist Party, 239
Hitler, Adolf, 284
Hoover, Herbert C., 378, 382
House of Representatives, United States, 99, 207, 212–13
Housewives in Workers party, 192–93
Howat, Alexander, 72, 181
Huiswoud, Otto E., 313, 320, 322, 326–27, 350, 353, 404, 425–26
Humbert-Droz, Jules, 134, 136, 286, 387
Hungarian foreign-language federation, 18, 59, 190
Hungary, 57–59; Red Army of, 58; revolution in, 16, 57; Soviet Republic of, 57–59; uprising in (1956), 441
Hyman, Louis, 222

I Confess, 6 *n.,* 207
Illegal party, 22–23, 26, 61, 174; *see also* Underground
Illinois, Farmer-Labor vote in, 30
Illinois Labor party, 115
Illinois State Federation of Labor, 76
Immediate demands, 13, 48, 175–76
"Impartial chairman," introduced by Comintern, 139–42
Imperialism, American, 259–60, 271, 277, 284, 312, 322, 397; British, 259
"Impossibilists," 92
Independent Communist League of Boston, 369
Independent Labor League of America, 430
Indians, American, 336
Industrial Committee of Communist party, 157; Industrial Department, 148
"Industrial registration" of 1924–25, 192–93
Industrial unionism, 14, 64–66, 71–72, 296; *see also* Syndicalism
Industrial Workers of the World, 13–14, 60, 62–64, 66, 68–69, 92, 150, 175, 178, 179–82, 201, 223, 311, 333
Industries, party strength in, 192–94
Industry's Coming of Age, 275
Information Conference, 1925, 167
Information Department, 112, 167
Institute of Red Professors, 343
Insurrection, armed, 14, 21–22, 54; *see also* Revolution
Intellectuals, Communist, 250–51, 358
Intercollegiate Socialist Society, 249, 252
International Association of Machinists, 30, 72, 100, 209, 233, 276
International Branch, *see* Nuclei, street
International Control Commission of Comintern, 146, 156, 313, 415, 435
International Labor Defense, 180–81, 184, 196, 204, 235, 363–64, 369, 371
International Ladies' Garment Workers' Union, 222, 232–33
International Publishers, 204, 479 *n.* 49
International Red Aid (M.O.P.R.), 173, 180, 393
"International Situation and the Tasks of the Comintern, The," 302
International Trade Union Educational League, 63
International Women's Department, 167
International Women's Secretariat, 177
International Workers Aid, 176, 204, 252
International Workers Delegation, 310
International Workers Order, 431
International Workers' Relief, 173, 176, 180
"Internationale," 244
Ireland, 338; Republican delegation of, 202
I.S.S., *see* Intercollegiate Socialist Society
Italian Bureau, 179
I.W.W., *see* Industrial Workers of the World
Izvestia, 202

Jakira, Abram, 23
Jansen, Carl, *see* Scott, Charles E.
Jefferson, Thomas, 274
Jeffersonianism, 83–84
Jenkins (Jenks), 167
Jewish Bund, 89, 168
Jewish Communist movement, 432
Jewish foreign-language federation, 22, 87, 190–91
Jewish Socialist federation, 89, 168
Jewish Workers Relief, 196
Jews, 191
Jim Crow, 334; Jim-Crowism, 348
Joffe, A. A., 202
Johannsen, Anton, 40–41
Johnson, Charles, *see* Scott, Charles E.
Johnson, Magnus, 99, 101
Johnson, Tom, 53–54
Johnston, William H., 30, 72
Johnstone, Jack W., 39, 41, 63, 71, 171, 178, 205, 219–20, 225, 230, 254, 263, 287–88, 294, 307, 310–313, 397, 400–401, 408, 412

Kamenev, Lev Borisovich, 105, 107–108, 131, 238–239, 301, 361
Kansas-Missouri district, Communist Labor party, 68
Karolyi, Count Michael, 57
Karsner, Rose, 369
Katayama, Sen, 14, 25, 67, 165, 170, 339, 348, 350
Katterfield, Ludwig E., 20, 43, 169
Kerensky, Alexander, 83; Kerensky Revolution, 83
Khitarov, 406
Knights of Labor, 316
Knights of the Nile, 319
Knudsen, William Ross, 71–72
Knutson, Alfred, 179, 205
Kolarov, 409
Kollontay, Alexandra, 14
Konikow, Antoinette, 368–69, 372
Kremlin, 166, 243–44, 258, 304, 334–335, 367
Krestintern, 173, 178, 184
Krivitsky, Walter G., 212
Krumbein, Charles, 39, 41, 77, 92, 149, 168
Krupskaya, 238, 360
Kruse, William F., 168, 236–37, 258, 274, 343, 350, 430
Ku Klux Klan, 83–84, 330
Kun, Bela, 57–58, 168, 407, 409
Kuusinen, Ottomar V., 134, 138, 236, 264, 345, 349–50, 406–407, 413–15, 418

Labor banks, 276
Labor Defender, The, 181
Labor Defense Council, 175, 180
Labor Herald, The, 39, 66, 71
Labor movement, American, 71, 106, 126, 138; *see also* American Federation of Labor, Trade unions
Labor party, 31, 36, 76, 80, 284, 297–298; and Comintern, 31–33, 70, 135, 137, 140; substituted for Farmer-Labor party, 137; *see also* Farmer-Labor party, Federated Farmer-Labor party, Third party
Labor party of 1919, in Chicago, 29–30; in Connecticut, 29; in New York, 29; national, 30–31
Labor Sports Union of America, 179–180
Labor Unity, 289
LaFollette alliance, *see* Third party
LaFollette movement, 28, 83–84, 91, 96, 98, 119–20, 129, 137, 374
"LaFollette revolution," 83–84, 118
LaFollette, Robert M., 83, 88, 91–92, 96–98, 101–104, 108–110, 114–16, 119–20, 123–26, 128, 130, 138, 150
Larkin, James J., 14
Latin America, 135, 383, 425
Latvian influence, 14
Lavoratore, Il, 179
Lawrence (Massachusetts) textile strike, 16
Leadership
American Communist: 4, 38–39, 41, 56–57, 67, 85, 95, 115, 117, 121, 125, 142, 162, 173, 175, 180, 185–186, 197–201, 208, 225–26, 228–230, 234, 244, 247, 283, 287, 291, 300, 355, 358, 385–86, 388, 390–392, 405, 408, 439–40; Browder and, 300–11, 431–32; and Comin-

tern, 112, 136–39, 143–44, 150, 163–64, 401–402; composite picture of, 200–201, 477–78 *n.* 33–35; Foster in, 431–32; Negro, 201, 332, 346; parity commission and, 148; post-Lovestone, 426, 430–36; post-Ruthenberg struggle for, 248, 253–257, 261, 266; reorganization of, 159–61
Canadian, 363; international, infallibility of, 151–52; of Left Wing, 18; national, control of by Comintern, 151–52, 413, 437–38; in needle trades, 233; Russian, 112, 145, 301–302, 309, 313, 365, 379, 386, 401, 420, 439–40; Socialist and Communist traditions of contrasted, 197–98; Stalinist, 241, 246
League of Struggle Against Prejudice and Racial Inequality, 346
League of Struggle for Negro Rights, 353
Left bloc, in trade-union policy, 217–219
"Left Bloc" Herriot regime, 109
"Left Communism," 133
Left danger, 227–28
Left Opposition of 1922, 419–20
Left Opposition of the underground Communist party, 22
Left Opposition (Trotsky), 306, 376
Left turn, 109, 125, 280–81, 284–85, 298, 300, 305–306, 375–76, 379–381, 386, 410
Left vs. Right, 24, 133, 375
"Left-Wing" Communism: An Infantile Disorder, 25
Left Wing émigrés, 14
Left Wing National Conference, 18–19
Left Wing, American traditional, 13, 15, 18–19, 26, 52, 54, 80, 122, 209; in American Federation of Labor, 286, 289, 292; Communist, 14–15; and Federated Farmer-Labor party, 86; in International Ladies' Garment Workers' Union, 222; in labor movement, 80, 219, 288, 295; in Negro history, 319; non-Communist, 53; pro-Bolshevik (pro-Communist), 87, 209, 250, 252, 390; in Socialist party, 14, 54, 62; Section, New York, 250; of third-party movement, 37; in United Mine Workers Union, 289; *see also* Dutch Left Wing
Legal party, 22–23, 26, 61
Lenin, V. I., 10–11, 15, 17, 59, 105–106, 110, 129, 172–73, 194, 246, 285, 294, 304, 379; and American Negroes, 320–21, 335–40, 344–45; labor-party policy of, 31–32, mausoleum of, 244; and socialism in one country, 131–32; testament of, 359; trade-union policy of, 67, 70; and Trotsky, 359
Lenin School, 58, 168–69, 205, 236–237, 293, 306, 334, 340, 343, 350, 366, 370, 373, 406, 418
Leninism, 14, 26, 134, 334, 375
Leninism, 301
Leninist party, 121, 124, 172–73
Lettish foreign-language federation, 18, 209
Lettish influence, 14
Lettish Left Wing, 209
Lettish Socialist federation, 14
Lettish Workers Society of Boston, 209
Lewis, John L., 51, 72, 206, 286, 290, 296
Libertador, El, 178
Liberator, The, 60, 82, 107, 359
Lincoln, Abraham, 273
Lippmann, Walter, 15
"Liquidators," 23, 26, 61
Literature and Revolution, 358
Literature Department, 210
Lithuanian foreign-language federation, 18
Lithuanian Workers' Literature Society, 44
"Liver and Onions," 413
Lominadze, Besso, 291, 304, 308
Lore, Ludwig, 15, 81, 98, 113, 123, 135, 145, 148, 236; and Cannon, 87–95; and Comintern, 110–11, 138–39; and Trotsky, 106–107, 357–58, 362, 368–69
Loreism, 106, 134–35

Lovestone, Jay, 19, 90–95, 103, 117, 121–22, 128, 142–43, 148, 167, 178, 180, 183, 188, 200, 205–207, 234–35, 242–43, 245–46, 248, 250, 253–59, 261–67, 294–99, 307–308, 355, 358, 366–67, 371–72, 375, 378–379, 391–92, 396–97, 401, 407–408, 410, 412–15, 418–20, 422–25, 431–434; and American capitalism, 268–281, 381–84; and Americanization, 273–75; background of, 249–50; and Bolshevization, 251, 274–75; and bourgeoisification, 277–79; and Bukharin, 258–59, 281, 309, 388–389, 401; and Comintern, 133–39, 151–52, 264, 313, 377–78, 380, 385–86, 398–404; in defeat, 405–430; expulsion of, 429; group formed by, 430; and Lozovsky, 285–287, 292–93, 309; and Negro question, 340–41, 345–48, 351; and Pepper, 61, 90–95, 111–12, 251–52, 391; in power, 265–67, 282; preparations for party take-over, 405–406, 416–17; pseud., "Powers," 134; reasons for downfall of, 436–40; and the Right danger, 307–309; and Stalin, 258, 311–13, 389; *see also* Communist Party of the U.S.A. (Opposition), Independent Labor League of America
Lovestone group, 264, 267, 311–12, 410; *see also* Lovestoneites
Lovestoneites, 253–54, 258, 261–62, 264–65, 267, 283, 293–94, 307, 311, 370, 395, 413, 429–30
Lovett, Robert Morss, 48
Lozovsky, A. (S. A. Dridzo), 70, 220–221, 285–90, 292–96, 299, 309, 343, 389, 402, 406, 409, 434

MacDonald, Duncan, 116–18
MacDonald, Jack, 362, 367, 373
MacDonald, James Ramsay, 109
Machinists' union, *see* International Association of Machinists
Machinists' union, Chicago, 39
McKay, Claude, 78, 321, 327, 335, 340
McNamara, J. B., 181
Magazine of Wall Street, 382
Mahoney, William, 100–104, 114–16, 118
Manhattan Lyceum, 243
Manifesto, Communist Party of America, 9, 16
Manley, Joseph, 45, 48, 75, 115–16
Mann, Tom, 310
Manuilsky, Dimitri, 35, 280, 406
Martens, Ludwig C.A.K., 175, 202
Martin, Alfred, *see* Tilton, Alfred
Marx, Karl, 10–11, 17
"Marxism and the National Question," 344
Maslow-Fischer leadership of German party, 227–28
Mass action, 13–15
Mass influence and political orthodoxy, 12, 17, 18, 20, 23, 55, 98, 119, 124, 213
Mass organizations, 171, 181–82; *see also* Fronts
Masses, The, 359
"Mecca," 255, 257
Membership application card, 162
Membership, party, and Bolshevization, 186–90, 194; and decision-making, 350; and depression, 187, 189, 192; and dual-stamp system, 187–88; East European and foreign-language proportions in, 19–20, 26–27, 190–92, 270; and Farmer-Labor movement, 188; fluctuations in, 188–90, 195–96; and LaFollette, 120–21; place of in party life, 194–197; social composition of, 192–94; *see also* Cadre, Rank-and-file
Membership estimates, 475 *n.* 1, 3, 8, 9; 476 *n.* 11, 12, 16; 494 *n.* 1, 3; 513 *n.* 93, 100; 1919, 19, 190; 1922, 26–27, 187, 203; 1923, 26–27, 90; 1925, 187; 1926, 188; 1927, 188–89; 1929, 188
Messenger, 319–20
Metal trades, and Workers party, 192, 216
Middle class, in Workers party, 192
Migration and the Negro question, 102, 347, 353, 356

Mikhailov, Boris, 170, 345, 406, 423, 430; pseud., "Williams," 345
Militant, The, 371
Military Revolutionary Committee of Petrograd, 141
Miller, Bert, 412, 430
Miller, Frank, *see* Sirola, Yrjo
Miller, William, 404
Mine workers and Workers party, 192
Miners' union, *see* United Mine Workers
Mingulin, I., 168
Mining, Communist strength in, 72, 192
Minnesota Farmer-Labor party, 99–101, 104
Minnesota Federation of Labor, 100
Minnesota Union Advocate, 100
Minor, Robert, 24, 61, 111, 169, 207, 231, 238, 258, 267, 328, 330–31, 361, 400–401, 405, 412–13, 416, 421, 423–24, 428, 430–31, 433
Minutes of top committees, 6
Model Statutes of Comintern, 159, 162
Moireva, 406
Molotov, V. M., 312, 388, 406, 409, 412–15
Monolithism, 125
Mooney, Tom, 181
Moore, *see* Ballam, John J.
Moore, Richard B., 205, 326, 346, 350, 353
M.O.P.R., *see* International Red Aid
Moriarty, Bill, 362
Moscow, 6, 27–28, 32, 38, 56–59, 67, 69–70, 73, 77–78, 103, 105, 108, 111–13, 123–24, 126, 133, 136–38, 140, 143–44, 148, 151, 165–69, 177, 180, 202, 206–208, 211–14, 217, 219–20, 226–30, 236–38, 243–45, 253–58, 261–67, 283–87, 291, 293, 296–97, 299–302, 310, 313–14, 321, 327–29, 331–33, 342, 344, 347–48, 350–51, 359, 361–62, 364, 366, 370–371, 373–74, 377, 385–86, 388–89, 391–92, 394, 402–407, 410, 412–17, 419, 423–25, 427–29, 431, 434–39; *see also* Comintern
"Moscow gold," 208
Mothers League of Boston, 177
Murray, Philip, 76
Mussolini, Benito, 179
Myerscough, Tom, 404

Nasanov, N., 170, 344–46, 350
Nation, definition of, 344; Negro consciousness of, *see* Negro "nation"
National Association for the Advancement of Colored People, 315
National Committee of the Opposition Bloc, 261–63
National Council for Protection of Foreign Born, 177, 184
National Council (Left Wing), 18, 19
National Defense Committee, 175
National Farmer-Labor Progressive convention, 461–62 *n.* 64, 462 *n.* 66, 74; *see also* Farmer-Labor party, Federated Farmer-Labor party
National Labor Union, 316
National Left Wing Conference, 18
National Miners' Union, 380
National Save the Miners Union Conference, 290, 297
National Textile Workers Union, 380, 434
Nationalism, Negro, 318–20
Nationalization, in Federated Farmer-Labor party platform, 30; in British Labour program, 48
Nearing, Scott, 122–23
Needle trades, 72, 88, 184, 189, 191–192, 216, 219, 222–23, 232–33, 268
Needle Trades Committee, 232–33
Needle Trades Workers' Industrial Union, 380
Negro Champion, The, 332
Negro Commission of Comintern, 327, 345, 348–50
Negro Department, set up by Fourth Convention, 160
"Negro Exodus," 317
Negro "nation," 317–18, 320, 323–24, 334, 346–48, 355, 505 *n.* 24
Negro, New, 319, 325
Negro People in American History, The, 338
Negro policy, 313–15, 320, 327–30, 337, 350–51; equality vs. self-de-

Negro policy (*continued*)
termination in, 329–30, 343, 345–347, 351–52
Negro question, 182, 314–56; *see also* South African Negro question
Negro Race Congress, 342
Negro Soviet Republic, 345, 347, 351–352
Negro workers (American) and Profintern Fourth Congress, 288
Negro World Congress, 327
Negroes, Communist position on, 313–315, 320, 327–30, 337, 350–51; at Far Eastern University, 168–69; fronts for, 174, 182, 331; history of in United States, 315–19; in party leadership, 201, 332, 346; right to self-determination of, 315, 322, 326–30, 333, 339–40, 343–56, 381; socialism and, 315–16; trade-unionism and, 316
Neumann, Heinz, 241, 291, 304, 308
"New capitalism," 275–78
New Deal, 38, 275
New International, The, 15
New Majority, The, 40
New Review, 15
New unions, *see* Unions
New York Times, 361, 424
New Yorker Volkszeitung, 87, 106, 368
New York Workers School, 88, 205, 253, 278
Nockels, Edward N., 29, 39–41
Nonfront organizations, 185; nonparty organizations, 155, 173
Noral, Alex, 404, 420, 425–26
Norge, 209
North Dakota, 179; Farmer-Labor party of, 115; labor party in, 29
"November theses" of 1923, 85–86
Nuclei, shop, 154–55, 157–61, 186, 191–93, 217–18, 223, 476 *n.* 20; *see also* Fractions
Nuclei, street, 157, 160–61, 191–92

Ochrana, 172
Office workers, in Workers party, 193
OGPU, 425
Olgin, Moissaye, 21, 87–88, 98, 105, 107, 110–11, 196, 358
Oneal, James, 273–74
Open Letter of Comintern to American party on Right danger, 311–13
Open Letter of Comintern (second), 411
Open Letter, from Comintern to Sixth Convention of American party, 392, 394–95, 398–99, 414
Open party, *see* Legal party
Opportunism, 11, 17, 23–24, 109
Opposition bloc (Cannon-Foster-Weinstone), 259, 261–64, 266, 366; National Committee of the, 261–63
Opposition bloc (Trotsky-Zinoviev-Kamenev), 361, 368, 371
Opposition (1923, Foster-Cannon-Bittelman), 81–82
Opposition (to Lovestone), 255–58, 294–96, 300, 307–14, 342, 377, 381, 397–404, 406–407
Opposition (Trotsky), 131–32
Organization Committee (Orgcom), 157
Organization Department, of E.C.C.I., 156, 159; set up by Fourth Convention, 160
Organizing the unorganized, 217, 224, 288
Orgburo, 155, 157, 166–67; conferences of, 158–59, 166
Orthodoxy, political, and mass influence, 12, 18, 20, 23, 55, 98, 125, 396, 432

Packing-house workers, Chicago, 63
Padmore, George, 349
Painters' union, Chicago, 39
Palmer raids, 20, 175, 189
Panken, Jacob, 298
Pan-Pacific Monthly, 310
Pan-Pacific Secretariat, 310; congress of, 435
Paquett, Joseph, *see* Tilton, Alfred
Parity commission, 139–46, 159–61
Party, conferences of and Comintern, 164–65; and fronts, 182–85; headquarters of, 90, 267; Leninist theory

of, 172; world, 165, 208; *see also* Communist Labor party, Communist party, Workers party
"Passaic policy," 225, 260, 288, 294; *see also* Dual unionism
Passaic (New Jersey) textile strike, 223–32, 266, 288, 433
Payroll of Communist party, 204–205
Peasant question, 134–35
Peasants' International, *see* Krestintern
"People's Republic" of Finland, 170
Pepper, John (Joseph Pogany), 38, 73–74, 85–91, 105–108, 110, 121, 123–25, 128, 133–39, 167, 226, 228, 238–39, 245, 246, 258, 261, 270, 284–86, 358, 366, 372, 374, 378–379, 381–83, 387, 389, 391, 394, 397, 402, 404, 406, 410–11, 414–15, 435–36; authority of, in American party, 26, 61, 170, 291–92, 297–99, 449 *n.* 24, 453 *n.* 19; background of, 57–60; as exile, 111–12; and Farmer-Labor party, 38, 40–45, 48–49, 77–82; and LaFollette, 83–86, 91–94, 102–103, 118, 121; and Lovestone, 61, 111–12, 251–52; on Negro question, 329, 341–42, 346–349, 351; at Sixth Comintern Congress, 308; "Swift," 291
Pepper-Ruthenberg group, 88, 90–95, 108, 111, 251
Perlman, Selig, 225
Persecution, governmental, 20–21, 52, 190
Petrovsky, D., 168, 309, 345, 348, 390–91; *see* Goldfarb
Phillips, H. V., 331, 346, 350
Piatnitsky, Ossip, 157–59, 208
Pittsburgh, 384; Pittsburgh "Save the Union" conference, 297
Platforms, 1924 and 1932, 499–500 *n.* 39; 1928, 298, 308, 380–81; Democratic and Republican, 379
Plenum, of American party, December 1925, 219, 225; end of 1926, 271; May 1927, 255–56; February 1928, 282, 363–64; May 1928, 294–97; December 1928, 371, 384, 388, 391, 394; of the Russian party, July 1926, 237–38; July 1928, 300; November 1928, 386, 389; April 1929, 408; *see also* Comintern, plenums of
Pogany, Joseph, *see* Pepper, John
Polish Catholic Union, 177
Polish foreign-language federation, 18
Politburo, Russian, 155–57, 165, 360, 368, 386
Political Bureau, 92, 161, 255
Political Commission of Comintern, 112, 270, 357
Political Committee (Polcom), 6, 38, 46, 61, 82, 85, 145, 148, 157, 160, 176, 183–85, 203, 205, 219–20, 229, 235–37, 243–44, 249, 253–56, 263–264, 266, 280, 282, 291, 331, 341, 350, 371–72, 381, 397, 400, 403, 423, 428–29
Political Secretariat, *see* Secretariat
Pollitt, Harry, 398
Popular Front, 3, 185, 192, 274, 432–433, 440
Populism and Farmer-Labor party, 30, 48
Powers, *see* Lovestone, Jay
Poyntz, Juliet Stuart, 19, 88, 143
Pravda, 386, 424
Present Economic Revolution in the United States, The, 275
Presidium of Comintern, 156, 158, 165, 259, 387–88, 393, 417–24, 426, 429, 440
Press, Communist, 167, 238, 298, 350, 360, 384, 428; *see also Daily Worker*
Printing trades, Communist strength in, 72
Professional revolutionaries, 172, 194, 197–201
Professionals in Workers party, 192
Profintern, 285, 293, 296, 343, 418; American representatives to, 69, 170, 229, 287, 310, 406; Anglo-American section of, 168; first congress of, 67, 69–70, 72; fourth congress of, 287–89; representatives of, 170–71, 210, 310, 387; subsidization by, 206; third congress of, 217; trade-union policy of, 216–21
Programs, Communist, 56, 250, 328, 477–78 *n.* 4; *see also* Platforms

Progressive group in American Federation of Labor, 216–17, 288, 295
Progressive party and results of 1924 election, 119, 137
Progressives in unions, 82, 190, 288, 397
Progressivism, American, 86; LaFollette, 122
"Proletarian delegation" of 1929, 403–405, 412, 416, 420–23, 428, 433, 435–40
Proletarian party, 44
Proletarian Women (Detroit), 177
Proletariat, 62, 83–84, 131, 146, 174, 241, 346, 349, 352, 379; Negro, 341–42, 352–53
Propaganda subdepartment of Comintern, 167
Publications, 1925, 184
Puerto Rico, 178

Radek, Karl, 35, 110, 112, 129, 334
Railroad unions, 30, 36, 72, 216
Railroaders' Next Step, The, 64
Rakovsky, Christian, 360
Ramsay County, Minnesota, Farmer-Labor party in, 100
Rand School of Social Science, 252
Rank and file, 120, 186, 194–97, 235, 266, 350, 413, 423–24, 436; *see also* Membership
Ravicb, 372
Real Situation in Russia, The, 368, 370
Reconstruction Program, British Labour party, 29
Recruiting and fronts, 182
Red Army, 33, 35, 244, 298; Fourth Department of, 211; Hungarian, 58
Red International of Trade Unions, *see* Profintern
Red Sports International, 173, 180
Reed, John, 19, 24, 27, 56, 69, 244, 320–21, 339, 346
Referenten, 167
Reformism, 13–14, 48–54
Reinstein, Boris, 26, 38, 170
Reiss, Mania, 416
Reorganization, 153, 159
Republican party, 96, 122
Research Department set up by Fourth Convention, 160
Resignations from Communist parties, 164
"Resolution of the Comintern on the American Question" of 1927, 259, 272
Resolution of Parity Commission, 146
Resolution on Bolshevization of the Party, 160
Revisionism, 13–14, 355
Revolution, Communist, 16; in America, 17, 60–61, 67, 69, 83, 368; in Austria, 16; in Bavaria, 16; in Bulgaria, 16; in Finland, 16; in Germany, 33, 58–59, 130, 240; in Hungary, 16, 57–59; Kerensky, 83; "LaFollette," 83–84; proletarian, 67, 83, 349, 351; in Russia, 14, 16, 18, 24–25, 27, 30, 40, 54, 57–59, 68–69, 83, 89, 110–11, 129, 131–32, 141, 154–155, 168, 199, 202, 209, 240–42, 274, 285, 323, 359, 361, 376; theory of, 11, 123, 132–33; in the West, 34, 131–32; world, 16–17, 129–32, 240–42, 335
Revolutionary Age (1929), 430
Revolutionary Age, The (1918–19), 15
Revolutionary movements, national, 135; of United States, 11–12
Right, attacked by Zinoviev, 130; vs. Left, 24, 133, 375; mistakes, 298, 313; Opposition, 420; turn, 125, 380
Right danger, 227, 306; in the American party, 306–308, 311–13, 342, 397, 407; the hunt for, 380–86; in the Russian party, 386
"Right Danger and Trotskyism, The," 391
"Right Danger in the American Party, The," 307
Right Wing, 13, 95, 149; of Brandler and Thalheimer, 387; Bukharinite, 279, 306; in Comintern, 304–307, 388; deviation, 398, 434; Finns, 145; German, 388; in I.L.G.W.U., 222; line in American party, 310; mis-

takes, 298, 313; of Rykov and Tomsky, 306; of Socialist party, 18; of third-party movement, 37
Riot Act, Passaic, 225
Rockefeller, John D., 273
Roosevelt, Franklin D., 99, 379
Roosevelt, Theodore, 379
Roots of American Communism, The, 5
Rosmer, Alfred, 360
Rothstein, Andrew, 345
Roy, M. N., 168, 271, 406
Rubin, Bertha and Samuel, 204
Rudas, Ladislaus, 58
Rumanian Progressive Club, 44
Russian émigrés, 14
Russian exceptionalism, 171–72
Russian foreign-language federation, 18–20
Russian influence, 14
Russian party, *see* Communist party of the Soviet Union
Russian Press Service, 105
Russian Workers party, 23
Russian Soviet Government Bureau, 175
Russians in America, 19, 27, 33, 190–191
Russification, and Bolshevization, 135, 153, 163, 440
Rust, William, 170
Rutgers, S. J., 14
Ruthenberg, Charles Emil, 15–17, 19–22, 24, 27, 36, 38, 41–50, 54–56, 60–61, 73–74, 77–80, 92–95, 97–98, 102–105, 108, 111–18, 125, 133–39; apotheosis of, 243–47; background of, 53–56; "C.E.," 244; death of, 243–44, 248, 272; and Pepper, 80–81, 85–90; pseud., "Sanborn," 134; upheld by Comintern, 148–51
Ruthenberg group, 21–23, 112, 140–144, 148–51, 227–30, 233, 294, 330; as majority, 229; as minority, 128, 138; *see also* Lovestone, Pepper
Ruthenberg Recruiting Drive, 243
Ruthenberg-Lovestone-Pepper group, 91, 150, 251, 253
Rykov, Alexis I., 239, 300, 305
Sabotage clause in Socialist party constitution, 54
Sacco, Nicola, 181
Sacco-Vanzetti demonstrations, 279–280, 313
St. Paul conference, 101
St. Paul, Minnesota, 100–101, 117; convention (1924), 102–105, 110, 114–16
St. Paul Trades and Labor Assembly, 100
Sanborn, *see* Ruthenberg, Charles Emil
Sandburg, Carl, 202
Saturday Evening Post, 212
"Save the Union," slogan, 285, 287–90, 297
"Save the Union Committee," 290
Scott, Charles E., 25, 67, 108, 169, 210, 363; pseud., Jansen, or Johnson, 210
Seattle general strike, 16
Secretariat, 214; American, 6, 129, 148, 157, 160, 182–83, 203, 205, 211–12, 229, 261, 403, 411–12, 415, 424, 427–28, 430–31, 434–35; Anglo-American, 168, 271, 307–308, 343, 345, 348, 389–90; of Comintern, 134, 156, 167–68, 351, 385, 423, 426–28; of C.P.S.U., 155
Sectarianism, 11, 23–24, 190
Self-determination of Negroes, 6, 322, 327–30, 333, 339–40, 343; in the Black Belt, 315, 326, 343–56, 381
Separatist movements, Negro, 352–54
Senate, United States, 64, 66, 99, 308
Senioren Konvent, 309, 365
Serra, 387
Shachtman, Max, 93, 143, 181, 363, 369, 371–74
Shannon, David A., 315
Sharecroppers, 354
Shiek, A., 346
Shipstead, Dr. Henrik, 99–101
Shop branches, *see* Nuclei
Shop Delegate League of 1919, 222
Simons, A. M., 273–74
Since Lenin Died, 360–61
Sinclair, Upton, 40

Sirola, Yrjo (Frank Miller), 170, 183
Siskind, G., 307
Sköglund, Karl, 372
Slavic foreign-language federations, 18, 190
Smith, Alfred E., 378–79
Smith, Stewart, 373
Smuggling of documents, 368
Social-Democracy, 33–34, 135, 168, 305
Social-Democratic parties, 109, 305
Social-Democrats, 35, 57, 284, 305
Social-fascism, 305
Social Forces in American History, 273
Social reformism, 395
Socialism, 9, 12–13, 20, 31, 54, 56, 62, 100, 109, 132, 165, 241, 252, 316; in one country, 130–33, 238–43, 271, 305, 374; through world revolution, 130–32
Socialist Labor party, 13, 15, 21, 150, 171, 249, 316, 378
Socialist-LaFollette-Gompers alliance, 120
Socialist party, 13–14, 18–20, 23, 30, 41, 54–56, 62, 68, 73, 116, 150, 171, 198, 201, 224, 235, 245, 249–250, 298, 313, 324, 378–79; of California, 381; Harlem branch of, 320; Malden branch of, 209; of Massachusetts, 14; and Negroes, 315–16, 341; structure of, 154
Socialist Propaganda League, 14, 209
Socialist Study Club, C.C.N.Y., 249
Socialist Trade and Labor Alliance, 171
Socialists, American, 30–31, 50, 90, 126, 179–80, 325, 395–96; European, 276; Finnish, 283; *see also* Social-Democrats
Society for Technical Aid to Soviet Russia, 175
Society of Old Bolsheviks and Former Political Exiles and Prisoners, 180
Soldiers' Council in Hungary, 57
Solntsev, 368–69
Sormenti, Enea, *see* Vittorio Vidali
South Africa, 345; delegation of to Comintern Congress, 326–27
South African Negro question, 348–49
South African party, 348–49
South Side branch, Chicago Party, 334
South Slavic foreign-language federation, 18, 190
Souvarine, Boris, 360
Soviet films, 204
Soviet House, 207, 257
Soviet intelligence service, 214, 414, 425; *see also* Agents, Soviet Military Intelligence
Soviet Military Intelligence, 211
Special Committee on Un-American Activities of the House of Representatives, 207, 212–13
Spector, Maurice, 362–67, 373, 438
Splits, 18–19, 21, 23, 33–34, 42–43, 85, 92, 97, 117–18, 142–43, 190, 416–17
Sport Department, set up by Fourth Convention, 160
Stabilization, capitalist, and socialism, 129–30, 133, 270, 279–81, 303, 305
Stachel, Jack, 149, 200, 205, 234–36, 267, 372, 400, 405, 412–13, 416, 421, 423–24, 427, 433, 437–39
Stalin, Joseph, 108, 123, 133, 138, 141, 155, 195, 208, 214, 222–28, 238–43, 246, 261, 282–83, 285, 291, 293, 301, 305, 310–12, 364, 375, 392, 400–404, 500 *n.* 7; and American factional struggle, 299, 388, 409; and American Negroes, 334, 342–45; and Bukharin, 133, 278–81, 300–307, 386–89; and death of Lenin, 105–107; emergence of, 105–106, 133, 459 *n.* 23; falsifications of in history, 368; and Lovestone, 258, 264, 309, 406–11, 413, 415, 418–20, 422–23, 427, 437, 439–40; and socialism in one country, 131–32, 239–43; solution of, to American problem, 409–12; and Trotsky, 133–135, 257, 359–60; and Zinoviev, 237–42
Stalin University of Peoples of the East, *see* Far Eastern University
Stassova, Eliena D., 393
State General Planning Commission (Gosplan), 436

Statistics and Information Department of Comintern, 156
Statutes of the Comintern, 25, 125, 156, 166; model, 159, 162
Steamfitters' union, Chicago, 39
Steel workers, strike of, 16, 63, 66
Steffens, Lincoln, 40, 276
Stoklitsky, Alexander, 18
Strikes, 16, 21, 29–30, 68, 184, 221, 223–33, 290
Strong, Anna Louise, 106
Subsidization, *see* Finance
Swabeck, Arne, 19, 39, 41, 77, 92, 115, 267, 372
"Swift," *see* Pepper, John
Sympathizers, 171, 184–85, 195
Syndicalism, 9, 12–13, 20, 33, 48, 63, 65, 68
Syndicalist movement, 33, 63, 171
Syndicalist League of North America, 63, 68, 201
Syndicalists, American, 12, 67, 69, 108, 126

Taft, Philip, 225
Technical Information Bureau, of Comintern, 156
Ten Days That Shook the World, 24
"Testament," of Lenin, 359, 361
Thaelmann, Ernst, 386–87, 398
Thalheimer, August, 165, 328, 387–88
Theses and Statutes of the Communist International, The, 338
"Theses on the National and Colonial Question," 321, 337
"Theses on the Negro Question," 327
"Theses on the Revolutionary Movement in the Colonies and Semi-Colonies," 349
Third International, *see* Comintern
Third party, 86, 98, 102, 119
Third-party alliance, 87, 91–92, 96–98, 109, 113–15, 119, 124, 126, 190; and Russian factional struggle, 109, 130
Third-party movement, 85
Third period, 302–306
Thomas, Norman, 225, 378
Thompson, A., 205
Tilton, Alfred (Alfred Martin, Joseph Paquett), 211
Titoism, 179, 440
Titus, Dr. William F., 62
Togliatti, Palmiro (Ercoli), 48, 72, 166, 241
Toiler, The (Kansas City), 68
Toiler, The (Cleveland), 69
Toledo, University of, 122
Tomsky, Mikhail P., 300, 306
Toohey, Pat, 290, 380
Trachtenberg, Alexander, 21
"Trade-union capitalism," 276
Trade Union Committee, 229, minutes of, 6
Trade Union Department, 218–19, 261, 267; set up by Fourth Convention, 160
Trade Union Educational League, 6, 21, 39, 64, 66, 70–72, 76–77, 91, 94–95, 98, 190, 206, 215–23, 229, 231, 233, 260, 266, 285, 288–89, 431, 433
Trade-union policy, 285–86, 292–93, 295–97, 309–10; and Lenin, 67–70
Trade-union support, and labor party, 137
Trade Union Unity League, 431
"Trade Union Work," American Commission, Eighth Plenum, 1927, 260
Trade unions, 30, 39, 41, 43–44, 50, 64–65, 72, 81, 172–73, 175, 215–16, 222–23, 227, 316, 396; Communists in, 186, 192, 194, 232–33; Russian, 155, 300; *see also* American Federation of Labor, Dual unionism, Unions, new, Trade Union Educational League
Transmission belts, 171, 173–74, 182
Trotsky, Leon, 14–15, 26, 58–59, 105–109, 113, 141, 213, 257–58, 261, 281, 283, 285, 305, 340, 357–71, 422, 438; assassination of, 179; criticism of Draft Program, 365, 374; expelled, 278–79; and socialism in one country, 131–33, 239–42, 374; and Stalin, 133, 135, 257, 359–60; and Zinoviev, 130, 238–39; *see also* Opposition

Trotsky-Zinoviev-Kamenev Opposition bloc, 361
Trotskyism, 104–109, 113, 135, 238, 365–67, 369–76, 385, 434; in American party, 357, 363–64; appeal of, 374–75; birth of American, 314, 357, 364–67; theory of, 374–75; *see also* Eastman, Lore
Trotskyist movement, 368, 372–73
Trotskyists, 301, 366, 368–72, 419, 429, 434
T.U.E.L., *see* Trade Union Educational League
Tugwell, Rexford Guy, 275
Turner, Bishop Henry M., 317
Twenty-One Points of admission to the Comintern, 25, 125, 472 *n.* 53
Tyomies, 88

Ugaroff, 229
Uj Elöre, 59
Ukrainian foreign-language federation, 18
Ulbricht, Walther, 407
Underground Communist parties, 20–23, 29, 31, 56, 161, 175–76, 190, 203–204, 374; structure of, 156–57
Underground convention, *see* Bridgman convention
Unemployed Council of Greater New York, 175–76
Unemployment, 122
Unemployment Conference of Greater New York, 175
U.N.I.A., *see* Universal Negro Improvement Association
Unification, 26–28
Union Labor Life Insurance Company, 276
Union Press, 205
Unions, new, 217, 286, 288–89, 293, 295–97, 299, 308–10, 380, 394–95; mine, 286–87, 289–90, 295, 299, 380; needle trades, 380; textile, 295, 380; *see also* Dual unionism
Unit, *see* Nuclei
United Cloth Hat, Cap and Millinery Workers International Union, 222
United Communist party, 21, 25, 68; program of, 447 *n.* 4
United Council of Working Class Women (Wives), 177
United Farmer, The, 178
United Farmers' Educational League, 178–79
United front, 32–38, 44, 90, 92, 102, 124–25, 140, 173, 179–80, 225, 228–229; from above, 34; from below, 34, 280, 304, 381; *see also* Farmer-Labor party, Third-party alliance
"United Front Committees," in textile centers, 223–25, 230–31
United Labor Council of New York and Vicinity, 216
United Mine Workers of America, 72, 76, 206, 216, 233, 286, 289–90
United Opposition Bloc of Trotsky and Zinoviev, 261
United States, 11–12, 14–17, 19, 24–26, 29, 32, 38, 47, 51, 53, 56, 58–60, 63, 67, 71, 74, 84, 87, 89, 100, 106, 108, 110–11, 121–23, 125, 135, 141, 158, 167–68, 170, 175, 178–79, 181, 191, 198, 201–202, 204, 207, 209–12, 217, 221, 223, 229–30, 242, 249, 252, 255–61, 269, 271–75, 278, 280–86, 289, 291, 298–300, 303, 317–18, 320, 322–23, 325, 327–30, 336, 339–41, 343–44, 346–47, 349, 352, 362–63, 367–69, 373, 379, 381–382, 387, 391–92, 397, 402, 410, 415, 422–23, 426–27, 435; *see also* House of Representatives, Senate
United Textile Workers, 223, 230–31
United Toilers of America, 22
United Workingmen Singers, 44
Unity Resolution, 150
Universal African Legion, 319, 333
Universal African Motor Corps, 319
Universal Black Cross Nurses, 319
Universal Negro Improvement Association, 318–19, 330, 333
Universal Socialist Co-operative commonwealth, 324

Valetski, H. (Walecki), 26, 38, 59, 170
Van der Lubbe, 213
Vanguard, 34–35; party, 172
Vanzetti, Bartolomeo, 181
Varga, Eugen, 130, 269–70, 447 *n.* 10

Vidali, Vittorio (Enea Sormenti, Carlos Contreras), 179
Viennese uprising, 1927, 279–80
Voice of Labor, The, 75, 210

Wachsoff, Victor, 167
Wage Workers party, 62
Wagenknecht, Alfred, 19, 88, 92, 176
Walecki, *see* Valetski, H.
Wallace, Henry A., 51, 119
Walling, William English, 315
Washington, 323; farmer-labor organization at Chicago convention, 47–48; farmer-labor vote in, 30; Federated Farmer-Labor party in, 116
Washington, George, 273–74
Weinstone, William Wolf, 19, 92, 221, 234, 236, 248–50, 252–57, 259, 265–267, 272, 313, 364, 400–401, 406, 408, 415–16, 423, 430–31, 435, 439
Weisbord, Albert, 224, 234, 288, 294, 380, 412, 416, 433; in Passaic textile strike, 224–26, 230–32
"Welfare capitalism," 276
Welsh, Edward, 404, 423, 425
Western Federation of Miners, 88
Western Progressive Farmers, 48, 178
What Is to Be Done? 172
Wheeler, Burton K., 116
Whitaker, Robert, 181
"White chauvinism," 434
White, William J., 404
Whither England? 358
Wicks, Harry, 22, 100, 170, 273, 366, 385, 406, 408, 415–16, 434–35
Williams, *see* Mikhailov, Boris
Williamson, John, 133
Wilson, William, 346
Wilson, Woodrow, 323
Winter, Ella, 276
Wise, Rabbi Stephen S., 225
Wittdorf, 386–87
Wives, *see* United Council of Working Class Women
Wolfe, Bertram D., 19, 169, 178, 196, 205, 234, 253, 267, 278, 283, 348, 363, 390, 398, 403, 406, 408, 416, 420, 422–23, 425–30, 438; and Americanization, 273–75; background of, 252–53; expelled, 429; representative to Comintern, 169, 385–86, 392–94
Wolfe, Mrs. Bertram D., 392, 425
Women's Bureau, Communist party, 177
Women's Departments, 160, 167, 177
Worker, The (Canadian), 367
Worker, The (New York), 40, 60, 210
Workers in American History, The, 273
Workers Center, New York, 406
Workers' Challenge, 22
Workers (Communist) Party of America, 160, 162, 379
Workers' Council, 21–22
Workers' and Farmers' Government, 178
Workers' government, as slogan, 35
Workers International Relief, 176–77
Workers Library Publishers, 204
Workers Monthly, 216, 238–39, 267, 358
Workers party of America, 22–23, 27, 80–82, 84–85, 87–88, 111, 120, 128, 137, 174, 216–17, 222–23, 234; branch life of, 196; in Chicago, 39; constitution of, 162; District No. 9, Minneapolis, 101; and Farmer-Labor party, 36–44, 75, 80; Fifth Convention of, 265–66, 277–78, 281, 492 *n.* 31, 492–93 *n.* 33; finances of, 203
Fourth Convention of: 140–47, 215, 217–18, 253, 340, 466–67 *n.* 35; and Bolshevization, 153, 159–62; and Comintern, 143–45, 147–50; name change at, 162
as legal party, 22–23, 26, 61; membership of, 26–27, 60, 90, 187, 190; and Negroes, 322, 328, 340; payroll of, 205; reorganization of, 159; Sixth Convention of, 392, 395, 398–404, 406–408, 412, 419, 424, 426, 429, 436–37; structure of, 157; Third Convention of, 77, 86, 90–95, 101, 104–106, 328, 456 *n.* 12, 457–58 *n.* 49; and third party, 97–98, 101–104, 109; *see also* Communist party
Workers' Sport International, 173

Workers Unemployment Council of America, 175–76
Workers' World, The, 68
World communism, *see* Communism
World Congress of the Communist International, *see* Comintern
World party, 165, 208
World War I, 14, 39, 54, 66, 100, 168, 170, 319, 333, 400; Negroes and, 322–23
World War II, 166, 179, 441
Wortis, Rose, 88, 222

Young Communist International, 345, 406; representatives of, to United States, 170, 344
Young Communist League, 235, 343; representatives of, to Young Communist International, 170; *see also* Young Workers League
Young People's Socialist League, 224
Young Worker, The, 92
Young Workers League, 92, 133, 137, 146, 148

Zack [Kornfeder], Joseph, 69, 149, 171, 293–94; in Negro work, 321, 325–26, 328, 343, 350
Zam, Herbert, 148, 430
Zetkin, Clara, 393
Zimmerman, Charles S., 88, 222, 430
Zinoviev, Gregory, 33, 35, 59, 87–88, 105–110, 124–25, 129–30, 133–35, 138, 153, 156, 173, 202, 237–42, 244, 247, 261, 265, 271, 278–79, 284–85, 293, 299, 301, 304, 359, 361, 364, 389, 413, 422
Zinoviev-Kamenev-Stalin alliance, 105, 107–108